California Mortgage Loan Brokering & Lending

FOURTH EDITION

Dr. D. Grogan
MBA, GRI, CRS, CPM

M. C. Buzz Chambers, Jr.
RECI, GRI

CENGAGE
Learning™

Australia • Brazil • Japan • Korea • Mexico • Singapore • Spain • United Kingdom • United States

**California Mortgage Loan Brokering &
Lending, Fourth Edition**
Dr. D. Grogan and M. C. Buzz Chambers, Jr.

Vice President/Editor-in-Chief: Dave Shaut

Acquisitions Editor: Sara Glassmeyer

Developmental Editor: Arlin Kauffman,
LEAP Publishing Services, Inc.

Editorial Assistant: Michelle Melfi

Senior Marketing and Sales Manager:
Mark Linton

Senior Art Director: Pamela A. E. Galbreath

Senior Frontlist Buyer, Manufacturing:
Charlene Taylor

Production Manager: Jennifer Ziegler

Content Project Manager: Sini Sivaraman,
PreMediaGlobal

Production Technology Analyst: Starratt
Alexander

Permissions Acquisition Manager/Photo:
Deanna Ettinger

Permissions Acquisition Manager/Text:
Mardell Glinski Schultz

Cover Designer: Jeff Bane, CMB Design Partners

Internal Designers: Patti Hudepohl and
PreMediaGlobal

Cover Image: © Photo 168; © Tom Schmucker;
© Mark Rasmussen/Dreamstime.com

For product information and technology assistance, contact us at
Cengage Learning Customer & Sales Support, 1-800-354-9706.

For permission to use material from this text or product,
submit all requests online at **www.cengage.com/permissions.**
Further permissions questions can be e-mailed to
permissionrequest@cengage.com

Library of Congress Control Number: 2010928360

Student Edition:

ISBN-13: 978-0-538-73959-7

ISBN-10: 0-538-73959-2

Cengage Learning
5191 Natorp Boulevard
Mason, OH 45040
USA

Cengage Learning is a leading provider of customized learning solutions
with office locations around the globe, including Singapore, the United
Kingdom, Australia, Mexico, Brazil, and Japan. Locate your local office at
www.cengage.com/global.

Cengage Learning products are represented in Canada by
Nelson Education, Ltd.

Purchase any of our products at your local college store or at our preferred
online store **www.cengagebrain.com.**

Printed in the United States of America
1 2 3 4 5 6 7 14 13 12 11 10

Brief Contents

Contents

5 LOANS: FINANCE DISCLOSURE AND OTHER REAL ESTATE DISCLOSURES 138

PART V   REGULATIONS AND OPERATIONS   397

Preface

With the mortgage meltdown and changes in the loan industry between 2007 and today, the real estate industry has seen the creation of new laws almost daily. While the fundamentals of financing and servicing residential loans have not changed, the practice of it has in order to adapt to the changing world surrounding mortgage lending. The first three editions of California Mortgage Loan Brokering & Lending were written for the licensed real estate agent who sought to gain knowledge as a mortgage broker, for those seeking to enter the loan business, and for people already actively working in the industry. These goals have not changed.

FOURTH EDITION

The fourth edition meets the volatile residential loan market head-on with a focus on the need for better performance from practitioners. There is new demand for knowledgeable loan officers, loan processors, loan underwriters, loan servicers, and others who meet the new federal and state regulations. The market calls for people who have the true knowledge of the loan business with strong academic backgrounds.

For the educators who must comply with mandatory legislation, a list of Student Learning Objectives (SLOs) is shown at the beginning of each chapter that states, "At the end of this chapter the student learning outcomes include" so students know what will be expected of them by the end of each chapter. The learner who reviews the chapter summary and knows the important terms listed at the end of each chapter should do well on the individual chapter quiz questions. Quiz answers are shown so the learner may review the content of the chapter.

Many forms that are used in the business were updated, and new laws regarding credit and privacy and disclosures were added. Much needed marketing ideas, personal traits for success in the field of real estate loans, updated loan programs, and guidelines for meeting the fierce competition in the mortgage loan brokering business have also been updated. All were written according to the guidelines as set forth by the California Real Estate Education Center (REEC), the Graduate,

Realtor Institute (GRI), the Certified Property Manager (CPM), and National Real Estate Educator's Association (REEA) writing guidelines for authors, instructors, and course materials, as acquired by the authors.

This edition has undergone significant revision and is current in terms, Internet resources, and the level of professional competence required to succeed in the business today. As the federal regulators and states individually change and evolve to comply with the federal mandates, many minor alterations are expected to meet compliance, yet this text remains the authority on current standards of professional practices that meet the goal of consumer protection for the public.

The world watched the U.S. mortgage loan market change the way business is conducted throughout the world. As conformity within the industry emerges and as guidelines and standards of practices are put into place to create uniformity, various states have either gone to the extreme of excess regulation and requirements of those working in the field or have pulled in the minimum that must be retained to comply with the federal laws. Thus, changes will continue to be seen. Almost every part of the loan business has changed to meet global changes, shifts in capital and financial markets, state civil codes and real estate laws, education-mandated SLOs and commissioner regulations—all to meet the federal statutes. Changes by chapter include the following:

NEW TO THE FOURTH EDITION

- Chapter 1: Web sites for current job salaries for various loan positions, new laws since 2005, the "Do Not Call" update, current graph showing information on housing starts, updated contact information for professional organizations, and added information about loan originators.

- Chapter 2: New section on referrals from other sources, and new regulations about license number required on all business cards and materials.

- Chapter 3: Raised maximum loan amounts for conventional and government-backed loans; updated charts and graphs for COFI, CMT, LIBOR, and prime rate indexes; added the steps for obtaining a RAM; separated condominium loan data; and 2009 foreclosure and delinquency rates in California showing government intervention.

- Chapter 4: FHA loans in California through 2009, new FHA down payment and maximum loan amounts, a first-time homebuyer chart, VA Benefit Improvement Act with higher loan limits, changes in the Cal Vet loan program, and added data about Small Business Administration loans.

- Chapter 5: Updated Truth in Lending Act (TILA), Reg Z, RESPA, Reg X, Home Mortgage Disclosure, Reg C, changes in CFL and CRMLA due to the S.A.F.E. Act, HOEPA loan information, the Mortgage Disclosure Improvement Act, Good Faith Estimate, HUD compliance, disclosure requirements for FHA and VA loans, HMDA disclosure for the Department of Corporations, the Department of Real Estate licensee disclosure, and FIRPTA update.

- Chapter 6: Newest January 2010 FNMA 1003 loan application form, updated FHA calculations and ratios, and updated insurance rates.

- Chapter 7: Credit and FICO scoring changes, ECOA and nontraditional credit reports, Housing Financial Discrimination Act and Fair Lending Notice current data.

- Chapter 8: Updated verification of employment, verification of deposit, and verification of rent/mortgage forms, eliminated forms no longer used, added homeowner association information, added mold and lead-based paint disclosures to the stacking order, and deleted the IRS Form 4506 that is no longer in use.

- Chapter 9: Escrow differences between Northern and Southern California, current wire transfer and bank transfer information for "Good Funds" practices, added condominium certificate, new FIRPTA affidavit, new language Statement of Information, Change in Ownership form and latest data about the Federal Housing Finance Agency, and appraisal management company (AMC) code changes.

- Chapter 10: Updated Web site addresses in underwriting and changed to the current FNMA form.

- Chapter 11: Newest addresses for the various loan software firms, and updated Loan Servicing Disclosure Statement.

- Chapter 12: New graph showing unemployment and the four-week moving average of initial unemployment claims, better explanation on four new graphs, new affordability chart, new Consumer Price Index, government deficit, institutional money funds, and Federal Reserve data on Depository Institution borrowing.

- Chapter 13: Added employment considerations, motivational data and book sources, time management and Blackberry data, added California Department of Real Estate Bulletin reference, sexual harassment training and education requirements, and current contact information for loan sources.

- Chapter 14: Updated DRE salesperson and broker license and renewal changes, added the required Risk Management data, S.A.F.E. Act loan broker federal license information, and list state-by-state comparison of loan broker license implementation.

- Chapter 15: Updated math loan amounts to meet more current prices; added California Department of Real Estate trust fund accounting laws, examples, and information.

- Appendix A: New FNMA 1003 loan application.

- Appendix B: New credit information.

- Appendix C: Current VOE, VOD, forms.

- Appendix D: New escrow instructions for 2009.

- Appendix E: New 2009 appraisal to comply with new URAR –FNMA 1005 form.

- Appendix F: Preliminary Title Report.

- Appendix G: New 2009 loan documents.

- Appendix H: Employment Application, Independent Contractor Agreement, and Policy & Procedures Manual.
- Appendix I: Wholesale Brokerage Agreements: Application, Agreement, Concurrent Funding Agreement.
- Appendix J: Updated Internet Web sites and addresses.

INSTRUCTIONAL SUPPORT

Instructors who adopt this book receive access to an online Instructor's Manual written by the authors. Each chapter has a 10-question Instructor Resource Quiz, plus two 50-question Mid-Term Exams and two 100-question Final Exams with answers, as well as a sample course syllabus.

Online WebTutor™ support for WebCT™ and BlackBoard® is also provided. Designed to accompany this textbook, WebTutor is an eLearning software solution that turns everyone in your classroom into a front-row learner. Whether you want to Web-enhance your class, or offer an entire course online, WebTutor allows you to focus on what you do best—teaching. More than just an interactive study guide, WebTutor™ is an anytime, anywhere online learning solution providing reinforcement through chapter quizzes, multimedia flashcards, e-mail discussion forums, and other engaging learning tools.

Classroom PowerPoint® presentation slides also support each chapter outlining learning objectives, emphasizing key concepts and highlighting real-world applications to help further engage learners and generate classroom discussion.

These instructional support materials are available online only to adopters from the text companion site www.cengage.com/realestate/grogan.

Acknowledgments

The materials contained within this book would not have been possible without the invaluable feedback and suggestions from numerous persons. Of all those who helped, we wish to specifically thank the following people for helping us put together this fourth edition of California Mortgage Loan Brokering & Lending.

The students from our mortgage brokering and lending classes at:

Coastline Community College, Fountain Valley, CA

El Camino Community College, Torrance, CA

Fullerton Junior College, Fullerton, CA

Long Beach City College, Long Beach, CA Joanne Ahmadi, president, Impact Credit/Mortgage Fax, Garden Grove, CA

Angeline Bevins, president, Grover Escrow Corp., Anaheim, CA

Charles Barger and Carlos Villegas, Bristol Home Loans, Bellflower, CA

Frank Capatosto, Paloma Mortgage Co., Rancho Santa Margarita, CA

Nick Gavrilas, On Time Appraisal, Anaheim, CA

Mike Ramirez, broker/owner, American Capital Loans, Garden Grove, CA

Chery Reid, underwriter, Flagstar Mortgage, Bellevue, WA

Greg Williams, underwriting manager, Bank of America, Phoenix, AZ

In addition to the industry experts, several administrative assistants have contributed to the typing, editing, and formatting of the materials and searching Internet Web sites. We offer our gratitude to Janet Tomey for work on the first edition, Gail Ohls for the second edition, and Sandra Saldana for the third edition.

Special thanks go to our significant others. Donna's husband, Pat Grogan, broker and a Certified Top Producer instructor, contributed not only support but also created most of the PowerPoint® presentation materials. Buzz's wife, the late Marion Chambers, CEO, CSEO, with 30 years in the escrow profession, who contributed to the first three editions, sacrificed significant family time and contributed in many areas. Without the support of these two individuals, the work could not have been completed for this edition, and earlier editions, in a timely manner.

This manuscript is also dedicated to Dennis McKenzie, a guru in the field of publishing real estate textbooks, author of numerous continuing education courses and seminars, dedicated humanitarian, and purest professional! He loved his daughters, travel to Holland, antique watches and expensive ink pens, but he was best known for his trivia humor about the presidents, coins, currency, and economics. Editor for the California real estate textbook series, he will be missed by all those whose life he gently touched but were left with a legacy of memories, both professional and personal, to be cherished. Dennis also used to quote presidents and stories about currency. One of his favorites is from Thomas Jefferson:

> *"I believe that banking institutions are more dangerous to our liberties than standing armies. If the American people ever allow private banks to control the issue of their currency, first by inflation, then by deflation, the banks and corporations that will grow up around the banks will deprive the people of all property until their children wake-up homeless on the continent their fathers conquered."*
>
> *Thomas Jefferson, 1802*

We would also like to express our appreciation to those who served as reviewers and who provided insightful comments and valuable suggestions.

Carol Jensen
Cabrillo College

Jim Cunningham
Long Beach City College

Our heartfelt thanks go out to each of you.

Buzz Chambers, Mortgage Lender and Instructor
Dr. Donna Grogan, Author, Broker and Professor of Real Estate

About the Authors

Dr. D. Grogan Professor Grogan began real estate practice in 1974 as a sales associate before eventually owning two Century 21 franchise offices. After closing 100 escrows and completing the Graduate Realtors Institute (GRI) designation criteria in 1977, Grogan received the Certified Residential Specialist (CRS) designation in 1979. In 1985, the coveted Certified Property Manager (CPM) designation was conferred on D. Grogan. Having received two bachelor's degrees, one in business administration/management and one in real estate/finance, Dr. Grogan earned a master's degree from California Polytechnic University, Pomona, for completing a thesis on property management training and education in 1985 before receiving a doctoral degree from Pepperdine University for her dissertation on a needs assessment for the real estate assistant. Dr. Grogan is the full-time real estate professor at El Camino College in Torrance, California. An instructor since 1980 at Cerritos, El Camino, Glendale, Mt. San Antonio, Rio Hondo, and Saddleback California Community Colleges, and at Woodbury University, California State University–Los Angeles, California Polytechnic University, and the University of California–Los Angeles, Grogan has also written many publications. Books include California Property Management, California Escrow, Computer Applications in Real Estate, and Mortgage Loan Brokering and Lending, in addition to many of the California Community Colleges' student or instructor study guides, continuing education course materials, and curricula. Awarded the Norm Woest award by the California Real Estate Educators' Association (CREEA) as Most Outstanding Real Estate Instructor, Grogan has served as an officer and director for that organization and served on committees such as conference planning, curriculum, and Academic Senate, Budget and Planning. Dr. Grogan was selected for the California Department of Real Estate State Exam Review Committee and served on the Real Estate Commissioner's special education committee. You may send suggestions on this book or make contact at Donna@DonnaGrogan.com.

Buzz Chambers M.C. "Buzz" Chambers, Jr. has been a senior loan consultant for many years, specializing in residential loans for one- to four-unit properties, FHA and VA loans, in addition to numerous conventional loans. He has owned a mortgage company, sold real estate and worked as a title insurance representative, in addition to managing a real estate office sales force. Mr. Chambers has been associated with the real estate industry for more than 30 years. Mr. Chambers is an approved instructor for the California Association of REALTORS® and has earned certificates in real estate and escrow. He is also a real estate certified instructor (RECI), a member of both the California Real Estate Educators' Association (CREEA) and the California Association of REALTORS® (CAR). He has also earned the Graduate REALTOR® Institute (GRI) designation. To contact Buzz, e-mail him at buzzme@bigplanet.com.

PART I
Scope of the Business

Chapter

1

IMPORTANT TERMS

FHLB - Federal Home Loan Bank

FIRREA - Financial Institutions Reform, Recovery & Enforcement Act

GNMA - Government National Mortgage Association

Holder in Due Course

HUD - Housing and Urban Development

Loan originator

Patriot Act

PMI - Private Mortgage Insurance

RTC - Resolution Trust Corporation

Seller Carryback Loans (Soft Money)

Scope of Mortgage Loan Brokerage

PREVIEW

A career in real estate mortgage lending can be exciting and profitable if a person has energy and is self-motivated. The most predominant essentials you will need to succeed in achieving your goals are the following six traits: (1) PMA = positive mental attitude, (2) P + P = patience and persistence, (3) time management, (4) a strong "WORK" ethic, (5) a business plan, and (6) a comprehensive marketing plan. These items are further discussed in Chapter 13.

Mortgage loan professionals help potential real estate buyers and existing property owners obtain financing to either purchase a property and/or place a refinance loan on an existing parcel. Along the way, mortgage loan professionals provide a great service by informing borrowers about the costs and terms that can be found in the variety of loan packages that exist in the marketplace.

The demand for the services of a well-trained mortgage loan professional is high, but to achieve success will take not only dedication and hard work but also a commitment to continuous training and education. No sooner does a mortgage loan representative learn everything about 20 types of loan packages than 30 totally new kinds of loan programs hit the marketplace. Not only the ability to adapt to change but the personality to thrive on the opportunity to learn something new every day will often make the difference between success and failure.

In short, the mortgage brokerage business is fiercely competitive, but it offers an opportunity for a high income and personal rewards if an individual has a good work ethic, which is often referred to by the acronym WORK, as shown below. This textbook will describe in detail the workings of the mortgage loan business and gives you the preview that you need to help you decide if this is the business for you. If you are already in the mortgage business, this book will give you ideas to make you more successful.

W = Wealth

O = Opportunity

R = Rewards

K = Knowledge

CHAPTER OBJECTIVES

At the end of this chapter, the student learning outcomes include:

1. Understand the structure of the book.
2. Describe the history of real estate lending in the United States.
3. Explain some current and future trends in real estate lending.
4. Learn about career opportunities in the mortgage loan brokerage field.
5. Differentiate between a mortgage broker and a mortgage banker.

1.1 OVERVIEW OF THE BOOK

This book begins with a table of contents to help you find topics by subject name and is followed by a table of figures so you can locate a specific form, illustration, or chart. The book is divided into five parts: scope of the business, loans, processing, the secondary money market, and regulations and operations. Figure 1.1 gives an overview of the book. It may be helpful for you to go to a website, such as www.salary.com or similar, to determine the various different income levels for the many related, but different, jobs within a career in mortgage loan brokering.

The first section of the book, Part 1, consists of Chapter 1, which covers the historic background that has led to present-day operations of the mortgage loan business. This is followed in Chapter 2 with information on career opportunities. Originating loans and developing business contacts are also discussed. Developing sources for your loan business will mean learning techniques and methods that separate you from your competition to create a marketing strategy that must also comply with all regulations.

Part 2 consists of three chapters that review real estate loan information. Chapter 3 is on the types and characteristics of the various conventional loans, plus loan features and mortgage insurance. Chapter 4 discusses both government loans and other loans. In this chapter, the basic details of the Federal Housing Administration (FHA), the Department of Veterans Administration (DVA), and the California Department of Veterans Affairs (Cal Vet) loan programs are covered from the viewpoint of the mortgage loan broker. Because not all loans

FIGURE 1.1 Overview of the book.

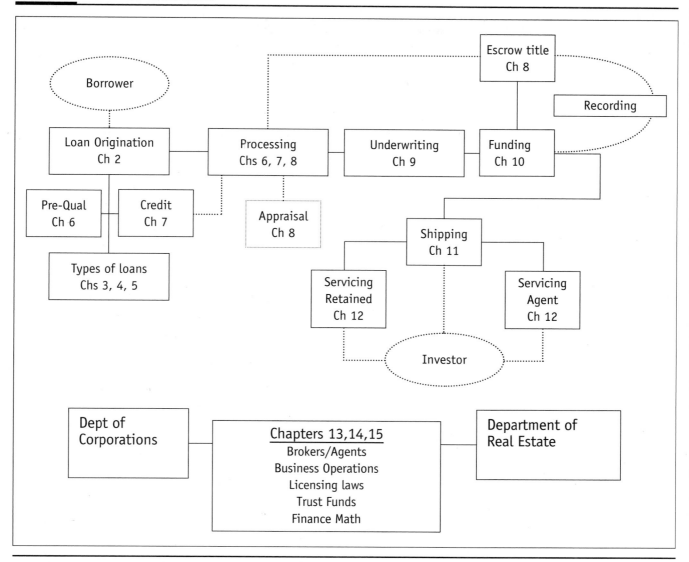

in the mortgage loan business involve institutional or government loans, this chapter also discusses such loans as junior liens, refinance and equity loans, Title I loans, and loans termed subprime loans. The last chapter in this section, Chapter 5, covers loan disclosures and compliance.

Part 3 of this text covers the bulk of the loan business, called processing. Once the loan has been originated or obtained, detailed steps are required to consummate the transaction. The first chapter in this section, Chapter 6, explains the first step in processing the loan application, often referred to as prequalification, or prequal. The reader will be furnished with a detailed explanation on how to complete the loan application, known as the Uniform Residential Loan Application (URLA), or the Federal National Mortgage Association (FNMA) form number 1003 (pronounced 10-0-3), as shown in Appendix A. From the application form, the mortgage loan broker is able to calculate income-to-debt and loan-to-value (LTV) ratios to begin matching the borrower to the various types of loans that are discussed in Part 2, as shown in the Calculating Ratios form in Chapter 6. A prospective borrower will usually qualify for more than one type of loan, so the mortgage loan broker will need to discuss the options available to the applicant.

The next chapter in processing the loan is Chapter 7, which covers the credit bureaus, how to establish credit, how to read a credit report, as shown in Appendix B, and how to interpret the credit FICO score ratings for determining a borrower's creditworthiness and information on compliance with both credit laws and fair lending practices. Chapter 8 covers the part of the processing in which the various verifications are handled, in addition to documentation required from the prospective borrower. Chapter 8 also discusses the stacking order required for loan submission to the investors by the mortgage loan broker. This chapter includes the processor's stacking order as required by the lender.

Chapter 9 describes the coordination between the mortgage loan broker and related real estate professionals to process the loan to closure. The chapter discusses escrow, or settlement, as shown in Appendix D; the appraisal, as shown in Appendix E; and the title reports, as shown in Appendix F. Escrow prorations and closing statements, the impound account, the title company Statement of Information (SI), the title policy binder, and the appraisal report are all important documents for the mortgage loan broker to review.

This is followed in Chapter 10 by the underwriting guidelines for FNMA and FHLMC. The mortgage loan broker is always concerned about the issues covered in the section on quality control and fraud audit. The last chapter of this section, Chapter 11, completes the loan-processing portion of the mortgage loan brokerage business with the loan documents, called loan docs, as shown in Appendix G, and is followed by information on the funding and closing of the loan.

Part 4 is about investment money markets and covers topics about the secondary money market and securities. Chapter 12 explains shipping and servicing of the loan. Whether the loan is kept in the originating lender's own portfolio or the loan is packaged and sold to other investors, knowledge about calculating yields, discounting notes, and the proper transfer of documents used to secure loans on real property is reviewed.

The last section of the text, Part 5, is about the various regulations and operations of the business. Chapter 13 begins with discussion of the office business operations, including the employment application, as shown in Appendix H.1, and the independent contractor's agreement that is between the mortgage loan broker individual employee and the mortgage brokerage firm, as shown in Appendix H.2, as well as the Policies and Procedures Manual of the brokerage firm, as shown in Appendix H.3. The wholesale broker agreement between the mortgage loan broker and the investor is shown in Appendix I. Chapter 12 then discusses the Department of Corporations (DOC) for loan brokers licensed under the Corporation Commissioner for those brokers handling Consumer

Finance Lender (CFL) loans. In addition, license law for loan agents under the Department of Real Estate (DRE) license laws are described with both the similarities and the differences between the two regulatory agencies, including topics of compensation, referral fees, and regulations. The distinction between real and personal property used as the collateral for the loan is included in this chapter.

Chapter 14 details broker supervision, agency law, recordkeeping, trust fund handling, and licensing laws under the California DRE regulations for brokers and salespersons. Chapter 15 is devoted to real estate finance mathematics that cover the various ratios, use of a payment factor chart, and calculating the annual percentage rate (APR), including the key strokes for various financial calculators. This chapter covers the number one area where a DRE licensee violates the law and has his or her license revoked, restricted, or otherwise censured. This financial area is where licensees have the most trouble with the state licensing agencies: handling client trust funds, including threshold reporting, compensation, and similar recordkeeping elements.

The appendices include various Internet sites, as shown in Appendix J, and a comprehensive glossary of terms, as shown in Appendix H. This text includes typical forms that are used in the mortgage loan business in English and some other languages, such as Spanish, followed by the index.

1.2 HISTORIC PERSPECTIVE

In the Beginning

Many of the current lending practices are based on the foundations carried forward from Roman times to the European governments, as shown in Figure 1.2.

FIGURE 1.2   Early history of finance.

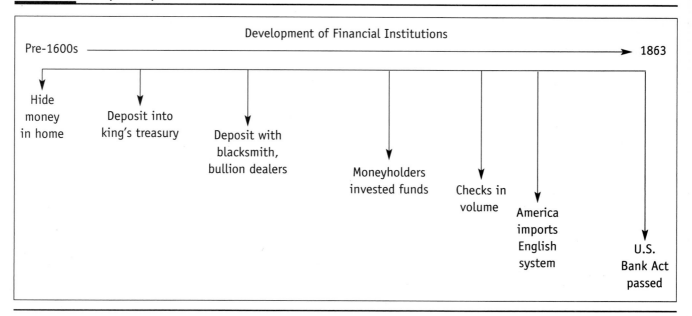

These standards of practice were brought to the United States by the early settlers and were included in the laws of the newly formed government on the East Coast. There were virtually no institutional or government loans available for residential properties during these early years. Home loans came from friends or family members.

Early Progress

Figure 1.3 shows the progression of major acts affecting real estate lending. The Federal Reserve Act was enacted in 1913. It made real estate loans available through federally chartered commercial banks. California enacted legislation in 1919 to become the first state to license persons who practice real estate activities. The other states followed, and virtually all states today require much of the real estate activity to be performed by a licensed real estate agent, including those acts of the mortgage loan broker. Most states today exempt actions that an owner does directly on their own property, such as renting or selling their own home. Also often exempt are persons working directly for a federal banking operation.

The early 1920s were times when real estate values increased by as much as 50 percent until the collapse of the optimistic real estate market in 1927. The stock market crash soon followed the real estate market crash. Congress enacted many new acts during the 1930s designed to prevent a similar future market crash.

The **Federal Home Loan Bank (FHLB)** Act of 1932 set up the Federal Home Loan Bank System under the Federal Home Loan Bank Board, found at www.fhlbsf.com, which established a board and 12 regional banks to provide loans and a central credit clearinghouse for home finance institutions. California, Arizona, and Nevada are located in the 12th district. Some real estate loans are tied to the 12th FHLB district cost of funds.

The Home Owner's Loan Act of 1933 began the first chartered savings and loan associations under the Federal Home Loan Bank Board, requiring members to be part of the Federal Home Loan Bank System and the Federal Savings and Loan Insurance Corporation (FSLIC).

The National Housing Act created the Federal Housing Administration (FHA) in 1934. The FNMA, found at http://www.fanniemae.com, became authorized to provide a secondary money market for FHA loans. This provided liquidity for real estate loan investments. An explanation of how to fill out the loan application is described in Chapter 6.

1940—1959

Toward the end of World War II, in the mid-1940s, the Serviceman's Readjustment Act created the DVA (formerly referred to as VA) with a home loan program. The period from 1945 to 1965 had only a few major real estate or lending laws pertaining to private sector economic growth.

In 1952 the savings and loan associations became subject to federal income tax and filing requirements that they had been exempt from since the 1939

FIGURE 1.3   Chronology of lending regulations.

1910s	Federal Reserve Act
	California Real Estate License (DRE) (1919)
1930s	Federal Home Loan Bank Act of 1932 (FHLB)
	National Housing Act-Home Owner's Loan Act of 1933
	Federal Housing Administration (FHA)
	Federal National Mortgage Association (FNMA)
1940s	Serviceman's Readjustment Act
	Veterans Administration (VA)
	(Note: 1990s, VA changed to DVA, Department of Veterans Affairs)
1950s	Federal Deposit Insurance Act of 1950 (FDIC)
	Bank Holding Company Act of 1956
1960s	Housing and Urban Development Act (HUD)
	Fair Housing Act
	Interstate Land Sales Full Disclosure Act
	Consumer Credit Protection Act (Truth-in-Lending Act [Reg Z and HOEPA])
	Fair Credit Reporting Act
	National Environmental Policy Act
	Government National Mortgage Association (GNMA) of 1968
1970s	International Banking Act of 1978
	Emergency Home Finance Act
	Flood Disaster Protection Act
	Real Estate Settlement Procedures Act (RESPA)
	Equal Credit Opportunity Act (ECOA)
	Home Mortgage Disclosure Act
	Fair Lending Practices Act
	Community Reinvestment Act (CRA)
	Housing and Community Development Amendments
	Financial Institution Regulatory and Interest Rate Control Act of 1978 (FIRIRCA)
1980s	Depository Institutions Deregulation and Monetary Control Act of 1980 (DIDMCA)
	Omnibus Reconciliation Act
	Garn–St. Germain Depository Institutions Act of 1982
	Depository Institution Act of 1982
	Deficit Reduction Act
	Competitive Equality Banking Act
	Financial Institutions Reform, Recovery, and Enforcement Act (FIRREA)
1990s	Federal Deposit Insurance Corporation Improvement Act of 1991 (FDICIA)
	Housing and Community Development Act of 1992 (HCDA)
	RTC Completion Act
	Community Development and Regulatory Improvement Act of 1994
	Interstate Banking and Branching Efficiency Act of 1994
	Economic Growth and Regulatory Paperwork Reduction Act of 1996
	Gramm-Leach-Bliley Act of 1999
2000s	Fair Credit Reporting Act (FCRA) (2002)
	Homeland Security Act (2002)
	Predatory Lending Law (2001)
	Telephone Solicitations for California
	Finance Lenders Law and California Residential Mortgage Lending Act (2003)
	California Financial Information Privacy Act (2005)
2010s	AB 759 Buyer's Choice for escrow and title companies (Oct 11, 2009)
	SB 237 Registration of appraisal management companies (Jan 1, 2010)
	SB 239 Penal Code Felony for fraud on loan application (Jan 1, 2010)
	AB 329 Reverse Mortgage Elder Protection Act of 2009. (Jan 1, 2010)
	AB 260 Higher-Priced Mortgage Loans (DRE)(DOC) (July 1, 2010)
	AB 1160 Document written in same language loan negotiated (July 1, 2010)
	SB 36 Mortgage Loan Originator real estate license endorsement & Nationwide Licensing System and Registry (CFL)(RMLA)(DRE broker) (July 1, 2010)

Source: Federal Deposit Insurance Corporation.

Internal Revenue Code. The FDIC Act of 1950 revised and consolidated earlier legislation, and the Bank Holding Company Act of 1956 required FDIC approval for establishment of a bank holding company. Bank holding companies headquartered in one state were prohibited from acquiring a bank in another state. An equilibrium point was reached in 1957 when the demand for housing needs most nearly matched the supply of housing available. This act has been updated and codified effective October 2009.

The Revenue Act of 1962 ended savings and loan association income tax exemption, and the Tax Reform Act of 1969 made significant changes in income tax that they became subjected to. From the mid-1960s forward, however, many changes have occurred. The **Housing and Urban Development (HUD) Act** in 1965 created HUD to consolidate many federal programs. During this time, the HUD Act of 1968 moved FNMA from government to private authority and created the **Government National Mortgage Association (GNMA)**. In 1966, the Freedom of Information Act (FOIA), as seen at http://www.usdoj.gov/index.html, was established and is administered under the Department of Justice (DOJ); it has been amended several times since its inception.

Before 1970, the Fair Housing Act, the Interstate Land Sales Full Disclosure Act, the Consumer Credit Protection Act (Truth-in-Lending Act [Reg Z and HOEPA]), the Fair Credit Reporting Act (FCRA), and the national Environmental Policy Act (EPA) were all put into place during the period when national interests were directed toward protecting consumers. The Tax Reform Act of 1976 raised the minimum tax rate from 10 percent to 15 percent, and the minimum tax rate exemption was reduced.

1960—1979

As employment was relatively stable and the economy grew during the 1970s, more legislation was enacted. Both the Real Estate Settlement Procedures Act (RESPA), first passed in 1974, and the FCRA, became law. In addition, the Emergency Home Finance Act, the Flood Disaster Protection Act, and the Fair Lending Practices Act were enacted.

In 1977, the Community Reinvestment Act (CRA) became law to encourage financial institutions to help meet the credit needs of their communities, including low- and moderate-income neighborhoods. The CRA requires federal financial institution regulators to access the record of each bank and thrift institute in helping to fulfill its obligations to the community and to consider that record in evaluating applications for charters or for approval of mergers, acquisitions, and branch openings. The federal financial institution regulators are Office of the Comptroller of the Currency, Board of Governors of the Federal Reserve System, Federal Deposit Insurance Corporation (FDIC), and Office of Thrift Supervision (OTS).

In 1978, two important federal acts became law. The International Banking Act brought foreign banks within the federal regulatory framework and required deposit insurance for branches of foreign banks engaged in U.S. retail banking.

The Financial Institutions Regulatory and Interest Rate Control Act (FIRIRCA) created major statutory provisions regarding electronic fund transfers and established limits and reporting requirements of banks.

1980—1999

Home prices began to increase in value, sustaining the real estate market activity for the next 25 years. Even though prices dipped in the early 1970s, 1980s, and early 1990s, the overall growth rate was about 4 percent per year until 1990. This created a demand for real estate loans.

The Emergency Home Finance Act provided for both secondary loan support for funding by thrift institutions and for FNMA to purchase conventional loans, rather than only VA or FHA loans.

Other acts began at this time. The Flood Disaster Protection Act required flood insurance for loans in flood hazard areas. RESPA, the Equal Credit Opportunity Act (ECOA), the Home Mortgage Disclosure Act (HMDA), the Fair Lending Practices Regulations, the CRA, and the Housing and Community Development Amendments received congressional approval.

In 1980, Congress passed the Depository Institutions Deregulation and Monetary Control Act (DIDMCA), which changed many practices. The act extended federal overrides of state usury ceilings, simplified Truth-in-Lending Act (Reg Z and HOEPA) eased geographical lending restrictions, and created jumbo loans. This act granted new powers to thrift institutions and raised the deposit insurance ceiling to $100,000.

The **Omnibus Reconciliation Act** limited housing revenue bond tax exemptions. The Garn-St. Germain Depository Institutions Act of 1982 phased out interest rate differentials and preempted state due-on-sale restrictions by lenders. The Deficit Reduction Act changed loan interest reporting procedures and extended the tax exemption for certain loan bonds. The Competitive Equality Banking Act (CEBA) kept Savings Bank Life Insurance and gave flexibility to thrifts.

The Tax Reform Act of 1986 removed most tax benefits from real estate that had formerly attracted investors. Savings and loan associations took back property from builders and developer foreclosures. The 1980s ended with a crash in the real estate market that exceeded the late 1920s disaster. Consequently, most loans over 80 percent of value require some form of mortgage insurance in the event of loan default, such as **private mortgage insurance (PMI)**. In 1989 FSLIC became insolvent and FDIC took over their insurance obligations.

The most important of the laws at that time was the enactment of the **Financial Institutions Reform, Recovery and Enforcement Act (FIRREA)**, which created the Office of Thrift Supervision (OTS) under the Treasury Department, and the **Federal Housing Finance Board (FHFB)**, abolishing the Federal Home Loan Bank Board (FHLBB). The FHLBB had 12 district banks, similar to the Federal Reserve System, but the district number was not the same for both. California is in the 11th District Cost of Funds for loan and for lease purposes. The act formed the **Resolution Trust Corporation (RTC)**, a temporary agency to liquidate defaulting assets of member banks. If a savings bank did not meet the Qualified Thrift Lender (QTL) guidelines, the FHLB closed the bank and transferred management to the RTC. In 1995, the RTC is no longer an active agency. The Savings Association Insurance Fund (SAIF) was created to replace FSLIC; the Bank Insurance Fund (BIF) was created to cover banks.

In 1991, BIF was recapitalized by borrowing from the Treasury to strength FDIC funds. The act put new capital requirements for banks and created new Truth in Savings provisions. In the following year, the Housing and Community Development Act was established to regulate the structure for Government-Sponsored Enterprises (GSEs) to combat money laundering.

In 1994, this act established the wholly owned government corporation that provides financial and technical assistance to CDFIs. The Interstate Banking and Branching Efficiency Act permitted bank holding companies to acquire banks in another state, thus allowing mergers.

The Home Ownership and Equity Protection Act of 1994 requires disclosures and clamps restrictions on lenders of high-cost loans. The Act was codified in Regulation Z and only applies to non-purchase money transactions.

The law gives the Federal Reserve Board broad powers to adjust regulations.

The California Mortgage Lending Act (CRMLA) was created in 1994 and became operative in 1996. This allowed a mortgage loan broker either to initiate the loan as a lender or to act as the loan servicer, or to do both functions. This act authorizes licensees to make federally related mortgage loans, to make loans to finance the construction of a home, to sell the loans to institutional investors, and to service such loans or to purchase a servicing portfolio.

This era ended with the Gramm-Leach-Bliley Act of 1999, which repealed the last of the Glass Steagall Act of 1933. This act allows affiliation between banks and insurance underwriters. The law creates new financial holding company legislation authorizing engagement in commercial and merchant banking, investment in and developing real estate, and other complimentary activities. All financial institutions must provide customers the opportunity of not sharing non-public information with unaffiliated third parties as of July 1, 2001.

Beyond 2000

In 2001, the **Patriot Act** was enacted, which requires the mortgage broker to obtain information about the borrower. Thus, the loan broker should ask the borrower(s) for identification, such as a driver's license (photo), social security card, and a passport. For further information, go to http://www.epic.org/privacy/terrorism/hr3126, subsection 351-358.

The FCRA, enacted in 2002, covers a person who intends to use the information contained in a credit transaction involving the consumer about whom the information is to be furnished and involves the extension of credit in connection with a valuation of payment risk with a business transaction. The full code section law may be seen at http://www.ftc.gov/os/statutes/fcra.htm#604.

Also in 2002, Section 204 of the Homeland Security Act, as shown at http://www.whitehouse.gov/deptofhomeland/bill, was set up to encourage the sharing of information with the Department of Homeland Security (DHS) by the private sector, state and local governments, and individuals. The provision provides for information voluntarily provided to the DHS that relates to infrastructure vulnerabilities terrorism and may be forwarded by the DHS to other federal departments or agencies.

State and federal regulations were put in place to require telephone solicitors to comply with an individual's right to put a telephone number on a "do not call" list, which has had a negative effect on both real estate sales agents and mortgage loan brokers. The Attorney General enforces the right for telephone subscribers to be placed on the list so they do not receive unwanted telephone calls from telephone solicitors. Effective January 1, 2003, a civil penalty of $1,000 for each violation of the provision was imposed. The document may be viewed at http://www.leginfo.ca.gov/pub/bill/sen/Sb_33_bill_20031911_chaptered. html. The California Financial Information Privacy Act became operative on January 1, 2005, and may be viewed at http://www.leginfo.ca.gov/pub/bill/sen/sb_1_bill_20030828_chaptered.html, which prohibits a financial institution from disclosing a consumer's nonpublic personal information to nonaffiliated third parties, unless the consent of the consumer is obtained. A list of specific information that may not be given is spelled out within the code section of this law. To put your phone on the "do not call" list, go to http://www.donotcall.gov.

By June 2007, about one-half of the sub-prime loans made in 2006 were based on stated income, with no verification through documentation. The Federal Reserve Board say the sub-prime lending industry reflects record numbers of foreclosures with greater numbers of people headed that direction. Other regulations addressed starter or teaser rate loans to require better disclosures for borrowers. New regulations address adjustable rate mortgage issues so that borrowers may have up to 60 days to refinance a loan before their interest rate goes up. Key to these regulations is that the borrower may refinance without penalty, because about three-quarters of all sub-prime loans had prepayment penalties.

The Emergency Economic Stabilization Act of 2008 is commonly referred to as a bailout of the U.S. financial system. Both foreign and domestic banks are included in the program The subprime mortgage market crisis reached a critical stage during September 2008, and this act was enacted October 3, 2008. The federal government did a takeover of Fannie Mae and Freddie Mac, in addition to other financial transactions. In the Troubled Asset Relief Program (TARP) of late 2008, the federal government buys up illiquid mortgage backed securities (MBS) with the intent to increase the liquidity of the secondary mortgage markets and to reduce potential losses encountered by financial institutions owning the securities. The idea is that the federal government will be able to sell the MBS in the future at a price sufficient to recover the funds expended to make purchases. The banks that hold the MBS were naturally reluctant to accept the asset write downs. Some banks became distressed with the devaluation of their asset holdings. The bulk of the $700 million bailout was used to purchase mortgage backed securities, backed by American homeowners, that the government could later sell at a profit providing that the dollar does not collapse or that hyperinflation does not occur as a result.

The bill authorizes the Secretary of the Treasury to establish TARP of 2008 to purchase troubled assets from financial institutions. The Office of Financial Stability was created within the Treasury Department as the agency through which the Secretary will run the program. The Secretary is required to consult with the Board of Governors of the Federal Reserve System, the Federal Deposit Insurance.

Corporation, the Comptroller of the Currency, the Director of the Office of Thrift Supervision, and the Secretary of Housing and Urban Development when running the program. For mortgages involved in assets purchased by the Treasury Department, the Treasury Secretary is required to:

- Implement a plan to seek to maximize assistance for homeowners.
- Encourage the servicers of the underlying mortgages to take advantage of the HOPE for Homeowners Program of the National Housing Act or other available programs to minimize foreclosures.

The Secure and Fair Enforcement for Mortgage Licensing Act of 2008 (SAFE) that is effective July 31, 2009 requires the states to adopt the following measures:

- Provide for the uniform licensing of mortgage loan originators through a nationwide Internet-based system, termed the Nationwide Mortgage Licensing System (NMLS)
- Improve accountability
- Track mortgage loan originators
- Enhance consumer protection
- Reduce fraud
- Provide consumers with easily accessible information about the professional mortgage loan originators (MLOs)

The NMLS provides for minimum standards for licensing of mortgage loan originators, which include:

- No mortgage license revocation
- No felony conviction in the last seven (7) years preceding application date, or EVER involving financial fraud
- Demonstration of financial responsibility, character and fitness to warrant operating honestly, fairly. and efficiently
- Pass a written pre-licensing test
- Complete twenty (20) hours of NMLS approved education, including:
  - Federal law and regulations
  - Ethics
  - Training related to nontraditional mortgage lending

AB 957, effective October 11, 2009, is the Buyer's Choice Act, giving the power to choose the escrow and title companies to the buyer, which is discussed in Chapter 9.

Many laws resulted from the mortgage meltdown that were legislated in 2009 and became effective in 2010. Other laws the California governor signed were:

- SB 237, effective January 1, 2010 and discussed in Chapter 9, creates a program that requires registration of appraisal management companies.

- AB 329, effective January 1, 2010, the Reverse Mortgage Elder Protection Act of 2009, imposes new disclosure requirement for reverse mortgages, as discussed in Chapter 3.

- SB 239 modifies the Penal Code to create a new crime, a felony, for those who commit loan application fraud, as discussed in Chapter 6.

- SB 36, for July 1, 2010, requires a real estate license endorsement from DRE, or DOC for CFL or RMLA lenders, and submission of data to the Nationwide Licensing System and Registry, discussed in Chapter 14.

- AB 260 establishes a new category of regulated loans for "higher-priced mortgage loans" with many stipulations, especially for DRE licensees, as discussed in Chapter 3 (loans) and Chapter 14 (licensing).

Unstable Market

The real estate market often appears to be a bouncing ball, and it seems that no one can control the height that a ball will bounce, nor when it will come to a stop. The real estate financial markets are often compared to the stock market: uncontrollable, unpredictable, and volatile. Changes create opportunities and new programs for the mortgage loan broker.

The transition period from the late 1980s through 1990s reflected the reaction to the vast regulatory changes. As the various acts were implemented, the industry kept adjusting strategies on how to comply, yet stay competitive. Along the way, many existing loan representatives and firms ceased operation. Also, new firms emerged with technology aids to handle understaffed peak demands and formerly overstaffed nonpeak periods. In Figure 1.4, new home starts from 1993 to 2009 are shown in graph form that clearly depict the market downturn from 2006 to 2008. When demand decreases builders stop producing new units. The top line shows the total units, which include multi-family units. The bottom line is single-family homes.

While Figure 1.4 showed new home starts for both single-family homes and multifamily dwelling units from 1993 to 2009, over the long run the number of multifamily starts remained fairly constant up to 2005, while single-family home starts had more drastic fluctuations. Since 2006 both have drastically declined because of significantly lower prices for property, competition with existing foreclosures in the 2006-2010 marketplace, and lack of profit incentive to begin construction on residential projects.

Figure 1.5 shows the short-term view from only 2000 to 2005 for new housing starts. Single-family homes have averaged about 1,300 thousand units per year in the United States. During the same period, the total new units started in the United States have averaged about 1,600 thousand. Clearly, single-family

FIGURE 1.4   Housing starts for multifamily and single-family units.

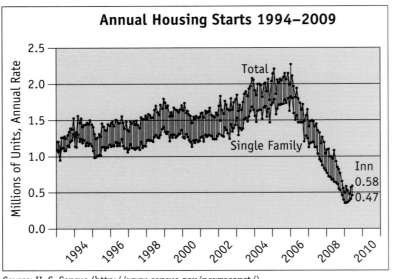

Source: U. S. Census (http://www.census.gov/newreconst/)

FIGURE 1.5   New housing units started in the United States, 2000-2005.

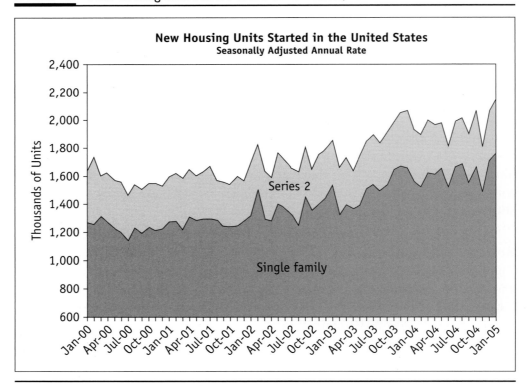

home units lead the total of new housing starts. This increases the supply-side inventory of housing stock and increases the number of future resale homes for real estate salespersons and new loan or refinance opportunities for the loan broker.

Today

As the real estate industry reaches the 21st century, lenders have become more competitive and specialized as a result of several factors: the real estate recession of the early 1990s, technology, and the market dominance of minority purchasers. Some lenders specialize exclusively in commercial shopping centers, such as http://www.clender.com, while others seek only less creditworthy borrowers, referred to as subprime lenders. As the government has tried to increase home ownership, new programs have emerged for the first-time homebuyer. This has led to loan professionals merging into firms with individuals who specialize in a particular type of loan. Firms employ multilingual loan agents to aid multicultural homebuyers.

Technology has also changed the way business is handled. Loan agents can now sit at a "for sale" open house with a real estate sales agent and take the loan application on their portable laptop computers, calculate the loan qualification ratios, and run a credit report, all without being at "the office."

The mortgage loan brokerage field now combines many aspects of the people-oriented real estate professional with the technical banking aspects to offer many career opportunities. As long as people need to borrow funds, loan arrangers will be in demand.

1.3 BASIC INFORMATION

Hard Money versus Seller Carryback Money

Hard money loans are deemed to be any institutional or noninstitutional loans for which the lenders placed their cash funds on the table in a transaction. The lenders' funds could be from their depositors, from the sale of their assets, or from funds borrowed against their assets. Private individuals, corporations, and investors may have a mortgage broker place his or her funds on a hard money, real estate-backed loan. The funds actually change hands, and upon default, the lenders could lose some or all of their cash, even if the property held as collateral were sold to try to retire the debt.

Because of the higher risk involved for certain types of loans, some hard money lenders place more weight on the equity in the property rather than the borrower. Typically residential loan investors rely most heavily on the borrower's ability to repay the loan. The LTV is often lower when relying only on the equity in the property. The lender must be able to show that the borrower has a reasonable chance to repay the loan. If the mortgage broker does not document that the borrower has a good chance of repaying the loan, the transaction could fall under the "predatory" lending rules, as discussed in Chapter 5.

A higher-than-normal yield may be demanded by hard money investors, over the rate they could receive in a safe and secured bank savings account to offset the higher risk and nonliquidity for real estate loans. However, all loans tend to revert to the normal yield for the specific type of loan, called market yield. This is the amount typical investors would pay in the market for the particular type of loan. The courts view these hard moneylenders as investors who gave up cash on the good faith expectation that the borrower would repay all funds.

Seller carryback loans, or soft money loans, are typically an extension of credit from a seller to a buyer. No funds are taken out of a bank account, nor are any assets sold to raise any capital to make the loan to the buyer. The loan amount may have been originated on the note for reasons other than banking or investor criteria. Often, these loans are made without the basic requirements that an institutional lender would use, such as a credit application, credit report, or property appraisal. In Chapter 15, "Math for Loan Agents," an example shows the benefit to the parties.

Some seller carryback loans may be generated to cover costs that the seller is initially paying for the buyer, such as an amount to buy down an interest rate, points, or loan fees. Seller carryback loans often have features such as more favorable terms. They typically do not have loan fees, loan origination points, prepayment penalties, and similar provisions, although they could have these. Mortgage insurance on the loan and similar items, if handled by a hard moneylender, would often result in the parties' being unable to qualify or obtain a loan.

After the close of escrow, seller carryback loans may be sold at a discount to a third party, who becomes the new lender beneficiary. The purchaser of the loan is usually a private individual termed the **holder in due course**. In a foreclosure procedure, should the sale proceeds fall short of covering all the loan amounts owed, the judicial system usually views hard money and seller carryback lenders differently. In case of default on any loan, it is very important for the borrower to consult a specialized real estate tax advisor to determine if there is any tax write-off or tax liability.

Careers in Mortgage Loan Brokerage

The various persons or entities who are involved in the real estate lending business at different stages of the loan process can appear confusing to the novice. Some individuals are licensed, while others are not required to have any state regulatory license. Most direct employees are not licensed and have very specific job duties and assignments according to a company policies and procedures manual. Licensed loan personnel are paid most often on a commission-only basis and are usually independent contractors, that is, his or her employing broker or business entity does not direct daily work activity. The licensee is compensated for the end result of having the loan accepted by the lender and the borrower, and the loan broker is not directed on the method of obtaining the loan. A contract and a sample copy of a policies and procedures manual for independent contractors are found in Appendix H and are discussed in Chapter 13, describing business operational practices.

A marketing department may have telemarketers, computer-generated form solicitation, advertising personnel, and key networking personnel. A loan processor may verify loan application information according to prescribed steps. This person or loan assistant may prepare computer-generated disclosure forms, credit reports, and work with title company records. The mortgage loan broker file must contain certified copies of escrow instructions obtained from the escrow officer; see Appendix D. The appraisal report must be ordered, as shown in Appendix E. Buyer's insurance information must be received.

An individual may be licensed by one or more government-regulated agencies. Those loan firms licensed by the California Department of Corporations (DOC) have different governing regulations, but they package loans in similar ways to DRE licensees to comply with secondary money market requirements. An individual licensed by the California DRE, such as a licensed real estate salesperson, must work under a licensed real estate broker. Both the broker and that salesperson may be an employee of a financial institution, such as a loan officer working for a bank. The institution is regulated by another form of government agency, such as the bank examiners and auditors who work for the Federal Reserve or the Office of the Comptroller of the Currency.

Loan Originators

The loan originators are those entities that solicit others to obtain applications for loans. **Loan originators** in California are usually DRE salesperson licensed real estate agents who create a loan in the normal course of their real estate activity while performing loan duties under a DRE broker. Some individuals are employees who work under a corporation commissioner-licensed office as described in Chapter 14 and may not need to be licensed by DRE.

Loan originators obtain the funds they loan from financial intermediaries, which fall into two groups: (as shown in Figure 1.6) Institutional lenders and noninstitutional lenders. Institutional lenders consist of commercial banks, life insurance companies, and thrifts. Commercial banks are places such as Bank of America, Chase, Citibank, Wells Fargo, and Union Bank. Life insurance companies are institutions such as New York Life Insurance Company, Prudential, Mutual of Omaha, Travelers, and Mutual of New York. Thrifts formerly were mainly savings and loan associations, but today they consist of savings banks, mutual savings banks, and credit unions. Noninstitutional lenders include mortgage loan bankers, mortgage loan brokers, investment companies, private individuals, nonfinancial institutions, and real estate investment trusts (REITS).

Loan originators predominantly fall into the following groups: (1) mortgage broker, (2) mortgage banker, (3) commercial banks or thrift institutions, (4) credit unions, and (5) loan correspondents. In Figure 1.7, only single-family residential loan originators are shown for only conventional loans with the Notes section explaining definitions for each category. The FHA, VA, and nonresidential lenders are not shown in this table. Note that in 1990, the savings and loans had above 40 percent of market share. After the market adjusted to the S & L crisis, after which many of these institutional lenders merged with other lenders or reformed as the new Thrift Institutes, their

FIGURE 1.6   Financial Intermediaries.

INSTITUTIONAL LENDERS:

1. Commercial banks
2. Life insurance companies
3. Thrifts
    a. Savings & loan associations
    b. Savings banks
    c. Mutual savings banks
    d. Credit unions

NON-INSTITUTIONAL LENDERS:

1. Mortgage loan banker
2. Mortgage loan broker
3. Investment company
4. Private individuals
5. Non-financial institutions
6. Real estate investment trusts (REITs)

market share was cut in half by 2000 to only about 20 percent. The commercial banks changed from just below 30 percent to about 20 percent of market share. Independent mortgage companies doubled market share by increasing from just above 10 percent to above 25 percent, which consists of mortgage brokers and mortgage bankers. Credit unions remained the same. The mortgage company subsidiaries, also known as loan correspondents, act as an in-state, direct lender from only one out-of-state investor, such as a life insurance company chartered in another state.

A mortgage banker acts much like a bank and receives revenue from the loan originator. Mortgage bankers may lend their own funds. They may also act as local, regional, or national representatives for an institutional lender. Thus, mortgage bankers may retain a loan in their own portfolio or they may transfer ownership of the loan to another. They may also sell the loan on the secondary money market to investors or to another lender. If they sell the loan, they generate funds to make more loans. The mortgage banker may retain the servicing of the loan so that the borrower often does not notice any difference. This also enables the mortgage banker to continue to receive ongoing revenue from loan-servicing fees.

Mortgage brokers do not lend any of his or her own funds. The mortgage broker is a party who connects a lender and a borrower, for which a fee is received. Many borrowers do not know that mortgage brokers often obtain wholesale rates that the borrower could not get directly from the same lender. A discussion of wholesale versus retail loans is found in Chapter 13. Many lenders cannot find an adequate number of borrowers at a particular time and welcome the mortgage broker for placing idle funds. A mortgage broker does not retain the loan servicing.

FIGURE 1.7 Mortgage-origination activity by lender type.

	Savings Institution	Commercial Bank	Mortgage Co. Subsidiary	Independent Mortgage Co.	Credit Union	**Total Volume**
	Market Share	Market Share	Market Share	Market Share	Market Share	($ Billions)
1999	21%	21%	29%	26%	3%	**962**
1998	23%	17%	30%	27%	2%	**1,165**
1997	25%	19%	26%	27%	3%	**632**
1996	25%	21%	25%	26%	3%	**558**
1995	25%	22%	25%	26%	2%	**447**
1994	26%	22%	19%	31%	2%	**536**
1993	22%	20%	19%	37%	2%	**834**
1992	40%	24%	19%	25%	2%	**610**
1991	33%	26%	17%	22%	2%	**341**
1990	41%	27%	18%	11%	3%	**268**

Lender Share of Single-Family Conventional Originations

Market share figures are based on annual dollar volume of residential loan origination reported under the Home Mortgage Disclosure Act (HMDA).

Savings institutions and *commercial banks* refer to federally regulated, deposit-taking institutions, or their service corporations, with assets exceeding an inflation-indexed, minimum threshold, which changes annually. The asset-level cutoff is set by the Federal Reserve Board based on changes in the consumer price index (CPI). The threshold was $28 million in 1997, $29 million in 1998 and 1999, $30 million in 2000, and $31 million for 2001.

Credit union refers to a federally regulated, deposit-taking institution that meets the asset and lending threshold tests for covered savings institutions and banks.

Mortgage company subsidiary refers to the mortgage-origination arm of the holding company for an HMDA-covered savings institution or bank when the parent company owns a minimum 50% interest in the subsidiary.

Independent mortgage company refers to a nondepository lender that (a) had assets, including those of parent corporation, exceeding $10 million (unadjusted for inflation) on the preceding Dec. 31 or (b) originated at least 100 home-purchase or refinancing loans in the preceding calendar year. (Before 1993, a small independent mortgage company with assets of $10 million or less was exempt from reporting to HMDA, even if it had originated 100 or more loans in the preceding year.)

Source: MBA.

From 1980 to 1995, mortgage bankers and brokers have dominated the single-family conventional market with between 35 percent and just under 60 percent of market share. Although thrift institutions reached a high of almost 40 percent in the mid 1980s, their market share has continued to decrease steadily to just about 15 percent of market share by the mid 1990s. Commercial banks hold a relative steady market share of about 20 percent; as Figure 1.8 indicates, savings institutions have decreased from about 40 percent to 20 percent of market share in the 1990s, while independent mortgage companies have grown from about 10 percent to almost 30 percent, and subsidiary mortgage companies have grown from under 20 percent to about one-third of the market.

FIGURE 1.8   Originators.

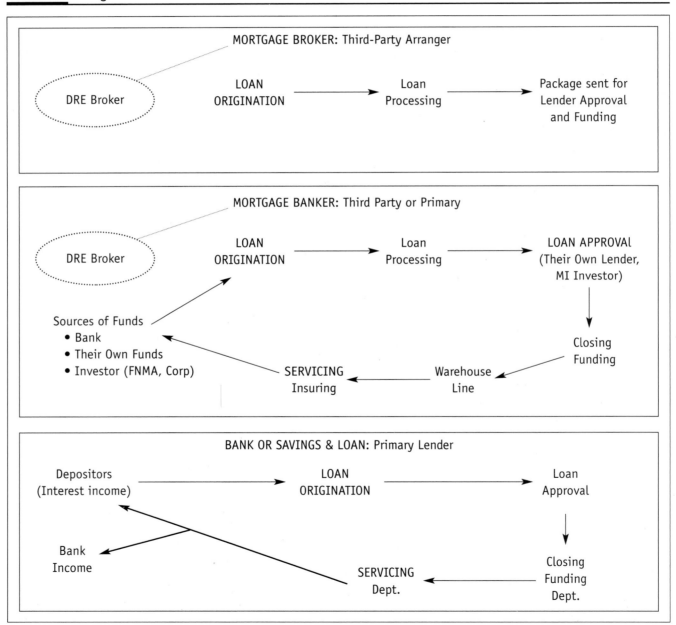

1.4 LICENSES AND PROFESSIONAL ORGANIZATIONS

Legal and Licensing Requirements

The loan business in involved with large amounts of money; thus, many regulations govern activities intended to protect the general public when borrowing funds. The California mortgage loan broker is regulated by the California DRE, which covers both the broker and the salesperson licenses. The mortgage company and mortgage banker may be licensed under the California DOC, such as the CFL, or may be an agent for a California institutional lender and fall under the banking regulations of the parent company. Both federal and state institutional lenders are heavily regulated, and their direct employees may handle loans where the individual as an employee of that firm may not be required to hold a government agency license. The details of license requirements are covered in greater detail in Chapter 14.

Professional Organizations

Real estate mortgage loan specialists have formed various local, state, and national trade associations. These associations go far beyond the mere social needs of its members to provide service in the areas of community outreach, educational courses, and the promotion of legislative interests affecting the business and political needs of the industry. These organizations establish codes of ethics to guide their members and to protect the public.

For more information on activities in the Mortgage Loan Business, you may wish to contact:

* California Association of Mortgage Brokers
  950 Glenn Drive, Suite 150
  Folsom, CA 95630
  Phone (916) 448-8236
  Fax (916) 443-8237
  http://www.cambweb.org
* National Association of Mortgage Brokers
  9700 West Park Drive, #T309
  McLean, VA 22101
  Phone (703) 342-5900
  Fax (703) 342-5905
  http://www.namb.org
* National Association of Professional Mortgage Women
  P.O. Box 140218
  Irving, TX 75014-0218
  Phone (800) 827-3034
  Fax (469) 524-5121
  http://www.napmw.org/

- Mortgage Bankers Association
  1331 L Street, NW
  Washington, DC 20005-2766
  Phone (202) 557-2700
  http://www.mbaa.org

SUMMARY

Lending practices go back to Roman times. Early U.S. loan activity was founded on traditions brought from Europe. Pioneer days had little real estate loan activity prior to the 1920s. Today, the loan business is heavily regulated by many different state and federal laws.

The lending industry views hard money as the primary market.

Private lender credit extension activity is viewed as the seller carryback market.

A loan arranger may be an individual agent, a principal, or a financial lending company. The originator is a third party to a real estate transaction, and is usually a broker. A common originator is the mortgage loan broker, who brings together a borrower and a lender for a fee. The mortgage loan banker may also be an originator, using its own funds or those of another. An originator may be able to locate funds from many sources, thus giving the borrower a better choice of various loan appointments. A mortgage loan banker may be able to make a loan on a property that is kept in the bank's own portfolio and not sold on the secondary money market, whereas the mortgage broker could not make the loan because it would not conform to the requirements of the secondary money market.

REVIEWING YOUR UNDERSTANDING

1. Loan originators predominantly fall into the following groups except:
   A. The mortgage broker
   B. The mortgage banker
   C. Commercial banks or thrift institutions
   D. Others

2. What was created as a consequence of the 1980 crash in the real estate market?
   A. California Mortgage Lending Act (CRMLA)
   B. Flood insurance requirements
   C. Requirement for mortgage Insurance for loans over 80% of value
   D. Depository Institutions Deregulation and Monetary Control Act (DIDMCA)

3. The term "holder in due course" is indicative of:
    A. Seller carryback loans may be sold at a discount to a third party, who becomes the new lender beneficiary
    B. Extension of credit from a seller to a buyer
    C. Loan tends to revert to the normal yield for the specific type of loan
    D. None of the above

4. In 2001, what act was enacted requiring the mortgage broker to obtain information about the borrower(s); driver's license (w/photo), social security card, passport, etc.?
    A. California Mortgage Lending Act
    B. Patriot Act
    C. RESPA
    D. HMDA

5. The first federal banking act that was passed is the:
    A. Federal Deposit Insurance Act
    B. Federal Reserve Act
    C. Federal Home Loan Bank Act
    D. Depository Institutions Deregulation and Monetary Control Act

6. Seller carryback loans are often referred to as:
    A. Investor loans
    B. Institutional loans
    C. Hard money loans
    D. Soft money loans

7. Which act limited housing revenue bond tax exemptions?
    A. Omnibus Reconciliation Act
    B. Financial Institutions Reform, Recovery and Enforcement Act (FIRREA)
    C. Home Mortgage Disclosure Act
    D. Community Reinvestment Act

8. The acronym "PP" stands for:
    A. People & Profit
    B. Pure Procrastination
    C. Patience & Persistence
    D. Practice makes Perfect

9. The primary reason for affiliation with a professional organization is to aid members in:
    A. Fulfilling social needs
    B. Keep common-interest groups together
    C. Meet educational, legislative, and political goals
    D. Make the public aware of the individual's level of education

10. Which of the following factors made lenders more competitive?
    A. Technology
    B. A real estate recession
    C. Specialization, such as dominance of minority purchasers
    D. All of the above

ANSWERS TO REVIEWING YOUR UNDERSTANDING

1. D (p. 19)   4. B (p. 12)   7. A (p. 11)   9. C (p. 23)
2. D (p. 11)   5. B (pp. 8-9)   8. C (p. 3)   10. D (p. 17)
3. A (p. 18)   6. D (p. 18)

Chapter

2

Affiliation media

Direct mail
  advertising

Federal Trade
  Commission (FTC)

Marketing

Networking group

Public Employees
  Retirement System
  (PERS)

Sources of Business

PREVIEW

Once the mortgage loan broker has become affiliated with a business operation and has completed some training, the main focus is on generating business. The entry-level person will want to concentrate on what will bring income to the individual. To accomplish this, the individual must know a great deal about marketing and advertising to solicit prospective borrowers. See http://marketplan.us/images/marketing_plan.pdf on "What is a marketing plan?" Initially, the key element to success will be the ability to get out and devise ways to obtain leads. This chapter concentrates on the various methods of marketing and discusses some legal requirements for advertising.

CHAPTER OBJECTIVES

At the end of this chapter, the student learning outcomes include:

1. Discuss marketing and advertising goals and image.
2. Identify the steps in the advertising process.
3. List the type of advertising media available for the mortgage loan broker.
4. Describe how advertising creates action.
5. Differentiate among various types of advertising.

2.1 GETTING STARTED

Many mortgage loan brokers come from real estate–related fields. Some come from banking, where they worked in servicing, processing, document preparation, or as a bank loan representative. Because the bigger financial institutions have more funds to spend on advertising, the employee loan representatives act more like order takers. Most new business came to the individual without much additional solicitation required. For this reason, many potential mortgage loan brokers are not successful, and they need to learn how to start over on their new business to realize their goals.

Other individuals enter the field from nonbanking positions. The most common of these is from the real estate sales field. Formerly acting as independent contractors, these individuals realize that even though some institutional advertising creates name recognition for the company, income results from the efforts of individual actions. Some people in this group come from escrow, title, appraisal, or similar fields relating to real estate. Initially, this group lacks the specifics of product knowledge of the various types of loans, but with good company training and concentrated study by the individual, it may be only a short time until the detailed skills of the mortgage loan brokerage business can be mastered.

With experienced loan brokers and bankers already in the industry, some people may feel that there is little chance for the novice to succeed. Nothing could be further from the truth. Because time changes all things, whatever the competition did yesterday to be successful will not be the formula for success tomorrow. Many experienced individuals do not continue to reinvent themselves, and they fall into ruts that eventually do not generate new business or income. New loan agents enter the business with enthusiasm and new ideas on *marketing* to new sets of buyers and cut a path through former marketing techniques to stand out on their own.

The study of the history of advertising shows that a very long time ago, a coat of arms was displayed to attract attention to the family, clan, or picture relating to the product. Then came town criers licensed to act as verbal signs, attracting attention to a business. The first written advertising was often placed on the walls of houses or on the windows of shops. Parts of the world still use these prebillboard forms by writing on walls, trees, buildings, and similar surfaces. Later, written newspaper advertising became the industry standard for marketing for many centuries. As people's reading interests focused, so did the campaigns that contributed to specialty magazines, the first large-scale attempt at marketing to a specific target market. With improvements in printing, photography, and graphics, the messages have been greatly enhanced. Radio added sound and television added motion to the message. Today, new advertising *media* include home page, Web boards, e-mail, and much more.

Marketing efforts transformed information from cold and matter-of-fact to dramatic human-interest characterizations. Campaigns are run in series using several types of media under the same theme. The public is inundated. Advertising sometimes became exaggerated. Along with this came a concerted effort and a series of laws for consumer protection in marketing under the **Federal Trade Commission (FTC)**, with established rigid rules regarding advertising and labeling. This has led to much of the current disclosure legislation, including the "do not call" list as the newest real estate business action to curtail use of the telephone in marketing and advertising campaigns.

Advertising effectiveness that led to today's methods came about largely because of the advertisement of a loan program begun in World War I. The outstanding effectiveness of the large-scale advertising campaign for the Federal Liberty Loan Program showed business people the new possibilities that could be accomplished through advertising. Some mortgage loan brokers still use these old methods but will not be as effective as the individual entering the loan brokerage business with new ideas, working with tomorrow's borrowers.

The world of technology is moving all business to new ways of reaching a specific target audience. At no time in history have marketers been better able to reach specific target markets than today. The census data and other government reports give specific information on the characteristics of groups of potential customers down to specific census tract areas. It is now possible to know the median age, average income, and buying characteristics of people in a particular area. When a loan broker works closely with a title company representative, the loan agent can obtain government and property record information in a format that is easier to use. The local title representative can furnish a property profile on a specific property. The title representative can also furnish a complete database file, usually referred to as a "farm" package, which can generate mailing labels and other useful items. Thus, new mortgage loan brokers should begin his or her marketing efforts by studying how to do research and real estate economics.

The new mortgage loan broker will also need to study computer technology. The ability for lenders and individual mortgage brokers to create his or her own home page allows the opportunity to give color, graphic, and photographic images to the world about the services, loan specialization areas, and things that make them stand out from the crowd. A list of facts, such as loan rates, will no longer be acceptable to obtain new business. Very personalized, professional messages can span the globe, which creates the need for the mortgage loan broker to study the basics of foreign languages and multicultural studies to meet the needs of tomorrow's consumers. For many loans today, the applicant is local but the cosigner is in another part of the United States or in another country.

The person who enters the field today can cut a path through the competition. To stand out from the existing lenders who keep doing things the way they have always done them, the new loan representative needs to market to today's buyers. Many of the borrowers whom the existing loan representatives formerly marketed to will no longer seek any new loan. This audience often consists of those who are retired, live in senior housing, live or travel in a motor home. Some live with children who will qualify and obtain a new loan. Many new loan applicants are first-time home buyers who have been raised on MTV and computer graphics. They expect the mortgage loan broker to use technology. The loan representative who comes to the applicant's home will perform the following with a portable laptop computer:

- type the borrower's credit information into the computer.
- run the credit report on the spot.
- determine credit rating (see "B" paper information at the end of Chapter 4).
- pull up a list of loan types for which the borrower would qualify.
- print a comparison of the various loan types, contrasting down payment, monthly payment, ratios, closing costs such as points, and similar loan options.
- print the URLA 1003, which loan applicant and loan broker agree on for signatures and submittal to the lender.

- do a database computer search for comparables to support the requested loan-to-value (LTV).
- transmit by computer the comparable sales and 1003 to the lender for submission with loan documents.

2.2 MARKETING

Marketing is any type of message that promotes communication of a product, service, or idea. For many mortgage loan brokers, the only way to reach potential loan applicants is to direct communications to specific target groups of individuals with common or similar characteristics. To increase business, it is important to create interest by gaining public recognition for the company name. The lenders create the image of the financial institution to make the individual mortgage loan broker who handles the loans better gain access to potential customers, called leads.

From the time the contact is made, however, it is important for the individual to be well trained on how to respond to leads that are provided by the company. Types of media are discussed in depth below, but the emphasis must be first placed on the training of the loan representative or loan consultant to be ready to handle the activity, which begins by clearing away trivial busy work from one's mind and desk to be ready to access new contacts. Practice on responding to new business also helps build confidence about the ability to handle new business professionally, making for effective use of advertising dollars spent to create business.

In addition to the company creating opportunities to obtain new business, the individual must know the image created for himself or herself. A business would flounder from one idea to another, jumping around between many concepts. Individuals who do not have a business degree may not know how to develop a business plan, a marketing plan, an advertising budget, or a financial forecast. Each of these may be found by using an Internet search engine for the topic to locate thousands of resources. A Web page for a business plan was developed by the founder of the Yum-Yum Donut Company, found at *http://www. myownbusiness.org,* which has a test for an individual to take to aid in making business decisions. Without a strong foundation, most individuals would not know how to put together a marketing plan, advertising budget, or financial forecast. Study the methods used by big business to promote a product and try to follow the same successful steps. If you cannot create your own campaign to have a successful image in the business, hire a professional who specializes in image advertising to assist you from the beginning. The goal is to make you generate business. It may be a wise investment to spend a little extra initially to create a positive public image, with name recognition for you and your company. A sample letter, prompted by the laws prohibiting telephone solicitation, is shown in Figure 2.1, to be sent to persons on the "do not call" list.

Start with the five W's. *Who* is your target market; who are you trying to reach? Be specific about income level, age group, industry in which they work, area in which they would want to obtain a loan, and similar groupings. *What* is

FIGURE 2.1   Letter to "do not call" list.

Company Logo

PLEASE CALL ME because I think that I can help you.

With the federal "do not call" list in effect, I am not able to contact you directly, so **PLEASE CALL ME** at my toll-free number, (800) 555-1212, ext. 105, because I think that I can help you in your current financial situation.

If you are receiving unwanted calls from others, please let me assist. You may visit the Web site of www.donotcall.gov or phone 1-888-283-4236 to register your number. California consumers, under federal law, may register to be placed on the list. It is illegal for most telemarketers to call your number after you have registered.

I hope you will let me help you in many other ways, especially for your real estate and loan finance needs. I can only do this if **YOU** take a moment to pick up the phone and call me so that we can put our heads together to resolve your present challenge. With more than 20 years of experience in helping people with their financial needs, I look forward to the opportunity of helping you.

I have money for you to use now, so please call me.

Thank you for your time.

Respectfully,

Buzz Chambers, Mortgage Broker – DRE license #123456789

the product you have to offer? Be specific about the types of loans you actually know and for which you can obtain funds to close. If you are concentrating on doing fewer loans and working the high-end properties with a view or at the beach, you should not spend a lot of time and money to learn about how to package low-end loans. *Where* are your clients? If you determine that you want to work with government employees because you have heard about loan programs that use retirement funds, such as the **Public Employees Retirement System (PERS)**, and you do not know anyone who works for the government, it may be difficult for you to be successful. Why would anyone want to do business with your firm? *Why* would anyone want the type of loan you can offer? Why would someone do business with you? *When* does your *lead* want to act? Some prospects want to know what they will qualify for after they sell their home. Thus, you need to prioritize your time to maximize your efforts in the scarce time available. After the initial prequalification, the mortgage loan broker needs to work with prospects ready to act now, rather than waiting for their home to sell. Know when the borrower wants to take action.

If you cannot answer these questions, you will probably have no loan applicants. Make a list of as many positive features for each of these points as you can. They may be the central core of your new marketing campaign. When can you give good service? Are you a struggling beginner on a part- time basis? Are you available nights and weekends? If real estate licensees call you to prequalify his or her prospective buyers, are you ready to go to work for them, *now*?

The marketing process is a step-by-step analysis of how to outline the objectives of your *promotional campaign* to gain results. The first step is to select the goal by listing the end result you would like to obtain. Goal setting must contain specific, measurable items that have concrete timelines tied to each. A goal stating that the mortgage loan broker will close one loan every week is far better than one saying that the mortgage loan broker hopes to get some loans soon.

The second step involves establishing your target market. It is unwise to try to solicit the world or to have a vague goal of trying to market to everyone. Tunnel down by using a set of filters. Start by making a list of your personal successes and interests and concentrate on people who relate to these, which will include your strongest personality traits and characteristics. It will also include a list of your hobbies, pastimes, sports interests, and similar activities. Next, list the characteristics of the group of people who best relate to you. Include his or her level of education, interests, and activities. Match the areas that are similar to find where to concentrate your efforts. Then identify these types of individuals or groups as your target audience and specialize on this segment.

While completing the second step, the successful mortgage loan broker also needs to identify two other areas; one is the *competition*, the other is the specific area in which your business will concentrate. If everyone is soliciting to the same market, then your efforts will not stand out from the crowd. If you find a *market niche* that few loan brokers are targeting, then you increase your chances for success. For example, if you target recent college graduates who completed studies in construction technology or architecture, the competition may be marketing first-time home-buyer programs to these individuals. You, however, may get the loan because instead you discuss the various loans that allow construction financing so the borrower can get a fixer-upper and be able to finance remodeling costs.

The third step is to select the media that are most appropriate for your target audience. Part 2.4 of this chapter details each type, but remember that the goal is to reach the greatest number of people who will do business with you. If the wrong media are used, the target market will not be reached, so the mortgage loan broker's goals will not be met. Research the appropriate media to use for your audience. If you want to reach young Latino families, it would be unwise to advertise in an English newspaper that has a subscriber audience of non-Latino senior citizens.

The fourth step is to design the actual marketing plan. An Internet search engine with the caption "How to Develop a Marketing Plan" will yield thousands of sites to explore. See Chapter 13 for more details. A set of steps that will accomplish your goals must be laid for each part of your marketing plan, which usually involves deciding the media to use, selecting a slogan for your marketing campaign, designing the messages, and implementing some form of end evaluation to determine the effectiveness of your efforts. The entire campaign must end with a call for action.

2.3 ADVERTISING

Advertising has many purposes. In basic real estate principles courses, the mortgage loan broker learns that AIDA is the acronym used for advertising, using the following:

*A*ttention. The ad image must attract attention to your media advertising.

*I*nterest. The media ad must stimulate enough interest to keep the viewer attentive to the balance of the image you created.

*D*esire. The ad must create desire in the product or services you offer.

*A*ction. The goal of the campaign is to make the customer act.

The ultimate aim of advertising is to increase your business. The following is a list of the various reasons for advertising:

- *To get nearer to the customer.* In this case, the mortgage loan broker would want a booth at the local REALTOR® trade fair and at the local city street fair to talk directly with the public and with people in the industry who refer loans.

- *To create interest and desire on the part of the prospective applicant.* Recent *television advertising* has seen Fannie Mae making direct appeals to the general public. Large franchise firms advertise on national television. The mortgage loan broker with a lesser budget can still use mass media recognition with local cable television and local radio stations.

- *To create demand.* Instead of relying solely on real estate sales agents to refer business to the mortgage loan broker, it is wise to create and extend services directly to the public. This is especially true if you have identified that your efforts will be primarily for refinances or for construction and equity loans in which intermediaries may not be involved.

- *To familiarize the customer with your services.* A borrower may have an existing loan that has a higher interest and should be refinanced at a lower rate. Direct mail to reference the existing loan may trigger action by the consumer based on your campaign. Figure 2.2 shows a door hanger that is a general ad inviting potential customers to call a telephone number for additional information.

- *To stress the exclusive features of your services.* Any bank or savings and loan is able to make loans. All mortgage loan brokers and bankers are in the business to make loans. What distinguishes you from your competition?

This is where specialization in a market niche is most important. If you make loans on half-acre to one-acre properties for which the value is not greatly increased because of the large amount of land, advertising in *The Truck Stop News* might increase your business if truck owners are looking for a place to park their

FIGURE 2.2   Door hanger.

big rigs. The key is to determine what you do differently and let the world know you offer that service.

- *To fill needs that change with styles and customs.* Most of the advertising world has planned obsolescence. Many homes offered for sale are dated by the color of the carpet and style of many features of the homes, especially in the kitchen and bath areas. The mortgage loan broker who recognizes that people would like to have modern looks but do not know how to finance the improvements could target the home improvement loan market, such as is shown in Figure 2.3. A brochure showing "before" and "after" shots of kitchens summarizing the little amount of cash out of pocket, the low monthly payments, and the increased tax advantage may generate new business opportunities.

- *To get leads to enter your place of business.* The reason so many mortgage loan broker firms have such gala open houses is to get the real estate community to know where the business is located and to literally get them in the door.

- *To offer "leaders" to generate business.* Lenders often offer "no points" and "no costs" loans to attract business. The problem is that only the best borrowers qualify for these low- or no-cost loans, as seen in Figure 2.4. The bulk of the

FIGURE 2.3   Remodel ad.

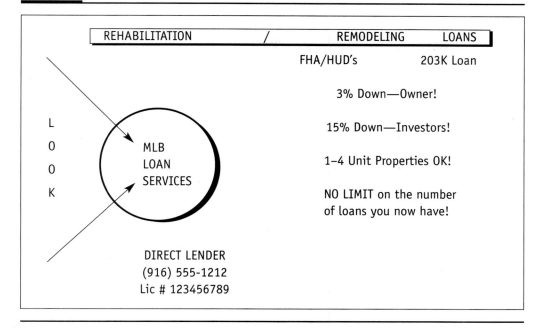

people with lesser credit ratings make contact with the firm and do generate loans for the company at higher rates and terms.

- *To assist newcomers.* In retail business, the welcome wagon offered discounts to local businesses when a new family came into the area. In the mortgage loan broker business, new agents come into offices on a regular basis. Most

FIGURE 2.4   Leader ad.

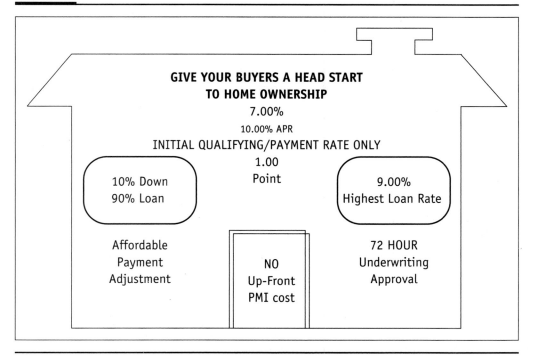

FIGURE 2.5   Licensee training ad.

```
┌─────────────────┐   JOIN OUR BREAKFAST CLUB
│  ATTENTION      │   LEARN AND EARN—FREE !!
│  NEW AGENTS     │
└─────────────────┘

At MLB Loan Services we've learned that for many new agents, the FIRST-TIME HOME-
BUYER market is their bread and butter. No one has more experience with First-Time
Buyers than we do. Join us at The Breakfast Club so that together we can turn bread
and butter into steak! Bring a Friend. (916) 555-1212 for reservations.
```

new agents do not understand that the key to successful sales conclusions is knowing financing. Thus, many mortgage loan brokers offer free classes and training to teach the newcomers the details on programs that the lender is offering, as shown in Figure 2.5.

- *To create goodwill.* Some lenders do not mention any particular type of loan program but simply show certain policies or statements about the company to create goodwill on the part of the public. These ads say things like "Our savings & loan has assets of over $1 trillion."

- *To get a list of prospects.* This is usually where the mortgage loan broker or banker offers to send a free booklet of information concerning loan qualification, home ownership, or types of loans available. The purpose is to get the names of persons who have expressed an interest or desire for more knowledge about your services. The names of persons answering such advertisements are called leads.

- *To prepare the way for the salesperson.* The ultimate goal of the marketing efforts and advertising campaigns is to close loans; the actual sale is usually completed by the salesperson. The purpose of advertising is to pave the way so that the work of the salesperson will be easier and more productive than it would have been without the marketing. The intent is that the advertising has prepared the way for the salesperson to close the sale. Figure 2.6 says "For REALTOR® use only" to introduce information to a target market before the mortgage loan broker does a follow-up call.

- *To emphasize a name or slogan.* The object is to make the name, symbol, or slogan so well known to the public and the industry that when a loan is needed, your name will unconsciously come to mind. Name recognition is important.

- *To increase the relationship to a line of products.* Many banks, savings and loans, insurance companies, and the like have funds available to borrowers. Consumers and industry know to seek these lenders out to obtain new first loans when handling a purchase. However, these same lenders often offer many types of secondary financing of which consumers are not aware. A mortgage loan broker could merely market to existing borrowers to increase opportunities to create new business.

- *To increase activity during off-season periods.* The typical sales period has historically run from Easter or Memorial Day through Labor Day. To generate more activity during the winter, a mortgage loan broker might specialize in refinances, loan consolidations, or the like.

FIGURE 2.6 Preparation ad.

MLB Loan Services
Presents

THE **BIG** LOAN

**A fixed rate jumbo loan with competitive rates,
large loan limits, and a variety of processing styles.**

- Loan amounts to $2,000,000
- 10- to 30-year terms in 5-year increments
- LTV's as high as 90%
- Ratios as high as 33/38
- Temporary and permanent buydowns available
- No income (quick) processing available

Call your local MLB Broker Services representative for current rates.

- *To introduce a new service.* New loan programs have recently been enacted that allow agents to offer new programs to prospective borrowers. Each new program has a specific set of guidelines that must be followed. Once these qualifications are mastered through training on the new program, the mortgage loan broker can run massive marketing efforts to boast the benefits of and availability of the new loan, as seen in Figure 2.7.
- *To urge hesitating prospects to take action.* A flurry of activity in sales always generates the rumor that rates are going up or that the market has turned and that you had better buy now at the current rates and market conditions before things get worse. Newspaper headlines generate the illusion of highs and lows.

FIGURE 2.7 Specific loan ad.

ATTENTION PERS MEMBERS!

Are you trying to buy a home but short on the down payment?

Would "PERS **100%" FINANCING**" help you?
(95% PERS Fixed Rate 1st Loan + 5% Personal Loan)

CALL MLB LOAN SERVICES at (916) 555-1212

PERS offers:

Competitive Interest Rates

60-Day Rate Lock with Float-Down Feature

Limited Fees

2.4 OTHER SOURCES OF BUSINESS

Referrals from REALTORS®

It is common that licensed real estate agents constantly need to work closely with a mortgage loan agent to prequalify the numerous contacts made with the public. Some agents have the loan agent accompany them to an open house so that prospective clients can have practically on-the-spot loan preapproval. Figure 2.8 shows a referral letter to thank the agent for the business. The second page of the form can be customized to your particular taste on the various areas of needs.

FIGURE 2.8   Agent referral letter.

Company Logo

Date

Name
Address
City, Zip

RE: Thank you!

One of the best ways to build any business is through referrals from those with whom we work in the business. But I know that when dealing with the business of life, it is easy to forget to make such connections. I have included a memory jogger with some suggested categories that hopefully will increase your business. In the past, these have made good referrals for me. If any names occur to you, please just jot them down and fax this sheet back to me at **(800) 555-1212** or furnish me your e-mail address so I can send you the form online for easy fill-in and return.

I've also included some of my business cards for you to have on hand. I believe I also need to keep your business card in my file for those clients who contact me directly. Perhaps you can pass along my cards to your friends, coworkers, or family members when you are thinking about real estate loans. As you know, my business is built on referrals from satisfied customers and agents who have the trust and confidence that I can close their loan.

Again, thank you so very much for the trust and confidence you have shown in selecting me for your real estate loan assistance. Hopefully, there will be many more opportunities for us to work together so I can help in your continued success.

Sincerely,

Loan Agent Name, DRE license #123456789

FIGURE 2.8   (*Continued*)

I'm expanding my business and I need your help.
Please fax or e-mail your referrals to: (800) 555-1212 or my name@getloan.com

Who do you know who . . .   Name   Phone

Is getting ready to retire?   _____ (____)_____

Has owned a home over 3 years?   _____ (____)_____

Just had a baby?   _____ (____)_____

Just got a promotion?   _____ (____)_____

Earns over $ 70,000 a year?   _____ (____)_____

Has a child going to college?   _____ (____)_____

Talked about refinancing?   _____ (____)_____

Referrals from Other Sources

Referrals from lenders and referrals to lenders is a common practice. This area would include banks, loan brokers, appraisers, escrow companies, title representatives, and similar tradespeople who work within the peripheral of the real estate industry and have contact with the public who inquire about obtaining financing. A divorce attorney, probate/estate attorney, and Certified Public Accountant (CPA) tax preparer would each be a referral source. There are various laws prohibiting the payment between the parties for referral fees in some of the business dealings. In other practices there is no prohibition. The mortgage loan broker must ask the other source the rules of their field of practice.

Referrals from the Public

The highest compliment a mortgage loan broker can receive is when a client refers a friend to you for a loan, which naturally requires a written thank-you to acknowledge that the friend is being assisted with loan information. A sample client referral letter is shown in Figure 2.9.

Testimonial

Many past clients are often happy to attest to the excellent job you have performed for them. When a difficult loan closes, it is a good time for you to have

FIGURE 2.9   Client referral letter.

Company Logo

Date

Name
Address
City, Zip

RE: Thank you!

Dear [Name of past client]:

Thank you so very much for your referral of [Name of person referred]. I respect the trust and confidence that this represents and just wanted you to know how much it is appreciated. As you know, I base the largest part of my entire business on direct recommendations from satisfied clients and other active professionals.

You may need a few more of my business cards, which I am enclosing. Perhaps you will consider passing them along to other friends, coworkers, or family members when they discuss real estate loans or financing. I'd really appreciate the opportunity to earn your continued confidence, and theirs.

Again, thank you for your referral. I hope to be able to have the continued opportunity to answer questions you and your friends may have, in addition to being the resource for an actual loan. Hopefully, there will be many more transactions with you as you continue with your success.

Sincerely,

Loan Agent Name, DRE Lic # 123456789

---

your client write comments in his or her own words as a testimonial for your ability to solve problems and finish the loan. However, any time you use the name of a client, it requires a written authorization release. Figure 2.10 shows a sample form.

2.5 TYPES OF MEDIA

Affiliation

Affiliation media are sometimes referred to as tie-ins because they tie to or connect with other business operations. The mortgage loan broker who is an active member of the Chamber of Commerce, with the Apartment Association, with the Escrow Association, will generate more people in the industry for referral contacts. Much of the mortgage loan business is generated from the sales agent, the insurance agent, or other non-real estate business ties. Networking groups

FIGURE 2.10   Testimonial release.

I, _____, do hereby authorize Mortgage Loan Broker Services (MLB) to use the statement below as a testimonial to their services. The information submitted may be used by MLB to market and promote loan business in any advertising media that it sees fit to use. I specifically release MLB from any and all liabilities regarding the use of this testimonial. I also understand that there is no monetary compensation.

I declare that all information on this document is true and correct to the best of my knowledge.

_____   ___/___/___
Signature   Date

_____   ___/___/___
Signature   Date

Testimony: _____

_____

_____

_____

_____

are becoming increasingly popular, such as Toastmasters, Mastermind groups, or Soroptimists. The mortgage loan broker would do well to check the local newspaper for meeting dates and locations in your area.

Billboards, Benches, Buses

Name recognition or awareness is best when displayed on very large exterior written signage, and the key is for the company name and telephone number to be very large. The reader should be able to remember the information while traveling at about 40 miles per hour when passing the sign. Lots of details are unnecessary, so fine print should be eliminated. An 800 number or an easily identifiable number is important, such as a telephone number that spells out "M-O-N-E-Y-4-U" or "E-Z-L-O-A-N-S." In addition, the mortgage loan broker may wish to consider similar items such as posters, painted bulletins, and similar ads such as shopping center kiosks. Figure 2.11 shows such an ad.

FIGURE 2.11   Name recognition ad.

GMAC

Your Affordable Housing Lender

(800) 555-GMAC

Committed to making the dream of homeowner a reality!

Direct Advertising

This type includes all those forms of advertising that are addressed to prospects individually. It differs from other media forms because it is not directed at mass, general, public consumer groups. Specific material is placed in the hands of designated individuals who are deemed to have a potential need for the mortgage loan broker's services. The material may include flyers to real estate agents, letters to people who have existing loans that may be refinanced at a lower rate, or to upper-end renters who likely could afford to buy. An example is shown in Figure 2.12, which appears to be an official government letter, yet is merely a loan broker using several government agencies' data to solicit homeowners for common, existing loan programs. The letter uses mail merge for the property owner's name and the property address. This type of letter is meant to lead the readers to believe they qualify for a special type of government loan program.

Direct Mail Advertising

Direct mail advertising is carried on through the mails, such as U.S. Postal Service, FedEx, or private mail delivery services. Because the mail system is subject to many regulations, the campaign must conform to the mail requirements. The message can be timed to reach the customer at a particular time, such as when property or income taxes are due or at Christmas. You pay only for the talking to prospects you want to reach in the language they understand on a more personal basis that extends your personality beyond the limits of impersonal contact. Mailing lists are sold that identify specific target markets. Figure 2.13 illustrates a direct mail letter.

Internet

In the age of technology the mortgage broker should have a Web page, which can be an excellent means of staying in contact with previous clients and advertising to new potential clients.

Magazines

A wide variety of magazines, catering to the different interests and tastes of the public, are published in millions of copies every month. General, class, trade, technical, or professional magazines are published weekly, bimonthly, monthly,

FIGURE 2.12   Direct advertising letter.

<u>FAIR LENDING REVIEW CENTER</u>
Phone 1 (800) 555-1212   OFFICIAL BUSINESS

Second Notice

                                        Eligibility Number: LLGOV-7711-MAR

John G. and Mary S. Martinez
7711 Pleasant Drive
Anytown, USA

Your property at 7711 Pleasant Drive may be eligible for specific government-sponsored loan programs from a government-sponsored institution, such as the Federal Housing Administration, the Veterans Administration, Fannie Mae, Freddie Mac or Ginnie Mae. Your census tract is currently being targeted by our Fair Lending Review Center for loans from major depository institutions without the usually restrictions on credit history, income, or employment status.

If you are the legal property owner of the above property, you may benefit from the above-cited government approved lending programs created by such Federal Agencies such as Fannie Mae (established in 1938) and Freddie Mac (established in 1970).

If you are not the legal owner, please forward this official notice immediately to the owner or return to the sender so official business contact may be made through an alternative method of delivery.

The legal owner of 7711 Pleasant Drive may benefit from lower monthly payments, cash out, fixed-rate loans, home-improvement funds, and elimination of mortgage insurance and cash out through a refinance loan.

If you have not taken advantage of this program within the past ninety days through an assigned Fair Lending Specialist for Anytown, please contact the local business office at:

1 (800) 555-1212

or visit the official secure Web site at www.OfficialFairLoans.com and reference your eligibility number as shown above.

Our records indicate that you have not responded to our previous attempts to notify you of your eligibility. You must contact us on or before the first of the next calendar month or you may lose your eligibility status.

This product or service has not been approved or endorsed by any government agency, and this offer is not being made by any agency of the government.
P.S.: When applying online, you will be provided a FREE copy of your credit report for allowing us to compute your monthly savings, your FICO credit score, and your qualifying loan ratios. Note: Consult your tax, legal, and real estate advisory. Official Fair Loans is licensed by the California Department of Corporations under CRMLA as a mortgage loan banker, state license #BRBR-5551212.

FIGURE 2.13 Direct mail letter.

Phone: (916) 555-1212   *MLB Loan Services*   Fax: (916) FAX-1212
                                    555 Sacramento Avenue
                                    Sacramento, California

January 2, 2XXX

Dear Investor,

   You have been hard to reach over the holidays so I have compiled a list of loans we currently have available for investments. I am looking forward to giving you more detailed information on any of the loans that interest you. If you do not find anything on the list, just call and let me know what loan type you are looking for. After I better understand your investment needs, I will be better able to immediately contact you with opportunities that fit your guidelines.

<u>Commercial</u>

- 1st Mortgage
- 55% LTV
- Loan amount = $ 520,000; $ 500K available
- Office building, owner-occupied + 2 tenants
- 15,000 SF lot with 6,000 SF improvements

- 14% Interest
- 3-Year term
- Borrower has strong income
- $100,000 Recent office remodel
- Adjacent 28,000 SF lot sold for $ 1 Mil

<u>Residential</u>

- 1st Mortgage
- 44% LTV
- Loan amount = $ 800,000
- Single-family resident on large lot
- Anytown location

- 13% Interest
- 2-Year term
- Excellent credit
- Purchase money loan
- Borrower bringing in cash $$$

<u>Residential Apartments</u>

- 1st Mortgage
- 62.5% LTV
- Loan amount = $ 750,000; $100K available
- 5 Units (1 house + 4-plex)
- Prestigious location

- 12.25% Interest
- 5-Year term
- $ 5,200 Gross monthly income
- Borrower has owned since 1975
- Only 1% vacancy in over 20 years

   Thanks for taking the time to look over these excellent investment opportunities. These loans will be sold quickly, so call soon for details at 1 (800) 555-1212.

Sincerely,

D. Grogan
Account Executive, DRE lic # 123456789

P.S.: Tell your friends about our services and we will thank you with a referral gift.

or quarterly. Detailed descriptions of the magazine's circulation are available to compare to the audience the mortgage loan broker is trying to reach. An ad in a home decorating magazine showing new kitchen cabinet fronts may be a good place to advertise the financing for a loan that could be used to accomplish completion of the remodel. Excellent advertising media sources would include newsletters such as, to name a few examples, those found at various homeowner associations (HOA), in sports publications such as golf and cycling, or in religious bulletins.

News Releases

If a firm has a favorable reputation and is a known name, prospects will make inquiries. The real estate sales agent has enough problems educating buyers with information that doing business with your firm is one fewer struggle if your name recognition alone gets an applicant's approval to begin processing a loan from the time of prequalification, referred to in the business as "prequal." Thus, regular press releases about you and your firm build a favorable image. The item submitted must have genuine news value, be correctly prepared, and meet the guidelines of the paper. The information should be keyboarded and double-spaced and include a picture, if possible. The material should include information on who, what, where, why, and how. Review other press releases in the paper to which you are submitting your ad to determine the desired format.

Newspapers

Publishers will have some type of information about their audience. Before purchasing ad space, be sure to research the subscribers. Weekend or daily papers constitute the largest segment of printed advertising. Present-day newspapers have something of interest to every member of the family. The mortgage loan broker could run ads that market to all segments of the family. Remodel loans showing the kids playing basketball with Dad could say "We got our loan with XXX to play hoops on our own court" to entice family members into helping the decision makers call about a construction or remodel loan. An ad showing a person in a graduation cap and gown getting into a new car with a big bow around it could say "Dad used his home and a loan with XXX to give me a big start in life" to solicit refinance or equity loans. Showing the benefits after obtaining the loan may be more important in picture advertising than listing the features of a particular loan.

Office Supplies

Letterhead stationery and envelopes, message pads, and business cards are all forms of advertising. They should reflect good taste and honest advertising and include the firm's logo, photograph of the loan agent, designated broker, and any company motto or slogan. The quality of the paper and printing is a strong part of the image for both the company and the mortgage loan broker.

Promotional Materials

There is only limited value to the purchase of pens, pencils, calendars, date books, newsletters, key chains, coffee cups, baseball caps, and similar items that bear the company name and logo. The mortgage loan broker is attempting to keep his or her name and phone number readily available and in front of the real estate agent or other user. If mass-distributed blindly, there seems to be little benefit for this advertising expense. But if limited to the target market audience, greater return is given and real advertising value may be realized.

Radio

Stations have identified their target market, just as newspapers have information on their audience. Most radio stations have set their programming into classifications such as music, drama, education, talk show/audience participation, news, or sports. The mortgage loan broker company records may indicate the characteristics of previous borrowers. This information can be used to match with the radio stations that have the same audience.

REALTORS®

A large source of business will come from licensed real estate agents who specialize in the sale of homes or from contractors who build to sell to the public. The mortgage loan broker must spend a great deal of time to develop ties with the real estate community. This may mean holding seminars in real estate offices to educate the agents, availability for quick turnaround time for prequalifications, joining the agent at an active open house to give loan information to prospects, or making a long-term commitment to the office management to establish an ongoing relationship with the office.

Telemarketing

A mortgage loan broker who is skilled in the use of the telephone can achieve success despite interest rates, the competition, or current market conditions because of the diverse kinds of loans that are available. The mortgage loan broker should prepare and organize before telephoning. Practice is needed to develop the skills that will increase sales. A written presentation should be developed with a prepared script and a list of common objections with positive responses. Developing good listening skills and gaining education on both effective communications and improving your speech are recommended for success. The various telephone carriers have specialists that can aid the mortgage loan broker in telephone skills. Figure 2.14 describes one example of the steps necessary to prepare a script to increase profits by using prospecting by phone; Figure 2.15 is an example of lead-in dialogue that may be developed as part of your actual telephone script. The loan agent might use the information as a guide when talking to potential clients about reducing credit card debt to help them qualify for a loan at a future date.

Television

Commercial television in the past held advertising captive with high prices to reach mass audiences. In the future, however, many alternatives will be more affordable. A local cable station may televise an educational presentation should the

FIGURE 2.14   Preparing a telephone script.

Step 1: Precall Planning:
    1. Establish criteria for screening prospects.
        Motivation. Why is the prospect considering a loan?
        Procurement time. Rate which loan type is fastest and easiest.
        FHA, VA, assumption, conventional, equity second, notice of default (**NOD**)
    2. Develop a list of prospects.
        What is the typical financing on the average home in your area?
        What are the socioeconomic/political/psychological profiles of
        area borrowers?
    3. Prepare an opening statement.
        Identify yourself and your firm.
        Establish rapport with the prospect.
        Make an interest-creating comment. Has the prospect been prequalified?
    4. Prepare fact-finding questions.
        How soon does the prequal applicant want to act?
        Use open-ended questions. Would the prospect like to be prequalified?
    5. Prepare your sales message.
        Deliver your message.
        Give information on several available loan programs.
    6. Prepare your request for an appointment.
        Ask for an appointment.
        Overcome objections.
        Confirm the appointment.
        Express your thanks.

mortgage loan broker be able to conduct a "first-time home buyer seminar" with some how-to's, available programs, and a small audience question format. Because you know your target market is interested in housing, placing an ad before, during, or after a related programmed show may be very effective, such as a "home improvement" or "fixer-upper seminar" or "how to buy a house using other people's money" seminar. Many specialized stations are available with real estate having its own REALVISION. Stations for real estate agents including educational seminars should have mortgage loan broker advertisers. Investigation into the numerous choices available will help mortgage loan brokers consider how to include some of these types of media into the marketing plan now and in the future.

Trade Shows

An excellent location for a loan booth is in an area in which related businesses are marketing to the general public. Most geographic locations have large home improvement shows, gardening shows, and construction/building shows. The people attending these shows will need financing to accomplish their desired goals. Broad, general information brochures that contain loan prequalification for later contact on a more personal basis are probably best when marketing to the general public. Business trade shows such as the local real estate trade fairs develop leads

FIGURE 2.15   Script dialogue.

PHONE SCRIPT FOR CREDIT CARD DEBT.....

I HAVE INFORMATION THAT **YOU** HAVE A LARGE AMOUNT OF CONSUMER CREDIT CARD DEBT. I MAY BE IN A POSITION TO HELP YOU MAXIMIZE YOUR INCOME TAX BENEFITS. WOULD YOU GIVE ME A MOMENT OF YOUR TIME?

WHAT IF I COULD LOWER YOUR MONTHLY PAYMENT ON YOUR CREDIT CARD DEBT?

WOULD YOU LIKE TO ELIMINATE YOUR CREDIT CARD DEBT?

I AM IN A POSITION TO HELP YOU TO REDUCE YOUR DEBT AND MAXIMIZE YOUR TAX BENEFITS. MAY I HAVE 90 SECONDS OF YOUR TIME?

THE INFORMATION THAT I CAN FURNISH **YOU** COULD SAVE YOU A LOT OF MONEY NOW AND IN THE FUTURE. MAY I HAVE 90 SECONDS OF YOUR TIME?

THE INFORMATION I HAVE FOR YOU IS WORTH MONEY TO YOU.

THE INFORMATION I HAVE WILL SAVE YOU A LOT OF MONEY.

WE ARE AT THE END OF THE 90 SECONDS AND I KNOW YOUR TIME IS VALUABLE. MAY I CONTINUE? I WILL BE HAPPY TO CONTINUE TO GIVE YOU OPTIONS THAT MAY BE AVALIBLE TO YOU? YES OR NO?

WOULD IT BE BETTER FOR ME TO CALL YOU LATER THIS EVENING OR WOULD TOMMOROW BE BETTER? WHEN WOULD BE A BETTER TIME FOR YOU?

MY NAME IS _____, AND I LOOK FORWARD TO SPEAKING TO YOU LATER THIS EVENING OR TOMORROW. HAVE A NICE DAY.

I HAVE INFORMATION THAT YOU MAY HAVE CONSUMER DEBT. I MAY BE IN A POSITION TO HELP YOU. PLEASE CALL ME AT _____.

---

for new sources of business. Specific, detailed loan information can be distributed to this more sophisticated audience.

Networking Group

This group can be a very good source of business. A **networking group** is a body of business people who get together at a breakfast, lunch, or dinner meetings to share contacts, leads, and business information. Select a group of business people who do not have competing loan brokers as a substantial part of the network. A group could consist of insurance agents, tax preparers, financial planners, probate and trust attorneys, home cleaning service professionals, credit union members, pest control and termite repair people, and home painters or similar maintenance personnel.

Look into your local newspaper on Monday's edition, business section, to ascertain the location of the meeting place

2.6 ADVERTISING REGULATIONS

Advertisement is defined as a commercial message in any medium that directly or indirectly promotes a transaction in the financing of real property. Advertisement is defined by the California Department of Real Estate. It includes dissemination in any newspaper, circular, form letter, brochure or similar publication, display, sign, radio broadcast, or telecast. It concerns any use, terms, rates, conditions or amount of any loan, security, solvency, or stability of any person carrying on licensee activities.

Licensee Advertising

The question is often asked, "May a salesperson advertise without using the broker's name?" The DRE clearly says: "No." The real estate law is specific about disclosing to the general public that a licensee is acting on behalf of the broker in this transaction. Prior to 1995, if a salesperson uses his or her own name in any advertising, the employing broker's name must also be specified. The employing broker may be a corporate broker with a fictitious business license name. If a corporate licensee is the broker, then the name of the broker is the name of the office. If the salesperson does not use his or her own name in the advertising, there is no legal requirement that the employing broker's name be mentioned. In addition, the Real Estate Commissioner's Code of Ethics for all licensees requires that any time a salesperson uses his or her own name in any advertisement, the name of the real estate firm must also be set forth, and the relationship with the employing broker must be made clear. In this case, the name of the office must be present in any advertising. The penalty for false or misleading advertising under the DRE business and professional Code is that a violator is subject to an injunction and/or penalties as high as $2,500 per violation. A licensee may also face suspension or revocation of the DRE license.

Effective January 1, 1995, submission of mortgage loan advertising for DRE approval will be entirely voluntary. For brokers who wish to voluntarily submit advertising for approval, a fee to cover the costs of the review will be charged. The amount of the fee may be no more than $40 per ad. If approval is given, it will be only for a certain duration. California AB 3358 sets the length of time an ad approval will remain valid as five years.

License Number on Business Cards

Effective July 1, 2009, pursuant to Senate Bill 1461, real estate licensees must disclose their DRE license identification number on all solicitation materials intended to be a first point of contact with consumers, as well as on all real estate purchase agreements in transactions where the licensee is acting as an agent. These materials include business cards, stationery, advertising flyers, and other materials "designed to solicit the creation of a professional relationship between a licensee and a consumer." The law does not require the broker license number to be disclosed and excludes print ads, electronic media ads, for-sale signs, and classified rental ads.

Advance Fee Advertising

The real estate commissioner has the right to pre-approve advance fee advertising material. Advance fees will be discussed in Chapter 15. Any person who proposes to collect an advance fee must submit the advance fee agreement and all materials to be used in advertising, promoting, soliciting, or negotiating an agreement calling for the payment of an advance fee to the commissioner. The advertising and the agreement must be submitted for not later than five days before the publication or use of the material. The advance fee agreement must be in not less than 10-point type. After submission, the commissioner may determine that the materials may not be used. A violation is considered a misdemeanor. Typical material that would not be approved by the Commissioner includes the following:

1. False, misleading or deceptive representations.
2. Does not set forth a specific, complete description of the services to be rendered.
3. Does not set forth the total amount of the advance fee and date on which it should be due and payable.
4. Contains any provision that purports to relieve the person collecting the fee from an obligation to fulfill commitments made by employees of the person contracting for the advance fee.
5. Contains any provisions that give a guarantee that a loan will be obtained as a result of the services rendered by the person collecting the advance fee.
6. Does not set forth a definite date for full performance of the services promised under the advance fee agreement.

The most common violations cited in DRE audits of mortgage brokers are the failure of the broker to properly account for and handle up-front fees collected (see Chapter 15). Brokers must recognize that all moneys collected from a borrower, including appraisal and credit fees, are trust funds and must be handled accordingly.

Regulation Z Advertising Disclosures

The federal Truth-in-Lending Act (Reg Z and HOEPA) regulates disclosure of the terms and the costs of credit in consumer credit transactions. The federal regulation that implements the act details the advertising requirements. The real estate financing advertisements that are subject to this act are those that claim to "aid, promote, or assist" loan availability through cooperating creditors. The act defines advertisement as a commercial message in any medium that promotes a credit transaction directly or indirectly.

First, if the advertisement states a finance charge rate, it must state the rate as an annual percentage rate (APR), as discussed in Chapter 12. Second, the advertisement must not state any rate other than the simple annual rate or periodic rate that is applied to the unpaid balance. Third, if the annual percentage rate may be increased after the credit transaction is consummated, the advertisement must state that fact. In addition, other terms in the advertisement may trigger the need for additional disclosures regarding federal Regulation Z (Reg Z), such as shown in the classified ad in Figure 2.16 and the solicitation letter in Figure 2.17. The act applies if any advertisement contains any of the following terms:

1. The amount or percentage of any down payment.
2. The number of payments or period of repayment.
3. The amount of any payment.
4. The amount of any finance charge.

FIGURE 2.16   Classified advertising.

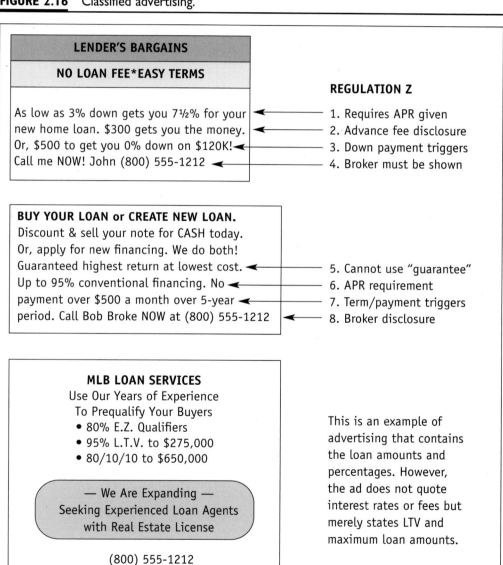

FIGURE 2.17   Solicitation letter.

CASH OUT ON RENTALS !

Dear Mr. and Mrs. Rental Property Owner:

Many lenders avoid making loans on your rental property or try to prevent you from getting the cash out you need from your income property.

Our firm likes rental property! Even if you have credit problems or your income is hard to prove, we can provide quality financing at affordable rates and terms for your rental property. Our program is specifically geared for 4 units or less and we guarantee you no more than 8% interest. Most banks expect you to have perfect credit. Most finance companies deal only with high-risk customers. We specialize in handling clients in the middle, without forcing you to take a loan with a balloon payment or high interest in excess of 8%. Borrowing is easier with our company because we offer:

* Fast 24-hour approval: You know right away how much cash you can count on because we guarantee results.

* Low-cost loan: To find out how much you qualify for with no risk to you, we charge only $300 for your pre-approval process.

* Easy qualification. We want to help you. We understand that not everyone is perfect. We know we can help you get a loan.

* Cash out for any purpose. Use your loan for debt payoff, home improvement, or reduction in your monthly payments. Increase your cash flow with a new loan from us!

Call us today at (800) 555-1212 to discuss your specific situation. Over the phone, pre-qualification and billing by credit card for the initial pre-approval will help you get your loan as soon as possible.

Sincerely,

Sam Stark, Lic # 123456789
Residential Lending Specialist

If any of the above is triggered, then the following must also be included as additional terms disclosed in the advertising:

1. The amount or percentage of the down payment.
2. The terms of repayment.
3. The annual percentage rate (must use the exact term).
4. The amount of any increase in annual percentage rate after the transaction is consummated.

From the previous *solicitation letter* example described in Figure 2.16, the following discrepancies can be found to trigger federal Regulation Z advertising requirements from the information contained in Figure 2.17:

When the 8 percent interest rate is quoted, the APR must also be quoted. Under the "Fast 24-hour approval," the indication that the borrower can receive cash does not make a qualifying statement that the loan amount is based on appraisal, net rental income, LTV, or creditworthiness of the borrower. Any reference to up-front fees, such as the "only $300 for your preapproval," must comply with the advance fee guidelines. Under the "Easy qualification" area, "We know we can help you get a loan" is misleading. DRE Regulation 2824 and Civil Code 449 listed examples that were considered to be false or misleading advertising, which include "guaranteed," "insured," "bonded," "sure," "safe," and "sound." The phrase "Increase your cash flow with a new loan" under "Cash out for any purpose" may be true if the former loans were at higher interest rates with higher monthly payments, but this blanket statement may not be true for every borrower and thus cannot be a universal statement. The last paragraph indicates up-front fees paid by credit card and would trigger advance fee disclosure. The letter does not disclose the name of the broker and would be in violation of real estate law.

Fair Housing Terminology

HUD has released a memorandum for acceptable verbiage for advertising terminology and for words or phrases that are not acceptable. However, always be alert for the many changes regarding current acceptability. Unlike newspaper advertising, in which the paper monitors verbiage compliance, flyers or brochures that you design do not have outside eyes to review the script. New regulations, court decisions, or hearings affect ongoing usage.

Before you take your brochure and flyers to the printers, be sure to double-check the compliance guidelines with the federal, state, and industry Fair Housing advertising terminology. On the one hand, the more inclusive the advertising is, the larger the potential market. On the other hand, the qualification guidelines for particular loans are so specific that if the advertising of a particular loan is too vague, you will waste time with applicants who will be unable to qualify or obtain that loan.

For example, HUD has indicated that it is not acceptable to say, "Adults only," yet the lender will not make a loan to a minor. However, using words relating to race, such as *black, white, Asian, or Latino*, is clearly prohibited. References to religious affiliation are also unacceptable, as is an advertising campaign to a *target market* associated with a specific temple, synagogue, church, or similar landmark. The problem areas for the mortgage loan broker are words related to specific groups of the public who are identified and separated from other groups. This segregation could be in violation of Fair Housing laws. For example, nonveterans cannot obtain a DVA or Cal Vet loan. Words that have also been terms unacceptable include *married, singles, senior citizens, and students*. Yet a reverse annuity mortgage (RAM, as discussed in Chapter 3) can be obtained only by a qualifying senior citizen. Remember that in advertising, the key for the mortgage loan broker is not to exclude any qualified applicant, even though the loan program mandates those who are and are not qualified.

SUMMARY

Once the mortgage loan broker begins working with a particular firm and after the sources of lender money are established so funds are available to lend, the most important concentration for the individual is to generate business that will bring income into the firm. Getting started may seem overwhelming in light of the competition and the vast amount of information to gain. Good training and ongoing education will give the mortgage loan broker the confidence to work hard. The sources to generate business come largely through the efforts of a long-range business plan and by use of various types of media advertising. Along with using the different media come a wide variety of regulations that are part of the advertising business and the mortgage loan broker business. Mastering the marketing skills will mean the difference between success and failure.

REVIEWING YOUR UNDERSTANDING

1. The marketing process includes the following steps:
   A. Select the goal by listing the end result to obtain
   B. Establish target market
   C. Select the media that is most appropriate for the target audience
   D. Design the actual marketing plan
   E. All of the above

2. In advertising, the AIDA formula does not include which of the following:
   A. Attention
   B. Image
   C. Desire
   D. Action

3. Preparation for telemarketing includes all of the following except:
   A. Prepared script
   B. List of common objections with positive responses
   C. Request for an appointment
   D. Promotional materials

4. The finance charge rate, APR, is required by:
   A. The California Department of Real Estate
   B. The California Department of Corporations
   C. The Federal Truth-in-Lending Act (Reg Z and HOEPA)
   D. HUD

5. Today the most used advertising media is:
   A. Walls on houses
   B. Trees and buildings
   C. Coat of arms related to a product
   D. Radio, T.V., home page, Web boards, etc.

6. The acronym used for creating successful advertising is:
   A. WORK
   B. AIDA
   C. KISS
   D. SCUBA

7. The first step in the marketing process is to:
   A. Establish your target market
   B. Select the appropriate media
   C. Select the goal
   D. Design the actual marketing plan

8. Which of the following is NOT one of the 5 W's of marketing:
   A. Who
   B. Where
   C. When
   D. Which

9. Effective January 1, 1995, the submission of mortgage loan advertising for DRE approval is:
   A. Partially voluntary
   B. Strictly enforced
   C. Entirely voluntary
   D. Relying upon the circumstances only

10. The ultimate aim in advertising is to:
    A. Stimulate enough interest
    B. Make the customer act
    C. Increase your business
    D. Create desire

ANSWERS TO REVIEWING YOUR UNDERSTANDING

1. E (pp. 31-32)   4. C (p. 50)   7. C (p. 32)   10. C (p. 33)
2. B (p. 33)   5. D (p. 28)   8. D (pp. 30-31)
3. D (p. 46)   6. B (p. 33)   9. C (p. 49)

PART II
Loans

Chapter

3

IMPORTANT TERMS

10- or 15-year mortgage

Adjustable Rate Mortgage (ARM)

B paper

Biweekly fixed-rate loan

California Housing Finance Agency (CHFA)

CalPERS

Conventional loan

Deferred interest

Desktop Underwriter (DU)

Economic Recovery Act (ERA)

Energy Efficiency Mortgage (EEM)

Energy Loan Tax Assessment Programs (ELTAP)

Equity loan

Fixed rate loan (FRL)

Home equity line of credit (HELOC)

Home Ownership Program (HOP)

Jumbo loan

Loan-to-value (LTV)

London Inter-bank Offering Rate (LIBOR)

My Community Mortgage Loan

Periodic Caps

Price level-adjusted mortgage (PLAM)

Property Assessed Clean Energy (PACE)

Public Employees Retirement System (PERS)

Rate lock

Reverse Annuity Mortgage (RAM)

Southern California Home Financing Authority (SCHFA)

T-bill rate

Variable Interest Rate (VIR)

Variable Rate Mortgage (VRM)

Loans: Conventional

PREVIEW

The mortgage broker should know something about the various types of loans before trying to match to the basic requirements of the borrower with the property. Thus, Part 2 of this text covers three chapters on loan information. The real estate mortgage loan broker is obligated to try to find the best available loan for an individual buyer.

Chapter 3 discusses the many types of conventional loan programs that are available and general loan information. Other loan information includes Small Business Administration (SBA), reverse mortgages, refinance loans, junior liens, equity loans, and B paper loans. Nongovernment loans are conventional loans with loan programs that usually follow the guidelines of FNMA, GNMA, or FHLMC.

Government loan programs are reviewed in Chapter 4. Government loans comprise three basic types: Department of Veterans Affairs (DVA), Federal Housing Administration (FHA), and California Veteran (Cal Vet). Chapter 5 discusses the loan disclosure information, such as federal and state compliance requirements.

This first chapter of Part 2 starts the mortgage loan broker on a road of lifelong learning of numerous loan programs. New and different variations are on the horizon as the financial communities try to make funds available for those who need real estate loans. Consumer needs change and investment markets change. Conventional loans, as described in Chapter 3, dominated the market from 1996 to 2008 and comprised the largest portion of the market because of the ability to obtain tailored loans to fit the property or borrower. Beginning in 2008 the market shifted away from conventional loans and the largest portion of the loan market became FHA loans, as discussed in Chapter 4.

CHAPTER OBJECTIVES

At the end of this chapter, the student learning outcomes include:

1. Compare and contrast the primary considerations used to select one conventional lender over another.
2. Differentiate among the various conventional loans for FNMA, GNMA, and FHLMC.
3. Describe the conventional loans features used to determine which loan best suits a particular borrower.
4. List and explain the components of various types of indexes for which a loan rate would be tied.
5. Describe conventional loan insurance programs, when such is required and the coverage.
6. Identify the loan criteria that serve as a match with buyer qualification.
7. Explain the nature of the various conventional programs.
8. Describe the elements of junior lien types.
9. Discuss subprime or B-paper loans.

3.1 HOW A MORTGAGE BROKER SELECTS A LOAN

One of the important decisions a borrower will make in the loan process is to select the right loan broker to handle the finance portion of his or her transaction. Equally important is making sure that the mortgage broker knows which loan programs to recommend to his or her clients. From 50 to 200 lenders are available to each loan broker. However, most brokers concentrate on five to ten specific lenders and work with only those loan programs that these few lenders offer. The broker works regularly with relatively few lenders and knows their programs well. Yet, these limited offerings may not give the consumers the best possible choices. Lenders typically specialize in only a certain number of programs. If the borrower fits one of these loan packages well, then the lender and borrower benefit. However, if the borrower is mismatched with a loan that does not best fit his or her needs, then the relationship is not good from the initial loan closing.

A mortgage loan broker receives rate sheets from lenders regularly or on request. The broker should begin with the lenders with whom they regularly deal. Ask for all the loan programs that these particular lenders typically fund. Then call other lenders and ask about their loan programs to gain a broader range of loan types available for your clients. Not every lender handles every type of loan. A borrower may fit a particular program perfectly, but it may require the mortgage loan broker to do some extra work to find a lender who knows of the program or who handles a particular type of loan. Other criteria to review on selecting a lender with the various loan types would include the following:

- What is the lender's ability to lock in an interest rate?
- What date or event will the loan rate tie to: application date, funding date, advertised rate?

- What loan points, fees, and costs go with which kind of loan?
- Will the lender give you references of other loan brokers who use this lender?
- What is the average time to close the loan once a processed loan is submitted?
- What loan terms and programs are available to the loan broker?
- What are the underwriting guidelines that the lender prefers for the loan package?

In addition to how the mortgage broker selects a type of loan and the criteria for selecting a lender, it should be noted that not all loans are available. Investors enact many loan programs, but lenders may choose not to offer the particular loan program. Lenders become familiar with certain loan programs in light of meeting the loan program criteria and on reviewing the foreclosure or slow payment record on the performance of that particular loan. Thus, the mortgage loan broker should check with different lenders in advance to see the availability of a particular loan program. It may be helpful to use a loan comparison checklist (see Figure 3.1) to assist in selecting the loan that best fits the borrower(s) needs and for which the lender will approve the borrower.

The primary consideration for selecting one conventional lender over another is often not the interest rate, fees, or programs that are available. The main criterion is often the quality of service provided by the lender, which is when an ongoing relationship can be most helpful to the mortgage loan broker. The following list may be helpful in considering the lender with whom to establish a regular working relationship:

- Will the lender's appraiser work with all parties: the property owner, REALTOR® etc.?
- Does the lender offer lock in loan commitments? For what period?
- What is the typical processing and underwriting time?
- Can you call regularly to check on the status of your loan and receive a friendly response?

3.2 CONVENTIONAL LOAN FEATURES

Any loan that is not a government loan is a **conventional loan**. What does this mean? A conventional loan is not guaranteed or insured by an agency of the federal government. It may, however, be insured by a private mortgage insurance (PMI) company, which is discussed later.

Comparison of FNMA and FHLMC underwriting guidelines is discussed later in Chapter 10. The guidelines for these conventional loans are set by the investor criteria, such as Fannie Mae (FNMA) or Freddie Mac (FHLMC), and are covered in more detail later in this chapter and in Chapter 12, which discusses the requirements for the secondary money market.

Most lenders prefer single-family, owner-occupied homes or condominiums. Conventional lenders, however, make the bulk of the loans on not only owner-occupied homes and one- to four-unit properties but also on larger complexes. Property types that conventional lenders normally make loans on include larger

FIGURE 3.1 Loan comparison checklist.

To make sure that the loan options are clearly conveyed to loan applicants, use the checklist below to organize loan options.

	#1	#2	#3
LENDER/AGENT	_____	_____	_____
LENDER PHONE	_____	_____	_____
STARTING NOTE RATE	_____	_____	_____
INDEX	_____	_____	_____
MARGIN	_____	_____	_____
"FULLY INDEXED" RATE	_____	_____	_____
FIRST RATE ADJUSTMENT	_____	_____	_____
SUBSEQUENT RATE ADJ.	_____	_____	_____
FIRST PMT. ADJUSTMENT	_____	_____	_____
SUBSEQUENT PMT. ADJ.	_____	_____	_____
RATE ADJUSTMENT CAPS	_____	_____	_____
PMT. ADJUSTMENT CAPS	_____	_____	_____
LIFETIME RATE CAPS	_____	_____	_____
LIFE CAP BASED ON	_____	_____	_____
LOAN FEE	_____	_____	_____
CONVERSION OPTION	_____	_____	_____
COST TO CONVERT	_____	_____	_____
QUICK QUALIFIER OPTION	_____	_____	_____
NEGATIVE AMORTIZATION	_____	_____	_____
LIMIT ON NEGAT. AMORT.	_____	_____	_____
RECAST FEATURE	_____	_____	_____
LOAN LIMITS: 95%	_____	_____	_____
90%	_____	_____	_____
80%	_____	_____	_____
75%	_____	_____	_____
70%	_____	_____	_____

apartment complexes, commercial shopping centers, office buildings, and industrial property. Just as many government lenders do not handle all programs, the same is true for conventional lenders, who prefer to work with only certain types of convention loan programs. No one conventional lender dominates the market; thus, mortgage loan brokers may take their borrowers' application files to more than one lender. If a loan is not approved by one lender, the mortgage loan broker may obtain approval at a second or third or fourth conventional lender because lenders set their own loan criteria.

The various conventional lenders have their own particular order that they want the loan file information to be placed in for submission, called stacking order, discussed in Chapter 8. The period for various loan functions will also vary from conventional lender to lender, but the mortgage loan broker can expect typical timelines to be as follows:

- 3 to 10 days to obtain a hard copy of a written appraisal from the date ordered
- 2 to 4 working days for underwriting (submission to investor, for approval)
- 1 to 4 working days to obtain loan documents
- 1 to 3 working days for funding

Loan Amounts

No maximum sales price is set by conventional lenders, but industry practice usually limits the amount of the loan to the FNMA/FHLMC/GNMA guidelines. Figure 3.2 shows the history for conventional loan limits from one to four units, including both first and second trust deeds. For example, FNMA announces each year the maximum loan amount. Loan agents should go to the FNMA Web site each month to determine the current maximum loan limits.

Loans that exceed these maximums are referred to as jumbo or nonconforming loans and command different rates and terms. The maximum loan limits have changed frequently during the past decade. See www.fanniemae.com for more information.

	9/24/01	1/1/08	1/1/09 General	1/1/09 High Cost Area
One unit	$275,000	$417,000	$417,000	$729,750
Two units	$351,950	$533,850	$533,850	$934,200
Three units	$425,400	$645,300	$645,300	$1,129,250
Four units	$528,700	$801,950	$801,950	$1,403,400

The Housing and **Economic Recovery Act (ERA)** of 2008 changed Fannie Mae's charter to expand the definition of a "conforming" loan. Effective November 2008 that is to begin January 1, 2009, high cost area, maximum loan amounts changed.

This was a result of the changes made under the American Recovery and Reinvestment Act (ARRA) for loans originated in 2009, which modified the high-balance eligibility requirements, clarified the Field Review requirement for loans in excess of $625,500, and added appraisal requirements for Refi Plus or DU Refi Plus loans for high-balance loans. This applies to loans dated October 1, 2008 or later.

Fannie Mae and Freddie Mac offer "super-conforming" loans if the borrower has good credit. **Jumbo loans** carry higher rates than conforming loans because they are not eligible for purchase and are not guaranteed by Fannie Mae and Freddie Mac. Jumbo loans run 1 percent to 1.5 percent higher than conforming loans of less than $417,000. In between the conforming and jumbo loans are the new so-called super-conforming loans that exceed the $417,000 conforming loan limits, but they are still eligible for purchase or guarantee by Fannie and Freddie. These super-conforming loans may carry slightly higher interest rates

FIGURE 3.2 Fannie Mae historical conventional loan limits.

Fannie Mae
Historical Conventional Loan Limits
(Excludes Alaska, Hawaii, the U.S. Virgin Islands and Guam)

Year	1 Unit	2 Units	3 Units	4 Units	Seconds
1980	93,750	120,000	145,000	180,000	N/A ***
1981	98,500	126,000	152,000	189,000	98,500 ***
1982	107,000	136,800	165,100	205,300	107,000 ***
1983	108,300	138,500	167,200	207,900	108,300 ***
1984	114,000	145,800	176,100	218,900	57,000
1985	115,300	147,500	178,200	221,500	57,650
1986	133,250	170,450	205,950	256,000	66,625
1987	153,100	195,850	236,650	294,150	76,550
1988	168,700	215,800	260,800	324,150	84,350
1989	187,600	239,950	290,000	360,450	93,800
1990	187,450	239,750	289,750	360,150	93,725
1991	191,250	244,650	295,650	367,500	95,625
1992	202,300	258,800	312,800	388,800	101,150
1993	203,150	259,850	314,100	390,400	101,575
1994	203,150	259,850	314,100	390,400	101,575
1995	203,150	259,850	314,100	390,400	101,575
1996	207,000	264,750	320,050	397,800	103,500
1997	214,600	274,550	331,850	412,450	107,300
1998	227,150	290,650	351,300	436,600	113,575
1999	240,000	307,100	371,200	461,350	120,000
2000	252,700	323,400	390,900	485,800	126,350
2001	275,000	351,950	425,400	528,700	137,500
2002	300,700	384,900	465,200	578,150	150,350
2003	322,700	413,100	499,300	620,500	161,350
2004	333,700	427,150	516,300	641,650	166,850
2005	359,650	460,400	556,500	691,600	179,825
2006	417,000	533,850	645,300	801,950	208,500
2007	417,000	533,850	645,300	801,950	208,500
2008*G	417,000	533,850	645,300	801,950	208,500
2008*HC	729,750	934,200	1,129,250	1,403,400	208,500
2009*G	417,000	533,850	645,300	801,950	208,500
2009**HC	729,750	934,200	1,129,250	1,403,400	208,500
2010*G	417,000	533,850	645,300	801,950	208,500
2010**HC	729,750	934,200	1,129,250	1,403,400	208,500

Notes:

*Beginning in 2008, there are two sets of loan limits - "General" and "High-Cost". The "High-Cost" areas are determined by Fannie Mae's regulator, the Federal Housing Finance Agency (FHFA).

The Economic Stimulus Act of 2008 temporarily increased the loan limits in high-cost areas. Then, the Housing and Economic Recovery Act of 2008 permanently changed Fannie Mae's charter to expand the definition of a "conforming loan" to include "high-cost" areas on loans originated on or after January 1, 2009.

**Pursuant to the American Recovery and Reinvestment Act of 2009, beginning January 1, 2009 through December 31, 2009 Fannie Mae may purchase loans up to $729,750 for a one-unit dwelling in designated high-cost areas. In October 2009, Congress extended the $729,750 limit through the end of 2010.

Please refer to FHFA's Web site or Fannie Mae's for the loan lookup table to see the limits by location.

The maximum "general" and "high-cost" limits in Alaska, Hawaii, U.S. Virgin Islands and Guam are 50% higher than the "general" and "high-cost" limits for the rest of the U.S.

*** Prior to 1984, second mortgage limits were the same as first mortgage limits. Subsequent legislation reduced the limits to 50% of first mortgage limits. Fannie Mae had no second mortgage program before 1981.

Updated: November 12, 2009   Prepared by Executive Communications

than conforming loans, about 25 to 30 basis points, but they are less costly than jumbo loans that Fannie and Freddie cannot buy or guarantee.

(A basis point = one hundredth of a percent.)

As of January 1, 2009, the upper limit for super-conforming loans was rolled back from $729,750 to $625,500, but the economic stimulus bill signed into law Feb 17, 2008, restored the higher limit for single-family homes in high-cost markets that was in place for much of 2008. For loans up to $417,000, the borrower must have three months' reserves, meaning that the new house payment times three must be kept in cash. This amount may not be used for the down payment or the closing costs and must be available after the close of escrow as a borrower's reserve. For loans from $417,000 to $1 million, the borrower must hold six months of house payments as a reserve. For loans that are $1 million and above, a minimum of twelve (12) month's reserves are required. The different types of loans that are in demand, over time, are shown below:

The FHA/VA shown in Figure 3.3 indicates the Federal Housing Administration and Veterans Administration government loans that are discussed in Chapter 4. The Conv/Conf is for standard conventional loans. The jumbo loans are for loans above conforming and above super-conforming. Subprime are conventional loans where the borrower often used stated income to qualify and almost no back-up documentation was required. All adjustable rate loans are not Alt-A loans. Generally, Alt-A are made to borrowers with good credit, but the loans lack some of the features of prime loans (no income verifications, small down payment), or involve riskier repayment terms (interest only, option ARM). The Alt-A loans may be fixed or adjustable. Many adjustable loans have a rate increase when the loan is five years or seven years old. When the loan adjusts higher, the borrower may be unable to make the increased payment, therefore this type of loan increases foreclosures. During the mortgage meltdown of the 2000s, these loans were targeted for restructuring the terms to keep the payment from going into foreclosure. The HEL is a Home Equity Line of credit. These are variable rate loans on the equity in an owner-occupied home.

FIGURE 3.3 Types of loans in demand (1990–2008).

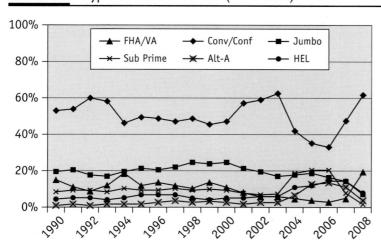

Eligibility Requirements for High-Balance Loans

Fannie Mae has re-evaluated existing high-balance guidelines and applied the following list for requirements for high-balance loans:

- Loans must be conventional first loans ONLY.
- One- to four-unit properties are eligible.
- Loans may be fixed rate or adjustable rate, but NO balloon payment is permitted.
- Loans may be underwritten manually or with **Desktop Underwriter (DU)**.
- Loans must meet the loan-to-value (LTV), combined loan-to-value (CLTV), and home equity combined loan-to-value (MCLTV) ratio requirements. See Figure 3.4.
- Borrowers must meet the minimum credit score requirements.
- All borrowers must have a credit score.
- Financed borrower-purchaser loan insurance is permitted; however, the maximum grow LTV cannot exceed 90 percent.
- All high-balance loans must meet all standard Fannie Mae eligibility and delivery requirements.

Loan-to-Value Ratio

For owner-occupied loans, the **Loan-to-value (LTV)** ratio for conventional loans goes up to 95 percent of the appraised value of the property or the purchase price, whichever is lower. Some lenders have allowed a conventional loan for 100 percent of appraised value, depending on the FICO credit score, as discussed in Chapter 7, Processing: Credit and Disclosures. Other types of property will typically restrict loans to 80 percent LTV. Interest rates and loan fees will vary not only on the LTV but also the duration of the loan. Each lender sets its own guidelines for LTV, with math calculations shown in Figure 15.1.

Loan Payment

The loan payment consists of many different components, the most common being the repayment of the principal and amount of interest due on the unpaid balance of the loan. Naturally, payments of interest only, termed a straight note, may consist of no principal paid with the loan payment. The principal may be all due and payable at the end of the term of the loan. Or, the principal may be due periodically, such as a lump sum once per year. The terms of the note dictate the loan payment component. Further, the loan payment may be made monthly, quarterly, annually, or at any other agreed-upon period of time, which is also stated in the note. The table shown in Figure 3.5 indicates the monthly payment for the principal and interest only for a 30-year fixed loan. A discussion of the payment factor chart is shown in section 15.1 of Chapter 15.

In addition, some loans have an amount impounded monthly and added to the payment to cover such items as property taxes and insurance. The insurance policies may include hazard, mortgage, earthquake, flood, or other types.

FIGURE 3.4   Qualifying ratios and debt ratios.

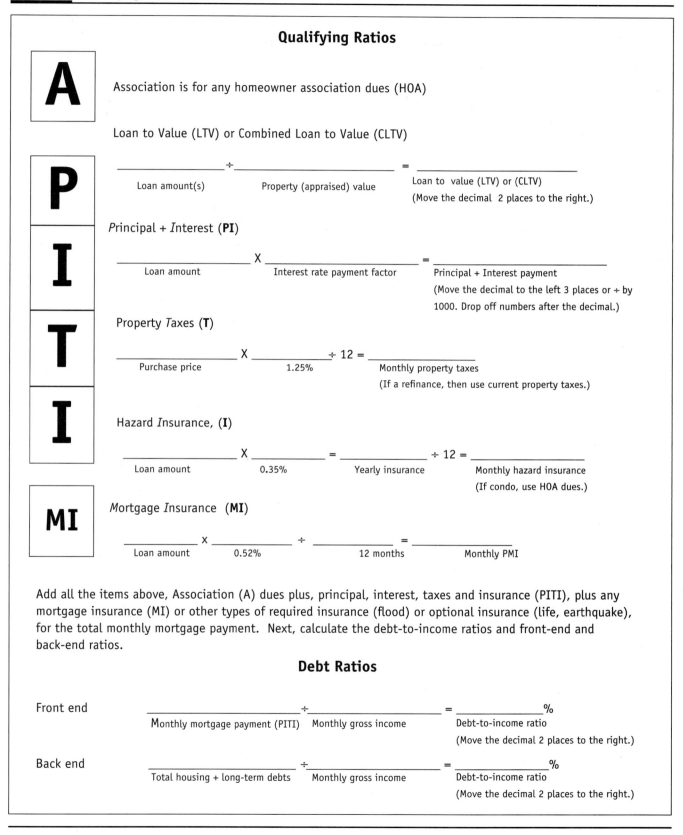

Qualifying Ratios

A   Association is for any homeowner association dues (HOA)

P   Loan to Value (LTV) or Combined Loan to Value (CLTV)

_____ ÷ _____   =   _____
Loan amount(s)   Property (appraised) value   Loan to value (LTV) or (CLTV)
                                                                            (Move the decimal 2 places to the right.)

Principal + *Interest* (**PI**)

_____ X _____   =   _____
Loan amount   Interest rate payment factor   Principal + Interest payment
                                                                            (Move the decimal to the left 3 places or ÷ by
                                                                            1000. Drop off numbers after the decimal.)

Property *Taxes* (**T**)

_____ X _____ ÷ 12 = _____
Purchase price   1.25%   Monthly property taxes
                                                                            (If a refinance, then use current property taxes.)

I   Hazard *Insurance*, (**I**)

_____ X _____ = _____ ÷ 12 = _____
Loan amount   0.35%   Yearly insurance   Monthly hazard insurance
                                                                                                    (If condo, use HOA dues.)

MI   *Mortgage Insurance* (**MI**)

_____ X _____ ÷ _____ = _____
Loan amount   0.52%   12 months   Monthly PMI

Add all the items above, Association (A) dues plus, principal, interest, taxes and insurance (PITI), plus any mortgage insurance (MI) or other types of required insurance (flood) or optional insurance (life, earthquake), for the total monthly mortgage payment. Next, calculate the debt-to-income ratios and front-end and back-end ratios.

Debt Ratios

Front end   _____ ÷ _____ = _____ %
                    Monthly mortgage payment (PITI)   Monthly gross income   Debt-to-income ratio
                                                                                            (Move the decimal 2 places to the right.)

Back end   _____ ÷ _____ = _____ %
                    Total housing + long-term debts   Monthly gross income   Debt-to-income ratio
                                                                                            (Move the decimal 2 places to the right.)

FIGURE 3.5   Monthly loan payment.

Loan Amount	(30-Year Fixed-Rate Principal and Interest) Interest Rates									
	5.0%	5.5%	6.0%	6.5%	7.0%	7.5%	8.0%	8.5%	9.0%	9.5%
$ 70,000	$ 376	$ 397	$ 420	$ 442	$ 466	$ 489	$ 514	$ 538	$ 563	$ 589
80,000	429	454	480	506	532	559	587	615	644	673
90,000	483	511	540	569	599	629	660	692	724	757
100,000	537	568	600	632	665	699	734	769	805	841
110,000	591	625	660	695	732	769	807	846	885	925
120,000	644	681	719	758	798	839	881	923	966	1,009
130,000	698	738	779	822	865	909	954	1,000	1,046	1,093
140,000	752	795	839	885	931	979	1,027	1,076	1,126	1,177
150,000	805	852	899	948	998	1,049	1,101	1,153	1,027	1,261
160,000	859	908	959	1,011	1,064	1,119	1,174	1,230	1,287	1,345
170,000	913	965	1,019	1,075	1,131	1,189	1,247	1,307	1,368	1,429
180,000	966	1,022	1,079	1,138	1,198	1,259	1,321	1,384	1,448	1,514
190,000	1,020	1,079	1,139	1,201	1,264	1,329	1,394	1,461	1,529	1,598
200,000	1,074	1,136	1,199	1,264	1,331	1,398	1,468	1,538	1,609	1,682

When the lender requires a specific type of insurance policy, they also usually require that policy to be included in the monthly payment and impounded. If the borrower elects to have insurance that is not required by the lender, the insurance policy premium may be paid outside of escrow and not impounded, such as a life insurance that would pay off the unpaid loan balance at the time of death of the borrower.

Some practitioners remember the acronym of "It is A PITI to have to make the payment" where the A refers to the homeowner association dues (HOA), and the P represents the principal paid, the I is any interest paid on the loan, the T is for property taxes, and the I represents any and all insurance policies. Other practitioners use the acronym of "PITI MI" (pronounced "pity me") where the PITI is the same as above, but the MI represents the mortgage insurance.

Fixed Rate Loan

The interest rate for a **Fixed Rate Loan (FRL)** stays the same over the life of the loan. These loans are generally for 30 years. They may be either fully amortized or contain a provision for a shorter due date, referred to as the call date. The shorter the duration, the better the rate and terms that are offered to the borrower. Amortization comparisons for various fixed-rate loans are shown in section 15.5 of Chapter 15, in which Example 1 in Figure 15.2 is a 15-year loan and Example 2 in Figure 15.3 is a 30-year loan.

One variation of loan duration could be a 30/5 loan. This means that the loan is amortized over a 30-year period to calculate the monthly payment, but the entire unpaid loan balance is due at the end of 5 years. The lender would be required to give written notice to the borrower 90 days prior to the due date of the then-unpaid balance, called a balloon payment. Private party lenders must give 60 days' notice, but it may not be delivered more than 150 days before the payment is due (Civil Code Section 2924(I) and 2966). The mortgage banker and a direct lender must comply with the balloon payment notice, but mortgage loan brokers do not have to comply with requirements to give notice of a balloon payment and are not covered under this law. A second type of a 30/5 loan is that for the first five years, the borrower makes interest-only payments. Beginning in the sixth year, the borrower makes fully amortized payments so that the remaining term of the loan would pay off the loan in full with no remaining balance, no balloon payment, as shown in Figure 15.6 of Chapter 15.

Biweekly Fixed-Rate Loans

The **Biweekly fixed-rate loan** shortens the life of the loan because the principal is decreased faster. The borrower makes 26 payments per year (every two weeks) rather than 12 payments per year (once per month). Making a payment more frequently means that the payment is applied to decrease the unpaid balance on the loan every two weeks. Because interest can be charged only on the unpaid loan balance, the amount of each payment is first applied to the unpaid interest due, and then the remaining amount directly reduces the principal. See Figure 3.6 for a comparison of monthly to biweekly payments for a 30-year loan used for amortization to see the savings realized over the life of the loan. Note that FNMA, as of September 22, 2009, no longer will purchase the biweekly loan because of the lower amount of interest earned by the investor. However, a borrower may continue to set up a biweekly program through private companies.

The 10- or 15-Year Mortgage

The **10- or 15-year mortgage** is popular among borrowers because it has a lower interest rate and shorter duration, producing a savings in total interest

FIGURE 3.6   Fixed-rate loan comparison of monthly to biweekly payments.

Frequency of payment	Monthly	Biweekly
Loan amount	$200,000	$200,000
Interest rate on loan	8%	8%
Each payment amount	$1,467.53	$733.77
Number of payments per year	12	26
Total of amount paid per year	$1,467.53 × 12 = $17,610.35	$733.77 × 26 = $19,078.02
Term of the loan	30 years	21 years 9 mo
Total of all payments	$17,610.35 × 30 = $528,310.49	$19,078.02 × 19 = $ 417,808.64
Minus principal borrowed	−200,000.00	−200,000.00
Total interest paid	$328,310.49	$ 217,808.64
Amount of interest *saved*	$328,310.49 − $217,808.64 =	$ 110,501.85

paid. Some borrowers agree to a 30-year loan instead and merely increase the loan payment by 1/12 each month to make a thirteenth payment each year. Example 3, shown in Figure 15.4, calculates the math for paying one extra payment a year, which would pay off the loan in 21 years and 9 months rather than in 30 years. The 4.5 percent formula may also be used. With this formula, the borrower makes the regular monthly payment for the first year and then increases the payment by 4.5 percent a year from the second year through the remaining balance of the loan until payoff. This strategy should also pay the loan off in 15 years. Example 4, shown in Figure 15.5, calculates the math for paying an extra 4.5 percent a year after the first year.

Adjustable-Rate Mortgages

Adjustable-Rate Mortgages (ARMs) are loans that do not have a fixed interest rate but have interest rate adjustment periodically to some predetermined index. A **Variable-Rate Mortgage (VRM)** and a **Variable Interest Rate (VIR)** are ARM loans, with one being by a state-chartered institution and the other by a federal. ARMs began in the early 1970s with California state-chartered savings and loans, and loans generally are no longer referred to as VRM or VIR. However, existing borrowers may use the terms for the last loan they obtained (perhaps many decades ago), for the new ARM loan that they are obtaining or they are assisting their children or grandchildren in obtaining, often as a co-borrower or as gifting the down payment. If the mortgage loan broker does not know the antiquated terms by which the borrowers refer to an existing loan there will likely be miscommunication between the parties. The interest rate is adjusted according to the terms of the contract note, usually with an annual maximum (cap) and a maximum rate for the entire contract (lifetime cap), as shown in Figure 3.7.

FIGURE 3.7   Interest rate adjustments (1% annual cap, 5% lifetime cap).

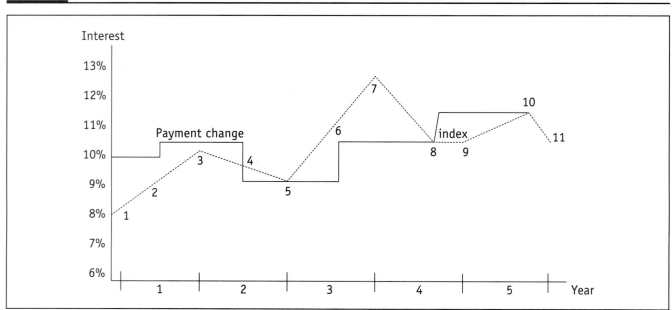

Index

Lenders have a preference about the index to which their loan is tied. They are not limited to only the 11th District COFI, T-Bill rate, prime rate, LIBOR, or Moving-Average Indexes. Each investor selects the index at which they will agree to loan funds according to the rate of return for the specific index for which the loan is tied.

In Figure 3.7, the vertical axis represents the year of the loan, as year 1, year 2, etc. The horizontal axis is the interest rate of the index and the interest rate on which the loan payment is charged. Thus, points 1, 2, and 3 show the index increasing by 1 percent at each point. Because of the increase at point 1 and 2, the payment increased and was changed at point 2. The index declined at points 4 and 5 to the payment changed to a lower rate, from 10 percent down to 9½ percent at point 4. Again, for 5, 6, and 7 the index went up 1 percent at each point. The payment increased at point 6 due to the increase in the index rate from point 5 to point 6. Thus, by the end of 5 years, at point 11, the index decreased by 1 percent so it would be projected and expected that the payment change would be incurred that would reduce the payment after point 10.

Eleventh District Cost of Funds Index (COFI)

This rate is the combined business index rate as compiled for the Western District of the Federal Reserve System located in San Francisco (Figure 3.8). This rate is defined as the monthly weighted average of the cost of borrowings for the Eleventh District savings institutions as made available on or near the last Friday of each month, indicating the cost for the previous month. See Figure 3.9 and Figure 3.10 for rate comparisons.

Treasury Bill Rate

The **T-bill rate** is used as an indicator of the cost of money that the government is paying on interest for borrowed money. T-bills are sold at weekly auctions. An

FIGURE 3.8   Cost of Funds Index (COFI).

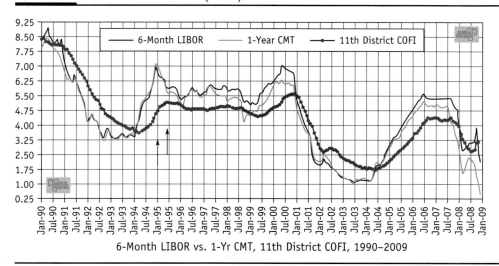

6-Month LIBOR vs. 1-Yr CMT, 11th District COFI, 1990–2009

FIGURE 3.9   Mortgage rates and federal fund rates.

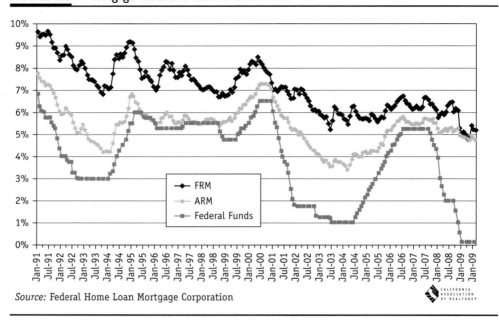

Source: Federal Home Loan Mortgage Corporation

FIGURE 3.10   Prime rate vs. 1-year CMT (2004-2009).

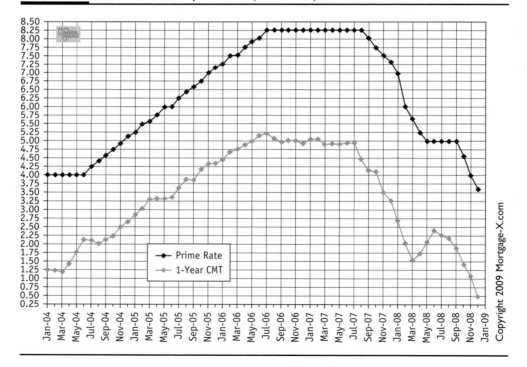

investor may use the average of the 6-month, 1-year, 26-week, or the 3- and 5-year T-bill rates. This rate is defined as the weekly average. Yields on actively traded Treasury securities are adjusted to a constant maturity of 1, 3, or 5 years, as issued by the Federal Reserve Board.

Prime Rate

The lenders average the prime rate during a specific period and add an interest rate to that rate to arrive at an offer rate. Figure 3.10 shows the historic prime rate from 1956 through 2004.

LIBOR

The **London Inter-Bank Offering Rate (LIBOR)** is an international rate compiled in London by using the ARMs sold in Europe. It is also an average of the interest rate on dollar-denominated deposits, also known as Eurodollars, traded between banks in London. The Eurodollar market is a major component of the international financial market. London is the center of the Euromarket in terms of volume. The LIBOR is an international index that follows the world economic condition. It allows international investors to match their cost of lending to their cost of funds. The LIBOR compares most closely to the 1-Year CMT index and is more open to quick and wide fluctuations than the COFI rate, as shown on our graph. There are several different LIBOR rates widely used as ARM indexes: 1-, 3-, 6-Month, and 1-Year LIBOR. The 6-Month LIBOR is the most common. See Figure 3.11.

Moving Average Index

Many ARM loans are tied to a moving average of a particular index. For example, if an ARM loan is tied to the 26-week average of the 6-month T-bill, the result will be a more stable index, which will not be subject to extreme volatility that can occur weekly.

FIGURE 3.11   London Inter-Bank Offering Rate vs. Constant Maturity Treasuries.

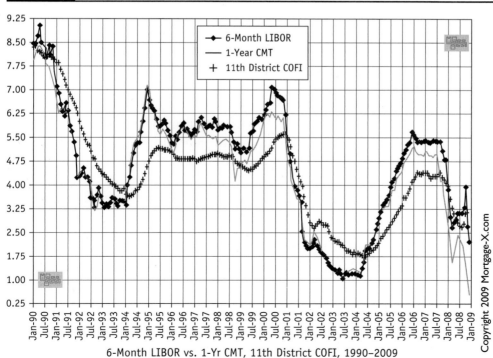

6-Month LIBOR vs. 1-Yr CMT, 11th District COFI, 1990–2009

Copyright 2009 Mortgage-X.com

The borrower rarely has the option of negotiating which index the investor chooses to tie the loan to in determining the interest rate. Most indexes run approximately at the same overall increase and decrease rate when the overall picture of the fluctuations is viewed.

Adjustable-rate loans often have specific qualifications because of the changes in the monthly payment by the *borrower*. For example, if the loan exceeds a 70 percent LTV and has longer than 15 years left and if the annual adjustment is at least 2 percent, then the mortgage loan broker must qualify the borrower at that adjustment at the end of the first year. Thus, a loan with 6 percent ARM start rate that could adjust by 1 percent every six months could be at 8 percent at the end of the first year. The borrower would need to qualify at 8 percent, not at 6 percent.

In addition to the index, ARMs also have a **margin**, also known as *basis points*, which is the lender's profit after covering the operating expenses. A margin is the "spread" that is added to the index to determine the note rate.

Index + Margin = ARM Interest Rate

ARMs usually have caps on the interest rates. Two types of caps are commonly used: the lifetime cap on the interest rate and the adjustment payment cap. **Periodic caps** are those that limit the interest rate increase from one *adjustment period* to the next, such as 2 percent. A lifetime cap is one that limits the interest rate increase during the life of the loan, such as 5 percent. The lower the start rate, the higher the cap rate. The higher the start rate, the lower the cap. A "teaser rate" is one for which the lender advertises a lower initial rate to attract the borrower. When the rate increases, the initial loan payments will not cover the interest due when the rate increases. Caps can be made on the interest rate, the payments, or both.

The amount accrued and unpaid is called **Deferred interest**, or negative amortization. There are California restrictions under AB 260 that prohibit negative amortization on higher-priced mortgage loans. See Financial Code § 4995.2(g). As a mortgage loan broker, it is unlikely that you will generate a new loan with negative amortization, because both government and conventional loans prohibit these types of new loans. However, it is highly likely that the mortgage broker will be asked to refinance an existing loan included negative amortization. Therefore, it is important to know the general terms of such loan when discussing the amount of payoff with the trustor and take into account that the loan amount may exceed the original loan amount generated at the inception of the loan. For a refinance the loan broker must include not only all the costs associated with obtaining a new loan, but also cover the amount of existing loans that are to be paid off.

For a negative amortized loan, the loan documents state how negative amortization is to be handled during the life of the loan. Some loans allow the payment to remain the same, but the term of the loan would be extended. Other loans require increased loan payments to offset some of the unpaid interest. To protect the investor from having a loan amount that far exceeds the future appraised value when deferred payments are added to the unpaid principal loan amount, lenders generally will not allow the loan to exceed more than 125 percent of the original loan amount ($100,000 original loan × 125% = $125,000 maximum loan amount). If the loan reaches this point, the lender will recast the loan, which is the making of a whole new loan.

The adjustment period can be based on the interest rate or the payment. The adjustment interval is usually either at six months or annually but could be as often as monthly.

A **convertible loan** is one that can be converted from an adjustable-rate loan to a fixed-rate loan or vice versa. These loans can usually be converted in months 13 through 60, normally at the anniversary date of the loan. Typically, the interest rate is higher than the market interest rate at conversion. A charge of one point is typical to convert the loan.

The Two-Step Mortgage

The two-step mortgage is an ARM loan program in which the interest rate is adjusted only once, usually five or seven years after origination. The new rate then remains in effect for the balance of the loan term. This loan carries a lower initial interest rate. This program is best for borrowers who will move within a short period and repay the loan prior to the step in the loan payment.

The two-step mortgage is useful when a borrower has a problem, even though the property qualifies with a current appraisal. Without this type of program, the mortgage broker may have to reject a loan package because the borrower has one of the following problems: (1) number of late loan payments within the last twelve months, (2) low FICO score, (3) higher income-to-debt ratio, or (4) too short a length of time on the job. When a borrower falls into one or more of these groups, the loan is termed a subprime or B-paper loan. Section 15.5 in Chapter 15 shows an example of the math calculations in Example 8.

Price Level—Adjusted Mortgage

The **Price Level—Adjusted Mortgage (PLAM)** is a mortgage loan program in which the monthly mortgage payment is at the same rate as the increased inflation rate, as measured by an index such as the Consumer Price Index. The outstanding principal balance is adjusted in constant dollars, with adjustment in both the monthly payment and the outstanding principal annually.

Reverse Annuity Mortgage

The **Reverse Annuity Mortgage (RAM)** is a loan in which the borrowers, who must be 62 years or older, are equity rich but cash poor. The source of the supplemental income is the loan program that may be either a lump-sum loan or a line of credit. The entire balance must be paid on the death of the borrower or the sale of the property.

Since 1995, FNMA purchases conventional RAM loans from mortgage loan brokers. The government loan program for the FHA reverse mortgage program is discussed in Chapter 4. Not every lender offers this type of loan program. One good source for home loan programs designed for seniors can be found by contacting http://rmc.ibisreverse.com//rmc_pages/rmc_aarp/aarp_index.aspx.

Types of reverse mortgages usually fall into the following categories:

- Single-purpose reverse mortgage that is used for only one specified purpose, such as to pay property taxes or make a home repair.
- Federally insured reverse mortgage that may be used for any purpose and is available throughout the United States, providing the largest advances that are conventional, insured loans.
- Proprietary reverse mortgage that may be used for any purpose and is designed for advances where the property value is substantially more than the median home value in the country, called high-cost areas.

Think of a reverse mortgage as the opposite of a conventional mortgage. With a conventional mortgage, the homeowner borrows a large sum of money and makes monthly payments. As payments are made, the loan balance gets smaller and the equity grows. With the RAM loan, in contrast, the balance increases during the life of the reverse mortgage while the equity decreases. Instead of using income to gain equity, the reverse mortgage borrower is using equity to increase income.

Payment options and limits include the following:

(1) ARM Payment Options
- Borrower(s) may receive monthly payments for a fixed period they select.
- Borrowers may receive monthly payments until they no longer occupy the property as their principal residence.
- Borrowers may set aside a portion of the loan proceeds as a line of credit that may be drawn upon at any time, and receive the rest of the principal limit in the form of equal monthly payments for a fixed period.
- Borrowers may set aside a portion of loan proceeds as a line of credit that may be drawn upon at any time and receive the rest of the principal limit in the form of equal monthly payments that continue until they no longer occupy the property as their principal residence.
- Borrowers may draw up to a maximum amount of cash at times and in amounts of their choosing until the principal limit is reached.
- Borrower may change from one payment option to another, for a fee authorized by HUD for each request, up to the maximum principal limit.

(2) Fixed-Rate Single Payment Option
- Borrower must draw down the entire line of credit on the day of closing.
- Future draws or other access to equity are allowed only for repairs and servicing fees.
- FNMA will only fund closed-end, fully drawn, fixed-rate HECMs that comply with all relevant HUD regulations and guidance.

Some RAM loans contain a clause in which the balance of the loan proceeds, if not given to the borrower, may go either to the estate and heirs of the borrower or to the lender. Be sure the borrower receives full disclosure on which of the different loan types they are signing for and giving a commitment to repay. For more information, call FNMA at (800) 732-6643 or use the Web site of https://www.efanniemae.com/sf/mortgageproducts/pdf/hecmlenderinfosheet. pdf. The steps for obtaining a reverse mortgage are as follows:

- Awareness: Go online to learn about reverse mortgage for general information.
- Action: Contact a reverse mortgage lender or NRMLA.
- Counseling: Obtain counseling from a HUD approved counseling agency or AARP-trained counselor. Counseling is mandatory, regardless of which program is chosen.
- Application: The homeowner completes an application and selects the payment option: fixed monthly payments, lump-sum amount, line of credit, or combination.
- Processing: Loan broker orders title and lien payoffs. Financial institution orders appraisal to determine the property value and physical condition of the property.
- Underwriting: Loan broker finalizes loan parameters with the homeowner and submits the loan package to an underwriter for final loan approval.
- Closing: After the loan is approved and the closing date is scheduled for the signing of the final loan documents, the loan closes escrow. The initial and expected interest rates are then calculated and the final figures are prepared. Once completed, the homeowner signs the new loan papers.
- Funding: The homeowner has three business days to cancel the loan. After the three days, the loan funds are disbursed.
- Payments: The homeowner does not make any monthly loan payment to the lender during the life of the loan. The loan is due upon death or sale.

The difference between a traditional second trust deed or an equity line of credit and a reverse mortgage is the borrower is required to have sufficient income to qualify for each type of loan, except the reverse mortgage, and the borrower will have to make monthly payments on all loans except the reverse mortgage. The reverse mortgage instead pays the homeowner, regardless of current income. With no payments, and the loan not due as long as the house is the principal residence, the homeowner may use the funds to make repairs, pay property taxes and utilities, or replace inefficient fixtures, such as an old floor furnace or drafty windows or a worn-out roof. The owner does not face foreclosure and is not forced to vacate their home because they miss a payment, since no payments are due.

When the home is no longer the primary residence, the borrower or the heirs of the estate must repay the cash received from the reverse mortgage, plus all interest and finance charges on the loan. The balance of the proceeds goes to the homeowner or the estate for all remaining equity in the home. The homeowner retains ownership and passes no debt on to heirs.

AB 329, referred to as the Elder Protection Act of 2009, has the following provisions:

- Prohibiting referrals between reverse mortgage lenders and companies that provide annuity contracts

- Requiring lenders to give a prospective borrower a list of at least 10 HUD approved reverse mortgage counseling agencies
- Requiring lenders, prior to counseling, to provide a prospective borrower with a written checklist pertaining to the risks and suitability of a reverse mortgage

FNMA and FHLMC Loan Programs

In today's market, many mortgage loan companies have taken the lead in offering loans with low down payments to qualified borrowers or even interest-only loans. The typical down payment required on many of these loans ranges from 3 percent to 10 percent. Many loans also offer reduced loan origination fees and expanded debt-to-income ratios. Although they are the lending network of banks, thrift institutes, and mortgage loan bankers, the National Mortgage Association (Fannie Mae or FNMA, http://www.fanniemae.com), the Federal Home Loan Mortgage Corporation (Freddie Mac or FHLMC, http://www.freddiemac.com), and the Government National Mortgage Corporation (Ginnie Mae or GNMA, http://www.ginniemae.com) offer various programs with as little as 3 percent to 5 percent down payment, of which 3 percent may be a gift. Thus, financial options make homes more affordable for more people.

Because so many loan types are available, it is often helpful to refer to a loan matrix chart to distinguish between the various programs. The chart, as shown in Figure 3.8, may be used by the mortgage loan broker, the processor, and the underwriter to ensure that the property and the borrower fit the criteria of a particular loan type. Additional matrix charts for other loans are discussed later. The following is a summary of some Fannie Mae and Freddie Mac loan programs, as shown in Figure 3.12.

Jumbo loans have similar guidelines. The primary difference is the maximum loan amount. In addition, it is highly recommended that the mortgage loan broker check with the individual investor to determine the particular lending guidelines that are acceptable.

In addition, the mortgage credit certificate (MCC) is a loan program in which 15 percent of the interest paid on the loan is a direct credit on federal taxes, which allows some borrowers to qualify for a loan that they might otherwise not be able to obtain. The MCC loan and similar programs come and go frequently in the marketplace. The mortgage loan broker usually needs continual training on the variety of new loan programs available at any particular time.

Condominium Loans

Although most loan terms are the same for owner-occupied single-family residences and for owner-occupied condominium units, there are a few differences that should be noted. If the borrower has a 20 percent down payment, the project that the individual unit is located within must be 51 percent or more owner occupied. When a loan has PMI, such as for a 90 percent loan or for an 80-10-10 (80 percent new first, 10 percent second, with 10 percent cash down payment),

FIGURE 3.12 FNMA & FHLMC loan matrix chart.

	FNMA & FHLMC			
	30/30	**15/15**	**30/7**	**30/5**
Max loan	See Figure 3.2 SFR's, PUD's, Condos—$417,000			
	Second mortgage—$208,500	same	same	
	2 units—$533,850	same	same	same
	3 units—$645,300	same	3 & 4 units $0	3 & 4 units $0
	4 units—$801,950	same		
Max LTV: Purchase	SFR, PUD, Condo—up to 90%	same	up to 90%	up to 80%
	2 units—80%	same	80% same	
	3 & 4 units—80%	same		
Max LTV: Refi same	SFR,PUD,Condo—up to 90%	same	up to 90%	up to 80%
	2 units—80%	same	80%	up to 80%
	3 & 4 units—80%	same		
Max LTV: Cash out	SFR,PUD,Condo-up to 80%	same	up to 75%	up to 65%
	2 units—75%	same	70%	65%
	3 & 4 units—75%	same		
	No cash-out max up to guidelines	same	same	
Second Home	Purchase & Refi—up to 90%	same	up to 80%	up to 80%
	Rate & Term refi—up to 90%`	same	70%	80%
	Cash out refi—up to 65%	same	60%	60%
	No 2–4 units	same	same	same
Non-Owner	Purchase & Refi—up to 70%	same	not available	not available
	Cash out refi on SFR—up to 65%	same	not available	not available
Seasoning	Less of appraisal or sales price(12 mo)	same	same	same
	Junior lien (12 mo) is cash-out	same	same	same
	24 month required on nonowner occ.	same	not applicable	not applicable
Qualifying	Use start rate	same	same	same
Assumability	Due on sale	same	same	same
Buy Downs	3-2-1, 2-1 & 1-0 on primary res—90%	same	2-1&1-0-resid	2-1&1-0/res/purchase

then FNMA requires 70 percent owner-occupied rate for the entire complex. In addition, if 15 percent of the total homeowner association dues are delinquent, FNMA will not approve the loan.

A condominium qualifies for a reverse mortgage program, with similar requirements as for a single-family home, so long as it is the borrower's principal residence. Also qualifying are manufactured homes, mobile homes, and condominiums in planned unit developments (PUDs).

3.3 MORTGAGE INSURANCE

Mortgage insurance is coverage against loss written by a private company to protect the mortgage lender in case of foreclosure. The premium amount is paid by the borrower and may be made as a cash, up-front, lump-sum payment or may be financed as part of the loan and paid as an impound amount. The insurance plan was devised to greatly reduce loss on conventional loans, with the goal to eliminate risk of loss. The conventional-guaranteed mortgage is insured with a private mortgage insurance (PMI) plan for up to 95 percent of the property's appraised value. The entire loan is not insured. On a 95 percent loan, the top 25 percent of the loan is insured. When the **LTV ratio** is 78 percent, the monthly mortgage insurance premium (MIP) may be taken off the loan if lender approval is obtained. The insurance companies deal only with approved lenders who comply with standardized criteria for both the borrower and the property. For PMI on conventional loans, Fannie Mae and Freddie Mac have premiums that cover the loan until the insurer's risk ceases. Should the property greatly appreciate or the LTV reach 80 percent, then the PMI is no longer liable for losses due to default because, under the terms of the PMI insurance certificate, for any default on a loan for 80 percent or less LTV, the lender must proceed with the steps for a foreclosure to retire the loan.

In the case of a single premium payment, the borrower pays the entire premium at the beginning of the loan. The lump-sum payment usually covers the lender's risk for ten years.

When the PMI is financed, an initial premium is paid at the beginning of the loan period by the borrower, and then an ongoing monthly premium amount is collected by the lender so that the annual premium can be made.

For example, if a loan is made to a borrower who places 10 percent cash down payment and receives a 90 percent LTV for $300,000, the monthly PMI would be as follows:

$$\$300,000 \times 0.0067 = \$2340 \div 12 \text{ months} = 195 \text{ per month.}$$

The monthly premium is based on the LTV as:

LTV	Annual Premiums
80.1%—90.0%	0.0067
90.1%—95.0%	0.0078
95.1%—100%	0.0122

The Mortgage Guaranty Insurance Corporation (MGIC) began in 1957 after a Wisconsin law was passed in 1956 and was the largest mortgage insurer for many years. Genworth Mortgage Insurance Company, http://mortgageinsurance.genworth.com, formerly GE Capital Mortgage Insurance Company of Raleigh, North Carolina, is a larger insurer today, as well as UGI and PMI Mortgage Insurance Company of San Francisco. The products offered by Genworth include borrower paid mortgage insurance (MI), lender paid MI, investor affordable housing programs and pledged asset mortgages. The Emergency Home Finance Act of 1970 authorized Fannie Mae and Freddie Mac to purchase conventional loans, and since that time, PMI has been a key element to conventional mortgages. This part of the insurance industry has developed actuarial reserves to reduce risk. In addition, specific regulations have led to greater regulatory control. The FNMA and FHLMC coverage for loans in excess of 80 percent require PMI coverage.

Example 6 in section 5.5 of Chapter 15 shows the cost to the borrower who has a 10 percent cash down payment and obtains a 90 percent conventional loan that requires PMI in comparison with a borrower who places 10 percent down and obtains a 10 percent second trust deed and an 80 percent first trust deed.

Additional sources for educational publications and seminars may be found by contacting MGIC, with the vice president of corporate training and development located at (800) 558-9900; or visit their Web site at www.mgic.com for locations of their offices and phone numbers. Available publications from mgic.com or fanniemae.com (http://www.acow-wa.org/FNMAforms.html) may include:

1. Evaluating the Loan Application
   a. Transmittal Summary (FNMA 1008)
   b. Uniform Residential Loan Application (FNMA 1003)
   c. Credit Report
   d. VOD (FNMA 1006)
   e. VOE (FNMA 1005)
   f. Uniform Residential Appraisal Report (FNMA 1004)
   g. Residential Offer to Purchase
2. Conquering the Paper Mountain (A Step-by-Step Approach to Evaluation of the Self-Employed Borrower)
   a. MGIC Presents Evaluating the Self-Employed Borrower SOFTWARE
   b. Self-Employed Borrower Documentation Checklist
3. Affordable Housing Guide
   a. Affordable Housing Underwriting Guidelines Reference
4. Straight to the Point: Everything You Need to Know about Evaluating an Appraisal
5. Manufactured Housing Guidelines
6. Fraud Alert: Detecting Fraud and Misrepresentation (see Chapter 10)
7. MGIC seminars cover the following topics:
   a. Time Management
   b. Team Building, TQM, Re-engineering, Customer Value Management
   c. Straight to the Point: Evaluating an Appraisal

California law contains provisions detailing both disclosure and cancellation requirements for PMI. Under Civil Code 2954.6, a disclosure statute, the regulation states that a lender that requires PMI as a condition of funding must notify the borrower within 30 days after the close of escrow about the right to cancel the PMI. The notice must be in writing in at least 10-point bold print and must contain the following:

- any information necessary to permit the borrower to communicate with the insurer or the lender concerning the borrower's PMI (telephone number, address to request termination, etc.)
- any conditions that must be satisfied before the lender will permit termination of PMI (minimum LTV, required appraisal, etc.)
- the procedure the borrower must follow to terminate the PMI.

The code also requires the lender or servicer to provide borrowers with an annual notice concerning the right to terminate PMI. The written notice must include either the same information required in the up-front disclosure discussed above or a clear and conspicuous written statement informing the borrower about the ability to cancel the PMI according to factors such as appreciation. If a loan does qualify for termination, the borrower's right to termination is still not absolute. Termination of PMI is mandated, according to Civil Code 2954.7, only if the

- borrower's request is in writing.
- the loan is at least two years old.
- the original loan was for personal, family, household, or purchase money purposes and is secured by a one- to four-unit, owner-occupied, residential property.
- the LTV is less than 75 percent of either the original purchase price, provided that the current fair market value of the property is equal to or greater than the original appraised value, or the current fair market value; and the borrower has not been delinquent on any payment more than 30 days during a 24-month period immediately preceding the request and that all payments are current at the time of the request.

3.4 CALIFORNIA LOAN PROGRAMS

California Housing Finance Agency

California Housing Finance Agency (CHFA) was created by the California legislature in 1975 to help low- to moderate-income persons and families obtain affordable housing. There are three programs: Program #1 Economically Distressed Area (EDA); Program #2 with Maximum Sales Price of $110,000 (MSP); and Program #3 for First-Time Homebuyer Low Income Limits.

The funds are obtained from the sale of bonds and are loaned through participating private lenders to qualified persons and families for home ownership. CHFA, a 30-year-old state agency, was formed to help first-time home buyers and provides interest rate mortgage capital through the sale of tax-exempt notes and mortgage revenue bonds (MRBs). Because the interest is exempt from federal and state income tax, the funds are marketed at favorable interest rates that are passed on to the home buyers. The notes and bonds are not state obligations.

The agency debt is not repaid with tax dollars but solely from revenues derived through repayment of the mortgage loans. In June 2004 the agency financed $1.24 billion in California, alone, and in 2008 CHFA financed $1.4 billion in home loans.

Recently, state housing banks in Rhode Island, Virginia, and Wisconsin have offered programs aimed at those who cannot initially afford a full payment.

These consumers fear even higher rising prices, such as in California, and seek to buy a property sooner. CHFA generally extends 18-month commitments to developers and builders to obtain the necessary permits and construction financing and to build and market a unit for delivery on a sales-price-competitive basis. When construction is completed, the developer makes below-market-rate mortgage financing available to first-time home buyers by using the services of private lenders. The agency then purchases each loan made by the lending institution. Agency interest rates are usually 1.5 percent to 3 percent below the prevailing market interest rates. CHFA does not charge points to the buyer, but the lender may charge up to 1 percent for a loan origination fee plus $350 for processing fees, such as the appraisal, credit report, and recording fees. For example, a buyer who obtains a $300,000 home loan would have monthly payments of $1,656 with a non-CHFA loan. With a qualifying loan, the buyer would instead pay $1,312 a month for the first 5 years, initially saving $344 per month, thus allowing a borrower to buy a property now to avoid a higher price at a later date.

The primary purpose of the single-family program is to provide home mortgage financing to low- or moderate-income first-time home buyers for the purchase of newly constructed or existing owner-occupied housing. To qualify for a loan, an applicant must be a first-time home buyer, unless exempt for certain targeted areas. CHFA multifamily loans are fully amortized, fixed at a below-market interest rate for 30 to 40 years for a first loan. In addition to single-family and multifamily housing, CHFA has strong commitment toward participation by minority and women borrowers, as well as disabled veterans business enterprises.

However, CHFA has recently lowered the maximum income limit for a borrower to qualify under the terms of this program. Now, fewer individuals and families can use this loan program. Also, a borrower who has a home-based business cannot obtain a CHFA loan. CalHFA purchases the loans within 90 days after the originating lender funds the loan. For each of the three programs, some basic criteria are the same, including:

- Eligible properties include new single-family detached homes, townhomes, and condominium units. Two- to four-unit buildings are excluded.
- The amount of down payment assistance is calculated using a portion of the school facility fees paid by the building, and it uses the square footage of the home.
- An application must be completed.
- Building permit is required, dated after January 1, 1999.
- There must be a School District Certificate of Compliance/receipt for fees paid.
- There must be Builder/Developer School Facility Fee Acknowledgement.

  Program #1, for an Economically Distressed Area (EDA), is for the purchase of a new home located in the counties listed March 1 of each year (starting 1999) based on rates of unemployment in each county. The sales price may not exceed 175 percent of the average median sales price of homes over the previous five years. This program requires:
- Sales contract signed by the buyer and the seller shows that the sales price does not exceed the county maximum limit.

- Signed agreement states that the borrower will occupy the home for five years; if less than five years, the borrower must repay a pro-rata share of the down payment assistance, based on the number of months of actual occupancy.

    Program #2, with maximum sales price (MSP) of $110,000 for a new home requires:

- Sales contract signed by the buyer and the seller shows that the sales prices does not exceed $110,000.

    Program #3, for first-time home buyers with low income limits, requires that the borrower not have owned a principal residence for the previous three years (as evidenced by copies of the income tax returns). This program requires:

- Current income verification or pay stubs identifying Employer and Employee
- 1040 tax returns for the last three years
- IRS Form 4506T

Southern California Home Financing Authority

The **Southern California Home Financing Authority (SCHFA)** was created in 1988 by the Community Development Commission (CDC) in a joint authority consisting of Orange and Los Angeles Counties. SCHFA provides tax-exempt, single-family mortgage revenue bonds that provide financing for first-time homebuyers in the two counties. These tax revenue bonds are sold to Fannie Mae because the loans must conform to FNMA flexible underwriting guidelines and below-market financing.

Hope for Ownership of Single-Family Homes

HOPE provides home ownership opportunities to lower-income persons by providing federal assistance to carry out or finance the acquisition and rehabilitation of single-family properties for sale and occupancy by families at affordable prices.

Home Investment and Affordable Housing

HOME provide federal assistance for use by participating jurisdictions for housing rehabilitation, assistance to first-time home buyers, and new construction when a jurisdiction is determined to need new rental housing.

Public Employees' Retirement System

Public Employees' Retirement System (PERS) is a California program for employees of public entities, such as a city, the state, or a public school. Eligible parties include those who are active, inactive, or annuitant members of the California PERS, the Legislators' Retirement System (LRS), or the Judges' Retirement System (JRS). The borrower must also have a PERS retirement fund.

A retired or inactive member may request a loan for a purchase or refinance of a home. Information on eligibility is available at (888) Cal-PERS 1-888-225-7377 or 1-877-801-PERS (7377). Information a loan application is available at (800) 874-7377. The general information for CalPERS member home loan program is found at http://www.californiaemployeeloans.com/program-details. html.

The borrower may obtain a loan for up to 100 percent of the purchase price. Some lenders offer a streamline-reduced documentation CalPERS loan for members with as little as 2 percent down payment. Basic loan feature options are many, with the ability to have a conventional fixed and jumbo financed loan for a purchase or a refinance. The program can offer up to 100 percent financing up to $350,000 and loan amounts up to $1,290,800.

One feature of the **CalPERS** loan is that most non-CalPERS loans charge extra for their rate locks and either do not offer a flat down option or charge extra for this benefit. The interest rate is lower at loan approval, and when the documents are drawn up for signing, a lower rate may be available. If the rate goes up, the borrower is protected because the interest rate is locked for a 60-day or 90-day rate lock at no extra charge.

With the CalPERS ACCESS Program a borrower may get down payment and/or closing cost assistance, up to 7 percent of the sales price of the home. The borrower may get into the home with as little as $500 from their own funds. Naturally, some restrictions apply to such a program. In addition, CalPERS has set maximums on some of the fees involved with a home loan, making it more affordable. Many non-CalPERS loans have higher closing costs.

A 95 percent loan is placed on the property and a 5 percent personal loan is secured by the borrower's retirement fund. A portion of the interest paid on the loan is reinvested into PERS. These loans are funded through approved PERS lenders. The personal loan is borrowed against the CalPERS retirement account of the borrower. The amount may be up to 5 percent of the home's value, up to 50 percent of what borrowers have already contributed into their own retirement accounts, or $18,421, whichever is less. In addition, the borrower continues to earn interest on the retirement funds. To use this option, the borrower must have at least $2,000 in the retirement fund.

Available loans include 10- to 30-year fixed-rate mortgages or 30-year ARMs. An individual may finance up to 95 percent of the value of a home to a maximum of $350,000 for a purchase. A PERS loan may be used on one- to four-unit, owner-occupied residences, condominiums, and PUDs. For single-family dwellings, a 100 percent financing operation is available. If the borrower wants to refinance an existing loan, a PERS loan for up to 95 percent LTV is available or 75 percent LTV if the borrower wants cash back.

The interest rate is set daily by PERS, and the loan fees are controlled:

PERS has set maximums on some of the fees involved with a home loan. PERS has a set maximum allowable loan origination fee of 1.25 percent of the loan amount. This program limits loan fees and may offer a reduced mortgage insurance cost. The following is a list of the approximate various costs associated with obtaining a PERS loan:

Appraisal costs	$350
Credit report	50
Processing	200
Tax service	65
Title charges	based upon size of loan
Underwriting fees	375

State Teacher Retirement System

Similarly, since 1986 a CalSTRS home loan program has been available in California for members who belong to the California State Teacher Retirement System. This program is often offered with as little as 5 percent down payment (3 percent from the borrower's own funds; 2 percent may be a gift or a grant), with limited loan fees for conventional financing loans with conforming and nonconforming units, no points, and no fees so that the borrower has lower up-front, out-of-pocket expenses at purchase, if the borrower wants to give up the rate buy-down option. Both 15- and 30-year terms are available.

One feature of the CalSTRS loan is the float-down option. When the borrower applies for the loan, the interest rate is locked in for 445 days. If the interest rate is *lower* during the 45-day lock period at any time prior to signing of the loan documents, the borrower receives the lower rate. If, on the other hand, the rate goes up, the borrower is protected with the original rate quoted. No extra charge is made for this feature under this program.

Home Ownership Program (HOP)

HOP is a loan program under the CDC of the County of Los Angeles, created to provide home ownership opportunities to low-income households. Financial assistance may be granted to qualified first-time home buyers and is secured by a second trust deed. The program falls under the Development Block Grant Program. Eligible purchasers must not have had ownership in a primary residence in the last three years and must agree to occupy the property. Generally, 3 percent to 5 percent of the purchase price or appraised value is required of the borrowers, plus closing costs. Home buyers must complete an educational course on home ownership. Gross annual income of the household cannot exceed 80 percent of the annual median income of the Los Angeles–Long Beach metropolitan statistical area, adjusted for household size, as established by HUD. Additional program requirements are that on sale, transfer, refinance, or default, the CDC will share up to a maximum of 25 percent of the appreciation of the property, determined by the number of years the home buyer occupied the property. Home buyers are required to sign an agreement giving the CDC the first right of refusal as an option to purchase the property in event of sale, transfer, or foreclosure. The deferred loan interest rate is 0 percent, and no monthly payments are required. All unpaid principal and interest on the loan will be forgiven, provided the purchaser(s) have complied with the provisions of the loan agreement for a period of 20 years from the date of the initial property purchase.

My Community Mortgage Loan

The **My Community Mortgage Loan**, is an FNMA community home-buyer loan that offers low mortgage insurance, with no additional loan-level price adjustment (LLPA) with 18 percent coverage for 97 percent LTV, and 6-18 percent coverage for other LTVs above 80 percent. The loan also has interest-only options, 40-year loan terms, and 3 percent or 5 percent down payment for two- to four-unit owner-occupied properties. The matrix shown in Figure 3.13 summarizes the loan features.

Energy Efficient Mortgage (EEM)

EEM is a loan program intended to make the existing home stock more efficient through the installation of energy-saving improvements. Typical items used for improvements include insulation, central air conditioning, energy-efficient glass windows, solar panels, new energy-efficient water heaters, window sunscreens, pool/spa covers, and changes to fluorescent lighting.

Fannie Mae, single-family energy loan tax assessment programs, as of July 2009, refer to certain state and county-sponsored programs that make loans available to residential homeowners for energy efficiency improvements tied to tax assessments. These loans are generally treated as special assessments and are levied and collected in the same manner as real property tax assessments. The resulting energy loan has priority over all existing liens, other than liens related to real property taxes.

These energy efficiency loan programs are sometimes referred to as **Property Assessed Clean Energy (PACE)** programs, or as **Energy Loan Tax Assessment Programs (ELTAPs)**. The specific implementation (maximum loan amount, permitted purpose, etc.) differs from county to county. Typically, homeowners repay ELTAP loans via their property tax bill. In the event of non-payment, the ELTAP has priority over a Fannie Mae lien. The **ELTAP** is a loan made by a government or private entity to fund improvements to the borrower's private residence, and the total obligation is generally considerably higher. ELTAPs are not eligible for sale to Fannie Mae.

Other Loan Programs

Some lenders offer specific loans that have a low starting monthly payment to assist individuals who are expected to have a future increase in income. One such program is the interest-only programs now available under fixed and fixed-period ARM programs. An interest-only loan is one in which the borrower makes a monthly payment of interest on the loan, with no principal amount paid, for a predetermined initial period. The initial, interest-only period is followed by a second period in which the borrower pays some interest and some principal payment each month, usually requiring the loan to be paid off completely over the remaining term.

FIGURE 3.13 MyCommunityMortgage.

FannieMae

MyCommunityMortgage®

Bringing Homeownership within Reach

Affordable Financing to Serve Low- to Moderate-Income Borrowers

		MCM 1-Unit (Max LTV 97%)[1]	MCM 2- to 4-Unit (Max LTV 95% for 2-, 3-, or 4-unit)[1]
Key Features	**Minimum Borrower Contribution** (own funds)	$0	3%
	Acceptable Sources for Flexible Funds	A gift from a family member; or a grant or loan from a nonprofit organization, municipality, or employer. Cash-on-hand (1-unit only)	
	Borrower Income Limits	100% of AMI; higher for high-cost areas; 115% in non-metro areas; no income limit in FannieNeighbors® areas	
	Prepurchase Home-Buyer Education and Counseling Requirements	If all borrowers are first-time home buyers, and/or if all borrowers are relying solely on nontraditional credit to qualify for the mortgage loan (regardless of loan product or home-buyer status), at least one borrower must complete prepurchase home-buyer education and counseling. All education and counseling must be provided by a third party that is independent of the lender and must adhere to the National Industry Standards for Homeownership Education and Counseling or those of comparable quality established by other organizations.	
Eligibility	**Loan Purpose, Eligible Products, and Term**	Purchase or LCOR Fully amortizing FRM, terms to 40 years 5/1, 7/1, and 10/1 ARMs (CMT or LIBOR), terms to 40 years Interest-only (IO) options: 30- or 40-year FRM with 10-year IO period; 30-year 5/1 ARM (2/2/5 caps) with 10-year IO period *3- and 4-unit properties not eligible for ARMs*	
	Occupancy and Property Type	Owner-occupied principal residence, including eligible condos, co-ops, and PUDs; no manufactured housing	Owner-occupied principal residence (no condos, co-ops, or manufactured housing)
	Mortgage Insurance (MI) Coverage	18% for 95.01–97% LTV • 16% for 90.01–95.00% • 12% for 85.01–90.00% • 6% for 80.01–85.00% (MCM loans not subject to the LLPA for minimum MI coverage.)	
	Financed MI	Up to 97% LTV *including* the financed MI	Not available
	CLTV Limits and Subordinate Financing	CLTV max. 105% with Community Seconds only; CLTV max. 97% with subordinate financing (non–Community Seconds)	
Underwriting	**Desktop Underwriter® (DU®)**	Available through DU using the "Additional Data" screen; select "MyCommunityMortgage." DU recommendations of Approve/Eligible and EA-I/Eligible are eligible for MCM. IO loans require Approve/Eligible recommendation. Qualifying ratios, reserves, and income requirements are determined by DU.	
	Manual Underwriting (Limited waiver of representations and warranties does not apply.)	Use manual underwriting if (1) the DU recommendation is other than Approve/Eligible or EA-I/Eligible; (2) there is not at least one borrower with a traditional credit history; or (3) Community Solutions™ or Community HomeChoice™ flexibilities are needed to qualify the borrower.** IO loans not eligible for manual underwriting.	
		Representative minimum credit scores for manual underwriting (or use enhanced credit evaluation):	
		660	680
		Benchmark qualifying ratio for manual underwriting: 43%. Maximum qualifying ratio of 45% allowed with strong compensating factors	
		Reserves for manual underwriting:	
		None	2 months of PITI (may not be gifted)
Underwriting (cont'd)	**Exceptions to Minimum Credit Score Requirements**	• If the borrower has a credit score below the minimum required based on an insufficient traditional credit history ("thin files") as documented by reason codes on the credit report, the lender may supplement the thin file with an acceptable nontraditional credit profile. SFC 818 must be used to identify loans with thin files (for manually underwritten loans only). • If a borrower has a credit score below the minimum required, but has sufficient traditional credit sources listed on the credit report, the lender may not establish a nontraditional credit profile to supplement the borrower's traditional credit history. • If the borrower's credit history was heavily influenced by credit deficiencies that were the result of documented extenuating circumstances, the minimum credit score requirement must be met, or the credit score must be no less than the greater of 620 or 40 points below the minimum required threshold as outlined in the Eligibility Matrix.	
	Temporary Interest Rate Buydown	2-1 temporary buydowns allowed (not allowed on 5/1 ARM products)	2-1 temporary buydowns allowed for 2-unit only (not allowed on 5/1 ARM products)
		The borrower must be qualified based on the greater of the note rate or the fully indexed rate, as applicable, considering the borrower's current obligations and other mortgage-related obligations (i.e., PITIA).	
	Other Income	Up to 30% of qualifying income can come from (1) boarder income (relatives or nonrelatives); or (2) income from an occupying co-borrower without a credit history (49% for DU)	Same as 1-unit; Plus, add projected rental income to qualifying income: 75% for 2-unit; 65% for 3- or 4-unit
	Interested Party Contributions	Standard guidelines per the *Selling Guide* – generally 3% for CLTVs above 90%	
	Ownership of Property	Borrower may not own another residence at the time of closing	
Pricing, Committing, and Delivery	**Loan-Level Price Adjustments (LLPAs)**	LLPAs apply. Refer to the Loan-Level Price Adjustment Matrix and Adverse Market Delivery Charge Information document on eFannieMae.com for details.	
	Special Feature Codes (SFCs)	• SFC 460 for all manually underwritten MCM loans and DU Version 8.0 MCM loans delivered on or after January 1, 2010. • SFCs 480, 481, 519, and/or 612 can be used for MCM loan casefiles underwritten with DU Version 7.0 and DU Version 7.1, or manually underwritten MCM loans meeting credit score eligibility requirements in place prior to November 1, 2009 (must be delivered on or before April 30, 2010). • In addition to SFC 460, SFC 574 continues to be required for MCM loans with financed MI, and SFC 818 is required for MCM loans with borrowers who have "thin" traditional credit files.	
Additional Flexibilities with Borrower Options	**Community Solutions** (teachers, police officers, firefighters, health care workers, military personnel)	Manual underwriting: Gifted reserves, consideration of part-time and overtime income with 12-month history	Options available for 2-unit (not available for 3- or 4-unit)
	Community HomeChoice (borrower or family member with a disability)	DU or manual underwriting: ○ Borrower income limit 115% of AMI ○ Non-occupying co-borrowers allowed Manual underwriting: Gifted reserves	

(1) Maximum LTV is reduced to 95% for manually underwritten loans or borrowers with a nontraditional credit history.

12.3.2009

These loans have a low interest-only monthly payment for a fixed period for owner-occupied and second-home properties. Some loans have the interest-only period for 3, 5, 7, or 10 years. The loan term may be 30 or 35 years and may be either a fixed-rate or an adjustable-rate loan. Thus, the borrower's monthly payment increases significantly once the principal starts to be paid off.

One such program, the 1-month/6-month interest-only ARM, allows for interest-only payments for the first 10 years for owner-occupied and second homes on a purchase or a cash-out transaction. For example, on a $300,000 conventional, 30-year, fixed-rate loan at 5.75 percent, the interest-only payment would be $1,438 a month. For a 5/25 loan, the payment would increase at the beginning of year 6 (the 61st monthly payment) to fully pay off the loan during the remaining 25 years. The monthly payment would go up from the $1,438 to $1,887, an increase of $449 per month. The buyers assume that their income will increase in the future to offset the increased cost of their home loan payment. If that loan were a 5/1 ARM, at the end of the fifth year, if the interest rate adjusted upward to 7 percent, the payment would jump to $2,120, or a $682-per-month increase.

This type of loan aids home ownership. In 2001, only 1.4 percent of California homes were purchased with an interest-only, adjustable-rate loan. This number increased in 2002 to just under 10 percent and then again in 2003 to just over 20 percent. However, by 2004, the percentage of California homes bought with an interest-only adjustable-rate loan had risen to just under 50 percent, at 47.8 percent. This kind of program helped increase the number of homeowners, whereas in 1984, only 53.7 percent owned a home, and in 2004, 59.7 percent of California households owned a home.

Other lenders have several streamline or reduced-documentation loans. Many of these loans offer 10-, 15-, 20-, and 30-year terms with fixed and fixed-period ARM programs. A stated income/stated asset loan often may simplify the application process because no documentation is required. This type of loan would require higher qualifying ratios and may even begin with an interest-only feature on owner-occupied and second homes.

Rate Lock

A **rate lock** or rate commitment is the lender's promise to hold a certain interest rate and a certain number of points on a loan for a specified period of time while the loan application is being processed. A lender may allow a rate lock for virtually any type of loan—conventional, FHA, DVA, fixed, adjustable, federal loan programs or privately funded loans, and state programs. When the loan is originated, the borrower may lock in a rate or let the rate float until the close of escrow. The borrower may choose between the rate float and the flat-down option. Since rates may vary widely between when the application is taken and the escrow actually closes escrow, the different considerations are an integral part of the loan options.

A *rate float* is a delay of the decision to fix the interest rate. An interest rate change from 1/8 percent to 1/4 percent usually only changes the payment by $10 or $20 per month. A borrower with a larger loan amount would benefit from floating the interest rate. A *float-down option* is the ability to lock in a rate today and take advantage of any drop in the interest rate before the loan closes.

The cost for this feature and all rate lock policies varies greatly among lenders. The longer period of time the rate lock is made for, the more risk that the lender takes, and therefore, the more expensive the rate lock fee. Interest rates tend to move down slowly but increase quickly. The cost of the rate lock is relatively small when compared to the cost of a rapid interest rate increase. As an example, a lender might charge an additional 1/4 percent for a 90-day rate lock.

3.5 REFINANCE, EQUITY AND JUNIOR OR SUBPRIME LOANS

Refinance Loan (Refi)

The borrower will usually ask the mortgage loan broker whether to refinance. A general rule of thumb that many consumers have heard is that if the new interest rate is 2 percent lower than the existing interest rate, then a refinance is well worth the costs that would be incurred with a new loan. However, the mortgage loan broker is expected to know more than rule of thumb before recommending a refinance. The objective for many prospective refinance borrowers is to cut the net out-of-pocket loan costs as quickly as possible. Thus, the fewer points the borrower has to pay, the better. The mortgage loan broker should shop around for a zero-point, zero-closing-cost loan, if available at the time and in the area where the loan is requested. To get the lower-cost loan, in exchange for a rate that is slightly higher—generally 3/8 percent to 1/2 percent—than what would be paid for a loan that comes with points and closing costs, the borrower can obtain a loan with virtually no costs. Zero costs means no points, no appraisal fee, no document preparation charges, no credit report fee, no title insurance charge, and no junk fees. Other items that may be asked of the mortgage loan broker include whether the new loan exposes the borrower to a higher lifetime or worst-case rate cap.

Most refinance borrowers do not want to have any cash outlay to obtain the new loan. Thus, the costs must be figured into the new loan amount. The new loan must be for the existing loan payoffs, the fees and charges for paying off the old loan, and all costs and expenses associated with obtaining the new loan. Figure 3.14 shows the calculation formula worksheet to determine the necessary loan amount for a refinance. If the property would not appraise for an amount equal to or greater than this calculation, it may not be in the best interest of the borrower to refinance the loan.

As an example, suppose that your applicants bought a home five years ago with a 30-year, $100,000 mortgage at an interest rate of 10 percent. The monthly payment of principal and interest is about $878. As the mortgage loan broker, suppose you propose to the applicants that they refinance with a new 30-year loan at 7 percent. The remaining balance on the original loan after 5 years of payments is $96,574. Refinancing this unpaid loan amount of $96,574 on a new loan would have a new monthly payment of $642.00 instead of the current $878. The savings each month would be about $236.00 per month. The total savings would be $32,280, consisting of the savings during the 25-year

FIGURE 3.14   Refinance loan amount calculation.

I. <u>Calculation of Base Loan Amount</u>

$ _____ Current 1st T.D. principal balance
$ _____ Estimate of interest owed (1 mo. payment)
$ _____ Estimate of demand & reconveyance fee
$ _____ Current 2nd T.D. principal balance (if any)
$ _____ Estimate of interest owed (1 mo. payment)
$ _____ Estimate of demand & reconveyance fee
$ _____ Total revolving & installment debt to be paid
$ _____ Taxes, liens, or other debts to be paid
$ _____ Cash out desired

$ _____ TOTAL BASE LOAN REQUIRED

II. <u>Calculation of Closing Cost on:</u>

	A. BASE LOAN	B. FINAL LOAN *
	$ _____	$ _____
Points _____ % _____	$ _____	$ _____
Underwriting	_____	
Appraisal	_____	
Credit report	_____	
Tax service	_____	
Appraisal review fee	_____	
Processing fee	_____	
Loan document prep. fee	_____	
Title insurance	_____	_____ *
Escrow fee	_____	_____ *
Subescrow fee	_____	
Recording fee	_____	
Prepaid interest @ _____%	_____	_____ *
Property taxes	_____	_____ *
Hazard insurance	_____	_____ *
Mortgage insurance (PMI)	_____	_____ *
Flood insurance	_____	_____ *
Termite report	_____	

TOTAL CLOSING COSTS: $ _____
  Plus BASE LOAN: + _____
  Subtotal: $ _____
  Plus safety buffer   + _____
TOTAL LOAN REQUIRED: * $ _____
  CLOSING COSTS ON ACTUAL LOAN REQUIRED: $ _____

period ($70,800), including the deduction for the additional costs during the five-year period ($38,520). The new savings would be calculated as follows: First, determine the difference ($236 × 12 months 25 years = $70,800) during the 25 years remaining until the original mortgage would be paid off. Under the refinancing, there are still 5 additional years of mortgage payments on the new loan at $642.00 per month ($642 × 12 months × 5 years = $38,520). These five additional years total $38,520. The net saving on the new loan is $70,800 − $38,520 = $32,280. Because the amount saved is $32,280 with the new refinance loan, it is advisable for the mortgage loan broker to recommend the refinance.

Fannie Mae continues to permit lenders to manually underwrite loans with an interest-only (IO) feature as the new Streamlined Refinance Option A for existing Fannie Mae borrowers. The existing loan being refinanced may still be an Interest-Only (IO) loan under Streamlined Refinance Option B, but the new loan for an Option B loan may NOT have an Interest Only (IO) feature.

Junior Liens

The mortgage loan broker is often asked to obtain additional financing above existing loans that are already placed on the property. The new loan being requested may be in secondary position, called a second, or in a third position, called a third.

Junior liens fall into their own special group with distinct characteristics. Seller carry loans have special rules that must be followed for disclosures when the loan is made and different notification time at payoff than institutional or conventional lenders must follow. Home equity loans are a large part of the junior lien market.

Many borrowers do not qualify for regular loans due to poor credit or other difficulties. These are referred to in the business as subprime borrowers and may be handled by either the mortgage loan broker, licensed by the Department of Real Estate, or a licensed consumer finance lender, licensed by the Department of Corporations, which is discussed in Chapter 14. Less creditworthy borrowers command a whole separate area of the mortgage loan business. See Figure 3.15.

Home Equity Line of Credit

A **Home Equity Line of Credit (HELOC)** is a form of revolving credit in which the property serves as collateral. The borrower is allowed to obtain multiple advances, at the discretion of the borrower, up to an amount that represents a specified percentage of the borrower's equity in the property at the time of the original loan appraisal. Because the home is likely to be a consumer's largest asset, many homeowners use their credit lines only for major items such as education, home improvements, or medical bills, and not for day-to-day expenses. The interest rate may be tax deductible on the HELOC that is used to pay off non-tax deductible loans, such as an auto loan or a credit card debt.

With a home equity line, the borrower is approved for a specific amount of credit limit, meaning the maximum amount that can be borrowed at any one time while the plan is in effect. Many lenders set the credit limit on a home equity line by taking a percentage (usually 75%) of the appraised value of the home and subtracting the balance owed on the existing mortgage. This loan may be an **equity loan** when the borrower receives a checkbook for a line of credit rather than a check at the close of escrow. Some lenders allow the rate to start as low as at the prime rate. As an example, suppose a home appraises for $250,000 and the homeowner owes $100,000. An equity loan for $87,500 could be placed on the

FIGURE 3.15   Qualifying parameters for rating loan types.

Qualifying Parameters	A+	A	B	C	Preapproval only D
Mortgage History	0 × 30 Last 12 months	1 × 30 Last 12 months	2 × 30 Last 12 months	4 × 30 Last 12 months	6 × 30 Last 12 months No 60-day ever
Minimum FICO Score: From Primary Wage Earner and Repository	720	680 to 719	640 to 679	600 to 639	580 to 599
Open Collection Accounts, Charge offs, Tax Liens	Any balance affecting title must be paid off at closing. Other unpaid balances may not exceed $1,000 in aggregates or $250. individually.				
Bankruptcy, Foreclosures, or Deed in Lieu	None allowed	None allowed	None allowed	None in the last 2 years	None in the last 2 years
Max Cash out	10%	10%	10%	N/A	N/A
D1 Ratio Gross annual Up to $30,000 35% $30,000 to $50,000 40% $50,000 to $75,000 45% $75,001 & Over 50%	50%	50%	45%	45%	40%

property. The borrower would be charged the costs for obtaining an $87,500 loan, such as credit report, appraisal fee, and costs for title and recording. The lender would record a loan for $87,500, but the current unpaid balance would amount to only the closing costs, such as $1,000. The borrower could write a check for $9,000 to pay off credit cards, $20,000 for a room addition, and $20,000 for a new car. Then, the unpaid loan balance would be $37,500 on the $87,500 equity loan.

Loans for Subprime Borrowers

Loans for subprime borrowers are rated according to the quality of the loan by the mortgage loan brokerage industry, such as the example shown in Figure 3.15. As with school grades, the borrower with the highest quality is referred to as A+. For a loan that has a borrower with poor credit and a history of delinquency, foreclosure, and bankruptcy, the lending community would consider the loan poor risk, so the loan is rate below A, maybe as a B paper borrower or even as a subprime loan, termed as C paper or D paper. The Fair, Isaac Company (FICO) score information will be discussed in more detail in Chapter 7 about credit.

Thus an A+ borrower would have no delinquent payments during the past 12 months, and an A paper loan is generally determined by the quality of the borrower and the property and the class of the lender. These are conforming loans that do not exceed the maximum FNMA or FHLMC limits for sale into the "institutional" secondary market. The **B paper** loans are similarly determined by the quality of the borrower and the property. Such loans, however, are generally not acceptable for sale into the institutional secondary market and are typically maintained in the portfolio of the originating lender. The unacceptability may be due to the loan being in nonconformance, such as a jumbo loan, or due to the inability of the borrower or property to meet underwriting guidelines imposed by the institutional secondary market. Most of these loans are placed with private lenders, rather than institutional lenders, by the mortgage loan broker who connects the parties for a fee.

The C paper and D paper loans indicate that the quality of the borrower or the property is beneath any institutional lender or quasigovernmental agency standard. The loan may be acceptable to the lender or broker making or arranging the loan, may not be subject to direct regulation or supervision by institutional lenders, and may be made by private parties directly or through a real estate licensee. The D paper loan might be for a borrower who shows six late payments during the past 12 months but with no payment as late as 60 days.

For E paper or F paper loans, the borrower may be subject to a notice of default, may be a petitioner in a bankruptcy, or may be otherwise subject to significant credit defects. Or the property to be secured as collateral for the loan may be atypical and fail to conform to any standards generally required by makers and arrangers of A through D paper loans. These loans have higher risks, and the investor therefore asks for higher charges and a higher yield. It is not unusual for a particular investor to specialize in a particular niche market, such as mini-warehouse storage facilities or secondary financing for a mobile home.

Defaults

The financial institutions and individuals are both falling delinquent on loan obligations or are going out of business. Figure 3.16 shows the bank failures in 2008 and 2009. In 2008, 5 out of 25 were California financial institutions. As the number of financial institutions decrease, fewer choices are available for consumers. For California, 12 of the top 36 bank failures have added to the unemployment in the state and the amassing of smaller banks by larger banks, as is shown in Figure 3.17. Bank of America now has the assets of both Security Pacific Bank and Countrywide, while Chase has Washington Mutual. The banking industry is heading toward economic oligopoly, in which the market is dominated by a small number of providers. Because there are few competitors, each oligopolist is aware of the actions of the few others operating in the same field. This can lead to collusion and price-fixing.

The delinquency rate for loans in California is about 10 percent, with unemployment rising to almost 15 percent. This has caused the long-term foreclosure rate to leap up from about a 1 percent average to almost 6 percent. This 5 percent increase will continue until the five-year and seven-year ARM loans are either renegotiated or are added to the list of foreclosures. Figure 3.18 shows the history of the past two decades for foreclosures and delinquencies.

FIGURE 3.16 Bank failures in 2008.

Number	Date	Name of bank	City	State
1	Jan 08	Douglass National Bank	Kansas City	MO
2	Mar 08	Hume Bank	Hume	MO
3	May 08	ANB Financial, NA	Bentonville	AR
4	May 08	First Integrity Bank, NA	Staples	MN
5	**Jul 08**	**IndyMac Bank**	**Pasadena**	**CA**
6	Jul 08	First National Bank of Nevada	Reno	NV
7	**Jul 08**	**First Heritage Bank, NA**	**Newport Beach**	**CA**
8	Aug 08	First Priority Bank	Bradenton	FL
9	Aug 08	Columbian Bank & Trust Co	Topeka	KS
10	Aug 08	Integrity Bancshares Inc	Alpharetta	GA
11	Sept 08	Silver State Bank	Henderson	NV
12	Sept 08	Ameribank	Northfork	WV
13	Sept 08	Washington Mutual Bank & Washington Mutual Bank FSB	Henderson Park City	NV UT
14	Oct 08	Main Street Bank	Northville	MI
15	Oct 08	Meridian Bank	Eldred	IL
16	Oct 08	Alpha Bank & Trust	Alpharetta	GA
17	Oct 08	Freedom Bank	Bradenton	FL
18	Nov 08	Franklin Bank	Houston	TX
19	**Nov 08**	**Security Pacific Bank**	**Los Angeles**	**CA**
20	Nov 08	Community Bank	Loganville	GA
21	**Nov 08**	**Downey Savings & Loan**	**Newport Beach**	**CA**
22	**Nov 08**	**Pomona First Federal (PFF) Bank & Trust**	**Pomona**	**CA**
23	Dec 08	First Georgia Community Bank	Jackson	GA
24	Dec 08	Haven Trust Bank	Duluth	GA
25	Dec 08	Sanderson State Bank	Sanderson	TX

FIGURE 3.17   The largest U. S. bank failures in 2009.

Number	Year failed	Name of bank	Total Assets in billions	City	State
1	2008	Washington Mutual	$307	Seattle	WA
2	1984	Continental Illinois National Bank & Trust	$40	Chicago	IL
3	1988	First Republic Bank	$32.5	Dallas	TX
4	**2008**	**IndyMac Bank**	**$32**	**Pasadena**	**CA**
5	**1988**	**American S & L**	**$30.2**	**Stockton**	**CA**
6	2009	Colonial Bancgroup	$25	Montgomery	AL
7	1991	Bank of New England	$21.7	Boston	MA
8	1989	MCorp	$18.5	Dallas	TX
9	**1989**	**Gibraltar Savings & Loan**	**$15.1**	**Simi Valley**	**CA**
10	1988	First City National Bank	$12.8	Houston	TX
11	1988	Guaranty Bank	$13	Austin	TX
12	**2008**	**Downey Savings & Loan**	**$12.8**	**Newport Beach**	**CA**
13	2009	Bank United FSB	$12.8	Coral Gables	FL
14	**1992**	**Home Fed Bank**	**$12.2**	**San Diego**	**CA**
15	1991	Southeast Bank	$11	Miami	FL
16	1991	Goldome	$9.9	Buffalo	NY
17	2009	Corus Bank	$7	Chicago	IL
18	2008	Franklin Bank	$5.1	Houston	TX
19	2009	Silverton Bank	$4.1	Atlanta	GA
20	**2008**	**Pomona First Federal**	**$3.7**	**Pomona**	**CA**
21	2008	First National Bank of Nevada	$3.4	Reno	NV
22	2009	Irwin Union Bank & Trust	$2.7	Columbus	IN
23	2008	ANB Financial	$2.1	Bentonville	AR
24	2008	Silver Sate Bank	$2	Henderson	NV

FIGURE 3.17   (*Continued*)

Number	Year failed	Name of bank	Total Assets in billions	City	State
25	2009	New Frontier Bank	$1.9	Greeley	CO
26	2009	Georgian Bank	$2	Atlanta	GA
27	**2009**	**Vineyard Bank**	**$1.9**	**Rancho Cucamonga**	**CA**
28	**2009**	**County Bank**	**$1.7**	**Merced**	**CA**
29	2009	Mutual Bank	$1.6	Harvey	IL
30	2009	Community Bank of Nevada	$1.5	Las Vegas	NV
31	**2009**	**First Bank of Beverly Hills**	**$1.5**	**Calabasas**	**CA**
32	**2009**	**Temecula Valley Bank**	**$1.5**	**Temecula**	**CA**
33	2009	Security Bank of Bibb County	$1.2	Macon	GA
34	**2009**	**Alliance Bank**	**$1.1**	**Culver City**	**CA**
35	2008	Integrity Bank	$1.1	Alpharetta	GA
36	**2009**	**Affinity Bank**	**$1**	**Ventura**	**CA**

FIGURE 3.18   California mortgage foreclosures and delinquency rates.

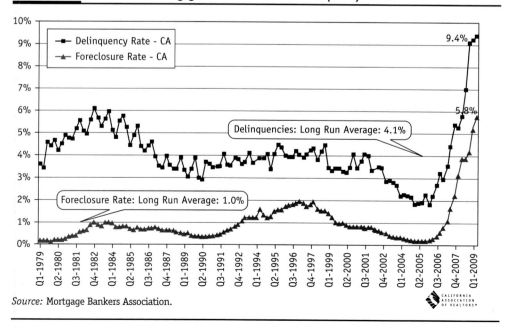

Source: Mortgage Bankers Association.

FIGURE 3.19 California foreclosure activity.

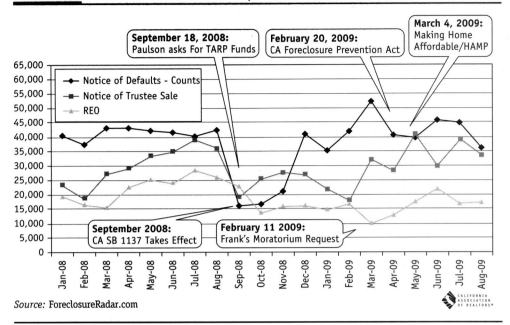

Source: ForeclosureRadar.com

Figure 3.19 shows that the government intervention is changing the loan market in an attempt to try to decrease foreclosure activity in California. The process begins with the Notice of Default being filed with the court, followed by the Notice of Trustee Sale when the property is taken away from the original borrower. Then the Trustee holds the property until there is a sale, referred to as Real Estate Owned (REO) for the foreclosed property. By the time the property reaches the REO stage, too often the property has been vacant too long and deferred maintenance awaits the purchaser. With deep discounts in the prices, sales activities has seen multiple offers by those who have the funds to purchase. For the most part, the high unemployment has kept many prospective purchasers from actually being able to close escrow. Investors or those with cash reserves are taking advantage of the low interest rates and the lower prices to make purchases.

SUMMARY

Conventional loan programs have differing loan components and criteria. The mortgage loan broker must know many kinds of loans before trying to match the borrower with the best program available. However, not all loan programs are available to the borrower; various lenders may offer only limited loan programs according to their investor criteria. The mortgage loan broker is responsible for seeking out lenders for the various loan programs.

Some borrowers do not qualify as a prime borrower in the conventional or government loan markets and must borrow at higher rates and with higher costs in the subprime market. These borrowers are often termed by the lending community as B, C, or D paper borrowers. Equity loans are one type of junior lien that the mortgage loan broker must become familiar with and have a source for when needed by a borrower.

REVIEWING YOUR UNDERSTANDING

1. How many payments would be made in one year on a biweekly loan?
   A. 6
   B. 12
   C. 24
   D. 26

2. A loan in which the borrower is a senior citizen who uses high home equity is:
   A. RAM
   B. PLAM
   C. HOPE
   D. HOME

3. The mortgage broker has ____ different lenders from which to find loans.
   A. 1–3
   B. 5–8
   C. 10–20
   D. over 25

4. PERS is the acronym for:
   A. Public and Employees Retirement System
   B. Personally Employed Retirement System
   C. Professional Employees Retirement System
   D. Public Employees Retirement System

5. An adjustable-rate mortgage has a margin or profit known as basis points and is calculated by:
   A. Index + Margin = APR
   B. Index + Margin = ARM
   C. Margin + APR = ARM
   D. ARM + APR = Margin

6. All of the following are indexes to which an adjustable rate mortgage may be tied, except:
   A. consumer price index
   B. LIBOR
   C. prime rate
   D. Eleventh District Cost of Funds

7. MRBs are _____ and exempt from _____ income tax.
   A. mortgage revenue bonds/federal
   B. mortgage revenue bails/state
   C. mortgage revenue bonds/federal and state
   D. mortgage revenue bonds/local and state

8. Mortgage insurance is written by:
   A. FNMA
   B. a private company
   C. the lender
   D. FHLMC

9. The 4.5% monthly payment formula on a 30-year fixed-rate loan would allow for a mortgage payoff in:
   A. 15 years
   B. 21 years and 9 months
   C. 30 years
   D. No early payoff will occur

10. The two-step mortgage is a:
    A. two-step fixed loan
    B. two-step ARM loan
    C. two-step ARM and fixed-rate loan
    D. any of the above

ANSWERS TO REVIEWING YOUR UNDERSTANDING

1. D (p. 69)
2. A (pp. 75-77)
3. D (p. 60)
4. D (p. 84)
5. B (p. 74)
6. A (p. 77)
7. C (p. 82)
8. B (p. 79)
9. A (p. 70)
10. C (p. 75)

Chapter

4

IMPORTANT TERMS

CAIVRS

CalVet

Certificate of Eligibility

DD214

DVA

EEM

FHA

FHA 203 (k)

FHA 207

FHA 221 (d) (2)

FHA 221 (d) (3)

FHA 221 (d) (4)

FHA 223 (e)

FHA 223 (f)

FHA 234

FHA 237

FHA 238

FHA 244

FHA 245

FHA 251 (ARM)

FHA 255 home equity conversion mortgage (HECM)

FTHB

Funding fee

Graduated equity mortgages (GEM)

Home Ownership Center (HOC)

Origination fee

Rate reduction refinance

SBA

Seller concessions

Streamline

Title I

Tribally Designated Housing Entities (TDHEs)

UPMIP

VA No-No

Loans: Government

PREVIEW

In addition to the various types of conventional loan programs that were discussed in Chapter 3, many other types of loans are prevalent in the marketplace. One group of loans is referred to as government loans because the agency administering the loans is a federal or state entity. The two major federal loan programs are those under the Federal Housing Administration (FHA) or the Department of Veterans Affairs (DVA). The state program is called the California Department of Veterans Affairs (CalVet).

Refinancing to consolidate bills or make home improvements and construction is a separate area in which some mortgage loan brokers specialize in bringing investors and borrowers together. These loans may be with private investors or can fall under government-backed programs. The Small Business Administration (SBA) helps entrepreneurs get the necessary capital for a business venture and act under the criteria set forth for government financing.

CHAPTER OBJECTIVES

At the end of this chapter, the student learning outcomes include:

1. Differentiate among the government loans: DVA, FHA, and CalVet.
2. List the components of the various government loans.
3. Identify which loan criteria would be required for a government loan.
4. Explain the nature of the various loan programs.
5. Describe SBA loan information.

4.1 FHA LOANS

Before the Great Depression of 1929, most lenders required a 50 percent down payment on a home purchase. This put home ownership out of reach for most Americans. Builders and lenders agreed that the key to stimulating home ownership was lowering down payment requirements without increasing the risk to the lenders, to protect the investor. To meet this identified need, Congress enacted the National Housing Act of 1934 that created the **FHA**, a government insurance agency. The FHA has taken on more than 34 million properties in the past 75 years.

The FHA is not a lender and does not make any loans directly to a borrower. Instead, it insures the loan to reduce the risk by the lender. Because of less risk, more investors are willing to make these types of loans. Specific criteria must be met in order for the FHA to approve these loans.

The loan requires that both the borrower and the property meet qualification criteria. The FHA sets the loan criteria for maximum loan amount, down payment requirements, and impound items such as insurance and property taxes. The borrower must fit into the guidelines for FHA-insured loans by meeting credit and income-to-debt guidelines. The property must have an FHA-approved appraisal and conform to minimum property standards for such items as room sizes, functioning access to utilities, and weatherproofing.

This section lists various FHA loan programs that legislation has approved. Not every lender has each type of loan program available at a specified time. One program may be offered today that was not formerly available; yet another program that a lender offered in the past may not be offered to the loan broker for consumer loan borrowing. The mortgage loan broker should review the programs that have been approved and call various lenders to determine which programs, if any, are available in the marketplace.

FHA loan characteristics generally include no secondary financing at the loan origination. These loans usually require a minimum down payment. However, the buyer must place 3.5 percent of the total funds needed (closing costs and down payment) into the transaction, and the seller may pay any amount above that requirement. The 3.5 percent down payment may be a gift from a relative of the buyer. The borrower cannot finance and must pay the amount required for reserves. Mortgage insurance premium (MIP) is always required. The interest rate, loan fees, and discount points, if any, are all freely negotiable so that either the buyer or the seller may pay the costs to obtain the original loan. The loans are subsequently assumable, with qualification requirements and no prepayment penalty. Figure 4-1 shows the market share for FHA loans in both the United States and for California. When the maximum loan amount increased, the number of loans in California increased.

The FHA loan amount may not exceed the FHA appraisal, called the conditional commitment, unless the loan program allows closing costs to be financed above the appraised value of the property. Often, less creditworthy borrowers may obtain an FHA loan. The less stringent qualifying standards make FHA loans attractive in areas in which the sales prices do not generally exceed the maximum loan amount. Figure 4-2 shows the change in demand, over time, for VA government guaranteed and FHA government insured loans. VA loans comprise only a small portion of the total loan programs, but they have recently risen to just under 5 percent of all first trust deed loans. During times of high prices and higher interest rates, the demand for FHA loans dropped to only about 3 percent

FIGURE 4.1   FHA loans in California and United States.

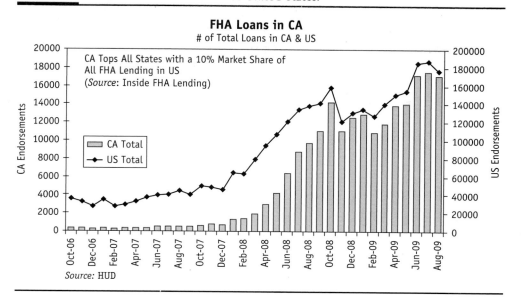

FHA Loans in CA
# of Total Loans in CA & US

Source: HUD

of loans. This was primarily because the maximum loan amount was equal to the amount of down payment needed by most borrowers. However, when the loan meltdowns began to occur in 2008, and the maximum loan amount was raised to meet the then current price of houses, FHA rose to a high of well over 30 percent of all first trust deed loans made.

One advantage of FHA-insured loans is that approved underwriters can approve these loans manually, even if the administration's automated underwriting system turns them down. Underwriters often err on the conservative side. Because of this, loan brokers don't have much wiggle room when it comes to making exceptions to FHA guidelines.

The Housing and Economic Recovery Act of 2008 makes it possible for FHA loans to be approved with the original note-holder taking a loss on principal. This funding may be difficult in cases where the initial loan carries previous insurance. Initial insurers may determine that it costs less to hold the loan as-is than to allow the borrower to refinance into an FHA-insured product.

The FHA mortgage amount types as of November 2, 2009, are shown in Figure 4-3.

Statutory Loan Amount Limits

The loan limits vary by program and by the number of family units for both purchase transactions and refinances. Some programs increase the total loan amount when the average housing costs for the county are higher to support higher limits. The National Housing Act specifies the maximum amount for each program.

The Department of Housing and Urban Development (HUD) has increased FHA loan limits as a percentage of the conforming loan limits. As of December 21, 2005, FHA's single-family loan limits are set by county and are tied to increases in

FIGURE 4.2   FHA and VA mortgages.

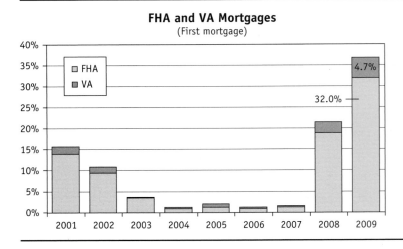

the loan limits established by Freddie Mac (http://www.freddiemac.com). In February 2009 the President signed documents that raised the maximum loan amounts. The final stimulus bill raised the FHA loan limit for insured reverse mortgages from $417,000 nationwide to $625,500 for the rest of the calendar year.

For high-cost areas (more than 100 U.S. counties), the limit varies by region. The limit is set at the lesser of 95% of the area median sales price, or the statutory ceiling, which is equal to an amount not to exceed 87% of Freddie Mac's conforming loan limit. The loan limits for Alaska, Hawaii, Guam, and the Virgin Islands will be higher than for the continental United States.

FIGURE 4.3   FHA mortgage amount types.

FHA Mortgage Amount Types					
Base Mortgage	Purchase Price or Appraised Value (whichever is lower) x the appropriate factor per the table above if borrower is paying their own closing costs				
	Origination Fee is calculated on the Base Mortgage Monthly MIP is calculated on the Base Mortgage				
Total Mortgage	Base Mortgage + the Up-front MIP				
	Discount Points are calculated on the Total Mortgage Yield Spread is typically calculated on the Total Mortgage FHA required repairs or allowable improvements can be added to the Base Mortgage for the Total Mortgage Qualifying is based on the Total Mortgage				
Mortgage Amount Calculation					
Purchase Price	$225,000	3.5% down	$7,875	Base Mortgage	$217,125
Calculating UFMIP – Up-front Mortgage Insurance Premium					
Base Mortgage	$217,125	X	2.25 UFMIP	$4,885.31	Base Mortgage + UFMIP	$222,000 Full Mortgage
Calculating Monthly MIP					
Base Mortgage	$217,125	X	.55%	$1,194.19	÷12 = Monthly MIP	$99.52
Calculating Origination Fee					
Base Mortgage	$217,125	X	1%	$2,171.25	Maximum of 1% Origination Fee	
Calculating Discount Points					
Full Mortgage	$220,924	X	1% Discount Point	$2,209.24		

Many lenders and real estate agent homepages today will often have information on the maximum loan amount limits and similar loan information. Note, however, that the most reliable and up-to-date information is the original source of current loan limits for FHA. The mortgage loan broker would use the Internet site found at http://www.hud.gov/fha to select the state, such as California, and then select the county. The site gives many areas of information, including maximum loan limits, MIP information, down payment requirements, closing costs, and credit guidelines. A summary of the primary FHA data is shown in Figure 4-4.

FHA 202

FHA 202 is called Supportive Housing for the Elderly and was enacted in 1959 but amended in 1990. This loan program provides assistance to expand the supply of housing with supportive services for elderly persons. The type of financing is based on development cost limits published periodically in the Federal Register. The property may be new construction or the rehabilitation of an existing building. The advances paid for the project are not required to be paid back as long as the housing remains available for occupancy by low-income, elderly persons for at least 40 years. The resident pays partial rent, but HUD subsidizes the rent and approves operating costs per unit. Under this program, it is the responsibility of the sponsor to arrange for the provision and funding of services appropriate for the assessed needs of the residents, for which HUD may share a portion of such funding.

FHA 203 (b) and FHA (i)

FHA 203 (b) and FHA (i) loans were established by the legislation in 1934 for one- to four-unit new and existing homes. This fixed-rate loan program is for new and existing homes. The borrowers non-reoccurring closing cost, including any up-front MIP (UPMIP), may be financed into the new loan amount. By insuring commercial lenders against loss, HUD encourages lenders to invest capital in the home loan market. HUD insures loans made by private financial institutions for up to 96.5 percent of the property value, up to a 30-year term on homes in urban and rural areas. The maximum loan amounts vary by area, with higher limits in areas with higher median home prices up to the maximum. Less rigid construction standards are permitted in rural areas.

HUD/FHA-insured homeowners threatened with foreclosure because of circumstances beyond their control, such as job loss, death, or illness in the family, may apply for assignment of the loans to HUD. If HUD accepts the assignment, it takes over the loans and adjusts the loan payments for a time until the homeowners can resume their financial obligations.

The seller in an FHA transaction is required to pay some of the fees that are not allowed to be paid by the buyer, including lender's processing fee, underwriting fee, document preparation fee, wire transfer fees, flood certification fee, tax service fee, funding fee, and sub-escrow fee. In addition to the listed fees, the buyer may be required to pay additional fees for notary service, prepaid interest on the loan, hazard insurance, and property taxes.

FIGURE 4.4 FHA Matrix.

FHA Matrix

LTV Matrix.						
Transaction	LTV	CLTV		Property Type	Loan Amount	High Cost (87% of FNMA)
Purchase or Rate and Term Refinance	97.75 Low Closing Cost States			Single Family/Condo	$172,632	$312,895
				2 Unit	$220,992	$400,548
	98.75 High Closing Costs States(<50,000)			3 Unit	$267,120	$484,155
				4 Unit	$331,968	$601,692
Cash Out	85%	N/A		SFD, Condo		

Program Offered	30, 20, 15, 10 year fixed (Sections 203b & 234c). 1 year ARM with 1/5 caps (Sec 251). Rehabilitation/Construction Permanent loan (Section 203k)		
	Mortgage Origination Date	Assumability Feature	
Assumability	12/15/89 – Present	Assumable by owner/occupant only for $500	

Mortgage Insurance	Loan Term		Up-Front MIP	Monthly Premiums Based LTV		
				90% or Less	90.01–95%	Over 95%
				None	.5 to .78LTV 25 to 78%	25 to 78%
	30 Year		1.5		25 to 78%	
	15 Year		1.5			

Automated Approval	FHLMC-Loan Prospector, FNMA-DU for FHA, and prniAURA System for FHA.
Refinancing	Streamline Refinance – With 12 month mortgage payment history and payment reduction, borrowers do not need to re-qualify. Loan amount can only be increased for closing costs with new approval.
Eligible Properties	SFD.2-4. C-c,ndo, & PUD units must be approved - http //entp.hud.gov/idapp/html/condlook.cfm

Income Restrictions	
Qualifying Ratios	29/41.ARMs and Buydowns Qualify at 2nd year rate if LTV is >95%
Documentation Types	Full and Alternative Documentation
Non-Occupant Co-Borrowers	No restrictions – may not be used for qualifying on 2–4 family properties
Self Employment	Minimum 2 years
Trailing Spouse	Not allowed

Asset Restrictions	
Cash Reserves	Although cash reserves after closing are not required on FHA insured mortgage transactions (except on 3–4 unit purchase
Gift Letters	Acceptable from any source. Must verify gift, and papertrail. Donor may borrow (secured) funds for down payment.
Seller Contributions	6% of Sales Price, including: buydowns, up-front Mortgage Insurance Premium and mortgage payment protection ins.
Required Contributions	Borrower MUST invest 3% cash in Transaction, including closing costs of down payment.
Borrowed Funds	Must be secured/counted for qualifying

Credit/Borrower. Restrictions	
Credit scores	Not considered
Non-Residential Aliens	The borrower must have a social security number and be eligible to work in the U.S.
Major Derogatory Credit	Significant Derogatory credit may be tolerated with documented extenuating circumstances. Bankruptcy Chapter 7-2 years from discharge; Chapter 13 – 1 year from discharge. Foreclosure – 3 years from discharge

Loan amounts vary depending on jurisdiction. See https://entp.hud.gov/idapp/html/hicostlook.cfm for current list.

To be eligible, a person must be able to meet the cash investment, the loan payments, and the credit requirements. The program is generally limited to owner-occupants. FHA normal qualifying ratios are discussed in more detail in Chapter 6, but the FHA 203 (b) program requires 31/43 for existing properties and 31/43 for new construction.

The closing costs for a buyer are broken down into two areas: recurring closing costs and nonrecurring closing costs. The recurring closing costs consist of property taxes, fire insurance, and MIP. Nonrecurring closing costs are one-time charges that consist of the title insurance policy, appraisal fee, credit report fee, loan commission or points, escrow or settlement costs, etc. Under this FHA loan program, the buyer's closing costs cannot be financed. Either the buyer or the seller may pay the nonrecurring closing costs.

The *MIP* can be financed with the loan amount. One exception is in the case of a refinance, in which both the closing costs and the MIP may be financed into the new loan amount. Two MIP amounts must be considered: the up-front mortgage insurance premium (**UPMIP**) charged on a single-family residence at 2.25 percent of the loan amount.

Because the FHA 203 (b) loan is the most common program, an example is shown in Figure 4-5 for calculating the loan amount. In the example, the property sales price is $310,000, and the buyer is financing the allowable closing costs and financing the MIP to obtain the maximum loan amount. A lender must calculate the maximum loan amount two ways. One method is if the closing costs are financed as part of the total loan amount. The second method is if the closing costs are not financed into the loan. The one that produces the greater down payment is the one the lender must use. Calculating maximum loan amounts is described in Chapter 6.

The sales price or appraised value is multiplied by 97 percent to determine the base loan amount. This figure is then multiplied by 101.5 percent in high cost areas to obtain the loan amount, which equals 98.455 percent for the loan to value (LTV).

Note that the total loan amount is figured as follows: *$318,930.16* (total acquisition cost) minus $24,250 (loan amount for first $25,000) minus $95,000 (loan amount of the next $100,000) equals *$199,680.16*. The balance above $125,000 is determined by taking that amount times *$199,680.16* × 90% = *$179,712.14.*

FHA rounds *down to the nearest fifty dollars in whole dollars* for the loan amount. The loan amount would not be *$298,962.14* but instead would be *$298,950*. Thus, the cash required to close escrow would require a slightly larger down payment.

FHA 203 (k)

FHA 203 (k) was established in 1961 as a rehabilitation mortgage insurance program for one- to four-family properties. HUD insures loans to finance (1) rehabilitation of an existing property; (2) rehabilitation and refinancing of the outstanding indebtedness of a property; and (3) purchase and rehabilitation of a property. An eligible rehabilitation loan must involve a principal obligation not exceeding the amount allowed under FHA 203 (b) insurance.

Any person able to make the cash investment and the loan payments meet the applicant eligibility requirements for this type of loan program. The loan-to-value ratios must fall between 95 and 97 percent for owner-occupied loans. The program offers either a 30-year fixed or a one-year adjustable-rate mortgage (ARM). The qualifying ratio is 31/43 for the borrower. The loan may not exceed the

FIGURE 4.5 COMSTAR: Buyer closing costs.

1. Calculating allowable BUYER closing costs (COMSTAR):

Credit report	$50	**(maximum of $50)**
Origination fee	2,959.91	**(see formula below*)**
Mortgage insurance **(MIP)**	4,439.25	**(1.5% of loanx $310,000)**
Settlement/escrow	592	
Title insurance	474	
Appraisal fee	375	
Recording fees	40	
	$8,930.16	Closing Costs Financed

2. Determining base loan amount

Step 1: Calculate the total acquisition cost

$310,000.00 **Sales price** = appraised value

+   8,930.16 Allowable financed closing costs (COMSTAR)
$318,930.16 Total Acquisition Cost

Step 2: Determine the total loan amount

Acquisition Cost	If the Closing Costs Are Financed	If Costs NOT Financed	Calculation of Loan Amount
$50,000 or less	97%		
More than $50,000	97% of the first $25,000 95% of the next $100,000	98.75%	$25,000 x 97% = $24,250.00 $100,000 x 95% = $95,000.00
	90% of the balance, up to the maximum loan amount	97.75%	$199,680.16 x 90% = $179,712.14
			Total Loan Amount $298,962.14

maximum FHA loan amount for the property geographical area. An FHA 203(k) loan worksheet is shown in Figure 4-6.

FHA 207

FHA 207 is a program designed to facilitate the construction or rehabilitation of manufactured home parks when the spaces are available for rent and not purchase. Projects must incorporate amenities and services found in competing parks and located in a HUD-approved area in which a need exists.

The mortgagor may be an investor, builder, developer, contractor, or cooperative. The maximum loan term is 40 years when repayment is a level annuity monthly plan with equal monthly payment to principal with interest. The loan limit is $9,000 per home space, with $15,750 per space available in high-cost areas. HUD defines a manufactured home as a transportable structure composed of one or more modules, each built on a chassis, with or without permanent foundation, designed for occupancy as a principal residence by a single family.

FIGURE 4.6   Maximum loan amount worksheet for FHA 203 (k) loan.

Borrower's Name and Property Address (including street, city, State, and zip code)	FHA Case Number:	No. Units:	HUD Owned Property ☐ Yes ☐ No
	Commitment Stage: ☐ Conditional ☐ Firm	Type: ☐ Owner-Occupant ☐ Investor	☐ Purchase ☐ Refinance ☐ Escrow Commitment

A. Property Information	1. Contract Sales Price or ☐ Existing Debt	2. "As-Is" Value	3. After-Improved Value	4. 110% After-Improved Value	5. Estimated Closing Costs

B. Rehabilitation and Other Allowable Costs
1. Total Cost of Repairs (Line 36, HUD-9746-A) $
2. Contingency Reserve on Repair Costs (_____%) (10 to 20% of B1) $
3. Inspection Fees (____x $ _____ per inspection) + Title Update Fee (_____ x $ _____ per draw) $
4. Mortgage Payments Escrowed (_____ months x $ _____) if vacant $
5. Sub-Total for Rehabilitation Escrow Account (total of B1 thru B4) $
6. Architectural and Engineering Fees (Exhibits) $
7. Independent Consultant Fees $
8. Permits and Other Fees (Explain in Remarks) $
9. Plan Reviewer Fees (including mileage, if applicable: _____ miles @ $ _____ per mile) $
10. Sub-Total (Total of B5 thru B9) $
11. Supplemental Origination Fee (greater of $ 350 or 1.5% of B10) $
12. Discount Points on Repair Costs and Fees (B10 x _____ %) $
13. Sub-Total for Release at Closing (total of B6 thru B9 + B11 and B12)** $
14. Total Rehabilitation Cost (total of B5 and B13) $

C. Mortgage Calculation for Purchase Transactions (See Note below)
1. Lesser of Sales Price (A1) or As-Is Value (A2) (or PD Contract Price) $
2. Total Rehabilitation Cost (B14) $
3. Lesser of Sum of C1 + C2 ($_____) or 110% of After-Improved Value (A4) $
4. Estimated Closing Costs (A5) + Allowable Prepaids for HUD-Owned Property ($_____) $
5. Maximum Mortgage Amount: Sum of C3 + C4 ($_____) x 85% (Investor) or 97/95% (Owner-Occupant) or Less Allowable Downpayment/HUD-Owned Property ($_____) $

D. Mortgage Calculation for Refinance Transactions (See note below)
1. Sum of Existing Debt (A1) + Rehabilitation Cost (B14) + Estimated Closing Costs (A5) + Discount on Refinance (_____% on $_____)*** $
2. Lesser of Sum of As-Is Value* (A2) + Rehabilitation Costs (B14) ($_____) or 110% of After_Improved Value (A4) $
3. Estimated Closing Cost (A5)*** $
4. Sum of D2 + D3 ($_____) x 85% (Investor) or 97/95% (Owner-Occupant) $
5. Maximum Mortgage Amount: Lesser of D1 or D4, not to exceed Statutory Amount $

E. Mortgage Calculation for Escrow Commitment Procedure
1. Maximum Mortgage Amount: After-Improved Value (A3) = Estimated Closing Costs (A5) x 97/95% (Owner-Occupant Assumptor) $
2. Enter the Value Established in C5 or D5 $
3. Total Escrow Commitment: E1 minus E2**** (Investor's Required Escrow plus loan proceeds) $

Remarks

*   If owned less than 1 year, use lesser of A2 or Original Acquisition Cost.
**   These Allowable Costs may be released at closing, provided paid receipts or contractual agreements requiring payment are obtained
***   Discount Points on Rehabilitation already included in B12. Include Discount Points only on refinance portion. Points are the same for both.
****   Release when an acceptable owner-occupant assumes the mortgage.

Preparer's Signature	Title	Date

Note: Mortgage Insurance Premium Paid Monthly: OTMIP does not apply

Source: HUD.

FHA 221 (d) (2)

FHA 221 (d) (2) was established in 1954. It is a HUD program that allows the Department of Transportation and Commerce to pay the HUD MIP on behalf of service members on active duty under jurisdiction. The loans may finance single-family dwellings and condominiums insured under standard HUD home mortgage insurance programs. To be eligible, the applicants must be service personnel or qualified service personnel who are on active duty in the U.S. Coast Guard or employees of the National Oceanic and Atmospheric Administration who have served on active duty for two years.

FHA 221 (d) (3)

FHA 221 (d) (3) is a HUD program designed to assist in financing projects for occupancy by low- and moderate-income families, principally by nonprofit mortgagors. Projects may be new construction or substantial rehabilitation and must have five or more residential units in which dining facilities are not provided. The mortgagor must demonstrate control of the site prior to applying as fee-simple ownership, an acceptable leasehold, or an option to purchase with at least an additional one-year renewal.

FHA 221 (d) (4)

FHA 221 (d) (4) is designed to aid in providing rental housing for families of moderate income. The project must contain five or more residential units and may not contain a dining facility. Individuals, partnerships, corporations, or similar approved entities are eligible, including profit-motivated sponsors, nonprofit, limited dividend, cooperative, and public mortgagors.

FHA 223 (e)

FHA 223 (e) was enacted by the legislation in 1968. It is a mortgage insurance program to purchase or rehabilitate housing in older, declining urban areas. In consideration of the need for adequate housing for low- and moderate-income families, HUD insures lenders against loss on loans to finance the purchase, rehabilitation, or construction of housing in older, declining, but still viable urban areas in which conditions are such that normal requirements for MIP cannot be met. The property must be in a reasonably viable neighborhood and an acceptable risk under the mortgage insurance rules. The terms of the loan vary according to the HUD/FHA program under which the loan is insured. HUD determines whether a project should be insured under Section 223 (e) and become an obligation of the Special Risk Insurance Fund. This program is not separate. It supplements other HUD mortgage insurance programs.

To be eligible, the applicant must be a home or project owner ineligible for FHA mortgage insurance because property is located in an older, declining urban area.

FHA 223 (f)

FHA 223 (f) is a program authorized by the National Housing Act, as amended by the Housing and Community Development Act of 1994. The purpose of this program is to help secure financing for existing multifamily rental housing projects, either on transfer of ownership or refinance of an outstanding indebtedness. The property must consist of eight or more complete living units at least 3 years or older, with at least a 10-year remaining economic life. The loan term may not be less than 10 years or more than either 35 years or 75 percent of the estimated remaining economic life of the physical improvements. The loan amount is usually 85 percent LTV.

FHA 234

FHA 234 was established in 1961 by the legislature as a federal loan insurance program to finance the construction or rehabilitation of multifamily housing by sponsors who intend to sell individual units and to finance acquisition costs of individual units in proposed or existing condominiums. HUD insures loans made by private lending institutions for the purchase of individual family units in multifamily housing projects under Section 234 (c). Sponsors may also obtain FHA-insured loans to finance the construction or rehabilitation of housing projects that they intend to sell as individual condominium units under Section 234 (d). A project must contain at least four dwelling units; they may be in detached, semi-detached, row, walk-up, or elevator structures. The maximum loan amount for a unit mortgage insured under Section 234 (c) is the same as the limit for a Section 203 (b) mortgage in the same area.

The applicant eligibility is that any qualified profit-motivated or nonprofit sponsor may apply for a blanket mortgage covering the project after conferring with the local HUD/FHA field office. Any creditworthy person may apply for a loan on individual units in a project; however, it is generally limited to owner-occupants with qualifying ratios of 31/43 percent.

The FHA Section 234(c) program is specifically geared toward those who purchase housing units in a condominium building. FHA insurance is important for low- and moderate-income renters who wish to avoid the risk of being displaced when the apartment in which they reside is converted into a condominium. FHA Condominium Loans are designed to encourage lenders to intend affordable loan credit to those who have non-conventional forms of ownership. The Section 234 (c) program insures a loan for 30 years to purchase a unit in a condominium building. The building must contain at least four dwelling units of detached or semidetached units, row houses, walk-ups, or an elevator structure. The program allows borrowers to finance up to 97 percent of the appraised value and some of the closing costs may be financed, further reducing up-front cash costs. There are limits on the size of the loan. At least 80 percent of the units must be owner occupied. The insurance may NOT be provided unless:

- The conversion occurred more than one year prior to the application for insurance.
- The potential buyer or co-buyer was a tenant of that rental housing unit.
- The conversion of the property is sponsored by a tenant's organization that represents a majority of the households in the project.

FHA 237

FHA 237 is a special credit risks program that was enacted in 1968. HUD insures lenders against loss on home loans to low- and moderate-income families who are marginal credit risks. HUD is also authorized to provide budget, debt-management, and related counseling services to these families when needed. These services are performed by local HUD-approved organizations.

Applicants may seek credit assistance under most FHA home mortgage insurance programs. The eligible applicant is a low- or moderate-income household with credit records indicating ability to manage his or her financial and other affairs successfully if given budget, debt-management, and related counseling.

FHA 238

FHA 238 is an active program for housing in areas affected by military installations. It is inactive with respect to multifamily programs. The nature of the program is mortgage insurance for single-family housing available under various insurance sections of Title II of the National Housing Act. This insurance is available in a community only if the Secretary of Defense certifies the need for additional housing and if the HUD secretary can show that the benefits of the insurance outweigh the risk of probable cost to the government. Such loans are the obligation of the Special Risk Insurance Fund.

For the applicant sponsor, eligibility will be determined by the section of the National Housing Act under which applications are made, which is generally Section 221 (d).

FHA 244

FHA 244 was established by the legislation in 1974 and is called single-family home mortgage coinsurance. The joint mortgage insurance by the federal government and private lenders is used for home ownership financing. HUD offers an additional and optional method of insuring lenders against losses on loans that they make to finance the purchase of one- to four-family homes. In return for the right to expedite their own preliminary processing procedures, lenders assume responsibility for a portion of the insurance premium. Thus, coinsurance is expected to result in faster service to the buyer and to improve quality of loan origination and servicing.

For borrowers, the program operates like full insurance programs. The major differences affect the lending institution, which performs the property disposition functions normally carried out by HUD alone. Qualifying ratios are 31/43 percent. Any mortgagee approved under the full insurance programs may apply for inclusion in this program. The coinsuring lender, according to the characteristics of the property and the credit qualification for the borrower, decides whether to make the loan.

FHA 245

FHA 245 was established in 1974 as federal mortgage program for graduated payment mortgages. HUD insures loans to finance early home ownership for households that expect their incomes to rise substantially. These "graduated payment" mortgages allow homeowners to make smaller monthly payments initially and to increase their payment amount gradually. The loan may have a negative amortization for the first 5 to 10 years, depending on which payment plan the borrower selects. The lender is required to disclose a projected worst-case scenario to the borrower.

Five plans are available, varying in length and rate of increase. Larger-than-usual down payments are required to prevent the total amount of the loan from exceeding the statutory LTV ratios. In all other ways, the graduated payment mortgage is subject to the rules governing ordinary HUD-insured home loans. **Graduated equity mortgages (GEM)** are insured under the same statutory authority, and the difference is that the interest rate is a fixed-rate loan tied to the one-year T-bill rate. HUD is considering eliminating GEM and removing its regulations.

All FHA-approved lenders may make graduated payment mortgages; creditworthy owner-occupant applicants with reasonable expectations of increasing income may qualify for such loans. The seller pays the major portion of the costs. Buyers are not allowed to pay document fees, tax service, processing, warehousing, or excessive points charged by some lenders. Although the program is available for one- to four-unit dwellings, one unit must be owner occupied. Income ratio qualifications are 26/38. The LTV ratio may be up to 95.5 percent, with only 4.5 percent down.

FHA 251 (ARM)

FHA 251 (ARM) was enacted in 1983 as a federal mortgage insurance for ARMs. Under this HUD-insured loan, the interest rate and monthly payment may change during the life of the loan. The initial interest rate, discount points, and the margin are negotiable between the buyer and lender. Qualifying ratios are 31/43.

The one-year Treasury Constant Maturities Index is used for determining the interest-rate changes. One percentage point is the maximum amount the interest rate may increase or decrease in any one year. Over the life of the loan, the maximum interest rate change is five percentage points from the initial rate of the loan.

Lenders are required to disclose to the borrower the nature of the ARM loan at loan application. In addition, borrowers must be informed at least 25 days in advance of any adjustment to the monthly payment. All FHA-approved lenders may make ARMs to creditworthy applicants.

FHA 255 (HECM)

FHA 255 home equity conversion mortgage (HECM) was established in 1987 under Section 417 of the Housing and Community Development Act (HCD) that added Section 255 to the National Housing Act. Under the HECM insurance demonstration program, FHA insures reverse mortgages that allow older homeowners to convert their home equity into spendable dollars. Reverse mortgages provide a valuable financing alternative for older homeowners who wish to remain in his or her homes but have become "home-equity rich and cash-poor." Any lender authorized to make HUD-insured loans may originate reverse mortgages.

Being eligible for Social Security income at age 62 qualifies a homeowner for an FHA-insured Home Equity Conversion Mortgage (HECM). The MIP which is required and paid to insure the lender also guarantees the borrower that the funds will be available if the lender is not able to make payments. HUD carefully monitors the homeowner's interest. Features of the loan include:

- No credit qualification
- No income restriction
- Pays off all existing loans
- No monthly payment
- Receive monthly cash flow
- No prepayment penalty
- No change in title for home ownership
- Increased equity may provide additional income
- The income is tax free
- The income does not reduce any Social Security payments
- May be used for a home purchase
- Current investment of the home does not have to be disturbed

Borrowers may select from five payment options: (1) tenure, in which the borrower receives monthly payments from the lender for as long as the borrower lives and continues to occupy the home as a principal residence; (2) term, in which the borrower receives monthly payments for a fixed period selected by the borrower; (3) line of credit, in which the borrower can make withdrawals up to a maximum amount, at times and in amounts of the borrower's choosing; (4) modified tenure, in which the tenure option (1) is combined with a line of credit (3); and (5) modified term, in which the term option (2) is combined with a line of credit (3).

The borrower retains ownership of the property and may sell the home and move at any time, keeping the sales proceeds in excess of the unpaid loan balance. A borrower cannot be forced to sell the home to pay off the loan, even if the loan balance grows to exceed the value of the property. An FHA-insured reverse mortgage need not be repaid until the borrower moves, sells, or dies. Should the homeowner need to be hospitalized or moved into a health care facility, the homeowner must provide the appropriate notification that is required to HUD and FNMA for the absence from the home. When the loan is due and payable, if the loan exceeds the value of the property, the borrower (or the heirs) will owe no more than the value of the property. FHA insurance will cover any balance due the lender.

All borrowers must be at least 62 years of age. Any existing lien on the property must be small enough to be paid off at settlement of the reverse mortgage.

FHA Title I

The Property Improvement Loan insurance program of FHA **Title I** was established in 1934 to federally insure loans to finance property improvements. HUD insures loans to finance improvements, alterations, and repairs of individual homes

(20-year loan), manufactured home on permanent foundation ($17,500 with real property taxes for 15 years), manufactured house ($7,500, personal property with DMV tax bill for 12 years), apartment buildings (15-year loan), and nonresidential structures. The structure must have been completed and occupied for 90 days if the FHA Title I loan is for new residential structure.

For improving a multifamily structure, the maximum loan amount is $12,000 per family unit, not to exceed a total of $60,000 for the structure. These are fixed-rate loans, for which lenders charge interest at market rates. The interest rates are not subsidized by HUD. A Title I loan may also finance new construction of nonresidential buildings. Title I loans may be used to finance permanent property improvements that protect or improve the basic livability or utility of the property—including manufactured homes, single-family and multi-family homes, nonresidential structures, and the preservation of historic homes. The loans can also be used for fire safety equipment.

Loans on single-family homes and nonresidential structures may extend to 15 years and 32 days. Loans on apartment buildings may be based on a per unit amount. The total for the building may not exceed the maximum loan amount. The term may not exceed 15 years. The FHA insures private lenders against the risk of default for up to 90 percent of any single loan. The annual premium for this insurance is $1 per $100 of the amount advanced. Lenders process these loans. Loans for more than $5,000 require that a mortgage or deed of trust be placed on the improved property. Title I loans can be in second, third, or fourth position. No equity, title insurance, or appraisal is needed. Title I loans can not be used to consolidate revolving debt into a new loan. For more information, visit www.calfha.com.

The Section 2 program of FHA Title I is part of the National Housing Act and was established by the legislation in 1969 to federally insure loans to finance the purchase of manufactured homes. HUD insures loans to finance the purchase of manufactured homes or lots. The loans are made by private lending institutions. The maximum loan amount is $40,500 for a manufactured home, $54,000 for a manufactured home and a suitable developed lot, and $13,500 for a developed lot. The maximum limits for combination of home and lot loans may be increased up to 85 percent in designated high-cost areas. The maximum loan term varies from 15 to 25 years.

Any person who is able to make the cash investment and the payments is considered an eligible applicant. Title I applications should be sent to U.S. Department of HUD, Lender Approval and Rectification Division, 451 7th Street, S.W., Room 9146, Washington, D.C. 20410-8000; (202) 708-4464. Lenders may contact the FHA's Home Mortgage Insurance Division at (202) 708-2121 for information about how to participate in the Title I loan insurance program. Consumers can register complaints about Title I lenders or contractors by contacting the Home Mortgage Insurance Division or state or local consumer protection agencies.

Energy-Efficient Mortgage (EEM)

EEM is a loan program intended to make the existing home stock more efficient through the installation of energy-saving improvements, as was described in

Chapter 3 for conventional loans. The EEM loan may be a 15- or 30-year fixed-rate or adjustable-rate (ARM) loan from an FHA-approved lender. Again, the FHA requires at least a 3.5 percent cash investment on the property, based on the sale price. The amount of the loan is based on the value of the home, plus the projected cost of the energy-efficient improvements. For FHA and DVA loans, however, the program may be used for one- to four-unit single-family homes and townhomes. The EEM may also be used for condominiums, though certain restrictions apply. Debt ratios are typically the same as for regular FHA requirements. Typical improvements that are made using an EEM loan include replacing a furnace or cooling system; fixing or replacing a chimney; insulating an attic, crawl space, or pipes and air ducts; replacing doors or windows; and installing active and passive solar technologies. Several HUD programs can help with financing solar energy systems. For example, FHA mortgage insurance is available for solar energy systems in these three ways:

1. The EEM Program (from 1995), which recognizes that the improved energy efficiency of a house can increase its affordability by reducing operating costs. Energy improvements must be identified with a home energy rating. The resulting cost-effective improvements may not be valued at more than 5 percent of the property value (not to exceed $8,000) or $4,000, whichever is greater. The EEM may be used on new and existing one- to four-unit properties in conjunction with FHA 203 (b), FHA 203 (k), 221 (d) 2, 234 (c), and 203 (h) loans for purchases and refinances.

2. Mortgage Increase for Solar Systems (from 1978) allows the FHA to exceed by 20 percent the maximum loan limit under 203(b) and 203 (k), which allows for installation of solar heating and domestic hot water systems. A 100 percent operational conventional backup system must be in place to act as a passive and active solar hot water system.

3. Title I allows up to $25,000 for single-family homes that may be used to finance energy-efficient improvements.

4.2 FHA LOAN CONSIDERATIONS

FHA vs. First-Time Home-Buyer Programs (FTHB)

Although the mortgage loan broker needs to be familiar with many different loan programs, it is often difficult to distinguish between FHA and FTHB loans. Because many borrowers have less than perfect credit, FHA will allow a qualifying ratio of 31/43, even with derogatory credit, whereas **FTHB** loans are usually more strict on the ratios for poor credit.

Congress enacted a tax credit to help the housing market during the mortgage meltdown, and over 1.5 million people took advantage of the program, according to the Internal Revenue Service. This projected $15 billion program has created a large demand for lower-priced homes to aid first-time homebuyers. As can be seen in Figure 4-7, FTHB loans average just under 40 percent of home sales. The tax stimulus, along with lower prices and lower interest rates, has pushed the average to about half of all sales.

FIGURE 4.7   First-time homebuyers (1981-2009).

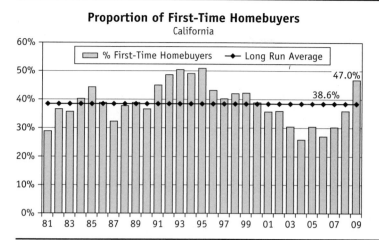

The number of first-time homebuyers would represent an even higher number of buyers, but over half the home purchasers are competing with each other and with investors to acquire the property. Just under 20 percent of all buyers are paying all cash and not requiring any loan financing. When a government loan buyer requires the seller to comply with the loan requirements for the property, called minimum qualifications, a seller may take less total sales price for a short escrow period, often less than two weeks, with no work requirements on their part. About 10 percent of all purchases are for rental investment purposes, with another 5 percent representing vacation second homes. When first-time homebuyers have to compete against these other groups, fewer FTHB loans are made. Naturally, the requirements for a non-owner occupied investment rental property or a second home have higher down payments, and lower loan amounts. The larger down payment looks like a stronger buyer to a seller and makes it less likely the buyer will default and the more the lender is willing to take the risk for the loan. It could also be the deciding factor if there is more than one offer made on a particular home. As you can see in figure 4-8, many homes in 2009 received multiple offers.

The FHA down payment requires a minimum of 3.5 percent of the total funds needed and will allow a gift from a family member for the entire down payment. FTHB loans require at least 3.5 percent of a 5 percent down payment to come from the borrower's own funds. FHA allows non-owner occupant co-borrowers, even if the co-borrower is out of state, whereas FTHB loans will allow co-borrower only if the primary borrower(s) occupy the subject property. In addition, FHA allows 3.5 percent to 8 percent down payments for loans up to 4 units, whereas FTHB financing requires a minimum of 10 percent down on three- and four-unit property.

FHA MIP

FHA insures lenders against loss on FHA loans. The lender makes the loan according to the FHA guidelines, and the loan is insured by FHA. The MIP must

FIGURE 4.8   Home percentages with multiple offers (1999-2009).

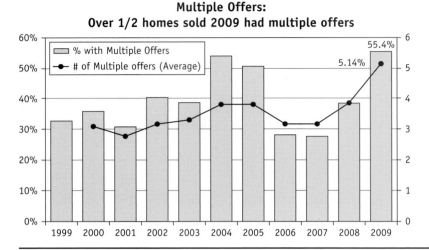

be paid on all FHA loans, regardless of LTV. The MIP is paid by the borrower and may be paid as follows: For a 30-year FHA loan on a single-family residence as of April 15, 2010, the borrower will pay 2.25 percent of the loan amount (as an up-front premium (UFMIP), plus 1/2 of 1 percent as the annual renewal premium. If the property is a condominium, no UFMIP fee is required, but the monthly premium is still applied. Congress mandated that private mortgage insurance (PMI) automatically be terminated when the LTV reaches 78 percent based on the original value of the property. The annual premium is also eliminated when the homebuyer's equity reaches 22 percent according to the original property value, not current appraisal. Figure 4-9 shows the FHA MIP data:

FIGURE 4.9   Federal housing mortgage data.

Up-front premiums are added to the base FHA mortgage and financed into the loan			
Purchase Money Mortgages and Full Qualifying Refinances	2.25%		
Streamline Refinances All Types	1.50%		
FHA Secure Delinquent Mortgagors	3.00%		
Annual premiums will be charged based on the initial LTV ratio and length of the mortgage (except for FHASecure delinquent mortgages)			
Purchase Money Mortgages, Full-Qualifying Refinances, and Streamline Refinances			
LTV	Annual for Loans Over 15 years	LTV	Annual for Loans 15 years of Less
LTV ≤ 95%	.50	LTV ≤ 90%	None
LTV > 95%	.55	LTV > 90%	.25
FHASecure delinquent mortgagors Annual premiums for all loans regardless of term			
LTV ≤ 95%		.50	
LTV > 95%		.55	

FIGURE 4.10   Calculating FHA monthly and up-front MIP.

FHA up-front MIP (UFMIP)
UFMIP based on MIP Chart Up-front MIP + Base Mortgage = Full Mortgage Full Mortgage and Base Mortgage must be different LTV is calculated on the **Base** Mortgage Amount
$175,000 x 2.25% = $3,937.50 (.50 will be paid in cash at closing) $175,000 + $3937.50 = $178,937 Full Mortgage
FHA monthly MIP
Base Mortgage x Monthly factor ÷ 12 = Monthly MIP
$175,000 x .55% ÷ 12 = $80.21 monthly MIP
Most FHA loans require both UFMIP and monthly MIP—check the appropriate MIP chart for loan perimeters.

As an example, if the loan amount is for $155,250 the front fee amount would be calculated: $155,250 × 2.25% = $3493.13 up front. The monthly MIP amount would be calculated: $155,250 × 0.5% = $776.25/12 months = $64.69 per month until the LTV is 78%. The up-front fee may be paid in one of four ways: (1) in cash by the buyer, (2) in cash by the seller, (3) split between the buyer and seller in any proportion, or (4) added to the loan amount and paid over the life of the loan. Figure 4-10 shows how to calculate FHA monthly and FHA up-front MIP.

Cancellation of Annual MIP

For mortgages with terms greater than 15 years, the annual MIP will be cancelled when the LTV reaches 78 percent based on the original value of the loan, provided the borrower has paid the annual MIP for at least five years. For mortgages with terms of 15 years of less, the annual MIP will be cancelled when the LTV reaches 78 percent.

The borrowers cannot request that it be removed once they feel they have reached 20 percent equity. The borrowers would have to refinance to have it removed before then.

The annual MIP of .50 percent will be collected the *entire duration* of the loan for *condos and 203k* loans closed prior to January 1, 2006, regardless of the term or LTV.

FHA mortgage insurance may have an unclaimed refund due to a previous FHA loan homeowner. If an individual had a previous HUD/FHA insurance loan, he or she may be eligible for a refund on part of the insurance premium or a share of the earnings. To search FHA records to determine qualification, see http://www.hud.gov/offices/hsg/comp/refunds/.

FHA Streamline Loan (Rate Reduction)

To obtain this loan, the borrower must have an existing FHA loan. The purpose is to lower the interest rate and the monthly payment without all the costs associated with obtaining a completely new loan. This loan does not allow any cash out for the borrower. The necessary costs that will be incurred for items such as recording may be paid in cash or added to the unpaid loan amount. No appraisal is required because FHA is merely restructuring the existing loan. To qualify for this loan, irrelevant of the credit history, the borrower may not have had any late payment during the previous 12 months. Effective in 2010, FHA **streamline** refinances require documentation of both income and assets and require an appraisal if the closing costs are financed.

Other FHA Features and Loan Programs

The loan **origination fee** is based on the loan amount, not including MIP, but the discount points are based on the total amount financed, including any MIP. A buyer must pay his or her own impound account for property taxes and insurance. If an FHA loan is paid off, a refund of MIP may be requested. Each item below is an FHA-approved feature or program; however, there may be no lender currently offering the feature or the program. Lenders are free to offer or NOT offer conventional, FHA, or VA programs according to the policy of the lender, the market conditions, and the investor criteria.

Secondary Residence

A borrower may have a secondary residence in addition to his or her primary, principal residence. For FHA these are only permitted when the appropriate **Home Ownership Center (HOC)** agrees that an undue hardship exists, meaning that affordable rental housing that meets the needs of the family is not available for lease in the area or within reasonable commuting distance to work, and the maximum loan amount is 85% of the lesser of the appraised value or the sales price. Direct Endorsement (DE) lenders are not authorized to grant hardship exceptions. All of the following conditions must be met:

- The secondary residence must NOT be a vacation home or otherwise used primarily for recreational purposes.
- The borrower must obtain the secondary residence because of seasonal employment, employment relocation, or other circumstances not related to recreational use of the residence.
- There must be a demonstrated lack of affordable rental housing meeting the needs of the borrower in the area or within a reasonable commuting distance of the borrower's employment. Documentation to support this must include:
  - A satisfactory explanation from the borrower of the need for a secondary residence and the lack of available rental housing in the area that meets the need.
  - Written evidence from local real estate professionals who verify a lack of acceptable rental housing in the area.

FHA Housing Loan Programs

1. *Hope for Homeowners (HOPE).* Like a conventional loan program: The FHA offers a new 30-year, fixed rate loan that is insured by FHA. The program is designed for people at risk of losing their home due to default and foreclosure.

2. *Indian Home Loan Guarantee Program Section 184.* The program provides home ownership opportunities through a guaranteed mortgage for Native Americans, tribes, **Tribally Designated Housing Entities (TDHEs)**, and Indian Housing Authorities on Indian land. This loan is specifically for American Indian and Alaska Native families, tribes, Alaskan villages or tribally designated housing entities. Congress established this program in 1992 to facilitate homeownership in Native American communities. The borrowers can purchase a home with a low down payment, no monthly mortgage insurance, and flexible underwriting.

- 2.25% down payment requirement for loans over $50,000;
- 1.25% down payment requirement for loan under $50,000;
- No monthly mortgage insurance
- A one-time, 1% loan guarantee fee that can be added to your financed loan.

The program may be used to purchase an existing home, construction of a home (stick-built or a manufactured home on a permanent foundation), rehab loans, purchase and rehab, or refinance (rate and term, streamline, and cash out).

HUD guarantees the mortgage loan made to eligible borrowers. The loan guarantee assures the lender that its investment will be repaid in the event of a foreclosure. The borrower pays a 1 percent loan guarantee fee at closing which may be financed in the mortgage or paid in cash. The borrower applies for the loan with a participating lender. If leasing tribal land they work with the tribe and the Bureau of Indian Affairs to obtain an approved 50-year lease. The lender then evaluates the necessary loan documentation and submits the loan for approval to the HUD Office of Loan Guarantee.

4.3 VETERANS' LOANS

Veterans Administration (DVA) loans, which began in 1944, are those loans that contain a provision in which the U.S. **DVA** guarantees the loan up to a maximum amount. The purchase allows financing of 100 percent of the purchase price with no down payment, provided that the Certificate of Reasonable Value (CRV = DVA appraisal) is equal to or greater than the loan amount. The maximum loan term is 30 years. DVA loans may be on property containing one to four units, but the veteran is required to occupy the premises. Even with no down payment required, the borrower still must qualify for the loan amount according to income. When an initial veteran borrower places no down payment and no closing costs on an original purchase, the loan is referred to as a **"VA No-No."** The loan is assumable with specific qualifications to a subsequent purchaser. DVA loans carry no prepayment penalty. Although VA does not have a maximum sales price, the VA has set a maximum loan amount that is guaranteed. For a loan of $417,000, for the no down payment option, the VA funding fee is not included. A loan of $450,000 with a small down payment of 5 percent is referred to as the VA Jumbo Loan.

Figure 4-11 shows the percent of buyers with zero down payment for both the first-time homebuyer and for repeat buyers. Although many of these buyers financed the down payment and obtained a conventional loan, as discussed in **Chapter 3**, the veteran no-money-down loan program would be part of these

FIGURE 4.11   Percent of buyers with no down payment.

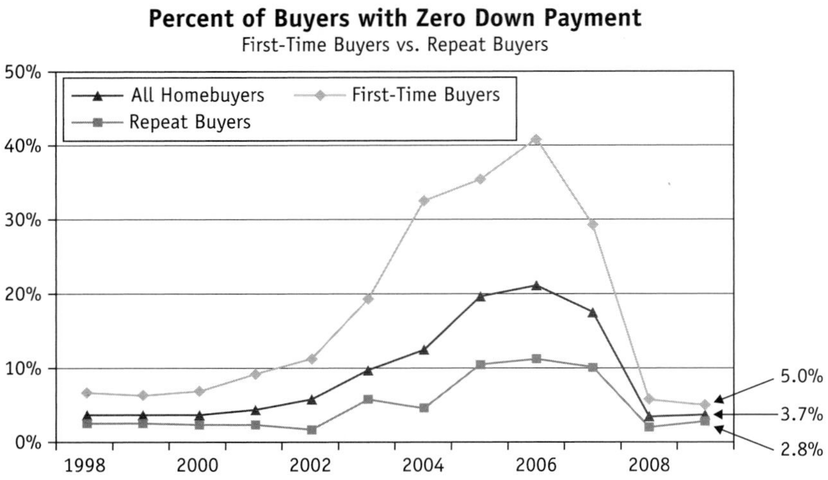

loans. Historically, less than 10 percent of all loans were made with no down payment. The subprime meltdown and stated income with financing of the entire purchase price has led to the rise to about 40 percent of buyers with no money down at the height of this type of market, in 2006, before returning back to normal no down market conditions, for which the majority of no-money-down loans are VA.

The mortgage loan broker should ensure that the applicant will qualify on the various aspects required for a DVA loan. One such requirement is the possession of the DVA separation papers form **DD214** and **Certificate of Eligibility**, which shows the eligible dates of inclusive service. Should the applicant not have a copy of this form, the mortgage loan broker may wish to have the veteran apply for a copy (see Figure 4-12). For example, since 1980, an enlisted person needed 24 months of active service to qualify. Because of budget constraints, many military personnel were discharged after 23 months and three weeks and would not be eligible to qualify under the 24-month rule.

FIGURE 4.12   VA matrix grid.

VA Matrix

	LTV Matrix				
Transaction	Owner Occupied	2nd Home	Investor	Property Type	Loan Amount at 100%
	LTV CLTV	LTV	LTV		
Purchase or Rate and Term Refinance	100%	N/A	N/A	Single Family, Condo, 2-4 Family	$417,000 To $729,750
Cash Out	90%	N/A	N/A	Single Family, Condo	$417,000 To $729,750
Refinancing	Streamline Refinance—with 12-month mortgage payment history and payment reduction, borrowers do not re-qualify. Loan amount can only be increased for closing costs with new appraisal.				

FIGURE 4.12 (*Continued*)

Programs Offered	Fixed Rate Mortgages and GPM and in some areas, GEM's		
Mortgage Insurance	VA funding fee is in lieu of insurance. See "Risk-Based" Premium charts		
Eligible Properties	SFD, 2-4, Condo, PUD—Condo's and PUD units must be approved		
	ERA	Dates	Time Required
	WW 11	9/16/40—7/25/47	90 days
	Post WW II	7/26/47—6/26/50	181 days
	Korean	6/27/50—1/31/55	90 days
	Post Korean	2/1/55—8/4/64	181 days
	Vietnam	8/5/64 — 5/7/75 Note: The Vietnam Era began 2/28/61 for those individuals who served in the Republic of Vietnam	90 days
Eligible Borrowers	Post Vietnam	5/8/75—9/7/80 5/8/75—10/16/81 9/8/80—8/1/90 10/17/81—8/1/90	Enlisted—181 days Officers—181 days Enlisted—2 years** Officers—2 years**
	Persian Gulf	8/20/90—Present	2 years **Note: The veteran must have served 2 years or the full period, which called or ordered to active duty (at least 90 days during wartime and 181 during peacetime.)
Secondary Financing	Allowed. Note must be at least 5 years in length. Since VA is no money down formula, 2nd mortgage would be used to exceed the maximum financing of $240,000/$322,700		
Automated Approval	FHLMC-Loan Prospector, FNMA-DO/DU, and pmiAURA System for VA		
Assumability	$500 Fee and the Borrower must qualify. No release of liability		
•	**Income Restrictions**		
Qualifying Ratios	41/41		
Documentation Types	Full, Alternative Documentation		
Non-Occupant Co-Borrowers	Veterans and their spouse only. Eligible veterans have served continuous active duty for at least the time frames listed and have an honorable release or discharge,		
Self-Employed	Minimum 2 years		
	Asset Restrictions		
Cash Reserves	None required		
Gift Letters	May come from any source not involved in the transaction. Must verify donor, transfer and receipt of funds.		
Seller Contributions	4% of sales price, not including points. Transaction may be structured so that borrower pays no money at closing, but borrowers may not receive cash back at closing.		
Borrowed Funds	Funds may be borrowed—must be counted for qualifying		
	. Credit Restrictions		
Multiple Properties	Number of VA loans is limited by entitlement		
Credit Scores	Not considered		
Major Derogatory	Significant derogatory credit may be acceptable with extenuating circumstances		

Spouses of service persons missing in action (MIAs) or listed as prisoners of war (POWs) for at least 90 days are eligible to purchase under DVA. It is generally required to have an honorable discharge to receive DVA benefits. However, an exception is that an applicant may apply to the DVA adjudication board for a Certificate of Eligibility if his or her discharge was other than honorable. Figure 4-12 shows a matrix for the Veterans Administration loan information.

Persons who have already used a DVA loan may be eligible for partial entitlement. A borrower may have used a DVA loan in the past and still have a partial or full entitlement remaining. To determine the applicant's current eligibility status, contact the DVA office to obtain a current Certificate of Eligibility. Eligible applicants must conform to dates of service, as discussed in Chapter 6, Figure 6-5.

The loan may be fixed rate or variable rate. The law requires that the VA be paid a funding fee with guaranteed loans, except for veterans receiving compensation for service-connected disabilities and surviving spouses of veterans who had a service-connected death. All DVA loans have a **funding fee**, as shown in Figure 4-13, which may be paid as follows: (1) the seller may pay the fee, (2) the veteran may pay the fee, or (3) the fee may be added to the DVA loan amount, over and above the purchase price for a loan in which the veteran puts no money down, provided that the combined total does not exceed the maximum loan amount.

DVA guarantees the lender will be protected against loss in the event of foreclosure up to a maximum amount on a tiered guaranty structure as of December 22, 1989. The lender would not incur a loss when making a loan to a veteran. Only the top portion of the loan is guaranteed, The lender obtains an independent appraisal for the property. There is little risk of loss because the property would most likely sell at an auction for higher than the lender's loan amount and the guarantee portion.

For example, if a property appraised for $200,000 and the lender made a loan to a veteran for $200,000, the guaranty would cover the top 25% of the loan, or $50,000. If a foreclosure were to take place, the guaranty would cover up to $50,000, so the property would have to sell for below $150,000 before the lender would incur any loss. If the property sold for $180,000, the VA guarantee would

FIGURE 4.13   DVA funding fees.

ALL FIXED-RATE and ARM LOANS		
LOAN TYPE	FUNDING FEE (Active Duty or Vet)	FUNDING FEE (Nat'l Guard/Reserve)
Purchase (first time use of eligible)		
less than 5% down payment	2.0% (subsequent use 3.0%)	2.75% (subsequent use 3.0%)
5%, but less than 10% down	1.5%	2.25%
10% or more down	1.25%	2.0%
Interest Rate Reduction Refinance	0.50%	0.50%
Regular Refinance (of DVA loan)	3.0%	3.0%
(of non DVA loan)	2.0%	2.0%

FIGURE 4.14 DVA loan program codes.

Program Code	Program Description
V-01	30 Year, Fixed Rate
V-02	15 Year, Fixed Rate
V-03	30 Year, Fixed Rate with Buydown
V-03V21S	30 Year, Fixed Rate with Combo Buydown
V-06	30 Year, GPM, Existing Construction
V-07	30 Year, GPM, New Construction
V-09	30 Year, ARM
V-10	30 Year, ARM with Lender Subsidized Compressed Buydown
V-13	20 Year, Fixed Rate
V-14	25 Year, Fixed Rate
V-19	30 Year, ARM with Seller Subsidized Compressed Buydown
V-20	30 Year, ARM with P&I Seller Subsidy
V-21	30 Year, Fixed Rate with P&I Seller Subsidy

cover the $20,000 loss that the lender would have had if the loan were not a VA guaranteed loan.

DVA loans previously offered only 30-year fixed-rate loans. During recent changes in all loan programs, a variety of more flexible programs has replaced the former DVA loan programs. Figure 4-14 shows the current loan programs.

Veterans Regulated Closing Costs

The cost for obtaining the loan is regulated such that a veteran may pay reasonable and customary amounts for any of the following items:

1. Credit report.
2. Appraisal fee for VA-approved appraisal report.
3. Recording fees.
4. Insurance: Title policy and hazard policy and prorations for an impound account.
5. VA funding fee.
6. Survey, inspection report, or similar veteran-requested items.
7. Federal Express, Express Mail, or similar service when the saved per diem interest cost to the veteran exceeds the cost of the special handling.

The lender may charge the veteran a flat fee, called the loan origination fee. The fee may not exceed 1 percent of the loan amount and must be in lieu of all other charges relating to costs of origination, including appraisal, inspections, escrow or settlement fees, documentation preparation fee, conveyance fees, attorney or title insurance, photographs, postage and mailing charges, notary fee, assignment or related commitment or marketing fees, trustee fees, loan application and processing fees, Truth-in-Lending Act (Reg Z and HOEPA) and disclosure statement fees, tax service fee, and any charges by a loan broker, finder, or third party affiliated with the lender.

DVA Loans with Second Trust Deeds

The Veterans Administration will allow a second trust deed with a DVA loan. The following is a list of the major criteria required. Although this information is believed to be accurate, it cannot be guaranteed.

1. The total amount of the first trust deed and second trust deed cannot exceed the CRV.
2. The buyer must qualify for the payments on both the first and second trust deeds.
3. The interest rate of the second trust deed cannot exceed the rate of the first trust deed.
4. The second trust deed cannot have a prepayment penalty clause.
5. The second trust deed must be assumable and may not contain an alienation clause.
6. The second trust deed can include a balloon payment; the amortization period may be for any period of time.
7. Late payment charges are allowable on the second trust deed, as they are on the first trust deed.
8. The second trust deed may be carried by anyone.
9. Points may be allowed on origination of the second trust deed: (a) the seller cannot charge points; (b) any other qualified source[**] may charge points, to be approved by DVA, which are set at submission.
10. The second trust deed can be for any portion of the total financing.[†]
11. The second trust deed may be written on a DVA-approved (and modified) first trust deed and note, or other forms will be acceptable, providing the wording meets DVA requirements.
12. A copy of the second trust deed must be submitted for approval at the time the loan application package is submitted to DVA for approval.
13. There is no maximum amount on the second trust deed set by the DVA.
14. The second trust deed must carry this endorsement on the face of the deed of trust and on reverse side of the note:
    "This note and deed of trust are subordinated to the note and first deed of trust date _____ in favor of _____ as beneficiary."

DVA Refinances

Rate Reduction Refinances

When interest rates decline, a veteran may wish to lower the amount of the loan payments by applying for a **rate reduction refinance**. Under this program, the

---

[**] Qualified source is defined as a lender who is able to negotiate the note within the parameters of the California usury laws.

[†] The DVA's position is to provide maximum benefits to the veteran but also to protect him or her from unexpected situations. The DVA will allow and encourage reasonable terms of the second and will work to ensure that the veteran receives the best financing available.

veteran may transfer the amount of entitlement used on the existing DVA loan to the new DVA loan, provided there are no cash proceeds to the veteran.

The new loan is limited to the amount of the outstanding balance on the existing DVA loan plus allowable closing costs for the new loan. The payoff of an existing second loan cannot be included when the new loan amount is computed. The loan must meet investor requirements with regard to credit and equity and the DVA's normal guarantee requirements.

Standard Refinance

The veteran may refinance an existing loan with a new DVA loan and receive cash proceeds. However, the new loan amount is limited to 90 percent of the CRV and *must meet normal investor guarantee requirements* (75 percent of the appraised value of the property, plus the remaining entitlement, up to the maximum entitlement, which is $89,912 as of 2005).

Usually, a veteran cannot refinance an existing DVA loan with a new DVA loan under this program, because only *unused* entitlement over and above the entitlement used on the existing loan, if any, may be applied to the new DVA loan. Unlike the rate reduction refinance, the *entitlement used on the existing loan cannot be transferred to the new DVA loan* because the veteran is receiving cash proceeds.

In order for the veteran to restore the entitlement on the existing DVA loan, the loan has to be paid in full and the property sold or disposed of in some way, such as by fire (see DVA information: "one-time restoration of entitlement").

Again, the loan is subject to investor requirements wherein the veteran's entitlement or equity must equal at least 25 percent of the CRV and also must meet DVA normal guarantee requirements.

DVA Jumbo Loan

In October 2008 Public Law 110-289, the Veterans' Benefit Improvement Act of 2008, was enacted. This law allows $0 down payment in qualified counties to go up to $729,750 on loans closed through December 2011. Qualifying customers apply for a regular VA loan with $0 down, up to the $417,000 maximum loan amount that lenders will use due to the maximum guaranty limit.

Qualifying customers can now apply for a VA Jumbo Loan up to $1,000,000 using the VALoans.com Super Max program. The qualified borrower can apply for a home loan with no money down under new VA Loans Maximum Guaranty Amount guidelines:

1. No money down for qualified borrowers for home loans up to a maximum of $417,000 or the higher limits for certain counties.
2. The VA guarantees the loan up to a maximum guaranty amount of 25 percent of the loan.

The VA guaranty amount is calculated based on the total amount of the home loan excluding higher amounts for certain counties.

Example Not Using Higher Limit Counties: If the borrower wants the maximum no money down $417,000 VA home loan amount, the VA guaranty amount would be the maximum $104,250.

The same no-money-down rules apply for the first $417,000 of the loan.

1. Borrower pays a 25 percent down payment only on the amount above $417,000.
2. Borrower pays the funding fee in cash for loans between $417,000 and $1,000,000.

Example Using Higher Limit Counties: If the borrower wants the maximum no-money-down $729,750 VA home loan amount, the VA guaranty amount would be the maximum $182,438.

The same no-money-down rules apply for the first $729,750 of the loan.

1. The same no-money-down rules apply for the first $417,000 of the loan.
2. Borrower pays a 25% down payment only on the amount above $417,000.
3. Borrower pays a funding fee in cash for loans between $417,000 and $1,000,000.

VALoans.com Super Max example in counties with maximum $0 down loan of $417,000 using a sample loan amount of $690,000:

- The first $417,000 of the loan = $0 down.
- Any amount in excess of $417,000 = 25 percent down payment on that amount.
- A total loan of $690,000 would be $273,000 over the no-money-down limit of $417,000.
- Borrower pays a 25 percent down payment on that $273,000 = $68,250.
- Borrower pays a funding fee in cash up front.

VALoans.com Super Max example in counties with maximum $0 down loan of $729,750 using a sample loan amount of $1,000,000:

- The first $729,750 of the loan = $0 down.
- Any amount in excess of $729,750 = 25 percent down payment on that amount.
- A total loan of $1,000,000 would be $270,250 over the no money down limit of $729,750.
- Borrower pays a 25 percent down payment on that $270,250 = $67,563.
- Borrower pays a funding fee in cash up front.

Additional information on all Super Jumbo VA Loans:

1. Minimum FICO score of 680 required for loans above $650,000.
2. Manufactured homes are not eligible for VALoans.com Super Max program.
3. Funding fees cannot be financed above conforming loan limits.
4. 2- to 4-unit purchase transactions and all refinance transactions will remain at conforming loan limits. They are not available under this VA Jumbo Program.
5. Refinance transactions remain at conforming loan limits.
6. The funding fee must be paid in cash either by the veteran or the seller.
7. The VA Loans.com Super Max program is for fixed-rate loans only.
8. Other terms and conditions may apply.

Veteran's EEM (DVA EEM)

Veterans who purchase an existing home (more than one year old) or veterans who currently own and occupy a dwelling are eligible to include energy-conservation improvements in the financing.

Appraisals issued for existing properties notify the veteran of the options available for energy-conservation improvements.

The loan may be increased up to $3,000 solely according to the documentation costs, or up to $6,000, provided the increase in the monthly loan payment does not exceed the likely reduction in monthly utility costs. In either case, a local utility company or qualified firm will complete a home energy audit.

For a refinance loan, the loan may not exceed 90 percent of the CRV plus the cost of the energy-efficient improvements (CRV $\times$ 0.90 + cost of improvements).

The funding fee must be calculated on the full loan amount, including the cost of improvements.

Seller Concessions

Effective July 1, 1990, on a DVA loan, the seller may pay for all of the veteran's normal closing costs. The veteran cannot be charged an escrow fee. For DVA purposes, a seller concession is defined as anything of value added to the transaction by the seller/builder for which the buyer pays no additional amount and which the seller is not customarily expected or required to pay or provide. Any concession or combination of **seller concessions** that exceed 4 percent of the established reasonable value of the property will be considered excessive for DVA loan purposes. Normal discount points and any closing costs that are customarily paid by the seller will not be considered a concession.

Any closing costs that are customarily paid by the seller, or closing costs equally likely to be paid by either buyer or seller (such as discount points), will not be considered a concession for purposes of determining whether the total concessions are within the established limit. Examples of items that would be considered concessions are funding fee, recurring closing costs, seller paying off buyer's debts to qualify, and large-cost items purchased by the seller on behalf of the buyer, such as a television or spa.

The Veterans Administration allows the interest rate and discount points to be negotiated between the buyer and the lender. There are no maximum interest rates as of October 28, 1992, within reasonable limits set by the DVA.

FHA or DVA Loan Approval

The mortgage loan broker should determine whether the source of the loan funds will come from a DVA Automatic Lender or an FHA Direct Endorsement lender, which means that a loan may be processed, approved, and closed before being sent to the DVA or FHA. To close the loan, the loan package must be completed. An FHA-DVA comparison chart is shown in Figure 4-15.

FIGURE 4.15 FHA–DVA comparison chart.

Buyer Characteristics	FHA	DVA
Eligibility	Any qualified borrower	Qualified veterans only
Owner-occupant loans only	Yes	Yes
Citizenship requirement	None	None
Property units	1–4 units	1–4 units
Loan characteristics		
Maximum loan	$78,660 to $261,609 depending on region (Fig. 4.1)	$240,000 ($60,000 x 4)
Maximum interest rate	Negotiated by borrower and lender	Set by DVA; negotiated by borrower and lender
Down payment required	Yes	No
Buyer permitted to pay points (negotiable)	Yes	Yes plus maximum 1% loan fee
FHA MIP or DVA fee	1.5% UPMIP ½ of 1% MIP to 78% LTVR	1.25–2% funding fee (see Fig. 4.5)
Secondary financing allowed	Yes	Yes
Secondary financing for down payment	No	Yes
Assumable loans (no due-on-sale)	Yes—with qualification	Yes—with qualification
Prepayment	No	No
Lender protection	Insured to full extent of losses from default	Maximum $60,000 guarantee (1-1-02)

Note: Neither FHA nor DVA loans may exceed appraised value.

4.4 CREDIT ALERT INTERACTIVE VOICE RESPONSE SYSTEM (CAIVRS)

All FHA and DVA loans must be cleared through the CAIVRS system before the loan may receive loan approval and close escrow. The purpose of this law is to ensure that the prospective borrower does not have additional debts that may not have been revealed to the lender.

The **CAIVRS** is a federal government database of delinquent federal debtors that allows federal agencies to reduce the risk to federal loan and loan guarantee

FIGURE 4.16 CAIVRS record sources.

Department of Housing and Urban Development (HUD)	Federal Deposit Insurance Corporation (FDIC)	Department of Justice (DOJ)
Department of Agriculture (USDA)	Department of Education (DOC)	Small Business Administration (SBA)

programs. CAIVRS alerts participating federal lending agencies when an applicant for credit benefits has a federal lien, judgment, or a federal loan, such as a student loan, in default or foreclosure. CAIVRS also reports when an individual has had a claim paid by a reporting agency. Since 1987, this system has saved the taxpayers more than $12 billion in potential claims and more than $4 billion in potential losses. Additionally, the United States Department of Agriculture (USDA), for farm and crop loans, and DVA have also realized significant saving in excess of $6 million.

CAIVRS allows authorized employees of participating federal agencies to access a database of delinquent federal borrowers for the purpose of prescreening direct loan applicants for creditworthiness. CAIVRS also permits approved private lenders acting on the government's behalf to access the delinquent borrower database records for the purpose of prescreening the creditworthiness of applicants for federally related loans. The list of database sources is shown in Figure 4-16.

Authorized users may access CAIVRS via the Internet or by touch-tone telephone where the user is prompted to enter their CAIVRS access code (an agency-assigned identification number or lender identification). The system will verify the authorization number and then prompt the caller to enter the social security number (SSN) of the applicant. If the applicant's SSN is not in the database, the caller will receive a clear confirmation code. If there is a record of default for the borrower whose SSN was entered, the caller will be given the name of the agency reporting the default, the case number of the defaulted debt, the type of delinquency (default, claim, foreclosure, lien, or judgment), and a telephone number to call for further information or assistance.

Federal law prevents "delinquent federal debtors from obtaining federal loans or loan insurance guarantees." CAIVRS provides a single repository of delinquent federal debtor records, with easy access through a variety of media for prescreening applicants for federal benefits. Most credit bureau reports do not identify insured debts as being delinquent federal debts. By participating in CAIVRS, federal lending agencies have ready access to an interdepartmental database of delinquent federal debts that provides federal financial managers with the information necessary to comply with the U.S. code requirements.

4.5 CALVET

The **CalVet** program was enacted in 1921 and is funded through the sale of general obligation, tax-exempt bonds, backed by the state of California until 1980. Demand for funds exceeded the ability to fund the general obligation bonds. The first CalVet revenue bonds were sold in 1980, also repaid by CalVet loan holders. Federal laws and regulations resulting from the Mortgage Subsidy Bond Tax Act of 1980, the Deficit Reduction Act of 1984, the Tax Reform Act of 1986, and subsequent amendments have affected how CalVet bond funds may be used.

In recent years, the U.S. Supreme Court in *Del Monte* ruled that all United States veterans with California residency may be eligible to apply for CalVet loans. The veteran need not have been a California resident prior to service. Peacetime-era veterans are also eligible. Typically, the veteran must have served 90 consecutive days on active duty and received a discharge under honorable conditions. Active-duty personnel are eligible. An applicant must have a DVA Certificate of Eligibility.

CalVet loans have short escrows, usually under 30 days, with liberal qualifying criteria. Secondary financing is allowed, subject to CalVet approval. The property must be owner occupied at all times, with the exception that it may be rented to a direct family member if written CalVet approval is obtained. The down payment can range from 0 to 20 percent, depending on the program for which the veteran qualifies. One very common program is the CalVet97 program, which requires a 3 percent down payment. The loan period is usually for 30 years but may be extended for up to 40 years. Loan amounts vary between counties, up to a maximum loan amount of $359,650 as of January 1, 2005. The loans have a variable interest rate with no cap, as set by CalVet. Any adjustments to the loan payment are made as of March 1 each year. And if needed, the loans are also reusable. Thus, if a veteran pays off a CalVet loan, the veteran may get a new CalVet loan. The property may be a single-family residence, condominium, or mobile home, and it may even be a farm. CalVet qualifications include income limits, as shown in Figure 4-17. A CalVet loan may be used again and again, so long as the previous loan has been fully paid off. The new loan must contain the then current features, eligibility, and financial qualifications. Figure 4-18 shows the loan programs for various property types as of October 2009.

FIGURE 4.17   Family income limitations.

Statistical Area	Income Limit		Statistical Area	Income Limit
	Nontargeted	Targeted		Nontargeted
Los Angeles–Long Beach	$ 71,898	$ 77,560	Santa Cruz–Watsonville	$70,955
Oakland (Alameda and			Santa Rosa (Sonoma Co.)	66,815
Contra Cos.)	77,740	94,640	Vallejo–Fairfield–Napa	63,710
Orange Co. (Napa and Solano Cos.)	80,040	97,440	Ventura (Ventura Co.)	78,775
San Francisco (San Francisco,			All other areas	63,710
San Mateo, and Marin Cos.)	86,135	104,860		
San Jose (Santa Clara Co.)	100,050	121,800		

Source: Cal Vet, http://www.cdva.ca.gov.

FIGURE 4.18   Loan programs.

Interest Rates

Loan Programs and Applicable Property Types & Fees			
Loan Programs	CalVet/VA (VA Certificate of Eligibility for full entitlement required.)	CalVet 97	CalVet 80/20
Maximum Loan	$ 521,250 (Includes the funding fee, if financed, for *all* loan programs.) [1]		
Property/ Program Type	New & Existing Homes (including VA-approved Condominiums), PUDs, and Mobile Homes on land.	New or Existing Homes including Condominiums, PUDs, Construction Loans, Rehabilitation Loans, Mobile Homes on land, and Mobile Homes in parks. [1]	New or Existing Homes including Condominiums, PUDs, Construction Loans, Rehabilitation Loans, Mobile Homes on land, and Mobile Homes in parks. [1]
Down Payment	0%	3%	20%
Funding Fee	1.25–3.30% (*may* be financed) [2]	0.63–1.38% (*must* be paid in escrow)	None
Loan Origination Fee	1%	1%	1%

In the past, the mortgage loan broker could not handle the CalVet loan program, and the borrower had to apply directly to the CalVet office. However, the mortgage loan broker is now encouraged to originate CalVet loans. For 1999 to 2000, mortgage loan brokers accounted for 50 percent of all CalVet loans. Training and a manual of reference material is available for those who desire to follow the required processing guidelines and forms used for a CalVet loan. The mortgage loan broker can receive the 1 percent loan origination fee that is charged on all loans in escrow and may also receive a processing fee of up to $350 if paid by the seller in escrow. CalVet loans may be processed with the standard DVA guidelines and forms as used for a regular DVA loan. Because of the many differences of CalVet financing, the mortgage loan broker may wish to show the borrower a comparison with alternative loans, including FHA, DVA, and FTHB programs. Figure 4-19 shows the CalVet maximum loan amounts as set forth for both targeted and for non-targeted areas throughout California.

With CalVet loans funded with revenue bonds after January 1, 1991, the contract purchaser may be liable for an additional tax. When the residence is sold to repay the federal government for some of the benefit of the federally subsidized CalVet home loan, this additional tax is called the recapture tax. The tax may have to be paid if the CalVet financed property is disposed of within the first full nine years after the funding date. There is no recapture tax if the disposition is by reason of death of the veteran [Section 143 (m) IRC, as amended by the 1990 Tax Act].

CalVet loan features includes low, flexible interest rate, with an even lower rate for qualified first-time homebuyers but usually 1 percent higher for mobile homes in parks. The maximum loan amount is up to $359,650 if the property is appraised for at least that amount in 2005; and, the maximum loan amount has been raised to $521,250 as of January 1, 2010. Figure 4-20 shows the specifications for various CalVet programs.

FIGURE 4.19   CalVet maximum loans.

Statistical Area	Average area purchase price, Safe Harbor limitations, Single-family residences, revenue bond–funded loans only Nontargeted Areas		Targeted Areas	
	New Residence	Existing Residence	New Residence	Existing Residence
Anaheim–Santa Ana (Orange Co.)	$345,436	$245,863	$422,199	$300,500
Bakersfield MSA (Kern Co.)	169,109	98,521	206,688	120,414
Chico (Butte Co.)	169,109	109,031	206,688	133,260
Fresno (Fresno and Madera Cos.)	169,109	115,112	206,688	140,693
Inyo County	169,109	144,448	206,688	176,547
Los Angeles–Long Beach (L.A. Co.)	281,902	219,683	344,547	268,502
Mendocino Co.	169,109	154,266	206,688	188,547
Modesto (Stanislaus Co.)	169,109	122,411	206,688	137,392
Nevada Co.	177,890	184,970	217,421	226.075
Oakland (Alameda and Contra Costa Cos.)	353,341	239,982	431,862	293,311
Redding MSA (Shasta Co.)	169,109	111,113	206,688	135,804
Riverside–San Bernardino Cos.	196,463	160,248	240,122	195,859
Sacramento (Sacramento, Placer, and El Dorado Cos.)	190,076	147,930	232,315	180,803
Salinas–Monterey (Monterey Co.)	239,380	292,528	292,575	357,535
San Benito Co.	237,374	208,689	290,123	255,064
San Diego (San Diego Co.)	283,603	217,167	346,626	265,426
San Francisco (San Francisco, San Mateo, and Marin Cos.)	394,808	421,040	482,543	514,605
San Jose (Santa Clara Co.)	412,505	347,915	504,172	425,230
San Luis Obispo–Atascadero–Paso Robles	208,914	202,109	255,339	247,022
Santa Barbara–Santa Maria–Lompoc	236,364	235,065	288,889	287,302
Santa Cruz–Watsonville (Santa Cruz Co.)	324,999	295,321	397,221	360,948
Santa Rosa (Sonoma Co.)	257,187	219,373	314,340	268,122
Stockton–Lodi (San Joaquin Co.)	171,105	122,132	209,128	149,273
Vallejo–Fairfield–Napa (Napa and Solano Cos.)	234,968	174,219	287,183	212,934
Ventura County	322,660	216,258	394,363	264,315
Visalia–Tulare–Porterville (Tulare Co.)	169,109	120,806	206,688	147,651
Yolo County	220.257	161,204	269,203	197,027
All other areas	169,109	143,914	206,688	175,895

Source: Cal Vet, http://www.cdva.ca.gov.

For earthquake and flood coverage, the deductible is only $250, provided that the buyer wanted to pay for this coverage. Mandatory life insurance to retire the debt in case of death of the borrower also increases the total costs but may benefit those unable to obtain life insurance because of health reasons. Applicants must be under age 62 when the loan is funded to receive the life insurance coverage.

The main office may be contacted at California Department of Veteran Affairs, 1227 O Street, Sacramento, CA 95814. For details on CalVet loan programs, go to the Web site at http://www.cdva.ca.gov, or call (800) 952-5626 for more detailed and current information.

FIGURE 4.20   CalVet programs.

	Cal Vet / VA	Cal Vet 2000/97	Cal Vet 80/20
Property or program type	Existing home Condominium PUD	New home Existing home Condo or PUD Construction loan Rehabilitation loan Mobile home on land Mobile home in park	New home Existing home Condo or PUD Construction loan Rehabilitation loan Mobile Home on land
Down payment	2%	3%	20%
Funding fee	1.25%–3% may be financed	1.25%–2% must be paid in escrow	None
Loan origination fee	1%	1%	1%
Other requirements	VA Cert. of Eligibility for full entitlement		
Targeted toward	Vets and active duty	Vets and active duty	Vets and active duty

Source: Cal Vet, http://www.cdva.ca.gov.

4.6 SBA

SBA loans are a special segment of the market. The SBA Web site, found at http://www.sba.gov, provides detailed information, has tutorials, and shows outlines for a business plan and financing data.

The qualifications are unique and focus primarily on the loan applicant's character, credit, and reliability. The primary consideration is a good history for prompt payment of debts. A cosigner is allowed. A significant factor is the likelihood that the expected earnings will be sufficient to pay the obligation and that the business has a good chance of success. Common requirements include purpose of the loan, history of the business, financial statements for three years (existing businesses), schedule of term debts (existing businesses), aging of accounts receivable and payable (existing businesses), projected opening-day balance sheet (new businesses), lease details, amount of investment in the business by the owner(s), projections of income, expenses and cash flow, signed personal financial statements, and personal resume(s).

Although the loan uses private lender funds, the SBA will guarantee up to 90 percent of the loan up to $100,000. The loan may be either a fixed or variable rate, tied to the prime rate. Loans are usually for 10 years and may not exceed 25 years for real property acquisition. The SBA maximum interest rates are set as follows:

Loan Amount	Due up to 7 years	Matures 7 years +
$1 – $25,000	Prime + 4-1/4%	Prime + 4-3/4%
$25,000 – $50,000	Prime + 3-1/4%	Prime + 3-3/4%
$50,000 – $100,000	Prime + 2-1/4%	Prime + 2-3/4%

The SBA can guaranty up to 85 percent of a small business loan; however, the lender must agree to loaning the money with the SBA guarantee. The lender will then forward the loan application and a credit analysis to the nearest SBA District Office. After receiving all documentation, the SBA analyzes the entire application, then makes its decision. The process may take up to 10 days to complete.

Home and Property Disaster Loans. If the property is in a declared disaster area and if the borrower is a victim of a disaster, the applicant may be eligible for financial assistance from the U.S. Small Business Administration (SBA).

- Real Property Loan: A homeowner may apply for a loan of up to $200,000 to repair or restore their primary home to its pre-disaster condition. The loan may not be used to upgrade the home or make additions to it. If, however, city or county building codes require structural improvements, the loan may be used to meet these requirements. Loans may be increased by as much as 20 percent to protect the damaged real property from possible future disasters of the same kind.

- Personal Property Loan: This loan can provide a homeowner or renter with up to $40,000 to help repair or replace personal property (e.g., clothing, furniture, automobiles) lost in the disaster. As a rule of thumb, personal property is anything that is not considered real estate or a part of the actual structure. This loan may not be used to replace extraordinarily expensive or irreplaceable items (e.g., antiques, collections, pleasure boats, recreational vehicles, fur coats).

SUMMARY

The two major federal types of loans are the FHA and the DVA programs. Both programs have loans predominantly for one- to four-unit properties, with specific guidelines for buyer qualification, including income and LTV. The FHA loan program MIP insures the loan for the investor so that low- to moderate- income families can acquire housing. The DVA loan program guarantees the top portion of the loan to attract investor funds to make loans available to qualified veterans or his or her families, with up to 100% financing.

The major state loan program is available through the sale of bonds, with tax advantages for investors. The mortgage loan broker may process, approve, and fund CalVet loans to qualified California veterans.

Other loans may be government or conventional for residence or business purposes. A large part of the market is refinance loans, especially when rates fall; thus, they become a greater or lesser portion of the mortgage loan broker business with interest-rate fluctuations. The SBA helps entrepreneurs get the needed capital for a business venture.

A thorough understanding of the various types of conventional loan programs discussed in Chapter 3 and the government and other types of loans explained in Chapter 4 will make the mortgage loan broker more competitive.

The ability to have variety in loans and a working knowledge of the requirements for each loan will enhance career opportunities.

REVIEW YOUR UNDERSTANDING

1. The UFMIP Premium is calculated at:
   A. 1.5% of the Sales Price
   B. 1.5% of the Loan Amount
   C. 2.25% of the Sales Price
   D. 2.25% of the Loan Amount

2. Which one of the following ls the most common FHA loan for a single-family residence:
   A. FHA 203 (b)
   B. FHA 203 (k)
   C. FHA 221 (d) (2)
   D. FHA 245

3. The MIP and Closing Cost may be financed into the new loan amount on a:
   A. Sale Transaction
   B. Refinance Transaction only
   C. Any type of a FHA transaction may include the MIP and Closing cost in the new loan amount.
   D. At no time can you include the MIP and Closing cost in an FHA loan amount.

4. FHA loans are:
   A. Insured.
   B. Guaranteed
   C. Either A or B
   D. Neither A nor B

5. The _____ of 2008 makes it possible for FHA loans to be approved with the original note-holder taking a loss on principal:
   A. Real Estate Settlement and Procedures act.
   B. Housing and Economic Recovery Act.
   C. The Loan Guarantee Act.
   D. The National Housing Act.

6. The Supportive Housing for the Elderly loan program is also known as:
   A. FHA 203 (b)
   B. FHA 207
   C. FHA 202
   D. FHA 223 (e)

7. Under a DVA loan the veteran separation papers in known as:
   A. DD412
   B. DD 142
   C. DD 241
   D. DD 214

8. Under the DVA Jumbo Loan, the veteran can borrower up to a loan amount of:
   A. $729,750
   B. $792,570
   C. $927,570
   D. $929,750

9. Under Cal Vet loans the Veteran must have served at least:
   A. 45 consecutive days on active duty
   B. 60 consecutive days on active duty
   C. 90 consecutive days on active duty
   D. 180 consecutive days on active duty

10. What does the acronym HECM stand for?
    A. HUD equity conversion mortgage
    B. Home equity continuation mortgage
    C. Home equity conversion mortgage
    D. Home equity condominium mortgage

ANSWERS TO REVIEWING YOUR UNDERSTANDING

1. D (p. 102)   4. A (p. 100)   7. D (p. 120)   10. C (p. 111)
2. A (p. 103)   5. B (p. 101)   8. A (pp. 120 & 125)
3. C (p. 103)   6. C (p. 103)   9. C (p. 130)

Chapter

5

IMPORTANT TERMS

Annual Percentage Rate (APR)

Article 7

Consumer Credit Protection Act

Environmental hazards

Federal Emergency Management Agency (FEMA)

Federal Reserve Board

Flood disaster insurance

Good Faith Estimate (GFE)

Hazard insurance

House and Urban Development (HUD)

Lead-Based Paint

Mortgage Loan Disclosure Statement

Predatory lending

Real Estate Settlement Procedures Act (RESPA)

Regulation C

Regulation X (Reg X)

Regulation Z (Reg. Z)

Section 32

The Home Mortgage Disclosure Act (HMDA)

The Home Mortgage Disclosure and Regulation C

Truth in Lending Act (TILA)

Loans: Finance Disclosure and Other Real Estate Disclosures

PREVIEW

When real estate mortgage brokers act as lenders or on behalf of lenders, they must be in compliance with all the applicable regulations. The broker may find conflicts between federal and state laws and has to be cognizant of all regulations regarding finance, licensing, and real estate contract law. A mortgage lender or mortgage broker operating on a multistate level faces the continual challenge of legal compliance, with ever-increasing costs of both compliance and the consequences of noncompliance. Even the government regulators charged with oversight of the lending industry are hard pressed to keep up with the new laws. The American Association of Residential Mortgage Regulators (AARMR) (http://www.aarmr.org/) was formed in the early 1990s to address the need for shared information at the state agency level; there are more than 30 state agencies participating.

At the federal level three laws that have become implemented as regulations that are most common to the loan industry:

(1) The Federal Truth-In-Lending Act (TILA), referred to as Regulation Z;
(2) The Real Estate Settlement Procedures Act, known as "RESPA";
(3) Regulation X, called Reg X;
(4) Home Mortgage Disclosure Act (HMDA);
(5) The Home Mortgage Disclosure, Regulation C.

The **Truth in Lending Act (TILA)** of 1968 is a United States federal law (www.occ.treas.gov/handbook/til.pdf) designed to protect consumers in credit transactions, by requiring clear disclosure of key terms of the lending arrangement and all costs. The statute is contained in Title I of the Consumer Credit Protection Act, as amended (15 U.S.C. § 1601 et seq.). The regulations implementing the statute, which are known as "Regulation Z," are codified at 12 CFR Part 226. The act does not regulate the charges that may be imposed for consumer credit but does require uniform and standardized disclosure of costs and charges to that the consumer may shop different loans and compare the costs. The act imposes limitations on home equity plans and certain higher-cost home loans. The regulation prohibits certain acts or practices in connection with credit secured by a consumer's principal residence.

The **Real Estate Settlement Procedures Act (RESPA)** was passed by the United States Congress in 1974. It is codified at Title 12, Chapter 27 of the United States Code, 12 U.S.C. § 2601–2617 (www.hud.gov/offices/hsg/sfh/res/respa_hm.cfm). The purpose of the act is to reduce the costs to the consumer by not allowing extra fees, such as undisclosed referral fees and kickbacks to other service providers in a real estate transaction. It is also intended to curtail bait-and-switch tactics on the price of the real estate fees. This is geared toward lenders, real estate sales agents, construction companies, and title insurance companies. The ACT prohibits kickbacks between lenders and third-party settlement service agents according to Section 8 of RESPA. The ACT was updated in 2009 to add substantial "meat," which were a result of the November 2009 final rule. Basically, the borrower must be provided estimated closing costs within three days of loan application that must match the actual costs that will be charged at the close of escrow. The old practices of quoting one price, then switching to higher costs at the time of closing, is being strictly enforced so that RESPA's principal goal of consumer protection is the final rule.

Regulation X (Reg X) extends to borrowers the provisions of regulations governing the extension of credit by brokers and dealers and by banks and other lenders for the purpose of purchasing or carrying securities. This Act is primarily to clarify the treatment of stock future and similar securities futures. Those dealing with the buying and selling of loans, selling loans at a discount, purchasing loan notes due in the future would need to comply (www.federalreserve.gov/bankinforeg/regxcg.htm).

The Home Mortgage Disclosure Act (HMDA) of 1975 requires financial institutions to maintain and annually disclose data about home purchases, home purchase pre-approvals, home improvement and refinance applications that involve one to four unit and multi-family dwellings. The Act is designed to identify discriminatory lending practices. The **Federal Reserve Board** oversees this law including the adjustment effective January 1, 2005 (www.hmda.net).

The Home Mortgage Disclosure and Regulation C: The lender and mortgage loan broker would need to have the loan comply with the adjustable rate mortgage loan disclosure and Regulation C. This act revises the rules for reporting price information on higher-priced loans. It conformed the definition of "higher-priced mortgage loan" language adopted under Regulation Z.

Contained within these laws are various disclosures for the annual percentage rate (APR) and the good faith estimate (GFE) of closing costs. The Consumer Credit Protection Act and the Right of Privacy Act are discussed in Chapter 7.

For California, both the California Department of Corporations (DOC) commissioner and the California Department of Real Estate (DRE) commissioner oversee the activities of lenders, including laws found in both the Business and Profession's Code and California Real Estate Law. Other real estate disclosure laws that must be complied with in a real estate transaction by the licensed mortgage loan broker include disclosure of a death on the premises, environmental and earthquake, energy, fire, foreign investor, flood, hazard insurance, lead-based paint, Mello Roos, real estate owned (REO), smoke detector, tax on real estate sales proceeds, title insurance, transfer disclosure statement, utility service, and water heater bracing. However, the Predatory Lending Laws recently enacted to protect California consumers have had the most significant impact on mortgage loan brokers.

Most of these disclosures are thought to be for only the DRE licensee who handles the seller or the buyer. However, as many transactions do not involve any licensed sales agent, if the mortgage loan broker is licensed by DRE, compliance with the various disclosures should be checked. If a DRE licensee closes a refinance or a home equity loan or handles the buyer's new loan when the transaction is a "for sale by owner" and no sales agent gives the parties any disclosure statements, then a burden is placed on the DRE licensee who handles the loan. No transaction in California may close without smoke detector compliance and the hot water strap bracing. The DRE licensed loan agent should check with their employing broker, the legal counsel for the firm with which they are employed and directly with the licensing agency. Should any party in the transaction sue any other party for any issue, even if not related to any part of the loan, the DRE licensee can expect to have to appear in court and to defend their compliance with the state license agency laws and regulations.

CHAPTER OBJECTIVES

At the end of this chapter, the student learning outcomes include:

1. Indicate the components of the Federal TILA, HMDA, Regulation Z, Regulation C compliance requirements.
2. Describe APR.
3. Discuss the elements of federal HUMDA RESPA provisions, Regulation X.
4. List California disclosures used for a real estate loan transaction.
5. Distinguish between federal and state laws involving the loan broker and the loan originating lender.

When the mortgage loan broker is acting as the lender or on behalf of the lender, potential conflicts arise between the various laws and regulations. Not only do the differences in wording between federal and state regulations place the loan broker in conflict but also differences between the two major federal regulations, TIL and RESPA, may cause confusion. Similarities and differences exist between the two state licensing agencies, the Department of Corporations (DOC) and Department of Real Estate (DRE), discussed in detail in Chapter 14. The DOC regulates consumer finance lenders (CFL) and the California Residential Mortgage Lending Act (CRMLA). The DRE regulates licensed brokers and salespersons on real estate loans.

With the enactment of Secure And Fair Enforcement for Mortgage Licensing Act of 2008 (SAFE) federal law adds another layer of regulations, and with state legislation in 2009 implementing SAFE, changes will continue to be made, especially in terminology and definitions. For example, the "loan originator" is defined as "an individual who takes a residential mortgage loan application or offers or negotiates terms of a residential mortgage loan for compensation or gain." When the loan originators are individually licensed and registered under SAFE, that would include both the loan broker and the employees of that broker. Currently, HUD defines a "loan originator" under RESPA as including both the lenders and the mortgage brokers. Thus, the future will continue to have differences between regulations, with the hope that consistency will eventually be brought about between the various laws.

A lender is the party referred to as an entity who regularly extends credit and to whom the debt arising from the consumer credit transaction is initially payable on the face of the evidence of the indebtedness. A lender may be a federal depository institution, a private party, a corporation, or any other global investor with funds to lend. The lender is the entity who funds the money and is referred to under law as the loan originator. The mortgage loan brokers do not lend their own funds and are therefore not the lender.

5.1 FEDERAL TIL: REGULATION Z

This regulation, known as **Regulation Z (Reg. Z)**, became effective July 1, 1969. It was issued by the Board of Governors of the Federal Reserve System to implement the federal TIL and Fair Credit Billing Acts, contained in Title I of the Consumer Credit Protection Act, as amended (15 U.S.C. 1601 et seq.); including Title XII, section 1204 of the Competitive Equality Banking Act of 1987 (Pub. L. 100-86, 101 Stat. 552), as approved by the Office of Management and Budget. Lenders who must comply with this federal regulation include those who are federal depository institutions and others who regularly extend credit and to whom the initial debt is payable on the face of the indebtedness if arising from a consumer credit transaction.

The purpose of Reg. Z is to promote the informed use of consumer credit by requiring disclosures about its terms and cost. The regulation also gives consumers the right to cancel certain credit transactions that involve a lien on their principal dwelling, regulates certain credit card practices, and provides a means for fair and timely resolution of credit billing disputes. It imposes limitations on home equity plans and credit where the finance charge is payable by a written agreement in more than four installments.

The Federal Reserve regulations amended TILA. to require that the loan cost disclosures now be as follows:

- The borrower must be given the disclosure at the time of loan application, OR within three days of loan application.

- The borrower must be given the disclosure BEFORE any fees are incurred, except a reasonable credit report fee.
- This is a change from BEFORE credit is extended.
- This regulation puts limitations on higher priced loans.
- This regulation prohibits deceptive loan advertising.
- Amended May 2009: requires a period of at least SEVEN (7) days between loan application date and closing date.

For closed-end loans, where the borrower cannot increase the original loan amount and the amount of the loan is fixed at the time of loan origination, the Federal Reserve has proposed many other changes, including changing the disclosure forms, requirement of a new disclosure booklet, and disclosures for more types of closing costs and fees within the definition of what is included as "finance charge." The lending industry and the consumer advocates are locking heads over the proposed prohibition of yield spread premiums. See http://edocket.access.gpo.gov/2009/pdf/E9-18119.pdf for the final outcome, when it becomes available.

The Home Ownership and Equity Protection Act (HOEPA), 60 FR 15452 of 1995 requires special disclosures and substantive protections for home-equity loans and refinancing with APRs or points and fees above certain statutory thresholds. Numerous other amendments have been made over the years to address new loan products, such as abusive lending practices in the home loan and home-equity markets. In 2007 the Federal Reserve Board proposed rules under HOEPA for higher-priced loans to prohibit certain unfair or deceptive lending and servicing practices in connection with closed-end real property loans. The final rules in July 2008 require creditors to provide consumers with transaction-specific disclosures early enough in the transaction to be able to use the information to shop for a loan.

In May 2009 the Mortgage Disclosure Improvement Act of 2008 was implemented with the final rules for the timing of the disclosures for closed-end real property loans. Loans secured by dwellings, even when the dwelling is not the consumer's principal dwelling, require a waiting period between the time when the loan disclosure fees are given and when the loan may be consummated specifically to allow consumers time to check loan fees with other loan providers.

Those who must comply with Reg. Z include any creditor who

1. extends credit more than five times in a calendar year and uses a dwelling as the security.
2. extends consumer credit more than 25 times a year.

Those who are excluded from compliance with Reg. Z include

1. licensed real estate brokers who are the arranger of credit between a buyer and a seller, such as when a seller carries back a loan on the property being sold.
2. credit extended primarily for a business, commercial, or agricultural purpose.
   a. Business purposes includes property not intended to be owner occupied, regardless of the number of units.
   b. If the property contains more than two family units and the purpose of the loan is to acquire the property, the credit is deemed to be for a business purpose.

The purpose of the act is to promote the informed use of consumer credit by requiring disclosures about the terms and costs of the loan. The regulation also gives consumers the right to cancel certain credit transactions that require a lien on a consumer's principal dwelling. The law does not regulate the amount of the charges for consumer credit but rather requires disclosure to the borrower of what the total loan costs will actually be. For applications seeking home equity loans or for loans with variable interest rates, additional disclosures must be provided to the consumer. Some disclosure items include the following:

- A brochure indicating the timing of the disclosure.
- The duties of the third parties.
- Retention of information.
- A statement of any change due to fluctuations in a variable-rate index.
- Default data.
- Acceleration clause.
- Extension or reduction in future limit.
- Charges, terms, APR, and fees.

In addition, the loan broker is responsible for checking that the lender gives to the borrower a written GFE indicating negative amortization and tax implications. The amount financed and the creditor must be disclosed (Section 226).

Neither the loan broker nor the lender nor any other person may impose a nonrefundable fee in connection with an application until three business days after the consumer receives the disclosure and brochure required by Reg. Z. The TIL law also requires a notice to the creditor for any fees paid by the consumer to anyone in connection with an application, such as a referral fee or commission paid to a licensee or a nonlicensee.

For persons other than the creditor, such as the loan broker, who provide closed-end credit transactions for real estate loans, Reg. Z requires as many as 18 disclosures. The mortgage loan broker or lender shall disclose to the borrower the following items in the terminology that is consistent with the clauses and words used on the periodic statement (Code 226.5 open-end credit) (Code 226.17 closed-end credit).

1. Identify of the creditor
2. Amount financed
3. Itemization of amount financed
4. Finance charge, which must include
   a. Interest
   b. Loan fees, assumption fees, finder's fees, and buyer's points
   c. Investigation and credit report fees
   d. Premiums for loan guaranty insurance
   e. Borrower-paid loan broker fees
   f. Fees for title examination, abstract of title, title insurance, or property survey
   g. Fees for preparing loan-related documents

    h. Notary, appraisal, credit report, pest report, flood hazard inspection

    i. Escrow or trustee account fees

    j. Third-party closing agents (attorney, escrow, or title company)

  5. APR

  6. Variable rate, including

    a. Circumstances under which the rate may increase

    b. Limitations on the increase

    c. Effect of the increase

    d. Sample of the payment terms that would result from an increase

  7. Payment schedule and payment plan information

  8. Total of payments

  9. Demand feature

10. Total sale price

11. Prepayment penalties and rebates

12. Late payment charge

13. Security interests (consumer's dwelling is collateral)

14. Insurance

15. Certain security charges, such as disclosure of taxes and fees paid to a public official

16. Reference to contract terms, such a nonpayment, default, and lender's right to accelerate the maturity of the obligation

17. Assumption policy

18. Require deposit statement of billing rights (when borrower may terminate a plan)

The loan broker or lender must also furnish the borrower with a periodic statement that discloses the following items (Code 226.7):

  1. Previous unpaid loan balance

  2. Identification of each transaction

  3. Billing cycle information, including payment date and closing date

  4. Amount of billing payment

  5. Periodic rate

  6. Balance on which finance charge is computed

  7. Amount of finance charge for the billing cycle

  8. APR during the billing cycle

  9. Grace period: time that payment may be made within to avoid additional finance charges

10. Address for notice of billing error

Examples of finance charges include the following required disclosure information regarding the transaction (Code 226.4):

  1. Transaction account charges, including service charges and overdraft fees

  2. Assumption fees

3. Credit loss insurance, including mortgage-guaranty insurance, holder-in-due course insurance, and repossession insurance

4. Residual-value insurance

5. Preexisting, new, or substitution of insurance policies

6. Discounts for payments, cash discounts, and determination of regular price

7. Participation fees and exclusions for nonrecurring fees

8. Lost interest

9. Interest, any time price differential, and any amount payable under an add-on or discount system of additional charges

10. Insurance for life of the borrower, accident, loss of income, or health

11. Charges imposed by another person for purchasing or accepting a borrower's loan if the charges are passed through to the borrower, such as referral fees or kickbacks.

5.2 APR

The Federal **Consumer Credit Protection Act**, commonly known as the **TIL**, became effective in May 1968. The act requires that the borrower be clearly shown how much he or she is paying for the loan, both in the dollar amount and in percentage terms. Both must be disclosed to and approved by the borrower before he or she is committed to the loan. The borrower is given the right to rescind the transaction in certain instances that complies with the new regulations as previously discussed.

The **Annual Percentage Rate (APR)** combines the interest rate with other costs of the loan into a single figure that shows the true annual cost of borrowing. This is one of the most helpful features of the law because it gives the prospective borrower a standardized figure to compare financing from different sources. The act requires consumer loans to comply with the regulations on loans pertaining to real property loans, as well as other types of personal property loans.

Lenders are required to make many disclosures to borrowers. The four principal disclosures required for APR, as shown in Figure 5.1, are:

1. Amount financed—the amount of credit provided to the borrower

2. Finance charge—the total dollar amount the credit will cost the borrower during the life of the loan, including interest, borrower prepaid discount points, loan fees, loan finder fees, loan service fees, required life insurance, and mortgage guarantee premiums

3. APR—the cost of credit

4. Total payments—the amount in dollars the borrower will have paid after making all the payments as scheduled. This amount does not include actual payments made during the life of the loan, which may include late fees or other costs (see Figure 5.2).

An example of determining the APR by using various calculators is shown in Chapter 15 (Reg. Z, Section 226.22: Determination of APR).

FIGURE 5.1   Frequently asked TIL questions.

ANNUAL PERCENTAGE RATE The cost of your credit at a yearly rate	Finance Charge The dollar amount the credit will cost you	Amount Financed The amount of credit provided to you or on your behalf	Total of payments The amount you will have paid after you have made all payments as scheduled
A	**B**	**C**	**D**

Q: What is the Truth-in-Lending disclosure, and why must the borrower receive it?

A: The disclosure is designed to give borrowers information about the costs of their loan so that they may compare the costs with other loan programs by various lenders.

Q: What is the annual percentage rate? (Box A above)

A: The annual percentage rate (APR) is the cost of the credit expressed as an *annual* rate. The borrower may be paying loan discount points and other prepaid finance charges at closing. The APR disclosed is often higher than the stated interest rate on the loan. This APR disclosure can be compared to the APR on other loans to give a consistent means of comparing rates among lenders for various programs.

Q: Why is the APR different from the interest rate that the borrower was quoted?

A: The APR is computed from the amount financed. It is based upon what the proposed payments will be on the actual loan amount credited to the borrower at settlement.

Q: What is the finance charge? (Box B above)

A: The finance charge is the cost of credit expressed in dollars. It is the total amount of interest calculated at the interest rate over the life of the loan, plus prepaid finance charge and the total amount of any required mortgage insurance charged over the life of the loan.

Q: What is the amount financed? (Box C above)

A: The amount financed is the loan amount applied for minus prepaid finance charges. Prepaid finance charges include items paid at or before settlement closing, such as loan origination fee, commitment or discount fees (points), adjusted interest, and initial mortgage insurance premium. The amount financed is lower than the amount of the loan that is applied for because it represents a *net* figure.

Q: Does this mean I will get a smaller loan than I applied for?

A: No. If the loan is approved in the amount requested, the borrower will receive credit toward the home purchase or refinance for the full amount for which the borrower applied.

Q: What is the total of payments? (Box D above)

A: This figure represents the total amount the borrower will have paid if the minimum required payment is made for each payment over the entire period of loan. This includes principal, interest, and mortgage insurance premiums but does *not* include payments for real estate taxes or property insurance premiums.

Q: The disclosure says that if the borrower pays the loan off early, no refund will be given for any part of the finance charge. What does this mean?

A: This means that all that will be charged is interest on the unpaid loan amount during the time that the funds were borrowed. Generally, the prepaid finance charges are not refundable nor is any interest that has already been paid.

FIGURE 5.2   APR example.

Assume the mortgage loan broker obtains a loan for a borrower for $162,400 at 9%. For the first year, the borrower owes $162,400 plus $14,616 in interest. The APR is the same as the interest rate, shown as:

$$\frac{\text{Interest}}{\text{Money Received}} = \frac{\$14,616}{\$162,400} = 9.0\%$$

If the bank collected a $1,624 service charge in advance, the borrower would only have received $160,776 and not $162,400. Therefore, the borrower would have the use of $160,776 for one year, not $162,400. The APR would be calculated as follows:

$$\frac{\text{Interest} + \text{Service Charge}}{\text{Money Received}} = \frac{\$16,240}{\$160,776} = 10.10\%$$

If the terms previously used are applied, the formula would look like this:

$$\frac{\text{Interest} + \text{Prepaid Finance Charge}}{\text{Loan Amount} - \text{Prepaid Finance Charge}} = \frac{\text{Finance Charge}}{\text{Amount Financed}} = \text{APR}$$

5.3 SECTION 32 LOAN GUIDELINES

The loans that fall under this particular section of the TIL regulations require special processing and closing procedures. The **Section 32** rule applies only to refinances of loans secured by the borrower's principal residence and if the loan meets either of two tests:

1. APR Test: If the APR shown on the TIL exceeds the applicable Treasury security rate by 10 percent or more
2. Points and Fees Test: If the points and fees exceed 8 percent of the amount-financed section of the required APR form

It is necessary to determine what the APR is for the actual, final loan terms in order to determine whether the loan is within this law. The applicable Treasury security rate is the rate, as of the fifteenth of the month preceding the month in which the borrower applies for the loan, for the Treasury security with the same maturity (15-year, 30-year) term as the borrower's loan. In addition, any item paid by the borrower that cannot be definitely identified as not being included in the list shown in Figure 5.3 must be included in the calculation and must be based on actual closing dollar amounts as disclosed in a proposed HUD-1 settlement statement.

The mortgage loan broker would need to use some form of a worksheet to determine whether the loan falls under Section 32 of Reg. Z, as shown in

FIGURE 5.3 Section 32 points, fees, and costs.

INCLUDED	NOT INCLUDED (unless paid to an affiliate, lender, or broker)
Origination fee	Per diem interest
Discount points paid by borrower	Appraisal fee
Broker administrative or processing fee	Credit report fee
Broker document preparation fee	Termite/pest control inspection
All other broker fees paid by borrower	Title search/abstract of title
Courier or FedEx fee	Title insurance/policy of title insurance
Settlement/escrow/closing agent/ attorney fees	Attorney fees (if representing borrower, not lender)
Underwriting fee	Survey expense
Tax service fee	Yield spread premium paid by lender
Assignment recording fee	Recording fees/document stands for recording trust deed or mortgage
Flood certification	Hazard insurance premium and escrow
PMI collected at closing	Property taxes
PMI escrow/impound	

Figure 5.4 for high-cost area loans. The worksheet shows the amount financed plus the costs and charges affiliated with obtaining the loan.

5.4 FEDERAL RESPA, REGULATION X

The RESPA is enforced by HUD, which implements RESPA with regulations known as Regulation X. The purpose of this law is to (1) provide the borrower with likely costs associated with the loan transaction, (2) help consumers become better shoppers for settlement services, (3) eliminate kickbacks and referral fees that unnecessarily increase the costs of certain services, and (4) put limits on escrow accounts.

Regulation X requires lenders to provide loan applicants with five types of disclosures relating to settlement costs in connection with applications for federally related mortgage loans used to purchase or refinance one- to four-unit residential property and the principal residence of the borrower. The first item is a booklet entitled *Settlement Costs: A HUD Guide*, published by HUD.

The second item is a **Good Faith Estimate (GFE)** statement of settlement costs, which must be provided to a loan applicant either at application or within three business days after submission of an application. The good faith estimate form will be discussed in more detail later in the chapter. The third item is the servicing disclosure statement that must give a written statement when the lender expects that someone else will be collecting the loan payments. The third is the affiliated business arrangement in which the lender must inform the borrower that he or she may use any other provider of services and is not required to use

FIGURE 5.4 Worksheet for Section 32, federal Reg. Z, high-cost-area loan.

SECTION 32 OF FEDERAL REGULATION Z
"High Cost Loan" Worksheet
Must be completed, reviewed and retained in ALL loan files prior to funding.

PLACE LABEL HERE

Application No. _____
Date of Federal Truth-in-Lending
Disclosure: _____

PART I   Is this a REFINANCE of the borrower's primary residence?
            YES _____ NO _____   If YES, complete PARTS II and III.

PART II   ANNUAL PERCENTAGE RATE (APR)
    1. Date loan application made to lender: _____
    2. Loan Maturity: 10 years 15 years 30 years
    3. Treasury index for the (a) 15th day of the month prior   _____ 10 Yr
       To the date of application in Line 1 above   _____ 20 Yr
       (b) Treasury Index with maturity matching loan term   _____ 30 Yr
       (if 15 yr loan term, use lower of 10 yr or 20 yr Treasury Index)
    4. SECTION 32 *Trigger Rate* (line 3b + 10%)   _____ + 10%_____
    5. ANNUAL PERCENTAGE RATE (APR) as listed on the
       Federal Truth-In-Lending Disclosure: _____
    6. Is the APR (line 5) more than the SECTION 32 *Trigger Rate*   _____
        (Line 4)?   Yes [ ]   No [ ]

PART III POINTS, FEES AND COSTS OR SECTION 32 FINANCE CHARGES:
    7. Add the Prepaid Finance Charges listed on the Federal Truth-in-Lending Disclosure, except prepaid per
       diem interest (MUST include ALL money paid directly to the Broker unless documented as an equivalent
       pass-through 3rd party charge):

Lender Points   _____   Appraisal Review _____
Broker Points   _____   Tax Service Fee   _____
Underwriting Fee _____   Flood Cert. Fee   _____
Doc Prep Fee   _____   Application Fee   _____
Closing Fee   _____   Other Broker Charges _____
Processing Fee   _____   Other Lender Charges _____

            Total SECTION 32 Finance Charges: $_____

    8. Per Diem ("odd days") interest _____

    9. Subtract both the Total Section 32 Finance Charges and the Prepaid Per Diem interest from the loan
       amount = Section 32 Total Loan Amount:
       Loan Amount $_____- (minus) Section 32 Charges (Line 7) $_____- (minus) prepaid per
       diem interest (Line 8) $_____ = Section 32 Total Loan Amount $_____. (To Line 10)

    10. Divide Section 32 Finance Charges by Section 32 Total Loan Amount:
        Total Section 32 Finance Charges (Line 7) $_____ ÷ Section 32
        Total Loan Amount (Line 9) $_____ x 100 = _____%

    11. Os the % in Line 10 greater than 7.99%?   Yes [ ]   No [ ]

SECTION 32 DETERMINATION:
If the answer to either PART II or PART III is "Yes" then the loan must be classified as a "SECTION 32
HIGH COST MORTGAGE" and the special "SECTION 32" disclosure must be provided to and signed by and
dated by the Borrower(s) at least three (3) business days (INCLUDING Saturdays) before the loan documents
and "Three-Day Right to Cancel" are signed.

Prepared and reviewed by: _____   Date: _____

Reviewed prior to Funding by: _____   Date: _____

ATTENTION FUNDING DEPARTMENT
If hazard insurance is being provided by the Lender or affiliated insurance brokers, then the amount of the
premium paid or collected must be added to the Total SECTION 32 finance charges in Line 7 above and
Lines 9 and 10 must be recalculated and reviewed.

If YES, what is the recalculation for Line 11:   _____ %

Points and Fees Worksheet:

Enter "Amount Financed" equal to amount to be shown on final TIL (not loan amount):   (1) _____

Enter the total amount of the points and fees as per the table above.   (2) _____

Divide (2) by (1). If the result is 8% or more, the loan falls within the Section 32 loan regulations. Either
the parties must (a) agree to reduce fees below the 8% level, or (b) the loan must be redisclosed including a
new period for the three day right of recission.

SEC32 2/99

the services of affiliates that are controlled or owned by a common corporate parent, such as the sales firm or the escrow company. The fourth item is a final statement of settlement costs (either the HUD-1 or the HUD-1A form), which must be available for review at an applicant's request at least 7 days prior to settlement. All financial institutions that are either regulated by or whose deposits are insured by an agency of the federal government are lenders who must comply with RESPA http://thismatter.com/money/real-estate/real-estate-closing.htm. The fifth item is the escrow account operation and disclosure statement. Either at the close of escrow or within the next 45 days, the loan servicer must provide an initial escrow account statement showing all payments expected to be deposited into the impound account and all expected disbursements for the year ahead.

If the borrower believes there is an error in the mortgage account, a qualified written request may be made to the loan servicer. The written request must identify the borrower by name and account, and include a statement of reasons why the borrower believes the account is in error. The servicer must acknowledge receipt of the request within 20 business days. The servicer then has 60 business days from the request date to take action on the request. If the servicer fails to comply, the borrower is entitled to actual damages, up to $1,000 of additional damages if there is a pattern of noncompliance, costs and attorney fees.

Borrowers often confuse the GFE and the actual closing statement received from the escrow officer or settlement agent. The GFE estimates typical, not actual, fees. The GFE covers the costs when obtaining financing and does not necessarily show the costs if a purchase is also involved, rather than obtaining only a loan, such as is the case with a refinance. If a buyer paid all cash for a property or if a buyer's only loan was with the seller, many of the costs would remain the same (such as title insurance), but many of the costs would not exist (such as loan origination fee).

Most costs are paid at closing, so borrowers would need advance notice of the amount they would need to close escrow, in addition to the down payment. Some borrowers finance all or a portion of the closing costs in addition to the loan, and the borrower would need to know the additional amount to be financed because this additional amount would affect both the additional monthly payment and the amount of loan for which the borrower would qualify. Figure 5.5 shows the breakdown of typical costs paid at closing that are required to be disclosed to the borrower on the HUD-1 form. The federal HUD GFE is not used instead of the California state DRE RE 883 form, but both may be required for a real property transaction. Practitioners in the field of loans must comply with both federal law and California law, so typically both forms would be used. The DRE commissioner had legislation in 2005 change the form for the GFE and amended Section 2840.1 to read:

(a) The commissioner approves the use of the following form and the form contained in Section 2840 of these regulations for the statement required by Section 10241 of the Business and Professions Code.

Regulation X defines a lender as the secured creditor named as such in the debt obligation for secondary market transaction purposes. RESPA covers loans secured with a mortgage placed on a one- to four-family residential property. These include most purchase loans, assumptions, refinances, property

FIGURE 5.5   GFE of borrower closing costs.

STATE OF CALIFORNIA
DEPARTMENT OF REAL ESTATE
Serving Californians Since 1917

MORTAGE LOAN DISCLOSURE STATEMENT/ GOOD FAITH ESTIMATE NONTRADITIONAL MORTGAGE PRODUCT (ONE TO FOUR RESIDENTIAL UNITS)

RE 885 (Rev. 8/08)

Borrower's Name(s): _____

Real Property Collateral: The intended security for this proposed loan will be a Deed of Trust on (street address or legal description) _____

This joint Mortgage Loan Disclosure Statement/Good Faith Estimate is being provided by _____ , a real estate broker acting as a mortgage broker, pursuant to the Federal Real Estate Settlement Procedures Act (RESPA) if applicable and similar California law. In a transaction subject to RESPA, a lender will provide you with an additional Good Faith Estimate within three business days of the receipt of your loan application. You will also be informed of material changes before settlement/close of escrow. The name of the intended lender to whom your loan application will be delivered is:

☐ Unknown   ☐ _____ (Name of lender, if known)

GOOD FAITH ESTIMATE OF CLOSING COSTS

The information provided below reflects estimates of the charges you are likely to incur at the settlement of your loan. The fees, commissions, costs and expenses listed are estimates; the actual charges may be more or less. Your transaction may not involve a charge for every item listed and any additional items charged will be listed. The numbers listed beside the estimated items generally correspond to the numbered lines contained in the HUD-1 Settlement Statement which you will receive at settlement if this transaction is subject to RESPA. The HUD-1 Settlement Statement contains the actual costs for the items paid at settlement. When this transaction is subject to RESPA, by signing page four of this form you are also acknowledging receipt of the HUD Guide to Settlement Costs.

HUD-1	Item	Paid to Others	Paid to Broker
800	*Items Payable in Connection with Loan*		
801	Lender's Loan Origination Fee	$ _____	$ _____
802	Lender's Loan Discount Fee	$ _____	$ _____
803	Appraisal Fee	$ _____	$ _____
804	Credit Report	$ _____	$ _____
805	Lender's Inspection Fee	$ _____	$ _____
808	Mortgage Broker Commission/Fee	$ _____	$ _____
809	Tax Service Fee	$ _____	$ _____
810	Processing Fee	$ _____	$ _____
811	Underwriting Fee	$ _____	$ _____
812	Wire Transfer Fee	$ _____	$ _____
		$ _____	$ _____
900	*Items Required by Lender to be Paid in Advance*		
901	Interest for ____ days at $_____ per day	$ _____	$ _____
902	Mortgage Insurance Premiums	$ _____	$ _____
903	Hazard Insurance Premiums	$ _____	$ _____
904	County Property Taxes	$ _____	$ _____
905	VA Funding Fee	$ _____	$ _____
		$ _____	$ _____
1000	*Reserves Deposited with Lender*		
1001	Hazard Insurance: ____ months at $_____ /mo.	$ _____	$ _____
1002	Mortgage Insurance: ____ months at $_____ /mo.	$ _____	$ _____
1004	Co. Property Taxes: ____ months at $_____ /mo.	$ _____	$ _____
		$ _____	$ _____
1100	*Title Charges*		
1101	Settlement or Closing/Escrow Fee	$ _____	$ _____
1105	Document Preparation Fee	$ _____	$ _____
1106	Notary Fee	$ _____	$ _____
1108	Title Insurance	$ _____	$ _____
		$ _____	$ _____
1200	*Government Recording and Transfer Charges*		
1201	Recording Fees	$ _____	$ _____
1202	City/County Tax/Stamps	$ _____	$ _____
		$ _____	$ _____
1300	*Additional Settlement Charges*		
1302	Pest Inspection	$ _____	$ _____
		$ _____	$ _____

Subtotals of Initial Fees, Commissions, Costs and Expenses $ _____ $ _____

Total of Initial Fees, Commissions, Costs and Expenses $ _____

Compensation to Broker (Not Paid Out of Loan Proceeds):
Mortgage Broker Commission/Fee $ _____
Any Additional Compensation from Lender   ☐ No   ☐ Yes $ _____
(Approximate Yield Spread Premium or Other Rebate)

FIGURE 5.5   (*Continued*)

ADDITIONAL REQUIRED CALIFORNIA DISCLOSURES

I. Proposed Loan Amount: $ _____

    Initial Commissions, Fees, Costs and
       Expenses Summarized on Page 1: $ _____

    Payment of Other Obligations (List):
       Credit Life and/or Disability Insurance (see XIV below) $ _____

    _____ $ _____

    _____ $ _____

    Subtotal of All Deductions: $ _____

    Estimated Cash at Closing   ☐ To You   ☐ That you must pay $ _____

II. Proposed Loan Term: _____   ☐ Years   ☐ Months

III. Proposed Interest Rate: _____%   ☐ Fixed Rate   ☐ Initial Adjustable Rate

    If the Fixed Rate Box is checked in Section III immediately above, proceed to section X. Do not complete sections IV through IX.

IV   Initial Adjustable Rate in effect for _____ Months

V. Fully Indexed Interest Rate _____%

VI. Maximum Interest Rate _____%

VII. Proposed Initial (Minimum) Loan Payment $_____ Monthly

VIII. Interest Rate can Increase _____% each _____ Months

IX. Payment Options end after _____ Months or _____% of Original Balance, whichever comes first

X. After _____ months you will not have the option to make minimum or interest only payments and negative amortization (increases in your principal balance), if any, will no longer be allowed. Assuming you have made minimum payments, you may then have to make principal and interest payments of $_____ at the maximum interest rate in effect for the remaining _____ months of the loan. *These payments will be significantly higher than the minimum or interest only payments.*

XI. If your loan contains negative amortization, at the time no additional negative amortization will accrue, your loan balance will be $_____ assuming minimum payments are made.

XII. The loan is subject to a balloon payment: ☐ No ☐ Yes. If Yes, the following paragraph applies and a final balloon payment of $_____ will be due on ___/___/___ *[estimated date (month/day/year)].*

    NOTICE TO BORROWER: IF YOU DO NOT HAVE THE FUNDS TO PAY THE BALLOON PAYMENT WHEN IT COMES DUE, YOU MAY HAVE TO OBTAIN A NEW LOAN AGAINST YOUR PROPERTY TO MAKE THE BALLOON PAYMENT. IN THAT CASE, YOU MAY AGAIN HAVE TO PAY COMMISSIONS, FEES, AND EXPENSES FOR THE ARRANGING OF THE NEW LOAN. IN ADDITION, IF YOU ARE UNABLE TO MAKE THE MONTHLY PAYMENTS OR THE BALLOON PAYMENT, YOU MAY LOSE THE PROPERTY AND ALL OF YOUR EQUITY THROUGH FORECLOSURE. KEEP THIS IN MIND IN DECIDING UPON THE AMOUNT AND TERMS OF THIS LOAN.

XIII. Prepayments: The proposed loan has the following prepayment provisions:

    ☐ No prepayment penalty (you will not be charged a penalty to pay off or refinance the loan before maturity)

    ☐ You will have to pay a prepayment penalty if the loan is paid off or refinanced in the first _____ years. The prepayment penalty could be as much as $_____. Any prepayment of principal in excess of 20% of the

        ☐ original loan balance or

        ☐ unpaid balance

    for the first _____ years will include a penalty not to exceed _____ months interest at the note interest rate but not more than the interest you would be charged if the loan were paid to maturity.

    ☐ Other – you will have to pay a prepayment penalty if the loan is paid off or refinanced in the first _____ years as follows:

    _____

    _____

XIV. Taxes and Insurance:

    ☐ There will be an impound (escrow) account which will collect approximately $_____ a month in addition to your principal and interest payments for the payment of ☐ county property taxes* ☐ hazard insurance ☐ mortgage insurance ☐ flood insurance ☐ other.

    ☐ If there is no impound (escrow) account you will have to plan for the payment of ☐ county property taxes* ☐ hazard insurance ☐ mortgage insurance ☐ flood insurance ☐ other_____ of approximately $_____ per year.

    * In a purchase transaction, county property taxes are calculated based on the sales price of the property and may require the payment of an additional (supplemental) tax bill from the county tax authority by your lender (if escrowed)

FIGURE 5.5   (*Continued*)

XV.   Credit Life and/or Disability Insurance: The purchase of credit life and/or disability insurance by a borrower is NOT required as a condition of making this proposed loan.

XVI.   Other Liens: Are there liens currently on this property for which the borrower is obligated?   ☐ No   ☐ Yes
If Yes, describe below:

Lienholder's Name	*Amount Owing*	*Priority*

Liens that will remain or are anticipated on this property after the proposed loan for which you are applying is made or arranged (including the proposed loan for which you are applying):

Lienholder's Name	*Amount Owing*	*Priority*

NOTICE TO BORROWER: Be sure that you state the amount of all liens as accurately as possible. If you contract with the broker to arrange this loan, but it cannot be arranged because you did not state these liens correctly, you may be liable to pay commissions, costs, fees, and expenses even though you do not obtain the loan.

XVII.   Article 7 Compliance: If this proposed loan is secured by a first deed of trust in a principal amount of less than $30,000 or secured by a junior lien in a principal amount of less than $20,000, the undersigned broker certifies that the loan will be made in compliance with Article 7 of Chapter 3 of the Real Estate Law.

     A.   This loan ☐ may ☐ will ☐ will not be made wholly or in part from broker controlled funds as defined in Section 10241(j) of the Business and Professions Code.

     B.   If the broker indicates in the above statement that the loan "may" be made out of broker-controlled funds, the broker must inform the borrower prior to the close of escrow if the funds to be received by the borrower are in fact broker-controlled funds.

XVIII.   This loan is based on limited or no documentation of your income and/or assets and may have a higher interest rate, or more points or fees than other products requiring documentation: ☐ No ☐ Yes

NOTICE TO BROKER

If any of the columns in section XIX, Comparison of Sample Mortgage Features, on page 4 of this RE 885 form, are not completed, you must certify to the following:

CERTIFICATION

I, _____, hereby certify (or declare) that the failure to complete the information in any or all of the columns (with the exception of the last column "Proposed Loan" in the Typical Mortgage Transactions portion of this RE 885) is either because (1) after a diligent search, I have determined that the product specified in that column is not available to consumers from mortgage lenders, or (2) the borrower to whom this form applies does not qualify for that particular product.

I certify (or declare) under penalty of perjury under the laws of the State of California that the foregoing is true and correct.

_____	_____
Signature of Broker	Date

Intentionally Blank

FIGURE 5.5   (Continued)

XIX.   Comparison of Sample Mortgage Features (One to Four Residential Units)

TYPICAL MORTGAGE TRANSACTIONS

PROPOSED LOAN AMOUNT $ _____ ___-YEAR TERM	Principal and Interest *Fully Amortizing* ☐ Not Offered*	Interest Only *Fully Amortizing* ☐ Not Offered*	5/1 ARM *Fully Amortizing* ☐ Not Offered*	Interest Only *Fully Amortizing* ☐ Not Offered*	Option Payment *Fully Amortizing* ☐ Not Offered*	Proposed Loan Type of Loan: _____ Type of Amortization: _____
	Fixed Rate (_____%)	**Fixed Rate** (_____%) **Interest Only for First 5 Years**	**Fixed Rate for First 5 Years; Adjustable Each Year After First 5 Years** (Initial rate for 1 to 5 is_____%; Maximum Rate is _____%)	**Interest Only and Fixed Rate for First 5 years; Adjustable Rate Each Year After First 5 Years** (Initial rate for 1 to 5 is_____%; Maximum Rate is _____%)	**Adjustable Rate for Entire Term of the Mortgage** (Rate in month 1 is _____%; Rate in month 2 through year 5 is _____%; Maximum Rate is_____%)	**Explanation of Type of Proposed Loan Product:**

Payment Scenarios

Minimum Monthly Payment Years 1-5 except as noted	$ _____ **	$ _____	$ _____	$ _____	$ _____ **** (1st year only)	$ _____
Monthly Payment in Year 6 with no change in rates	$ _____	$ _____ ***	$ _____	$ _____	$ _____	$ _____
Monthly Payment in Year 6 with a 2% rise in rates	$ _____	$ _____	$ _____	$ _____	$ _____	$ _____
Minimum Monthly Payment	$ _____	$ _____	$ _____	$ _____	$ _____	$ _____
Your Gross Income	$ _____	$ _____	$ _____	$ _____	$ _____	$ _____
Difference	$ _____	$ _____	$ _____	$ _____	$ _____	$ _____
Maximum Monthly Payment in Year 6 with a 5% rise in rates	$ _____	$ _____	$ _____	$ _____	$ _____	$ _____
Your Gross Income	$ _____	$ _____	$ _____	$ _____	$ _____	$ _____
Difference	$ _____	$ _____	$ _____	$ _____	$ _____	$ _____

Loan Balance Scenarios

How much will be owed after 5 years?	$ _____	$ _____	$ _____	$ _____	$ _____	$ _____
Has the loan balance been reduced after 5 years of payments?	**Yes** The loan balance was reduced by $ _____	**No** The loan balance was not reduced	**Yes** The loan balance was reduced by $ _____	**No** The loan balance was not reduced	**No** The loan balance **increased** by $ _____	**No/Yes** The loan balance: **did not change/ increased/decreased** by $ _____

*   "Not offered" indicates the broker does not offer the comparison loan product.

The information provided for the products not offered was obtained from sources deemed reliable. ☐ Yes ☐ No

**   This illustrates an interest rate and payments that are fixed for the life of the loan.

***   This illustrates payments that are fixed after the first five years of the loan at a higher amount because they include both principal and interest.

****   This illustrates minimum monthly payments that are based on an interest rate that is in effect during the first month only. The payments required during the first year will not be sufficient to cover all of the interest that is due when the rate increases in the second month of the loan. Any unpaid interest amount will be added to the loan balance. Minimum payments for years 2-5 are based on the higher interest rate in effect at the time, subject to any contract limits on payment increases. Minimum payments will be recast (recalculated) after 5 years, or when the loan balance reaches a certain limit, to cover both principal and interest at the applicable rate.

IMPORTANT NOTE: Please use this chart to discuss possible loans with your broker or lender

If a mortgage loan broker licensed by the California Department of Real Estate is acting as your agent in connection with your home loan/mortgage, the agent owes you certain fiduciary duties, and California statutory law imposes other duties.

XX.   NOTICE TO BORROWER: THIS IS NOT A LOAN COMMITMENT. Do not sign this statement until you have read and understood all of the information in it. All parts of this form must be completed before you sign. Borrower hereby acknowledges the receipt of a copy of this statement.

_____ *Name of Broker*	_____ License #	_____ *Broker's Representative*	_____ License #
_____ *Broker's Address*			
_____ *Signature of Broker*	_____ *Date*	OR _____ *Signature of Representative*	_____ *Date*
_____ *Borrower*	_____ *Date*	_____ *Borrower*	_____ *Date*

Department of Real Estate license information telephone number: (916) 227-0931, or check license status at www.dre.ca.gov

FIGURE 5.5   (Continued)

STATE OF CALIFORNIA
DEPARTMENT OF REAL ESTATE
Serving Californians Since 1917

INSTRUCTIONAL GUIDE FOR NONTRADITIONAL LOAN DISCLOSURE (PAGE 4)
(ONE TO FOUR RESIDENTIAL UNITS)

PROPOSED LOAN AMOUNT ① ① EAR TERM	P I ___ Fully Amortizing ☐ Not Offered* F R (②)	I O Fully Amortizing ☐ Not Offered* F R (③) I O F	/ ARM Fully Amortizing ☐ Not Offered* F R F A A E A F (I ④ M ④ R ④)	I O F R Fully Amortizing ☐ Not Offered* A F E F (I ④ M ④ R ④)	O P Fully Amortizing ☐ Not Offered* A R E T M (R ⑤ R M ⑤ R ⑤)	P L T L ㉕ T A ㉖ E T P L P ㉖
Payment Scenarios						
Minimum Monthly Payment Years 1-5 except as noted	$ ⑥ **	$ ⑦	$ ⑧	$ ⑦	$ ⑨ **** (1st year only)	$ ㉖
Monthly Payment in Year 6 with no change in rates	$ ⑥	$ ⑩ ***	$ ⑪	$ ⑫	$ ⑬	$ ㉖
Monthly Payment in Year 6 with a 2% rise in rates	$ ⑥	$ ⑩	$ ⑭	$ ⑮	$ ⑯	$ ㉖
Minimum Monthly Payment	$ ⑥	$ ⑦	$ ⑧	$ ⑦	$ ⑨	$ ㉖
Your Gross Income	$ ⑰	$ ⑰	$ ⑰	$ ⑰	$ ⑰	$ ⑰
Difference	$ ⑱	$ ⑱	$ ⑱	$ ⑱	$ ⑱	$ ⑱
Maximum Monthly Payment in Year 6 with a 5% rise in rates	$ ⑥	$ ⑩	$ ⑲	$ ⑳	$ ㉑	$ ㉖
Your Gross Income	$ ⑰	$ ⑰	$ ⑰	$ ⑰	$ ⑰	$ ⑰
Difference	$ ㉒	$ ㉒	$ ㉒	$ ㉒	$ ㉒	$ ㉒
Loan Balance Scenarios						
How much will be owed after 5 years?	$ ㉓	$ ㉓	$ ㉓	$ ㉓	$ ㉓	$ ㉓
Has the loan balance been reduced after 5 years of payments?	The loan balance was reduced by $ ㉔	N The loan balance was not reduced	N The loan balance was reduced by $ ㉔	N The loan balance was not reduced	N The loan balance by $ ㉔	N / The loan balance: / by $ ㉔

① Proposed loan amount and term.

② Current interest rate for fixed rate loan.

③ Current interest rate for fixed rate loan that is interest-only for first 5 years.

④ Current fixed interest rate for first 5 years and maximum rate based on 5% maximum increase.

⑤ Current initial interest rate for month 1; interest rate for month 2 through year 5 based on current fully-indexed interest rate; maximum rate based on 5% maximum increase.

⑥ Fixed rate loan payment (see *).

⑦ Interest-only payment based on fixed rate for first 5 years.

⑧ P&I payment based on fixed rate for first 5 years.

⑨ Minimum option payment based on month 1 rate for first year only(see ***).

⑩ P&I payment for remaining term (see **).

⑪ P&I payment for remaining term (same as #8).

⑫ P&I payment for remaining term.

⑬ P&I payment based on increased principal balance for remaining term.

⑭ P&I payment for remaining term based on decreased principal balance at 2% increase in interest rate.

⑮ P&I payment for remaining term based on original principal balance at 2% increase in interest rate.

⑯ P&I payment for remaining term based on increased principal balance at 2% increase in interest rate.

⑰ Borrower's gross income from loan application.

⑱ Subtract minimum monthly payment from gross income.

⑲ P&I payment for remaining term based on reduced principal balance at maximum interest rate.

⑳ P&I payment for remaining term based on original principal balance at maximum interest rate.

㉑ P&I payment for remaining term based on increased principal balance at maximum interest rate.

㉒ Subtract maximum monthly payment from gross income.

㉓ Calculate loan balance after 5 years based on minimum monthly payments for years 1 through 5.

㉔ Calculate the amount the loan balance has increased or decreased after 5 years.

㉕ Insert type of proposed loan product.

㉖ Insert applicable information for each scenario.

*   "Not offered" indicates the broker does not offer the comparison loan product. The information provided for the products not offered was obtained from sources deemed reliable. ☐Yes ☐ No

**   This illustrates an interest rate and payments that are fixed for the life of the loan.

***   This illustrates payments that are fixed after the first five years of the loan at a higher amount because they include both principal and interest.

****   This illustrates minimum monthly payments that are based on an interest rate that is in effect during the first month only. The payments required during the first year will not be sufficient to cover all of the interest that is due when the rate increases in the second month of the loan. Any unpaid interest amount will be added to the loan balance. Minimum payments for years 2-5 are based on the higher interest rate in effect at the time, subject to any contract limits on payment increases. Minimum payments will be recast (recalculated) after 5 years, or when the loan balance reaches a certain limit, to cover both principal and interest at the applicable rate.

Rev. (8/08)

improvement loans, and equity lines of credit. This law covers required disclosure at various times: at the time of the loan application, before closing occurs, at settlement and after settlement. Enforcement may be brought about with a civil law suit in addition to filing a complaint with the Housing and Urban Development (HUD) Office of RESPA, and with Interstate Land Sales. There are many sections to this complicated law with which the mortgage loan broker must comply, but specific sections are intended to be aimed at consumer protections and to prohibit specific practices. For example, Section 8 covers kickbacks, fee-splitting, and unearned fees. Section 9 regulates that the seller is required to furnish title insurance. Section 10 puts limits on escrow accounts.

At the time of loan application for a purchase transaction, the lender must furnish the borrower with a special information booklet which contains the various real estate settlement services. For all transactions, a Good Faith Estimate (GFE) must be given to the buyer that lists charges that are likely at closing. In addition, all transactions must disclose to the borrower whether the lender intends to service the loan or transfer it to another lender. This Mortgage Servicing Disclosure Statement provides information about complaint resolution. The Settlement Statement Instruction booklet was created in March 1986 and is referred to as the HUD-1 form. In February 1994 the HUD-1A Settlement Statement was required. From this Act, numerous forms were generated by HUD from 2001 through 2007, such as HUD 1041 through 1047, HUD 11, and HUD 11600 through 11710. Effective December 2, 1992, California concluded that a "table funded" or "concurrent funded" transaction is brokering and must be treated as brokering for dis- closure purposes. In addition, RESPA imposes special disclosure requirements relating to loan servicing, the transfer of loan servicing, required escrow accounts, controlled business arrangements, and computerized loan originations. RESPA imposes limitations on the payment of unauthorized referral fees (kickbacks) and regulates how affiliated entities may refer business/transactions to each other when those activities are subject to RESPA. Loan types included under the RESPA requirements are:

1. Long-term financing used on construction of residential property (not the short-term, two-years-or-less construction loan).
2. Any loan made by a lender whose deposits are insured by an agency of the federal government (not private, owner-carryback loans).
3. Any loan intended to be sold on the secondary money market (such as FNMA, GNMA, FHLMC, or FHA).
4. Any lender who makes more than $1 million in residential real estate loans in one calendar year (including temporary financing, junior liens, and multi-family loans).
5. A "dealer"-originated loan made by a mortgage loan broker to be assigned to a lender.

The definition expressly includes reverse mortgages and home equity conversion loans made by a lender. The following transactions are expressly exempted from RESPA coverage:

1. Loan secured by vacant land, unless the loan proceeds will be used to construct a home on the property.

2. Any loan secured by property of 25 or more acres, even if it contains a residence.

3. Any business, commercial, or agricultural loan, except one- to four-unit residential property rented to other persons, whether to acquire, maintain, improve, or refinance.

4. A loan assumption for which the lender has no right to prohibit the person assuming the loan from becoming the borrower.

5. A bona fide transfer of a loan in the secondary market.

A lender, defined for the purposes of being obligated to make adjustable rate loan disclosures and to deliver the booklet entitled *Consumer Handbook* on *Adjustable Rate Mortgages*, is any person, association, corporation, partnership, or other business entity that makes more than 10 loans in any 12- month period. Lender is also defined to include those who make credit sales secured by residential real property of one to four units (Title 12 Code of Federal Regulations Part 29 of Chapter 1 and/or 563 of Chapter V; CC 1921).

The RESPA Settlements Procedures Act further defines inclusive services and the costs relating to the loan and must be given to the parties. The fees, commissions, costs, and expenses are an estimate, and the actual charges may be more or less. The HUD-1 Settlement Statement contains the actual costs, charges, and adjustments for items paid at close of escrow, called settlement. The form may be used in transactions in which its use is not legally required under Section 4 of RESPA and Regulation X of the *Department of Housing and Urban Development* (*HUD*) (24 CFR part 3500).

The HUD-1 form is shown in Figure 5.6. As of January 1, 2010, the new three-page HUD-1 must be used. This HUD-1, Uniform Settlement Statement form requires a comparison of the actual costs to the estimate in the Good Faith Estimate (GFE), shown in Figure 5.7, that was given to the borrower within three days of the original loan application. This new third page of the form lists certain loan terms and costs. This act prohibits increases in lender-controlled costs and limits increases in other costs to an increase of 10 percent over the amount originally shown on the GFE.

The settlement agent must complete the form to itemize all charges imposed on the borrower and the seller, if any by the lender and all sales commissions, whether paid at close of escrow or outside of escrow. Charges to be paid or already paid outside of settlement are to be marked "P.O.C." for "paid outside of closing" and are not included in computing totals, and the item is placed on the appropriate line next to the columns.

Blank lines are provided in Sections J, K, and L for items not listed. Section J, which relates to the borrower, may be left blank on the copy furnished to the seller. Section K, which relates to the seller, may be left blank on the borrower's copy.

The second page of the form itemizes broker commissions, loan fees, impounds, prorations and reserves, title charges, government recording and transfer fees, and other common charges, such as pest control, home protection policy, or

FIGURE 5.6   HUD-1 final settlement statement.

OMB Approval No. 2502-0265

A. Settlement Statement (HUD-1)

B. Type of Loan

1. ☐ FHA 2. ☐ RHS 3. ☐ Conv. Unins.	6. File Number:	7. Loan Number:	8. Mortgage Insurance Case Number:
4. ☐ VA 5. ☐ Conv. Ins.			

C. Note: This form is furnished to give you a statement of actual settlement costs. Amounts paid to and by the settlement agent are shown. Items marked "(p.o.c.)" were paid outside the closing; they are shown here for informational purposes and are not included in the totals.

D. Name & Address of Borrower:	E. Name & Address of Seller:	F. Name & Address of Lender:
G. Property Location:	H. Settlement Agent:	I. Settlement Date:
	Place of Settlement:	

J. Summary of Borrower's Transaction		K. Summary of Seller's Transaction	
100. Gross Amount Due from Borrower		**400. Gross Amount Due to Seller**	
101. Contract sales price		401. Contract sales price	
102. Personal property		402. Personal property	
103. Settlement charges to borrower (line 1400)		403.	
104.		404.	
105.		405.	
Adjustment for items paid by seller in advance		**Adjustments for items paid by seller in advance**	
106. City/town taxes to		406. City/town taxes to	
107. County taxes to		407. County taxes to	
108. Assessments to		408. Assessments to	
109.		409.	
110.		410.	
111.		411.	
112.		412.	
120. Gross Amount Due from Borrower		**420. Gross Amount Due to Seller**	
200. Amounts Paid by or in Behalf of Borrower		**500. Reductions In Amount Due to Seller**	
201. Deposit or earnest money		501. Excess deposit (see instructions)	
202. Principal amount of new loan(s)		502. Settlement charges to seller (line 1400)	
203. Existing loan(s) taken subject to		503. Existing loan(s) taken subject to	
204.		504. Payoff of first mortgage loan	
205.		505. Payoff of second mortgage loan	
206.		506.	
207.		507.	
208.		508.	
209.		509.	
Adjustments for items unpaid by seller		**Adjustments for items unpaid by seller**	
210. City/town taxes to		510. City/town taxes to	
211. County taxes to		511. County taxes to	
212. Assessments to		512. Assessments to	
213.		513.	
214.		514.	
215.		515.	
216.		516.	
217.		517.	
218.		518.	
219.		519.	
220. Total Paid by/for Borrower		**520. Total Reduction Amount Due Seller**	
300. Cash at Settlement from/to Borrower		**600. Cash at Settlement to/from Seller**	
301. Gross amount due from borrower (line 120)		601. Gross amount due to seller (line 420)	
302. Less amounts paid by/for borrower (line 220)	( )	602. Less reductions in amount due seller (line 520)	( )
303. Cash ☐ From ☐ To Borrower		**603. Cash** ☐ To ☐ From Seller	

The Public Reporting Burden for this collection of information is estimated at 35 minutes per response for collecting, reviewing, and reporting the data. This agency may not collect this information, and you are not required to complete this form, unless it displays a currently valid OMB control number. No confidentiality is assured; this disclosure is mandatory. This is designed to provide the parties to a RESPA covered transaction with information during the settlement process.

FIGURE 5.6 *(Continued)*

L. Settlement Charges				Paid From Borrower's Funds at Settlement	Paid From Seller's Funds at Settlement
700. Total Real Estate Broker Fees					
Division of commission (line 700) as follows:					
701. $			to		
702. $			to		
703. Commission paid at settlement					
704.					
800. Items Payable in Connection with Loan					
801. Our origination charge		$	(from GFE #1)		
802. Your credit or charge (points) for the specific interest rate chosen $			(from GFE #2)		
803. Your adjusted origination charges			(from GFE A)		
804. Appraisal fee to			(from GFE #3)		
805. Credit report to			(from GFE #3)		
806. Tax service to			(from GFE #3)		
807. Flood certification			(from GFE #3)		
808.					
900. Items Required by Lender to Be Paid in Advance					
901. Daily interest charges from to @ $ /day			(from GFE #10)		
902. Mortgage insurance premium for months to			(from GFE #3)		
903. Homeowner's insurance for years to			(from GFE #11)		
904.					
1000. Reserves Deposited with Lender					
1001. Initial deposit for your escrow account			(from GFE #9)		
1002. Homeowner's insurance months @ $	per month	$			
1003. Mortgage insurance months @ $	per month	$			
1004. Property taxes months @ $	per month	$			
1005. months @ $	per month	$			
1006. months @ $	per month	$			
1007. Aggregate Adjustment		−$			
1100. Title Charges					
1101. Title services and lender's title insurance			(from GFE #4)		
1102. Settlement or closing fee		$			
1103. Owner's title insurance			(from GFE #5)		
1104. Lender's title insurance		$			
1105. Lender's title policy limit $					
1106. Owner's title policy limit $					
1107. Agent's portion of the total title insurance premium		$			
1108. Underwriter's portion of the total title insurance premium		$			
1200. Government Recording and Transfer Charges					
1201. Government recording charges			(from GFE #7)		
1202. Deed $ Mortgage $		Releases $			
1203. Transfer taxes			(from GFE #8)		
1204. City/County tax/stamps Deed $		Mortgage $			
1205. State tax/stamps Deed $		Mortgage $			
1206.					
1300. Additional Settlement Charges					
1301. Required services that you can shop for			(from GFE #6)		
1302.		$			
1303.		$			
1304.					
1305.					
1400. Total Settlement Charges (enter on lines 103, Section J and 502, Section K)					

FIGURE 5.6 (*Continued*)

Comparison of Good Faith Estimate (GFE) and HUD-1 Charges		Good Faith Estimate	HUD-1
Charges That Cannot Increase	**HUD-1 Line Number**		
Our origination charge	# 801		
Your credit or charge (points) for the specific interest rate chosen	# 802		
Your adjusted origination charges	# 803		
Transfer taxes	#1203		

Charges That in Total Cannot Increase More Than 10%		Good Faith Estimate	HUD-1
Government recording charges	# 1201		
	#		
	#		
	#		
	#		
	#		
	#		
Total			
Increase between GFE and HUD-1 Charges		$	or %

Charges That Can Change		Good Faith Estimate	HUD-1
Initial deposit for your escrow account	#1001		
Daily interest charges	# 901 $ /day		
Homeowner's insurance	# 903		
	#		
	#		
	#		

Loan Terms

Your initial loan amount is	$
Your loan term is	_____ years
Your initial interest rate is	_____ %
Your initial monthly amount owed for principal, interest, and and any mortgage insurance is	$ _____ includes ☐ Principal ☐ Interest ☐ Mortgage Insurance
Can your interest rate rise?	☐ No. ☐ Yes, it can rise to a maximum of ___%. The first change will be on _____ and can change again every _____ after _____ . Every change date, your interest rate can increase or decrease by ___%. Over the life of the loan, your interest rate is guaranteed to never be **lower** than ___% or **higher** than ___%.
Even if you make payments on time, can your loan balance rise?	☐ No. ☐ Yes, it can rise to a maximum of $ _____ .
Even if you make payments on time, can your monthly amount owed for principal, interest, and mortgage insurance rise?	☐ No. ☐ Yes, the first increase can be on _____ and the monthly amount owed can rise to $ _____ . The maximum it can ever rise to is $ _____ .
Does your loan have a prepayment penalty?	☐ No. ☐ Yes, your maximum prepayment penalty is $ _____ .
Does your loan have a balloon payment?	☐ No. ☐ Yes, you have a balloon payment of $ _____ due in ___ years on _____ .
Total monthly amount owed including escrow account payments	☐ You do not have a monthly escrow payment for items, such as property taxes and homeowner's insurance. You must pay these items directly yourself. ☐ You have an additional monthly escrow payment of $ _____ that results in a total initial monthly amount owed of $ _____ . This includes principal, interest, any mortgage insurance and any items checked below: ☐ Property taxes ☐ Homeowner's insurance ☐ Flood insurance ☐ _____ ☐ _____ ☐ _____

Note: If you have any questions about the Settlement Charges and Loan Terms listed on this form, please contact your lender.

FIGURE 5.7   Good Faith Estimate (GFE)

OMB Approval No. 2502-0265

Good Faith Estimate (GFE)

Name of Originator		Borrower	
Originator Address		Property Address	
Originator Phone Number			
Originator Email		Date of GFE	

Purpose

This GFE gives you an estimate of your settlement charges and loan terms if you are approved for this loan. For more information, see HUD's *Special Information Booklet* on settlement charges, your *Truth-in-Lending Disclosures,* and other consumer information at www.hud.gov/respa. If you decide you would like to proceed with this loan, contact us.

Shopping for your loan

Only you can shop for the best loan for you. Compare this GFE with other loan offers, so you can find the best loan. Use the shopping chart on page 3 to compare all the offers you receive.

Important dates

1. The interest rate for this GFE is available through _____. After this time, the interest rate, some of your loan Origination Charges, and the monthly payment shown below can change until you lock your interest rate.

2. This estimate for all other settlement charges is available through _____

3. After you lock your interest rate, you must go to settlement within _____ days (your rate lock period) to receive the locked interest rate.

4. You must lock the interest rate at least _____ days before settlement.

Summary of your loan

Your initial loan amount is	$
Your loan term is	years
Your initial interest rate is	%
Your initial monthly amount owed for principal, interest, and any mortgage insurance is	$ per month
Can your interest rate rise?	☐ No ☐ Yes, it can rise to a maximum of %. The first change will be in
Even if you make payments on time, can your loan balance rise?	☐ No ☐ Yes, it can rise to a maximum of $
Even if you make payments on time, can your monthly amount owed for principal, interest, and any mortgage insurance rise?	☐ No ☐ Yes, the first increase can be in and the monthly amount owed can rise to $. The maximum it can ever rise to is $
Does your loan have a prepayment penalty?	☐ No ☐ Yes, your maximum prepayment penalty is $
Does your loan have a balloon payment?	☐ No ☐ Yes, you have a balloon payment of $ due in years.

Escrow account information

Some lenders require an escrow account to hold funds for paying property taxes or other property-related charges in addition to your monthly amount owed of $ _____ .

Do we require you to have an escrow account for your loan?

☐ No, you do not have an escrow account. You must pay these charges directly when due.

☐ Yes, you have an escrow account. It may or may not cover all of these charges. Ask us.

Summary of your settlement charges

A	Your Adjusted Origination Charges (See page 2.)	
B	Your Charges for All Other Settlement Services (See page 2.)	
A + B	Total Estimated Settlement Charges	$

Good Faith Estimate (HUD-GFE) 1

FIGURE 5.7 *(Continued)*

Understanding your estimated settlement charges

Your Adjusted Origination Charges

1. **Our origination charge**
   This charge is for getting this loan for you.

2. **Your credit or charge (points) for the specific interest rate chosen**
   ☐ The credit or charge for the interest rate of [   ] % is included in "Our origination charge." (See item 1 above.)

   ☐ You receive a credit of $ [   ] for this interest rate of [   ] %.
   This credit **reduces** your settlement charges.

   ☐ You pay a charge of $ [   ] for this interest rate of [   ] %.
   This charge (points) **increases** your total settlement charges.
   The tradeoff table on page 3 shows that you can change your total settlement charges by choosing a different interest rate for this loan.

A | Your Adjusted Origination Charges | $

Your Charges for All Other Settlement Services

Some of these charges can change at settlement. See the top of page 3 for more information.

3. **Required services that we select**
   These charges are for services we require to complete your settlement. We will choose the providers of these services.

Service	Charge

4. **Title services and lender's title insurance**
   This charge includes the services of a title or settlement agent, for example, and title insurance to protect the lender, if required.

5. **Owner's title insurance**
   You may purchase an owner's title insurance policy to protect your interest in the property.

6. **Required services that you can shop for**
   These charges are for other services that are required to complete your settlement. We can identify providers of these services or you can shop for them yourself. Our estimates for providing these services are below.

Service	Charge

7. **Government recording charges**
   These charges are for state and local fees to record your loan and title documents.

8. **Transfer taxes**
   These charges are for state and local fees on mortgages and home sales.

9. **Initial deposit for your escrow account**
   This charge is held in an escrow account to pay future recurring charges on your property and includes ☐ all property taxes, ☐ all insurance, and ☐ other [   ] .

10. **Daily interest charges**
    This charge is for the daily interest on your loan from the day of your settlement until the first day of the next month or the first day of your normal mortgage payment cycle.
    This amount is $ [   ] per day for [   ] days (if your settlement is [   ]).

11. **Homeowner's insurance**
    This charge is for the insurance you must buy for the property to protect from a loss, such as fire.

Policy	Charge

B | Your Charges for All Other Settlement Services | $

A + **B** | Total Estimated Settlement Charges | $

Good Faith Estimate (HUD-GFE) 2

FIGURE 5.7   *(Continued)*

Understanding your estimated settlement charges

Your Adjusted Origination Charges

1.   Our origination charge
This charge is for getting this loan for you.

2.   Your credit or charge (points) for the specific interest rate chosen

☐ The credit or charge for the interest rate of [   ] % is included in "Our origination charge." (See item 1 above.)

☐ You receive a credit of $ [   ] for this interest rate of [   ]%.
This credit **reduces** your settlement charges.

☐ You pay a charge of $ [   ] for this interest rate of [   ]%.
This charge (points) **increases** your total settlement charges.
The tradeoff table on page 3 shows that you can change your total settlement charges by choosing a different interest rate for this loan.

| **A** | Your Adjusted Origination Charges | $ |

Your Charges for All Other Settlement Services

Some of these charges can change at settlement. See the top of page 3 for more information.

3.   Required services that we select
These charges are for services we require to complete your settlement. We will choose the providers of these services.

Service	Charge

4.   Title services and lender's title insurance
This charge includes the services of a title or settlement agent, for example, and title insurance to protect the lender, if required.

5.   Owner's title insurance
You may purchase an owner's title insurance policy to protect your interest in the property.

6.   Required services that you can shop for
These charges are for other services that are required to complete your settlement. We can identify providers of these services or you can shop for them yourself. Our estimates for providing these services are below.

Service	Charge

7.   Government recording charges
These charges are for state and local fees to record your loan and title documents.

8.   Transfer taxes
These charges are for state and local fees on mortgages and home sales.

9.   Initial deposit for your escrow account
This charge is held in an escrow account to pay future recurring charges on your property and includes ☐ all property taxes, ☐ all insurance, and ☐ other [   ] .

10. Daily interest charges
This charge is for the daily interest on your loan from the day of your settlement until the first day of the next month or the first day of your normal mortgage payment cycle.
This amount is $ [   ] per day for [   ] days (if your settlement is [   ]).

11. Homeowner's insurance
This charge is for the insurance you must buy for the property to protect from a loss, such as fire.

Policy	Charge

| **B** | Your Charges for All Other Settlement Services | $ |

| **A** + **B** | Total Estimated Settlement Charges | $ |

special reports. The total for the column of the buyer and the total for the seller are shown on line 1400. The total from line 1400 is the amount paid by the borrower, and the amount is carried to line 203 on the first page of the form. The line 1400 total for the seller is carried to the first page on line 502. The first page is a summary of the gross amount to or from the borrower or the seller and includes adjustments for items paid in advance by either party, amount paid by someone else on behalf of the party, seller loan payoff of existing encumbrances, and adjustments. The first page also contains the names of the parties, including borrower, seller (if any), lender, escrow or settlement agent, type of loan, loan number, mortgage insurance case number, and date of close of escrow.

5.5 HMDA, REGULATION C

The Board of Governors of the Federal Reserve System issued regulations to financial institutions to provide the public with loan data regarding meeting the housing needs of their communities. This information helps government officials make public-sector investments to attract private investors to areas where funds are needed. This regulation also assists in identifying possible discriminatory lending patterns.

The mortgage loan broker, in this case, is not responsible for completion of the reporting forms but should be aware of the requirements that the lender must meet when a borrower asks questions regarding the question on the loan document forms. To meet federal regulations, the originating lender who actually funds the loan is responsible for compliance.

Regulation C applies to banks, savings associations, credit unions, and other mortgage lending institutions. The lender must collect data from loan applications each calendar year and report the findings (two copies) to the federal government by March 1 of the following calendar year. The data must be available to the public for review no later than March 31 for requests made before March 1 and within 30 days if made after March 1. If a loan broker submits a loan to a direct lender or investor and that lender or investor turns down the loan, the loan broker does not have to submit an HMDA report. However, if a lender turns down 100 or more loans in one year, a HMDA report is required. The following must be included:

1. A number for each application
2. The type and purpose of loan
3. Owner-occupied status
4. Amount of the loan
5. Property location with census tract and county code (no street address)
6. Race or national origin of borrower and coborrower
7. Sex of borrower and coborrower
8. Income relied on in processing the application
9. Investor code for the entity purchasing the loan

The board amended Regulation C to make compliance mandatory for collection of data that begins on January 1, 2003, which must be submitted to supervisory agencies no later than March 1, 2004. The amendment expands coverage of nondepository centers by adding a $25 million volume test to the existing percentage-based coverage test. The amendment requires lenders to report items related to loan pricing. The lender will report the spread or difference between the APR and the Treasury yield. Lenders must report whether a loan is covered by the Home Ownership and Equity Protection Act (HOEPA) and whether the loan involves a manufactured home.

For brokered loan applications forwarded through a correspondent, the institution reports as originations those loans that it approved and subsequently acquired per a pre-closing arrangement (whether or not the loan closed in the institution's name). The institution reports the data for all applications that did not result in originations; that is, applications the institution denied or that the applicant withdrew during the calendar year.

An oral application constitutes an application received for purposes of this law. It is typical to log the basic information with some type of record. An example of a mortgage loan broker loan status form is shown in Figure 5.8. Also mandated is the type of action taken and the date such action is taken.

The Credit Card Accountability, Responsibility and Disclosure Act (CARD), which was implemented in February 2010, has set new limits on interest rates and fees, and credit card statements must include more information about the extent of a consumer's debt. The biggest change for most consumers is a ban on hiking interest rates for existing balances in most cases.

FIGURE 5.8   Loan status information.

LOAN STATUS INFORMATION

Loan Number _____   Loan Status _____

Disposition _____   Denial _____

Commitment Number _____   Investor _____   Investor ID # _____

Price _____   Expiration Date _____   Service Rate _____

Offered to Investor _____   Shipped _____   Purchased _____

Approved by Investor _____   Funded _____   Audit _____

Due to Investor _____   Remarks _____

Housing Authority Date _____   Status _____

Documentation Type _____

LOAN SOURCE/BROKERS: Loan Source

LOAN SOURCE REPRESENTATIVE _____

Listing Agent Name _____   Phone _____

Selling Agent Name _____   Phone _____

The CARD Act will force credit card companies to issue credit more carefully, screening out potential defaulters who raise cost for everyone. Issuers will be required to verify income and consider a person's assets and current financial obligations before doling out a line of credit.

Any person under the age of 21 must now show that they are the sole support of themselves. If they are not able to do so, they must have a co-signer.

5.6 GOVERNMENT LOAN DISCLOSURES

REQUIRED DISCLOSURES FOR FHA LOANS

- *Addendum to the uniform residential loan application.* Includes a variety of certifications by the lender and the applicant.

- *Important notice to home buyer.* Informs the applicant that FHA does not warrant the condition or value of the property. It states that FHA does not set the interest rates or the discount points, which are negotiated with the lender. It warns of the penalties of loan fraud; and, it discusses discrimination. It includes a disclosure regarding prepay, in that any prepayment must be received on the installment due date.

- *Lead paint disclosure.* Explained elsewhere/self-explanatory.

- *Assumption notice*—release of liability. Provides a release of personal liability from FHA, ensuring that the borrower is NOT responsible for making payments after an assumption takes place.

- *Informed consumer choice disclosure notice.* Compares the cost of an FHA loan with a conventional loan, including the cost of the PMI mortgage insurance.

- *Real estate certification.* Certifies the terms of the real estate purchase contract. Both the buyer and the seller are required to sign the form.

- *Social Security Number certification.* Self-explanatory.

- *FHA identity of interest certification.* Requires the borrower to disclose whether he or she has any relationship to the seller of the property.

- *Notice to the home buyer (home buyer summary).* Provided by the FHA appraiser to disclose whether the home meets minimum FHA property standards.

- *For your protection.* Explains that an appraisal is NOT an inspection, and advises the borrower to obtain an inspection.

REQUIRED DISCLOSURES FOR DVA LOANS

- *Addendum to uniform residential loan application.* Same as for FHA, this addendum includes a variety of certification.

- *VA debt questionnaire (Form 26-0551).* Asks the veteran about previous foreclosures, judgments, defaults or present delinquencies on any federal debts (including student loans).

- *Interest rate and discount statement.* States that the interest rate and points are not set by VA and are negotiable between the borrower and the lender.
- *Federal collection policy notice.* Informs the veteran of actions the government can take if scheduled payments are not made.
- *Assumption of VA-guaranteed mortgages.* Provides a release of personal liability from the VA, ensuring that the veteran is not responsible for making payments after an assumption of the loan.
- *Borrower's acknowledgments of disclosures.* Acknowledges receipt of the good faith estimate.
- *For home built prior to 1978*—notice of possible lead-based paint. Self-explanatory.
- *Counseling checklist for military homeowners.* Active-duty applicants must sign to certify that they have received homeownership and loan obligation counseling.

5.7 CALIFORNIA DISCLOSURES

California Corporations Commissioner's Regulations 1460 became effective July 29, 1991, and were set forth in Chapter 3, Title 10, California Code of Regulations for licensees acting under Financial Codes (FFL Lenders). Lenders are defined as entities that approve the loan (accomplish the underwriting functions) in which they are the beneficiary of the promissory note. They also provide funding for the loan from sources exclusive of any advances received from an institutional investor committed to or who purchased the note.

The California DRE currently distinguishes an agent from a lender according to whose funds are involved. If the funds are the broker's or sources the broker is obligated to repay, then lending activity is involved. The form of broker obligation may be that of a credit line. This DRE regulation includes a broker acting as an agent of the borrower as a factual matter. Under DRE law, table or concurrent funding loans are not a lending activity but are subject to Articles 5, 6, and 7 of the Real Estate Law Section 4. The DOC has disclosures, just as all mortgage lenders must comply with the numerous regulations. The DOC mortgage broker is not required to file the Home Mortgage Disclosure Act (HMDA) form (Figure 5.9).

Mortgage Loan Disclosure Statement

As of 1993, DRE requires completion of Form RE 882 according to Section 10241 (j) of the Business and Professions Code. The broker must disclose whether any part of the loan is made from broker-controlled funds. When a licensee receives separate compensation for making loans with his or her own funds, the licensee must provide the **Mortgage Loan Disclosure Statement** (see Figure 5.10). The document details the total costs of a loan to the borrower,

FIGURE 5.9 Residential mortgage loan report and information.

STATE OF CALIFORNIA
RESIDENTIAL MORTGAGE LOAN REPORT
HDN 1 (REV 1/09)

DEPARTMENT OF CORPORATIONS
FINANCIAL SERVICES DIVISION

REPORT ENTITY - NAME & LICENSE NUMBER	ENFORCEMENT AGENCY (*FOR THIS REPORTING ENTITY*) -- NAME **DEPARTMENT OF CORPORATIONS**	CENSUS TRACT SERIES USED **2000**	REPORT FOR LOANS MADE IN (YEAR) **2008**
ADDRESS & TELEPHONE NUMBER	ADDRESS **320 West Fourth Street, Suite 750 Los Angeles, CA 90013**	MSA (*LOCATION OF PROPERTY*)	

Section 1 - Originations   Loans On Property Located Within Those MSAs In Which Lender Has Home or Branch Offices

CENSUS TRACT (*in numerical sequence*) where property located	LOANS ON 1-TO-4 UNIT DWELLINGS						Non-Occupant Home Improvement Loans on 1-TO-4 Unit Dwellings D	
	Home Purchase Loans		Home Improvement Loans C					
	FHA, FmHA, and VA A	Other (Conventional) B						
	Number of Apps. / Loans	Principal Amount (Thousands)	Number of Apps. / Loans	Principal Amount (Thousands)	Number of Apps. / Loans	Principal Amount (Thousands)	Number of Apps. / Loans	Principal Amount (Thousands)
MSA TOTAL								

Section 2 - Originations   Loans On All Property Located Elsewhere In California

RESIDENTIAL MORTGAGE LOAN REPORT INFORMATION

HDN 1A

WHO MUST FILE

1. This form must be filed by lenders that:

    a) Regularly make qualifying loans on 1 to 4 unit residential real estate property which total at least 10% of the loans made during the preceding calendar year.

    b) have total assets of 10 million dollars and less; and

    c) who do not report to a federal or state regulatory agency as provided by the Home Mortgage Disclosure Act of 1975.

WHEN AND WHERE TO FILE

1. The lender must send two copies of the loan report to the office of its state enforcement agency no later than March 31st following the calendar year for which the loan data is compiled.

2. The lender also must make its loan report available for examination by the public no later than March 31st of each year.

INSTRUCTIONS FOR COMPLETION OF FORM

Data to be shown

1. The lender must show the data on residential purchase and home improvement loan applications and loans that were originated during the calendar year covered by the report.

2. Data for each category on the statement must show the number of applications taken, the number made and the total dollar amount of loans made.

3. Dollar amounts are to be rounded to the nearest thousand ($500 will be rounded up), and show in terms of thousands.

Data to be Excluded

1. Do not report loans that, although secured by real estate, are made for purposes other than the purchase of residential real estate or home improvement (for example, a loan secured by residential real property for the purpose of financing education, a vacation or business operations.)

2. Also exclude from the report: construction loans and other temporary financing; loans made by the lender acting in a fiduciary capacity (by the lender's trust department, for example); loans on unimproved land; and refinancing of loans originated by the lender that involved no increase in the outstanding principal (providing the parties to the loan remain the same.

Geographic Itemization   (*Grouping of loan data by MSA, census tract or county; and outside-MSA*)

1. Loan data is to be reported separately for each MSA in which the lender has a home or branch office. A separate page must be used for each MSA (See item #4 below for treatment of loans on property outside such MSAs). The lender must use the MSA boundaries as defined by the U.S. Department of Commerce on January 1 of the calendar year for which the loan data is compiled.

2. Loan data on property within an MSA shall be further itemized in Section 1 by the census tract in which the property is located except that the loan data shall be itemized by the county instead of the census tract when the property to which the loan is related is located in a county that has not been assigned an MSA.

3. To determine census tract numbers and MSA boundaries, the lender should consult the Census Bureau's census tract outline maps.

4. For loans secured by properties located outside MSAs in which the reporting lender has a home or branch office, the loan data should be listed as an aggregate sum in Section 2 of the form; no geographic itemization is necessary.

5. If duplicate census tract numbers are encountered in an MSA, the lender must indicate the county name in addition to the census tract.

Type of Loan Itemization   (*Itemization of each geographic grouping into loan categories*)

Column A – FHA, FmHA and VA loans on 1 to 4 unit dwellings. This category includes loans that are secured by liens (both first and junior liens) and that are made for the purpose of purchasing residential real property and that have FHA, FmHA and VA insurance or guarantee. It includes refinancings (see Item #2 under *Data to be Excluded*). It may include, at a lender's option, first lien loans for home improvement purposes if the lender normally classifies first lien loans as purchase loans. It does not include FHA Title I loans, which are to be entered in column C.

Column B – Other home purchase loans (conventional loans) on 1 to 4 unit dwellings. This category includes loans secured by liens (both first and junior liens) and made for the purpose of purchasing residential real property, other than FHA, FmHA and VA loans. It includes refinancings (see item #2 under *Data to be Excluded*). It may include, at a lender's option, first lien loans for home improvement purposes if the lender normally classifies first lien loans as purchase loans.

Column C – Home improvement loans on 1 to 4 unit dwellings. This category is limited to any loan, including a refinancing, that is to be used for repairing, rehabilitation or remodeling a residential dwelling and that is recorded on the lender's books as a home improvement loan.

Column D – Non-occupant loans on 1 to 4 unit dwellings. This is an addendum category for reporting those home purchase and home improvement loans on 1 to 4 unit dwellings (recorded in columns A, B and C) that were made to a borrower who did not at the time of the loan application, intend to use the property as a principal dwelling.

FIGURE 5.10   Mortgage loan disclosure statement (borrower).

MORTGAGE LOAN DISCLOSURE STATEMENT (RE882)
INFORMATIONAL SHEET

WHEN TO USE THIS FORM

TRADITIONAL LOAN PRODUCTS – This form may be used when the loan product being offered to the consumer ***DOES NOT*** allow the borrower to defer repayment of principal or interest. Each payment includes the full amount of interest and principal due for that installment. ***THIS FORM CANNOT BE USED FOR LOAN PRODUCTS THAT ALLOW THE BORROWER TO DEFER REPAYMENT OF INTEREST OR PRINCIPAL AND ARE SECURED BY A 1 – 4 UNIT RESIDENTIAL PROPERTY. FOR THOSE LOANS THE MORTGAGE LOAN DISCLOSURE STATEMENT/GOOD FAITH ESTIMATE – NONTRADITIONAL MORTGAGE PRODUCT (ONE TO FOUR UNIT RESIDENTIAL UNITS) - RE885 MUST BE USED.   REFER TO THE DEFINITION OF A NONTRADITIONAL MORTGAGE PRODUCT IN COMMISSIONER'S REGULATION 2842 AVAILABLE ON THE DRE WEB SITE AT WWW.DRE.CA.GOV.***

SECURED BY REAL PROPERTY – This form may be used when the loan is secured by real property (raw or unimproved land or parcels, commercial, multi-family, 1 to 4 unit residential, or any other interest in real property).

TIPS ON COMPLETING THIS FORM

Section I (B) (4) – Additional Compensation – This section is completed to disclose any compensation received by the broker from a lender in the form of a yield/spread premium, service release premium or any other rebate or compensation.

Section II (A) – PROPOSED LOAN INFORMATION – The form contains four (4) boxes for the purpose of providing loan terms and information to the consumer. Depending on the loan product being offered to the consumer, select the appropriate box and complete the information specified in that box. The Real Estate Law requires the disclosure of all material terms of the loan. In situations where the proposed loan terms cannot be accommodated in one of the four (4) boxes, an addendum, signed and dated by the borrower(s) and the broker (or broker's representative), should be attached to the form. The addendum must include all material information on the proposed loan. A real estate broker who wishes to use a form other than the approved RE882 must obtain the prior written approval of the Department.

IF THE LOAN PRODUCT IS A NONTRADITIONAL MORTGAGE LOAN PRODUCT YOU ARE USING THE WRONG FORM. THE RE885 MUST BE USED.

Other than the non-applicable boxes in Section II, do not leave any lines or spaces blank.

After completion, the form must be signed by the broker or broker's representative and provided to the borrower within THREE (3) DAYS OF RECEIVING THE BORROWER'S COMPLETED WRITTEN LOAN APPLICATION.

A COPY OF THE FORM SIGNED BY THE BORROWER MUST BE RETAINED BY THE BROKER FOR A PERIOD OF THREE (3) YEARS.

FIGURE 5.10 (*Continued*)

STATE OF CALIFORNIA
DEPARTMENT OF REAL ESTATE
Serving Californians Since 1917

MORTGAGE LOAN DISCLOSURE STATEMENT (BORROWER)

RE 882 (Rev. 6/09)

Name of Broker	Business Address

I. SUMMARY OF LOAN TERMS
    A. PRINCIPAL AMOUNT .... $ _____
    B. ESTIMATED DEDUCTIONS FROM PRINCIPAL AMOUNT
        1. Costs and Expenses (See Paragraph III-A) .... $ _____
        2. Broker Commission/Origination Fee (See Paragraph III-B) ... $ _____
        3. Lender Origination Fee/Discounts (See Paragraph III-B) ...... $ _____
        4. Additional compensation will/may be received from lender not deducted from loan
            proceeds.   ☐ YES $_____ *(if known)*   ☐ NO
        5. Amount to be Paid on Authorization of Borrower (See Paragraph III-C) ... $ _____
    C. ESTIMATED CASH PAYABLE TO BORROWER (A LESS B) .... $ _____

II. GENERAL INFORMATION ABOUT LOAN
    A.   PROPOSED LOAN INFORMATION
    1. Proposed loan term   ☐ Years   ☐ Months

☐ FIXED RATE LOAN	☐ ADJUSTABLE RATE LOAN (EXAMPLE 6-MONTH ARM; 1-YEAR ARM)
Fixed rate loan_____% payable at $_____ month	Proposed interest rate:____% Fully indexed rate _____% Proposed monthly payment $_____ Maximum interest rate _____% Interest rate can increase_____% each_____months Maximum loan payment can be $_____after_____months
☐ INITIAL FIXED RATE LOAN (EXAMPLE 2/28; 3/1; 5/1) Proposed initial fixed interest rate:____% Initial fixed interest rate in effect for____months Proposed initial monthly payment $_____ Adjustable interest rate of _____% will begin after fixed rate period ends Monthly payment can increase to $____after fixed rate period ends Fully indexed rate _____% Maximum interest rate _____% Interest rate can increase _____% each _____ months Maximum loan payment can be $_____ after_____ months	☐ INITIAL ADJUSTABLE RATE LOAN (EXAMPLE LOW ENTRY RATE ARM) Proposed initial adjustable interest rate ____% Initial interest rate in effect for_____months Proposed monthly payment $_____ Fully indexed rate _____% Maximum interest rate _____% Interest rate can increase_____% each _____months Monthly payment can increase to $____after initial adjustable rate period ends Maximum loan payment can be $_____ after _____ months

2. This loan is based on limited or no documentation of your income and/or assets and may have a higher interest rate, or more points or fees than other products requiring documentation: ☐ No ☐ Yes.

3. The loan is subject to a balloon payment: ☐ No ☐ Yes. If Yes, the following paragraph applies and a final balloon payment of $_____ will be due on __/__/__ *[estimated date (month/day/year)]*.

NOTICE TO BORROWER: IF YOU DO NOT HAVE THE FUNDS TO PAY THE BALLOON PAYMENT WHEN IT COMES DUE, YOU MAY HAVE TO OBTAIN A NEW LOAN AGAINST YOUR PROPERTY TO MAKE THE BALLOON PAYMENT. IN THAT CASE, YOU MAY AGAIN HAVE TO PAY COMMISSIONS, FEES AND EXPENSES FOR THE ARRANGING OF THE NEW LOAN. IN ADDITION, IF YOU ARE UNABLE TO MAKE THE MONTHLY PAYMENTS OR THE BALLOON PAYMENT, YOU MAY LOSE THE PROPERTY AND ALL OF YOUR EQUITY THROUGH FORE- CLOSURE. KEEP THIS IN MIND IN DECIDING UPON THE AMOUNT AND TERMS OF THIS LOAN.

B. This loan will be evidenced by a promissory note and secured by a deed of trust on property identified as (street address or legal description):

_____

_____

C. 1. Liens presently against this property (do not include loan being applied for):

Nature of Lien	Priority	Lienholder's Name	Amount Owing

    2. Liens that will remain against this property after the loan being applied for is made or arranged (include loan being applied for):

Nature of Lien	Priority	Lienholder's Name	Amount Owing

NOTICE TO BORROWER: Be sure that you state the amount of all liens as accurately as possible. If you contract with the broker to arrange this loan, but it cannot be arranged because you did not state these liens correctly, you may be liable to pay commissions, fees and expenses even though you do not obtain the loan.

D. Prepayments: The proposed loan has the following prepayment provisions:
    ☐ No prepayment penalty (you will not be charged a penalty to pay off or refinance the loan before maturity)

    ☐ You will have to pay a prepayment penalty if the loan is paid off or refinanced in the first _____ years. The prepayment penalty could be as much as $_____. Any prepayment of principal in excess of 20% of the

FIGURE 5.10   (*Continued*)

RE 882 — Reverse

☐   original loan balance or
☐   unpaid balance
for the first _____ years will include a penalty not to exceed _____ months interest at the note interest rate but not more than the interest you would be charged if the loan were paid to maturity.
☐   Other – you will have to pay a prepayment penalty if the loan is paid off or refinanced in the first _____ years as follows:

_____

_____

E.   Taxes and Insurance:
  ☐   There will be an impound (escrow) account which will collect approximately $_____ a month in addition to your principal and interest payments for the payment of ☐ county property taxes**☐ hazard insurance ☐ mortgage insurance ☐ flood insurance ☐ other_____.

  ☐   If there is no impound (escrow) account or if your escrow (impound) account does not include one or more of the payments described above, you will have to plan for the payment of ☐   county property taxes** ☐   hazard insurance ☐ mortgage insurance ☐ flood insurance ☐ other_____ of approximately $_____ per year.

  **   **In a purchase transaction, county property taxes are calculated based on the sales price of the property and may require the payment of an additional (supplemental) tax bill from the county tax authority by your lender (if escrowed) or you (if not escrowed)**

F.   Late Charges: ☐ YES, see loan documents   ☐ NO

G.   The purchase of credit life and/or credit disability insurance by a borrower is not required as a condition of making this loan.

III.   DEDUCTIONS FROM LOAN PROCEEDS
  A.   Estimated Maximum Costs and Expenses of Arranging the Loan to be Paid Out of Loan Principal

	PAYABLE TO:	Broker	Others
1. Appraisal fee		_____	_____
2. Escrow fee		_____	_____
3. Title insurance policy		_____	_____
4. Notary fees		_____	_____
5. Recording fees		_____	_____
6. Credit investigation fees		_____	_____
7. Other costs and expenses:		_____	_____
_____		_____	_____
_____		_____	_____
Total Costs and Expenses		$ _____	

  B.   Compensation
1. Broker Commission/Origination Fee	$ _____
2. Lender Origination Fee/Discounts	$ _____

  C.   Estimated Payment to be Made Out of Loan Principal on Authorization of Borrower

	PAYABLE TO:	Broker	Others
1. Fire or other hazard insurance premiums		_____	_____
2. Credit life or disability insurance premiums (See Paragraph II-G)		_____	_____
3. Beneficiary statement fees		_____	_____
4. Reconveyance and similar fees		_____	_____
5. Discharge of existing liens against property		_____	_____
_____		_____	_____
6. Other:		_____	_____
_____		_____	_____
Total to be Paid on Authorization of Borrower		$ _____	

Article 7 Compliance: If this loan is secured by a first deed of trust on dwellings in a principal amount of less than $30,000 or secured by a junior lien on dwellings in a principal amount of less than $20,000, the undersigned licensee certifies that the loan will be made in compliance with Article 7 of Chapter 3 of the Real Estate Law.

➤   This loan may/will/will not *(delete two)* be made wholly or in part from broker-controlled funds as defined in Section 10241(j) of the Business and Professions Code.

IV.   **NOTICES TO BORROWER:**

  1.   This disclosure statement may be used if the broker is acting as an agent in arranging the loan by a third person or if the loan will be made with funds owned or controlled by the broker. If the broker indicates in the Article 7 compliance immediately above, that the loan "may" be made out of broker-controlled funds, the broker must notify the borrower prior to the close of escrow if the funds to be received by the borrower are in fact broker-controlled funds.

  2.   THIS IS NOT A LOAN COMMITMENT. Do not sign this statement until you have read and understood all of the information in it. All parts of this form must be completed before you sign. Borrower hereby acknowledges the receipt of a copy of this statement.

Name of Broker		*License #*		*Broker's Representative*		*License #*

Broker's Address						

Signature of Broker		*Date*	OR	*Signature of Representative*		*Date*

Borrower		*Date*		*Borrower*		*Date*

Department of Real Estate license information telephone number: 877-373-4542, or check license status at www.dre.ca.gov

RE 882 — Page 2 of 2

Source: Reproduced with permission of California Department of Real Estate.

including data regarding interest rate, balloon payments, security documents, and costs and commissions to licensees. All items are to be completed by the broker and signed along with the real estate license number before the borrower signs the document. Immediately after the borrower signs the document, a signed copy is to be delivered to the borrower. For advertising disclosure, DRE requires the broker to put the broker's license number and the DRE telephone number, (916) 227-0931, so that the borrower may make a complaint.

DRE Article 7 [Section 10131 (d) and 10240 (a)] requires loan disclosure to be given to a borrower within 3 business days of receipt of the application or before the borrower becomes obligated for the loan, whichever is earlier. The DRE form RE882 is in addition to the federal GFE. In California, both must be used.

When a broker can and does make a loan from the broker's personal funds or from funds controlled by the broker, disclosure must be made to the borrower. The disclosure must be done no later than the day after the election to use "broker-controlled funds." Funds included under this provision are those owned by the broker, by a spouse, child, parent, grandparent, brother, sister, father-in-law, mother-in-law, brother-in-law, sister-in-law, or an entity in which the broker has more than 25 percent ownership interest.

5.8 CALIFORNIA LICENSEE NON-LOAN DISCLOSURES

The California licensee is responsible for ensuring that the borrower has received disclosures for many items under both state and federal laws and regulations. Even when the mortgage loan broker is not the agent handling the sales transaction as an agent representing the seller, and when the mortgage loan broker is not the sales agent for the buyer, the California Department of Real Estate (DRE) licensed agent who is acting as the real estate loan agent is the ONLY licensee in the transaction and should make sure that the legislated disclosures are complied with in the transaction. Some disclosures are made from the seller to the buyer. Others are made from the buyer to the seller. Some will be requirements that the appraiser will request that the primary lender will not allow the loan to fund or close escrow until meeting compliance. When no other licensed agent is involved, the licensee does not have any DRE regulation or law that exempts the licensee from liability in the event of a legal suit that may arise from any part of the transaction. Although not responsible for handling many of the disclosures, it is strongly advised to get specific clarification from the legal department of the firm with which the mortgage loan broker is affiliated, and additional a written request and answer from DRE. The particulars for a property may be provided by the seller to the buyer through escrow, by another real estate licensee acting as sales agents in the transaction, or by outside firms, such as home inspection or pest control companies. The loan broker, however, needs documentation that the borrower has received the disclosure, no matter who has provided the documentation. It is not uncommon for a transaction to have no other licensee except the person handling the loan; for example, if neither the buyer nor the seller uses a licensed real estate salesperson, as an agent. The borrower often made contact directly with the loan officer, who is a DRE licensee. The following items are listed in alphabetic order for disclosures required for a transaction in California:

Appraisal Disclosure

The appraisal disclosure information may be found in Chapter 9, including who is entitled to receive a copy of a real property appraisal.

Credit and Fair Lending Disclosure

Regulations protect the rights of the borrower about several issues on credit and credit reporting and are covered in more detail in Chapter 7.

Death or Acquired Immunodeficiency Syndrome (AIDS)

As of June 1990, California Civil Code 1710.2 required a transferor, agent, seller, or lessor of all real property to disclose to a buyer, tenant, or borrower whether a death has occurred within 3 years of the date of the offer or loan application. No voluntary disclosure need be made regarding affliction or death from AIDS; however, a licensee must disclose such information if requested.

Earthquake Disclosure

Pursuant to the Alquist-Priolo Earthquake Fault Zoning Act, the agent must disclose to the buyer that the property is or may be situated in an earthquake fault zone. This disclosure is made on the Natural Hazard Zone Disclosure Statement. In addition, the Seismic Safety Commission developed a Homeowner's Guide to Earthquake Safety and a *Commercial Property Owner's Guide to Earthquake Safety* for distribution. For a one- to four-unit property built prior to January 1, 1960, which are of conventional light-frame construction; any masonry building with wood-frame floors or roofs built before January 1, 1975; and commercial buildings after 1975, the licensee must provide the Earthquake Disclosure Booklet and Regulation Guide. This regulation became effective January 1, 1993, for transfers to buyers. Because most purchasers require some financing, the loan broker should ascertain compliance.

Energy Conservation Retrofit and Thermal Insulation Disclosure

State law prescribes a minimum energy conservation standard for all new construction, without which a building permit may not be issued. Some local ordinances impose energy retrofitting as a condition of the sale of an existing home. Federal law requires a "new home" seller to disclose in every sales contract the type, thickness, and R-value of the insulation that has been or will be installed in the house.

Environmental Hazards Disclosure

Business and Professions Code 10084.1 requires DRE and the State Department of Health Services to have a consumer education booklet concerning **environmental hazards**. The DRE, the Department of Toxic Substances Control, and the Office of Environmental Health Hazard Assessment developed the Environmental Hazards: A Guide for Homeowners, Buyers, Landlords and Tenants booklet, which identifies common environmental hazards. The January 1, 1991, law includes the significance of common environmental hazards and what can be done to mitigate those hazards. Civil Code 2079.7 (a) provides that if the booklet is delivered to the transferee, then the seller and broker are not required to provide additional information. Areas of concern may include asbestos, radon gas, urea-formaldehyde foam insulation, ground water and soil contamination, safe drinking water, abandoned wells, military or explosive hazards, air quality, hazardous waste dumps, landfills, chemical plants, refineries, and similar disclosures. The licensee should obtain a signed receipt from the transferee for the booklet (see Figure 5.10, RE851 Mortgage Loan Disclosure Statement (borrower), and Figure 5.11, DRE Form RE 882 Lender/Purchaser Disclosure Statement).

Fire Hazard Areas (State Responsibility Areas)

To obtain funding of the loan, the borrower must have fire insurance on the property. However, certain California real property is designed as a "wildland area" in which the state, not local or federal government, has the primary financial responsibility for fire prevention. The seller must disclose to the buyer that there exists a risk of fire and state the imposed duties such as maintaining weed-free fire breaks and the fact that the state may not provide fire protection services for the property.

Flood Disaster Insurance

Flood disaster insurance is required by federal regulations for all loans on property identified as being in special flood hazard areas. This requirement is defined by the **Federal Emergency Management Agency (FEMA)** in accordance with the Flood Disaster Protection Act of 1973. As of September 23, 1994, all property located in a flood hazard area indicated on maps published by the FEMA must be disclosed to buyers, lessees, and borrowers. Federal law requires flood insurance as a condition of obtaining financing on most structures located in an identified special flood hazard area. The disclosure must be made on the Natural Hazard Zone Disclosure Statement.

Foreign Investment in Real Property Tax Act (FIRPTA) and CAL-FIRPTA

Federal law requires a buyer of real property to withhold and send to the Internal Revenue Service (IRS) 10 percent of the seller's gross sales price if the seller of the real property is a "foreign person." Exemptions include if the sales price is less

FIGURE 5.11   Lender/purchaser disclosure statement: loan origination.

STATE OF CALIFORNIA

DEPARTMENT OF REAL ESTATE
MORTGAGE LENDING

LENDER/PURCHASER DISCLOSURE STATEMENT
(Loan Origination)

RE 851A (Rev. 6/09)

DISCLOSURE STATEMENT SUMMARY		

Note: If this is a multi-lender transaction and more than one property secures the loan, you should also refer to the attached Lender/Purchaser Disclosure Statement Multi-Property (Cross Collateralization) Addendum (RE 851D).

AMOUNT OF THIS LOAN *(SEE PART 3)*	MARKET VALUE OF PROPERTY (SEE PART 8)	TOTAL AMOUNT OF ENCUMBRANCES SENIOR TO THIS LOAN *(SEE PART 9)*
$	$	$
TOTAL AMOUNT OF ENCUMBRANCES ANTICIPATED OR EXPECTED TO BE JUNIOR TO THIS LOAN *(SEE PART 9)*	PROTECTIVE EQUITY (MARKET VALUE MINUS THIS LOAN AND TOTAL SENIOR ENCUMBRANCES)	TOTAL LOAN TO VALUE (SEE PART 10G)
$	$	%

PART 1	BROKER INFORMATION	

NAME OF BROKER	REAL ESTATE LICENSE ID#
BUSINESS ADDRESS	TELEPHONE NUMBER

NAME OF BROKERS REPRESENTATIVE

PART 2	BROKER CAPACITY IN TRANSACTION

THE BROKER IDENTIFIED IN PART 1 OF THIS STATEMENT IS ACTING IN THE FOLLOWING CAPACITY IN THIS TRANSACTION: (CHECK AS APPLIES)

☐ A. Agent in arranging a loan on behalf of another

☐ B. Principal as a borrower of funds from which broker will directly or indirectly benefit other than through the receipt of commissions, fees and costs and expenses as provided by law for services as an agent.

☐ C. Funding a portion of this loan. *(Multi-lender transactions are subject to Business and Professions Code Section 10238.)*

IF MORE THAN ONE CAPACITY HAS BEEN CHECKED, PROVIDE EXPLANATION HERE.

IF "B" HAS BEEN CHECKED, THE BROKER INTENDS TO USE FUNDS FROM THE LENDER/PURCHASER IN THIS TRANSACTION FOR:

PART 3	TRANSACTION INFORMATION	

(CHECK IF APPLICABLE)

☐ THERE IS MORE THAN ONE PROPERTY SECURING THE LOAN. IF MULTI-LENDER LOAN, YOU SHOULD ALSO REFER TO ATTACHED RE 851D.

TERM OF LOAN	PRIORITY OF THIS LOAN (1ST, 2ND, ETC.)	PRINCIPAL AMOUNT	YOUR SHARE IF MULTI-LENDER TRANS.
		$	$
INTEREST RATE % ☐ VARIABLE ☐ FIXED	(CHECK ONE) ☐ AMORTIZED ☐ PARTIALLY AMORTIZED	☐ INTEREST ONLY	***THE TRUST DEED WILL BE RECORDED.***
PAYMENT FREQUENCY ☐ MONTHLY ☐ WEEKLY	APPROXIMATE PAYMENT DUE DATE	AMOUNT OF PAYMENT $	YOUR SHARE IF MULTI-LENDER TRANS. $
BALLOON PAYMENT ☐ YES ☐ NO	APPROX. BALLOON PAYMENT DUE DATE	AMOUNT OF BALLOON PAYMENT $	YOUR SHARE IF MULTI-LENDER TRANS. $

Balloon Payment — A balloon payment is any installment payment (usually the payment due at maturity) which is greater than twice the amount of the smallest installment payment under the terms of the promissory note or sales contract.

The borrower/vendee may have to obtain a new loan or sell the property to make the balloon payment. If the effort is not successful it may be necessary for the holder of the note/contract to foreclose on the property as a means of collecting the amount owed.

There are subordination provisions. ....   ☐ Yes   ☐ No

If YES, explain here or on an attachment.

FIGURE 5.11   (*Continued*)

PART 4	MULTI-LENDER TRANSACTIONS	

NAME OF ESCROW HOLDER	ANTICIPATED CLOSING DATE

ADDRESS OF ESCROW HOLDER

ESTIMATED LENDER COSTS		ESTIMATED BORROWER COSTS — *Broker will provide you a copy of the "mortgage loan disclosure statement" given to the borrower or a separate itemization of borrower's costs.*
_____	$ _____	
_____	$ _____	
_____	$ _____	
TOTAL	$ _____	TOTAL $ _____

Servicing

You will be a joint beneficiary with others on this note and you should request a list of names and addresses of the beneficiaries as of the close of escrow from the broker or servicing agent. The beneficiary(ies) holding more than 50% interest in the note may govern the actions to be taken on behalf of all holders in the event of default or other matters. See Civil Code Section 2941.9.

Loan To Value

GENERALLY the aggregate principal amount of the notes or interests sold, together with the unpaid principal amount of any encumbrances upon the real property senior thereto, shall not exceed the following percentages of the current market value of the real property as determined in writing by the broker or qualified appraiser.

Single-family residence, owner-occupied 80%

Single-family residence, not owner-occupied 75%

Commercial and income-producing properties 65%

Single-family residentially zoned lot or parcel which has installed off-site improvements including drainage, curbs, gutters, sidewalks, paved roads, and utilities as mandated by the political subdivision having jurisdiction over the lot or parcel...65%

Land which has been zoned for (and if required, approved for subdivision as) commercial or
Residential development 50%

Other real property 35%

The percentage amounts specified above may be exceeded when and to the extent that the broker determines that the encumbrance of the property in excess of these percentages is reasonable and prudent considering all relevant factors pertaining to the real property. However, in no event shall the aggregate principal amount of the notes or interests sold, together with the unpaid principal amount of any encumbrances upon the property senior thereto, exceed 80 percent of the current fair market value of improved real property or 50 percent of the current fair market value of unimproved real property, except in the case of a single-family residentially zoned lot or parcel as defined above, which shall not exceed 65% of current fair market value of that lot or parcel. A written statement shall be prepared by the broker that sets forth the material considerations and facts that the broker relies upon for his or her determination which shall be disclosed to the lender or note purchaser(s) and retained as a part of the broker's record of the transaction.

NOTE: If more than one property secures this loan, you should also refer to attached RE 851D.

FIGURE 5.11 *(Continued)*

PART 5	SERVICING ARRANGEMENTS

If the loan is to be serviced by a real estate broker you must be notified within ten (10) days if the broker makes any advances on senior encumbrances to protect the security of your note. Depending on the terms and conditions of the servicing contract, you may be obligated to repay any such advances made by the broker. (Note: There must be a servicing agent on multi-lender transactions.) The broker may not guarantee or imply to guarantee, or advance any payments to you unless a securities permit is obtained from the Department of Corporations.

CHECK APPROPRIATE STATEMENTS

☐ THERE ARE NO SERVICING ARRANGEMENTS *(Does not apply to multi-lender transactions.)*   ☐ BROKER IS THE SERVICING AGENT
☐ ANOTHER QUALIFIED PARTY WILL SERVICE THE LOAN   ☐ COPY OF THE SERVICING CONTRACT IS ATTACHED

IF BROKER IS NOT SERVICING AGENT, WHAT IS THE RELATIONSHIP BETWEEN THE BROKER AND SERVICER?

COST TO LENDER FOR SERVICING ARRANGEMENTS *(EXPRESS AS DOLLAR AMOUNT OR PERCENTAGE)*

PER ☐ MONTH ☐ YEAR   PAYABLE ☐ MONTHLY ☐ ANNUALLY

NAME OF AUTHORIZED SERVICER, IF ANY

BUSINESS ADDRESS | TELEPHONE NUMBER

PART 6	BORROWER INFORMATION

SOURCE OF INFORMATION
☐ BORROWER   ☐ BROKER INQUIRY   ☐ CREDIT REPORT   ☐ OTHER (DESCRIBE)

NAME	CO-BORROWER'S NAME
RESIDENCE ADDRESS	CO-BORROWER'S RESIDENCE ADDRESS
OCCUPATION OR PROFESSION	CO-BORROWER'S OCCUPATION OR PROFESSION
CURRENT EMPLOYER	CO-BORROWER'S CURRENT EMPLOYER
HOW LONG EMPLOYED?	AGE	HOW LONG EMPLOYED?	CO-BORROWER'S AGE

SOURCES OF GROSS INCOME *(LIST AND IDENTIFY EACH SOURCE SEPARATELY.)*	MONTHLY AMOUNT	CO-BORROWER SOURCES OF GROSS INCOME *(LIST AND IDENTIFY EACH SOURCE SEPARATELY.)*	MONTHLY AMOUNT
Gross Salary	$	Gross Salary	$
OTHER INCOME INCLUDING: Interest	$	OTHER INCOME INCLUDING: Interest	$
Dividends	$	Dividends	$
Gross Rental Income	$	Gross Rental Income	$
Miscellaneous Income	$	Miscellaneous Income	$

TOTAL EXPENSES OF ALL BORROWERS *(DO NOT COMPLETE IF BORROWER IS A CORPORATION)*

Payment of Loan being obtained	$	Spousal/Child Support	$
Rent	$	Insurance	$
Charge Account/Credit Cards	$	Vehicle Loan(s)	$
Mortgage Payments *(include taxes and property insurance)*	$	Other *(federal & state income taxes, etc.)*	$
TOTAL GROSS MONTHLY INCOME OF BORROWER(S) $		TOTAL MONTHLY EXPENSES OF BORROWER(S) $	

FIGURE 5.11   *(Continued)*

The borrower has filed for bankruptcy in the past 12 months. .... ☐ Yes   ☐ No

If YES, the bankruptcy has been discharged or dismissed. .... ☐ Yes   ☐ No

❖ *THE FOLLOWING STATEMENTS ONLY APPLY IF THE BORROWER IS A CORPORATION, PARTNERSHIP OR SOME OTHER FORM OF OPERATING BUSINESS ENTITY.*

Copies of a balance sheet of the entity and income statement covering the indicated period have been supplied by the borrower/obligor and are attached. If no, explain on addendum. .... ☐ Yes   ☐ No

If YES, Date of balance sheet .... _____

Income statement period *(from-to)* .... _____

Financial Statements have been audited by CPA or PA. .... ☐ Yes   ☐ No

Additional information is included on an attached addendum .... ☐ Yes   ☐ No

PART 7	PROPERTY INFORMATION

Identification of property which is security for note. *(If no street address, the assessor's parcel number or legal description and a means for locating the property is attached.)*

(CHECK IF APPLICABLE)
☐ THERE IS MORE THAN ONE PROPERTY SECURING THE LOAN. IF MULTI-LENDER LOAN, YOU SHOULD REFER TO ATTACHED RE 851D.

STREET ADDRESS	OWNER OCCUPIED
	☐ NO ☐ YES

ANNUAL PROPERTY TAXES	ARE TAXES DELINQUENT?	IF YES, AMT. REQUIRED TO BRING CURRENT
$ ☐ ACTUAL ☐ ESTIMATED	☐ NO ☐ YES	$

SOURCE OF TAX INFORMATION

PART 8	APPRAISAL INFORMATION

Estimate of fair market value is to be determined by an independent appraisal, copy of which must be provided to you prior to you obligating funds to make the loan. Note: You may waive the requirement of an independent appraisal, in writing, on a case by case basis, in which case the broker must provide a written estimate of fair market value. The broker must provide you, the investor, with the objective data upon which the broker's estimate is based. **In the case of a construction or rehabilitation loan, an appraisal must be completed by an independent, qualified appraiser in accordance with the Uniform Standards of Professional Appraisal Practice (USPAP).**

(CHECK IF APPLICABLE)
☐ THERE IS MORE THAN ONE PROPERTY SECURING THE LOAN. IF MULTI-LENDER LOAN REFER TO ATTACHED RE 851D.

FAIR MARKET VALUE (ACCORDING TO APPRAISER) *(Place this figure or brokers estimate of fair market value on line "F" of Part 10.)*	DATE OF APPRAISAL
$	

NAME OF APPRAISER (IF KNOWN TO BROKER)	PAST AND/OR CURRENT RELATIONSHIP OF APPRAISER TO BROKER (EMPLOYEE, AGENT, INDEPENDENT CONTRACTOR, ETC.)

ADDRESS OF APPRAISER

DESCRIPTION OF PROPERTY/IMPROVEMENT	IS THERE ADDITIONAL SECURING PROPERTY?
	☐ YES IF YES, SEE ADDENDUM.
	☐ NO

AGE	SQUARE FEET	TYPE OF CONSTRUCTION

IF THE PROPERTY IS CURRENTLY GENERATING INCOME FOR THE BORROWER/OBLIGOR:

ESTIMATED GROSS ANNUAL INCOME	ESTIMATED NET ANNUAL INCOME
$	$

FIGURE 5.11   *(Continued)*

PART 9	ENCUMBRANCE INFORMATION

Information is being provided concerning senior encumbrances against the property, to the extent reasonably available from customary sources (excluding the note described on page 1 Part 3). **Note:** You have the option to purchase a policy of title insurance or an endorsement to an existing policy of title insurance to insure your interest. You are entitled to a copy of a written loan application and a credit report to obtain information concerning all encumbrances which constitute liens against the property. This information may help determine the financial standing and creditworthiness of the borrower.

(CHECK IF APPLICABLE)

☐ THERE IS MORE THAN ONE PROPERTY SECURING THE LOAN. IF MULTI-LENDER LOAN, YOU SHOULD REFER TO ATTACHED RE 851D.

SOURCE OF INFORMATION

☐ BROKER INQUIRY   ☐ BORROWER   ☐ OTHER *(EXPLAIN)*

Are there any encumbrances of record against the securing property at this time?................... ☐ YES   ☐ NO

A. Over the last 12 months were any payments more than 60 days late? .... ☐ YES   ☐ NO

B. If YES, how many? .... _____

C. Do any of these payments remain unpaid? .... ☐ YES   ☐ NO

D. If YES, will the proceeds of subject loan be used to cure the delinquency? .... ☐ YES   ☐ NO

E. If NO, source of funds to bring the loan current. .... _____

Encumbrances remaining and/or expected or anticipated to be placed against the property by the borrower/obligor after the close of escrow (excluding the note described on page 1).

ENCUMBRANCE(S) REMAINING *(AS REPRESENTED BY THE BORROWER)*

PRIORITY (1ST, 2ND, ETC.)	INTEREST RATE %	PRIORITY (1ST, 2ND, ETC.)	INTEREST RATE %
BENEFICIARY		BENEFICIARY	
ORIGINAL AMOUNT $	APPROXIMATE PRINCIPAL BALANCE $	ORIGINAL AMOUNT $	APPROXIMATE PRINCIPAL BALANCE $
MONTHLY PAYMENT $	MATURITY DATE	MONTHLY PAYMENT $	MATURITY DATE
BALLOON PAYMENT ☐ YES ☐ NO ☐ UNKNOWN	IF YES, AMOUNT $	BALLOON PAYMENT ☐ YES ☐ NO ☐ UNKNOWN	IF YES, AMOUNT $

ENCUMBRANCES EXPECTED OR ANTICIPATED *(AS REPRESENTED BY THE BORROWER)*

PRIORITY (1ST, 2ND, ETC.)	INTEREST RATE %	PRIORITY (1ST, 2ND, ETC.)	INTEREST RATE %
BENEFICIARY		BENEFICIARY	
ORIGINAL AMOUNT $	MATURITY DATE	ORIGINAL AMOUNT $	MATURITY DATE
MONTHLY PAYMENT $		MONTHLY PAYMENT $	
BALLOON PAYMENT ☐ YES ☐ NO ☐ UNKNOWN	IF YES, AMOUNT $	BALLOON PAYMENT ☐ YES ☐ NO ☐ UNKNOWN	IF YES, AMOUNT $

Additional remaining, expected or anticipated encumbrances are set forth in an attachment to this statement. .... ☐ Yes   ☐ No

FIGURE 5.11   *(Continued)*

PART 10	LOAN TO VALUE RATIO

(CHECK IF APPLICABLE)

☐ THERE IS MORE THAN ONE PROPERTY SECURING THE LOAN. IF MULTI-LENDER LOAN, YOU SHOULD REFER TO ATTACHED RE 851D.

A. Remaining encumbrances senior to this loan *(from part 8)*....... $_____

B. Encumbrances expected or anticipated senior to this loan
    (from part 9) ....   + $_____

C. Total remaining and expected or anticipated encumbrances senior to this loan ....   = $_____

D. Principal amount of this loan from page 1 part 3 ....   + $_____

E. Total all senior encumbrances and this loan ....   = $_____

F. Fair market value from page 4 part 8 ....   ÷ $_____

G. Loan to value ratio ....   = _____ %

Note: See Part 4 if multi-lender transaction.

BROKER VERIFICATION

The information in this statement and in the attachments hereto is true and correct to the best of my knowledge and belief.

SIGNATURE OF BROKER OR DESIGNATED REPRESENTATIVE	BROKER/CORPORATION ID#	DATE
➢		

ACKNOWLEDGMENT OF RECEIPT

The prospective lender/purchaser acknowledges receipt of a copy of this statement signed by or on behalf of the broker.

SIGNATURE OF PROSPECTIVE LENDER/PURCHASER	DATE
➢	

**For licensing information, please refer to the Department of Real
Estate's Web site located at www.dre.ca.gov.**

or

**You may call the DRE licensing information telephone number at
877-373-4542.**

Source: Reproduced with permission of California Department of Real Estate.

---

than $300,000, or if the buyer intends to reside in the property as their primary residence, or if the seller provides a nonforeign affidavit and a U.S. taxpayer identification number. The agents and buyers must make sure that the sellers sign an "Affidavit of Non-Foreign Status" where they attest under penalty of perjury that they are not foreigners. And the seller must furnish the social security number or tax identification number on the form.

Sellers often do not want to give buyers or agents their confidential tax identification information. HR3221 became effective July 2008 allows the seller to provide that no federal withholding is required if the seller furnishes the Affidavit of Seller to a "qualified substitute" rather than to the buyer or the agents. A qualified substitute can be any person responsible for closing the transaction, such as a title insurance or escrow company. Seller already furnish the confidential information on the statement of information form (see Chapter 9, Figure 9.5).

The buyer must also withhold $3\frac{1}{3}$ percent of the total sale price as stated income tax and deliver the sum withheld to the California State Franchise Tax Board. See http://www.ftb.ca.gov/forms/2009/09_1016.pdf. Escrow is required to notify the buyer of this responsibility. Transactions subject to the law are those in which the seller shows an out-of-state address or sale proceeds are distributed to a financial intermediary of the seller, the sales price is more than $100,000, or the seller does not certify being a resident of California, as defined in Internal Revenue Code (IRC) 1034. Those who are subject to the withholding include a corporate seller with no permanent place of business in California (out-of-state corporation), and a non-California partnership. Federal withholding tax would apply no matter which state was involved for the individual or the business.

The California withholding tax laws requires that everyone must be subject to the withholding, except if the property sold meets the primary residence test under IRC §121.

Government Compliance Disclosure

Many areas require a city inspection or some release that the property confirms to acceptable use for the premises. Some transactions require the following items to be checked:

1. Retrofit: Local government compliance that includes installation of low-flow showerheads and gallon-restricted flush toilets.
2. Inspection and necessary repairs of septic systems: Testing of any well for potability and production; local law requirement of connection to a sewer system.
3. Violations and inspections: The seller is to make disclosure of any knowledge of any notice of violation of any building, zoning, fire or health laws, regulations, or ordinances. Some areas require a "city inspection" prior to close of escrow to see whether the property conforms to health and safety regulations.

Hazard Insurance Coverage

The State of California AB 1673 (Johnston), 1992, Civil Code 2955 states that no lender may require a borrower to provide **hazard insurance** coverage on the property being used to secure the loan in any amount that would exceed the replacement value of the improvements. The value of the replacement cost of the improvements is established by the property insurer that the borrower selects.

Language of the Agreement

Any person engaged in a business who negotiates primarily in Spanish orally or in writing in the course of entering into a loan or extension of credit for use primarily for personal, family, or household purposes when such loan or extension of credit is subject to the provisions of Article 7, Section 10240, Chapter 3, Part 1,

Division 4 of the Business and Professions Code or Divisions 7, 9, or 10 of the Financial Code, shall, upon the request of any party to such contract or agreement and prior to execution, deliver an unexecuted Spanish- language translation of the contract or agreement and make available upon request a Spanish-language translation of the statement to borrower.

Lead-Based Paint

If the house the borrower is purchasing was built before 1978, a **Lead-Based Paint** Notice must be given to the borrower on or before the date the borrower executes the sales contract or application for financing or refinancing. It must be signed and dated by the borrower and a copy provided to the lender when the borrower applies for mortgage financing. This law applies to all contracts and applications as of October 1, 1992.

Under federal and state superfund laws, an owner in a chain of title of a property could be liable for the cost of removing contamination of toxic substances on a property. A lender who takes the property back at a foreclosure sale is the owner. Potential lenders, such as sellers extending credit or hard-money lenders, should consult an attorney about his or her possible liability.

The federal Environmental Protection Act (EPA) publishes the *Protect Your Family From Lead in Your Home* booklet, which is required to be delivered to a prospective purchaser before a contract is formed.

Local Option Disclosure Statement

Any city or county may require additional disclosure statements focusing on local conditions that may materially affect the use and enjoyment of the property.

Supplemental Property Taxes Disclosure

Assembly Bill 459 requires that, beginning January 1, 2006, sellers of most residential properties up to four units, or his or her agents, must disclose to prospective buyers that they may owe supplemental taxes. Also, Senate Bill 565 requires that, beginning with the lien date for the 2006–2007 fiscal year, any transfer between registered domestic partners will not trigger property tax reassessment. As a result, registered domestic partners will be treated the same as spouses under California property tax laws.

Mello-Roos Disclosure

The Mello-Roos Community Facilities Act of 1982 authorized the formation of community facilities districts, the issuance of bonds, and the levying of special taxes on real property to finance public facilities and services. Civil Code Section 1102.6 requires disclosure to a buyer of one- to four-unit dwellings.

Methamphetamine-Contaminated Properties

Assembly Bill 1078 requires that on January 1, 2006, a property owner must disclose in writing to a prospective buyer or tenant if local health officials have issued an order prohibiting the use or occupancy of a property contaminated by methamphetamine laboratory activity. The owner must also give a copy of the pending order to the buyer or tenant to acknowledge receipt in writing. Failure to comply with these requirements may subject an owner to, among other things, a civil penalty up to $5,000. Aside from disclosure requirements, this new law also sets forth procedures for local authorities to deal with methamphetamine-contaminated properties, including the filing of a lien against a property until the owner cleans up the contamination or pays for the cleanup costs.

Pest Control

Delivery to a transferee of a copy of a structural pest control inspection report prior to transfer of title is required pursuant to Section 8516 of the Business and Professions Code if the report is a requirement imposed as a condition of financing.

REO Property (REO)

The mortgage loan broker may be asked to finance a property for a borrower who obtained ownership not from a seller but rather through a fore- closure action. The disclosure requirement is different for the trustee or sheriff than for a seller, and thus the borrower may not have received the information when he or she acquired title to the property. This information must be provided to the lender. As of September 1995, the following list is a summary of disclosures that the REO seller does not need to comply with Transfer Disclosure Statement (TDS), Mello-Roos District, *Homeowner's Guide to Earthquake Safety*, Environmental Hazards Booklet, and Energy Efficient Booklet. The REO seller must still comply with the following disclosures: Earthquake Fault Zones and Seismic Hazard Zones, Flood Insurance Disclosure and Special Flood Hazard Areas, Lead-Based Paint Notice, Water Heater Compliance Statement, and State Fire Responsibility Areas.

Smoke Detector Compliance

As of September 2, 1992, California Health and Safety Codes 13113.7, 13113.8, and 18029.6 require all existing dwelling units to have an operable smoke detector centrally located outside each sleeping area. New construction or modifications of more than $1,000 require hardwired smoke detectors if the permit is obtained after August 14, 1992.

Title Insurance Advisory

If no title insurance is to be issued, the buyer must receive written notice as a separate document in an escrow stating that it is advisable to obtain title insurance.

Transfer Disclosure Statement (TDS)

California Civil Code Section 1102.3 requires a prospective buyer of one to four residential units to receive a written disclosure statement concerning the condition of the property, based on a reasonably diligent inspection of the property. Exemptions include a transfer under a court order, by foreclosure, by settling of an estate, between co-owners, or by government entity, such as the state comptroller or tax collector.

Utility Line Extensions

As of July 1, 1995, the Public Utilities Commission (PUC) adopted a Stipulation and Settlement Agreement for electric and gas lines. Water and telephone lines are excluded. The new rule imposes a per-foot charge to bring in gas or electricity from the source. For financing of construction in rural areas, the loan broker should determine whether the cost of extending power to the property by the developer or builder and borrower has been part of the total calculations.

Water Heater Bracing

Health and Safety Code 19211 became effective January 1, 1996. Water heaters must be braced, anchored, or strapped to resist falling or horizontal displacement caused by earthquake motion. A law in 2000 requires that braces be placed on the water heater, one that is one-third up from the bottom and another that is one-third down from the top. A written certification is required in which the seller acknowledges to a prospective purchaser that this law has been complied with.

Lender/Purchaser Disclosure Statement

These forms have been designed by the DRE to better accommodate the loan transaction. The previous single disclosure statement did not adequately serve the purposes for which it was intended. The disclosure statement pertains to a specific type of transaction, such as loan origination, collateral loan, and sale of existing note (see Figure 5.11). The DRE has three forms for its Form 851 as of February 1990, and all are still current.

5.9 OTHER LOAN DISCLOSURES

Article 7

The DRE has various provisions with which the loan broker must comply. They may be found in state laws that explain the licensee's responsibility. **Article 7** is most often used for small loans, rather than the large first trust deed, and it may be found in Sections 10240 to 10248 of the Business and Professions Code. Included under these sections are provisions that every broker must comply with when negotiating a loan secured directly or collaterally by a lien on real property. The specific areas should cover late fees, insurance limitations, the appraisal report, and maximum charges and expenses, in addition to prepayment penalty and liability.

Within three business days after the loan broker receives a completed loan application or before the borrower becomes obligated on the note, a written statement must be made that contains certain disclosures. The broker and the borrowers must sign the form and the borrowers must receive a copy. The borrower is not to sign the form unless all items are completed. The broker must retain a copy of the form for four years. Under this law, the term broker includes all licensees working under the broker license, including salespersons or brokers and those parties who solicit borrowers or cause borrowers to be solicited using the services of the broker.

The law mandates the content of the written statement to include:

1. The estimated maximum costs and expenses of making the loan for appraisal fee, escrow fees, title charges, notary fees, recording fees, and credit fees.

2. Total brokerage or commission for original fees, points, bonuses, and other charges in lieu of interest received by the broker if broker is the lender rather than the agent.

3. Senior or subordinate loans to the lien being secured.

4. Estimated amount that borrower will pay for fire insurance premiums, loan payoffs, other creditor payoffs, fees for transfer, assumption, forwarding, and beneficiary statement.

5. Amount of ultimate cash to the borrower after all deductions.

6. The original, unpaid amount of the principal.

7. The rate of interest and APR.

8. The loan term, number of payments, amount of each payment, and the approximate unpaid balance when the loan becomes due plus a 10-point bold capitalized "**NOTICE TO BORROWER**".

9. Name of the broker, business address, and DRE license number.

10. Disclosure of whether the funds are "broker-controlled funds" rather than lender funds; if the former, they must be disclosed within one business day or before close of escrow.

11. Terms of prepayment penalty.

12. Statement that credit life insurance is not required for the loan.

13. Statement that fire and hazard insurance are required to protect against loss and that borrower may obtain his or her own policy or the lender is authorized to add such.

14. Notice of balloon payment information and loan extension data (effective as of July 1, 1995) including 10-point bold capitalized specific disclosure wording.

15. Late charges cannot (1) exceed 10 percent of the installment due, (2) be less than $5. No late charge may be imposed if paid within 10 days from the scheduled due date.

16. Prepayment penalty during first 7 years of the loan calculated on 80 percent of the unpaid loan amount charged at 6 months' interest.

Prepayment Penalty

This is the amount that a lender charges as a penalty because the borrower pays off all or a substantial portion of the loan in advance of the scheduled payment date. The investor was promised a certain return on his or her capital during a certain period, which cannot be obtained if the loan is paid off. The lender placed the original loan with the expectation of the borrower paying specific installments at specific dates for a specific period. The lender had calculated the return to the investor and costs associated with placing the original loan. On receiving the loan funds paid back to the lender in advance of the due date, the lender is obligated to replace the funds. When the lender must find a new place to use the funds, there are costs associated with doing this new business. Thus, the lender charges the borrower for these expected additional costs and expenses.

Different lenders have set varying amounts for their prepayment penalty, which can be anywhere from no charge up to the maximum allowed by law. Different lenders call the prepayment penalty by other names, such as a "transaction fee." Many institutional lenders who are state chartered fall under the guidelines that charge a maximum fee of six months' interest on the unpaid loan amount after first deducting 20 percent from the principal for the current year. If the loan is paid off after seven years, some laws do not allow a prepayment penalty. In the case of federally chartered lending institutions, this rule usually does not apply. The prepayment penalty may be for the life of the loan. A borrower must always check with his or her tax preparer because the prepayment penalty, although called by some "prepaid interest," may not be tax deductible.

When a borrower pays off a loan after a natural disaster, the rules are different. If a state of emergency has been declared by the governor and when the property is an owner-occupied dwelling that is made not habitable or safe, no prepayment may be charged. Hurricanes, tornadoes, excessive flooding, earthquakes and most FEMA loans fall into this category.

Liability

The borrower may be liable for the payment of one-half of the charges of the brokerage fees, points, and commission if the loan is not consummated because the prospective borrower failed to disclose the amount of the outstanding liens of record. The same is true if the vested title is misrepresented by the prospective borrower. The borrower may also have to pay for the title search expenses, escrow fee, appraisal report, credit check, and other charges. The borrower may not be committed to the broker in a signed employing authorization, called an exclusive agreement, for more than 45 days.

Loan Terms

A loan carried back by the seller is exempt from complying with this law. Three categories of loan limitations are outlined:

1. Due date under three years: Requires equal installment payments. The final payment may not be greater than twice the amount of the smallest installment payment (Section 10244).
2. Due date under six years, owner occupied: No installment may be greater than twice the amount of the smallest installment.
3. Loan amounts: If the loan is a first trust deed for more than $30,000 or a second trust deed for more than $20,000, the loan would not fall under the provisions of Article 7.

Maximum Charges

The maximum amount of all costs and expenses under the Real Estate Law Article 7, exclusive of actual title charges and recording fees, shall not exceed $390 or 5 percent of the principal amount of the loan, whichever is greater. No loan fee may exceed a total of $700. The total amount may not exceed the actual

FIGURE 5.12   Article 7 maximum allowable costs and charges.

First loans	5%	Less than 3 years
	10%	More than 3 years
Junior loans	5%	Less than 2 years
	10%	2 years
	15%	3 years or more

costs and must comply with the maximum amount of charges under this DRE regulation (see Figure 5.12).

No interest may be charged for any period prior to the borrower's access to the funds, either directly to the borrower or deposited into an intermediary such as an escrow account. In addition, a borrower may not be held to any clause, rule, or form containing provisions that waive the borrower's rights.

5.10 PREDATORY LENDING LAW

California adopted a **predatory lending** law in 2001, which became effective July 1, 2002. The law applies to certain high-cost, high-rate "covered loans" of $250,000 or less secured by one- to four-unit residential real property located in California that is intended to be used or occupied as the borrower's principal dwelling. The $250,000 cap is subject to adjustment every five years according to changes in the California consumer price index (CPI) (Cal. Fin. Code x 4970 et seq.).

A loan is deemed to be a covered loan if the APR exceeds the interest rate on comparable U.S. Treasury securities by more than 8 percent or the total points and fees exceed 6 percent of the total loan amount. The California definition of points and fees is similar to the definition of points and fees under the federal HOEPA except that California law does not require the inclusion of fees paid to an affiliate for a fee that is otherwise excludable from the finance charge under 12 C.F.R. x 226.4 (c)(7) of Reg. Z.

Disclosure

The predatory lending law requires that certain disclosures be provided to borrowers at least three days prior to the signing of a covered loan [Cal. Fin. Code x 4973(k)(1)].

Prohibited Loan Terms

The predatory lending law imposes the following limitations on loan terms:

- Prepayment penalties. A prepayment penalty may not be charged on a covered loan after the first 36 months after the consummation of the loan. A prepayment penalty may be charged during the first 36 months of the loan if (1) the person who originates (that is, makes, arranges, or negotiates) the loan has also offered the consumer a choice of a product without a prepayment penalty; (2) the person who originates the loan has provided the consumer with a written disclosure about the prepayment penalty terms and the rates, points, and fees available to the consumer if the consumer accepted a loan without a prepayment penalty; (3) the prepayment penalty is limited to an amount not to exceed the payment of six months' advance interest, at the contract rate or interest then in effect, on the amount prepaid in any 12-month period in excess of 20 percent of the original principal amount; (4) the loan does not impose the prepayment penalty if the lender accelerates the loan due to default; and (5) the person who originates the loan will not finance a prepayment penalty through a new loan that is originated by the same person [Cal. Fin. Code x 4973(b)(1)].

- Balloon payments. Balloon payments are not allowed for covered loans with a term of five years or less [Cal. Fin. Code x 4973(b)(1)].

- Negative amortization. Negative amortization is not allowed unless the covered loan is a first mortgage and the person who originates the loan disclosed to the consumer that the loan contains a negative amortization provision [Cal. Fin. Code x 4973 .1].

- Call provisions. Call provisions permitting the lender to accelerate the indebtedness at his or her discretion are prohibited [Cal Fin. Code x 4973(i)].

Prohibited Practices

The following practices, among others, are regulated in connection with covered loans.

- Regard for repayment ability. A lender is prohibited from making a covered loan if it does not reasonably believe that the borrower will be able to make the scheduled payments to repay the obligation according to a consideration of the borrower's current and expected income, current obligations, employment status, and other financial resources, other than the consumer's equity in the dwelling securing the loan. For ARM loans subject to adjustment within 37 months from the date of application, this evaluation must be based on the fully indexed interest rate calculated as of the date of the application. Repayment ability must be verified by the credit application, the borrower's financial statement, a credit report, and other reasonable means. The borrower is presumed to be able to repay the obligation if the borrower's total monthly debts do not exceed 55 percent of the borrower's gross monthly income [Cal. Fin. Code x 4973(f)].

- Identifiable benefit. A lender is prohibited from refinancing or arranging for the refinancing of a covered loan if the new loan would be a covered loan that is made for the purpose of refinancing, debt consolidation, or cash out that does not result in an identifiable benefit to the borrower, considering the borrower's stated purpose for seeking the loan, fees, interest rates, finance charges, and points [Cal. Fin. Code x 4973(j)].

- Steering. A borrower may not be steered, counseled, or directed to accept a covered loan with a risk grade less favorable than the risk grade that the borrower would qualify for based on the lender's current underwriting guidelines. Likewise, a loan broker may not steer a borrower to a covered loan at a higher cost than that for which the borrower could qualify for based on the loans offered by the lenders with whom the broker regularly does business [Cal. Fin. Case x 4973(l)].

- Credit insurance. A lender may not finance as part of a covered loan single premium credit life, credit disability, credit property, or credit unemployment insurance or single-payment debt cancellation or suspension agreements [Cal. Fin. Code x 4979.7].

- Financing points and fees. A lender may not make a loan that finances points and fees in excess of $1,000 or 6 percent of the original principal balance exclusive a points and fees, whichever is greater [Cal. Fin. Code x 4979.6].

Penalties and Corrective Action

A knowing and willful violation of the predatory lending restrictions may result in a license suspension of not less than six months and not more than three years. The state regulator who supervised the lender may assert a penalty of not more than $2,500 for each violation. A willful and knowing violation can result in a civil penalty of up to $25,000 for each violation. Even an unintentional violation may cause a lender to be civilly liable to the consumer in an amount equal to actual damages, plus attorney's fees and costs or, if greater, $15,000 plus attorney's fees and costs [Cal. Fin. Code x 4979.6].

Any compliance failure that was not willful or intentional and resulted from a bona fide error may be corrected within 45 days after receipt of a complaint or discovery of the error. A person who originates a covered loan is not administratively, civilly, or criminally liable for a bona fide error corrected within the 45-day period [Cal. Fin. Code x 4974].

Balloon Payments

All loans that do not fully amortize will have a balloon payment. A balloon payment is a scheduled payment at maturity (the date the entire unpaid balance is due) that is more than twice the amount of the smallest regular payment [CC 2957 (f)]. In the case of any balloon payment, the law requires the holder to give prior notice to the borrower in writing to inform the borrower that the large amount is becoming due [CC 2966]. Some loans are exempt, such as construction loans and open-end credit loans [CC 2924i (b)]. The required notice must include the following:

1. Name and address to whom the payment must be made.
2. The due date.
3. The estimated amount that will be due.
4. The terms of a refinance, if any.
5. The amount of all interest, principal, and charges due between the date of the notice and the due date, assuming all payments are made until payoff.

The due date notice must be within the specified period or the notice will have to be redelivered. Figure 5.13 shows the notice period.

FIGURE 5.13   Balloon payment notice period.

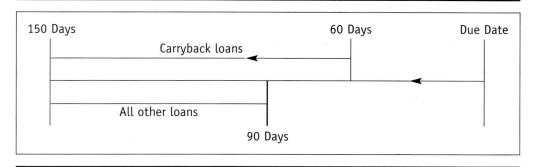

For example, to calculate the balloon payment at the end of five years, using a Texas Instruments financial calculator, the remaining balance would be the remaining unpaid principal balance plus the last month's payment.

	Key Sequence	Display
Step 1:	30 × 12 = [N]	360
Step 2:	10/12 = [% i]	0.83
Step 3:	25000 [PV]	25000.00
Step 4:	[2nd] [PMT]	219.39
Step 5:	219.39[PMT]	219.39
Step 6:	[2nd][N]	360.03
Step 7:	5 × 12 = [2nd][K][x = y]	24143.80

5.11 GOOD FAITH ESTIMATE (GFE)

The Good Faith Estimate (GFE) for nontraditional loan products must be used when the loan product being offered to the consumer allows the borrower to defer repayment of principal or interest and is secured by a one- to four-unit residential property whether owner or non-owner occupied.

Commissioner's Regulation 2842 defines a nontraditional loan product as a loan that allows borrowers to defer repayment of principal or interest. Such products include, but are not limited to, interest-only loans where the borrower pays no loan principal for a period of time and payment option loans where one or more of the payment options may result in negative amortization. A nontraditional loan product does not include reverse mortgages or home equity lines of credit.

The California Department of Real Estate Form RE885 (Figure 5.5) is a four-page document that must be completed for nontraditional loans. Page 1 is the compensation to the broker that is not paid out of the loan proceeds. This section is completed to disclose any compensation received by the broker from the lender in the form of a yield/spread premium, service release premium or any other rebate or compensation.

Page 2, Section III is used if the initial adjustable rate box is checked, then sections IV through XI must be completed. If the fixed-rate box is checked and the loan has an interest-only or negative amortization payment feature, sections IV through IX are skipped, and sections X and XI are completed. Section XIX is the Certification. If any or all of the columns, with the exception of the last column, termed proposed loan, are used in the typical mortgage transactions portion of the form are not completed, the broker MUST read and complete the Certification on page 3. Page 4, section XIX is the comparison of sample mortgage features for one to four residential units. This part uses the Instructional Guide for nontraditional loan disclosure (page 4) found on the DRE Web site at www.dre.ca.gov/frm_forms.html and go to Mortgage Lending Brokers. If the broker does not offer one or more comparison loan products, the box "not offered" is checked. The broker must provide the required information in all columns except those for which the broker has executed the Certification on page 3 of the RE885.

No blanks may be left blank. After completion, the form must be signed by the borrower within three days of receiving the borrower's completed written loan application. The broker must retain the form for a period for three years.

SUMMARY

The mortgage loan broker has many state and federal disclosure regulations that must be complied with. All states must comply with the federal laws such as the Consumer Credit Protection Act, the Truth-in-Lending Act, Reg. Z, Regulation X, and RESPA. The APR statement alone requires 14 disclosures. These laws require disclosures of finance charges, rates of interest, loan terms, and fees. Many disclosures require giving a booklet to a prospective borrower that describes information about certain issues that may be of concern to the applicant. In California, licensees must disclose matters such as lead-based paint, environmental issues, insurance, and similar lender requirements. Both DRE and CFL licensees must comply with the many disclosure laws, including institutional and private lenders. New laws have been enacted to protect consumers from predatory lending.

REVIEWING YOUR UNDERSTANDING

1. California Civil Code requires an agent to disclose to a buyer or borrower whether a death has occurred within _____ years of the offer or loan application?
   A. 3
   B. 4
   C. 5
   D. Not required to be disclosed

2. The APR does NOT include:
   A. Origination fee
   B. Buy down points
   C. Lender services charges
   D. Title Insurance fee

3. A good faith estimate (GFE) is given:
   A. Only if the borrower requests it
   B. Within three business days after submission of the loan application
   C. Within three days of funding the loan
   D. Only if the loan is non-conforming

4. The regulation that requires mortgage lending institutions to collect data from loan applications each calendar year, and report the findings to the federal government for public review is:
   A. Federal Real Estate Settlement Procedures Act (RESPA) Regulation X
   B. Federal Truth In Lending (TIL) Act, Regulation Z
   C. Consumer Credit Protection Act of 1968
   D. Home Mortgage Disclosure Act (HMDA), Regulation C

5. In which disclosure should you find the thickness and the "R" value of the insulation that has been or will be installed in the house?
   A. Energy Conservation Retrofit and Thermal Insulation Disclosure
   B. Environmental Hazard Disclosure
   C. Earthquake Disclosure
   D. Fire Hazard Areas

6. Which type of sale does not require the seller to comply with disclosures such as Mello Roos District, Energy Efficiency, etc.?
   A. Short pay-off sale
   B. Banks REO sale
   C. Sale by the owner
   D. None of the above

7. The amount that a lender charges as a penalty because the borrower pays off the loan in advance is called:
   A. Prepayment fee
   B. Prepayment charge
   C. Prepayment penalty
   D. Prepayment sub-charge

8. The document that contains the actual costs, charges and adjustments for items paid at close of escrow is called:
   A. The HUD-1 Settlement Statement
   B. The Credit Report
   C. The Mortgage Loan Disclosure Statement
   D. The Preliminary Report

9. The Section 32 rule includes the two-test rule:
   A. APR test and credit test
   B. ARM test and APR test
   C. APR test and points & fees test
   D. None of the above

10. What agency enforces RESPA?
    A. HUD
    B. FHA
    C. FEMA
    D. FDIC

ANSWERS TO REVIEWING YOUR UNDERSTANDING

1. A, (p. 172)   4. D, (p. 138)   7. C, (p. 184)   10. A, (p. 147)
2. D, (pp. 144–146) 5. B, (p. 172)   8. A, (p. 156)
3. B, (p. 147)   6. B, (p. 182)   9. C, (p. 146)

PART III
Processing

Chapter

6

Processing: Prequalification and Loan Application

PREVIEW

For most people, the money involved for the purchase of a home is the largest single transaction in their life and, thus, an emotional commitment. For most lenders, loaning money is their normal daily work and just another routine business transaction. The mortgage loan broker can bridge the gap between the differing emotional versus business point of view. Although lenders receive funds to loan from investors and thus must have criteria by which they lend, the service the mortgage loan broker gives means a great deal to a prospective borrower by way of explanation on what seems like a complicated process. In addition, the mortgage loan broker or banks not only aid in the basic paperwork and forms for the borrower but also provide valuable service to the investor or lender by freeing the time needed to prepare the loan for funding that might otherwise cost direct employee time and overhead, thus reducing lenders' expenses.

This chapter discusses the prequalification process of taking a prospective borrower from thinking about borrowing to some basic initial guidelines and ratios that will determine the ability to obtain a loan. The uniform residential loan application (URLA), referred to as the 1003 (pronounced 10-0-3), is also reviewed in detail.

CHAPTER OBJECTIVES

At the end of this chapter, the student learning outcomes include:

1. Complete buyer qualification data to determine qualifying ratios.
2. Differentiate between acceptable ratios for Federal Housing Administration (FHA), Department of Veterans Administration (DVA), and conventional financing.
3. Outline basic DVA eligibility criteria for veterans.
4. Explain the sections of the URLA 1003, loan application.

6.1 LENDER/PURCHASE STATEMENT

The mortgage loan broker should collect as much information as possible at the beginning of the transaction. The licensee can help get the offer accepted by the seller by assisting in the transaction to have the prospective purchaser complete a loan application and have a credit report completed. The information obtained can be used to determine the prequalification of the borrower. These data can be typed on a letter or stated on a computer printout form at the early stages of the purchase.

The lender and purchaser then have a statement to present to the selling agent and the seller that gives the indicated value for which the borrower may obtain financing. Often in a transaction, the borrower qualifies after the initial loan application and creditworthiness are determined. However, the property may not qualify because the appraised value can end up lower than the price negotiated between the buyer and the seller or the loan asked for is higher than the lender is able to loan. Figure 6.1 is a checklist for a borrower to furnish the mortgage loan broker when the original loan application is completed.

Before taking the loan application, the mortgage loan broker should obtain a **property profile** on the subject property. The report can be requested by a telephone call or by using a password with a title company program to access the information. The customer service department of a local title insurance company can be helpful to the loan agent gathering initial information for a prospective loan. For any type of loan, the information needed will prove to be invaluable. Pertinent information will include the names of the current title holders of the property, a legal description, status on payment of property taxes, lien documents, the grant deed, each recorded deed of trust, comparables (comps), property information for pricing the property to determine loan-to-value status, assessors parcel number (APN), and year built. Obtaining this information in advance will save you a great deal of time later in the process, which is explained in more detail in Chapter 9.

6.2 DISCLOSURE OF HOME OWNERSHIP COUNSELING

The prequalification step in the loan process may include the necessity for the borrowers to receive **home ownership counseling**. Certain types of loans require this step prior to the loan processing. The intent is for the borrower to have a clear understanding of the costs and responsibilities of what home ownership involves. The purpose for the program is based on the concept that the more a borrower knows about home ownership, the better the borrower can make realistic and wise decisions. The seminar may be given by the lender, the mortgage loan broker, or some other entity.

The first part of the home ownership seminar is whether home ownership is right for the attendee. Then the prospective borrower learns how much loan he or she can afford, followed by the financial loan costs for obtaining the loan.

FIGURE 6.1   Checklist for borrower's loan application.

_____ Check for $_____ to cover the cost of the credit report, made payable to_____.

_____ Copy of most recent pay stub for all borrowers, driver's license, and Social Security card.

_____ List of all residence addresses for the last 2 years and name and address of past and current landlord(s) or loan payment information.

_____ If not a U.S. citizen, a copy of the green card.

_____ Copy of W-2 statements for all employment for all borrowers for this year and last year. Note: Complete 1040s required if additional income other than W-2 income is used.

_____ Copy of three months' bank statements, all pages, all accounts, all borrowers. Include IRA, CD, stocks, bonds, investment funds, 401K, TSA, retirement plans, etc.

_____ Provide written, detailed letter of explanation for any credit problems, signed and dated by the borrower (signed in _blue_ ink).

_____ If self-employed: For sole proprietor, include year-to-date profit and loss statement, signed and dated (in _blue_ ink). Note: Must be supported by previous year's tax returns. Provide three months' bank statements on the business account.

_____ If self-employed, for corporation, S corporation, partnership: Provide all tax returns for this year and last year, K1s, 1120s, year-to-date profit and loss statement for the business income.

_____ If self-employed: For commission income, provide 1040s for last year and this year and a year-to-date profit and loss statement.

_____ Provide a copy of all current rental agreements and the 1040s or Schedule E for last year and this year.

_____ For any cash-out refinance loan: Include a letter, signed (in _blue_ ink) by all borrowers and dated, stating the intended purpose of the loan and the cash. (See Figure 8.9.)

_____ Include a copy of the most recent monthly statement for all automobile loans, recurring monthly expenses, revolving debt, etc.

_____ If using alternative credit, when no established credit has been established: Copy of last year's (12 months) utility bill for cable or dish television, telephone, gas, electric, and water company.

_____ If subject property is a condominium: Provide name, address, and telephone number of the homeowners association and the property management company.

_____ If divorced, a copy of the final divorce decree, including all pages.

_____ If applicable, a copy of any bankruptcy, including all pages.

Several loan types are presented, as was discussed in Chapter 3 and 4, so the borrower can see how to stretch his or her borrowing power through a variety of financing options and with flexible lending programs.

Many important topics are reviewed by the home ownership seminar attendee, such as the following concepts:

• How much money will be needed to consummate the transaction, including the down payment, closing costs, and the reserves?

- What does the credit history indicate about the future ability to make the loan payments?
- What questions should the borrower ask when shopping for a loan to obtain attractive terms?
- Can the borrower budget for the cost of home ownership to obtain the tax advantages of home ownership?

6.3 RESIDENTIAL LOAN APPLICATION

Most lenders will insist on completion of the standard **URLA**, commonly referred to as the 1003 by mortgage loan brokers. It is not unusual to have this form computer generated, with the name of the lender or the name of the mortgage loan brokerage firm printed on the top of the form.

The form is used to provide information to determine the creditworthiness of the borrowers by determining their net worth. It also establishes the amount of debt that the borrowers have and will have after the loan is funded. Filling in all of the boxes on the loan application gives your processor a strong sense of direction about the loan. The information is used to determine the ratios established for a particular type of loan, which will be discussed in the next section. The form is usually completed twice. The first 1003 form is completed by the borrower or loan officer at the initial loan application. The second 1003 form is completed by the processor close to the actual submission for final loan approval.

The FNMA form 1003, the loan application, has been updated recently and the January 2010 version must be used as of that date, replacing the July 2005 form that was required to be used after January 2006. The new form, shown in Figure 6.2, is broken down into sections, with explanations corresponding to the circled numbers indicated on the form. The circled numbers require detailed and accurate information for each item giving complete data or else the loan will not be approved. The lender pays fees to the mortgage loan broker to make sure that the information is correctly obtained and completed before submission for loan approval. An FNMA 1003 in English and in Spanish is shown in Appendix A.

6.4 QUALIFYING RATIOS

Two ratios are predominantly used by most lenders. The first is referred as the **front-end ratio**, and the second is called **back-end ratio**. Portfolio lenders that use their own funds may have different guidelines, but these two ratios are the most common and industry-accepted criteria that the mortgage loan broker must use to have the loan accepted by the secondary money market and by the funding lender. Subprime lenders may also have different debt ratios.

Both the front-end ratio and the back-end ratio use the borrower's monthly gross income. However, the data that are provided to the loan broker often do not show monthly figures but may instead be indicated in weekly or monthly

FIGURE 6.2 Loan application: FNMA 1003.

Uniform Residential Loan Application

This application is designed to be completed by the applicant(s) with the Lender's assistance. Applicants should complete this form as "Borrower" or "Co-Borrower," as applicable. Co-Borrower information must also be provided (and the appropriate box checked) when ⊙ the income or assets of a person other than the Borrower (including the Borrower's spouse) will be used as a basis for loan qualification or ⊙ the income or assets of the Borrower's spouse or other person who has community property rights pursuant to state law will not be used as a basis for loan qualification, but his or her liabilities must be considered because the spouse or other person has community property rights pursuant to applicable law and Borrower resides in a community property state, the security property is located in a community property state, or the Borrower is relying on other property located in a community property state as a basis for repayment of the loan.

If this is an application for joint credit, Borrower and Co-Borrower each agree that we intend to apply for joint credit (sign below):

Borrower Co-Borrower (1)

1. This is an application for joint credit, Borrower and Co-Borrower each agree that we intend to apply for joint credit (sign above):

I. TYPE OF MORTGAGE AND TERMS OF LOAN

Mortgage Applied for:	⊙ VA ⊙ Conventional ⊙ Other (explain): (2) ⊙ FHA ⊙ USDA/Rural Housing Service	Agency Case Number (3)	Lender Case Number (4)
Amount $ (5)	Interest Rate (6)	No. of Months (7)	Amortization Type: ⊙ Fixed Rate ⊙ GPM ⊙ Other (explain): ⊙ ARM (type): (8)

At the top of the form, the borrower is asked to check a box about whether income or assets of a person other than the borrowers will be used *or* whether income or assets of the borrower's spouse will not be used as basis for loan qualification. Check the appropriate box. The new wording listed above now states that you must use the debts of the other party if they live in a community property state. The parties must sign at the top of page one.

I. Type of Mortgage and Terms of Loan

2. Enter the type of mortgage applied for: VA, FHA, conventional, USDA/rural housing service, or other.
3. Agency case number is used for VA or FHA loans.
4. Lender case number is used by the lender submitting the loan request (mortgage broker).
5. Enter the dollar amount of the loan request.
6. Enter the interest rate.
7. Enter the term of the loan, in months: 15 years is 180 months, 20 years is 240 months, 30 years is 360 months, and 40 years would be 480 months.
8. Enter the amortization type.

II. PROPERTY INFORMATION AND PURPOSE OF LOAN

Subject Property Address (street, city, state & ZIP) (9)	No. of Units (10)		
	Legal Description of Subject Property (attach description if necessary) (11)		Year Built (12)
Purpose of Loan ⊙ Purchase ⊙ Construction ⊙ Other (explain): ⊙ Refinance ⊙ Construction-Permanent (13)	Property will be: ⊙ Primary Residence ⊙ Secondary Residence ⊙ Investment (14)		

Complete this line if construction or construction-permanent loan. (15)

Year Lot Acquired	Original Cost $	Amount Existing Liens $	(a) Present Value of Lot $	(b) Cost of Improvements $	Total (a + b) $

Complete this line if this is a refinance loan. (16)

Year Acquired	Original Cost $	Amount Existing Liens $	Purpose of Refinance	Describe Improvements Cost: $	⊙ made	⊙ to be made

Title will be held in what Name(s) (17)	Manner in which Title will be held (17)	Estate will be held in: ⊙ Fee Simple ⊙ Leasehold (show expiration date) (17)
Source of Down Payment, Settlement Charges, and/or Subordinate Financing (explain) (18)		

II. Property Information and Purpose of Loan

9. Enter the property address for which the loan is being requested. Be sure to include the five- or nine-digit zip code.
10. Enter the number of units: SFR, two units, three units, etc.
11. Enter the lot, tract, book, and page number of the legal description of the subject property. Be sure to include the AP number (Assessor's Parcel Number). (This information can be obtained from your local title insurance company, customer service department.)
12. Enter the year built. (This information is generally on the property profile that can be obtained from your local title insurance company.)
13. Purpose of the loan. Mark the appropriate box.
14. Property will be . . . . Mark the appropriate box.
15. Complete this section only if you are applying for a construction-permanent loan.
16. Complete this line if applying for a refinance loan.
17. Show how the borrowers' names will appear on legal documents. Also include how they will be taking title and if the property (the land) is fee simple or leasehold.
18. Enter the source of the down payment, i.e., savings, sale of current residence, gift.

FIGURE 6.2   *(Continued)*

Borrower		III. BORROWER INFORMATION		Co-Borrower		
Borrower's Name (include Jr. or Sr. if applicable) (19)				Co-Borrower's Name (include Jr. or Sr. if applicable) (20)		

Social Security Number (19)	Home Phone (19) (incl. area code)	DOB (mm/dd/yyyy) (19)	Yrs. School (19)	Social Security Number (20)	Home Phone (20) (incl. area code)	DOB (mm/dd/yyyy) (20)	Yrs. School (20)

☉ Married ☉ Unmarried (include ☉ Separated single, divorced, widowed) (19)	Dependents (not listed by Co-Borrower) (19) no. ages (19)	☉ Married ☉ Unmarried (include (20) ☉ Separated single, divorced, widowed)	Dependents (not listed by Borrower) (20) no. ages (20)

Present Address (street, city, state, ZIP) ☉ Own ☉ Rent ____No. Yrs. (21)	Present Address (street, city, state, ZIP) ☉ Own ☉ Rent ____No. Yrs. (21)
Mailing Address, if different from Present Address (22)	Mailing Address, if different from Present Address (22)

If residing at present address for less than two years, complete the following:

Former Address (street, city, state, ZIP) ☉ Own ☉ Rent ____No. Yrs.	Former Address (street, city, state, ZIP) ☉ Own ☉ Rent ____No. Yrs.

III. Borrower Information

19. Complete all the information regarding the primary borrower. Be sure to include middle initial, social security number, home telephone, with the area code. DOB: you must show the month, day, and the full year of birth (example: 06/21/1940). Years of school (high school + college)
20. If there is a spouse, complete all the information regarding the *coborrower*. If your co-borrower is *not* a spouse, you need to complete a separate 1003 loan application.
21. You will need to show two years (24 months) of residence. Be sure to indicate whether the borrower owned or rented and for how long.
22. Mailing address. If different from Present Address. Complete as needed.

Borrower		IV. EMPLOYMENT INFORMATION		Co-Borrower	
Name & Address of Employer (23)	☉ Self Employed	Yrs. on this job	Name & Address of Employer (23)	☉ Self Employed	Yrs. on this job
		Yrs. employed in this Line of work/profession			Yrs. employed in this line of work/profession
Position/Title/Type of Business	Business Phone (incl. area code)		Position/Title/Type of Business	Business Phone (incl. area code)	

If employed in current position for less than two years or if currently employed in more than one position, complete the following:

Name & Address of Employer (23)	☉ Self Employed	Dates (from – to)	Name & Address of Employer (23)	☉ Self Employed	Dates (from – to)
		Monthly Income $			Monthly Income $
Position/Title/Type of Business	Business Phone (incl. area code)		Position/Title/Type of Business	Business Phone (incl. area code)	
Name & Address of Employer	☉ Self Employed	Dates (from – to)	Name & Address of Employer	☉ Self Employed	Dates (from – to)
		Monthly Income $			Monthly Income $
Position/Title/Type of Business	Business Phone (incl. area code)		Position/Title/Type of Business	Business Phone (incl. area code)	

IV. Employment Information

23. Complete all information as requested for the borrower and the coborrower. Be sure to take into consideration that you need to verify two full years (24 months) of employment for each party. If the former employer is no longer in business, complete this section and furnish a pay stub or W2 from the former employer.

FIGURE 6.2   (Continued)

Gross Monthly Income	Borrower	Co-Borrower	Total	Combined Monthly Housing Expense	Present	Proposed
Base Empl. Income*	$	$	$	Rent	$	
Overtime				First Mortgage (P&I)		$
Bonuses				Other Financing (P&I)		
Commissions				Hazard Insurance		
Dividends/Interest				Real Estate Taxes		
Net Rental Income				Mortgage Insurance		
Other (before completing, see the notice in "describe other income," below)				Homeowner Assn. Dues		
				Other:		
Total	$	$	$	Total	$	$

* Self Employed Borrower(s) may be required to provide additional documentation such as tax returns and financial statements.

Describe Other Income *Notice:* Alimony, child support, or separate maintenance income need not be revealed if the Borrower (B) or Co-Borrower (C) does not choose to have it considered for repaying this loan.

B/C		Monthly Amount
		$

V. Monthly Income and Combined Housing Expense Information

24. Borrower's and coborrower's monthly base income (salary).
25. Overtime is to be averaged over a minimum of two years (24 months), using W-2 forms and current pay stubs.
26. Bonuses are handled the same as overtime.
27. Commissions are averaged over two years (24 months), using check stubs, W-2 forms, or 1099 forms and tax returns (1040s).
28. Dividends/interest are averaged over two years (24 months), using the same documents as for overtime, bonuses and commissions.
29. Net rental income: Take off 25% from the monthly gross income for maintenance, utilities, and vacancy. On older property, you may need to deduct 35% to 50%.
(Example: If your monthly gross rent is $1,000 × 75% = $750 net rent, and if the mortgage payment on the rental property is $900 a month principal, interest, taxes, and insurance (PITI), you would have a negative cash flow of $150 per month, which would be considered a "long-term" debt on the part of the borrower.) You would also need to insure that the borrower has atleast a 30% equity position in the property.
30. Use this space to describe any other "effective income." See the note in the space (#30) below.
31. Total: Add each column, borrower, coborrower and total.
32. Describe any other "effective income" listed in space 28.
33. Combined monthly housing expense: Add all items applicable to arrive at the total monthly payment (present) and include homeowners association dues, when needed.
34. Add all items applicable to arrive at the total monthly payment (proposed).

VI. ASSETS AND LIABILITIES

This Statement and any applicable supporting schedules may be completed jointly by both married and unmarried Co-Borrowers if their assets and liabilities are sufficiently joined so that the Statement can be meaningfully and fairly presented on a combined basis; otherwise, separate Statements and Schedules are required. If the Co-Borrower section was completed about a non-applicant spouse or other person, this Statement and supporting schedules must be completed about that spouse or other person also.

Completed ⊙ Jointly ⊙ Not Joi

ASSETS Description	Cash or Market Value	Liabilities and Pledged Assets. List the creditor's name, address, and account number for all outstanding debts, including automobile loans, revolving charge accounts, real estate loans, alimony, child support, stock pledges, etc. Use continuation sheet, if necessary. Indicate by (*) those liabilities, which will be satisfied upon sale of real estate owned or upon refinancing of the subject property.		
Cash deposit toward purchase held by:	$			
List checking and savings accounts below		LIABILITIES	Monthly Payment & Months Left to Pay	Unpaid Balance
Name and address of Bank, S&L, or Credit Union		Name and address of Company	$ Payment/Months	$
Acct. no.	$			Acct. no.
Name and address of Bank, S&L, or Credit Union		Name and address of Company	$ Payment/Months	$
Acct. no.	$			Acct. no.
Name and address of Bank, S&L, or Credit Union		Name and address of Company	$ Payment/Months	$
Acct. no.	$			Acct. no.

Freddie Mac Form 65 7/05 Page 3 of 5 Fannie Mae Form 1003 7/05

FIGURE 6.2   *(Continued)*

VI. ASSETS AND LIABILITIES (cont'd)				
Name and address of Bank, S&L, or Credit Union	Name and address of Company	$ Payment/Months		$
Acct. no.		$		Acct. no.
Stocks & Bonds (Company name/ number & description) ㊳	$	Name and address of Company	$ Payment/Months	$
Acct. no.				
Life insurance net cash value Face amount: $ ㊴	$	Name and address of Company	$ Payment/Months	$
Subtotal Liquid Assets		$		
Real estate owned (enter market value from schedule of real estate ㊵	$			
Vested interest in retirement fund ㊶	$			
Net worth of business(es) owned (attach financial statement) ㊷	$			Acct. no.
Automobiles owned (make and year) ㊸	$	Alimony/Child Support/Separate Maintenance Payments Owed to: ㊻		$
Other Assets (itemize) ㊹	$	Job-Related Expense child care, union dues, etc.) ㊼		$
Total Monthly Payments		$		
Total Assets a.	$	Net Worth (a minus b) ㊽	$	Total Liabilities b. $ ㊾

VI. Assets and Liabilities

35. Mark the appropriate box: Completed ___ Jointly ___ Not Jointly.
36. Cash deposit toward purchase held by: Enter the amount the borrowers have deposited and who holds the deposit. Be sure to include the name, address, and telephone number of the person or company that holds the deposit.
37. Enter the name, address, zip code, account type, and account numbers of all checking, savings, certificates of deposit (CDs), or IRAs the borrower may have. Obtain three months' bank statements, all pages, for all accounts.
38. Stocks and bonds: Describe and include a total amount of value.
39. Enter the face amount of the policy and the cash value.
40. Enter the total value of all properties owned by the borrower. (Include present home, even if sold, but for which borrower has not received the proceeds of the sale. See page 3 under Schedule of Real Estate Owned.)
41. Enter amount, if applicable. Furnish a copy of the most current statement.
42. Attach a current profit and loss statement (drawn up by a CPA) and include the total market value of the business.
43. List all automobiles owned and leased; include their market value. If the vehicles are less than five years old and paid off, you may need to furnish a photocopy of the

44. List all other assets the borrower may have: (household goods, boat, jet-ski, recreational vehicle, art collection, etc.)
45. List any open or closed revolving or installment debts the borrower may have, such as automobile loans, student loans, credit cards, and real estate loans. Include all account numbers.
46. For this section, you may wish to obtain a full copy of the divorce decree. Enter the amount the borrower is to pay for alimony/child support.
47. Review pay stubs and 1040s for "job-related" expenses and enter the amount in this space. (This will be a monthly expense.)
48. To obtain the net worth, take the total amount of assets and subtract the total liabilities (a minus b).
49. Total the amount owed of the unpaid bills.

FIGURE 6.2 (Continued)

VI. Assets and Liabilities (cont.)

50. List all real estate owned by the borrower. If needed, attached a schedule of real estate owned. List current residence, even if it is being sold.
51. List any additional names under which credit has been received and indicate appropriate creditor names and account numbers (e.g., maiden names, former married names, aliases).

VII. Details of Transaction

52. If the transaction is a purchase, enter the purchase price.
53. Enter only if being done prior to the close of the transaction.
54. Enter only if applicable.
55. Enter all loans and closing cost that are being paid through the closing.
56. See prepaid items you listed on the good faith estimate.
57. See items you listed on the good faith estimate.
58. Enter only if being paid by the borrower.
59. Enter only if being paid by the borrower.
60. Enter total cost (add items a through h).
61. Have the borrowers read these questions very carefully and check the yes or no boxes. Those questions answered with a yes may need a letter of explanation or any applicable documentation (e.g. full copy of any bankruptcy papers, including discharge, divorce decrees, with a filed final decree.)
62. List any junior liens.
63. List any items that the seller is going to pay.
64. List any other credits to the borrower and explain.
65. List the new loan amount (excluding PMI, MIP, Funding Fee-Financed).
66. List PMI, MIP, Funding Fee Financed.
67. List the loan amount (add m and n).
68. List the amount of money the borrowers need to bring into the escrow or the loan proceeds be received by the borrowers under a cash-out refinance.

FIGURE 6.2   (*Continued*)

VIII. Declarations

69. Have the borrowers read these questions very carefully and check the yes or no boxes. Those questions answered with a yes may need a letter of explanation or any applicable documentation (e.g., full copy of any bankruptcy papers, including discharge, divorce decrees, with a filed final decree).

IX. ACKNOWLEDGEMENT AND AGREEMENT

Each of the undersigned specifically represents to Lender and to Lender's actual or potential agents, brokers, processors, attorneys, insurers, servicers, successors and assigns and agrees and acknowledges that: (1) the information provided in this application is true and correct as of the date set forth opposite my signature and that any intentional or negligent misrepresentation of this information contained in this application may result in civil liability, including monetary damages, to any person who may suffer any loss due to reliance upon any misrepresentation that I have made on this application, and/or in criminal penalties including, but not limited to, fine or imprisonment or both under the provisions of Title 18, United States Code, Sec. 1001, et seq.; (2) the loan requested pursuant to this application (the "Loan") will be secured by a mortgage or deed of trust on the property described in this application; (3) the property will not be used for any illegal or prohibited purpose or use; (4) all statements made in this application are made for the purpose of obtaining a residential mortgage loan; (5) the property will be occupied as indicated in this application; (6) the Lender, its servicers, successors or assigns may retain the original and/or an electronic record of this application, whether or not the Loan is approved; (7) the Lender and its agents, brokers, insurers, servicers, successors, and assigns may continuously rely on the information contained in the application, and I am obligated to amend and/or supplement the information provided in this application if any of the material facts that I have represented herein should change prior to closing of the Loan; (8) in the event that my payments on the Loan become delinquent, the Lender, its servicers, successors or assigns may, in addition to any other rights and remedies that it may have relating to such delinquency, report my name and account information to one or more consumer reporting agencies; (9) ownership of the Loan and/or administration of the Loan account may be transferred with such notice as may be required by law; (10) neither Lender nor its agents, brokers, insurers, servicers, successors or assigns has made any representation or warranty, express or implied, to me regarding the property or the condition or value of the property; and (11) my transmission of this application as an "electronic record" containing my "electronic signature," as those terms are defined in applicable federal and/or state laws (excluding audio and video recordings), or my facsimile transmission of this application containing a facsimile of my signature, shall be as effective, enforceable and valid as if a paper version of this application were delivered containing my original written signature.

Acknowledgement. Each of the undersigned hereby acknowledges that any owner of the Loan, its servicers, successors and assigns, may verify or reverify any information contained in this application or obtain any information or data relating to the Loan, for any legitimate business purpose through any source, including a source named in this application or a consumer reporting agency.

Borrower's Signature (70)	Date	Co-Borrower's Signature	Date
X		X	

IX. Acknowledgment and Agreement

70. Each borrower must sign and date (month, day, year) the loan application after it is completed by either the loan agent or the prospective borrower.

X. INFORMATION FOR GOVERNMENT MONITORING PURPOSES

The following information is requested by the Federal Government for certain types of loans related to a dwelling in order to monitor the lender's compliance with equal credit opportunity, fair housing and home mortgage disclosure laws. You are not required to furnish this information, but are encouraged to do so. The law provides that a lender may not discriminate either on the basis of this information, or on whether you choose to furnish it. If you furnish the information, please provide both ethnicity and race. For race, you may check more than one designation. If you do not furnish ethnicity, race, or sex, under Federal regulations, this lender is required to note the information on the basis of visual observation and surname if you have made this application in person. If you do not wish to furnish the information, please check the box below. (Lender must review the above material to assure that the disclosures satisfy all requirements to which the lender is subject under applicable state law for the particular type of loan applied for.)

BORROWER ☉ I do not wish to furnish this information	CO-BORROWER ☉ I do not wish to furnish this information
Ethnicity: ☉ Hispanic or Latino ☉ Not Hispanic or Latino	**Ethnicity:** ☉ Hispanic or Latino ☉ Not Hispanic or Latino
Race: ☉ American Indian or ☉ Asian ☉ Black or African American Alaska Native ☉ Native Hawaiian or ☉ White (71) Other Pacific Islander	**Race:** ☉ American Indian or ☉ Asian ☉ Black or African American Alaska Native ☉ Native Hawaiian or ☉ White Other Pacific Islander
Sex: ☉ Female ☉ Male **Sex:**	☉ Female ☉ Male

To be Completed by Interviewer	Interviewer's Name (print or type)	Name and Address of Interviewer's Employer
This application was taken by: ☉ Face-to-face interview ☉ Mail ☉ Telephone (72) ☉ Internet	(72)	(73)
	Interviewer's Signature Date	
	Interviewer's Phone Number (incl. area code)	

X. Information for Government Monitoring Purposes

71. This information is to be completed by the loan agent.
72. This information is to be completed by the loan agent; print and sign your name and list your telephone number, including the area code.
73. Name and address of interviewer's employer are generally computer generated from the software system that is being used by the employer.
74. This is a continuation sheet of the loan application, if needed.

FIGURE 6.2 (*Continued*)

CONTINUATION SHEET/RESIDENTIAL LOAN APPLICATION		
Use this continuation sheet if you need more space to complete the Residential Loan Application. Mark **B** f or Borrower or **C** for Co-Borrower.	Borrower:	Agency Case Number:
	Co-Borrower:	Lender Case Number:

(74)

I/We fully understand that it is a Federal crime punishable by fine or imprisonment, or both, to knowingly make any false statements concerning any of the above facts as applicable under the provisions of Title 18, United States Code, Section 1001, et seq.

Borrower's Signature	Date	Co-Borrower's Signature	Date
X		X	

numbers. Different employers pay their employees at different times of the month. To convert the information about income to the needed monthly income, the loan broker would make the converting computations as shown in Figure 6.3.

The front-end ratio is used to determine the financial ability of the borrower to meet the obligation to repay the loan. The front end ratio is the total housing expense. The total gross income from all sources for the borrower and co-borrower is first derived. Then the total house payment, including PITI plus homeowners association dues and mortgage insurance, is totaled for the housing

FIGURE 6.3 Salary conversion chart.

Weekly	$\dfrac{\text{Gross pay amount} \times 52}{12}$	=	monthly income
Biweekly	$\dfrac{\text{Gross pay amount} \times 26}{12}$	=	monthly income
Semimonthly	Gross pay amount $\times$ 2	=	monthly income
Annually	$\dfrac{\text{Gross pay amount}}{12}$	=	monthly income
Hourly	$\dfrac{\text{Hourly wage} \times \text{\# of hours worked per week} \times 52}{12}$	=	monthly income

The number of hours worked per week must be noted by the employer on the Verification of Employment (VOE). If the employer did not state the applicable hours on the VOE, a separate letter from the employer and pay stubs covering the most recent 30-day period will be necessary. *Never* assume an applicant works 40 hours per week. When the number of hours worked is less than full time (40 hours) or a guaranteed minimum, a 24-month average of the past and year-to-date earnings will be used to calculate the monthly income used qualify the borrower.

Also, if the employer provides a range of hours worked, the low range is used in the calculation, or a 24-month average of the borrower's actual earnings could be used. Comparison to year-to-date earnings should always be made to identify any discrepancies greater than 20%.

expense. To determine the ratio, the total housing expense is divided by the total gross income. The front-end ratio may be a different percentage with private lenders than the new revised FNMA and Freddie Mac guidelines benchmark ratios, which were often formerly based upon LTV but are more uniform and consistent under the rules for the future.

The different loan types, such as government loans discussed in Chapter 4, handle ratios similar to the conventional LTV ratios, but they are a separate set of guidelines.

$$\text{FRONT-END RATIO} = \frac{\text{PITI} + \text{HOA} + \text{MI}}{\text{GROSS INCOME (GI) MONTHLY}}$$

The back-end ratio is used to let the lender see the borrower's total financial obligations. The ratio is determined by dividing the total housing debt plus all long-term debt. Long-term debt is usually considered to be any debt that has 10 months or more remaining. The type of debt depends, in part, on the type of debt. For example, a car lease payment of 10 months is handled differently than another type of debt. Another consideration is if the debt is large enough to significantly affect the borrower's ability to repay the loan, such as a payment on dental work of $25 a month for 12 months that has an entire unpaid remaining balance of only $300.

FIGURE 6.4 ARM income-expense ratios.

	Housing Expense	Total monthly Debt service
FNMA (LTV 90% or more)	26%	33%
FNMA (LTV 90% or less)	28%	36%
FHLMC (exceeds cap and discount guidelines)	25%	33%

The gross income used is the same as the amount used for the front-end ratio. The expense portion of the formula uses the same housing expense information but adds non-housing consumer loans, such as auto, furniture, and credit card loans. Again, the ratio varies, depending on loan type.

Prior to the mortgage meltdown and the new guidelines set forth in 2009, the ratios were tied to the LTV. For example, Figure 6.4 shows the ARM income-expense ratio for FNMA and FHLMC before the 2009 changes when Fannie Mae and Freddie Mac were taken over by the federal government and then put in place under new administrative practices with the Federal Reserve.

$$\text{BACK-END RATIO} = \frac{\text{PITI + HOA + MI + DEBTS}}{\text{GROSS INCOME (GI) MONTHLY}}$$

For example, if one borrower makes $52 per hour and the coborrower makes $4,265 per month, and they have a car payment of $350 per month and a credit card payment of $500 per month ($350 + $500 = $850), a basic prequalification for a 90% conventional LTV would be:

Borrower: $52 × 40 hours per week = $2,080 per week × 52 weeks per year = $108,160/yr/12 months per year = $9,013.33 per month

Coborrower: $4,265 per month × 12 months per year = $51,180 per year/12 month = $4,265/mo
$9,013.33 + $4,265 = $13,278.33 total income

Front-end ratio: $13,278.33 × 28% = $3,717.93 (28% is for a 90% LTV)

Bank-end ratio: $13,278.33 × 36% = $4,790.20 − $850 = $3,930.20 (36% is for 90% LTV)

The maximum payment they qualify for would be the lower of the two: $3,717.93 per month. (PITI)

To determine the amount of loan a prospective borrower could afford, the mortgage loan broker would begin with the above calculation to determine the maximum loan amount for which the borrower would qualify. In addition to the principal and interest (P & I), the borrower would also pay taxes and insurance. As a rule of thumb, the loan broker would take 22% of PITI ($3,717.93) for payment of taxes and insurance. Then, the PITI times 78% ($3,717.93 78%) would leave a P & I payment of $2,370. Using a financial calculator, enter the $2,370 for the PMT key and then 30 g n or TERM, and then the interest rate (such as 5.5%) 5.5 g I or INT and enter PV or L/A, which equals $417,408. Press 1.8 (for a loan of 80% LTV) for a sales price of $519,000; or 1.9 (for a loan of 90% LTV) for a sales price of $460,000.

Compensating factors could offset debt or add income or mean different things that might be taken into consideration; for example, a borrower who has accumulated a large savings almost exclusively from earnings and savings is demonstrating to the lender a strong ability to manage his or her finances. If a borrower places a very large cash down payment, such as proceeds from the sale of another property, the risk to the lender is relatively low. Other factors that can compensate for poor credit may be a strong cosigner when the borrower has indicated a history of a credit problem on some item that is now gone. An example is when a borrower has filed bankruptcy because of large medical bills incurred because of a premature baby who now is a normal, healthy three-year-old.

The new April 1, 2009, Fannie Mae Selling Guide instruction book does not use a front-end ratio. Fannie Mae uses 36% as the back-end ratio for manually underwritten loans. The § B3-6-02, Debt-to-Income Ratios for the Fannie Mae Selling Guide do not show different benchmark ratios based upon LTV.

Freddie Mac lists its benchmark qualifying ratios, that became effective 10/1/2009, as 25%–28% and 33%–36%. The Freddie Mac Seller/Servicer Guide §§ 37.15 and 37.16 allow the back-end ratio to go to a maximum of 45% if there are substantial compensating factors.

6.5 DEPARTMENT OF VETERANS ADMINISTRATION (DVA) QUALIFICATION

A basic course in real estate finance would take the mortgage loan broker through many details of the DVA loan. The portion discussed here is to determine the prequalification criteria that must be met before a DVA borrower would be able to obtain a loan from a lender.

When working with a DVA borrower, the mortgage loan broker must obtain two items at the onset: (1) DD form 214, Report of Release or Discharge from Active Duty (see Figure 6.5), and (2) original certificate of eligibility (see Figure 6.6). At the bottom of Figure 6.6, do NOT tear off the perforated portion, but complete and keep it together. Should the borrower not have these documents, Form 180, Request Pertaining to Military Records and Application for DD form 214 (see Chapter 4, Figure 4.3) should be completed by the veteran. In some circumstances, the borrower may need to complete Form 26-1817, Request for Determination of Loan Guaranty Eligibility—Unmarried Surviving Spouses.

To ascertain whether the veteran is eligible for DVA benefits, the mortgage loan broker should first determine the eligibility requirements. Each conflict

FIGURE 6.5 Service period criteria.

ERA	DATES	LENGTH OF SERVICE
World War II	09/16/40–07/25/47	90 days active duty
Peacetime	07/26/47–06/26/50	181 days continuous active duty
Korean Conflict	06/27/50–01/31/55	90 days active duty
Post-Korean	02/01/55–08/04/64	181 days continuous active duty
Vietnam	08/05/64–05/07/75	90 days active duty
Post-Vietnam	05/08/75–09/07/80	181 days continuous active duty
Enlisted	09/08/80–08/01/90	2 years (24 months) active duty
Officers	10/17/81–08/01/90	2 years (24 months) active duty
Persian Gulf	08/02/90–undetermined	24 months or period called to active duty, not less than 90 days
Veteran is still on active duty		181 days continuous service

period has specific dates that the military determined as the beginning date and an ending date for benefits, even though the individual may have served for a longer period. One of the most troubling areas for the mortgage loan broker is the post-Vietnam conflict period from September 1980 to August 1990. It is imperative to ascertain whether the veteran served a full 24-month period of active duty (23 months and 10 days does not qualify). Figure 6.5 shows the DVA table for the military service period. The **DD 214** form will show the time served for the veteran.

The borrower may be the veteran or may be the spouse of an MIA veteran and should obtain the qualifying eligibility form. Should this not be the case, the DVA Form 26-1880 Request for Determination of Eligibility and Available Loan Guaranty Entitlement must be completed (see Figure 6.6) and returned to the lender for processing. Many individuals who have already used the benefits for a DVA loan may be entitled to the remaining loan benefits. The prior DVA loan may have been assumed at the time of past sale and been paid off at a later time, of which the veteran had no knowledge. The only way to determine whether it was paid off is by having a current eligibility statement showing the status of benefits, if any.

Once these two items have been obtained, the loan may proceed. To determine the **maximum loan amount** a DVA borrower may be eligible for, a basic prequalification sheet should be completed. (See Figure 6.7.)

It should be noted that there is no one single figure that is now used as a maximum DVA loan amount. The DVA does not have a statutory maximum loan

FIGURE 6.6 Request for determination of eligibility.

	TO	DEPARTMENT OF VETERANS AFFAIRS ATTN: LOAN GUARANTY DIVISION
Department of Veterans Affairs **REQUEST FOR DETERMINATION OF ELIGIBILITY AND AVAILABLE LOAN GUARANTY ENTITLEMENT**		

NOTE: Please read information on reverse before completing this form. If additional space is required attach separate sheet

1. FIRST - MIDDLE - LAST NAME OF VETERAN	2A ADDRESS OF VETERAN (No., Street or rural route, City or P.O. State and ZIP Code)

2B. VETERAN'S DAYTIME TELEPHONE NO. (Include Area Code)	3. DATE OF BIRTH	

4. MILITARY SERVICE DATA (ATTACH PROOF OF SERVICE – SEE PARAGRAPH F. ON REVERSE)

PERIODS OF ACTIVE SERVICE		NAME (Show your name exactly as it appears on your separation papers or Statement of Service	SERVICE NUMBER	SOCIAL SECURITY NUMBER	BRANCH OF SERVICE
DATE FROM	DATE TO				
A.					
B.					
C.					
D.					

5A. WERE YOU DISCHARGED, RETIRED OR SEPARATED FROM SERVICE BECAUSE OF DISABILITY OR DO YOU NOW HAVE ANY SERVICE-CONNECTED DISABILITIES? ☐ YES ☐ NO (If "Yes," complete Item 5B)	5B. VA CLAIM FILE NUMBER C –	6. IS A CERTIFICATE OF ELIGIBILITY FOR LOAN GUARANTY PURPOSES ENCLOSED? ☐ YES ☐ NO (If "No," complete Items 7A and 7B)

7A. HAVE YOU PREVIOUSLY APPLIED FOR A CERTIFICATE OF ELIGIBILITY FOR VA LOAN PURPOSES? ☐ YES ☐ NO (If "Yes," give location of VA office(s))	7B. HAVE YOU PREVIOUSLY RECEIVED SUCH A CERTIFICATE? ☐ YES ☐ NO (If "Yes," give location of VA office(s) and complete item 7c.)	7C. COMPLETE THE FOLLOWING CERTIFICATION IF YOU HAVE PREVIOUSLY RECEIVED A CERTIFICATE OF ELIGIBILITY WHICH IS NOT ENCLOSED AND THIS IS A REQUEST FOR A DUPLICATE CERTIFICATE. ☐ THE CERTIFICATE OF ELIGIBILITY PREVIOUSLY ISSUED TO ME HAS BEEN LOST OR STOLEN. IF RECOVERED, IT WILL BE RETURNED TO VA.

8. HAVE YOU PREVIOUSLY ACQUIRED PROPERTY WITH THE ASSISTANCE OF A GI LOAN? (If "Yes," complete Items 9 through 18. Please attach a separate sheet if more than one loan is involved. If "No," skip to Items 19 through 22) ☐ YES ☐ NO	9. ADDRESS OF REGIONAL OFFICE(S) WHERE LOAN WAS OBTAINED (City and State)

10. STATE TYPE(S) AND NUMBER OF LOAN(S) (Home, Manufactured Home, Condominium, Direct, Farm, Business, etc.)	11. ADDRESS(ES) OF PROPERTY PREVIOUSLY PURCHASED WITH GUARANTY ENTITLEMENT	12. DATE YOU PURCHASED THE PROPERTY(IES)

13. DO YOU NOW OWN THE PROPERTY DESCRIBED IN ITEM 11? ☐ YES ☐ NO (If "Yes," do not complete Items 14 and 15)	14. DATE(S) THE PROPERTY WAS SOLD	15. IS THERE ANY UNDERSTANDING OR AGREEMENT WRITTEN OR ORAL, BETWEEN YOU AND THE PURCHASERS THAT THEY WILL RECONVEY THE PROPERTY TO YOU? ☐ YES ☐ NO

NOTE: It will speed processing if you can complete Items 16, 17, and 18.

16. NAME AND ADDRESS OF LENDER(S) TO WHOM LOAN PAYMENTS WERE MADE	17. LENDER'S LOAN OR ACCOUNT NUMBER
	18. VA LOAN NUMBER(S)

I CERTIFY THAT the statements herein are true to the best of my knowledge and belief.

19. SIGNATURE OF VETERAN	20. DATE SIGNED

FEDERAL STATUTES PROVIDE SEVERE PENALTIES FOR FRAUD, INTENTIONAL MISREPRESENTATION, CRIMINAL CONNIVANCE OR CONSPIRACY PURPOSED TO INFLUENCE THE ISSUANCE OF ANY GUARANTY OR INSURANCE BY THE SECRETARY.

21. THIS SECTION FOR VA USE ONLY

21A DATE CERTIFICATE ISSUED AND DISCHARGE OR SEPARATION PAPERS AND VA PAMPHLETS GIVEN TO VETERAN OR MAILED TO ADDRESS SHOWN BELOW.	21B. TYPE OF DISCHARGE OR SEPARATION PAPERS RETURNED	21C. INITIALS OF VA AGENT	21D. NAME AND ADDRESS TO WHOM CERTIFICATE MAILED

VA FORM 26-1880, NOV 1993   DO NOT DETACH

IMPORTANT – You must complete Item 22 since the Certificate of Eligibility along with all discharge and separation papers will be mailed to the address shown in Item 22 below. If they are to be sent to you, your current mailing address should be indicated, or if they are to be sent elsewhere, the name and address of such person or firm should be shown in Item 22.

The amount of loan guaranty entitlement available for use is indicated on the enclosed Certificate of Eligibility. This certificate must be returned to VA at the time a loan application or loan report is submitted.

NOTE–PLEASE DELIVER THE ENCLOSED PAMPHLETS AND DISCHARGE OR SEPARATION PAPERS TO THE VETERAN PROMPTLY.

VA FORM NOV 1993 **26-1880**   SUPERSEDES VA FORM 26-1880, OCT 1991, WHICH WILL NOT BE USED.   • U S G.P.O. 1993-381-967

22. PLEASE BE SURE THAT NAME AND ADDRESS ARE ENTERED IN THE SPACE INDICATED TO INSURE PROMPT DELIVERY OF DOCUMENTS

FIGURE 6.7   Maximum DVA loans: Calculating the sales price/loan amount gross income.

Maximum DVA loans: Calculating the sales price/loan amount gross income

Multiply by   Gross Income
X   41%
Total debt service, including housing expense

Subtract   monthly installment/revolving debts
Total debt allowed for PITI

Subtract   figure for monthly taxes and insurance/Homeowners association dues(HOA)
Total debt for principal and interest

Divide by   P & I factor for current allowable interest rate
Maximum loan amount borrower may receive

EXAMPLE: $ 10,851 gross income
X   41%
$ 4,489
−   850 monthly installment debts
$ 3598.91
−   150 taxes and insurance/HOA
$3,448.91   total P & I

Divide by   7.337646 payment factor for 8.0% interest rate for 30 yrs.
$470,029   Loan Amount/Sales Price

THE PREQUAL FOR ACTUAL TAXES AND INSURANCE/HOA IS BASED ON THE ESTIMATED
SALES PRICE: ($470,029).

limit. The DVA has several types of loan programs, such as the loan program that allows up to 100% LTV for a purchase, and up to 90% on a refinance. The actual maximum loan amount is determined by the entitlement of 25% of the VA limit, by individual county. For example, in Chapter 4 the DVA government loan showed the various different maximum loan amounts. In 2009 for Los Angeles County, for example, the DVA allows up to $737,500. Remember that lenders may impose their own maximum loan amounts.

The mortgage loan broker must determine the loan amount that the veteran would qualify for using the DVA required criteria. First, the monthly **gross income** from all sources is included before deducting the **liabilities**. Then the monthly expenses are deducted. The balance is the amount of funds the veteran loan applicant has available for family support. The DVA **qualifying worksheet**

FIGURE 6.8   DVA loan prequalification worksheet.

VA LOAN PRE-QUALIFY WORKSHEET

Prequalification For _____   **Date** _____

☐ Purchase   ☐ Refinance   ☐ Fixed Rate   ☐ ARM

INCOME

	Borrower	Co-Borrower	TOTAL
Base	$ _____	$ _____	$ _____
O / T	_____	_____	_____
Commission	_____	_____	_____
Other	_____	_____	_____
GROSS INCOME	$ _____	$ _____	$ _____ [1]

deduct Fed. Inc. Tax withholding (use 20%)   < _____ >

deduct State Inc. Tax withholding (use 3%)   < _____ >

deduct Soc. Sec. or Retirement withholding (7.65%)   < _____ >

NET TAKE-HOME PAY $ _____ [2]

LIABILITIES

Payable To	Bal. Due	Mo. Pymt.	Payable To	Bal. Due	Mo. Pymt.
_____	$ _____	$ _____	_____	$ _____	$ _____
_____	_____	_____	_____	_____	_____
_____	_____	_____	_____	_____	_____
_____	_____	_____	_____	_____	_____

TOTAL MONTHLY DEBT PAYMENTS   (10+ months to pay) $ _____ [3]

RATIO CALCULATION

Loan Amount $ _____ @ _____ % Interest Rate = $ _____ Monthly P + I

Monthly P + I $ _____

est. Monthly Prop. Taxes   _____   (use CHARTS and FACTORS)

est. Monthly Hazard Ins.   _____   (use CHARTS and FACTORS)

est. HOA   _____

TOTAL MONTHLY P I T I $ _____ [4]

TOTAL MONTHLY DEBT PAYMENTS [3]   _____

TOTAL PITI + MONTHLY PAYMENTS $ _____ ÷ GROSS INCOME [1] $ _____ = [_____ %]

SHELTER EXPENSES

TOTAL MONTHLY P I T I   [4] $ _____

est. Maint. + Utilities   _____

EST. SHELTER EXPENSE $ _____ [5]

RESIDUAL INCOME - BALANCE AVAILABLE FOR FAMILY SUPPORT

NET TAKE-HOME PAY [2] $ _____

deduct MONTHLY PAYMENTS [3]   < _____ >

deduct SHELTER EXPENSE [5]   < _____ >

BALANCE AVAILABLE FOR FAMILY SUPPORT $ _____   vs. GUIDELINE * of $ _____

☐ Sufficient   ☐ Insufficient

for WEST Region - Loan Amounts over $69,000

Family Size	1	2	3	4	5	6 to 7
Amount	$491	$823	$990	$1,117	$1,158	add $80 per family member

is then used to determine the income ratio, which may not exceed 41%, as shown in Figure 6.8. The ratio can have offsetting factors that may be used in calculating the final outcome of the qualification information. Note that for a DVA loan only one ratio is used to determine qualification, not both a front-end ratio and a back-end ratio.

The DVA considers several primary factors to qualify a purchaser. The 41% income ratio and the residual income of a borrower are both the major loan criteria used by the lender, along with the credit history report and property appraisal, to determine the loan amount. The **residual income** is determined by the DVA and gives specific lists of dollar amounts based on the number of family members and the geographic region where the property is located, as shown in Figure 6.9.

Many persons receiving DVA or other income have arranged for automatic deposit of income funds. Likewise, the expense of the monthly loan payment may also be automatically deducted. Some lenders offer a lower interest rate if the borrower has the payment automatically deducted from his or her checking account.

To handle the workload, the DVA has assigned the files for specific veteran cases for particular states to regional offices, as shown in Figure 6.10. When processing a veteran loan, it is important for the mortgage loan broker to submit data to or request data from the appropriate regional office. This avoids the additional delays for internal transfers between the veteran offices.

For example, the mortgage loan broker may wish to verify whether the veteran qualifies for specific loan benefits, which may include whether the veteran is exempt from the DVA funding fee or other benefit-related indebtedness. One way to do this, if the borrower is receiving DVA income benefits, is by completion of the Verification of V.A. Benefits Related Indebtedness (see Figure 6.11).

FIGURE 6.9   Table of residual income by region.

For loan amounts *below* $79,999:				
Family Size	Northeast	Midwest	South	West
1	$390	$382	$382	$425
2	$654	$641	$641	$713
3	$788	$772	$772	$859
4	$888	$868	$868	$967
5	$921	$902	$902	$1,004
Over 5	Add $75 for	each additional	member up to a	family of 7

For loan amounts *above* $80,000:				
Family Size	Northeast	Midwest	South	West
1	$450	$441	$441	$491
2	$755	$738	$738	$823
3	$909	$889	$889	$990
4	$1,025	$1,003	$1,003	$1,117
5	$1,062	$1,039	$1,039	$1,158
Over 5	Add $80 for	each additional	member up to a	family of 7

FIGURE 6.10   Geographic region used for DVA regions.

Northeast	Connecticut Maine Massachusetts	New Hampshire New Jersey New York	Pennsylvania Rhode Island Vermont
Midwest	Illinois Indiana Iowa Kansas	Michigan Minnesota Missouri Nebraska	North Dakota Ohio South Dakota Wisconsin
South	Alabama Arkansas Delaware District of Columbia Florida Georgia	Kentucky Louisiana Maryland Mississippi North Carolina Oklahoma	Puerto Rico South Carolina Tennessee Texas Virginia West Virginia
West	Alaska Arizona California Colorado Wyoming	Hawaii Idaho Montana Nevada	New Mexico Oregon Utah Washington

6.6 FEDERAL HOUSING ADMINISTRATION (FHA) QUALIFICATIONS

The discussion here is limited to the loan broker FHA forms needed for calculating the maximum loan amount and the borrower's loan qualification information. The following information is not an all-inclusive introduction to all FHA financing. Chapter 4 discussed many FHA loan programs and the general guidelines for each loan type.

The first step for the mortgage loan broker is to calculate the maximum loan amount from the gross income, with an example shown in Figure 6.12. When the form is followed step by step, the result will be the maximum loan amount as set by FHA, which the lender will use as the basic loan guideline. For more specific loan guidelines, a loan broker would go to the FHA Web page, type in the state in question, and finally review the loan limits for the specific region. The borrower should furnish the mortgage loan broker with proof of total verifiable income from all sources and the total monthly expenses that would continue six months after the loan would close. The broker then includes the new loan debt into the formula to derive the maximum monthly payment, which is used to calculate the maximum loan amount at the current prevailing interest rate.

The qualifying ratios must also be determined. The front-end ratio according to FHA guidelines must not exceed a maximum of 31%, unless the borrower has compensating factors, such as cash reserves or extensive equity in other assets. The total housing payment is divided by the total gross income. The back-end ratio consists of dividing the total housing payment plus any long-term debts by

FIGURE 6.11 Verification of DVA benefits.

VA	Department of Veterans Affairs	VERIFICATION OF V.A. BENEFIT—RELATED INDEBTEDNESS

PRIVACY ACT INFORMATION: This information is to be used by the agency collecting it in determining whether you qualify for the V.A. loan benefit. This information request is authorized by Title 38, U.S.C., Chapter 37. Responses may be disclosed outside the V.A. only if the disclosure is authorized under the Privacy Act, including the routine uses identified in V.A. system of records, 55VA26, Loan Guaranty Home, Condominium and Manufactured Home Loan Applicant Records, Specially Adapted Housing Applicant Records, and Vendee Loan Applicant Records - V.A., published in the Federal Register.

INSTRUCTIONS TO LENDER

Complete Items 1 through 6. Have veteran complete Items 7 and 8. Forward to the Finance Officer (24) at the local V.A. office to determine whether the veteran has any V.A. benefit-related indebtedness. If a debt is found to exist, the home loan must not be closed until the veteran presents evidence showing that the debt has been cleared or an acceptable repayment plan has been established with V.A. After completion by the Finance Officer, this form will be returned to the lender at the address shown. V.A. Form 26-8937 is a required exhibit to accompany home or manufactured home loans closed on the automatic basis and prior approval submissions.

TO: NAME AND ADDRESS OF LENDER

1. NAME OF VETERAN *(First, middle, last)*

2. CURRENT ADDRESS OF VETERAN

3. DATE OF BIRTH

4. V.A. CLAIM FOLDER NUMBER *(C-File No.)*   5. SERVICE NUMBER   6. SOCIAL SECURITY NUMBER

I HEREBY CERTIFY THAT I ☐ DO ☐ DO NOT have a V.A. benefit-related indebtedness to my knowledge. I authorize V.A. to furnish the information listed below.

7. SIGNATURE OF VETERAN   8. DATE SIGNED

FOR V.A. USE ONLY

☐ The above named veteran does not have a V.A. benefit-related indebtedness.   ☐ The veteran has the following V.A. benefit-related indebtedness.

V.A. BENEFIT — RELATED INDEBTEDNESS *(if any)*

TYPE OF DEBT(S)	AMOUNT OF DEBT(S)
	$
	$
	$

TERM OF REPAYMENT PLAN *(if any)*

☐ Veteran is exempt from funding fee due to receipt of service-connected disability compensation of $ _____ monthly. (Unless checked, the funding fee must be remitted to V.A. with V.A. Form 26-1820, Report and Certification of Loan Disbursement.)

☐ Veteran is not exempt from funding fee due to receipt of nonservice-connected pension of $ _____ monthly. **LOAN APPLICATION WILL REQUIRE PRIOR APPROVAL PROCESSING BY V.A.**

☐ Veteran has been rated incompetent by V.A. **LOAN APPLICATION WILL REQUIRE PRIOR APPROVAL PROCESSING BY V.A.**

☐ Insufficient information. V.A. cannot identify the veteran with the information given. Please furnish more complete information, or a copy of a DD Form 214 or discharge papers. If on active duty, furnish a statement of service written on official government letterhead, signed by the adjutant, personnel officer, or commanding officer. The statement should include name, birth date, service number, entry date and time lost.

SIGNATURE OF AUTHORIZED AGENT   DATE SIGNED

RESPONDENT BURDEN: Public reporting burden for this collection of information is estimated to average 5 minutes per response, including the time for reviewing instructions, searching existing data sources, gathering and maintaining the data needed, and completing and reviewing the collection of information. Send comments regarding this burden estimate or any other aspect of this collection of information, including suggestions for reducing this burden, to the V.A. Clearance Officer (723), 810 Vermont Ave., NW, Washington, DC 20420; and to the Office of Management and Budget, Paperwork Reduction Project (2900-0406), Washington, DC 20503. Do NOT send requests for benefits to these addresses.

---

the total gross income, which should not exceed 43%. The lenders rarely vary from the FHA ratio guidelines.

Once the maximum loan amount has been derived, the cash down payment is added to calculate the total maximum sales price. The amount of cash down payment is in excess of the cash needed for any closing costs that must be paid prior to the close of escrow. The estimated closing costs may be a guide to the amount of cash the borrower will need.

It is then a good idea to complete a worksheet showing FHA qualifying information. The gross income from all sources is shown, along with total debts and long-term obligations. The monthly payment includes principal, interest,

FIGURE 6.12   Maximum FHA loan amount.

	$ _____ Gross income
Multiply by	× _____ 43% Back-end ratio
	Total debt service including housing expense
Subtract	monthly installment/revolving debts
	Total income allowed for PITI
Subtract	figure for monthly taxes and insurance/HOA
	Total income for principal and interest
Divide by	P & I factor for interest rate (varies with point structure—buydown)
	Maximum loan amount borrower may obtain
ADD	CASH DOWN PAYMENT
Total Price	Total Sales Price

Example $ **10,851** gross income
              ×   43%
              $ **4,666** total available for debt service
              −   850 monthly installment debts
              $ **3,816**
              −   150 taxes and insurance/HOA
              $ **3,666** total P & I (total)
Divide by   7.337646 payment factor for 8.0% interest rate for 30 yrs.
              $469,905 (round down to $**469,900**)

FINE TUNE YOUR PREQUAL FOR ACTUAL TAXES AND INSURANCE/HOA AFTER THE SALES PRICE HAS BEEN ESTABLISHED.

REMEMBER: FHA also has a front-end ratio of 31%. After establishing your estimated loan amount, check your front-end ratio for compliance with FHA guidelines.

Example: Using figures from above

              $ **3,666** Total allowable housing expense = **33.78%** - Front-end ratio
Divide by $ **10,851** Gross Income

This **33.78**% exceeds our 31% guideline. With "compensating factors," this may still be acceptable to FHA.

---

taxes, insurance, homeowners association dues, and mortgage insurance that may be required for FHA loans. The **housing expense** total is divided by the total gross income to determine the front-end ratio, and the fixed payment is divided by the total gross income to arrive at the back-end ratio, which is shown in Figure 6.13.

FIGURE 6.13 FHA qualifying worksheet.

MONTHLY GROSS INCOME

Borrower's Base Income $ _____

Other $ _____

Coborrower's Income $ _____

Other $ _____

       TOTAL MONTHLY INCOME (Gross) $ _____ (A)

DEBTS AND OBLIGATIONS

Installment Debt (10 mo. or longer–Car, Student Loans, Etc.) $ _____

Revolving Debt (Credit Cards) $ _____

       TOTAL MONTHLY OBLIGATIONS $ _____ (B)

MONTHLY PAYMENTS

Prin. and Int. $ _____

    Loan Amount $_____ + MIP_____ $ _____

Homeowners Assoc. (Monthly Dues) $ _____

    Not Covered_____ (i.e., fire, flood, etc.)

Hazard Insurance (Fire Only) $ _____

Property Taxes @ _____% of the purchase price $ _____

      TOTAL HOUSING EXPENSES $ _____ (C)

TOTAL HOUSING EXPENSE (C) $_____ ÷ Total Gross Income (A) $_____ = _____%

TOTAL FIXED PAYMENTS (B) + (C) $_____ ÷ Total Gross Income (A) $_____ = _____%

Ratio Guidelines are 31%/43%. These ratios may be exceeded by up to 2% if the property is "Energy Efficient" (built after 1976).

Cash-Out Refinance: No compensating factors allowed, ratios as stated, 29%/41%, CANNOT BE EXCEEDED.

6.7 CONVENTIONAL QUALIFICATIONS

The mortgage loan broker should assume that most lenders will use FNMA or FHLMC guidelines as the industry standard unless given different information when asking about the original arrangement.

Prequalification of the borrower must include not only the P & I but also the taxes and insurance, even though the borrower may choose to make his or her own payments for these items rather than have the lender set up an impound account with the loan servicing. The down payment requirement for conventional loans usually exceeds the amount required for either FHA or DVA loans. The benefits for conventional financing are that many more lenders are available to fund these loans, and the loan amount is greater, which allows the borrower a wider range of properties to purchase. The loan programs for DVA and FHA have a maximum loan amount whereas conventional jumbo loans may be double that of the maximum government loans.

There are reserve requirements for all conventional loans. Just as the banks have a *reserve requirement* under their bank regulations that sets the minimum reserves each bank must hold to customer deposits and notes, new loan criteria are now requiring that borrowers also have a reserve. For the banking system, the reserve ratio is sometimes used as a tool in the monetary policy, influencing the country's economy, borrowing, and interest rates. For individual borrowers, the reserve is used as an indicator of financial stability for the loan that the lender will be placing on the property.

The amount of the reserve often depends upon the price of the property. One guideline used in Fall 2009 is that if the loan amount is $417,000 or less, the borrower must have two to three months of the principal, interest, taxes, and insurance held as a cash reserve that is documented before the close of escrow. If the loan amount is between $417,000 and $729,750, the lender requires proof of three to six months reserve requirements at the close of escrow. If the loan amount is over $1 million, the borrower must show proof of reserve requirements for 12 months.

Loan amount is determined in much the same manner that has been illustrated. Note that according to the same income and debt for a DVA loan, the maximum sales price was $470,029, rounded down to $470,000. For an FHA loan, the maximum loan amount was $469,900. For conventional financing, the maximum loan amount is only $396,039, rounded down to $396,000 after placing a 10% cash down payment, for a total sales price of $440,044, rounded to $440,000. See Figure 6.14 for an example of how to calculate the FNMA front-end ratio prior to the 2009 FNMA changes.) The initial step remains the same in that the mortgage loan broker must obtain the borrower's total gross income from all sources to begin the qualifying process. The total housing expenses must be determined, which includes principal, interest, taxes, insurance, association dues, and mortgage insurance, if any. In addition to the gross income and gross expense calculation that has been computed for DVA, FHA, and conventional loan, the mortgage loan broker must additionally obtain the borrower's assets and liabilities, which consist of long-term debt that the borrower would have 10 months after the loan begins. The front-end ratio is calculated by dividing the housing expense by the gross income. The back-end ratio is determined by dividing the total of both the housing expense and liabilities by the gross income, which is shown in Figure 6.15, as an example of how a FNMA back-end ratio is calculated prior to the 2009 FNMA and Freddie Mac changes.

The ratios remain the same for all loan types for both the front-end and back-end calculations. There are several differences, however, including the equity position of the owner for that property and for the owner's other property, the LTV, and the interest rate charged for the loan. For example, for a conventional loan on an owner-occupied, single-family residence in which the borrower has a 20% equity position, the lender is funding only 80% of value loan, which would entitle the borrower to favorable loan terms with a good interest rate in the prevailing market. If the loan were for the same borrower's fourplex, the lender would use only 75% of the gross scheduled income to add to the borrower's income and would not use 100% of the rental income toward the loan indebtedness (debt service). The lender would typically require 25% to 50% equity position by the borrower, and the interest rate would likely be 0.5% to 1% higher than for

FIGURE 6.14   Maximum conventional loan amount.

CALCULATING THE SALES PRICE/LOAN FROM GROSS INCOME

Multiply by	Gross Income
	×_____36% (33, 36, 38% back-end ratios based on the LTV)
	Total debt service including housing expense
Subtract	monthly installment/revolving debts
	Total allowed for PITI
Subtract	figure for monthly taxes and insurance/HOA
	Total allowed for PI
Divide by	P & I factor for interest rate (varies with points charged)
	Maximum loan amount borrower may obtain
Divide by	loan to value percentage (0.95, 0.90, 0.80)
	Sales price borrower may purchase

Example	$ **10,851** Gross Income
	×_____36%
	$ **3,906** Total available for debt service
	−_____850 monthly installment/revolving debts
	$ **3,056**
	−_____150 taxes and insurance/HOA
	$ **2,906** Total available for P & I
Divide by	7.337646 payment factor for 8.0% interest rate for 30 yrs.
	$ 396,039 Loan amount the borrower may obtain
Divide by	_____.90 Borrower has a 10% down payment
	$ 440,044 Sales price the borrower may purchase

PREQUALIFICATION SHOULD BE DETERMINED FOR ACTUAL TAXES, INSURANCE, AND HOA. ALSO BE SURE THAT THE BORROWER HAS THE AMOUNT NECESSARY FOR THE DOWN PAYMENT AVAILABLE.

REMEMBER: Conventional loans qualify with a front-end ratio too. Be sure to take this into account during your final calculations.

Example: Using figures from above

	$ **2,906** Total allowable housing expense
Divide by	$ **10,851** Gross Income
	26.78% front-end ratio

This **26.78%** is within the guideline for a FNMA 90% LTV.

FIGURE 6.15   Prequalify worksheet: conventional/FHA loan.

☐ Conventional   ☐ FHA

Prequalification for _____ **Date** _____

☐ Purchase   ☐ Refinance   ☐ Fixed Rate   ☐ ARM

INCOME	BORROWER	COBORROWER	TOTAL
BASE	$_____	$_____	$_____
O/T	$_____	$_____	$_____
COMMISSIONS	$_____	$_____	$_____
OTHER	$_____	$_____	$_____
TOTAL INCOME	$_____ +	$_____	= $_____ [1]
			GROSS INCOME

DEBTS

Payable To	Bal. Due	Mo. Pymt	Payable To	Bal. Due	Mo. Pymt.
_____	$_____	$_____	_____	$_____	$_____
_____	$_____	$_____	_____	$_____	$_____
_____	$_____	$_____	_____	$_____	$_____

TOTAL DEBTS (10+ months to pay) $_____   =$_____ [2]

RATIO CALCULATIONS

Loan Amount $_____ @ _____% Interest Rate = $_____   Monthly P & I

Monthly P & I	$_____		
Add Other Financing	_____		
Add Est. Monthly Taxes	_____	(use CHARTS and FACTORS Chart 4 or Chart 5)	
Add Est. Monthly Ins.	_____	(use CHARTS and FACTORS Chart 5)	
Add Est. PMI or MMI	_____	(use CHARTS and FACTORS Chart 2 and Chart 5)	
Add Est. HOA	_____		**Front-End Ratio**
TOTAL MONTHLY PITI	$_____	**TOTAL INCOME [1]** $_____ =	⬜ %
Add TOTAL DEBTS Mo. Pymt. [2]	_____		
			Back-End Ratio
TOTAL PITI + DEBT	$_____	**TOTAL INCOME [1]** $_____ =	⬜ %

RATIOS SHOULD NOT EXCEED:

Conventional 95% LTV: 26/33 FHA: 31%43%   First-Time Home Buyer 45/45%
                90% LTV: 28/36   ADJUSTABLE–28/36
                80% LTV: 32/38   **Subprime may go up to a 55% back-end ratio**

---

owner-occupied. In addition, lenders are now calculating income property in which the rental income must support the **debt service**; that is, the net rent must cover the amount of P & I payment. Some lenders require that the net rents also cover the taxes and insurance.

Another example is when an owner of a single-family home decides to keep that property and then purchase another single-family home. The lender will require the owner to have at least a 30 percent equity position in the home they are leaving, if they are going to remain on title as the owner and not sell that property. The lender will also only use 75 percent of the projected gross scheduled rental income to add to the borrower's income for qualifying ratios. The owner will also be required to furnish the lender a copy of the rental agreement on the property that shows the tenant, the amount of rent, the property address, and other information. This is often the most difficult part of the transaction for trying to close the loan. The owner must furnish a rental agreement on the property they are occupying and that they own to the lender. However, this rental agreement is executed with a tenant before the owner moves out of the property because the new property that the owner will be moving into has not yet closed escrow and the owner most likely does not have possession of the new property yet. The specific requirements will differ among lenders. The mortgage loan broker must check the underwriting requirements well in advance with the lender to make sure the process is correctly followed.

6.8 OTHER QUALIFICATIONS

The mortgage loan broker must comply with many other lender and governmental requirements. The real estate disclosures were discussed in Chapter 5, and the appraisal report disclosure information will be discussed in Chapter 9. In addition, the credit report information is discussed in Chapter 7, which includes the Fair Lending Notice, which must be given to the borrower when the loan application is taken.

In addition to qualifying for DVA, FHA, or standard conventional loans, an entire market exists for the area of subprime loans, which have different criteria. These loans that do not fit into the standard FNMA/FHLMC guidelines are called subprime loans. This form of the business could equate to 40% of the mortgage broker's total business and therefore should not be overlooked as a feasible source of business.

The borrower or the property could cause the loan to fall into this category because

1. the structure does not conform to the zoning of the land (for example, a single-family residence is located on land that is zoned C-1, commercial, I-1, or industrial).
2. the borrower's mortgage payment record is slow and there have been three to four late payments in the last 12 months.
3. the property is being placed into foreclosure.
4. the borrower's length of time on the job does not meet FNMA/FHLMC guidelines.

Another type of chart that can be used in qualifying a borrower is shown in Figure 6.16.

FIGURE 6.16   Charts and factors.

CHARTS and FACTORS

CHART 1
Estimated TOTAL CASH TO CLOSE
(for Purchases)

Down Payment		$ _____
Pre-Paid Costs	(see below)	+ _____
Non-Recurring Costs	(see below)	+ _____
TOTAL CASH REQ'D		$ _____

Estimated PRE-PAID COSTS
(called "Pre-Paids")

Interest	Loan Am't X Int.Rate − 360 X 15 days	= $ _____
Hazard Insur.	Loan Am't X .0035 ÷ 12 X 14 mos	= $ _____
Prop Taxes	S P − $7000 X .0125 ÷ X No.Mos.in CHART 4 [1]	= $ _____
UFMIP (if FHA)	Loan Am't X 1 5%	= $ _____
Funding Fee (if VA)	Loan Am't X Fee shown in CHART 5	= $ _____
	TOTAL ESTIMATED PRE-PAIDS	$ _____

[1] if Mello-Roos. use 02

Estimated NON-RECURRING COSTS

Loan Costs.	Loan Am't X 1% [1]	= $ _____	−	$1750 [2]	= $ _____
Escrow	S.P − 1000 X $2	= $ _____	+	$450 [3]	= $ _____
Title	use Chart 8 on reverse	= $ _____	+	$225 [4]	= $ _____
Misc.	cushion for extra days of interest, title endorsements, etc				$ 250
	TOTAL ESTIMATED NON-RECURRING COSTS				$ _____

[1] use exact Loan Orig. Fee, if known
[2] includes Appraisal Proc Fee, "Junk" Fees, Cr Rept Flood Cert., Tax Srvc, Wire Transfer
[3] includes Loan Tie-In, Messenger, Notary
[4] includes Sub-Escrow Recording

CHART 2
PMI Factors

LTV	Annual Factor	Monthly Factor
80.1 - 90%	.0067	.00056
90.1 - 95%	.0078	.00065
95.1 - 100%	.0122	.00102

CHART 3
CLOSING COSTS Buyer Can Pay

"Allowable"	Con	FHA	VA
Credit Report	√	√	√
Appraisal	√	√	√
Escrow Fee	√	√	NO
Title Insur.	√	√	√
Recording	√	√	√
Notary	√	√	√
Loan Fee	√	√	√
"Non-Allowable"			
Sub-Escrow Fee	√	NO	NO
Loan Tie-In Fee	√	NO	NO
Processing Fee	√	NO	NO
Underwriting Fee	√	NO	NO
Doc Prep Fee	√	NO	NO

CHART 4
No.Months Tax Impounds

Closing Month	1st Pymt Month	# mo
Jan	Mar	6
Feb	Apr	2
Mar	May	2
Apr	Jun	3
May	Jul	4
Jun	Aug	5
Jul	Sep	6
Aug	Oct	7
Sep	Nov	8
Oct	Dec	3
Nov	Jan	4
Dec	Feb	5

CHART 5
FHA Mutual Mortgage Insurance (MMI)
paid in 2 parts and based on LOAN AMOUNT
1) Up Front Premium (UFMIP) =   Loan Amount x 1 5%
   [may be PAID IN CASH at closing or ADDED to the LOAN]
2) Monthly Premium =   Loan Amount X .005 ÷ 12

VA Funding Fee

Based on Ln Amt	0% Dn	5% Dn	10%+ Dn
1st Time User	2%	1.5%	1 25%
2nd Time User	3%	1.5%	1.25%

Monthly Property Tax Estimate

w/Mello-Roos	(Sales Price - $7,000) X .02 ÷ 12
no Mello-Roos:	(Sales Price - $7,000) X .0125 ÷ 12

Monthly Hazard Insurance Estimate
Loan Amount X .0035 ÷ 12

Escrow Fee Estimate (Purchases per Side)
$200 Base PLUS $2 per Thousand of Sale Price

CHART 6
Qualifying Ratios
GUIDELINES ONLY!

Conventional	Front	Back
to 80 0% LTV	32%	38%
80.1 - 90.0% LTV	28%	36%
90.1% +	26%	33%
FHA		
All LTVs	29%	41%
VA		
All LTVs	n/a	41%

CHART 7
Compensating Factors - for ratios exceeding Guidelines

- Excellent credit history	- Minimal increase in shelter expense
- Conservative use of credit	- Military benefits
- Minimal consumer debt	- Satisfactory prior homeownership
- Long-term employment	- High residual income
- Significant liquid assets	- Low debt-to-income ratio
- Sizable down payment	- Tax credits for child care
- Amount of equity	- Tax benefits of home ownership

over for CHART 8 - Title Insurance Rates

FIGURE 6.16 Charts and factors.

	**CHART 8**
	*ALTA Lender's Policy*
	**LOAN AMOUNT**	**PURCH**	**REFI**		**LOAN AMOUNT**	**PURCH**	**REFI**		**LOAN AMOUNT**	**PURCH**	**REFI**		**LOAN AMOUNT**	**PURCH**	**REFI**
100,000 -	105,000	315	446	325,000 -	330,000	490	851	550,000 -	555,000	630	1,178	775,000 -	780,000	765	1,493
105,000 -	110,000	320	455	330,000 -	335,000	493	859	555,000 -	560,000	633	1,185	780,000 -	785,000	768	1,500
110,000 -	115,000	324	464	335,000 -	340,000	496	866	560,000 -	565,000	636	1,192	785,000 -	790,000	771	1,507
115,000 -	120,000	328	473	340,000 -	345,000	500	873	565,000 -	570,000	639	1,199	790,000 -	795,000	774	1,514
120,000 -	125,000	332	483	345,000 -	350,000	503	880	570,000 -	575,000	642	1,206	795,000 -	800,000	777	1,521
125,000 -	130,000	336	492	350,000 -	355,000	506	888	575,000 -	580,000	645	1,213	800,000 -	805,000	780	1,528
130,000 -	135,000	340	501	355,000 -	360,000	509	895	580,000 -	585,000	648	1,220	805,000 -	810,000	783	1,535
135,000 -	140,000	344	510	360,000 -	365,000	512	903	585,000 -	590,000	651	1,227	810,000 -	815,000	786	1,542
140,000 -	145,000	348	520	365,000 -	370,000	515	910	590,000 -	595,000	654	1,234	815,000 -	820,000	789	1,549
145,000 -	150,000	352	529	370,000 -	375,000	518	917	595,000 -	600,000	657	1,241	820,000 -	825,000	792	1,556
150,000 -	155,000	356	538	375,000 -	380,000	521	924	600,000 -	605,000	660	1,248	825,000 -	830,000	795	1,563
155,000 -	160,000	360	547	380,000 -	385,000	525	932	605,000 -	610,000	663	1,255	830,000 -	835,000	798	1,570
160,000 -	165,000	364	557	385,000 -	390,000	528	939	610,000 -	615,000	666	1,262	835,000 -	840,000	801	1,577
165,000 -	170,000	368	566	390,000 -	395,000	531	947	615,000 -	620,000	669	1,269	840,000 -	845,000	804	1,584
170,000 -	175,000	372	575	395,000 -	400,000	534	954	620,000 -	625,000	672	1,276	845,000 -	850,000	807	1,591
175,000 -	180,000	376	584	400,000 -	405,000	537	962	625,000 -	630,000	675	1,283	850,000 -	855,000	810	1,598
180,000 -	185,000	380	594	405,000 -	410,000	540	969	630,000 -	635,000	678	1,290	855,000 -	860,000	813	1,605
185,000 -	190,000	384	603	410,000 -	415,000	544	976	635,000 -	640,000	681	1,297	860,000 -	865,000	816	1,612
190,000 -	195,000	388	612	415,000 -	420,000	547	983	640,000 -	645,000	684	1,304	865,000 -	870,000	819	1,619
195,000 -	200,000	392	621	420,000 -	425,000	550	991	645,000 -	650,000	687	1,311	870,000 -	875,000	822	1,626
200,000 -	205,000	396	631	425,000 -	430,000	553	998	650,000 -	655,000	690	1,318	875,000 -	880,000	825	1,633
205,000 -	210,000	400	640	430,000 -	435,000	556	1,006	655,000 -	660,000	693	1,325	880,000 -	885,000	828	1,640
210,000 -	215,000	404	649	435,000 -	440,000	559	1,013	660,000 -	665,000	696	1,332	885,000 -	890,000	831	1,647
215,000 -	220,000	407	658	440,000 -	445,000	563	1,020	665,000 -	670,000	699	1,339	890,000 -	895,000	834	1,654
220,000 -	225,000	412	668	445,000 -	450,000	566	1,027	670,000 -	675,000	702	1,346	895,000 -	900,000	837	1,661
225,000 -	230,000	416	677	450,000 -	455,000	569	1,035	675,000 -	680,000	705	1,353	900,000 -	905,000	840	1,668
230,000 -	235,000	419	686	455,000 -	460,000	572	1,042	680,000 -	685,000	708	1,360	905,000 -	910,000	843	1,675
235,000 -	240,000	423	696	460,000 -	465,000	575	1,050	685,000 -	690,000	711	1,367	910,000 -	915,000	846	1,682
240,000 -	245,000	428	705	465,000 -	470,000	578	1,057	690,000 -	695,000	714	1,374	915,000 -	920,000	849	1,689
245,000 -	250,000	431	714	470,000 -	475,000	581	1,064	695,000 -	700,000	717	1,381	920,000 -	925,000	852	1,696
250,000 -	255,000	435	724	475,000 -	480,000	584	1,071	700,000 -	705,000	720	1,388	925,000 -	930,000	855	1,703
255,000 -	260,000	439	733	480,000 -	485,000	588	1,079	705,000 -	710,000	723	1,395	930,000 -	935,000	858	1,710
260,000 -	265,000	443	742	485,000 -	490,000	591	1,086	710,000 -	715,000	726	1,402	935,000 -	940,000	861	1,717
265,000 -	270,000	447	752	490,000 -	495,000	594	1,094	715,000 -	720,000	729	1,409	940,000 -	945,000	864	1,724
270,000 -	275,000	451	761	495,000 -	500,000	597	1,101	720,000 -	725,000	732	1,416	945,000 -	950,000	867	1,731
275,000 -	280,000	455	770	500,000 -	505,000	600	1,108	725,000 -	730,000	735	1,423	950,000 -	955,000	870	1,738
280,000 -	285,000	459	780	505,000 -	510,000	603	1,115	730,000 -	735,000	738	1,430	955,000 -	960,000	873	1,745
285,000 -	290,000	463	789	510,000 -	515,000	606	1,122	735,000 -	740,000	741	1,437	960,000 -	965,000	876	1,752
290,000 -	295,000	467	798	515,000 -	520,000	609	1,129	740,000 -	745,000	744	1,444	965,000 -	970,000	879	1,759
295,000 -	300,000	471	807	520,000 -	525,000	612	1,136	745,000 -	750,000	747	1,451	970,000 -	975,000	882	1,766
300,000 -	305,000	474	815	525,000 -	530,000	615	1,143	750,000 -	755,000	750	1,458	975,000 -	980,000	885	1,773
305,000 -	310,000	477	822	530,000 -	535,000	618	1,150	755,000 -	760,000	753	1,465	980,000 -	985,000	888	1,780
310,000 -	315,000	481	829	535,000 -	540,000	621	1,157	760,000 -	765,000	756	1,472	985,000 -	990,000	891	1,787
315,000 -	320,000	484	836	540,000 -	545,000	624	1,164	765,000 -	770,000	759	1,479	990,000 -	995,000	894	1,794
320,000 -	325,000	487	844	545,000 -	550,000	627	1,171	770,000 -	775,000	762	1,486	995,000 -	1,000,000	897	1,801

SUMMARY

The more the mortgage loan broker knows at the beginning of the loan term relationship, the easier it will be to get to the end. Always remember that the completeness of the mortgage application determines the speed of the closing of the loan. Therefore, **prequalifying** elements are essential for a smooth loan process. It may take 20 minutes or 2 hours to prequalify the client, but it is worth every minute if that time helps consummate the loan. Make it easier by using the conventional, FHA, and DVA prequalifying forms as a guideline to ask the right questions of your borrower. Remember that the prequalification includes some disclosure statements. The subprime market is a feasible source of business for the mortgage broker.

REVIEWING YOUR UNDERSTANDING

1. The DVA uses what primary factor to qualify a purchaser:
   A. 41% income ratio
   B. Residual income of the borrower
   C. Maximum loan amount
   D. Both A and B

2. FHA's qualifying front-end ratio is _____ and the back-end ratio is_____.
   A. 31% , 43%
   B. 28% , 36%
   C. 26% , 33%
   D. 00% , 41%

3. The DVA qualifying worksheet uses only one income ratio to determine qualification. This ratio is:
   A. 28%
   B. 29%
   C. 36%
   D. 41%

4. The first step for the mortgage broker to qualify a borrower under FHA is:
   A. To calculate qualifying ratios
   B. To calculate the maximum loan amount from the gross income
   C. To calculate monthly payment
   D. None of the above

5. The property profile can be obtained from the:
   A. Title company
   B. Department of Real Estate
   C. Escrow company
   D. Loan originator

6. Under a DVA loan, initially the loan broker must obtain:
   A. DD214
   B. Original Certificate of Eligibility
   C. Form 1003
   D. A and B

7. Loans that do not fit into the standard FNMA/FHLMC guidelines are called:
   A. Ugly loans
   B. Emergency loans
   C. Non-conforming
   D. Personal loans

8. The DD214 is:
   A. Time served for the veteran
   B. Maximum loan amount
   C. Amount of loan and sales price
   D. None of the above

9. What is included in the housing expenses is:
   A. P & I
   B. PITI and mortgage Insurance
   C. PITI, HOA, and mortgage insurance, if any
   D. PITI, HOA, debts, and mortgage insurance, if any

10. For an FHA loan, the front-end ratio is 31% and the borrower's total housing expense is $4,500; therefore the monthly gross income of the borrower is:
    A. $10,714
    B. $12,500
    C. $14,516
    D. $17,428

ANSWERS TO REVIEWING YOUR UNDERSTANDING

1. D (p. 215)
2. A (pp. 216–217)
3. D (p. 241)
4. B (p. 216)
5. A (p. 198)
6. D (p. 210)
7. C (p. 223)
8. A (p. 211)
9. C (pp. 207–208)
10. C (p. 219)

Chapter

7

IMPORTANT TERMS

Credit authorization

Credit rating scores

Credit report

Equal Credit
   Opportunity Act
   (ECOA)

Fair Credit Reporting
   Act (FCRA)

Fair Lending Notice

Federal Deposit
   Insurance
   Corporation (FDIC)

FICO credit scoring

Nontraditional
   mortgage credit
   report

Processing: Credit and Disclosures

PREVIEW

The United States is predominantly a credit society, not a debit society; we consumers spend now and pay later. A credit society establishes individual records for the credit history of each borrower. A prospective lender may access the records to determine whether the borrower is creditworthy according to the lending policies established by the individual lender. Lenders now rely on more than just being able to read and interpret the credit report. Several rating score methods were devised to determine the creditworthiness of the borrower, with the FICO score being the most prevalent.

Not everyone has access to the credit records. Laws protect consumers from unauthorized individuals or entities accessing individual private records. Strict adherence to the credit laws is mandatory for the mortgage broker. In addition, fair lending practices laws have been established, with penalties for those who discriminate against borrowers.

CHAPTER OBJECTIVES

At the end of this chapter, the student learning outcomes include:

1. Describe credit bureau services.
2. Discuss how to establish credit.
3. Read a credit report and interpret the ratings.
4. Explain the facts about the FICO score and the rating.
5. Indicate the components of the Equal Credit Opportunity Act (ECOA).
6. Outline the anti-discrimination credit applicant provisions.

7.1 CREDIT

State and federal laws require specific disclosures to be made by the mortgage loan broker to a consumer seeking mortgage credit for a loan secured against real property. Although disclosures were discussed in Chapter 5, the credit laws are more universal and not generally specific to real property transactions. The general principles for obtaining credit are part of the body of knowledge from the study of real estate principles, and they are the "Four C's of Credit":

1. **CHARACTER**—Want or Intend to repay [Credit History]
2. **CAPACITY**—Ability to repay [Earning Power]
3. **CAPITAL**—Financial Strength to repay [Collateral]
4. **CONDITIONS**—Economic Environment [Economic Conditions]

A **credit report** demonstrates how well a borrower has handled credit and the pattern of how the borrower uses credit. A credit report is a listing of the accounts receivable as reported by various firms that have extended credit to a borrower. It shows when a bill was paid in relation to when the due date for the payment was expected. It lists debts, payment history, banks, credit card companies, and department stores. It shows the history of tax liens or a bankruptcy. A credit score is a computer-generated number that provides a snapshot of how likely a consumer is to repay a debt.

The mortgage industry uses a credit scoring method, called the FICO score, described in detail later in this chapter. This method is named after the company that first developed the credit scoring system, Fair, Isaac Company, Inc., in San Rafael, California. Another firm, Credit Reports, Inc. (CRI), of Tustin, California, began offering scoring in October 1993. Appendix B shows a sample credit report, along with an explanation for each area represented.

Personal credit rights come under the **Fair Credit Reporting Act** of 1971 (FCRA) and later amendments, such as the Fair and Accurate Credit Transaction Act 2003 update. The act guarantees consumer rights relating to credit information, including a prospective borrower's right to information about his or her own credit. The consumer should contact a credit report agency for further information regarding the credit report items. The act addresses many areas of consumer data reporting, such as

1. Federal Trade Commission (FTC) issues.
2. the rule on a consumer obtaining a free annual credit report.
3. alerts for initial, extended, and active duty.
4. mailing and street address mismatch indicators.
5. blocked data.
6. notification of modified and deleted data to data furnishers.
7. another scoring factor for mortgage lenders.

A consumer who feels his or her credit report contains a mistake and wishes to dispute or correct the mistake may contact the national credit repository that developed the report. Under the FCRA, the repository must complete an investigation of the disputed item within 30 days and provide a written notice of the results of the investigation within five days of completion, including a copy of the credit report, if it has changed according to the data found from the dispute. For copies and updates, go to the FCRA Web site at http://www.ftc.gov/os/statutes/fcrajump.shtm. The FTC is responsible for enforcing FCRA. Credit unions often do not report information to the credit bureaus. To verify that their records are correct, access the National Credit Union Administration through their Web site at http://www.ncua.gov.

No law requires reporting to a credit bureau. Credit laws frequently change. For example, a recently proposed law states that if a person writes a "bad" check (dishonored for payment by the institution), such notice may be placed with a credit bureau for up to five years.

The **Fair Lending Notice** is a separate form that must be kept in the broker's file (see Figure 7.1). This form notifies the consumer of various credit-related laws and the rights of the individual under each of these laws.

Three credit bureaus are primarily used, although several smaller agencies exist. To run a credit report, it is necessary to have the written authorization of each individual. Each lender usually has its own form. An example of a typical credit authorization is shown in Figure 7.2.

The mortgage broker is required to run a credit check through at least two credit bureaus to comply with requirements for later selling the loan on the secondary money market. Most lenders want three credit reports from the three primary agencies and will take the middle FICO score. As indicated above and as a quality control check, when the mortgage broker has forwarded the completed loan package to the actual lender, that lender will run a separate credit check. When lenders run a credit check on a borrower, they have access to at least 25 scoring models. Thus, the lender's credit score is often different from the score obtained by mortgage broker. The lender will use a bureau that the mortgage broker did not use to validate the authenticity of the credit bureau records for the prospective borrower.

Credit reports show payment history records for lenders who have reported the information to a credit-reporting bureau. No law requires a private lender to report credit. Typically, a seller who carries back financing rarely reports the loan payment history. Similarly, when a consumer obtains financing from a jewelry store, furniture store, department store, or some automobile dealers, no record of the amount borrowed, current unpaid loan amount, or the payment history is available. Landlords typically do not report slow payment of rents but a court-awarded judgment for an unlawful detainer eviction shows as a public record against the borrower. It is possible for a prospective borrower to have a long history of credit with organizations that do not show up on a typical credit report. The mortgage broker often must document these other sources in a different manner.

The borrower must give written authorization to spend funds on behalf of and for the benefit of the borrower obtaining the loan. Some items, such as the appraisal report and the credit check fee, are paid at the close of escrow from the funds of the borrower or the seller, depending on the transaction negotiations. Some lenders do not charge any fee for running the prospective borrower's credit. All fees are negotiable, except as prohibited by a specific loan program. The appraisal fee may be paid at service by either the buyer or seller and not paid through escrow. In this case, the amount paid would still appear

FIGURE 7.1   Fair Lending Notice.

RIGHT OF PRIVACY ACT: This is a notice to you as required by the Right to Financial Privacy Act of 1976 that the Department of Housing and Urban Development has a right to access to financial records held by a financial institution in connection with the consideration of assistance to you. Financial records will be made available to the Department of Housing and Urban Development without further notice or authorization, but will not be disclosed or released to another government agency or department without your consent except as required or permitted by law.

FAIR CREDIT REPORTING ACT: YOUR COMPANY NAME, as a part of the processing of your real estate loan, may request a consumer report bearing on your creditworthiness, standing, and capacity. This notice is given pursuant to the Fair Credit Reporting Act of 1971, Section 601 to Section 622, inclusive. You are entitled to such information within 60 days of written demand therefore made to the credit reporting agency pursuant to Section 606(b) of the Fair Credit Reporting Act.

EQUAL CREDIT OPPORTUNITY ACT: The Federal Equal Opportunity Act, 15 U.S.C. 1961cc., prohibits discrimination against credit applicants on the basis of sex and marital status. Beginning March 23, 1977, the act extends this protection to race, color, religion, national origin, age (provided the applicant has the capacity to contract), whether all or part of the applicant's income is derived from any public assistance program, or if the applicant has in good faith exercised any right under the Consumer Credit Protection Act. The federal agency which administers compliance with this law concerning this lender is the Federal Trade Commission, 450 Golden Gate Ave., San Francisco, CA 94102.

STATE OF CALIFORNIA FAIR LENDING NOTICE: Under the Housing Financial Discrimination Act of 1977, it is unlawful for a financial institution to refuse to make a loan, or offer less favorable terms than normal (such as higher interest rate, larger down payment, or shorter maturity) based on the following considerations:
1. Neighborhood characteristics (such as the average age of the homes or the income level in the neighborhood), except to the limited extent necessary to avoid unsafe and unsound business practices. 2. Race, color, sex, religion, marital status, national origin, or ancestry. It is also unlawful to consider, in appraising a residence, the racial, ethnic, or religious composition of a particular neighborhood whether or not such composition is undergoing change. To find out about your rights, contact The Department of Real Estate, 185 Berry St., Rm. 5816, San Francisco, CA 94107 or the Department of Real Estate, 107 S. Broadway, Rm. 8107, Los Angeles, CA 90012. If you file a complaint, the law requires that you receive a decision within thirty (30) days.

REFINANCES ONLY: When refinancing, (YOUR COMPANY NAME) advises you to seek tax counsel regarding the interpretation of any new tax reform rulings on interest deduction.

I/WE ACKNOWLEDGE RECEIPT OF A COPY OF THIS NOTICE:

_____   _____

SIGN HERE   (BORROWER)   DATE

_____   _____

SIGN HERE   (BORROWER)   DATE

FIGURE 7.2   Credit authorization.

I/We hereby authorize the lender to verify my/our past and present employment earnings records, bank accounts, stock holdings, and any other asset balances that are needed to process my/our mortgage loan application. I/We further authorize the lender to order a consumer credit report and to verify other credit information, including past and present mortgage and landlord references. It is understood that a copy of this form will also serve as authorization.

The information the lender obtains is only to be used in the processing of my/our application for a mortgage loan.

Borrower	Date
Borrower	Date
Coborrower	Date
Coborrower	Date

on the closing statement for disclosure purposes. If items are paid by escrow, the request to do so would need to be a written document, such as is shown in Figure 7.3.

Mortgage lenders are required to disclose credit scores to prospective borrowers (CC code 1785.20.2). Any person who uses a credit score in the making or arranging of a residential loan must provide the credit score information to the borrower as soon as is reasonably practicable. The law specifies the type of information that must be provided, which includes the

1. credit score.
2. range of possible credit scores under the model used.
3. key factors (up to four) that adversely affected the consumer's score in the model.
4. date the credit score was created.
5. name of the person or entity who provided the credit score.

The nation's largest credit bureaus operate services that sell the credit information to authorized parties. Direct marketers who pitch credit card offers, catalog sales firms, and others may purchase the list of names and addresses of consumers contained in the credit report database of the credit bureau. They do not, however, sell specific credit information—a credit report—without specific authorization from the actual consumer. To request that the consumer's name be

FIGURE 7.3   Authorization to pay by escrow.

National Mutual Savings
111 South Any Street
P.O. Box 000
Any Town, Any State, Zip Code
Phone: (xxx) 555-1212 Fax (xxx) 555-1213

EXPENSE AUTHORIZATION

Date: _____

To Whom It May Concern:

   This is written instruction regarding <u>Name of the borrower(s)</u>which authorizes the escrow/settlement agent to pay for the items listed below through escrow:

      Credit report fee of $ _____ , payable to:
          <u>Name of credit company   </u>.
          <u>Street address of credit company   </u>.
          <u>City, State, Zip Code of credit company   </u>

      Appraisal report fee of $ _____ , payable to:
          <u>Name of appraiser/appraisal company   </u>.
          <u>Street address of appraiser/appraisal company   </u>.
          <u>City, State, Zip Code of appraiser/appraisal company</u>.

   Should you have any further questions or concerns regarding this matter, please do not hesitate to contact me by the information in the above letterhead at extension 17.

Thank you,

Buzz Chambers
Loan Processor

Reprinted with permission of Experian.

---

removed from direct marketing agency purchasers, consumers may send written instructions to the following:

DIRECT MARKETING ASSN., INC.
Mail Preference Service
1111 19th St. NW, Suite 1100
Washington, D.C. 20036-3603
Fax: 202-955-0085

EXPERIAN TARGET MARKETING DIV.
Mail Preference Service
901 North International Parkway
Suite 191
Richardson, TX 75081

EQUIFAX OPTIONS
Customer Service Department
15450 Peachtree Street NE
P.O. Box 740123
Atlanta, GA 30309-2468
(404) 885-8000
http://www.equifax.com

TRANS UNION CORPORATION
Consumer Relations Department
TransMark Division
555 West Adams Street
Chicago, IL 60661-3631
(312) 382-1553
http://www.transunion.com

To obtain an actual credit report and meet the guidelines of the laws that pertain to credit, the mortgage broker must have the written authorization or verbal authorization from the individual. One spouse cannot sign to authorize a credit report on the other spouse. A friend or relative cannot authorize credit on a borrower. The only exceptions are the legal documents that the courts have established when one party can act for another, such as a power of attorney or guardianship documents. A record for each type of authorization must be maintained for a minimum of three years.

The mortgage loan broker must have an original signature in the file that would authorize the broker to run a credit report. The signed **credit authorization** (see Figure 7.2) should specify release of a photocopy of the authorization to a subsequent party, such as the actual lender who will run the backup credit check. Some credit forms authorize more than just the credit check and might include authorization for employment verification or bank account verifications.

Credit report bureaus charge various fees for obtaining a record of their information. The price for one individual or for a couple will vary between agencies. If a joint report is sought, the information needed to run the report must be obtained from both people. Agencies have different types of report information, such as personal credit, business credit, public record, and inquiries from other parties.

The primary credit agencies that perform credit-reporting bureau activities are listed below. The nationwide consumer reporting agencies, Experian, Equifax, and Trans Union, are required to provide consumers, on request, a free copy of their credit report once every 12 months. On June 4, 2004, the FTC issued its final rules regulating the process. The initial rollout to comply with the law is that consumers will become eligible to request their report during a regional rollout of the centralized source on the following schedule:

12/1/04—Alaska, Arizona, California, Colorado, Hawaii, Idaho, Montana, Nevada, New Mexico, Oregon, Utah, Washington, and Wyoming

3/1/05—Illinois, Indiana, Iowa, Kansas, Michigan, Minnesota, Missouri, Nebraska, North Dakota, Ohio, South Dakota, and Wisconsin

6/1/05—Alabama, Arkansas, Florida, Georgia, Kentucky, Louisiana, Mississippi, Oklahoma, South Carolina, Tennessee, and Texas

9/1/05—Connecticut, Delaware, DC, Maine, Maryland, Massachusetts, New Hampshire, New Jersey, New York, North Carolina, Pennsylvania, Rhode Island, Vermont, Virginia, and West Virginia

Should credit be denied, consumers are entitled to a free copy of their credit report if they write to the credit-reporting bureau within 30 days from the date of the denial. Further, if a consumer has been denied a job, insurance, or credit in the past 60 days, that individual may be entitled to a free credit report.

EXPERIAN
P.O. Box 949
701 Experian Parkway
Allen, TX 75013-2104 (800) 682-7654
http://www.experian.com

TRANS UNION
P.O. Box 1000
2 Baldwin Place
Chester, PA 19022
(800) 888-4213
http://www.transunion.com

Consumer Disclosure Center for Trans Union
P.O. Box 1000
Chester, PA 19022 (800) 888-4213
http://www.transunion.com

BEACON: EQUIFAX
Equifax Credit Information Services, Inc.
P.O. Box 105873
Atlanta, GA 30348
Equifax Check Services
P.O. Box 30032
Tampa, FL 33630-3033
(800) 237-4851 or (800) 685-1111
http://www.equifax.com

UNIQUOTE: FAIR, ISAAC AND COMPANY, INC. (FICO)
200 Smith Ranch Road
San Rafael, CA 94903-1996
(888) 342-6336
http://www.fairisaac.com

TELECHECK A First Data Company
6200 South Quebec Street
Greenwood Village, CO 80111
(800) 735-3362
http://www.telecheck.com

Credit bureau reports are not always accurate. A prospective borrower may have the same name as a parent or child. The data from these other individuals can be mixed into the credit of the person the mortgage broker is trying to obtain a loan. For very common names, it is not unusual for credit information to get into the wrong individual's database. It is imperative that consumers maintain accurate records of their credit history. Incorrect records may be due to a person having the same family name, adding "Jr.," or changing only the middle name. The loan broker must always include middle name, verify the correct spelling of a person's name (do not guess), and check to see whether the generation code (e.g., Sr., Jr., 3rd) is applicable.

Records can also be incorrect when a party intentionally uses someone else's credit because his or her own credit is blemished. The bureau may publish the information that was furnished to them, even though it may not be accurate. With today's computer technology, more volumes of data are being entered into records. The chance for data error increases as the volume increases. To correct errors, credit bureaus must follow "reasonable procedures" to ensure that information in the file is accurate. They must reinvestigate any item questioned unless they believe the inquiry is irrelevant. Inaccurate data or information that can no longer be verified must be deleted. For a copy of the FCRA of 1971, see www.ftc.gov/os/statutes/fcra.pdf or www.FTC.gov/os/statutes/fcra.htm.

Federal Trade Commission
Correspondence Branch
Washington, DC 20680

Federal Trade Commission
10877 Wilshire Boulevard
Los Angeles, CA 90024
(310) 824-4300

Federal Trade Commission
Public Reference Branch
6th & Pennsylvania Avenue, N.W.
Washington, DC 20850
(202) 326-2222
www.ftc.gov/bcp/consumer.shtm
www.ftc.gov/ftc/moreinfo.htm

It is advisable for consumers to have a credit report run at least once each year to check the records for accuracy. Consumers with extremely common names are advised to run their credit report more often, at least twice per year. With modern technology, consumers can request a credit report by telephone by giving their name and address by telephone. They will receive a form by mail to sign, complete, and return. The consumers will receive a copy of their own credit report and a detailed explanation on how to read the report information. Consumers can also check their own credit by going online at www.experian.com, www.equifax.com, and www.transunion.com. There is an additional charge if the consumer wants his or her FICO score.

To disprove bad credit information, the consumer can write a letter of explanation to keep on file with the credit bureau (see Figure 7.4). The

FIGURE 7.4   Credit dispute form.

Date: _____

Name: _____   Social Security Number: _____

Address: _____   Date of Birth: _____

City, State, Zip: _____

Experian	Transunion	Equifax
P.O.Box 2002	P.O.Box 1000	P.O.Box 740241
Allen, TX 75013	Chester, PA 19022	Atlanta, GA 30374
(888) 397-3742	(800) 916-8800	(800) 685-1111
http://www.experian.com	http://www.transunion.com	http://www.equifax.com

Attention: Consumer Compliant Division

   I am in disagreement with the following items listed below which appear on my credit report. These incorrect items are highly injurious to my credit rating and must be corrected immediately.

Subscriber Name: _____
Subscriber Number: _____   Account Number: _____

Reason for the disagreement:

_____ Account is paid. Account paid on _____
_____ Account does not belong to me.
_____ Account belongs to my former spouse.
_____ Account reported incorrectly.
_____ Account belongs to my son/daughter.
_____ Account belongs to my father/brother or mother/sister.

Other: _____
_____

Please forward an updated credit report after you have completed your credit investigation. Your cooperation is greatly appreciated.

Sincerely,

_____   _____

Reprinted with permission of Experian.

explanation can be up to 100 words and becomes part of the credit report that is printed. Should the report show information that is not the consumer's credit, the written explanation would state such. The consumer will need to have documentation to explain certain items. Consumers should keep at least three years of their canceled checks, along with receipts and tax returns, to substantiate their credit.

To run a credit report, the mortgage broker would need to obtain

1. original signed credit authorization, separate form, or documented verbal authorization, such as recorded telemarketing leads.
2. original signature on a loan application form (1003).
3. credit report fee statement indicating who pays if the loan closes or is denied.

Although the full loan application form has a great deal of data, not all of the information is needed to run a credit check. The following is the minimum information that would be needed to run a credit check:

1. Full name, including first, middle, and last, plus nickname and maiden name, if appropriate (the credit bureau accesses only the names that the consumer stated)
2. Date of birth (DOB)
3. Social Security number (SSN)
4. Current address (for the past two years)
5. Former address (for the past five years)

Mortgage loan brokerage firms often subscribe directly to credit bureau services. The clerical staff of the firm inputs the consumer credit information, and the report is sent over lines directly to the firm and is printed on their equipment. Anyone who knowingly obtains information from a credit bureau under pretenses may be fined up to $5,000, imprisoned for up to one year, or both. The same law applies to unauthorized disclosures made by officers or employees of a credit bureau or of a mortgage loan company.

7.2 CREDIT AND FICO SCORE

Computerized process credit scoring is an attempt to qualify a potential borrower with a single number. The intent is to aid lenders in determining the likelihood of repayment of a loan. It takes into consideration a consumer's record for paying bills, the total amount owed by that consumer, and other factors such as late payments and number of open credit accounts, to arrive at an estimate of creditworthiness. Scoring has been used in other types of consumer lending for more than 45 years but just recently became widely used by the real estate lending community. A repository credit risk score is a specific type of credit score that evaluates the information in a consumer's file at that credit repository. Several bills were introduced in Congress to force disclosure of a consumer's credit score that began to be available to consumers in 2001.

The mortgage industry uses the **FICO credit scoring** method, which is based on a point system that ranges from a low of 300 to a high of 850. The higher the score, the lower the chances are that the borrower will default on a mortgage payment; thus, the better the loan terms offered to the borrower.

The FICO scores are broken down into five specific areas. The approximate percentage used is shown below, along with the credit area.

Percent	Credit Area
35%	based on your payment history
30%	based on amounts owed
15%	based the length of time the credit history has been established
10%	based on new credit
10%	based on types of credit that are used

When borrowers want to improve their FICO score, they can do various things over time, that will increase the opportunity for extension of credit for housing. For example, the consumer needs to keep the balances low on revolving debt. The mortgage loan broker can aid the borrower in improving the FICO score by looking at the maximum loan balance allowed in each if the borrower's existing credit cards. If the borrower has two credit cards, of Card A having a maximum allowable balance of $800 and Card B with a maximum allowable balance of $2500, the amount owed on each should be reviewed. If the borrower owes $800 on a Card A and $0 on Card B, it would improve the FICO score to move the existing balance from Card A to Card B. The idea is to reduce the percentage owed on the card. Instead of owing 100 percent of the limit on that Card A ($800, $800), the percentage for Card B would show as only 32 percent of the allowable limit ($800, $2,500 = 32 percent). Changing the percentage owed from 100 percent to 32 percent would have a dramatic effect on the credit score.

The credit score also checks to see if the borrower is taking on a new debt, which is why good credit counseling at the beginning of the loan process helps the loan to close escrow. It is not uncommon when the borrower hears that the loan has been approved and is being submitted for loan documents, that the borrower thinks the loan will automatically close escrow. At this point, the borrower is anxious to get into his or her new home and may go shopping to obtain furnishings for that new home. When the mortgage loan broker submits the loan package that contains the initial credit report obtained at the beginning of the loan process to the lender for final approval, the lender runs another credit report just prior to final loan approval and funding of the loan. New debt for a household for new furniture will often decrease the FICO score to a point at which the loan will be denied at the last minute by the lender.

When the credit of a prospective borrower is examined, the FICO score is better if the credit shows that the borrower has established a healthy mix of the various types of credit available, such as a mix of retail sales, installment loan payment, finance company credit, bank credit cards, and real estate loans. Appendix B shows a credit report that has been broken down, with an explanation for each area represented.

After FNMA and FHLMC commenced the use of FICO credit scoring in 1993, it became the current industry standard (see Figure 7.5). Each credit repository has a name for its risk score: Experian uses Experian/FICO Score; Equifax uses Beacon; and Trans Union uses Emperica, as previously discussed.

FICO was developed by NextGen for lenders who desired a stronger tool for credit analysis than basic credit reports. Traditional lenders formerly generated only prime borrower loans and can now use the more refined assessment tool when considering minimal credit users, subprime borrowers, heavy revolvers, and others. Three main differences separate FICO scores from the former classic credit scores:

1. Multidimensional predictive variables, such as length of time of credit
2. Population segmentation scheme
3. Refined performance outcome classification

A FICO score rates a consumer's creditworthiness according to data in the individual's credit bureau files. A FICO score considers credit card, installment debt, and public records in giving the rating. One million borrowers nationwide were studied, and borrowers with FICO scores below 600 had a one-in-nine chance of falling seriously behind or defaulting on a real estate loan. Borrowers with scores above 800 had only a 1-in-1,293 chance of having trouble keeping mortgage loan payments current.

Credit bureau scorings evaluate such items as past delinquencies or derogatory payment behavior, current level of indebtedness, length of credit history, types of credit used, frequency of application for credit, and credit lines opened. The score reflects the relative risk of serious delinquency, default, foreclosure, or bankruptcy associated with the specific borrower. Three rules apply when a borrower wants to maintain a high FICO score:

1. Credit lines: Small balance on more cards is better than maximum balance debt on less lines of credit. Six credit cards with small balances are better than three cards with high unpaid balances.
2. Payment record: Pay everything on time.
3. Credit report: Order a copy and dispute any incorrect or derogatory information that drags down the score.

The higher the FICO score, the lower the risk of default. FNMA and Freddie Mac (FHLMC) tested the FICO scoring system on thousands of home loans funded in the previous 10 years. Those with FICO scores over 680 were still considered good credit risks. A borrower with a 660-to-680 FICO score had only a 1 percent chance of having a 60-day delinquency on their loan. Less than 10 percent of their current borrowers had a FICO score below 620. The small group that fell below 620 accounted for half of all defaults and experienced at least one 60-day delinquency. Thus, lenders were warned that borrowers rated below 620 were high risk, especially those with a very low down payment. Both FNMA and FHLMC now urge lenders to use credit scores in evaluating applicants when the loan is expected to be sold on the secondary money market.

FHLMC is now rejecting 50 percent more audited loans below the new standards. The new underwriting software systems are producing FICO scores along with LTV and debt-to-equity ratios automatically. In addition, the credit rating score is nondiscriminatory because it does not consider gender or ethnicity and only uses the FICO score as a rating stick.

FIGURE 7.5   Credit bureau risk factor reason codes.

Reason Statement	All Bureaus	Equifax	Empirica	UniQuote
Amount owed on accounts is too high	01	*	*	*
Level of delinquency on accounts	02	*	*	*
Too few bank revolving accounts	03	*		
Proportion of loan balances to loan amounts is too high	03	33	*	*
Too many bank or national revolving accounts	04	*		
Lack of recent installment loan information	04	32	*	*
Too many accounts with balances	05	*	*	*
Too many consumer finance company accounts	06	*	*	
Account payment history is too new to rate	07	*	*	*
Too many inquiries last 12 months	08	*	*	*
Too many accounts recently opened	09	*	*	*
Proportion of balances to credit limits is too high on banking revolving or other revolving accounts	10	*	*	*
Amount owed on revolving accounts is too high	11	*	*	
Length of time revolving accounts have been established	12	*	*	
Time since delinquency is too recent or unknown	13	*	*	*
Length of time accounts have been established	14	*	*	*
Lack of recent bank revolving information	15	*	*	*
Lack of recent revolving account information	16	*	*	*
No recent non-mortgage balance information	17	*	*	*
Number of accounts with delinquency	18	*	*	*
Too few accounts currently paid as agreed	19	*	27	27
Date of last inquiry too recent	19		*	*
Length of time since derogatory public record or collection is too short	20	*	*	*
Amount past due on accounts	21	*	*	*
Serious delinquency, derogatory public record, or collection filed	22	*	*	*
Number of bank or nation revolving accounts with balances	23	*		
No recent revolving balances	24	*	*	*
Length of time installment loans have been established	25	I/0		
Number of revolving accounts	26	I/0		
Number of bank revolving or other revolving accounts	26		I/0	
Number of retail accounts	27			
Too few accounts currently paid as agreed	27	19	*	
Number of established accounts	28	*	*	*

FIGURE 7.5   (*Continued*)

Reason Statement	All Bureaus	Equifax	Empirica	UniQuote
No recent bankcard balances	29		*	*
Date of last inquiry too recent	29		19	19
Time since most recent account opening is too short	30	*	*	*
Too few accounts with recent payment information	31	*		
Amount owed on delinquent accounts	31	34	I/0	*
Lack of recent installment loan information	32	*	04	04
Proportion of loan balances to loan amounts is too high	33	*	03	03
Amount owed on delinquent accounts	34	*	31	31
Payments due on accounts	36			
Length of time open installment loans have been established	36			
Number of consumer finance company accounts established relative to length of consumer finance history	37			
Serious delinquency, and public record or collection filed	38	*	*	*
Serious delinquency	39	*	*	*
Derogatory public record or collection filed	40	*	*	*
No recent retail balances	41			*
Length of time since most recent consumer finance company accounts established	42			*
Lack of recent mortgage loan information	43			*
Proportion of balances to loan amounts on mortgage loans is too high	44			*
Too few accounts with balances	45			*
Number of consumer finance company inquiries	47			
Lack of recent retail account information	50			*
Amount owed on retail accounts	56			*
Lack of recent auto loan information	97		I/0	
Length of time consumer finance company loans have been established	98		*	
Lack of recent auto loan information	98		97	
Length of time consumer finance company loans have been established	98			
Lack of recent auto loan information	98			
Lack of recent auto finance loan information	98	I/0		
Lack of recent consumer finance company account information	99	I/0	I/0	

FIGURE 7.6   Valid Social Security numbers.

Code Range	State	Code Range	State
001–003	New Hampshire	433–439	Louisiana
004–007	Maine	440–448	Oklahoma
008–009	Vermont	449–467	Texas
010–034	Massachusetts	468–477	Minnesota
035–039	Rhode Island	478–485	Iowa
040–049	Connecticut	486–500	Missouri
050–134	New York	501–502	North Dakota
135–158	New Jersey	503–504	South Dakota
159–211	Pennsylvania	505–508	Nebraska
212–222	Delaware	509–515	Kansas
223–231	Virginia	516–517	Montana
232–236	West Virginia	518–519	Idaho
237–246	North Carolina	520	Wyoming
247–251	South Carolina	521–524	Colorado
252–260	Georgia	525	New Mexico
261–267	Florida	526–527	Arizona
268–302	Ohio	528–529	Utah
303–317	Indiana	530	Nevada
318–361	Illinois	531–539	Washington
362–386	Michigan	540–544	Oregon
387–399	Wisconsin	545–573	California
400–407	Kentucky	574	Alaska
408–415	Tennessee	575–576	Hawaii
416–424	Alabama	575–579	District of Columbia
425–428	Mississippi	700	Railroad
429–432	Arkansas		

Reprinted with permission of Experian.

A risk score may not be accessible for an individual because of any of the following legitimate reasons:

1. The repository shows no credit activity within the past six months.
2. The repository reflects a credit history of less than six months' duration.
3. The file has a "deceased" indicator when the Social Security number appears on the deceased list or a trade file indicating the individual has died. See Figure 7.6 for the list of valid Social Security number identifiers. A Social Security number consists of nine digits, written as three fields separated by hyphens (AAA-GG-SSSS). The first three-digit number is the area number; the middle two-digit number is the group number; and the last four-digit field is the serial number. The process of assigning numbers was changed in 1965 and again in 1972. Comserv, Inc., is a firm that for a fee will verify the Social Security number.

Comserv, Inc.

7095 S E Twin Oaks Circle

Stuart, FL 34997-4729

(866) 937-2836

Fax (772) 781-9435

www.comserv-inc.com

FIGURE 7.7   Average credit card interest rate 1994–2009.

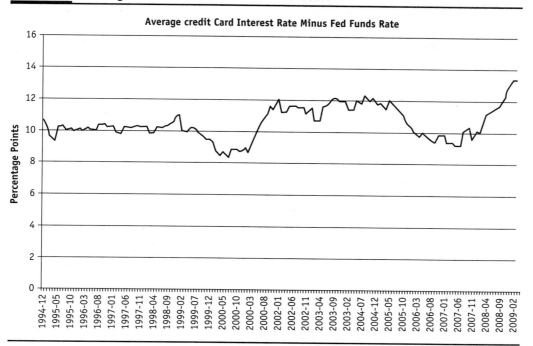

4. A consumer who has too much credit on file, usually exceeding 100 lines of credit, and inquiries is often not accessible. A score model is not available for consumers who fall into this area.

One reason for the concern by lenders has been the recent increase in consumer debt. Typically, the price of a new car has been equal to the amount of down payment and closing costs needed to purchase a home, and this has stayed about the same. But the amount of credit card debt has drastically risen since 1980 to the point at which prospective purchasers cannot qualify for home loans because of the amount of credit card debt. The goal is for credit card debt to be no greater than 10 percent to 15 percent of consumer income. For the past 15 years, however, credit card debt has averaged just under 20 percent, as shown in Figure 7.7.

With income taxes at 28 percent to 33 percent federally and state income tax about 9 percent to 11 percent, about 40 percent of the borrower's income is decreased from gross to net income. With 20 percent in credit card debt, only about 40 percent of income is left for transportation, general living expenses, medical, and housing. Clearly, no matter how low interest rates for home loans stay or how low home prices fall in the short run, borrowers would not be able to qualify for a home loan.

An example of credit rating grade (A paper, B borrower, C loan, D credit) and FICO scoring is shown in Figure 7.8. The lending industry refers to the credit grade to differentiate between a prime loan and a subprime loan. The rating is used for initial purchase loans, refinance loans, and home improvement (Title 1) loans. A typical Title 1 loan scoring matrix is shown in Figure 7.9. The program parameters vary among lenders. But as more lenders rely on scoring, similar worksheets will become more common.

FIGURE 7.8   Credit rating grade and FICO score.

	A+	A	B	C	D
Mortgage history	0 × 30 last 12 months	1 × 30 last 12 months	2 × 30 last 12 months	4 × 30 last 12 months	6 × 30 last 12 months, never a payment 60 days late
Minimum FICO score from primary wage earner and repository	720	680–719	640–679	600–639	580–599
100% Debt consolidation	Max. CLTV 125% Loan Amount $50,000	Max. CLTV 125% Loan Amount $40,000	Max. CLTV 125% Loan Amount $30,000	Max. CLTV 125% Loan Amount $25,000	Max. CLTV Loan Amount N/A
40% Home improvement, 60% debt consolidation	125% $75,000	125% $75,000	125% $50,000	125% $25,000	N/A
Title I	$25,000	$25,000	$25,000	$25,000	$25,000
Max. cash out	10%	10%	10%	5%	N/A
Bankruptcy foreclosures or deeds in lieu	None allowed	None allowed	None allowed	None in last 2 years	None in last 2 years
Gross annual income Up to 30,000	35%	35%	35%	35%	35%
30,000–50,000	40%	40%	40%	40%	40%
50,000–75,000	45%	45%	45%	45%	40%
75,000 & over	50%	50%	45%	45%	40%

Program	Term (years) Min. Max.		Security Position	Title Insurance	Appraisal Requirements	Use of Funds
All debts	1	25	1st or 2nd	Over $25,000 required	10 to 50K Driveby, 10K	Consolidation Max. cash out
60/40	1	25	1st or 2nd	Over $50,000 required	$50,000 = URAR 10 to 50K Driveby, 10K None	Improvement up to 60% debt Consolidation Max. cash out

Credit Policy

1. FICO scores are for primary wage earner, using preferred repository.
2. Credit file must contain *three* or more trade lines, with one opened at least 12 months, with a high credit of $1,000.00 and rated satisfactorily.
3. No trade presently 30 days or more past due.
4. Rate adjustments: add 0.25% for debt ratio over 40 up to 45; add 0.50% for ratios over 45 up to 50.
5. Rate adjustments: add 0.50% for self-employed.
6. VOE are optional for conventional loans.
7. VOE current pay stub showing year-to-date (12-month income). W-2s if less than 1 year. VOE is not required on A+ or A grades.
8. Bankruptcy is based on the discharge date of the bankruptcy.
9. Prior bankrupts may not be higher than a C grade, regardless of score.
10. First-time buyers (less than 6 months of mortgage credit history) may not be higher grade than A.
11. VOMs must contain at least 6 months of ratings. May use credit bureau history to verify.
12. HUD-1 may be used in place of driveby if less than 7 months old.
13. Owner-occupied properties only.
14. Collateral type may be single-family or PUD; no units or condos.

FIGURE 7.9 Title I scoring matrix.

TITLE I LOAN SCORING MATRIX

Borrower's Name _____

Address _____

Employer _____

Agent _____

Approved By _____

Circle/Insert Appropriate Number

1. Credit   FICO Score
   - A. Excellent _____ 641 and higher   35
   - B. Good _____ 600–640   (30)
   - C. Fair _____ 550–599   20
   - D. Limited or Marginal ___ 549 and lower   10

   [30]

2. Debit ratio
   - A. 34% or less   20
   - B. 35–40%   15
   - C. 40–44%   (10)
   - D. Over 44%   0
   - E. If over 44% but excess income > $2,000   10

   [10]

3. Employment
   - A. Present employer ___max 5 points (1 point for each full year of service)   5
   - B. Present occupation/profession__max 10 points   10
   - C. Retiree   15

   [15]

4. Residence (same metro area)
   - A. Over 5 years   10
   - B. 2–5 years   6
   - C. Less than 2 years   (4)
   - D. Deduct if previous renter in last two years   (2)

   [2]

Loan Classification
   - A. 64–80 = A
   - B. 56–63 = B
   - C. 44–55 = C
   - D. 43 or less = D
   -     35 or less = not acceptable

Total score: [57]
Loan classification: [B]

Review element	Excellent	Good	Fair	Limited/Marginal	Poor
Credit Definition					
History	5 yrs	3 yrs	2 yrs	>2 yrs	N/A
High credit (min 1 yr exprc) (other than home loan)	$5,000	$2,500	$2,000	>$2,000	N/A
Nonderogatory trades	5	3–5	3	1–3	N/A
Delinquency profile					
Currently delinquent	None	None	None	None	Yes
Prior 2 yrs revolving delinquency	None	2–30 day Now current	0–over 30	0–over 60	Over 60
Over 2 yr old installment Delinquency	2–30 day Now current	0–over 30	0–over 30	Over 30	Over 60
Over 2 yr revolving delinquency	2–30 day	0–over 30	0–over 60	Over 60	Over 90
If derogatory	5 nonderog	4 nonderog	3 nonderog	2 nonderog	None
Then derogatory must equal	1 derog	1 derog	1 derog	1 derog	
In last seven years					
Bankruptcy	No	No	No	No	Yes
Repossession	No	No	No	No	Yes
Foreclosure	No	No	No	No	Yes
Repossession	No	No	No	No	Yes
Charge-off (over $200)	No	No	No	No	Yes
If over 7 yrs and Yes, downgrade two grades					
Points	35	30	20	10	0

7.3 PRIVACY POLICY

Legislation that became effective July 1, 2001, requires providers to give their customers a written explanation of their privacy choices. The notice may contain the location of the personal information, such as:

1. Information received from an application for an extension of credit, such as the name, address, and telephone number of the prospective borrower.
2. Information about a transaction with the lender, the lender's affiliates, or nonaffiliated third parties, such as account balance, payment history, and account activity of a borrower.
3. Information received from a consumer reporting agency, such as a credit bureau, relating to creditworthiness of a borrower.
4. Information received from an applicant's employer or other third parties.

The privacy law requires disclosure of affiliates to whom the lender may disclose personal information, usually credit card, consumer finance, automobile financing, partner businesses of the lender, securities, or insurance firms affiliated with the lender. Consumers may be given options such as (1) sharing information among the affiliates described in the privacy policy; (2) sharing among partners for marketing purposes unrelated to partner programs; (3) a statement that the consumer does not wish to be contacted by mail for offers of products or services; and (4) a statement that the consumer does not wish to be contacted by telephone with offers of products or services (see Figure 7.10).

7.4 EQUAL CREDIT OPPORTUNITY ACT (ECOA)

The ECOA was originally enacted on October 25, 1975. Congress wanted to ensure that financial institutions that engage in the business of extending credit would be responsible for exercising fair and impartial practices. It was felt that this act would enhance the economic stability of the nation and strengthen competition among institutions. The main purpose of the act is to guarantee that credit is equally available to all creditworthy customers. Every lender should display the Fair Housing Emblem (see Figure 7.11).

The **ECOA** prohibits discrimination in any credit transaction on the basis of race, color, religion, national origin, sex, marital status, age, income source, or any good-faith exercise of any right under the Consumer Credit Protection Act. It is not a violation of ECOA to inquire about an individual's marital status as long as the information is used to determine the creditor's rights and remedies in the extension of credit. Determining the applicant's age for capacity to contract is allowed. Information on income derived from public assistance for the purpose of information to ascertain the amount and probable continuance of this income is also acceptable for credit history and financial elements of creditworthiness.

ECOA requires a creditor to notify an applicant within 30 days of receipt of a completed credit application of the action taken. If adverse action is taken, the creditor must inform the applicant for the reasons. Adverse action includes

FIGURE 7.10   Public notice disclosure.

ꀊ **National Mutual Savings** ꀊ
111 South Any Street
P.O. Box 000
Any Town, Any State, Zip Code
Phone: (area code) 555-1212 Fax (area code) 555-1213

To Our Customers:

This notification is in compliance with our obligations to comply with federal (and state) laws to safeguard your nonpublic information.

We collect nonpublic personal information about you from the following sources:

    1. Information we receive from you on applications or other forms

    2. Information about your transactions with us, our affiliates, or others involved in the processing of your transaction

    3. Information we receive from a consumer-reporting agency

We do not disclose any nonpublic personal information about our customers or former customers to anyone, except as permitted by law.

We restrict access to nonpublic information about you to those employees who need to know that information to provide products or services to you. We maintain physical, electronic, and procedural safeguards that comply with federal and state regulations to guard your nonpublic personal information.

I/We have read and received a copy of this notification as of the date listed below.

Date:

_____   _____

_____   _____

Public Notice Disclosure 06/01

denial, revocation of credit, a change in terms of an existing credit arrangement, or refusal to grant credit on substantially the amount or terms requested. The notification should be in writing as a normal course of business. The notice may be oral if the creditor does no more than 150 applications during a calendar year.

FIGURE 7.11   Equal housing opportunity.

EQUAL HOUSING OPPORTUNITY

We do business in accordance with the Federal Fair Housing Law
(The Fair Housing Amendments Act of 1988)

It is Illegal to Discriminate Against Any Person
Because of Race, Color, Religion, Sex,
Handicap, Familial Status, or National Origin

- In the sale or rental of housing or residential lots
- In advertising the sale or rental of housing
- In the financing of housing

- In the provision of real estate brokerage services
- In the appraisal of housing
- Blockbusting is also illegal

Anyone who feels he or she has been Discriminated against may file a Complaint of housing discrimination:
(800) 669-9777 (Toll Free)
(800) 927-9275 (TDD)

U.S. Department of Housing and Urban Development
Assistant Secretary for Fair Housing and Equal Opportunity
Washington, D.C. 20410

Previous editions are obsolete   from HUD-928.1A(8-93)

The Board of Governors of the Federal Reserve issues regulations to carry out the purpose of the act. The intent is to see that credit transactions do not circumvent or evade the purpose of the act and that adherence to the act is strictly followed. Lenders must keep records relating to such loans for a minimum of one year. The Board of Governors also established the Consumer Advisory Council to advise and consult in the exercise of its functions under the guidelines of the act and other consumer-related matters.

Compliance with ECOA requirements is enforced under (1) Section 8 of the Federal Deposit Insurance Act for national banks, (2) the Comptroller of the Currency for member banks of the Federal Reserve System, and (3) the Board of Directors of FDIC for banks insured by the **Federal Deposit Insurance Corporation (FDIC)**.

ECOA is also enforced under the Home Owner's Loan Act, Federal Home Loan Bank Act, Federal Credit Union Act, Packers and Stockyard Act, Farm Credit Act, Securities Exchange Act, Small Business Investment Act, and the Federal Trade Commission Act. The FTC has overall responsibility for compliance with the act.

Under ECOA provisions, a creditor can require the signature of both a husband and a wife for the purpose of establishing a valid lien, passing clear title, or waiving property rights. The federal law overrides any state law that prohibits separate extension of consumer credit to a married couple from the same creditor if they request that such credit be established. Under such circumstances, each party in the marriage is solely responsible for his or her own debts. When a married person voluntarily obtains his or her own credit with the same creditor, the separate accounts may not be combined to determine applicable finance charges or loan ceilings (Commerce and Trade—Title 15, Code Section 1691, Subchapter IV Equal Credit Opportunity).

7.5 NONTRADITIONAL CREDIT REPORTS

Fannie Mae announced guidelines for credit report information in mid-1995 to help develop a standard format for verifying nontraditional credit histories for consumers. This is consistent with the federal lending discrimination intent and Fannie Mae's longstanding desire to help mortgage applicants who do not have traditional credit histories to obtain financing when they need it, rather than having to wait until they establish such histories.

If the consumer has no credit, the mortgage loan broker may need to look to alternative sources to show that the consumer has established credit. The cultural differences of our society require the mortgage broker to be creative in establishing a credit payment history for a borrower. Sources could include a copy of the front and back of canceled checks for payment of:

1. Rent (matching rent receipts may also support payment, obtaining verification from the current and previous landlord)
2. Utilities (gas, electric, water, telephone, cable TV)
3. Insurance (life, automobile, health)
4. Personal property tax payments
5. Other regular payment records

Credit reporting agencies are establishing **Nontraditional Mortgage Credit Report** standards that will soon be available to lenders. This credit report may be used as a substitute for a traditional credit report for the borrower who does not have one or as a supplemental report to a traditional credit report that has insufficient number of credit references. This type of credit report is not to be used to offset an existing credit report showing negative information.

Lenders may immediately begin the use of such nontraditional credit reports, if available. As of January 1, 1996, it became mandatory to use a nontraditional credit report when needed. If the credit history that is developed does not include sufficient information for the lender to make a prudent underwriting decision, the lender should request the credit reporting agency to develop a nontraditional mortgage credit report. The lender must use its own judgment in determining whether the references on the standard credit report are sufficient for it to make an underwriting decision without ordering a nontraditional credit report.

When a lender requests a credit reporting agency to develop a nontraditional mortgage credit report, the agency should first verify that all three of the major credit repositories were checked in the initial attempt to verify the applicant's credit history. The agency considers only credit in which the applicants have shown that they have made regular payments at least quarterly. New reports that meet Fannie Mae nontraditional credit guidelines would establish three tiers. Tier I credit shows payments for rental housing and utilities. Tier II includes payments for medical, automobile, and life insurance coverage, excluding automatic payroll deductions. Tier III credit shows payments to local stores, such as department, furniture, appliance, and specialty stores, in addition to payments for school tuition and child care. The payment terms must be documented in a written agreement, and the borrower must provide copies of canceled checks to indicate that the payments are of a continual nature.

Tier I credit would be acceptable if it establishes at least four sources of credit. If fewer than four sources of credit have been identified, the credit reporting agency should contact the sources for the Tier II credit (and, if necessary, for the Tier III credit) until it is able to prepare a nontraditional mortgage credit report that includes a credit history that is developed by using four to six sources of credit.

To evaluate a nontraditional credit report, the lender should evaluate the credit history under the same standards that are used for a traditional credit history. However, if the source for the rental housing payments was a party other than a professional management company, the lender should ask the applicant to provide at least 12 months of canceled checks or other evidence of a timely payment of rent. Copies of bank statements may also be used to establish proof of regular, monthly payment of rent and other obligations.

7.6 THE HOUSING FINANCIAL DISCRIMINATION ACT OF 1977: FAIR LENDING NOTICE

According to the law, the lender must provide a Fair Lending Notice to the applicant (see Figure 7.1). This notice explains that it is illegal to discriminate in providing financial assistance because of race, color, religion, sex, marital status, national origin, or ancestry. The neighborhood composition or geographic area surrounding the property the applicant wants to borrow against cannot be a reason for denial of the loan. The lender cannot offer different terms and conditions for the loan from one neighborhood or area to another. The mortgage loan broker should write to obtain information about consumer rights from:

Office of Fair Lending
Business & Transportation Agency
1120 N Street
Sacramento, CA 95814

If the applicant is seeking funds from a credit union, it must comply with the provisions of the Federal ECOA (15 U.S.C. 1691, effective March 12, 1977), which also provides that there cannot be discrimination according to a credit applicant's race, color, religion, national origin, sex, marital status, or age (see Figure 7.12).

FIGURE 7.12 Sample housing financial disclosure notice.

National Mutual Savings Bank 🏦
Please Read and Return a Signed Copy with Your Completed Loan Application.
Retain a Copy For Your Records.

The Housing Financial Discrimination Act of 1977
Fair Lending Notice

It is illegal to discriminate in the provision of or in the availability of financial assistance because of the consideration of:

1. trends, characteristics or conditions in the neighborhood or geographic area surrounding a housing accommodation, unless the financial institution can demonstrate in the particular case that such consideration is required to avoid unsafe and unsound business practice; or

2. race, color, religion, sex, marital status, national origin, or ancestry.

It is illegal to consider the racial, ethnic, religious, or national origin composition of a neighborhood or geographic area surrounding a housing accommodation or whether or not such composition is undergoing change, or is expected to undergo change, in appraising a housing accommodation or in determining whether or not, or under what terms and conditions to provide financial assistance.

These provisions govern financial assistance for the purpose of the purchase, construction, rehabilitation, or refinancing of one- to four four-unit family residences occupied by the owner and for the purpose of the home improvement of any one- to four four-unit family residence.

If you have questions about your rights, or if you wish to file a complaint, contact the management of this financial institution, or

Department of Financial Institutions
111 Pine Street, Suite 1100
San Francisco, CA 94111-5613

Acknowledgement of Receipt
I (we) received a copy of this notice.

_____   _____

Signature of Applicant   Date

_____   _____

Signature of Applicant   Date

This law further states that the applicant does not have to disclose additional income received, unless the applicant is using that income to support repayment of the loan. This should include items such as child support and alimony or separate maintenance income. Additional credit union information may be obtained from:

National Credit Union Administration
2300 Clayton Road, Suite 1350
Concord, CA 94520

SUMMARY

The mortgage loan broker must establish an individual's credit history for the lender to evaluate approval to the loan terms and conditions. These terms are based on the record of the applicant's previous ability to meet payment obligations. The mortgage loan broker uses written credit reports obtained from credit bureau services. To comply with privacy and equal credit opportunities, the mortgage loan broker must understand the provisions of various state and federal laws regarding credit.

The mortgage loan broker is expected to verify information before forwarding a loan package to the lender. A standard of reasonableness is expected of the professional in which a reviewer would submit verifications of information. **Credit rating scores** are used to aid in determining the creditworthiness of borrowers.

REVIEWING YOUR UNDERSTANDING

1. The law requiring a private lender to report credit to a credit bureau is:
   A. Fair Credit Reporting Act
   B. Equal Credit Opportunity Act
   C. Federal Trade Commission
   D. None of the above; reporting is not required

2. A credit score is a generated number that:
   A. Predicts how likely a consumer is to repay a debt
   B. Is a non-discriminatory method of evaluating a consumer
   C. Can be affected by bounced checks
   D. All of the above

3. A nontraditional credit report, under FNMA guidelines are divided into how many tiers:
   A. One
   B. Two
   C. Three
   D. Four

4. Consumers are allowed a free credit report:
   A. Once a month
   B. Once every 6 months
   C. Once a year
   D. Never; they are not allowed free credit reports at any time

5. The ECOA requires a lending agency to notify the application of the action taken for:
   A. 5 days
   B. 10 days
   C. 15 days
   D. 30 days

6. Which of the following is NOT a major credit reporting agency?
   A. Experian
   B. Trans Union
   C. Equifax
   D. FICO

7. Which of the following pairs of credit areas has the most effect on your FICO score?
   A. Payment history and new credit
   B. Payment history and amounts owed
   C. Amounts owed and length of time the credit history has been established
   D. Amount owed and types of credit used

8. The upper and lower range of the FICO credit score is:
   A. 250 to 750
   B. 300 to 800
   C. 300 to 850
   D. 350 to 850

9. The mortgage broker is required to run credit check through at least _____ credit bureaus to comply with requirements for later selling the loan in the secondary market.
   A. One
   B. Two
   C. Three
   D. Four

10. Personal credit rights come under the _____ of 1971.
    A. FCRA
    B. DRE
    C. CAR
    D. FDIC

ANSWERS TO REVIEWING YOUR UNDERSTANDING

1. D (p. 231)	4. C (p. 237)	7. B (p. 240)	9. B (p. 231)
2. D (p. 230)	5. D (p. 248)	8. C (p. 239)	10. A (p. 230)
3. C (p. 252)	6. D (p. 236)		

Chapter

8

Processing: Verifications and Stacking Order

PREVIEW

The mortgage loan broker is an intermediary who brings the borrower and lender together in a loan transaction. The lender expects the broker to perform certain duties for and on behalf of the lender's investor. The investor's money is used to fund the actual loan, and each lender requires specific documentation before releasing the final loan payment to the escrow or title company. The details for the exact order of specific documents are important here. The mortgage loan broker may process the documents or may hire a specialist, called a processor, to ensure compliance with the loan package requirements.

This chapter discusses the work the loan processor performs. The flow of the loan is often determined by the experience of the processor. The work involves detailed paperwork and the talent for investigation. Although no license is required for the position of processor, the individual should be able to accurately complete all components of the loan package.

CHAPTER OBJECTIVES

At the end of this chapter, the student learning outcomes include:

1. Determine the tools a processor needs.
2. List the items the processor would have to obtain to complete a loan file.
3. Outline the guidelines used for a complete loan package, including borrower documentation and verifications.
4. Describe the criteria list that a lender requires in order to accept a loan package.

8.1 PROCESSING TOOLS

To accomplish any task, an individual must have the right tools. Loan processing is no different. Professional tools include internal supplies and external forms and reference materials. Although dialogue with different processors would provide various lists of the necessary tools, the following is a basic uniform basis from which to begin work. Internal setup for the loan office is discussed in more detail in Chapter 13, but this list will assist in the initial planning stages. Without these tools, processing time is delayed, and thus the funding of the loan is extended.

- **Computer.** A laptop with a high-speed modem is preferred. The capacity of the computer should be the maximum available at purchase. Add-ons, such as a PDA data transfer and removable drives with USB ports, are recommended. Basic packages of forms are readily available. The laptop is often used to take the loan application to the client's home, so wireless Internet is used to transmit and receive data such as a credit report.

- **Computer software** with loan processing forms. Decide what software will be needed. Determine what basic computer packages are needed, such as spell-check, artwork, and form design. Does the operation need basic bookkeeping, e-mail capacity, and the ability to draw loan docs? Is it compatible in format to underwriting standards, such as meeting FNMA guidelines? (See Chapter 13.)

- **Modem** with highest speed available. A loan processor will use his or her laptop with a modem, telephone access with built-in or internal satellite connection. The agent and the processor will then start typing the information directly to the main office or lender.

- **Laser printer/scanner.** The ability to make clear and sharp copies will be important. Many items may be scanned in and electronically forwarded as part of an electronic file.

- **Fax machine.** Some lenders will accept a fax copy for some documents, which speeds up the process of gaining the necessary data for submission of the loan package.

- **E-mail address.** Transmissions by e-mail will reduce the use of fax transmissions. Current practices include transmission of many loan documents via e-mail, such as escrow instructions, appraisal report, and the actual loan documents that are sent to the escrow company.

- **Web page.** Common forms, such as a prequalification loan application, can be placed on a Web page that is electronically sent to the office.

- **Copy machine** with sorter, collator, and automatic feed. Two copies are generally required to submit a loan file to a lender. If the loan uses PMI insurance, a third copy is needed. The ability to make multiple copies will save time and money.

- **Telephone** with speakerphone, memory, speed dial, and redial. Placing frequently called numbers in memory saves time. Hands-free telephones with a headset or ear piece allow the processor to turn pages in a file to locate documents while talking on the telephone.

- **Calculator** with paper printout. Many computers and newer keyboards come with a calculator keypad. Processors have to calculate LTV, income-to-debt ratios, net rents, income conversion, closing costs, and many other items.

- **Dictionary and thesaurus.** These books, CDs, or online references are used for writing letters of explanations and cover letters.

- **Desk calendar**. When the processor sends out the verification requests (VOD, VOM, VOE), credit request, appraisal request, beneficiary demand, or other documents, the desk calendar should be marked five to ten working days from the date sent as the follow-up request date to check the status on receipt of the data. Many processors use a computer calendar reminder program to accomplish this important task.
- **Self-stick and removable note pads**, printed with "sign and return," "notarize," and "original," are used to mark items in the file and on forms sent to others. These notes aid the parties in easily finding the necessary item on the tax returns, verifications, and similar documents.
- **Legal-size Rolodex**. Business cards do not fit on a standard-size Rolodex card unless part of the card is cut off. Most cards fit on a legal-size Rolodex, with additional room to write notes. A business card scanner program is often used. Online systems are also now available for maintaining a database, as well as handheld Blackberry, Palm or similar downloadable database systems that tie the individual's phone to the company computer. (Note: Should the employee no longer work at this firm, if all the data is stored only on the company computer system, the individual has no contacts. If the database is on the handheld, the company security personnel may allow the employee to keep the data, or they may remove all contacts from the portable system and from the company computer. A separate, back-up system of contacts is important for both the company and the individual loan broker.)
- **Highlighter pens**. Mark items in the file with a particular color to ease finding a section at a later date.
- **Pens, pencils, staple remover, tape, scissors, glue stick, stapler**, and any other items to make tasks easier.

External materials that will need to be collected from outside sources for the processor include the following:

- *Lane Guide* or MapQuest via Internet.
- FNMA Selling Guide (underwriting guidelines).
- FHLMC underwriting guidelines.
- Underwriting guidelines from your private investors.
- All legal forms, including 1003, VOD, VOM, VOE, to do the job properly.

8.2 THE PROCESSOR'S FILE

Then a loan file is turned over to the processor, the 1003 must be reviewed for completeness and accuracy. Chapter 6 detailed a complete loan application. Once this form is completed, it is time to "open" the file. Using the flowchart in Figure 8.1, begin the process by ordering the credit report and appraisal. The processor must also insure that the borrower has sufficient funds to cover the PITI, Association Dues, Down Payment, and Closing Cost and Reserves. The loan agent must be sure to have these client trust funds available to pay for the credit report and appraisal. The loan agent must also place a copy of any funds

FIGURE 8.1   Loan flow chart.

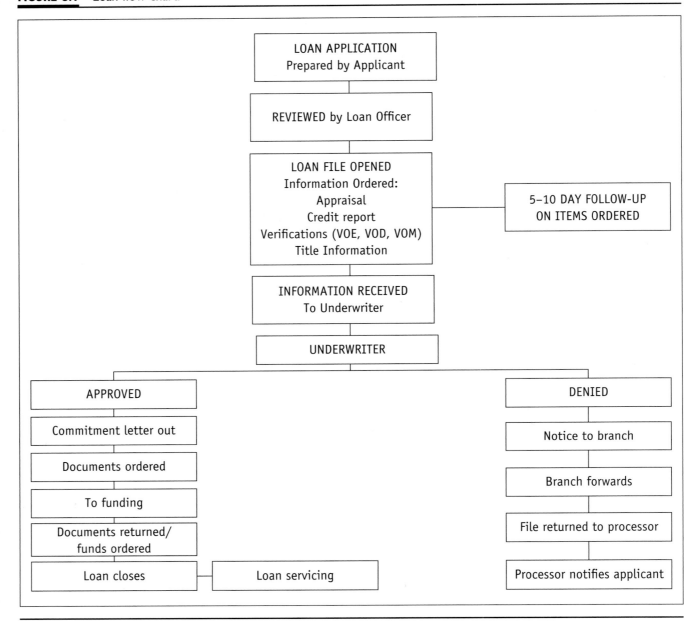

received to pay for these in the file as discussed in Chapter 15. It is common for lenders to not charge a fee for a credit report and to have the client pay the appraiser directly for the appraisal fee, thus relieving the loan agent from handling any trust funds.

The loan underwriting process often encounters delays in obtaining the financing because of some of the following reasons:

1. The borrower may be slow to return or complete all of the 1003 loan application form.
2. The borrower does not give a check to start the loan process

3. Creditors will not respond in a timely manner.

4. Creditors do not respond correctly.

5. Employers will not respond in a timely manner.

6. Employers do not complete the verification form properly.

7. An explanation is needed for any late payment.

8. Bad credit complicates the transaction and delays loan approval.

9. Income is less than what the prospective borrower reported on the application.

10. Additional creditors show up who were not reported on the loan application.

11. Appraisal value is lower than the sales price.

12. Property is unacceptable to the underwriter or the lender.

13. Inspections or repairs must be completed prior to the funding of the loan.

14. The file must be restructured because of a change in the loan type applied for.

15. Closing documents are incorrectly signed.

16. Closing requirements are not satisfied.

17. Workload backup, because of the market conditions, by the appraiser, underwriter, or lender.

Next, the most important form will be placed in the file, the **conversation sheet**, as shown in Figure 8.2. This sheet is used every time the processor speaks to

FIGURE 8.2   Conversation sheet.

| Borrower: _____ Loan #: _____ |

Date	Spoke With	Remarks	Employee's Name

All information that might have any bearing on the loan, the property, or the borrower, whether it be phone call, information received through other channels, or just knowledge, should be written down here.

WRITE IT DOWN NOW!!

any person in conjunction with the file. The processor logs a summary of the dialogue, along with the date, time, person spoken with, and that person's area code and telephone number. Often, the conversation log is included in many of the processing software systems that are available in the marketplace. Computer programs such as Goldmine or Top Producer can log every customer and client contact.

The processor uses a **file checklist** of some kind to keep track of the various aspects of the loan (see Figure 8.3). Many items in a loan happen concurrently, and it is difficult for the novice to keep track of these separate, simultaneous operations. The processor needs to log the date that items are ordered so he or she can follow up when the documents are not received, which may mean alerting the mortgage loan broker to telephone certain persons to assist in nudging others to return documents in a timely manner. It may mean that the processor will have to reorder a lost or misplaced document.

The next step is to mail out all verifications and any other items that need to be done at this time; experience is the best trainer on knowing what is needed. Until the processor has received the exposure to know what to look for, he or she must use the tools at hand provided at the place of employment. The blank forms listed below are commonly used when processing a file. Although the forms in this chapter are blank, Appendix C has a sample file with the forms filled in for a case study learning example.

- **Verification of employment (VOE)** on each borrower (see Appendix C)
- **Verification of deposit (VOD)** for each bank account, including savings and checking (see Appendix C)
- Credit authorization signed by each borrower and coborrower (see Figure 7.2)
- **Verification of Social Security number** (see Figure 8.4)

The loan processor will also need to verify other records about the borrower from the Department of Motor Vehicles (DMV), such as the driving record of the applicant (see Figure 8.5). Some lenders require a thorough background check for criminal records and other documentation that might affect the borrower's ability to repay the loan in the future or earn future income.

The *Lane Guide* is a helpful outside source that the processor needs to use. This publication provides the correct mailing address for a specific lender. The *Lane Guide* also maintains a master list of more than 36,000 closed lenders for locating the originator of a document for reconveyance of the subsequent trustee or assignee. The address provided in the guide is often not the same address that the borrower shows on his or her payment stub or where his or her monthly loan payment is sent. It is also not the same address that is listed in the telephone book as the local branch office. The database records that keep the loan information are usually centralized by most lenders.

The *Lane Guide* gives the complete street address and zip code of the verified address, fax numbers, 800 numbers, and special departments for collections, wholesale lending, REO, assumptions, and administrative offices. The *Lane Guide* can be obtained in print or CD-ROM or via the Internet. For information,

FIGURE 8.3 File checklist.

Branch:

Loan Officer:

Borrower:

Home Phone:

Work Phone:

Property Info:

Address:

Zip:

Tract:

SFR: Condo: PUD:

Number of Units:

Appraiser: Phone:

Escrow Co:

Escrow Officer:

Selling Broker:

Salesperson:

Listing Broker:

Salesperson:

Title Company:

Title Company Phone:

Total Points

Estimating Closing:

Purchase Info:

Owner: Non-Owner:

First: Type:

2nd: Type:

VA: Type: Pts

FHA: Type: Pts

Purchase: Equity:

Interest Rate:

Buydown:

Projected Source & Phone:

Address:

City, State, Zip:

Address:

City, State, Zip:

Address:

City, State, Zip:

Title Representative:

Processor

Loan Number:

Submit by:

LTV:

Sales Price:

Down Payment:

Seller Carryback:

New 1st:

Existing 1st:

New 2nd:

Existing 2nd:

Cash out: Yes   No

Escrow Number:

Home Number:

Work Phone:

Home Phone:

Home Phone:

Order Number:

Need	Document	Ord	Re-Ord	Rec	Need	Document	Ord	Re-Ord	Rec
	Cert of Eligibility					Deposit Receipt			
	VA Indebt/Off-base House					Escrow Instructions			
	DD214/1880					Receipt/Funds in Esc			
	Credit Report					Escrow Amendments			
	Supplement					Appraisal Funds			
	Credit Explanation					Hold Yes/No Due By:			
	Bankruptcy: Schedule E					442/Inspection			
	Divorce: Interlock/Final					Assignment			
	Driver's License					Reconsideration			
	Social Security Card					Seller Paying Costs			
	AKA Letter					Preliminary Title			
	Landlord Letter					C C & R's			
	Borrower:					Assn. Name/Phone			
	VOE (Present)					Budget/Bylaws			
	VOE (Prior)					Article of Incorpor			
	VOE (Prior)					DOC Letter			
	Add'l Income					Fidelity Bond			
	Coborrower:					Insurance: Decl.Pg			
	VOE (Present)					ECOA/State Notices			
	VOE (Prior)					Good Faith Est.			
	VOE (Prior)					ARM Disclosure			
	Add'l Income					Advance Disclosure			
	1040s					Termite/Completion			
	Profit & Loss Stmt					FHA/VA Assumption			
	Pay stubs					Sale of Servicing			
	W-2s					MIP Letter			
	Work History Expl.					FHA Disclosure			
						Lead-Based Paint			
	VOD					FHA/R.E. Certification			
	VOD								
	Gift Letter					Credit Report			
	Bank Statements (3 mo)					Appraisal			
	Source of Funds Explan.					442			
	Disposition of R.E.					Lock In			
	Sale Escrow Instructions					Remarks			

FIGURE 8.4 Verification of Social Security number.

Authorization for the Social Security Administration to
Release Social Security Number Verification

Printed Name _____ SSN_____

Date of Birth _____

I authorize the Social Security Administration to verify my Social Security number to
_____ through their agent, _____.

I understand that my consent allows no additional information from my social security
records to be provided to _____ and that the verification of my social
security number will be used for identifying the validity of my Social Security number.
I also understand that my Social Security number may not be used for any other purpose
other than the one stated above, including resale or redisclosure to other parties. The
only other redisclosure permitted by this authorization is for review purposes to insure
that _____complies with SSA's consent
requirements.

I am the individual to whom the Social Security number was issued or that person's legal
guardian. I declare and affirm under the penalty of perjury that the information contained
herein is true and correct. I know that if I make any representation that I know is false to
obtain information from Social Security records, I could be found guilty of a misdemeanor
and fined up to $5,000.

Signature _____ Date Signed _____

This consent is valid only for 90 days from the date signed, unless indicated otherwise by
the individual named above.

Contact information of individual signing authorization:

Address   _____

                 _____

Phone Number   _____

If consent is signed other than by the individual named above, indicate relationship:

                 _____

FIGURE 8.5 DMV Consent form.

I/We authorize the release of information regarding my/our record(s) for the purpose of processing a loan. I/We authorize that the mortgage loan broker and the lender may obtain information from the California Department of Motor Vehicles or any other agency or person, and I/We waive the requirements of Section 1808.21 of the California Motor Vehicle Code. I/We further authorize that a photocopy of this letter is to be considered as valid as the original document.

Print Name	Social Security/Taxpayer ID
Signature	Date
Print Name	Social Security/Taxpayer ID
Signature	Date

call (800) LANEGUIDE, or write to *Lane Guide*, 5450 Riggins Ct. # 1B, Reno, NV 89502-6577; fax (775) 826-5678; or http://www.laneguide.com.

The guide also provides the service center with information to obtain account ratings or verifications of deposit, payoff quotes, mortgage verifications, ratings, and schedule of fees, as well as rating policies, hours, and locations of installment loan accounts. For example, a prospective borrower may have a current loan with ABC Mortgage Corporation on a property in Kansas, with the loan originated by a mortgage loan broker in Kansas. Subsequently, the loan was sold in the secondary market (see Chapter 12) and is with a loan servicing firm located in California. What mailing address would be used for the VOM and for sending for the beneficiary demand? By using the *Lane Guide*, the processor would be able to ascertain that the mailing address for the loan servicing agent is 17671 Victory Blvd. #104, Tustin, CA 92680-3164. Without the *Lane Guide*, the processor may have sent the VOM to the Kansas office where the loan originated, and this detour would cause a delay in the processing time for the new loan.

Because insurance carriers that insure for loan default and government regulators try to reduce risk from loan default, the loan processor or the mortgage loan processor is often required to ensure that all documents received are the true and correct representations made to the lender (see Figure 8.6).

The processor will also need a copy of the borrower's income tax forms, which can be obtained form the IRS by completion of **Form 4506-T**. The form may be transmitted by fax or mail. The 1040 and W-2 information, plus

FIGURE 8.6 Loan processor document certification.

National Mutual Savings
111 South Any Street
P.O. Box 000
Any Town, Any State, Zip Code
Phone: (xxx) 555-1212 Fax: (xxx) FAX-LOAN

DOCUMENT CERTIFICATION

Date:

   I certify that the copies of exhibits described below are true and correct
copies of the original documents provided by the applicant(s). Subject originals do
NOT contain any "alterations, erasures or whiteouts." An employee of said lender
made copies of said original documents in the office of the originating lender.
This originating lender hereby certifies the above mentioned is true and correct,
per authorized signature on this form.

Exhibits submitted and certified:
[ ] Earnings statement, pay stubs (to cover the most recent 30-day period)
[ ] W-2s (2-year period)
[ ] Monthly bank statements (3 months most recent)
[ ] Canceled checks (front and back) (last 12 months)
[ ] Other: _____

                    _____

_____   _____
         Signature   Print Name and Title

---

attachments for various schedules, can be obtained, either free or for a fee. Special
instructions are given on the form if the copy must be certified for a court or administrative proceeding. The Form 4506-T (Request for Transcript of Tax Return, Figure 8.7) is used at no cost when the loan broker does not need the full tax return.

8.3 INCOME AND GUIDELINES FOR THE PROCESSOR

The mortgage loan broker's key responsibility is to make the job of the **underwriter** as easy as possible. In submitting a loan to the underwriter for approval, it helps to have a proven track record so the underwriter has confidence that the processor knows the guidelines for the particular loan program. The broker and processor's reputation should project to others that they have done a complete and thorough job with the loan package. The better the loan package, the faster

FIGURE 8.7 Tax return transcript request (IRS Form 4506-T).

Form **4506-T**
(Rev. January 2010)
Department of the Treasury
Internal Revenue Service

Request for Transcript of Tax Return

▶ **Request may be rejected if the form is incomplete or illegible.**

OMB No. 1545-1872

Tip. Use Form 4506-T to order a transcript or other return information free of charge. See the product list below. You can also call 1-800-829-1040 to order a transcript. If you need a copy of your return, use **Form 4506, Request for Copy of Tax Return.** There is a fee to get a copy of your return.

1a Name shown on tax return. If a joint return, enter the name shown first.

1b First social security number on tax return or employer identification number (see instructions)

2a If a joint return, enter spouse's name shown on tax return.

2b Second social security number if joint tax return

3 Current name, address (including apt., room, or suite no.), city, state, and ZIP code

4 Previous address shown on the last return filed if different from line 3

5 If the transcript or tax information is to be mailed to a third party (such as a mortgage company), enter the third party's name, address, and telephone number. The IRS has no control over what the third party does with the tax information.

Caution. *If the transcript is being mailed to a third party, ensure that you have filled in line 6 and line 9 before signing. Sign and date the form once you have filled in these lines. Completing these steps helps to protect your privacy.*

6 **Transcript requested.** Enter the tax form number here (1040, 1065, 1120, etc.) and check the appropriate box below. Enter only one tax form number per request. ▶

a **Return Transcript,** which includes most of the line items of a tax return as filed with the IRS. A tax return transcript does not reflect changes made to the account after the return is processed. Transcripts are only available for the following returns: Form 1040 series, Form 1065, Form 1120, Form 1120A, Form 1120H, Form 1120L, and Form 1120S. Return transcripts are available for the current year and returns processed during the prior 3 processing years. Most requests will be processed within 10 business days . . . . . . ☐

b **Account Transcript,** which contains information on the financial status of the account, such as payments made on the account, penalty assessments, and adjustments made by you or the IRS after the return was filed. Return information is limited to items such as tax liability and estimated tax payments. Account transcripts are available for most returns. Most requests will be processed within 30 calendar days. . ☐

c **Record of Account,** which is a combination of line item information and later adjustments to the account. Available for current year and 3 prior tax years. Most requests will be processed within 30 calendar days . . . . ☐

7 **Verification of Nonfiling,** which is proof from the IRS that you **did not** file a return for the year. Current year requests are only available after June 15th. There are no availability restrictions on prior year requests. Most requests will be processed within 10 business days . . ☐

8 **Form W-2, Form 1099 series, Form 1098 series, or Form 5498 series transcript.** The IRS can provide a transcript that includes data from these information returns. State or local information is not included with the Form W-2 information. The IRS may be able to provide this transcript information for up to 10 years. Information for the current year is generally not available until the year after it is filed with the IRS. For example, W-2 information for 2007, filed in 2008, will not be available from the IRS until 2009. If you need W-2 information for retirement purposes, you should contact the Social Security Administration at 1-800-772-1213. Most requests will be processed within 45 days . . . ☐

Caution. *If you need a copy of Form W-2 or Form 1099, you should first contact the payer. To get a copy of the Form W-2 or Form 1099 filed with your return, you must use Form 4506 and request a copy of your return, which includes all attachments.*

9 **Year or period requested.** Enter the ending date of the year or period, using the mm/dd/yyyy format. If you are requesting more than four years or periods, you must attach another Form 4506-T. For requests relating to quarterly tax returns, such as Form 941, you must enter each quarter or tax period separately.

Signature of taxpayer(s). I declare that I am either the taxpayer whose name is shown on line 1a or 2a, or a person authorized to obtain the tax information requested. If the request applies to a joint return, **either** husband or wife must sign. If signed by a corporate officer, partner, guardian, tax matters partner, executor, receiver, administrator, trustee, or party other than the taxpayer, I certify that I have the authority to execute Form 4506-T on behalf of the taxpayer. **Note.** *For transcripts being sent to a third party, this form must be received within 120 days of signature date.*

Telephone number of taxpayer on line 1a or 2a

Sign Here ▶

Signature (see instructions)

Date

▶ Title (if line 1a above is a corporation, partnership, estate, or trust)

▶ Spouse's signature

Date

For Privacy Act and Paperwork Reduction Act Notice, see page 2.

Cat. No. 37667N

Form **4506-T** (Rev. 1-2010)

FIGURE 8.7   *(Continued)*

Form 4506-T (Rev. 1-2010)   Page **2**

General Instructions

Purpose of form. Use Form 4506-T to request tax return information. You can also designate a third party to receive the information. See line 5.

Tip. Use Form 4506, Request for Copy of Tax Return, to request copies of tax returns.

Where to file. Mail or fax Form 4506-T to the address below for the state you lived in, or the state your business was in, when that return was filed. There are two address charts: one for individual transcripts (Form 1040 series and Form W-2) and one for all other transcripts.

If you are requesting more than one transcript or other product and the chart below shows two different RAIVS teams, send your request to the team based on the address of your most recent return.

Automated transcript request. You can call 1-800-829-1040 to order a transcript through the automated self-help system. Follow prompts for "questions about your tax account" to order a tax return transcript.

Chart for individual transcripts (Form 1040 series and Form W-2)

If you filed an individual return and lived in:	Mail or fax to the "Internal Revenue Service" at:
Florida, Georgia, North Carolina, South Carolina	RAIVS Team P.O. Box 47-421 Stop 91 Doraville, GA 30362
	770-455-2335
Alabama, Kentucky, Louisiana, Mississippi, Tennessee, Texas, a foreign country, or A.P.O. or F.P.O. address	RAIVS Team Stop 6716 AUSC Austin, TX 73301
	512-460-2272
Alaska, Arizona, California, Colorado, Hawaii, Idaho, Illinois, Indiana, Iowa, Kansas, Michigan, Minnesota, Montana, Nebraska, Nevada, New Mexico, North Dakota, Oklahoma, Oregon, South Dakota, Utah, Washington, Wisconsin, Wyoming	RAIVS Team Stop 37106 Fresno, CA 93888
	559-456-5876
Arkansas, Connecticut, Delaware, District of Columbia, Maine, Maryland, Massachusetts, Missouri, New Hampshire, New Jersey, New York, Ohio, Pennsylvania, Rhode Island, Vermont, Virginia, West Virginia	RAIVS Team Stop 6705 P-6 Kansas City, MO 64999
	816-292-6102

Chart for all other transcripts

If you lived in or your business was in:	Mail or fax to the "Internal Revenue Service" at:
Alabama, Alaska, Arizona, Arkansas, California, Colorado, Florida, Hawaii, Idaho, Iowa, Kansas, Louisiana, Minnesota, Mississippi, Missouri, Montana, Nebraska, Nevada, New Mexico, North Dakota, Oklahoma, Oregon, South Dakota, Tennessee, Texas, Utah, Washington, Wyoming, a foreign country, or A.P.O. or F.P.O. address	RAIVS Team P.O. Box 9941 Mail Stop 6734 Ogden, UT 84409
	801-620-6922
Connecticut, Delaware, District of Columbia, Georgia, Illinois, Indiana, Kentucky, Maine, Maryland, Massachusetts, Michigan, New Hampshire, New Jersey, New York, North Carolina, Ohio, Pennsylvania, Rhode Island, South Carolina, Vermont, Virginia, West Virginia, Wisconsin	RAIVS Team P.O. Box 145500 Stop 2800 F Cincinnati, OH 45250
	859-669-3592

Line 1b. Enter your employer identification number (EIN) if your request relates to a business return. Otherwise, enter the first social security number (SSN) shown on the return. For example, if you are requesting Form 1040 that includes Schedule C (Form 1040), enter your SSN.

Line 6. Enter only one tax form number per request.

Signature and date. Form 4506-T must be signed and dated by the taxpayer listed on line 1a or 2a. If you completed line 5 requesting the information be sent to a third party, the IRS must receive Form 4506-T within 120 days of the date signed by the taxpayer or it will be rejected.

Individuals. Transcripts of jointly filed tax returns may be furnished to either spouse. Only one signature is required. Sign Form 4506-T exactly as your name appeared on the original return. If you changed your name, also sign your current name.

Corporations. Generally, Form 4506-T can be signed by: (1) an officer having legal authority to bind the corporation, (2) any person designated by the board of directors or other governing body, or (3) any officer or employee on written request by any principal officer and attested to by the secretary or other officer.

Partnerships. Generally, Form 4506-T can be signed by any person who was a member of the partnership during any part of the tax period requested on line 9.

All others. See Internal Revenue Code section 6103(e) if the taxpayer has died, is insolvent, is a dissolved corporation, or if a trustee, guardian, executor, receiver, or administrator is acting for the taxpayer.

Documentation. For entities other than individuals, you must attach the authorization document. For example, this could be the letter from the principal officer authorizing an employee of the corporation or the Letters Testamentary authorizing an individual to act for an estate.

Privacy Act and Paperwork Reduction Act Notice. We ask for the information on this form to establish your right to gain access to the requested tax information under the Internal Revenue Code. We need this information to properly identify the tax information and respond to your request. You are not required to request any transcript; if you do request a transcript, sections 6103 and 6109 and their regulations require you to provide this information, including your SSN or EIN. If you do not provide this information, we may not be able to process your request. Providing false or fraudulent information may subject you to penalties.

Routine uses of this information include giving it to the Department of Justice for civil and criminal litigation, and cities, states, and the District of Columbia for use in administering their tax laws. We may also disclose this information to other countries under a tax treaty, to federal and state agencies to enforce federal nontax criminal laws, or to federal law enforcement and intelligence agencies to combat terrorism.

You are not required to provide the information requested on a form that is subject to the Paperwork Reduction Act unless the form displays a valid OMB control number. Books or records relating to a form or its instructions must be retained as long as their contents may become material in the administration of any Internal Revenue law. Generally, tax returns and return information are confidential, as required by section 6103.

The time needed to complete and file Form 4506-T will vary depending on individual circumstances. The estimated average time is: **Learning about the law or the form,** 10 min.; **Preparing the form,** 12 min.; and **Copying, assembling, and sending the form to the IRS,** 20 min.

If you have comments concerning the accuracy of these time estimates or suggestions for making Form 4506-T simpler, we would be happy to hear from you. You can write to the Internal Revenue Service, Tax Products Coordinating Committee, SE:W:CAR:MP:T:T:SP, 1111 Constitution Ave. NW, IR-6526, Washington, DC 20224. Do not send the form to this address. Instead, see *Where to file* on this page.

the file will be approved and the fewer the additional conditions, requirements, or limiting factors. The name of the game is to get the loan approved.

In training novices to the industry, one professional found that many loans were turned down by underwriters or the loan committee because the processor did not know the guidelines for the loan program under which that loan application had been submitted. Never challenge the underwriter by asking, "Why did you turn down this loan?" Rather, you can ask, "What can we do to put this loan together?" Do not personally challenge those who will be making the final decision in the loan process, because the mortgage loan broker and processor may be working with the same people in the future and should try to stay on their good side.

The processor will need to know which type of loan file the borrower has applied for to know what is needed for processing and what documents will be needed by the underwriter for final loan approval. The four basic forms of loan files are:

1. Full documentation file
2. Time-saver documentation file
3. Streamline documentation file
4. Subprime loan file

According to the FNMA Selling Guide, the information shown in Figure 8.8 should assist the processor in looking over a 1003 and supporting documents that are submitted in a loan file. A good processor commits to memory as many of these items as possible.

What Is Income?

The borrower must have a history of receiving stable **income**. There must be a reasonable expectation that the income will continue to be received in the foreseeable future. Salary and wage incomes are the easiest to determine and verify. Income from most other sources can be considered as qualifying income as long as it is properly documented. Income received from any source that the lender cannot verify is not acceptable for the purpose of qualifying borrowers. Special consideration may need to be given to income from sources other than wages and salaries.

Military Income

Military personnel may be entitled to various types of pay in addition to their base pay. Flight or hazard pay, rations, clothing allowance, quarters allowance, and proficiency pay are acceptable as part of stable income as long as the expectation that they will continue in the future can be established.

Commission Income

Commission income may be subject to fluctuation from year to year. Therefore, the lender will want the mortgage loan broker and processor to develop an

FIGURE 8.8   Loan limits (FNMA) as of 2009.

Units	Maximum Original Principal Balance (*Last Revised : January 12, 2009*)			
	Contiguous States, District of Columbia, and Puerto Rico		Alaska, Guam, Hawaii, and the U.S. Virgin Islands	
	General	High-Cost*	General	High-Cost*
1	$ 417,000	$ 625,500	$ 625,500	$ 938,250
2	$ 533,850	$ 800,775	$ 800,775	$ 1,201,150
3	$ 645,300	$ 967,950	$ 967,950	$ 1,451,925
4	$ 801,950	$ 1,202,925	$ 1,202,925	$ 1,804,375

Second Mortgages: The maximum original mortgage amount for a second mortgage is 50% of our conventional first mortgage limit for a single-family dwelling—$208,500 in the continental United States and $312,750 in Alaska, Hawaii, and the Virgin Islands.

Loan-to-Value Ratios: Use a SFR as an example in this chapter. Refer to the standard underwriting guidelines for additional information on 2 to 4 units.

Purchase Money Transactions: For purchase money transactions, the maximum allowable LTV ratio (CLTV or combined loan-to-value ratio) may be a factor of the type of loan, the method of amortization, the lien type, the number of dwelling units, the property's occupancy status, the borrower's residency status, and whether there is any subordinate financing.

Category	LTV (Loan to Value)	CLTV (Combined Loan to Value)
* Owner-Occupied Principal Residence(2)		
—Fully Amortizing Fixed-Rate First Mortgage	95% (5)	90% (6, 11)
—Balloon Fixed-Rate First Mortgage	90% (5)	90% (6, 11)
—Adjustable-Rate First Mortgage	90% (5, 7)	90% (6, 11)
—Cooperative Share Loan	90% (5)	—
—Second Mortgage	—	80% (8)

Footnotes: FNMA has eleven footnotes in its guideline. We will only cover the ones listed above.

(2) The following are eligible only as one-family owner-occupied principal residences: Cooperative share loans, balloon first mortgages, and two-step adjustable-rate first mortgages.

(5) The ratio is limited to 80% if the property secures a rehabilitation mortgage or 75% if it secures a mortgage to a nonpermanent resident alien.

(6) The ratio is limited to 80% if the property secures a rehabilitation mortgage or if the property seller provides the financing at a below-market interest rate and 75% if the property secures a mortgage to a nonpermanent resident alien.

(7) One version of the STABLE adjustable-rate mortgage may have a maximum loan-to-value ratio of 95%, as long as the property does not secure a cooperative share loan, a rehabilitation mortgage, or a mortgage to a nonpermanent resident alien.

(8) The ratio is limited to 75% if the property secures a mortgage to a nonpermanent resident alien.

(11) The first mortgage cannot represent more than 75% of the lesser of the sales price or appraised value.

Refinance Transactions: The guidelines are different for this type of loan. Refer to the underwriting guidelines.

Mortgage Insurance: Mortgage insurance is required for first mortgages if the loan is loan-to-value. ratios greater than 80%, and for second mortgages when the combined loan-to-value ratio for the first and second mortgages is greater than 70%. The mortgage insurance coverage must be obtained from one of the FNMA acceptable mortgage insurers.

http://www.fanniemae.com/

Reprinted with permission from Fannie Mae.

average of the last two years' (24 months') income to use in evaluating the borrower's income qualifications. If the borrower has had a bad year, the processor may be able to use three years (36 months) for income purposes. Fewer than two years of commission income will be acceptable only if significant compensating factors can be verified.

Overtime and Bonus Income

Overtime and bonus income can be used for qualification purposes if the employer verifies that the applicant has received this income for the past two years (24 months). The employer must also indicate whether any overtime or bonus income will, in all probability, continue.

Part-Time or Second-Job Income

Part-time or second-job income may be used if it can be verified as having been uninterrupted for the previous two years and if it has a strong likelihood of continuation.

Retirement Income

A copy of an award letter, tax returns, IRS W-2 form, or copies of the borrower's recent bank statements to confirm the regular deposit of the payments must be received and placed into the file.

Social Security Income

Receipt of a Social Security Administration's award letter or copies of the borrower's last 12 bank statements must confirm the regular deposit of the payments. Benefits that have defined expiration dates must have a remaining term of at least three years from the date of the mortgage application to be considered as income. Social Security income was not taxable up to a specific amount and only taxable above a certain amount. For example, $1,200 income from Social Security each month 125% means that $1,500 is counted as gross income because the $1,200 is the net amount received, and no income tax is taken from this amount, whereas the $1,500 gross monthly income would require income tax deducted from the gross amount. FNMA uses the 125% amount, and FHLMC uses 115%. Figure 8.9 shows what can be done online with the Social Security Administration (www.socialsecurity.gov).

Alimony or Child Support

For alimony or child support to be considered as income, it must continue for at least three years (36 consecutive months) from the date of the loan application. The borrower must provide evidence that the funds have been regularly received for at least the past 12 months, as may be found on a bank statement.

FIGURE 8.9   Social Security Administration information.

Apply for retirement/spouse's benefits	www.socialsecurity.gov/applyforbenefits
Apply for disability benefits	www.socialsecurity.gov/applyfordisability
Find out what benefits can be applied for	www.socialsecurity.gov/applyforbenefits
Use benefit planner to calculate future retirement, disability and survivor benefits	www.socialsecurity.gov/planners
Request a Social Security statement	www.socialsecurity.gov/statement
Request a Proof of Income letter	www.socialsecurity.gov/beve
Get a 1099/1042S benefit statement	www.socialsecurity.gov/1099
Get a password	www.socialsecurity.gov/password
Check information and benefits	www.socialsecurity.gov/pcyb
Direct-deposit information	www.socialsecurity.gov/pdd

Notes Receivable

FNMA requires a copy of the note to establish the amount and length of payment. Payments must continue for at least three years from the date of the loan application. Borrowers must provide evidence that they have received the funds for the last 12 months.

Interest Income and Dividends

May be used if the lender can develop an average of the income for the last two years.

The preceding sources of income are what FNMA and FHLMC will accept. The processor should always check with the underwriter for full details of what is acceptable income. Some other areas of income that may be used are:

1. Mortgage differential payments
2. Trust income
3. VA benefits
4. Welfare benefits (aid for dependents)
5. Rental income
6. Automobile allowances and expense account payments
7. Foster care income

Net Rental Income

Many borrowers believe that 100 percent of the gross rental income is used for loan qualifications. Most rental income property owners use between 25 percent and 50 percent of gross income for operating expenses. Typically, the owner uses the gross income, then subtracts the loan payment, then deducts the operating expenses. Operating Expenses (OE) consist of property Taxes, Insurance,

<u>M</u>aintenance and repairs, property <u>M</u>anagement, <u>U</u>tilities and <u>R</u>eserves for replacement (TIMMUR).

Some other owners use the IRS tax form method for calculating new rental income that is often available through computer software programs, such as Yardi, QuickBook, or Quicken. Yet another method to calculate rental income is the appraisal income approach to value, which does not take into consideration the existing or proposed debt on the property, using the following formula:

> Gross scheduled income (GSI)
> − Vacancy and bad debt (Vac/BD)
> = Effective gross income (EGI)
> − Operating Expenses (OE) = (TIMMUR)
> = Net Operating income (NOI)

These methods are not what is required for the calculations by the loan broker for qualifying the borrower for the loan. Instead, the following criteria are the FNMA loan requirements as explained on the loan application, Form 1003. First, the borrower needs to have at least a 30 percent equity position in the property, based upon a current appraisal. Second, from the gross scheduled income, if the property is older, deduct 35 percent to 50 percent for maintenance, utilities, and vacancy; and, if the property is newer, deduct 25 percent from the monthly gross income for maintenance, utilities, and vacancy. Should the results derive any negative cash flow after deducting the loan payment, the amount of negative cash flow is considered to be as long-term debt for the borrower in the loan qualification process and would be calculated as such.

8.4 BORROWER DOCUMENTATION

A processor should never place anything into the borrower's files without first reviewing the item and comparing it with the other data received to determine the accuracy and completeness of the information. Items include the credit report, appraisal, VOE, VOD, VOM, and preliminary title report. Once the types of income have been reviewed, the mortgage loan broker must look into other areas of which the processor should be aware.

Self-Employment

When a borrower is self-employed, in addition to verification of income from the federal or state government tax agencies, the loan broker must often obtain more documentation. The primary difference is that the borrower must have been self-employed for a minimum of two years (24 months) and be able to document the income. The processor will need to obtain a copy of a business card of the borrower and a copy of a business license issued by the city in which the company operates.

The processor will also need to check with the lender to determine whether the investor requires any additional documentation. It is common that the investor will require the bank statements for the past six months, along with proof of

FIGURE 8.10   Profit and loss statement.

For the period from ___/_____/____ to ___/____/____

Business Name: _____

Business Address: _____

Business Phone: _____ Business Fax: _____ Business e-mail: _____

Type of Business: _____

Business Tax Preparer: _____

GROSS INCOME $_____

OPERATING EXPENSES:

     Salaries (Excluding owners) $_____

     Rent $_____

     Supplies and Materials $_____

     Equipment (Auto, machines, etc.) $_____

     Taxes (Excluding income taxes) $_____

     License Fees and Insurance $_____

     Telephone and Utilities $_____

     Advertising $_____

     Repairs (Equipment, auto, etc.) $_____

     Gas, Oil and Transportation $_____

     Debt payments $_____

     Other: _____ $_____

     Other: _____ $_____

TOTAL OPERATING EXPENSES $_____

NET PROFIT $_____

I certify that the above is true and correct to the best of my knowledge and records.

BY: _____ Title: _____ Date: _____

quarterly tax estimates payment records. A current **profit and loss statement**, such as is shown in Figure 8.10, will have to be obtained by the loan processor before the loan package is submitted to the lender's underwriter for loan approval.

Gifts from a Relative

A borrower may use funds obtained as a gift from a relative to satisfy part of the cash requirement for closing. The borrower generally must use his or her own funds to cover the required minimum cash down payment, usually at least 5% of the sales price. When the loan-to-value ratio for the mortgage is 80 percent or less, the full down payment may come from a gift. Other guidelines apply to funds received by a gift from others, and the reader should refer to the FNMA guidelines or loan specifics. A sample gift letter is shown in Figure 8.11.

FIGURE 8.11   Gift letter.

To Whom It May Concern:

I/We _____ hereby certify that I/We have made a gift of
          Print Name(s) of Donor

$ _____ to my _____, _____.
                       Relationship   Name of Recipient

This gift is to be applied toward the purchase of the property located at:

_____
     Street Address, City, State

I/WE FURTHER CERTIFY THAT <u>NO REPAYMENT IS EXPECTED</u> OR IMPLIED OF THIS GIFT, EITHER IN THE FORM OF CASH OR FUTURE SERVICES.

NAME: _____   _____
      Print   Signature of Donor

NAME: _____   _____
      Print   Signature of Donor

ADDRESS: _____   PHONE (_____)_____
       Street number and name

_____   _____
  City   State   Zip   Relationship to the Borrower

THIS SIGNATURE AUTHORIZES THE RELEASE OF INFORMATION TO VERIFY THE FUNDS IN THIS GIFT LETTER.

These funds are currently deposited with:

Bank(s) Name: _____   Address _____

_____   _____

Account number(s) _____   Current Balance $ _____

_____   Current Balance $ _____

____ Evidence of receipt of transfer of the gift funds from donor's funds.

Undisclosed Debt

When the processor receives the credit report from the credit reporting agency and the report discloses that the borrowers did not disclose all of their debts on their original 1003, the borrowers must provide a written explanation for the omission. The item will have to be added to the required second 1003 prepared by the lender and signed by the borrowers before the loan is closed.

Revolving Debt

When revolving accounts with outstanding balances do not have stated minimum required payments, payments should be calculated at the greater of 5% of the outstanding balance or $10 per month.

Judgments, Garnishments, or Liens

Any judgments, garnishments, or liens, usually in excess of $2,500, must be paid in full before closing; however, check with your investor for any other guidelines.

Bankruptcy

A **bankruptcy** must have been fully discharged and the borrower must have reestablished good credit and demonstrated an ability to manage financial affairs before a lender will accept the loan. Under FNMA guidelines, the borrower must have at least four years (as of October 1998; formerly it was only two years, and FHLMC is still two years) between the discharge date of the bankruptcy and the loan application as sufficient time to reestablish credit. A shorter elapsed time may be justified if the lender is able to document that extraordinary circumstances caused the bankruptcy, such as the death of a spouse that left exorbitant medical debts. In addition, the mortgage loan broker, on discovering a prior bankruptcy, should determine which legal federal code section under which bankruptcy was filed: Chapter 7, a complete discharge for an individual on personal debts; Chapter 11, a bankruptcy by a business doing business as a corporation; or Chapter 13, known as credit card consolidation or reorganization, in which the creditor must accept virtually whatever the borrower can pay, as approved by the court, which is often substantially less than the contract agreement.

As of October 2005, new rules for filing bankruptcy are in effect. The filing party must meet certain guidelines, such as determining the filing parties' income. If the borrowers' income exceeds the median state income, then they must file under Chapter 13 and repay the obligation throughout a five-year period, which would show as long-term debt for the borrower when the income-to-debt ratio is determined for five full years.

Cosigner

When a borrower has a contingent liability as the result of having cosigned a loan to enable another party to obtain credit, the mortgage loan broker must establish several items. Typically, this method is used when the borrower cosigns for his or her child's automobile loan or a sibling cosigns for a student loan. In this case, the paperwork must show that the borrower is not the party who is actually repaying the debt by producing a copy of the contract showing the primary borrower's obligation and that person's payments on that loan. Most lenders will not require that this contingent liability be included in the borrower's long-term debt. The processor will need documentation to show that the primary borrower has been making the payments for at least 12 months, such as the past six months' bank statements for the individual who has actually been making the loan payments, if such is not the borrower for the current loan. A shorter payment history may be approved on a case-by-case basis. One item that will be needed is 12 months of canceled checks as proof of payment by the primary borrower.

In some cases, the reverse may be the case. The current borrower may be applying for a loan using a coborrower for some portion of the qualification process, such as length of time on the job, income, credit, or cash for down payment or closing costs. In this case, the **cosigner** is also treated as a co-mortgagor on the new loan, which may require that the coborrower be placed on title as co-owner of the property.

Student Loans

There are many types of student loans. Some student loans require repayment on graduation, and others may be deferred if the borrower is working on a graduate degree. The processor needs to ascertain which type of loan the borrower has by reviewing the loan contract. If the borrower is behind on the student loan payment, then it must be paid off before the close of escrow. Also, if a borrower has a deferred payment loan, the payment must still be counted as a long-term debt.

Loan Purpose

When a borrower refinances a property and requests cash out, it is common to include some statement of the purpose of the loan. Figure 8.12 is a sample of such a letter that would be part of the file.

8.5 SAMPLE LOAN FILE

The following samples have been included in this chapter for your review:

1. **Credit authorization**: May be used for any type of loan (VA, FHA, or conventional) (see Figure 7.2).
2. **Gift letter**: When the borrower is receiving part of the down payment from a relative (see Figure 8.11).
3. **Purpose of loan letter**: To explain the reason for the loan (see Figure 8.12).
4. **Child care statement**: Usually used on VA and FHA loans (see Figure 8.13).
5. **Cover letter**: To be used for all loan submissions (see Figure 8.14).

FIGURE 8.12   Purpose of loan letter.

To Whom It May Concern:

The purpose of this loan is to: _____

_____

_____

_____

_____   _____
Borrower   Date

_____   _____
Borrower   Date

_____   _____
Borrower   Date

6. **Underwriting "red flags"**: Things to look for as the processor compiles a loan file for submission to an (underwriter) investor, shown in Chapter 10.

7. **Homeowners association**: The processor must obtain various types of information from different sources when processing a loan that involves an association. Some data is available from the borrower, while other items must be received directly from the homeowners association. Because the mortgage loan broker and processor must rely on other people to get necessary information, the mortgage loan broker should assist in following up to get the data. The faster the information is obtained, the sooner the processor can forward the file to the underwriter for loan approval. Delays usually occur when there is a lack of follow-up. A request for homeowners association information is shown in Figure 8.15. Additional information may be found at http://www.hoa-sites.com/homeowners_association_website.php?gclid=COGWy8bzi6ECFctx5QodNw0xOA.

8. **File order**: To be placed as the number one item in the processor's submission file. Each investor may have its own format, as shown in Figure 8.16. The processor should ask for a copy of the investor's format, as found in Figure 8.17.

FIGURE 8.13 Child care statement.

Date _____

This is to state that during my/our working hours my/our children are cared for by:

_____

Name of Care Provider

_____

Address

_____

City/State/ZIP

_____

Telephone Number with Area Code

at a cost to us of $ _____ per day/week/month (circle one).

Comments: _____

_____   _____

Borrower   Date

_____   _____

Coborrower   Date

8.6 STACKING ORDER

First, the file contents are placed in the required order listed for the internal file purposes of the mortgage loan broker's firm (see Figure 8.17). Then, the file materials must be placed in a particular order, called the **stacking order**, for presentation to the lender so the underwriter can review the documentation. Should items be out of place or missing, the file will most likely be rejected when presented to the lender. Each type of loan has a separate criteria list; however, most of the same elements are requested for each type of loan (see Figure 8.17). Different lenders use different file formats. When a lender uses a left- and- right-side file, the format resembles Figure 8.17. If a right-side file is used, the format is more like Figure 8.16. A good loan processor who works for the loan broker knows the differences and knows how to compare and contrast the different styles to meet the lender requirements.

To get a current, approved stack order list, the mortgage loan broker and processor may wish to obtain a copy from the direct lender. Each lender that the mortgage brokers work with will have their own particular order. The office

FIGURE 8.14   Cover letter.

To Whom It May Concern:

Enclosed you will find a loan request under your loan program _____ in the amount of $ _____ for _____years with an interest rate of _____ (fixed) (variable, initial rate_____, cap _____)   at _____ points and fees.

I feel that this is a good loan for the following reasons. (List the positive features of the loan)
     1.
     2.
     3.
     4.
     5.

Items for your consideration. (List any items that may be of concern to the underwriter.)
     1.
     2.
     3.

If you have any questions regarding this loan request, please feel free to contact me at (900) 123-4567 or me at FAX number (900) 765-4321.

I look forward to your positive response.

Sincerely,

Buzz Chambers
Processor

---

location of FNMA and FHLMC to obtain current forms and underwriting books for the loan may be obtained from the following:

WESTERN REGIONAL OFFICE FOR FEDERAL NATIONAL MORTGAGE ASSOCIATION (FANNIE MAE)
http://www.fanniemae.com
135 North Los Robles Avenue, Suite 300 Pasadena, CA 91101-1707
Phone: (626) 396-5100
No Hotline Number.

An operator directs the call to an underwriter per the area code of caller.

WESTERN REGIONAL OFFICE FOR FEDERAL HOME LOAN MORTGAGE CORPORATION (FREDDIE MAC)
http://www.freddiemac.com
21700 Oxnard, Suite 1900
Woodland Hills, CA 91367
Phone: (818) 710-3000
Hotline (818) 710-3024

Hotline number is for underwriting questions only and generally referred to as the company's servicing number.

FIGURE 8.15   Directions for obtaining homeowners association (HOA) information.

I. <u>At the application time ask the borrower:</u> (obtained by Loan Officer)
  A. Do you pay Homeowner Association Dues?
    1. If so, how much are the monthly dues?
  B. NAME OF HOMEOWNER ASSOCIATION # 1
    Address: City   Zip
    Area code   Phone
  C. NAME OF HOMEOWNER ASSOCIATION # 2
    Address: City   Zip
    Area code   Phone
  D. NAME OF THE MANAGEMENT COMPANY (If any)
    Address: City   Zip
    Area code   Phone
  E. Phone number of HOMEOWNER ASSOCIATION, if no management company
    is involved:
    Address: City   Zip
    Area code   Phone
II. PROCESSING: OBTAINING NEEDED DOCUMENTS:
  A. Check with each individual lender on guidelines for items needed on CONDO,
    PUD, DE-MIN PUD, etc.
  B. NAME OF SUBJECT PROPERTY PROJECT: (See the Appraisal)
  C. Call MANAGEMENT COMPANY (If no management company, call homeowners'
    association). Ask for the ESCROW DEPARTMENT.
    1. Identify yourself and your company. State that you are doing a purchase or
      refinance loan for their association member.
    2. Ask what is the management company's (HOA's) policy for obtaining
      Association information.
      <u>Will they accept a written request letter from your company or must the
      request come from the Escrow company?</u>
    3. What are the fees for the following items: (charges)
      _____CCRs (Get this from the Title Insurance Co.) $ _____
      _____ Bylaws $ _____
      _____ Articles of Incorporation $ _____
      _____Current Budget & Balance Sheet for the HOA $_____
      _____ Evidence of Fidelity Bonding (for a Mgmt. Co.) $ _____
      _____ Dishonesty Coverage (for HOA) $ _____
    4. How can we obtain evidence of property & liability insurance for the
      Homeowners' Association?
      Name, address and phone of carrier.
      Policy number and insurer.

NAME & PHONE NUMBER OF INSURER FOR HOA & THE FEE $ _____

FIGURE 8.16 File order.

```
                              (TOP TO BOTTOM)

    (    )          COVER LETTER
    (    )          BROKER FEE REQUEST FORM
    (    )          1008 TRANSMITTAL SUMMARY
    (    )          APPLICATION (TYPED 1003)
    (    )          CREDIT REPORT
    (    )          CREDIT EXPLANATION LETTER
    (    )          VOES
    (    )          OTHER INCOME VERIFICATIONS (tax returns, W-2s, P&Ls,
                    interest, K-1s, 1065s, trust agreement, etc.)
    (    )          VODS
    (    )          GIFT LETTER
    (    )          ESCROW INSTRUCTIONS
    (    )          HUD 1 for the sale of existing property
    (    )          VOMS*
    (    )          RENTAL AGREEMENTS
    (    )          DEPOSIT RECEIPT/SALES AGREEMENT
    (    )          APPRAISAL (three photo sets, subject property and comps)
    (    )          RECERTIFICATION OF VALUE
    (    )          OPERATING INCOME STATEMENT
                    (Nonowner-occupied property)
    (    )          PRELIMINARY TITLE REPORT
    (    )          PROJECT APPROVAL LETTER, CC&RS, BYLAWS
    (    )          TERMITE REPORT, SOILS REPORT
    (    )          HANDWRITTEN APPLICATION (1003)
    (    )          FAIR LENDING STATEMENT
    (    )          RESPA (Good Faith) STATEMENT
    (    )          ADVANCED DISCLOSURE
    (    )          OCCUPANCY STATEMENT
```

* Unrated VOM must be supplemented with copies of 12 months of canceled checks, consecutive order, or year-end statement and checks to cover 12 previous months.

FIGURE 8.17   Loan stacking order.

Left Side of File	Right Side of File
_____ HUD 1 Settlement Stmt	_____ Loan Approval
_____ Recorded Deed of Trust	_____ Funding conditions
_____ Recorded Corp. Assignment	_____ MI Approval
_____ Recorded Intervening Assignments	_____ Investor Loan Approval
_____ Final Title Policy w/Endorsements	_____ Loan Submission Form
_____ Copy of PMI check	_____ Stack Order Form
_____ Copy of Executed PMI Remittance	_____ Lock-in Request
_____ Collateral Confirmation	_____ Final 1008
_____ Funding Sheet	_____ Final Typed & Signed 1003
_____ Conversation Log	_____ Handwritten 1003 Application
_____ Funding Checklist	_____ Green Card(s)
_____ Copy of Wire	_____ Silent Second Information
_____ Original Hazard Policy	_____ Purpose of Cash Out Refi
_____ Flood Certificate	_____ Credit Report Supplements
_____ Flood Insurance	_____ Credit Report
_____ Disclosures: Mold, Lead-based paint	
_____ Copy of MI Approval	_____ Business Credit Report
_____ Copy of Note	_____ Signed/Dated Inquiry Explan.
_____ Signed and dated Buydown Agreement	_____ Complete Bankruptcy Papers
_____ Certified Copy of Trust Deed/Riders	_____ Divorce Decree
_____ Certified Copy of Grand Deed	_____ Verifications of Loan (VOM)
_____ Final Truth-in-Lending Act	
(Reg Z and HOEPA)	_____ Copy of Note for Sub. Finan.
_____ Itemization of Amount financed	_____ Copy of Deed for Sub. Finan.
_____ Right to Cancel	_____ Processor's Certification
_____ W-9 Taxpayer I.D.	_____ Verif of Employment (VOE)
_____ ARM Disclosure	_____ Prior Employment Verif.
_____ Compliance Agmt, Est. pymt	_____ Employment History Explan.
_____ Copy of Loan Escrow Inst. to Title	_____ Current Y-T-D Pay Stubs
_____ Loan Escrow Instructions/borrower	_____ Verif. of Additional Income
_____ Other Misc. Closing Forms	_____ Self-Employed Inc. Analysis
_____ Underwriting Conversation Log	_____ Signed Profit & Loss
_____ Quality Control Audit Report	_____ Signed Balance Sheet
_____ MI Application Form	_____ Two (2) years' W2/1099 forms
_____ Underwriting Worksheet	_____ Signed/dated Tax Returns (2 yrs.)
_____ Copy of Und's corrected 1008/1003	_____ 1040/K-1 form (2 yrs.)
_____ Miscellaneous	_____ Corp (1120)/Partnership (1065)
	_____ Rental Agreements/Leases
	_____ Gift Letter

```
Green Label—Conventional
Red Label—FHA
Blue Label—DVA
```

Left Side of File	Right Side of File
_____ Evidence of transfer of funds	
_____ Source of funds letter	
_____ Verifications of Deposit (VOD)	
_____ Bank statements (2 months)	

Number of "Copy" packages required by investor _____ Sales escrow instructions
  to be sent to corporate. _____ Purchase Agmt/Counter Offers

FHMA/FHLMC 2	_____ Escrow Instr./Amendments
With MI 3	_____ HOA Certification/CC&R's
	_____ Complete Appraisal

Note: All documents are mandatory at funding. _____ Preliminary Title Report
_____ Reg. Z/Good Faith/Fair Lend. _____ Authorization to Release Info.
  _____ Servicing Trans. Discl. Notice

SUMMARY

Processing is a vital step in the successful closing of the loan. It takes the right equipment and attitude to prepare a loan file for submission to the underwriter in a short time. The most important form in the file may be the conversation sheet. A good working knowledge of the flowchart is required of the loan processor. Time on the job is the best way to truly learn processing. The loan broker should be, and the processor must become, computer literate. Good common sense is also an important tool for the professional processor.

REVIEWING YOUR UNDERSTANDING

1. If a borrower has a student loan with a deferred payment, the loan:
   A. Does not need to be included as a long- term debt
   B. Is always included as a long- term debt
   C. Is included only if payments start two years from the date of the loan application
   D. Is disclosed in the loan application but not included in the debt calculation

2. The document that shows the correct mailing address for a specific lender is the:
   A. 1003
   B. *Lane Guide*
   C. VOD
   D. FNMA Selling Guide

3. The mortgage loan broker's key responsibility is:
   A. To close as many loans as possible
   B. To make the job of the underwriter as easy as possible
   C. To reject as many loans as possible
   D. To assume that the borrower's documentation is always correct

4. Any judgment, garnishments, or liens more than $2,500:
   A. Must be paid in full before the loan closing
   B. Do not have to be paid in full to obtain a loan
   C. Do not have to be disclosed in the loan application
   D. Need to be disclosed but do not need to be paid off

5. Child support can be considered in the borrower's income if there is evidence that it has been regularly received for the past 12 months and will continue for at least:
   A. 12 months
   B. 24 months
   C. 36 months
   D. There is no minimum requirement

6. "Stacking order" means:
   A. The file contents are placed in the required order
   B. Presentation to the lenders
   C. The underwriter can review the documentation
   D. All of the above

7. The areas of income that may be used are:
    A. Interest income and dividends
    B. Mortgage differential payments, trust income, VA benefits
    C. Aid for dependents, rental income, automobile allowances and expense, foster care income
    D. All of the above

8. Generally, the minimum number of years that a lender would require to verify for a self-employed borrower is:
    A. One
    B. Two
    C. Three
    D. Four

9. Under FNMA guidelines, how many years must a bankruptcy be discharged before a lender could accept a re-established borrower's credit history?
    A. Two years
    B. Four years
    C. Six years
    D. Seven years

10. When the processor receives the credit report from the credit reporting agency and the report discloses that the borrower did not disclose all of his or her debt on original 1003:
    A. The mortgage broker/lender must enter these undisclosed debts on the original 1003 and initial it
    B. The loan is automatically denied
    C. The mortgage broker/lender must return the original 1003 to the borrower and tell him or her to shred it; the mortgage broker/lender then asks the borrower to submit a new 1003 with the disclosed debts and the undisclosed debts included
    D. The borrower must provide a written explanation for the omission and a second 1003 is required, prepared by the lender and signed by the borrower

ANSWERS TO REVIEWING YOUR UNDERSTANDING

1. B (p. 277)   4. A (p. 276)   7. D (p. 269)   9. B (p. 276)
2. B (p. 262)   5. C (p. 271)   8. B (p. 273)   10. D (p. 276)
3. B (p. 266)   6. D (p. 279)

Chapter

9

IMPORTANT TERMS

ALTA

American Banking Association (ABA)

Appraisal

Assessor's parcel number (APN)

Binder policy

Bond

Certified copy

CLTA

Contingencies

Covenants, conditions and restrictions (CC&Rs)

Depository Institutions Deregulation and Monetary Control Act (DIDMCA)

Escrow

Escrow instructions

Extended coverage

Financial Institution's Reform and Recovery Act (FIRREA)

Homeowners associations

Impounds

Mello-Roos

Memorandum Items

Office of Real Estate Appraisal (OREA)

Preliminary title report (Prelim)

Property profiles

Proposition 13 (Prop 13)

Proration

Statement of information (SI)

Title officer

Title insurance

Trust certification

Uniform Residential Appraisal Report (URAR)

Uniform Standards of Professional Appraisal Practice (USPAP)

Vesting

Wire transfer

Processing: Escrow Settlement, Title, and Appraisal

PREVIEW

The mortgage loan broker does not close the loan; the process is usually handled by an escrow agent and the title company. The escrow agent makes sure all necessary documents are prepared and properly signed, calculates the various charges to be assessed against each party, makes sure all the necessary funds have been deposited, and gives each party an itemized list of the costs, charges, and fees associated. The title company handles the existing loan payoff, if any, in addition to receiving the new loan proceeds, and records the necessary documents with the recorder's office. An **appraisal** is normally required for most loans. After all these items have been completed, the loan is then in a position to fund and close.

CHAPTER OBJECTIVES

At the end of this chapter, the student learning outcomes include:

1. Outline the what, why, who, and how of the escrow process.
2. Discuss escrow instructions, expenses handled by escrow and the impound account.
3. Describe title insurance, a preliminary title report, and a binder.
4. Differentiate between a title company and title insurance policies.
5. Review the appraisal report.

9.1 ESCROW

Escrow—what is it? In general, **escrow** is a neutral depository for things of value to be handled according to the terms and conditions of the mutually agreed upon escrow instructions given to the escrow agent or escrow officer. Such money and instruments include the down payment, deposits, deeds, and documents received by escrow that are deemed to be held "in escrow" until written mutual authorization is received to do something with the items. The escrow holder is actually an independent stakeholder. For reference in the following discussion, see the sample take sheet and sale escrow instructions (Appendix D), located at the end of the book, which may assist in the understanding of the escrow process.

All of the interested parties in an escrow must have an interest or lien, claim, or estate into or on the property being escrowed. Outside parties are not privileged to any information on the escrow, including basic information that there even is an open escrow, without the written authorization of the escrow parties. The escrow officer notes the deposit of the necessary documents and notifies the title insurance company, who releases the interest for a party and makes the payment of a certain sum of money or other consideration for said releases or conveyances, as the case may be.

In order to have a binding escrow, all parties must execute written escrow instructions and deliver these documents back to the *escrow holder*. The parties do not sign all the same documents. Each party signs his or her own separate set of **escrow instructions** because the agreement is not between the parties but between the escrow officer and each principal individually. The escrow instructions represent a written statement of instructions to the escrow agent. After receipt of the signed documents from all the parties, the escrow officer then indicates on a copy that a **certified copy** of escrow instructions is in the file. This is when escrow is officially "opened." If any individual to the escrow fails to return the signed documents within the specified period, there is no escrow, and that party may be held in breach of contract. In the case of a refinance, however, it is not required for the lender to sign and return escrow instructions. Because the borrowers must sign the loan documents and other items, only the borrower is required to sign the escrow instructions. In addition, all parties to an escrow must be legally competent to execute such instructions. The subject upon which the parties are contracting must be lawful. An interest rate that violates the usury law is unlawful.

Escrow practices differ in other states and between northern and southern California. In most states, not including the southwestern United States, such as California, escrow is conducted similarly to a mediation business transaction, in a roundtable method with all parties present. Loan documents and escrow instructions are signed at the same time, with the necessary paperwork passed around the table among the parties. The escrow agent is typically an attorney, such as an abstract attorney who may also search the title records. In this case, a separate policy of **title insurance** may or may not be used. Rather, the seller gives a warranty deed and warrants that the title is in good standing to give to the buyer. The governing body would be the legal bar association regulations covering escrow transactions handled by an attorney.

In northern California, most escrows are handled by the title insurance companies and some broker-owned escrow services. The same company that writes the title insurance policies also performs the duties of escrowing the transaction. The regulations for the escrow company in this case would fall under the California insurance commissioner.

In southern California, three primary escrow methods are used to escrow a real estate transaction:

1. Title insurance companies, escrow division, under the insurance commissioner, similar to northern California
2. Broker-owned escrow, under the DRE commissioner
3. Independent escrow services, under the corporation commissioner

The type of escrow company used determines which government agency has jurisdiction or responsibility for the procedures that must be followed. There are many differences in the records process and trust fund handling for the different types of escrow agents.

The insurance commissioner is the governing body that oversees the escrow operation for a title insurance company. Broker-owned escrow entities may fall under the jurisdiction of either the DRE real estate commissioner or the corporations commissioner. If the broker does not have the corporations commissioner escrow approval, the broker or his licensees must be a party to the transaction in order to handle the escrow. An independent, non-broker-owned escrow falls under the guidelines of the corporations commissioner.

To better understand the entire escrow process, it is often helpful to look at the big picture. The components are often complicated and depend on another party to furnish to the escrow officer, which may cause delays. An overview of a typical escrow is shown in flowchart form in Figure 9.1.

Why Is an Escrow Needed?

In today's society, it is not wise to hand a large sum of money directly to a person you believe is the property owner. The prudent person would want assurance that they receive a deed in exchange for their money. This is the function of escrow. If the person owns it, he or she may not have the ability to give you clear and marketable title because of other items recorded against the property or the person. If the money and the deed are deposited with a neutral party, it enables the third party to determine for the principals whether the person executing the deed is in fact the owner and is in a position to give good title to the property in question.

When opening escrow, either a purchase or refinance, by telephone, fax, e-mail, or in person, it helps the escrow run smoother and faster for the loan broker to provide a copy of the property profile (discussed in Chapter 6), the "take sheet" (see Appendix D), the existing grant deed, and the **assessor's parcel number (APN)**, to the escrow officer. The loan broker will also want a copy of any change in the escrow instruction. By providing answers to the list below, the loan broker will make the transaction easier for the escrow agent to handle.

1. What is the amount and who is holding the earnest money deposit?
2. What is the amount of the total purchase price?
3. How much is the down payment (5 percent, 10 percent, etc.)?
4. How long is the escrow period (30, 45, 60 days)?

FIGURE 9.1   Life of an escrow: escrow flowchart.

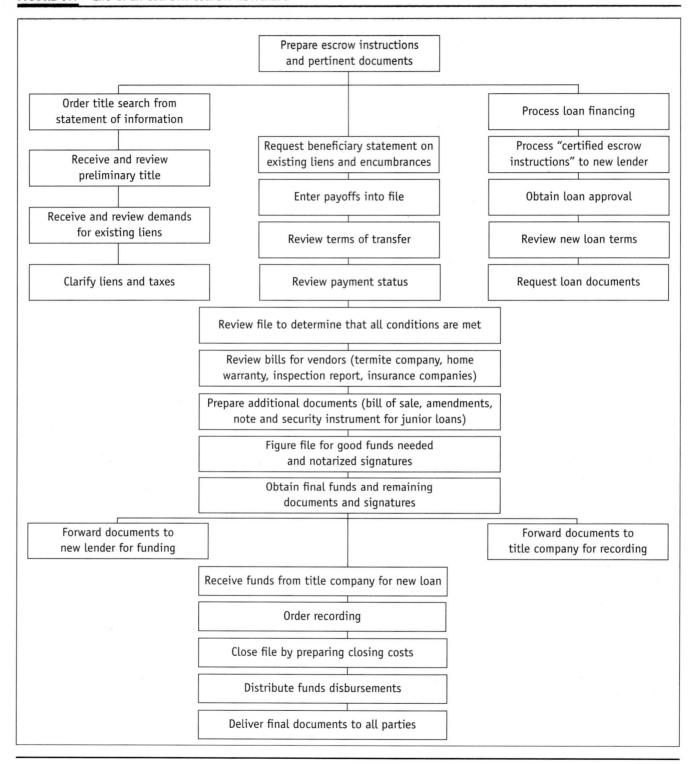

5. What is the legal description for the property in question? Only use the grant deed or a preliminary title report to obtain this information. Other documents, such as the tax deed, may be only a partial legal description.

6. Who is the seller? Get the full legal name(s), current mailing address, and forwarding address after the close of escrow (COE), along with zip code and telephone number, including area code, and e-mail address.

7. How will the buyer take title? Obtain the full legal name and mailing address, with zip code, area code, telephone number, and e-mail address. Be sure to have the exact spelling and how title to the property will be taken.

8. Who will pay the lender's fees and points (if any), or will all fees be deducted from the loan proceeds?

9. Will a termite inspection and completion notice be obtained through escrow?

10. Will the funds for the credit report and appraisal be released through escrow, and who will pay for each?

11. What is the possession date?

12. Who is the **title officer**? What is the title company name and telephone number?

13. Who is the new lender? Include the telephone number and address if possible.

14. What are the exact name, loan number, and telephone number of all lenders having existing liens recorded against the property, being paid off, and funding new loans?

What Is "Close of Escrow"?

The COE is the culmination of the transaction. It signifies the legal transfer of title to the buyer in a sale situation, or it is the completion of obtaining the loan for a borrow in a refinance situation. The event occurs after all written instructions to the escrow officer have been complied with and all documents and funds transferred.

Many events lead to the COE. From three days to about a week prior to the scheduled closing date, the buyer signs many documents, usually including loan documents. The borrower deposits the balance of the necessary funds with the escrow officer. The lender for any new loan usually requires 24 to 72 hours to review the final executed documents before releasing the loan funds to the title company.

After everyone else is finished, the escrow officer begins the work of performing the handling of all final accounting and the issuance of the official closing statements. Then the escrow agent makes the final disbursements and issues checks for remaining proceeds to the parties to the transaction.

Who Pays the Escrow Expenses?

Escrow is not required by law in California, but is always highly recommended, except in specific cases. An escrow is required for the following (acronym LIPS):

(1) transfer of a Liquor license, (2) where an Impound account is involved, (3) Probate, and (4) transfer of Securities. The costs of related services will vary

throughout the state and are always negotiable between the principals. Either party may pay the costs, except where specifically prohibited by a particular loan program. Figure 9.2 is a representation breakdown of the costs and the general guidelines for which of the parties is usually responsible for the payment through escrow. This would be a typical sales transaction for Southern California. If the property were a foreclosure transaction, most of the closing costs fees are passed along to the purchaser. If the property were in Northern California, many items

FIGURE 9.2   Typical buyer and seller debits and credits.

Debit to the parties	SELLER	BUYER
Conventional loan escrow fee	1/2	1/2
DVA loan escrow fee	X	
FHA loan escrow fee	X	X
Documentary transfer tax	X	
City transfer or conveyance tax	X	
Documentary preparation fee for deed	X	
Documentary preparation fee for loan		X
Drawing of grant deed	X	
Recording of grant deed	X	
Recording of new trust deed		X
Recording of reconveyance deed	X	
Drawing of 2nd trust deed and recording		X
Beneficiary demand statement	X	
Reconveyance fee	X	
Loan tie-in fee		X
Loan origination fee		X
Loan payoff of existing loan	X	
Assumption fee		X
Appraisal fee		X
Termite inspection and corrective work	X	
Termite preventive work		X
Homeowner's transfer fee		X
Home warranty policy	X	
Credit report		X
Survey		X
Unpaid liens	X	
CLTA title insurance policy	X	
ALTA title insurance policy		X
Preliminary title report		X
Sub escrow fee	1/2	1/2
<u>Credit to the parties</u>		
Initial deposit toward purchase		X
Balance of deposit placed into escrow at closing		X
Prepaid items (rents, taxes, association dues)	X	
Items paid in arrears (taxes, assumed loan interest)		X

are paid by the opposite person shown here, since the final agreement of who pays for what is often dictated by local custom and tradition, and are not legislated. For example, it is typical that the seller pay the CLTA title policy and the buyer pay the ALTA policy in Southern California. In Northern California, it is normal that the buyer would pay the CLTA.

The escrow fee charge will vary among firms and is negotiable among the parties, unless a government loan requirement specifies otherwise. Figure 9.3 illustrates a typical schedule of fees that might be expected in 2005.

Contingencies

It is imperative that the escrow officer obtain sufficient information to complete the escrow. If the completion of the escrow is contingent on the occurrence of a future event, the escrow officer should ascertain exactly what documentation will constitute the waiver or removal of the particular contingency. Typical **contingencies** are:

- Contingent upon the sale of another property
- Contingent upon the loan rate not to exceed X percent
- Contingent upon the appraised value to be not less than $XXX,XXX
- Contingent upon the loan amount to be $XXX,XXX
- Contingent upon the seller carrying back a second loan for $XXX,XXX

Memorandum Items

Certain agreements between parties are not the responsibility of escrow to comply with but are memorandum instructions. Such items normally

FIGURE 9.3 Typical schedule of escrow fees by type of escrow.

Escrow Type	Borrower	Seller	Buyer
Sale		$200 Base fee + $2 per $1,000 of price	$200 Base fee + $2 per $1,000 price
			Second set of loan docs $75
FHA loan		$200 Base fee + $2 per $1,000 of price	As per FHA chart
Refinance	$500 base fee (under $500,000) 500 + $1 per $1000 (over $500,000)		
Second trust deed loan	$175 base fee		
Courier fee/FedEx/ wire transfer		$20–$40	

pertain to the status of a property or structure. Typical **memorandum items** include:

- Personal property items included in the sale price.
- Working condition of utilities and appliances.
- Dates for transfer of physical possession.
- Any other agreement pertaining to an event that will happen outside the escrow or after the escrow closes.

Such items may be included in the escrow instructions under the heading of "As a matter of record only, with which escrow holder is to assume no liability or concern, but with which all parties do agree," as shown in the sample sale escrow instructions in Appendix D.

Supplemental/Additional Escrow Requirements

The mortgage loan broker is required to comply with many disclosures during the course of a loan, as is any DRE licensee. Likewise, the escrow agent or officer is also required by law to furnish various disclosures, depending on under which legal structure the escrow entity is acting, such as DRE or corporation commissioner. The following are common disclosures:

1. Foreign Investors Real Property Tax Act (FIRPTA)
2. Additional Tax Assessments
3. Preliminary Change of Ownership Report (PCOR)
4. Smoke Detector Requirements
5. Internal Revenue Code (IRC) Section 6045 (E)
6. Sections 18805 and 26131 of the Revenue and Taxation Code

Escrow Needs "Good Funds"

Once title has transferred between parties or once a new loan has been recorded against a property, it may not be unrecorded. Instead, a different document must be used to supersede the previous event that pays off the earlier lien or transfers the title. Thus, should the transaction close with a personal check that is found to lack sufficient funds, the document with the mistake was recorded without consideration and would be final. California's good funds law is found in the California Insurance Code 12413.1. For this reason, pursuant to SB 1550, effective January 1, 1985, escrow must have *good funds* that must be drawn on and payable through a California bank. To ensure that the funds are available for distribution, the escrow officer will require the demand funds to the placed into the escrow account or in the account of the title insurance company before the escrow officer will notify the lender for funding or the title company to affect recordation. This law covers funds received from the lender, as well as any principals. Disbursement may occur on the same day as deposit if the funds are deposited in cash or via wire transfer. Disbursement may occur on the day after deposit if the funds are deposited via cashier's check, certified check, or teller's check.

Although California Insurance Code 12413.1 does not apply to independent escrow companies (i.e., escrow companies not affiliated with title insurance companies), the standard set forth in 12413.1 has been accepted almost universally throughout California as the appropriate standard for disbursement.

A bank **American Banking Association (ABA)** number, such as the example shown below, must appear on the check. The ABA number is either separate or is part of the account number at the bottom of any check. If a locally paid cashier's check is not available through the borrower's bank, the most satisfactory way of depositing your funds into escrow is by wire transfer. An example of a California bank check would be 1210, 1211, 1220, 1222, and 3222.

A wire transfer enables the party to pay without writing a check. It works much like a direct deposit, in which funds are sent directly from a payee into the receiver's bank account. In a **wire transfer**, the funds are sent directly from bank to bank, which ensures that the funds are "good funds" (see Chapter 15) and that the transfer has been made, and it saves time because fewer intermediaries need to handle the funds.

Homeowners Association Information

On occasion, the escrow holder may be asked to obtain information from one or more **homeowners associations**. See Figure 9.4 for an example of an expedited procedure. Many associations charge a fee for this information and may even require up-front fees. The escrow instructions should state who pays for what fees and must give authorization for release of any funds to pay for such items. Go to *http://www.hoacerts.com* for further information.

Vesting

The escrow officer is often burdened with the problem of the manner of how the parties will take title to the property. The existing titleholders may change the way they take title on the new loan from the way they hold title on the existing loan. The deposit receipt sale agreement often states that title is "to be determined in escrow," which is meant to postpone the decision until the principals can research the various methods of holding title. The consequences for legal and tax purposes are significant. The escrow agent is prohibited from giving real estate advice, legal advice, and tax advice. The real estate licensees, including the loan broker, are also prohibited from giving legal or tax advice. However, title must be placed on the written instruments. Any delay in instructing the escrow officer as to the method of taking title often is an unnecessary delay in the escrow period.

The form of ownership taken is called the **vesting** of title. The method of taking title determines who may sign various documents involved in the property. The current and future rights of the parties involve the real property taxes, income taxes, inheritance and gift taxes, and transferability for creditor's claims. Title has significant probate implications upon death.

In sole ownership, one entity acquires title, such as an individual person or a single legal corporation. Common examples include taking title as "a single man" or as "a single woman" for a person who has never been legally married. Taking title as "an unmarried man" or as "an unmarried woman" is for a person who has

FIGURE 9.4   Association information request.

DATE:

TO ESCROW: REFERENCE:
                                                   HOMEOWNERS' ASSOCIATION:
                                                   1.
                                                   2.

ESCROW #   MANAGEMENT COMPANY:
ESCROW OFFICER:
BORROWER:

PROPERTY ADDRESS & UNIT #

Please forward the enclosed copy of this letter and HOA Information Form to the
Homeowners' Association/Management Company, which has been checked above for
the subject property.

The following items are **essential to loan underwriting and approval**. Please obtain
them from the Management Company and forward them to (Your Company Name), **as
soon as possible**.

1. Signed and completed Homeowners' Association Information Form.

2. The following items, which have been checked:

_____ Current Budget for HOA

_____ Current Balance Sheet for HOA

_____ Evidence of Fidelity Bonding and/or Directors & Officers Liability Insurance

   NOTE: Usually the management company has evidence of fidelity bond, but the
   hazard insurer will often have to be contacted for evidence of directors &
   officers liability insurance (if they have this additional coverage).

_____ CC&Rs
_____ Articles of Incorporation
_____ Bylaws of HOA

Thank you for your time and efficient assistance!
Cordially yours,

been married but is now legally divorced or is a widow or widower. Taking title as
"a married man as his sole and separate property" or as "a married woman, as her
sole and separate property" is for an individual who acquires title during a marriage but is keeping the title ownership to the property separate from the spouse.

In this case, if title insurance is used, the title company may require a specific disclaimer or relinquish of spousal rights in the property. In California the title company will require the spouse to sign a quit claim deed to relinquish any possible claim or interest in the property. A corporation is a single, legal entity, created under state law, with a separate existence from the shareholders. The title company and investor will usually require a copy of the legal documents verifying the right of the signature to act on behalf of the corporation.

Co-ownership is property held in title by two or more persons. As of July 1, 2001, title may be taken as "community property, with right of survivorship," which enables benefits for joint tenancy ownership under community property ownership.

Taking title as "community property" is for property acquired during a marriage and it is intended that the property be owned together. Both husband and wife own the property equally, and both must sign all agreements and documents of financial obligation and transfer of title.

Taking title as "joint tenancy" is for married or unmarried persons to acquire ownership with equal interest in the property and with the right of survivorship to the remaining, surviving joint tenants. Joint tenancy property is not subject to a will. Taking title as "tenancy in common" is for two or more individuals who seek an undivided fractional interest, which may be unequal in quantity or duration, and the ownership may arise at different times. Each co-owner may will his or her share separately.

Other ways are possible for vesting title to real property, including a partnership or trust. Taking title as a "partnership" is when two or more business persons hold title who are co-owners and are governed by the Uniform Partnership Act.

Taking title in a "trust" is an arrangement for legal title to real property to be held in the name of the trust, and documents to be executed by the trustee for the benefit of the beneficiaries of the trust. If the buyer or seller is or will be holding title in the form of one of the many types of trusts, the principal will be required to furnish a copy of the trust agreement to escrow, and a copy will be given to the lender. A copy of a **"trust certification"** stating that there are no changes to the trust or a copy of any addendums and amendments to the trust must be attached indicating that the trust is still in effect. The mortgage brokers should contact the investor to ascertain whether they will need all pages to the trust agreement or just the pages that pertain to the real estate.

It is strongly recommended that mortgage brokers advise their clients to consult a real estate attorney and an accountant on the manner of taking title to property.

9.2 STATEMENT OF INFORMATION

Both the escrow entity and the title insurance company will want a completed **statement of information**, or statement of identity, referred to as the SI. This document is very important in researching to confirm or release an item that may or may not belong to a buyer or seller. It is imperative that this form be entirely completed and returned to escrow for processing. The Social Security number and prior addresses could be the determining factor in removing a derogatory item from the borrower's permanent record. HR 3221 is the Foreign Investment in Real Property Tax Act (FIRPTA) which requires the seller to provide taxpayer identification number or Social Security number. Sellers often were unwilling to provide this confidential information to the buyer or the real estate agents. This new law allows the seller to furnish the Affidavit of Seller to a "qualified substitute" which is often the escrow company or the title insurance company, since they already obtain the tax identification number or Social Security number as part of the title search process (see Chapter 5 topic FIRPTA).

The SI is designed to protect the principals. The information is used to search public records for locating financial obligations against the individual. The data that may be found could be a specific lien or a general lien. The title company usually finds judgments, bankruptcies, divorces, and income-tax liens against persons with similar names. The individual who is a party to this transaction may have a name that is common or similar to that of many others. The SI is used to separate the information about this borrower from the information about others.

The title company may find items that create a "cloud" on the title because a lien is recorded on a property of an individual. This may be a mechanic's lien, nonpayment of child support or student loans, or similar.

The following points may help clarify the misconceptions about the SI that the borrower may have or may ask either the escrow officer or the mortgage loan broker:

- It is not intended to be an invasion of privacy.
- The information is kept in strict confidence.
- The information is not available for public examination.
- Receipt of the document early in the transaction helps escrow and title personnel close the escrow faster
- Accuracy is the most important item of information.
- The information is not used for credit-checking purposes.

The SI is a basic component of the escrow transaction. To process the escrow, the escrow officer will include the SI at the original time the escrow instructions are given to the principals or their agents. California, like most areas of the United States that have a high population, is a melting pot of many peoples. Thus, it may help the borrower to have the SI in multiple languages, such as Spanish, Chinese, Japanese, or French. An SI in English and Vietnamese Spanish is shown in Figure 9.5.

9.3 IMPOUND ACCOUNT

Impounds consist of items that are not part of the lender's principal and interest payment on the loan. The most common items in an impound account are the property taxes, the hazard/fire/earthquake insurance policy, and the mortgage insurance. The lender may require that the monthly payment include not only

FIGURE 9.5 Statement of information (English and Spanish).

STEWART TITLE OF CALIFORNIA, INC.

STATEMENT OF INFORMATION

CONFIDENTIAL INFORMATION STATEMENT TO BE USED IN CONNECTION WITH ORDER NO:
INFORMACION CONFIDENCIAL QUE SERA USADA EN CONECCION CON LA ORDEN NO:

COMPLETION OF THIS FORM WILL EXPEDITE YOUR ORDER AND WILL HELP PROTECT YOU. *COMPLETAR ESTA FORMA HARA MAS RAPIDO EL TRAMITE Y LE PROTEJERA.*

THE STREET ADDRESS of the property in this transaction is:
LA DIRECCION de la propiedad en esta transaccion es:

LEAVE BLANK (IF NONE) *(DEJE EN BLANCO SI NO TIENE DIRECCION)*

IMPROVEMENTS: __SINGLE RESIDENCE __MULTIPLE RESIDENCE __COMMERCIAL *MEJORAS: __CASA SOLA __MULTIFAMILIAR __COMERCIO*
OCCUPIED BY: __OWNER __LESSEE __TENANTS *CUPADA POR: __DUENO __ARRENDATARIO __INQUILINOS*
ANY PORTION OF NEW LOAN FUNDS TO BE USED FOR CONSTRUCTION __YES __NO *PARTE DEL PRESTAMO SERA DESTINADO A CONSTRUCCION __SI __NO*

- NAME ~ *NOMBRE* -

FIRST ~ *DE PILA* MIDDLE ~ *SEGUNDO* LAST ~ *APELLIDO*

BIRTHPLACE ~ *LUGAR DE NACIMIENTO* BIRTH DATE ~ *FECHA DE NACIMIENTO*

I HAVE LIVED IN CALIFORNIA SINCE *HE VIVIDO EN CALIFORNIA DESDE* SOCIAL SECURITY NUMBER *NUMERO DE SEGURO SOCIAL*

DRIVER'S LICENSE NO. ________ NUMERO DE LICENCIA

- NAME ~ *NOMBRE* -

FIRST ~ *DE PILA* MIDDLE ~ *SEGUNDO* LAST ~ *APELLIDO*

BIRTHPLACE ~ *LUGAR DE NACIMIENTO* BIRTH DATE ~ *FECHA DE NACIMIENTO*

I HAVE LIVED IN CALIFORNIA SINCE *HE VIVIDO EN CALIFORNIA DESDE* SOCIAL SECURITY NUMBER *NUMERO DE SEGURO SOCIAL*

DRIVER'S LICENSE NO. ________ NUMERO DE LICENCIA

WE WERE MARRIED ON ________ *CASADOS EL DIA* AT ________ *EN* WIFE'S MAIDEN NAME ________ *NOMBRE DE SOLTERA*

-RESIDENCE(S) FOR LAST 10 YEARS ~ *RESIDENCIA(S) DURANTE LOS ULTIMOS 10 ANOS*-

NUMBER AND STREET ~ *NUMERO Y CALLE*	CITY ~ *CIUDAD*	FROM ~ *DESDE*	TO / *HASTA*
NUMBER AND STREET ~ *NUMERO Y CALLE*	CITY ~ *CIUDAD*	FROM ~ *DESDE*	TO / *HASTA*
NUMBER AND STREET ~ *NUMERO Y CALLE*	CITY ~ *CIUDAD*	FROM ~ *DESDE*	TO / *HASTA*
NUMBER AND STREET ~ *NUMERO Y CALLE*	CITY ~ *CIUDAD*	FROM ~ *DESDE*	TO / *HASTA*

-OCCUPATION(S) FOR LAST 10 YEARS ~ OCUPACION(ES) DURANTE LOS ULTIMOS 10 ANOS-

HUSBAND ~ *ESPOSO*

PRESENT OCCUPATION ~ *EMPLEO ACTUAL*	FIRM NAME ~ *NOMBRE DE LA COMPANIA*	ADDRESS ~ *DIRECCION*	NO. YEARS ~ *CUANTOS ANOS*
PRIOR OCCUPATION ~ *EMPLEO ANTERIOR*	FIRM NAME ~ *NOMBRE DE LA COMPANIA*	ADDRESS ~ *DIRECCION*	NO. YEARS ~ *CUANTOS ANOS*
PRIOR OCCUPATION ~ *EMPLEO ANTERIOR*	FIRM NAME ~ *NOMBRE DE LA COMPANIA*	ADDRESS ~ *DIRECCION*	NO. YEARS ~ *CUANTOS ANOS*

WIFE / *ESPOSA*

PRESENT OCCUPATION ~ *EMPLEO ACTUAL*	FIRM NAME ~ *NOMBRE DE LA COMPANIA*	ADDRESS ~ *DIRECCION*	NO. YEARS ~ *CUANTOS ANOS*
PRIOR OCCUPATION ~ *EMPLEO ANTERIOR*	FIRM NAME ~ *NOMBRE DE LA COMPANIA*	ADDRESS ~ *DIRECCION*	NO. YEARS ~ *CUANTOS ANOS*
PRIOR OCCUPATION ~ *EMPLEO ANTERIOR*	FIRM NAME ~ *NOMBRE DE LA COMPANIA*	ADDRESS ~ *DIRECCION*	NO. YEARS ~ *CUANTOS ANOS*

-FORMER MARRIAGES ~ *MATRIMONIOS ANTERIORES* -

IF NO FORMER MARRIAGES, WRITE "NONE" ________
SI NO SE HA CASADO ANTERIORMENTE ESCRIBA "NINGUNO"

NAME OF FORMER SPOUSE ________
NOMBRE DE SU EX-ESPOSO(A)

IF DECEASED: DATE ________ WHERE ________
SI HA FALLECIDO: FECHA *DONDE*

HOMEOWNERS ASSOCIATION ________
PHONE NUMBER ( ) ________

- CURRENT LOAN ON PROPERTY -
~ *PRESTAMOS ACTUALES A ESTA PROPIEDAD* ~

PAYMENTS ARE BEING MADE TO:
ESTA HACIENDO SUS PAGOS A:
1.

2.

3.

4.

DATE ~ *FECHA* ________ **SIGNATURE ~ *FIRMA*** ________
HOME PHONE ~ *TELEFONO* ________ **BUSINESS PHONE ~ *TELEFONO DE OFICINA*** ________

DOCUMENT PROVIDED BY STEWART TITLE OF CALIFORNIA, INC. STATINFO.DOC

the principal and interest amount but also the taxes and insurance, called PITI, depending on the LTV amount. Impound accounts are appropriate when a relatively low down payment is made by the borrower and the lender has a higher degree of risk because of the higher loan amount. An impound account is a

FIGURE 9.6 Real estate property tax calendar.

July	1st	Beginning of Fiscal Tax Year
	1st	Delinquent properties sold to the state (five-year period to redeem)
	1st	Owners informed of new property value
August	25th	Sale number assigned for delinquent properties
September		
October	25th	Tax bills mailed to property owner
November	1st	First installment due
December	1st	Last day to file for 80% exemption (homeowner, veteran, senior citizen)
	10th	First installment delinquent
January	1st	Assessment date
February	1st	2nd Installment due
	10th	Last day to file for 100% exemption (homeowner, veteran, senior citizen)
March	1st	Taxes due on unsecured role
April	10th	2nd Installment delinquent
May		
June	8th	Publication date for delinquent taxes

reserve of money collected by a lender monthly to cover recurring expenses. The mortgage loan broker must use the entire PITI to qualify the borrower, as was discussed in Chapter 6 about prequalification. The escrow officer must collect the amount the lender requires at the COE to fill the reserves to the lender's required level, as shown in Figure 9.7.

Property Taxes

The largest portion of the impound account consists of the property tax and assessments:

- Base rate. Determined by California's **Proposition 13** of 1% of the sales price plus an increase of 2 percent per year and paid according to the fiscal tax year (see Figure 9.6).
- Special assessments for local bond revenue issues. Typically school taxes, public safety issues such as weed abatement, and health issues such as mosquito abatement.
- **Mello-Roos**. A public improvement special district bond; see Figure 9.8.
- Supplemental property taxes. Additional property tax on new construction on a property for an existing property owner and for all transfers for a new purchaser.

The escrow officer will need a copy of the current tax billing information to determine many items, such as calculating **prorations**, determining reserves (see Figure 9.7), and completing the transfer notice to the tax offices with the APN.

FIGURE 9.7   Impound schedule for property taxes.

Date of First Month's Payments	Tax Reserve to Be Collected
January	6 Months
February	2 Months
March	2 Months

Second Installment Taxes Should Now Have Been Paid

April	3 Month
May	4 Months
June	5 Months
July	6 Months
August	7 Months
September	8 Months
October	3 Months
November	4 Months

First Installment Taxes Should Now Have Been Paid

December	5 Months

To set up the impound account for the following items:

HAZARD INSURANCE	2 Months
FLOOD INSURANCE	2 Months
PRIVATE MORTGAGE INSURANCE (PMI)	2 Months
MORTGAGE INSURANCE PREMIUM (FHA-MMI)	2 Months

The information is not usually obtained directly from the property owner or borrower, however. The title insurance company typically gives the information to escrow in the form of the preliminary title report, which shows the recorded taxes that are a lien against the property. If the transaction involves a sale, it will be expected that the property taxes will change. However, because the new property taxes are not yet determined because the new purchaser is not the current owner, the escrow officer does not use the projected new tax amount to determine prorations.

As an example, a seller who purchased subject property in 1960 may have an existing annual tax of only $650. A buyer paying $700,000 for that property would be assessed at $700,000 × 1% for the base property tax of $7,000 a year, plus local special assessments. Escrow and title would use the existing, recorded $650 amount. The tax collector will mail a supplemental property tax bill for the increased amount due only after the new owner actually holds title ownership to the property, which is after recordation of the deeds at COE.

The date that the taxes are a lien on the property is not the date that the taxes are paid. In the case of personal income taxes, the income taxes are a liability at

FIGURE 9.8   Mello-Roos property assessment.

1. A Mello-Roos community facilities district (CFD) is formed. Mello-Roos is a method of financing government entities (cities, counties, school districts, and other special districts) to fund the cost of public improvements. Before government entities can form a CFD, they must either obtain permission from area landowners or hold an election of registered voters within the CFD.

2. The municipality sells bonds on behalf of the CFD. These bonds are sold to private investors, who purchase them for tax-free interest income. The money raised through the bond sale becomes the debt obligation of the CFD.

3. Bond proceeds are used to pay for public improvements within the CFD. The types of improvements that can be funded by a CFD are much broader than those types of improvements that can be funded by traditional assessment districts. For example, new schools, police stations, fire stations, and libraries can be constructed with CFD bond proceeds, as well as roadways, water lines, and other traditional types of public improvements. CFDs can also be formed for purposes of public facility maintenance.

4. Money is repaid to bondholders through the Mello-Roos special tax. The service for the bonds is repaid by the levy of a special tax on property within the CFD. The amount of the special tax is determined by each CFD's special tax formula and may vary between property types. The special tax revenue is used to repay principal and interest to bondholders. Taxation and repayment continue each year for the life of the bond issue, usually 20 to 40 years.

the time the wages are earned. However, most people usually do not pay income taxes more than quarterly or by April 15 of the following year. Similarly, for real property, taxes are due on one date and not usually paid until a different date. California allows property taxes to be paid in two installments. Because the state fiscal year runs from July 1 of one year to June 30 of the next year (616, 617 Revenue & Taxation Code and Government Code 20040), the first installment covers the period from July 1 to December 31 of the first year, with the property tax due November 1 of that year (2605, 2701 Revenue & Tax Code). The payment by most individuals and lender-paid impound disbursement is not actually made until just before the date it becomes delinquent, December 10 (2189, 2617, 2619, and 2704 Revenue & Tax Code). The second installment covers the period from January 1 to June 30 of the second year, with the taxes due February 1 (2606, 2700, and 2702 Revenue & Tax Code), and usually not paid until just before the delinquent date of April 10 (2618 and 2705 Revenue & Tax Code). For more information, go to *www.boe.ca.gov/prop taxes/pdf/r281.pdf.*

Because of the tax calendar on payments, the lender must ensure that sufficient funds are available to pay the taxes before they become delinquent. To ensure that the lender has adequate "clear" funds on hand, the impound account must have sufficient reserves. If the escrow is closing between November 1 and

April 1, then the taxes have usually not been paid. If the loan that is being paid off has an impound account, escrow must determine from that lender the amount that is in the reserve. This reserve can be a positive amount, or there may be a shortage that must be paid to the lender, along with the balance and payoff figures. The escrow officer may need verification from the borrower or current lender by receiving a copy of the latest loan payment stub, if the payment reflects the payment of taxes.

The amount of reserves required by the lender for an impound account is available in a chart used by the escrow officer (see Figure 9.7). The escrow agent determines the amount to be collected according to the date that the lender indicates that the first payment on the new loan will be due. The escrow officer may be directed by the lender to collect a specific amount rather than calculate the amount from a chart.

The supplemental real property tax was signed into law in July 1983. Two events trigger an increase in the existing tax that is already on the property: (1) new construction and (2) new owner of the property. For the first event, the property owner will receive a bill for the supplemental tax as of the date of completion of the new construction. For the second event, the new owner will receive a supplementary tax bill from three weeks to six months after escrow closes and the title has been transferred to a new buyer. The date of COE is used. The assessor appraises the property and advises the owner the supplemental assessment amount. The bill will identify the amount of the tax and the date the taxes become delinquent.

A formula is used to determine the amount of the tax bill. The total supplemental assessment will be prorated according to the number of months remaining until June 30, the end of the tax year. The tax becomes effective on the first day of the month after the month in which the change of ownership or completion of the new construction actually occurred.

If the effective date is not July 1, a proration factor is used (see Figure 9.9). For example, if the supplemental tax bill would be $1,000 for a full year and the

FIGURE 9.9   Supplemental property tax.

Effective Date	Proration Factor
January 1	0.50
February 1	0.42
March 1	0.33
April 1	0.25
May 1	0.17
June 1	0.08
July 1	0.00
August 1	0.92
September 1	0.83
October 1	0.75
November 1	0.67
December 1	0.58

escrow closed on September 15, the effective date would be October 1. The supplemental property tax would be subject to a proration factor of 0.75 of the $1,000, so the supplemental tax bill would be $750.

All supplemental taxes are payable in two equal installments. The tax is due on the date the bill is mailed and delinquent on specified dates, depending on the month the bill is mailed, as follows:

1. If the bill is mailed in July, August, September, or October, the first installment is delinquent on December 10 of the same year. The second installment is delinquent on April 10 of the next year.

2. If the bill is mailed in November, December, January, February, March, April, May, or June, the first installment is delinquent on the last day of the month after the month in which the bill is mailed. The second installment is delinquent on the last day of the fourth calendar month after the date the first installment is delinquent.

Escrow does not prorate the supplemental property tax bill because the increased amount is not yet a recorded lien on the property. In addition, the amount of the increased tax is not yet known until the assessor appraises the property. Unlike ordinary property taxes, the supplemental tax is a one-time tax that is due for the period from the date of new ownership or new construction only up to and until the end of that tax year, as of June 30. Even when the lender has set up an impound account to collect the taxes in monthly installments from the borrower and payment of the property taxes when due, the impound account will only cover the amount of existing property taxes recorded against the property, and the supplemental taxes will be billed separately and have to be paid or they will become an unpaid tax lien against the property. The borrower must be advised that the supplemental tax bill will be forthcoming. A loan broker would not want the borrower to miss a loan payment because the borrower has to pay a large, unexpected tax bill. Advising borrowers of this disclosure helps them plan their finances.

9.4 TITLE INSURANCE

Whenever purchasing real property, the buyer expects to acquire use of the property as well as to receive "title" and legal ownership. It is important to ascertain that the person representing himself or herself to be the seller is the property owner. Once that is determined, it is essential that the owner be in a position to give the buyer clear title. There are times when the current owner did not receive clear title. The owner may consequently not be legally entitled to sell or transfer title to the property to the purchaser.

Title insurers, unlike property or casualty insurance companies, operate under the theory of risk elimination. Title companies spend a high percentage of their operating income each year collecting, storing, maintaining, and analyzing official records for information that affects title to real property. The goal of title companies is to conduct such a thorough search and evaluation of public records that no claims will ever arise. Of course, this is impossible; we live in an imperfect world in which human error and changing legal interpretations make 100 percent risk elimination impossible.

When a proposed claim arises, professional claims personnel are assigned to handle the problem according to the terms of the title insurance policy. The rates charged by title companies are filed with the California Department of Insurance, and each company is required to publicly post its schedule of fees. As in all competitive business environments, rates vary from company to company, so you should make comparisons before selecting a particular title company or a specific type of policy coverage.

Title insurance protects the buyer and lender involved in a real property transaction against incompetent past action; clerical errors; incorrect marital status; undisclosed heirs; improper interpretation of wills; signature by an unauthorized person, a minor, or an insane person on an earlier deed; and any possible forgery in the entire chain of title signatures. It insures against claims made by third parties against the title. Title insurance guarantees that the ownership of the property one is buying or lending is as stated in the recorded documents. A flowchart of a typical title search is shown in Figure 9.10.

How important is title insurance? The following article was taken from the *Los Angeles Times* real estate section, dated September 3, 1995, by Robert J. Bruss:

"BUYER MUST PAY FOR TITLE INSURANCE POLICY ERROR"

QUESTION: We bought our home about six years ago. At the time, I recall having to pay for title insurance. Recently, the city informed us that it will be replacing the sewer line that runs through our back yard and beneath our detached garage. When we bought our home, we were never informed of any sewer line easement. Tearing down and rebuilding our garage will cost at least $5,000. Since the title insurance company failed to tell us about the sewer easement, shouldn't it pay for the cost? The company claims that we never bought an owner's title policy and that only the lender is insured. Is this correct?

ANSWER: It appears you did not buy an owner's title insurance policy. Instead, you apparently paid only for a lender's title policy to protect your mortgage company. Although the title insurance company should have discovered the recorded sewer-line easement through your back yard, since you didn't buy an owner's title policy you have no title protection. The previous owner who built the garage on top of the sewer line should have known better. Now that mistake is your loss. Your attorney can explain further.

Is there a difference between a title company and a title insurance company? Yes. Just as the mortgage loan broker is not the ultimate investor, so too most title companies are often not the ultimate insurer. A title company is underwritten by a title insurance company. This may come into play if you have a claim against the title company. The claimant will generally have to deal with the

FIGURE 9.10   Life of a title search.

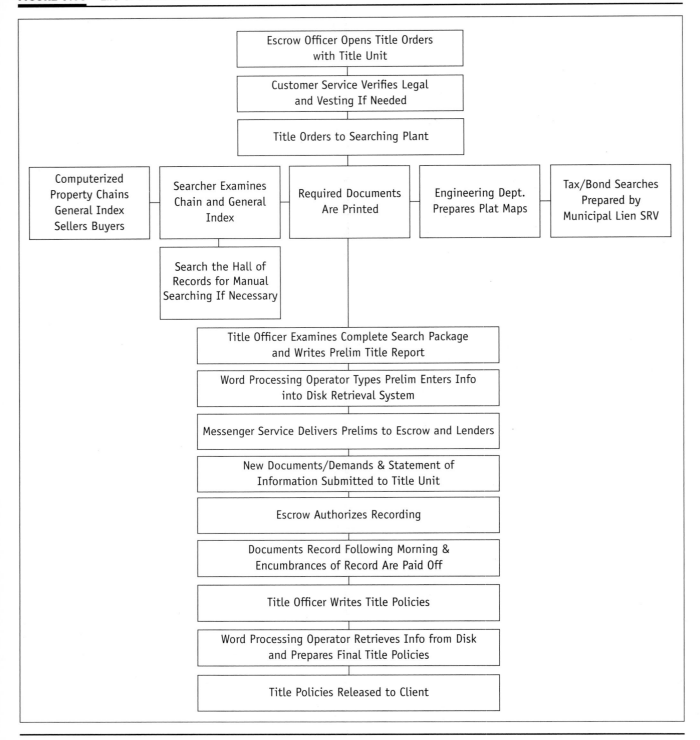

main office of the title insurance company that underwrote the title company regardless of the geographical location of the title insurance company.

Whether you are working locally, intercounty, or nationally, a title insurance company can be a great asset to the mortgage broker. With the many departments and individuals available, full use of a title insurance company is highly recommended. For example, the following title company personnel may assist the escrow agent and the mortgage loan broker:

- Advisory title officers (ATO)
- Title officers (TO)
- Title information department national title desk
- Inner counties department
- Customer services department
- Marketing department
- Sales department

As noted above in the escrow section, escrow and title insurance are not required by law in California. However, few lenders will fund the loan without title insurance. When private parties are handling a transaction for a loan and no institutional lender is involved, the individuals may feel they are saving money by not incurring the extra expense. The one-time, nonrecurring cost has been found to be well worth the reasonable expense. The institutional lenders, thus, will not fund the loan without having the coverage. A sample title insurance rate chart is shown in Figure 6.16 of this book.

An example of how a department can be of service to the mortgage loan broker is the customer service department, which may provide the following data:

1. Farm packages—information on a geographical area
2. Address labels—to be used for a marketing plan
3. **Property profiles**—documents of record
4. Legal and vesting(s)—existing method of holding title
5. Property information—liens, room count, lot size, **covenants, conditions and restrictions (CC&Rs)**, public records information (e.g., year built)

When a client wants a refinance on a property they already own, they must still complete the Change of Ownership form required by the tax assessor's office. It is important to note that when a person puts ownership to their property into a Limited Liability Corporation (LLC) and takes the title out of his or her existing name(s), this is a change of ownership and will most likely trigger the need for a new title insurance policy. This is often overlooked, and upon the change in ownership either the old policy is cancelled, or the coverage is no longer effective.

Another example of how the title company can be of service to the mortgage loan broker is the use of the national title desk department. If the client is purchasing a property in California and the down payment is coming from the proceeds of a sale of property in Virginia, the entire transaction can be handled from California by using the national title desk. All the necessary documents for the transfer of the funds and the encumbrance of the property in Virginia can be handled from California. Should non-California documents be needed, this desk can provide the necessary paperwork. An example may be when the Virginia transaction consists of the seller carrying back a lien on the Virginia property. Because California would normally use a deed of trust and note, the

California title insurance companies would not be expected to have a mortgage and a mortgage note that is used for a Virginia loan, which the national title desk could provide.

What Is a Preliminary Title Report?

A **preliminary title report** (prelim) is designed to provide an interim response to an application for title insurance. It is also intended to facilitate the issuance of a particular type of policy. The preliminary report identifies the existing title to the estate or interest in the described land. It also contains a list of defects, liens, encumbrances, and restrictions that would be excluded from coverage if the requested policy were to be issued as of the date of the report. Common CC&Rs are not reflected in a prelim. The mortgage loan broker should obtain a copy from the title insurance company or association (if any) or the seller and review the document.

Proof of payment of any liens that the borrower claims have been paid off may show on the prelim and will require documentation if there is a dispute. In this case, the principal will usually be required to post a **bond** from one and one-half times up to twice the face amount of the lien.

The California legislature has taken action to clearly define a preliminary report. In 1981, the legislature added Sections 12340.10 and 12340.11 to the Insurance Code. These define an abstract of title and preliminary report. Section 12340.11 reads:

> *Preliminary report, commitment and binder are reports furnished in connection with an application for title insurance and are offers to issue a title policy subject to the stated exceptions set forth in the reports and such other matters as may be incorporated by reference therein. The reports are not abstracts of title, or are any of the rights, duties or responsibilities applicable to the preparation and issuance of an abstract of title applicable to the issuance of any report. Any such report shall not be construed as, or constitute a representation as to the condition of title to real property, but shall constitute a statement of the terms and conditions upon which issuer is willing to issue its title policy, if such offer is accepted.*

Based on this definition, a prelim does not necessarily show the condition of title but merely reports the current vesting of title and items the title company will exclude from coverage if a policy should later be issued. The elements of this definition are threefold. First, a prelim is an offer to issue title policy. It may be revoked if later information is found that the title insurance company does not wish to cover. Not every property is able to obtain title insurance. Second, it is only a partial reporting of the chain of title and not a complete abstract of title. Third, it is a statement of the terms and conditions of the offer to issue a title policy. It is not a representation as to the condition of title.

A sample prelim may assist in understanding as shown in Appendix F. A review of the sample prelim is shown later in this chapter, noting the errors and discrepancies found by the mortgage loan broker upon checking the document. For learning purposes, we have placed a few deliberate errors in this prelim.

Types of Title Insurance Policies

When examination of title insurance is arranged between a title insurance company and a buyer, lending institution, or other party, various types of policies are issued. After the prelim on the condition of the title, the final policy supplants the prelim, and the issuer is bound to the title insurance policy contract. The basic types of policies available in California are the CLTA, ALTA, **extended coverage**, and binder policies.

The CLTA policy is often referred to as the standard coverage. The intent is to shield the new owner, buyer, from any valid and unforeseen claims against the property or prior owner, seller, based on matters of public record as of the date of recordation. This policy does not cover specified matters not disclosed by public records. Certain other types such as actual defects known to the insured when policy is issued are also excluded. The **CLTA** policy is known as an owner's policy, or joint protection policy.

The **ALTA** policy is the second major type of title insurance used in California. It provides coverage for the lender through elimination of the standard exceptions from the CLTA joint policy. For a mortgage loan broker, the ALTA policy is required for virtually every institutional lender loan. The extended coverage policy is a type of CLTA title insurance in which many of the exclusions from the standard policy are included, such as easements. This extended coverage policy includes valid liens not of public record, such as a mechanic's lien.

Binder Policy

A **binder policy** is issued as a policy of title insurance for cases in which a sale of the property is contemplated within the next two, four, or five years. A check with a local title company is ascertained for the duration of the binder policy. This type of insurance can be used on any type of property, whether owner occupied or not. In our example, when the property was purchased, the seller paid 100 percent of the basic-rate ALTA and the buyer paid an additional 10 percent. If the property is resold within a two-four-or five-year period, the original buyer, who becomes the future seller, will pay only the "binder" resale rate, which is the difference between the original cost and the resale price. The binder policy is a title insurance coverage with specifics to reduce the total cost of the premium by prepaying a sum that reduces the subsequent policy cost upon the future resale. In lieu of an owner's policy, a binder to insure a resale within 24 months of the date of closing may be issued for a fee. The fee is usually on a written rate chart, based upon the liability amount, and is often 10 percent of the base rate of the policy. This fee is in addition to the applicable fee for an owner's policy. Prior to its expiration, a binder may be extended for an additional 12 months for an additional fee of another 10 percent of the base rate. The binder may be reissued to reflect an interim transfer of title prior to the ultimate resale for an additional charge (usually 25 percent of a base rate fee) based on the binder amount. (See Figure 9.11.)

FIGURE 9.11   The binder policy.

Sales Price		ALTA Standard Owners Policy or CLTA Owners Policy
$150,000	Base rate	$862.00
	Additional 10%	86.20
	Total	$948.20

If the property is sold within 2 years for $425,500, the following would apply:

Sales Price		ALTA Standard Owners Policy or CLTA Owners Policy
$425,500	Base rate	$1,749.00
	Less original base rate	862.00
	New sale Total	$887.00

If the owners wish to extend the binder for one additional year, they must pay an additional 10% before expiration of the two-year binder.

Review of Sample Preliminary Title Report

The mortgage loan broker would need to review the prelim to look for red flags signaling a possible discrepancy in the information represented from the parties or from other sources that the mortgage loan broker might be liable for in the event of an internal audit, as reviewed by quality control. The following items are a review of the prelim, as presented in Appendix F:

No discrepancies noted for the first page and Schedule A. On Schedule A-1, items 1, 2, and 3, there are no discrepancies. However, for item 4 regarding the "Homeowners Exemption," the prelim shows $7,000. The mortgage loan broker should be aware that if this shows as "NONE" and the prelim indicates that the current owners have been on title for more than two years, this may or may not be an error. If the loan applied for is a cash-out loan in which the information indicates that the property has been owner occupied, the mortgage loan broker should note that this may be a red flag. If this is the only red flag found in the entire file, as shown on the list given in Chapter 10, the mortgage loan broker may wish to do nothing and pass the file along to the underwriter for approval. However, if this is one of a series of many ongoing items that do not match, the loan broker may wish to pass the file on to quality control for an audit.

On Schedule A-1, items 5, 6, 7, and 8 have no visible discrepancies, nor does Schedule B for items 1, 2, 3, and 4. However, item 5 on Schedule B indicates that the seller's existing loan amount on the property was obtained in October 1991 for $300,000, yet the escrow instructions in Appendix D indicate a current sales price for $425,500, which would signal the mortgage loan broker that the seller may have worked out a "short pay" with his or her existing lender to relieve the seller from the obligation. In these circumstances, the seller may not have sufficient funds to pay off the existing loan and pay his or her portion of the closing costs. In this case, the transaction could not close unless funds were received from some source to cover the expenses. If no funds are available from the new loan proceeds and the seller does not have the cash reserves to place funds into escrow to cover his or her costs, the buyer would be prohibited from paying these costs unless disclosed to the lender as part of the escrow and disclosure.

Schedule B, item 6, indicates an additional loan for $40,000. In conjunction with the information about item 5 regarding the first loan, the lender would want assurances that this junior lien would be paid in full with no future obligation by the buyer.

Schedule B, item 7, indicates an abstract of judgment lien from Cool Pool, Inc. The lender will need to know if this is for the subject property. If it is not, the title company or courts would need paperwork to release this lien. If it is a valid lien, it is required to show proof of payment prior to transfer of ownership.

Schedule B, items 8, 9, and 10, are all seller's tax liens. Each must have a release from the government showing payment in full or release from the property prior to the new loan being secured on the property.

Item 11 is a buyer's personal judgment lien for nonpayment of child support. Note that if the borrower has a common name, the lien may not be against our borrower. After first checking and determining that the lien is against the borrower in this transaction, then the mortgage loan broker would check the 1003 to see whether the borrower indicated any current payment of child support. The borrower may have a lien for former child support, but because the child is now an adult, no current or future payments may occur. Naturally, if the lien is against the borrower for past child support and is also liable for ongoing future payments that were not indicated on the 1003, the mortgage loan broker may wish to either deny the loan or forward the file to quality control. However, the borrower may have sufficient funds to pay off the entire judgment and still maintain the cash reserves required for the current loan. In this case, the mortgage loan broker would require a copy of the entire divorce decree to explain the complete terms of the future financial obligation of the borrower.

9.5 APPRAISAL

Background

The **Uniform Residential Appraisal Report (URAR)**, referred to as the 1004 (pronounced 10-0-4) form, has become standard in the industry, even though it has undergone many changes. The **Depository Institutions Deregulation and Monetary Control Act (DIDMCA)** of 1980 greatly expanded the activities of the financial institutions that set the level to $100,000 for federally insured accounts. With deregulation that followed, many problems arose with the mismanagement of some of the institutions. Significant changes were brought about in 1986 as a result of the **Financial Institution's Reform and Recovery Act (FIRREA)**. The **Uniform Standards of Professional Appraisal Practice (USPAP)** were generated, which included specific guidelines and appraisal ethics on most federally related transactions.

For example, the Federal Housing Finance Agency (FHFA) implemented a revised Home Valuation Code of Conduct effective May 1, 2009 between the Enterprises, the New York State Attorney General, and FHFA to improve the reliability of home appraisals. The code applied to lenders that sell single-family mortgage loans beginning May 1, 2009, to help assure that borrowers, homebuyers, and secondary mortgage market investors receive fair and independent property valuations. FHFA regulates Fannie Mae, Freddie Mac, and the 12 Federal Home Loan Banks. In December 2008 these government-sponsored enterprises provided more than $6.2 trillion in funding for the U.S. mortgage markets and financial institutions.

The March 2005 form consists of six pages, and the appraisal must cover the following five areas:

1. A complete visual inspection of the interior and exterior areas of the subject property
2. An inspection of the neighborhood
3. An inspection of each of the comparable sales on at least that particular street
4. Collection, confirmation, and analysis of data from reliable public or private sources
5. Recording of the analysis, opinions, and conclusions in the appraisal report

A new appraisal FNMA form 1004 was required as of November 2005, then revised for an effective date of January 2006. The form was updated and revised several times between January 2009 and May 2009. The newest form is required as of May 2009. During recent legislative hearings, the subprime mortgage market problems and the subsequent economic downturn were the reasons for the revised form. FNMA 1004c is the Manufacture Home Appraisal Report, effective March 2005. The FNMA 1004, also effective March 2005, is the Appraisal Update and/or Completion Report. The FNMA Form 1004mc is the Market Conditions Addendum to the Appraisal Report, effective March 2009.

For single residential properties, condominiums, planned unit developments (PUDs), and most one- to four-unit loans, the mortgage loan broker must submit to the lender an appraisal on the URAR form. For FNMA, FHLMC, FHA, DVA, FmHA, and similar loans, the URAR form is required.

HR 3221, the Federal Housing Finance Regulatory Reform Act (FHFRRA) created specific provisions that pertain to appraisals. For the HOPE for Homeowners Program:

• All appraisals must be conducted in accordance with Title XI of FIRREA and performed by an appraiser who meets the competency requirements of the Uniform Standards of Professional Appraisal Practice (USPAP).

• The FHA is authorized to contract for independent quality reviews of underwriting, including appraisal reviews and fraud detection, of mortgages insured under the HOPE for Homeowners program or pools of such loans.

The FHA Appraisal Reports also amends the FHA Appraiser Roster Requirements as follows:

Beginning on the date of enactment of the Federal Housing Finance Regulatory Act, an appraiser chosen or approved to conduct FHA appraisals shall:

- Be certified by the state in which the property to be appraised is located, or
- Be certified by a nationally recognized professional appraisal organization, and
- Demonstrate verifiable education in FHA appraisal requirements.

The FHFRRA prohibits all parties involved in a real estate transaction, including the mortgage lenders, mortgage brokers, mortgage bankers, real estate brokers, appraisal management companies, employees of appraisal management companies, or any other persons with an interest in a real estate transaction from improperly influencing an appraiser. This provision protects appraisers working under the HOPE for Homeowners Program and the FHA Appraiser Roster.

For portfolio loans, this form is optional; however, most lenders expect to see the URAR uniform appraisal form.

The new Home Valuation Code of Conduct (HVCC), covering one- to four-family conventional residential consumer loans, dictates certain practices lenders must follow with respect to appraisals related to loans intended to be sold to FNMA or Freddie Mac. The borrower must receive a copy of the completed appraisal not later than three business days prior to closing. The purpose of HVCC is to insulate the appraisal process from undue influences by placing tight controls and restrictions on the ordering of the appraiser, as well as guidelines for communicating with the appraiser using the process. The code is effective May 1, 2009. The code requires lenders to order appraisals themselves, rather than accept any appraisal completed by an appraiser who was chosen, hired, or paid by a mortgage broker, real estate agent, or other third party. The rules apply to in-house appraisers and their independents. The code allows an appraisal to be transferred from one lender to another.

The appraisal may be required by the lender's designed appraisal management company (AMC) so that the process is permissible provided all of the following criteria are met:

- The AMC is specifically authorized by the lender to act on its behalf and the AMC is not acting on behalf of the mortgage broker,
- The AMC selects, retains, and provides for the payment of all compensation to the appraiser on the lender's behalf,
- The appraiser's client is the lender and the appraiser correctly identifies the lender as the lender/client on the appraisal report,
- The lender has policies and procedures in place that comply with the code, and
- The lender ensures that the AMC has policies and procedures in place that comply with the code.

The penalty for violation of the code is suspension or termination of the lender's eligibility to sell loans to Freddie Mac if the lender fails to remediate violations.

The appraisal form is divided into specific sections laid out in bold print on the left side of each page of the form. The top section is for determining the purpose of the appraisal for the subject property. The next section is information about the neighborhood and site. Then a section gives a specific description of the improvements, including general description, foundation, exterior description, and interior, to complete the first page. The second page deals with subject sales history, sales comparison analysis, and reconciliation. The third page covers additional comments, cost approach to value, income approach to value, and project information if subject property is a condominium or for PUDs. The fourth page covers definitions and statement of assumptions and limiting conditions. The fifth page covers appraiser's certification, and the sixth is for the supervisory appraiser's certification. A new two-page section follows, covering definition of market value and a statement of limiting conditions and the appraiser's certification. This is followed by various exhibits: a building sketch, plat map, legal description map, location map, subject photo page, photograph addendum (showing interior photo shots), and comparable photo page.

In addition to FNMA form 1004, the mortgage broker or processor will need to ensure that the following items are included with each appraisal report:

1. Two sets of photos (front, rear, and street scene) for subject property
2. Two sets of comparable photos (front only)
3. Appraiser's addendum to the appraisal form (statement of limiting conditions) FNMA #1004B FHLMC #439
4. Building sketch giving exterior measurements and a rough room layout
5. Location map

In addition to the above items, all appraisals that will be submitted to investors must have a copy of the appraiser's license and a copy of the Errors and Omissions (E&O) Insurance policy.

There are several other factors surrounding an appraisal report that the mortgage broker or processor must take note of:

1. **Economic life remaining on the property.** (If the borrower requested a 30-year loan and the economic life remaining on the property is 20 years, then the processor must inform the mortgage broker another loan program must be located, such as a 15- or 20-year loan.)
2. **Land to value.** This value is figured by dividing the value of the land or the property by the final estimate of market value; land to value will be found in the cost approach section of the appraisal. If it exceeds 50 percent, then the appraiser should be asked to comment about whether this is a high land value or is typical of the area.
3. **Room additions.** If the appraiser has stated that a room addition was made, the mortgage broker should ask whether a building permit was obtained for the addition.
   (Note: Some lenders will not make a loan without building permits. Also, if the property is damaged from a fire that started in the room addition, the borrower will not be covered under the fire insurance policy.)
4. **Predominant value.** This value should not exceed the final value of the property.

Licensing

On February 20, 2004, the Appraiser Qualifications Board of the Appraisal Foundation adopted changes to the Real Property Appraiser Qualification Criteria that became effective January 1, 2008. These changes represent the minimum national requirements that each state must implement for individuals applying for a real estate appraiser license or certification. The major changes will be for a certified residential and certified general license. The certified residential license will require a minimum of an associate degree or higher, and the certified general will require a bachelor's degree or higher. You may also go to the AQR's Web page at *http://www.appraisalfoundation.org* for the latest information. See Figure 9.12.

The appraiser must be licensed in California. The **Office of Real Estate Appraisal (OREA)** has several levels of license, similar to the DRE separate salesperson and broker license. Above the trainee licensee, the entry-level license is the licensed appraiser, with a higher level of experience and knowledge needed to acquire the certified residential real estate appraisal license. The highest level is the certified general real estate appraisal license, in which 50 percent of the work consists of nonresidential appraisals. (Appraiser guidelines are available at *http://www.dpa.ca.gov*; steps at *http://www.isle.net*; agencies, *http://www.orea.ca.gov*.)

FIGURE 9.12   Appraisal license requirements.

LICENSING CRITERIA
EFFECTIVE JANUARY 1, 2008

OREA License Levels	Education Requirements	Experience Requirements	Scope of Practice
Trainee	150 hours, covering specific modules including the 15-hour *National USPAP Course* (or its equivalent as determined by the Appraiser Qualifications Board	None	Any property which the supervising appraiser is permitted to appraise
Residential	150 hours, covering specific modules including the 15-hour *National USPAP Course* (or its equivalent as determined by the Appraiser Qualifications Board	2000 hours and encompassing no less than 12 months of acceptable appraisal experience	Any non-complex 1–4 family property with a transaction value up to $1 million; and non-residential property with a transaction value up to $250,000
Certified Residential	200 hours, covering specific modules, including the 15-hour *National USPAP Course* and an Associate Degree. In lieu of a degree, 21 semester credits in specific subject matters may be substituted	2,500 hours and encompassing no less than 2.5 years (30 months) of acceptable appraisal experience	Any 1–4 family property without regard to transaction value or complexity; and non-residential property with a transaction value up to $250,000
Certified General	300 hours, covering specific modules, including the 15-hour *National USPAP Course* and a Bachelors Degree. In lieu of a degree, 30 semester credits in specific subject matters may be substituted	3,000 hours and encompassing no less than 2.5 years (30 months) of acceptable appraisal experience, of which 1,500 hours must be non-residential	All real estate without regard to transaction value or complexity

Borrower Copy

When the loan application is received, it is customary to order an appraisal. The borrower is entitled to a copy of the appraisal report if the buyer paid for it. Some lenders do not charge the borrower for the report and therefore do not have to furnish a borrower with a copy of the report. It is also common for the appraiser to be paid by the seller at the time of performance of the work.

In California, if the borrower pays for the appraisal, a DRE-licensed mortgage loan broker must provide a copy of the appraisal to the borrower and a copy to the lender at or before the closing of the loan transaction (Business and Professional Code 10241.3). (In some states, this is referred to as the B & P code). A statute requires the lender to provide a notice to loan applicants informing them that they have the right to a copy of the appraisal if the borrower paid for it. This notice must be given in 10-point bold type as a separate document no later than 15 days after the lender receives the written application for the loan. This notice must be received by the applicant, from the lender, no later than 90 days after the lender provides notice of the action taken, including application incompleteness or loan withdrawal. Release of the appraisal to the applicant may be conditioned upon payment of the cost of the appraisal. When the mortgage loan broker collects a fee from the prospective borrower to pay for the appraisal report, the borrower should sign a form such as that shown in Figure 9.13.

Lender Approval

When the appraiser has an approved state license and uses the URAR form the mortgage loan broker may now assume that the appraiser has been approved by the lender to meet the investor criteria for safety and risk. However, if the loan broker changes from one lender to another, a new appraisal report will need to be printed that shows the name of the new lender on the top of the report. Normally, there is an extra fee to make any changes to the appraisal report.

To become an approved appraiser of a specific lender, the individual must submit some common items including:

- copy of current state license
- current resume
- sample work
- references
- copy of errors and omissions insurance
- sample appraisal review

The appraiser compiling the sample appraisal report in Appendix E was asked to make a number of errors for the purpose of training the loan broker on details to look for when receiving a typical appraisal. The reader is asked to review the sample report first and then return to this page to continue reading the comments listed below. A completed URAR appraisal (FNMA Form 1004 and FHLMC Form 70) is shown in Appendix E for the property at 7711 Pleasant Drive. The processor should review the appraisal to ascertain discrepancies as submitted by the appraiser. Any errors discovered by the processor should be

FIGURE 9.13   Request for copy of appraisal report.

You have the right to a copy of the appraisal report or the property evaluation report to be obtained in connection with the loan for which you have applied for, provided you have paid for or are willing to pay for the appraisal. Unless you have selected a no closing cost or a home equity loan or a line of credit, you will be required to pay the cost of the appraisal or the property evaluation report before being provided a copy.

If you obtain a home equity loan or line of credit, a copy of the appraisal report or the property evaluation report will be mailed to you shortly after closing. If you do not receive a copy shortly after closing or if your loan does not close, please submit a written request to the following address:

> YOUR COMPANY NAME
> 1234 Any Street,
> Hometown, State 98765

YOUR COMPANY NAME cannot be held liable for any appraisal inaccuracies. We are providing this appraisal copy in accordance with Calif. SB 492. It is provided for informational purposes only. Further use of the appraisal is prohibited by you or any third party.

A written request must be received no later than 90 days after the closing of escrow. If the loan does not close escrow, a written request must be received within 90 days after notice that the action taken on the application is a denial for the loan request, or upon withdrawal of your loan application. When required, you must have paid the cost of the appraisal report or the property evaluation report before you are provided a copy.

The signature below acknowledges your receipt of this notice of your right to a copy of the appraisal report. Please keep this notice with your other loan records in a safe place.

_____   _____
SIGN HERE   (BORROWER)   DATE

_____   _____
SIGN HERE   (BORROWER)   DATE

shown to the mortgage loan broker or appraiser to make the necessary corrections prior to submitting the loan package to underwriting for final loan approval.

The items below are a review of the appraisal shown in Appendix E. The appraisal report pages are numbered from pages 1 to 6, plus pages 1 and 2 of Definition of Market Value.

Page 1

Under the bold heading "Contract" the appraiser is now required to review the purchase contract for any seller concessions. Under the bold heading "Improvements," under the subheading "General Description," the box is marked as a one-story home. Subject photo page shows the subject property as a two-story. Under "Foundation" is shown that the property has a crawl space. This property is on a concrete slab and would not be able to have a crawl space. Under "Exterior Description," "Pool" is not marked and shows none. The photos show a pool in the backyard. Under "Interior," "Garage" indicates a one-car garage, but the subject photos of the front of the property indicate a two-car garage.

Page 2

Under the bold heading "Sales Comparison Analysis," the appraiser indicated that comparable No. 1 is located 2.02 miles northwest of subject property as noted under subheading "Proximity to Subject." Without the appraiser's making any comments on why the comparable is so far away from subject property, this would exceed FNMA guidelines of all comparables being within one-half to one mile of the subject property. The appraiser may have included other tracts in the appraisal that are comparable, which may be acceptable to the lender if these are, in fact, similar properties. The lender may question, however, why the appraiser had to go so far to find a third comparable property without any notation in the comments section of the report. The loan approval may be delayed because the lender requests justification of this possible discrepancy. "Date of Sale/Time" for comp 3 shows 09/25/04. This sample appraisal was dated 08/16/05. That would make comp 3 eleven months old. Comparables should not be more than six months old. "Garage/Carport" shows a one-car garage, discussed previously. "Porch/Patio/Deck" shows a covered patio. On page 1, under "Improvements," the appraiser has noted that no value has been given to the enclosed patio because permits could not be verified (some lenders would require building permits for the enclosed patio as a condition of the loan).

Pages 3, 4, 5, and 6

Pages 3, 4, 5, and 6 have no discrepancies. Also, pages 1 and 2 have no discrepancies on the definition of market value.

Subject Photo Page

As noted before, the photos show a two-story structure, not a one-story. The street number on the curb does not look like 7711, which is the house number. The rear photo shows security bars on the windows. All bedroom windows must have safety releases. The appraiser covered this item on page 1 of the report under "Improvements."

Photograph addendum: If the loan scenario is for an owner-occupied cash-out refinance, not a sale, then the photos would be a possible red flag. Kitchen photos show no amenities, i.e., no small appliances on the counters. The bathroom has no mirror on the wall and no personal grooming items on the sink counter.

Building sketch indicates a one-car garage. This item will need to be clarified.

The plat map shows Pleasant Street not Pleasant Drive, indicating that the plat map may be wrong.

Appraisal Conditions

It is common for the appraiser to note items that must be completed for the property before a loan may be approved or funded. Government loans tend to have more specific property condition requirements than conventional loans, but all loans may be subject to the conditions found by the appraiser. The loan broker cannot finalize the loan and the escrow cannot close the loan until these items have been removed as a valuation condition. Therefore, a review with the parties to determine how these conditions will be handled is advised as early as possible after receipt of the report from the appraiser to avoid delays in the closing. An industry standard form is found in Figure 9.14.

Reconsideration

Often, an appraisal report may fall below the value needed to comply with the amount of the loan requested. It is not unusual to request a reconsideration of value. However, in order to entertain such a request, the mortgage loan broker needs to submit several items. First, a cover letter with an explanation and summary is in order. Second, documented closed escrow comparables or backup data, such as settlement statements for same or similar sales, are required. An appraiser usually does not determine one singular value for a property from the workup sheets but rather has a range of values, with a low and a high amount. If the reconsideration for a higher value falls within the range of values that the appraiser has already determined on the workup sheet, the appraiser is more likely to award the change. If the value requested is outside the range of values, then the original valuation report is not likely to change.

SUMMARY

Although the escrow process varies among geographic areas, the primary purpose is to have a neutral stakeholder control the funds and documents prior to release to the buyer or borrower in a real estate transaction. One of the main purposes for an escrow is to handle the prorations and impound funds.

Title may be taken in many forms, and the vesting determines future tax and legal consequences. Title search begins with the statement of information (SI). The prelim is the worksheet used to ascertain payoffs and other information. Title policies are available in many forms and with many different endorsements for various types of coverage.

The appraisal often determines the ultimate sales price and the amount of the actual loan. Part of the processing of the loan will be to review all aspects of the written appraisal report to determine the accuracy of the report and currency of the form. Major changes went into effect on January 1, 2008, regarding the level of education required for appraisers that affected their licensing. Both appraisal license laws and appraisal forms changed.

The mortgage loan broker must be aware of the functions of escrow, title, and the appraisal and must review the documents, such as escrow instructions, prelim, and appraisal report, in conjunction with the processing of the new loan.

FIGURE 9.14 Valuation conditions.

Department of Housing and Urban Development   OMB 2502-0536
Office of Housing: Federal Housing Commissioner   HUD-92564-VC

NOTICE TO THE LENDER

All required repairs must be completed in a professional manner, in compliance with HUD's guidelines and satisfied prior to closing. The lender is responsible for coordinating repairs. A professionally licensed, bonded, registered engineer, licensed home inspector or appropriately registered/licensed trades person, as applicable, must provide documentation that all deficiencies have been acceptably corrected upon completion of repairs. Check the appropriate response for readily observable evidence of or mark "Yes" for each observable deficiency noted below. Each item marked "Yes" constitutes a limiting condition on the appraisal. Each condition requires repair or further inspection and must be satisfied prior to closing the loan to be eligible for FHA mortgage insurance.

Site Considerations: VC-1 Site Hazards and Nuisances

       Hazards, as defined below, are conditions that endanger the health and safety of the occupants and/or the marketability of the property. Use these criteria to determine the extent of the hazard. If the required component is not visible during the site visit, provide a detailed comment.

Yes ___ a. Surface evidence of subsidence/sink holes.

Yes ___ b. Operating oil or gas wells within 300 feet of existing construction.

Yes ___ c. Operating oil or gas wells within 75 feet of new construction.

Yes ___ d. Abandoned oil or gas well within 10 feet of new/existing structure.

Yes ___ e. Readily observable evidence of slush pits.

Yes ___ f. Excessive noise or hazard from heavy traffic area.

Yes ___ g. New/proposed construction in airport clear zone.

Yes ___ h. High-pressure gas or petroleum lines within 10 feet of the property.

Yes ___ i. Overhead high voltage transmission lines within engineering (designed) fall distance.

Yes ___ j. Excessive hazard from smoke, fumes, offensive noises or odors.

Yes ___ k. New/proposed construction in Special Flood Hazards Areas without LOMA or LOMR

Yes ___ l. Stationary storage tanks with more than 1000 gallons of flammable or explosive material.

Property Considerations

VC-2: Soil Contamination. Evidence of environmental contamination

Yes ___ a. On-site septic shows observable evidence of system failure.

Yes ___ b. Surface evidence of an underground storage tank (UST).

Yes ___ c. Proximity to dumps, landfills, industrial sites or other locations that could contain hazardous materials.

Yes ___ d. Presence of pools of liquid, pits, ponds, lagoons, stressed vegetation, stained soils or pavement, drums or odors.

VC-3: Grading and Drainage. Evidence of topographical problems.

Yes ___ a. Grading does not provide positive drainage away from structure.

Yes ___ b. Standing water proximate to structure

VC-4: Well, Individual Water Supply and Septic. Response with regard to wells and systems. Note: Lender will require water testing for "yes" response. Estimate distance to sewer or water hook-up and whether hook-up is practical as connection should be made to public or community water/sewage disposal system.

Yes ___ a. Property lacks connection to public water

Yes ___ b. Property lacks connection to a public/community sewer system

VC-5: Wood Destroying Insects. Evidence of wood infestation.

Yes ___ a. Structure and accessory buildings are ground level and/or wood is touching ground.

Yes ___ b. The house and/or other structures within the legal boundaries of the property show obvious evidence of active termite infestation.

FIGURE 9.14   (*Continued*)

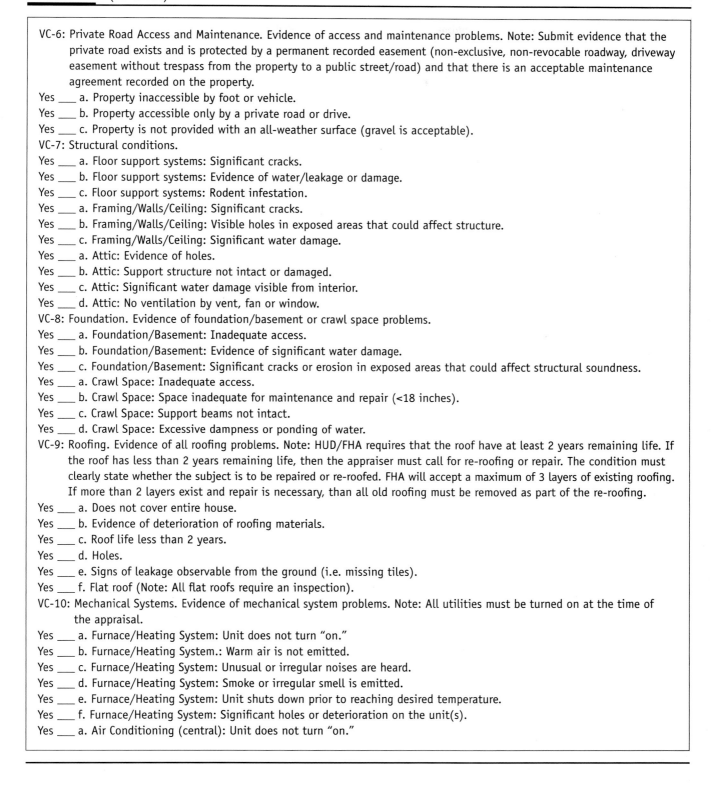

VC-6: Private Road Access and Maintenance. Evidence of access and maintenance problems. Note: Submit evidence that the private road exists and is protected by a permanent recorded easement (non-exclusive, non-revocable roadway, driveway easement without trespass from the property to a public street/road) and that there is an acceptable maintenance agreement recorded on the property.

Yes ___ a. Property inaccessible by foot or vehicle.

Yes ___ b. Property accessible only by a private road or drive.

Yes ___ c. Property is not provided with an all-weather surface (gravel is acceptable).

VC-7: Structural conditions.

Yes ___ a. Floor support systems: Significant cracks.

Yes ___ b. Floor support systems: Evidence of water/leakage or damage.

Yes ___ c. Floor support systems: Rodent infestation.

Yes ___ a. Framing/Walls/Ceiling: Significant cracks.

Yes ___ b. Framing/Walls/Ceiling: Visible holes in exposed areas that could affect structure.

Yes ___ c. Framing/Walls/Ceiling: Significant water damage.

Yes ___ a. Attic: Evidence of holes.

Yes ___ b. Attic: Support structure not intact or damaged.

Yes ___ c. Attic: Significant water damage visible from interior.

Yes ___ d. Attic: No ventilation by vent, fan or window.

VC-8: Foundation. Evidence of foundation/basement or crawl space problems.

Yes ___ a. Foundation/Basement: Inadequate access.

Yes ___ b. Foundation/Basement: Evidence of significant water damage.

Yes ___ c. Foundation/Basement: Significant cracks or erosion in exposed areas that could affect structural soundness.

Yes ___ a. Crawl Space: Inadequate access.

Yes ___ b. Crawl Space: Space inadequate for maintenance and repair (<18 inches).

Yes ___ c. Crawl Space: Support beams not intact.

Yes ___ d. Crawl Space: Excessive dampness or ponding of water.

VC-9: Roofing. Evidence of all roofing problems. Note: HUD/FHA requires that the roof have at least 2 years remaining life. If the roof has less than 2 years remaining life, then the appraiser must call for re-roofing or repair. The condition must clearly state whether the subject is to be repaired or re-roofed. FHA will accept a maximum of 3 layers of existing roofing. If more than 2 layers exist and repair is necessary, than all old roofing must be removed as part of the re-roofing.

Yes ___ a. Does not cover entire house.

Yes ___ b. Evidence of deterioration of roofing materials.

Yes ___ c. Roof life less than 2 years.

Yes ___ d. Holes.

Yes ___ e. Signs of leakage observable from the ground (i.e. missing tiles).

Yes ___ f. Flat roof (Note: All flat roofs require an inspection).

VC-10: Mechanical Systems. Evidence of mechanical system problems. Note: All utilities must be turned on at the time of the appraisal.

Yes ___ a. Furnace/Heating System: Unit does not turn "on."

Yes ___ b. Furnace/Heating System.: Warm air is not emitted.

Yes ___ c. Furnace/Heating System: Unusual or irregular noises are heard.

Yes ___ d. Furnace/Heating System: Smoke or irregular smell is emitted.

Yes ___ e. Furnace/Heating System: Unit shuts down prior to reaching desired temperature.

Yes ___ f. Furnace/Heating System: Significant holes or deterioration on the unit(s).

Yes ___ a. Air Conditioning (central): Unit does not turn "on."

FIGURE 9.14   (*Continued*)

Yes ___ b. Air Conditioning (central): Cold air is not emitted.

Yes ___ c. Air Conditioning (central): Irregular noises are heard.

Yes ___ d. Air Conditioning (central): Smoke or irregular smell is emitted.

Yes ___ e. Air Conditioning (central): Unit shuts down prior to reaching desired temperature.

Yes ___ f. Air Conditioning (central): Significant holes or deterioration on the unit(s).

Yes ___ a. Electrical System: Electrical switches do not turn "on" or "off."

Yes ___ b. Electrical System: Outlets do not function.

Yes ___ c. Electrical System: Presence of sparks or smoke from outlet(s).

Yes ___ d. Electrical System: Exposed wiring visible in living areas.

Yes ___ e. Electrical System: Frayed wiring.

Yes ___ a. Plumbing System: Toilet: Toilets do not function.

Yes ___ b. Plumbing System: Toilet: Presence of leak(s).

Yes ___ c. Plumbing System: Leaks: Structural damage under fixtures.

Yes ___ d. Plumbing System: Leaks: Puddles present.

Yes ___ e. Plumbing System: Sewer System: Observable surface evidence of malfunction.

Yes ___ f. Plumbing System: Sinks: Basin or pipes leak

Yes ___ g. Plumbing System: Sinks: Water does not run.

Yes ___ h. Plumbing System: Water: Significant drop or limitation in pressure.

Yes ___ i. Plumbing System: No hot water.

VC-11: Other Health and Safety Deficiencies. Evidence of health and safety deficiencies.

Yes ___ a. Multiple broken windows.

Yes ___ b. Broken or missing exterior stairs.

Yes ___ c. Broken or missing exterior doors.

Yes ___ d. Inadequate/blocked entrances or exits.

Yes ___ e. Steps without handrails.

Yes ___ f. The mechanical garage door does not reverse or stop when meeting reasonable resistance during closing.

VC-12: Lead-Based Paint Hazard. For any home built prior to 1978, check for evidence of defective paint surfaces, including peeling, scaling or chipping paint. For all FHA-insured properties, the seller is required to correct all defective paint in or on dwelling units built before January 1, 1978.

Yes ___ a. Evidence on interior.

Yes ___ b. Evidence on exterior.

VC-13: Condominiums and Planned Unit Developments (PUD)

Yes ___ a. This project is not on FHA's approval list.

Yes ___ b. The property does not meet owner-occupancy standards.

Yes ___ c. This property does not meet completion standards.

ADDENDA:

Yes ___ a. Provide the current full/market assessed value: $ _____.

Yes ___ b. Provide the summary of estimated repair costs: $ _____.

DESCRIPTION OF RESPONSES AND RELATED COMMENTS:

VC# ___ Section: ___   _____

VC# ___ Section: ___   _____

VC# ___ Section: ___   _____

VC# ___ Section: ___   _____

VC# ___ Section: ___   _____

VC# ___ Section: ___   _____

REVIEWING YOUR UNDERSTANDING

1. Which is not reflected in a preliminary title report?
   A. Common CC&Rs
   B. Existing title to the estate or interest in the described land
   C. A list of defects, liens, and encumbrances
   D. Restrictions that would be excluded from coverage, if the requested policy were to be issued at the date of the report

2. The title policy required for virtually every institutional lender is:
   A. ALTA
   B. CLTA
   C. CLTA extended coverage
   D. ALTA extended coverage

3. Escrow is:
   A. A neutral depository for the things of value to be handled to the terms and conditions of the mutually agreed upon instructions given to the escrow agent or officer
   B. A holder to transfer values
   C. A title insurance company
   D. None of the above

4. Escrow is required on:
   A. Transfer of a liquor License
   B. Probate sale
   C. Transfer of securities
   D. None of the above

5. A common item found in an impound account is:
   A. Property taxes
   B. Hazard insurance
   C. Mortgage insurance
   D. All of the above

6. Which of the following is NOT a license category for licensed appraisers?
   A. Certified Residential Appraiser
   B. Certified General Appraiser
   C. Certified Income Property Appraiser
   D. None of the above

7. The form number for the Uniform Residential Appraisal Report (URAR) is:
   A. 1030
   B. 1980
   C. 1004
   D. 1003

8. OREA stands for:
   A. Operation of Residential Estate Report
   B. Office of Real Estate Appraisal
   C. Office of Residential Estate Report
   D. Office of Real Estate Occupation

9. Who requires the "Statement of Information"?
   A. Both escrow and title insurance
   B. Only the escrow company
   C. Only the title company
   D. Only the escrow company, after the title company requests it

10. FNMA guidelines for sales comparisons in an appraisal say that comparable properties should be within _____ of the subject property.
    A. ½ mile
    B. 1 mile
    C. 3 miles
    D. 5 miles

ANSWERS TO REVIEWING YOUR UNDERSTANDING

1. A (p. 308)
2. A (p. 309)
3. A (p. 287)
4. D (p. 291)
5. D (p. 298)
6. C (p. 315)
7. C (p. 311)
8. B (p. 315)
9. A (p. 297)
10. B (p. 318)

Chapter

10

Approval with conditions

Auditing

Auditor

Automatic funding

Direct endorsement

Fraud audit form

Loan committee

Prior to funding conditions

Quality control

Red flags

Subject to conditions

Underwriter

Underwriting guidelines

Underwriting worksheet

Uniform Underwriting and Transmittal Summary Form (1008)

Zero tolerance

Processing: Underwriting and Quality Control

PREVIEW

After the mortgage loan broker completes his or her portion of the transaction, the file is sent from the processor to the loan underwriter. The underwriter reviews all items in the file to look for areas that need further information or do not meet the lending guidelines of the loan program. The underwriter sometimes finds discrepancies, referred to as red flags. Items that can be explained and documented are then added to the file for the lender. When the item appears to be a problem, the matter is handed to the quality control or auditing department for a fraud or misrepresentation audit. After the underwriting department has completed its work on the file and the contents have been reviewed by the audit personnel, the loan file is then forwarded to the funding department, where loan documents are prepared for the borrower to sign.

CHAPTER OBJECTIVES

At the end of this chapter, the student learning outcomes include:

1. Describe the underwriting process.
2. Name typical stages for conditional approval.
3. Differentiate between acceptable and problem red flag loan criteria.
4. Explain the audit department functions in the loan process.
5. Outline the major components of quality control.

10.1 UNDERWRITING

There are no loan underwriting schools where individuals may obtain a certificate or degree. Few colleges and private schools offer programs in underwriting. Yet, the **underwriter** is the last loan approval step in the loan process before the loan is forwarded to the loan document department to draw the loan documents. The underwriter is the last person to protect the investor. The underwriter approves or denies the loan and needs the highest level of expertise possible.

A person becomes an underwriter by working his or her way up through the ranks within the industry. A typical chain of progression is shown in Figure 10.1. The opportunities for promotion are based upon the amount of experience of the individual, the industry activity that leads to openings, and the structure of personnel of a particular business firm.

Common business operations within the banking community include the use of either an individual loan underwriter or the use of a **loan committee**. The committee is usually made up of loan underwriters and senior personnel of the lending institution, such as the vice president of loan operations.

A loan underwriter's experience increases over the years. As such, the lender places the loan underwriter in a position of high responsibility for the protection of the investor's funds by reducing the exposure the lender would have for liability if the loan is funded. One example of how underwriting often works is as follows:

- For loan amounts up to FNMA or similar maximum loan limits, the underwriter approves all loans submitted to the lender.
- For an FNMA maximum loan amount, two underwriters are required to deny the loan package, whereas only one is required to approve the loan.
- For jumbo loans, the file must be approved by the loan committee.

A loan committee is made up of one or more individuals, based upon their experience, that the lender has approved to act on behalf of the investor. Each lender has particular criteria for individual underwriters and for the loan committee personnel.

The mortgage loan broker and processor must be aware that the lender often requires a loan package to be submitted 48 to 72 hours in advance of the loan committee meeting to allow the lender time to determine the number of loans that the committee will need to review and the types of personnel needed for the loan committee that day. For example, if only residential loans are being reviewed on a particular day, the personnel may be different from those needed for reviews of loans submitted for construction, business building expansion, and mini-warehouses. Because the loan committee generally meets only once a week, the lender needs the advance time to prepare the files for the meeting.

FIGURE 10.1 Employment progression to underwriting.

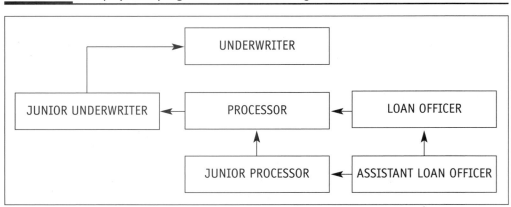

When the terms **direct endorsement** and **automatic funding** are used, they denote specific meanings within the lending community. Many lenders let individual underwriters approve loans up to a maximum FHA, DVA, or FNMA loan amount and only require loans in excess of the maximum to be approved by the loan committee. Individuals or lenders who have gained the proper approval are careful not to jeopardize their special position of confidence. For instance, FHA allows a lender to earn the approval for direct endorsement after having had 10 loans approved with no errors found in the file. The DVA automatic funding approval is much the same.

A helpful tool for the mortgage loan broker is quickly being able to access the underwriting loan criteria for the secondary market investors, such as the Freddie Mac and Fannie Mae Underwriting Comparison Guidelines. Contact your local lender for a comparison guideline chart. There are differences between the two types of loan programs. The two most common agencies are FNMA and FHLMC. One difference is when a prospective borrower's credit report indicates multiple Social Security numbers. For FHLMC, the comparison chart indicates that the agency will not accept the loan. How-ever, FNMA may accept the loan, pending a letter of explanation and completion of IRS Form 4506-T indicating verification of the correct Social Security number. FNMA guidelines can be found at: https://www.efanniemae.com/sf/guides/ssg/sgpdf.jsp. Click on the most current version of "Fannie Mae Selling Guide".

Before the loan application form is submitted to the lender for approval, the mortgage loan broker and the processor have checked the borrower's file for income, debts, bank and employment verifications, and property valuation. However, the underwriter does additional calculations for a final analysis before submission for approval. A typical **underwriting worksheet** to guide the underwriter through the steps to loan approval or denial is shown in Figure 10.2.

It is typical for a file to be neither approved nor denied. Most loans are approved with conditions. The most common conditions often originate from the appraisal report, such as the need for the termite inspection or building permits. Other times, the mortgage loan broker did not submit the paperwork with "original" signatures, such as on tax returns and W-2s. Three stages of "**approval with conditions**" are commonly found in the industry.

- Prior to docs—This is after loan submission to the lender and after the loan has been approved but before the lender draws loan documents. Examples include quality control audit, current/last pay stub, mortgage insurance approval, estimated HUD-1/good faith net proceeds from the sale of the borrower's existing property ownership, and final clearance on termite report.

- Prior to funding—This is after the loan is approved and loan documents have been drawn, but it is before the loan is funded by the lender. Examples are final clearance of work requirements cited on the appraisal report and satisfactory records of 12-month payment history.

- After funding—This is after the loan has closed but before the file is forwarded to the investor. Examples are original fire insurance policy, certified copy of HUD-1 closing statement on borrower's former property, and the original policy of title insurance.

FIGURE 10.2 Underwriting worksheet.

BORROWER _____
COBORROWER _____
COBORROWER _____
PROPERTY ADDRESS _____
_____
_____

SALES PRICE $ _____ LTV _____
APPRAISED VALUE $ _____ LTV _____

ORIGINATOR _____
PERSON TO CONTACT _____
TELEPHONE NUMBER _____
FAX NUMBER _____
LOAN TYPE/PROGRAM # _____ TERM _____
OWNER _____ NONOWNER _____ 2ND HOME _____
LOAN AMOUNT _____
INTEREST RATE _____ % QUAL RATE _____
PURCHASE _____ REFI _____ CASH OUT _____

CASH REQUIREMENTS

CLOSING COST	$ _____	
DOWN PAYMENT	$ _____	
1ST. TD P/I	$ _____	
2ND TD P/I	$ _____	
DEBT P/I	$ _____	
TOTAL CASH REQ.	$ _____	

VERIFICATION OF FUNDS:

CASH VERIFIED	$ _____
STOCKS & BONDS	$ _____
PRIOR HOME PROCEEDS	$ _____
OTHER _____	$ _____
DEPOSIT IN ESCROW	$ _____
TOTAL	$ _____
CASH RESERVES	$ _____

DEBT ANALYSIS

_____ + _____ + _____ + _____
_____ + _____ + _____ + _____

TOTAL DEBT PER 1003	$ _____
PRIMARY RESIDENCE	$ _____
NEGATIVE RENTS	$ _____
TOTAL LONG-TERM DEBT	$ _____

INCOME ANALYSIS:	**BORROWER**	**COBORROWER**
BASE PAY	$ _____	$ _____
OVERTIME ____ AVG	$ _____	$ _____
COMMISSION ___ AVG	$ _____	$ _____
NET RENTAL	$ _____	$ _____
OTHER	$ _____	$ _____
TOTAL	$ _____	$ _____

TOTAL EFFECTIVE INCOME: $ _____

PROPOSED MONTHLY PMNT. (SUBJ. PROP)

P & I 1ST	$ _____
P & I 2ND	$ _____
HAZ/HO	$ _____
TAX	$ _____
PMI	$ _____
HOA DUES	$ _____

TOTAL PROPOSED PAYMENT $ _____

QUALIFYING RATIOS:
PITI/STABLE MONTHLY INCOME _____
PITI & LTV/STABLE MO INCOME _____
PRIOR DEBT P/O RATIO, IF APPL _____

PROPERTY EVALUATION	**YES**	**NO**
IS APPRAISER APPROVED?		
APPRAISAL REVIEW DESK _____ OTHER _____		
IS NEIGHBORHOOD FREE OF ADVERSE INFLUENCES?	____	____
IS SITE CLEAR OF ADVERSE INFLUENCES?	____	____
IS PROPERTY LOCATED OUTSIDE A HUD-IDENTIFIED FLOOD AREA?	____	____
ARE ALL PROPERTY RATINGS AT LEAST AVERAGE?	____	____
REMAINING ECONOMIC LIFE MINUS LOAN TERM		
OBSOLESCENCE? TYPE _____ AMOUNT _____ FOR _____		
RATIO OF LAND VALUE _____ TO TOTAL VALUE _____		
ARE COMPARABLE ADJUSTMENTS EXPLAINED, REASONABLE AND CONSISTENT?	____	____
LOAN AMOUNT DOES NOT EXCEED 125% OF PREDOMINANT VALUE?	____	____
PRICE RANGE		

_____ LOW _____ HIGH _____ PREDOMINANT _____ 125% OF PREDOMINANT VALUE

_____
_____
_____

APPROVED BY: _____ DATE _____ ADVISED _____
APPROVED SUBJECT TO CONDS. BY: _____ DATE _____ ADVISED _____
DENIED BY: _____ DATE _____ ADVISED _____
SUPERVISOR: _____ DATE _____
RATE: _____ TOTAL POINTS _____ MKT _____ ORIGINATOR _____ FLOAT _____
LOCKED _____ DISCOUNT POINTS _____ ORIG. PTS _____ PAID BY _____ LOAN # _____

Each lender has specific requirements for **underwriting guidelines** or final loan approval. Lenders differ substantially on the criteria they use to approve a loan **subject to conditions**. The industry standard Uniform Underwriting and Transmittal Summary (FNMA) Form 1008 or FHLMC 1077 is shown in Figure 10.3. Both agencies use the same form, which is commonly known as the 1008 among the mortgage loan brokers. The 1008 comes to the underwriter from the processor, along with the loan package.

FIGURE 10.3   Uniform Underwriting and Transmittal Summary (FNMA Form 1008).

Uniform Underwriting and Transmittal Summary

I. Borrower and Property Information

Borrower Name _____   SSN _____
Co-Borrower Name _____   SSN _____
Property Address _____

Property Type
- ☐ 1 unit
- ☐ 2- to 4-units
- ☐ Condominium
- ☐ PUD   ☐ Co-op
- ☐ Manufactured Housing
  - ☐ Single Wide   ☐ Multiwide

Project Classification

Freddie Mac
- ☐ Streamlined Review
- ☐ Established Project
- ☐ New Project
- ☐ Detached Project
- ☐ 2- to 4-unit Project
- ☐ Reciprocal Review

Project Name _____

Fannie Mae
- ☐ P Limited Review New Detached   ☐ E PUD   ☐ 1 Co-op
- ☐ Q Limited Review Established   ☐ F PUD   ☐ 2 Co-op
- ☐ R Expedited Review New   ☐ T PUD   ☐ T Co-op
- ☐ S Expedited Review Established
- ☐ T Fannie Mae Review
- ☐ U FHA-approved
- ☐ V Refi Plus™

CPM Project ID# (if any) _____

Occupancy Status
- ☐ Primary Residence
- ☐ Second Home
- ☐ Investment Property

Additional Property Information
Number of Units _____
Sales Price $ _____
Appraised Value $ _____
Property Rights
- ☐ Fee Simple
- ☐ Leasehold

II. Mortgage Information

Loan Type
- ☐ Conventional
- ☐ FHA
- ☐ VA
- ☐ USDA/RHS

Amortization Type
- ☐ Fixed-Rate—Monthly Payments
- ☐ Fixed-Rate—Biweekly Payments
- ☐ Balloon
- ☐ ARM (type)
- ☐ Other (specify)

Loan Purpose
- ☐ Purchase
- ☐ Cash-Out Refinance
- ☐ Limited Cash-Out Refinance (Fannie)
- ☐ No Cash-Out Refinance (Freddie)
- ☐ Home Improvement
- ☐ Construction to Permanent

Lien Position
- ☐ First Mortgage
Amount of Subordinate Financing
$ _____
(if HELOC, include balance and credit limit)
- ☐ Second Mortgage

Note Information
Original Loan Amount $ _____
Initial P&I Payment $ _____
Initial Note Rate   _____ %
Loan Term (in months) _____

Mortgage Originator
- ☐ Seller
- ☐ Broker
- ☐ Correspondent
Broker/Correspondent Name and Company Name: _____

Buydown
- ☐ Yes
- ☐ No
Terms _____

If Second Mortgage
Owner of First Mortgage
- ☐ Fannie Mae   ☐ Freddie Mac
- ☐ Seller/Other
Original Loan Amount of First Mortgage
$ _____

III. Underwriting Information

Underwriter's Name _____   Appraiser's Name/License # _____   Appraisal Company Name _____

Stable Monthly Income

	Borrower	Co-Borrower	Total
Base Income	$ _____	$ _____	$ 0.00
Other Income	$ _____	$ _____	$ 0.00
Positive Cash Flow (subject property)	$ _____	$ _____	$ 0.00
Total Income	$ 0.00	$ 0.00	$ 0.00

Qualifying Ratios
Primary Housing Expense/Income _____ %
Total Obligations/Income _____ %
Debt-to-Housing Gap Ratio (Freddie) _____ %

Qualifying Rate
- ☐ Note Rate _____ %
- ☐ _____ % Above Note Rate _____ %
- ☐ _____ % Below Note Rate _____ %
- ☐ Bought-Down Rate _____ %
- ☐ Other _____ %

Loan-to-Value Ratios
LTV _____ %
CLTV/TLTV _____ %
HCLTV/HTLTV _____ %

Level of Property Review
- ☐ Exterior/Interior
- ☐ Exterior Only
- ☐ No Appraisal
Form Number: _____

Risk Assessment
- ☐ Manual Underwriting
- ☐ AUS
  - ☐ DU   ☐ LP   ☐ Other
  - AUS Recommendation _____
  - DU Case ID/LP AUS Key# _____
  - LP Doc Class (Freddie) _____
Representative Credit/Indicator Score _____
Underwriter Comments _____

Escrow (T&I)
- ☐ Yes   ☐ No

Community Lending/Affordable Housing Initiative   ☐ Yes   ☐ No
Home Buyers/Homeownership Education Certificate in file   ☐ Yes   ☐ No

Present Housing Payment: $ _____
Proposed Monthly Payments
Borrower's Primary Residence
First Mortgage P&I $ _____
Second Mortgage P&I $ _____
Hazard Insurance $ _____
Taxes $ _____
Mortgage Insurance
HOA Fees $ _____
Lease/Ground Rent $ _____
Other $ _____
Total Primary Housing Expense $ 0.00
Other Obligations
Negative Cash Flow (subject property) $ _____
All Other Monthly Payments $ _____
Total All Monthly Payments $ 0.00

Borrower Funds to Close
Required $ _____
Verified Assets $ _____

Source of Funds
No. of Months Reserves _____
Interested Party Contributions _____ %

IV. Seller, Contract, and Contact Information

Seller Name _____
Seller Address _____

Seller No. _____   Investor Loan No. _____

Seller Loan No. _____

Contact Name _____
Contact Title _____
Contact Phone Number _____ ext. _____

Contact Signature _____

Lenders typically do not use just loan approval or loan denial. Often a loan is approved subject to some conditions, restrictions, or limiting factors. One lender's checklist of conditions is shown in Figure 10.4. Before the loan is funded, certain items may need documentation, such as copies of permits or items may be required from the appraiser, such as an explanation of safety releases on subject-property window photos showing security bars.

The underwriter and **auditor** would need the following information in their quest to locate or confirm/verify the data to underwrite the loan:

I.D. Checking Guide
Drivers License Drive Company
P.O. Box 5305, Dept. 96
1492 Oddstad Dr.
Redwood City, CA 94063
(800) 227-8827
www.driverslicense.com

Credit Repair Quick & Legal
NOLO Press
950 Parker Street
Berkeley, CA 94710
(510) 704-2248

U.S. Immigration and
Naturalization Service
300 N. Los Angeles Street
Los Angeles, CA 90012
(800) 829-4477

Tax Rate Booklet for Orange County
County of Orange Tax Unit
Auditor/Controller
P.O. Box 567
Santa Ana, CA 91702

Social Security Verification Manual
Profit Protection, Inc.
Miami, FL
(305) 652-6953

Do It Yourself Credit File Correction
NCFE Nat'l Center for Fin. Educ.
P.O. Box 34070
San Diego, CA 92163
(619) 239-1401

10.2 RED FLAGS

The following are **red flags** in a loan package that may alert a processor or underwriter to possible fraud or misrepresentations. It should be emphasized that the presence of one or more of these items is not necessarily indicative of fraud; however, they should alert the processor or the underwriter to further review and document the file. These items may be perfectly legitimate when viewed separately, but when taken as a whole, a pattern may begin to emerge. In reviewing any loan file, the processor and underwriter should constantly ask the following questions (these guidelines are from FNMA):

1. Does this file make sense?
2. Who stands to gain in this transaction?

Loan Application

- Significant or unrealistic change in commute distance
- New housing not large enough to accommodate all occupants
- Buyer is downgrading from larger to smaller home (except empty-nesters)

FIGURE 10.4 Loan approval subject to the following conditions.

Approval Date _____   Borrower _____

Originator _____   Underwriter _____

1. _____ Satisfactory loan purpose letter from borrowers / Cash Out $ _____
2. _____ Satisfactory 12-month payment history from _____
3. _____ Transmittal summary and 1003 corrected as applicable.
4. _____ Loan application signed by all borrowers and loan agent with gov't monitoring information. Signed addendums, if applicable.
5. _____ Private mortgage insurance approved at _____ % of coverage.
6. _____ Prelim supplement re: _____
      _____
7. _____ Certified copy of final closing statement to net $ _____
      on property located at _____
8. _____ Certified copy of escrow amendment(s) re: _____
      _____
9. _____ Evidence of flood insurance _____   Flood Zone Letter _____
10. _____ Loan documentation no older than 120 days from note date _____
11. _____ No secondary financing
12. _____ Pay all existing liens currently of record
13. _____ Three (3) day right of rescission
14. _____ Final building permit or code compliance: _____
15. _____ Establishment of monthly tax and/or insurance impound account.
16. _____ Purchase agreement _____ Transfer disclosure statement (TDS) _____
17. _____ Termite report and final clearance, including completion of any work required by lender.
18. _____ Well _____ /Septic _____ certification by _____ local health authority or by _____ licensed contractor.
19. _____ All tax returns to be signed and dated by borrower(s) and sign Form 4506.
20. _____ Year-to-date profit-and-loss statement and balance sheet satisfactory to the underwriter, signed by _____
21. _____ Timesaver Cert. with certified paystubs and W-2s or VOE for_____
      _____
22. _____ Fair Lending _____ ECOA _____ Form 1097 _____ Good Faith/Reg. Z _____ .
23. _____ Certification of disclosure re: Reg. Z signed by processor.
24. _____ 442 _____ Photos _____ upon completion to be supplied by appraiser.
25. _____ Appraiser to comment _____
      _____
26. _____ Satisfactory explanation from borrower re: _____
      _____
27. _____ Condo Questionnaire _____ CC&Rs _____ Articles _____ Bylaws _____ Budget _____
      Balance Sheet _____ Fidelity Bond _____ in the amount of $ _____
28. _____ QUALITY CONTROL AUDIT
29. _____ _____
30. _____ _____
31. _____ _____
32. _____ _____
33. _____ _____
34. _____

- Buyer currently resides in property (purchased from landlord)
- Buyer intends to rent/sell current residence with no documentation
- Down payment other than cash
- Stocks, bonds (liquid assets) not publicly traded (may be closely held corporation)
- Face (not cash surrender) value of life insurance policy shown as liquid asset
- Personal property value exceeds one year's salary or high-income buyer has no personal property
- New housing expense exceeds 150% of current housing expense
- Inappropriate salary with respect to amount of loan
- Invalid Social Security number
- High income/no credit, high income/no cash
- High income, no other real estate owned and renter for substantial period
- Stock broker who does not own stock
- High income/finance company, furniture rental debt
- Self-employed but no entertainment-type credit cards
- Low income or young buyer with substantial cash in bank
- High income/little or no cash in bank
- Buyer has checking account but says source of funds is "cash on hand" because of lack of faith in banks
- Handwritten application shows no debt but typed application does
- Information on application inconsistent with other loan documents: credit report VOE vs. VOD, etc.
- Inconsistent buyer signature or handwriting throughout file
- Same person appearing throughout file such as landlord, seller, buyer, employer the same
- Excessive cash deposit
- Significant changes or contradictions from handwritten to typed loan application

Verification of Employment (VOE)

- Current and prior employment overlap
- No prior year earnings
- Round dollar amounts
- Date of hire is weekend or holiday (per perpetual calendar)
- Income is primarily commissions (self-employed)
- Employer used mail drop or post office box address
- Answering machine or service at place of business
- Prior employer out of business
- Borrower changed profession from previous to current employer
- Illegible signature with no further identification on VOE

- Business entity not in good standing or registered with applicable regulatory agencies
- Coborrower maiden name same as signature of employer (self-employed)
- VOE completed same day as ordered
- VOE says company car and application shows auto loan
- White-out, cross-outs, "squeezed-in" numbers
- If VOE not creased (folded), may have been hand carried
- Income out of line with type of employment

Verification of Deposit (VOD)

- Cash in bank not sufficient to close
- New bank account (verify previous)
- Bank account not in borrower's name
- Rounded dollar amounts (especially on interest-bearing accounts)
- Gift letter that is not backed up by bank statements or canceled checks
- Escrow closing check drawn on different depository from VOD
- Buyer has no accounts (doesn't believe in banks)
- IRA shown as liquid asset or as source of down payment
- Loan secured by checking or savings account
- Illegible bank employee signature with no further identification on VOD
- Significant changes in balance from prior two months to the day of verification
- Source of funds consists of unverified note, equity exchange, sale of residence
- Funds paid outside escrow
- Excessive balance in checking account
- Date of verification by bank is weekend or holiday (per perpetual calendar)
- VOD completed same day as ordered
- White-out, crossouts, "squeezed-in" numbers
- If VOD not creased (folded), may have been hand carried
- Seller has same address as employer
- Checking accounts with average two-month balance exactly equal to present balance
- Credit union for small employer

Appraisal

- Ordered by any party to transaction (buyer, seller, REALTOR®)
- Comps not verified as recorded (data source MLS, sales office, real estate agent, etc.)
- Tenant shown to be occupant on owner-occupant application
- Income approach not used on tenant-occupied SFDs
- Excessive adjustments in urban or suburban area where marketing time is under six months

- Distance of comps
- Comparison of square footage to value
- Photos do not match description of property
- High land value in urban areas
- Undesignated appraiser
- "For sale" or "for rent" signs in yard or windows
- Appraiser located outside of subject property area

Title Search

- Tax or similar liens against buyer
- Delinquent property tax

Tax Returns

- Real estate taxes or interest paid but no rental or owner-occupied property on application (or vice versa)
- Amount of source of income disagrees with other information in the loan file
- No dividends on stock
- Substantial cash in bank with no related interest income
- Gross income does not agree with total income on W-2s or 1099s
- Buyer shows interest expense but no related liability (business loans with personal liability)
- Buyer takes depreciation deduction for real estate not disclosed (or vice versa)
- Net income from rents plus depreciation does not equal cash flow as submitted by buyer
- Additional properties listed but not on loan application
- Buyer shows partnership income (may be liable as general partner for partnership's debts)
- Invalid employer ID number on W-2 (see Figure 10.5) FICA and local taxes (where applicable) exceed ceilings
- Copy submitted is not "employee's copy"
- Different tax preparer each year
- Low-income employee used tax preparer for 1040 short form
- If previous year shows preparer, is fee paid deducted on following year's return?
- Paid preparer handwrites tax return
- No interest expense; however, credit outstanding
- Dependents on loan application but not on tax return or vice versa
- No salaries paid on nonservice self-employed P & L
- No cost of goods sold on retail or similar operations
- Address and occupation differ from the application
- W-2 from large corporation handwritten
- Social Security number on return different from application or credit report
- Post office box for depository if not typical for area or company

FIGURE 10.5 Valid federal employer identification codes.

Alabama—Birmingham	63	Nebraska—Omaha	47
Alaska—Anchorage	92	Nevada—Las Vegas/Reno	88
Arizona—Phoenix	86	New Hampshire—Portsmouth	02
Arkansas—Little Rock	71	New Jersey—Newark	22
California—Laguna Niguel	33	New Mexico—Albuquerque	85
California—Los Angeles	95	New York—Albany	14
California—Sacramento	68	New York—Brooklyn	11
California—San Francisco	94	New York—Buffalo	16
California—San Jose	77	New York—Manhattan	13
Colorado—Denver	84	North Carolina—Greensboro	56
Connecticut—Hartford	06	North Dakota—Fargo	45
Delaware—Wilmington	51	Ohio—Cincinnati	31
Florida—Ft. Lauderdale	65	Ohio—Cleveland	34
Florida—Jacksonville	59	Oklahoma—Oklahoma City	73
Georgia—Atlanta	58	Oregon—Portland	93
Hawaii—Honolulu	99	Pennsylvania—Philadelphia	23
Idaho—Boise	82	Pennsylvania—Pittsburgh	25
Illinois—Chicago	36	Rhode Island—Providence	05
Illinois—Springfield	37	South Carolina—Columbia	57
Indiana—Indianapolis	35	South Dakota—Aberdeen	46
Iowa—Des Moines	42	Tennessee—Nashville	62
Kansas—Wichita	48	Texas—Austin	74
Kentucky—Louisville	61	Texas—Dallas	75
Louisiana—New Orleans	72	Texas—Houston	76
Maine—Augusta	01	Utah—Salt Lake City	87
Maryland—Baltimore	52	Vermont—Burlington	03
Massachusetts—Boston	04	Virginia—Richmond	54
Michigan—Detroit	38	Washington—Seattle	91
Minnesota—St. Paul	41	West Virginia—Parkersburg	55
Mississippi—Jackson	64	Wisconsin—Milwaukee	39
Missouri—St. Louis	43	Wyoming—Cheyenne	83
Montana—Helena	81	District of Columbia—Baltimore, Maryland	52

Credit Report

- No credit (possible use of alias)
- Variance in employment or residence data
- Several recent inquiries from credit card companies or other mortgage lenders
- Invalid Social Security number
- Length of time on file inconsistent with buyer's age
- Coborrower's maiden name shows data different from data on application
- Age over 25 with no credit history
- Personal data not consistent with handwritten application
- If late pays due to unemployment because of illness or layoff, is VOE income less during this period?

Note: Mortgage loan brokers have to create a written program that creates a policy for the office so that when an employee of the broker notices a fraud alert on a client's credit report, the mortgage broker would make sure the client was notified of this fact. Effective June 1, 2008, this federal law is a red flag of identity theft.

Closing Instructions

- Cash paid outside escrow
- Down payment paid into escrow upon opening
- Reference to another (double) escrow
- Related parties
- Unusual credits with no economic substance
- Right of assignment
- Power of attorney
- Seller is corporate (except for developers, RELO companies, or real estate owned (REO))

Sales Contract

- Seller is real estate agent or broker, relative, employer
- No real estate agent or broker
- Lease option
- Price substantially below market value
- Second mortgage
- Deposit checks have inconsistent dates
- Name and address on deposit check different from buyers'
- Deposit check, not cash

Payroll Check Stubs

- Debts reflect as deduction from pay (credit union loans, etc.) not disclosed on loan application
- Name spelled differently from loan application
- Social Security number different from tax return forms

Miscellaneous

- Require all borrowers to sign release of tax information form
- Do not accept incomplete handwritten applications
- Call borrower at work and at home at least once during loan processing
- Call employer on closing date to verify if still employed
- Run credit report on closing date to check for additional incurred debt

In addition, a check to match the correct federal employer identification codes, as shown in Figure 10.5, is often needed to verify the numbers shown on the W-2 forms and the tax return form attachments. The number is always nine digits. The first two digits represent the geographic area of the IRS district office that issued the identification number.

10.3 QUALITY CONTROL AND AUDITING

A file may be referred to **quality control** for **auditing** by the lender to audit the mortgage loan broker, the processor, or the underwriter. The lender, mortgage insurance company personnel, or the government loan agency may audit the loan broker. Files may be audited at random for a specific reason. The alleged concern for which the file was forwarded to the audit department may be determined to be unfounded. During the audit, however, the auditor may find other discrepancies. The auditor would be obligated to proceed with the investigation.

In most regions of the United States, all DVA and FHA loans are regularly audited, with less frequent periodic checks for conventional loans. This standard procedure is to ensure that the loans being forwarded to the secondary market (see Chapter 12) are of a consistent high quality.

When a loan goes bad, such as in the case of a foreclosure, quality control may review the file. The names of the underwriter, appraiser, loan officers, escrow agent, brokers, and processor are reviewed. The audit is to determine whether a pattern for specific individuals or firms has developed in the normal course of their business for which quality control should be concerned. If an individual is found to have a pattern of bad loans, various methods of action may be taken. An individual could lose his or her license. A claim against the errors and omissions insurance may be filed. A court action as either criminal or civil with recommended sentencing and fines may be instituted. Should an individual be prosecuted under a federal government loan program, such as DVA, the party may not move to another state to transact business. The national level of action taken would remain with the individual should loss of licensing or prosecution action result and would thus prohibit real estate activity in an individual state or region. One consequence of a fraudulent loan may be the requirement by the lender that the mortgage loan broker repurchase the loan and pay any loss of the mortgage insurance coverage.

Many lenders require the mortgage loan broker to sign an agreement that places the responsibility for quality control audit and content of the quality for each application taken and for each loan submitted. This is referred to as **zero tolerance**. Submission of false information is a crime, and the lender may take action to prosecute.

The types of loan fraud may include any of the following, as well as any items discussed in the previous section:

- Forgery or predominantly inaccurate information
- Incorrect statements about current occupancy or intent to maintain minimum continuing occupancy as stated in the security instrument (owner occupied)
- Submission of inaccurate information with false statements on the loan application and falsification of documents purporting to substantiate credit, employment, deposit and asset information, personal information, and ownership of real property
- Lack of due diligence by the mortgage loan broker, interviewer, or processor, including failure to obtain all information required by the application and

failure to request further information as dictated by borrower's response to other questions

- Unquestioning acceptance of documentation and statements, which are known, should be known, or should be suspected to be inaccurate
- Broker's nondisclosure of relevant information

In addition to consequences to the broker or other professionals, many avenues are available that may be taken against the borrower. If the broker has no knowledge of the fraud, no action will be taken against him or her. The borrower, however, often has no excuse for the submission of fraudulent documents and information. Any of the following may be applied against the borrower if fraudulent information is found:

- Acceleration of the debt. Foreclosure under this section would not allow the borrower the benefit of reinstatement to cure the default. The borrower must pay off the loan.
- Criminal prosecution.
- Civil action by the mortgage loan broker or other parties to the transaction, such as the licensee or seller.
- Employment termination.
- Loss of professional license, if any.
- Adverse effect on credit history.

A sample of a **fraud audit form** is shown in Figure 10.6. The auditor will review the various areas of the loan to substantiate the information and documents submitted.

Discrepancies are usually forwarded to the audit supervisor for a second opinion on the items found in question. The underwriter or other parties may be asked to review the audit data and to sign off on the information found. Again, each financial institution has its own particular procedure and process.

FNMA has identified a number of factors commonly associated with fraud. The following is a list of items commonly found during the foreclosure period:

- Early payment defaults, with 12 or fewer payments made on the loan
- Multiple unit defaults, with foreclosures within the same condo project, PUD, or subdivision
- Contiguous defaults by the same or different borrowers
- Scattered site defaults with recurring common names or other common factors
- Valuation variances of 20% or more between the original and the postforeclosure appraisal reports in an otherwise stable market
- Denial of the mortgage insurance claim because of alleged irregularities
- Undisclosed secondary financing extended to the buyer by the seller in lieu of cash needed to close ("silent second")
- Projected loss exceeding 25% of the original loan amount
- Double escrows, indicated in the instructions or settlement statement

FIGURE 10.6   Fraud audit form.

Corrs/Branch   Lender   Loan Type: Conv FHA DVA   Prepared by: Date IN

Purpose: Refi   Purchase   Date OUT

BORROWER

Name	Social Security number	Current pay stubs in file? Yes No
		Past 2 years W-2s? Yes No
Self-Employed	Current Employer Phone	Called info? Yes No

VOE   VOE sent to P.O. Box? Yes   No   VOE   Still employed?
No VOE One month current pay stubs?   Yes   No   Yes   No
Contact/Title   Position   Continued Empl?
                                                Yes   No

Authorized signature on VOE? Yes   No CNV Same as VOE? Yes   No
Tax Preparer   Phone   Called Info?
                                                Yes   No

Past 2 yrs tax returns?   Yes   No   Verified with tax preparer
Profit & Loss statement?   Yes   No   Number & Address Yes   No
Corporate return filed?   Yes   No   Confirmed tax returns? Yes   No

COBORROWER

Name	Social Security number	Current pay stubs in file? Yes No
		Past 2 years W-2s? Yes No
Self-Employed	Current Employer Phone	Called info? Yes No

VOE   VOE sent to P.O. Box? Yes   No   VOE   Still employed?
No VOE One month current pay stubs?   Yes   No   Yes   No
Contact/Title   Position   Continued Empl?
                                                Yes   No

Authorized signature on VOE? Yes   No CNV Same as VOE? Yes   No
Tax Preparer   Phone   Called Info?
                                                Yes   No

Past 2 yrs tax returns?   Yes   No   Verified with tax preparer
Profit & Loss statement?   Yes   No   Number & Address Yes   No
Corporate return filed?   Yes   No   Confirmed tax returns? Yes   No

CREDIT BUREAU

| Credit Bureau | Authorized Mtg Report Yes No | Repositories used? EFX TU FICO EXP |
| | No. of inquiries in past 90 days: ___ | In-house Report. Other: |

**LENDER
VERIFICATION**

Notes: Corres/Branch   Lender

Underwriter Only: I have reviewed this Fraud Audit Report. | Name
                   Underwriter: Date: |

Attachments included: None   Memo   CS-1   CS-2   CS-3   Other

- Blind assumptions (title transfers) shortly after loan closing
- Significant discrepancies on reverifications, such as employment, deposit, credit
- Related party transactions, whether disclosed or not
- Recommendation to "walk away" (no equity) from second trust deed holder
- Unusual liens or encumbrances on the foreclosure title report (TSG)
- Tenant-occupied properties, which were originally to be owner-occupied by the borrower
- Bankruptcy within one year of loan origination
- Statements made by borrower to the servicer during collection

SUMMARY

The underwriter has the ultimate responsibility for reviewing the file to clarify potential discrepancies before the file is funded and forwarded to the investor. When items appear to be a concern, the file is forwarded to quality control or the audit department for further scrutiny. After the underwriter and auditor complete their review, the loan file is forwarded to the loan document department, where loan documents are drawn for signatures before funding.

REVIEWING YOUR UNDERSTANDING

1. These are "red flags" that may alert an underwriter for possible misrepresentation or fraud, EXCEPT:
   A. VOE and 1003 matches accurately to the employment information
   B. Invalid Social Security number
   C. Income out of line with type of employment
   D. Bank account not in borrower's name

2. Types of loan fraud may NOT include:
   A. Forgery
   B. Zero tolerance disclosure for quality control audit
   C. Broker's nondisclosure of relevant information
   D. Lack of due diligence by the mortgage loan broker

3. The typical progression to an underwriter position of a financial institution employee is:
   A. Processor, loan officer, junior underwriter, underwriter
   B. Teller, processor, junior underwriter, underwriter
   C. Loan officer, processor, junior underwriter, underwriter
   D. Teller, loan officer, junior underwriter, underwriter

4. Which of the following may be applied against the borrower, if fraudulent information is found?
   A. Acceleration of the loan
   B. Criminal prosecution
   C. Loss of professional license, if any
   D. All of the above

5. Which of the following is NOT one of the three stages of "approval with conditions" commonly found in the industry?

A. Prior to docs

B. Prior to funding

C. After docs

D. After funding

6. When looking at a new loan file, to detect red flags the underwriter would ask:

A. Does this file make sense?

B. Who stands to gain in this transaction?

C. Any question the underwriter wishes to ask

D. A and B

7. When a prospective borrower's credit report indicates multiple Social Security numbers, _____ may accept the loan pending a letter of explanation.

A. DVA

B. CalVet

C. FNMA

D. FHLMC

8. In most regions of the United States, the most frequent auditing occurred in which type of loan?

A. FHA

B. DVA

C. Both FHA and DVA

D. Conventional (FNMA/FHLMC)

9. Who has the ultimate responsibility for reviewing the file to clarify potential discrepancies before the file is funded and forwarded to the investor?

A. Underwriter

B. Auditor

C. Loan broker

D. Borrower

10. A "silent second" is one that was:

A. Discounted and sold after the close of escrow

B. Not disclosed to the first trust deed lien holder

C. An owner carryback loan shown in the escrow instructions

D. An outside lender loan shown in the escrow instructions

ANSWERS TO REVIEWING YOUR UNDERSTANDING

1. A (pp. 326–331)

2. D (p. 337)

3. C (p. 326)

4. D (p. 338)

5. C (p. 327)

6. D (p. 330)

7. C (p. 327)

8. C (p. 337)

9. A (p. 340)

10. B (p. 338)

Chapter

11

Borrower's
certification

Closing

Conditions prior
to funding

Deed of trust

Drawing docs

Funder

Hardship letter

Impound account

Loan docs

Loan verifier

Occupancy affidavit

Prior to funding

Reviewer

Wire transfer

Processing: Docs, Funding, and Closing

PREVIEW

After completion of the work by the underwriter, the file is sent to the document department, which draws the loan documents. The computer-generated documents are printed and reviewed by a funder in the doc department. A complete set of loan documents is shown in Appendix G and reviewed in this chapter. After checking the accuracy of all the papers, the mortgage loan broker sends the loan documents to the escrow for signing by the borrower. The mortgage loan broker must see that all documents are returned to the lender's funding department so that the lender may have final review of the loan file to set up closing. If the file is approved, the lender notifies escrow and the title company as to when the loan will be funded. The funds are wire transferred to the title company from the lender. The title company notifies the lender and escrow upon receipt of the funds and advises both that they are in a position to record. Escrow instructs the title company to record. The loan records and the funder prepares the file to forward for shipping and servicing.

CHAPTER OBJECTIVES

At the end of this chapter, the student learning outcomes include:

1. Explain the loan document process from underwriting up to shipping and servicing.
2. Discuss reasons that the funder would review the loan documents.
3. Indicate examples of discrepancies the funder may find on loan docs.
4. Describe components of the various loan docs that the funder would verify.
5. Outline the steps involving the loan broker that lead to the loan being funded.

11.1 CONDITIONS PRIOR TO DOCS

The underwriter is often unable to approve the loan as it was submitted to the lender from the mortgage loan broker. Sometimes other parties to the transaction must complete various items. Typically, the termite clearance final report and insurance policy have not yet been received by escrow. Until these necessary documents are received, the loan may not be funded or recorded. Thus, the underwriter will approve the loan *subject to conditions*. Figure 10.2 shows a sample worksheet that the underwriter might use.

The first step for the underwriter's review would include verification or additional documentation before the loan is sent to the funder. The purpose is to collaborate evidence of information that the underwriter believes the lender may wish to have for additional review to substantiate the data. Before submission to the lender, who often requires additional verifications to protect the investor, the underwriter tries to ensure that the loan will not be rejected by the investor, PMI, or lender. Scrutiny and review of foreclosures by various government and private entities has revealed loan fraud, as discussed in Chapter 10, section 10.2.

As an example, on a loan refinance, the credit report should show the payment record for the previous 12 months. If the report does not show a loan rating for a 12-month period, the underwriter may require additional documentation. A Verification of Mortgage (VOM) indicating no late payments during the previous 12-month period and a copy of canceled checks for the past 12 months for the loan may be required.

Another typical condition by the underwriter may deal with the appraisal report. If the property shows alterations or additions, copies of the building permits may be requested. Any nonconforming property may need substantiation that the current use is not in violation of the city or county zoning. If security bars are shown on the windows of subject property in the appraisal photographs, the underwriter may ask for compliance with interior safety releases that comply with fire regulations. When security doors and alarm systems are indicated on the appraisal report, the underwriter may ask for documentation that the system meets current safety codes.

The underwriter knows that the lender will request information on condominium projects that neither the mortgage loan broker nor the appraiser may have furnished. It is not unusual to require the percentage and number of units that are owner occupied compared to those that are tenant occupied, in addition to how many units are vacant in the complex. A statement from the homeowners association or management firm may be needed, indicating that there is no evidence of pending litigation against the complex. Any special assessments levied for resurfacing or roofs for the complex or the building in which subject property is located may cause the loan to not be approved without additional documentation.

If all conditions required by the underwriter are not met, the loan will not fund. The industry refers to this by stating that the loan has been denied. When the underwriter's *prior to doc* conditions have been met, the file is forwarded to the document department with the list of conditions, which have not yet been received *prior to funding*, such as the termite report and insurance policy.

A typical example is a phrase in the documents that states "satisfy roof certificate by a licensed roofer verifying no leaks and guaranteeing roof for at least 2 years."

11.2 DRAWING DOCS

Drawing Docs is forwarding the loan file to the document department which is then completed by the funder. The individual who will complete the next steps on the loan package is referred to as the funder or the loan doc verifier.

Before loan docs are requested to be prepared, the loan doc verifier must make sure that the loan has been locked in, which means that the loan doc verifier checks with the lender to see whether the investor's funds are still available at the rate and terms that will be stated on the loan documents being prepared. It is not uncommon for the original loan commitment to have recently expired because of delays caused by the verifications and other paperwork in the loan process.

At this point, the loan doc verifier will verify all loan programs' details, borrower data, and property information by using a computer software program to generate the **loan docs**. This procedure entails having the details of the loan information available to complete the fields asked for by the program. Various software programs are available, such as DOC MGIC and Mortgage Professional (MORT PRO), as shown in Figure 11.1. Although the various software programs have similarities, the funder does not usually have a choice of which software program to use because the employer determines which system the firm uses. A funder who is proficient with one program and moves to a different company will most likely have to adjust to a different program.

11.3 CONDITIONS PRIOR TO FUNDING

If the conditions prior to funding have not been met or if the funder finds discrepancies, the loan will not fund, which the industry refers to as having the loan pulled. This means that the title company has been ordered not to record the documents, so recordation has been pulled.

This point of the process is called the prior to funding conditions and is critical for the loan because it is the last time the loan papers are thoroughly checked before the loan is funded and closed. Any errors on the forms become the permanent documents that may be enforceable throughout the life of the loan.

FIGURE 11.1 Lending Loan Origination Systems (LOS).

BYTE® Enterprises 11332 NE 122nd Way, Suite 100 Kirkland, WA 98034 1-800-695-1008	Genesis is now ELLIEMAE 4155 Hopyard Road Pleasanton, CA 94566 1-877-355-4362 www.elliemae.com
Calyx® Software 6475 Camden Avenue, Suite 207 San Jose, CA 95120 1-800-362-2599	Document Systems, Inc. 20501 South Avalon Blvd., Suite B Carson, CA 90746 (310) 323-1994 www.docmagic.com

The **reviewer** could check the credit, the source of funds, and vesting. The preliminary title report is analyzed to see whether all items are clear, such as tax liens and judgments. The documents are inspected to see whether the correct legal and unit numbers are shown. In almost every instance, a field review or desk review of the appraisal is checked. The reviewer will determine whether the comparable sales listed are within the last 12 months and whether property that is out of the area is not used for on the report.

Another area reviewed is to see whether the loan is for property that is occupied or rented. When a borrower has a property on the market for a long period and has been unable to make a sale, the reviewer double checks when the owner wants to refinance with a large cash-out loan. In this case, the borrower may let the property go into default after the new loan is placed. The investor will not buy the loan if the property has obvious initial problems.

Also, when the borrower obtains a new loan for a high amount after the property has been on the market for a while, the reviewer may suspect unusual financing for a subsequent borrower. The owner may have found a party interested in purchasing the property but who cannot qualify for a loan. The buyer may have the existing owner obtain financing and then merely try to assume that loan without lender approval of the new buyer. The reviewer does not want to put the investor at risk by placing a loan on a property that might be assumed in the near future by an unqualified borrower.

Any potential problems are to be worked out before the loan is funded. If everything appears to have been complied with, the file moves forward. When this audit is completed, the lender knows that the file has been reviewed to see whether it is correct. The actual loan documents have been drawn and are now ready to go to escrow. The delivery is typically by FedEx or messenger or is hand-carried between the parties. These important documents are almost never sent by the U.S. postal service.

The loan docs are good only until the rate expires or until the end of the calendar month. Thus, for a loan that has a lock-in rate at 8.5% that is good for 30 days, if docs were drawn on September 4 they would expire September 30, even though the rate would not expire until October 3. If the loan docs expire, they may be redrawn, but for this act there is usually an extra fee, and some of the loan commitment terms may also expire. For example, the interest rate may expire and only a more current rate may be available.

When the loan docs reach escrow, the borrower is notified to come in and sign the paperwork. At escrow, the loan docs are signed and notarized. However, before the loan docs are returned to the lender for funding, the escrow must see that the final instructions, called **prior to funding** conditions, have been met. The list may include having a final, typed 1003/loan application form signed and dated. It is not unusual that this form must also be signed by all parties, including the loan agent.

One condition might be to show proof that all the final funds are on deposit with escrow, which clarifies the source of the funds. Another typical condition is if there is evidence that an existing loan is still a lien against the borrower for another property, such as the house this borrower is selling in order to purchase the subject property. The borrower usually does not qualify for both the new loan and the existing loan. The old loan must be paid off.

A problem that may occur is that the funds for the down payment and closing costs are from a highly suspect source. Whatever is not verified in U.S. dollars and available to be reported to IRS is probably not allowed. Self-employed parties often have trouble explaining why they only report $10,000 annual income to IRS yet claim to make $100,000 a year when trying to borrow funds for a loan.

Most lenders require 48 to 72 hours' notice prior to funding that the loan will be **closing**. This time is used to set up the **wire transfer** of funds to the title company for last-minute checks on the file and to see that conditions have been met.

11.4 LOAN DOCUMENTS (SEE LOAN DOCUMENT PACKAGE LIST IN APPENDIX G)

A new law, effective July 1, 2010, or 90 days after issuance of a specified form requires a person in a trade or business, such as a supervised financial organization, that negotiates specified contracts or agreements primarily in the languages of Spanish, Chinese, Tagalog, Vietnamese, or Korean, prior to execution of the contract or agreement. In the course of entering into a contract or agreement for a loan or extension of credit secured by residential real property, a translation of the contract or agreement in the applicable foreign language must be delivered, prior to the execution of the contract or agreement, and no later than three business days after receiving the written application. The prospective borrower must receive a specified form in that language summarizing the terms of the contract or agreement, as specified. The law applies to Industrial Loan Law and California Financial Lenders Law. A complete set of loan documents is found in Appendix G.

Loan Document Package List

The loan document package cover sheet briefly lists which items are and are not included as part of the documentation. Notice that only a portion of the items are used for the sample loan package shown in Appendix G. Some items are contained in other chapters and will refer the reader to that chapter. Each item must be complied with or the loan will not be funded.

Conditions Prior to Funding

These conditions are put into the file until the loan docs are returned. The items listed in Appendix G would serve as a written notation to the funding department so they could review that each has been complied with. The form is called **conditions prior to funding** and shows the mortgage loan broker, borrowers, property address, and lender. In the case of the sample loan, the primary lender is T. J. Financial, Inc., who will receive this page and review it prior to funding the loan. The mortgage loan broker is Primera Mortgage Source, who must ensure that all conditions are met and that the completed loan package is given to T. J. Financial no later than 5:00 p.m. in order to fund the following day. This means that T. J. Financial requires no more than 24-hour prior funding notice. In the upper right-hand section of the form, the name of the funder would be placed. Also, the loan expiration date is filled in, and this represents the rate expiration date. The recession date is stated when the loan cannot fund until after a specific date because someone has the right to cancel the loan. This form also states the loan conditions that must be met.

The bottom portion of this form shows escrow conditions that must be met; for example, reviewing a copy of the grant deed, releases, or a proper notary. Loans are pulled at the last minute because the notary stamp is blurred and the funder knows that the recorder will reject the documentation for recordation.

The small check boxes at the very bottom of this form are important. The first indicates the method for the documents to go from the escrow to the mortgage loan broker to the lender for funding. The future assignment of the loan is often prepared at the original loan funding. The second box is a last-minute check before the loan is ordered to fund to make sure that the borrower is still employed and has not been laid off between the time of loan approval and the time of funding. The third box is to indicate information about the actual transfer of the funds.

The Loan Document Audit Sheet

The loan document audit sheet is shown as found in the loan package. This is an internal document that the borrower and the mortgage loan broker usually do not see. It is primarily used to double check items such as the borrower's name and vesting, legal description, and insurance endorsements. The special endorsements that the lender wants from the title company are common coverage items that protect the investor.

This lender document indicates the amount of both the appraised value and the sales price. The fees and charges are shown, including the amount for the appraisal, review appraisal, processing, underwriting, and drawing docs. Both the per diem amount for interest on the loan and the total for a 30-day period are shown. In the example, the mortgage loan broker is receiving the amount for the appraisal, credit report, processing, administration fee, and a one-point loan fee, shown under the column indicated "Fee to" and noted as "Bkr," which is Primera Mortgage Source. The lender, T. J. Financial, is receiving the funds for all other fees and charges shown. This software also generates amounts for an impound account, if any, showing the annual fee and reserves, in addition to any monthly amount. The impound account would cover property taxes and insurance for items such as mortgage insurance, flood, and hazard policies. The bottom of the form gives the monthly payments and calculation of both prepaid interest and financed finance charges, plus the total of all payments if paid over the life of the loan, in addition to the APR. The internal document also shows additional instructions to escrow that the lender will review when the signed, notarized loan docs are returned from escrow. If each item is not completed, the loan will not fund.

Lender Escrow Instructions to Title and Escrow

Lender escrow instructions to title and escrow are multiple instructions. Two pages are for the escrow company and two pages are for the title company. One copy is to be kept by them and one copy is to be signed by an authorized escrow and title representative. Page 6 is signed by the borrower to give escrow authorization to charge the fees and charges indicated. The items used on the internal page 3 are again shown on this external document with the title policy endorsements, vesting, prepaid charges and fees, and the amount of the loan. Using this document, the escrow officer obtains the amount per diem to charge to the borrower. It does show the one-point fee being paid to the loan broker. The balance of the other fees are not indicated or disclosed to the payee. The first payment due date and amount are also indicated. The box indicates that all documents must be with the lender at least 24 hours prior to disbursement of the loan funds. This external form also indicates the ALTA endorsements required for the title insurance coverage. The lender's processor and underwriter have reviewed the prelim and would indicate here which items will stay on record after the new loan is funded that will show on the new title insurance policy. The questions most often asked are what the various endorsements mean, so it is a good idea to keep a list of title company endorsements on hand.

Addendum to Escrow Instructions

The addendum to escrow instructions picks up the items that were on the internal page 4 document, which were the lender's instructions to escrow, to indicate that each item must be complied with or the loan will not fund. Each is indicated as being an item that has been met as a prior to closing condition. In addition, the lender's loss payee endorsement is given with instruction on the type of hazard insurance required. This instructs the maximum deductibles that will be allowed on the insurance policy.

Title Wire Instructions

Title wire instructions are the wire transfer information. This document will be manually filled in by the loan verifier. The **loan verifier** will call escrow and the title company to get their fees, which will be added to the lender's own fees. The total amount needed to cover all items that will be funded by the lender will be placed as the amount of the wire transfer. The lender, escrow, and title numbers are shown, along with the names of the originator, borrowers, and title officer. The amount of funds to be wire transferred from the lender to the title company will be completed, along with the bank routing information necessary to complete the transaction.

HUD Settlement

The settlement costs and fees that were discussed in Chapter 5 on disclosure and compliance are shown on the HUD-1 settlement statement. This document is prepared by the loan verifier and forwarded to the escrow company to complete. The final amount cannot be completed until the actual closing because the escrow officer will have the per diem charges and other items that the lender may not have known when drawing up the documents, such as courier fees or extra repair costs to complete the termite clearance report.

Note

This section shows the actual note for the loan, which is what the investor will eventually purchase and that the borrower will be bound by for the entire life of the loan. The loan verifier will carefully check to see whether the items shown are correct, such as the loan amount, payment, and due date, as well as maturity date. Both pages must be initialed by the borrower at the bottom of the document. The last page indicates that the person places his or her seal, which is the borrower's signature on the note, approving the terms and conditions for the debt. This is the instrument, which lists the clauses containing the late fee, conditions under which the loan may be accelerated, and giving notice.

Mortgage Loan Application Disclosure

The mortgage loan application disclosure example shown is for a fixed-rate loan. If the loan were a variable-rate loan, a similar form would be included in the loan package. This form gives details about any acceleration clauses, such as a due-on-sale clause, plus late fees and penalties. This form also explains that the escrow account, or impound account, is analyzed once a year so that adjustments may be made for deficits or overages if such an account is maintained by the lender.

Deed of Trust

The **deed of trust**, or trust deed, is the record security instrument available by public record. The trust note is not recorded or available by public record but may be the most important document in the entire file. The trust deed is the document that is signed by the borrower and notarized. It will be recorded to let the world have constructive knowledge that the borrower has agreed to a debt on his or her property. The loan verifier uses extra care to check this document when it is returned from escrow to the lender just prior to funding. The verifier knows that the county recorder will not record the document without the tax assessor's parcel number, APN, shown on the document. The recorder will not allow a notary seal that is smudged or illegible or that has an expired notary date. All items are reviewed one last time for accuracy of the names, title, address, legal description, and loan amount. The signature of borrower is checked to see whether the document is signed exactly as it is typed, not omitting full middle name, if given. The borrower cannot use a nickname or make any alterations to the document. The document requires the full legal name of the party agreeing to the debt.

Federal Truth-in-Lending Act (Reg Z and HOEPA) Statement and Itemization of Amount Financed

This document shows the Federal Truth-in-Lending Act (Reg Z and HOEPA) disclosure statement, as was discussed in Chapter 5. The APR and total amount financed are shown, along with the amount of each monthly payment, late fee, prepayment penalty, and assumption clause. The second page of the document shows what the charges are for. For technical guidance, information can be found by calling (800) 767-7468, going to the HUD Web site at http://www.hud.gov, or reviewing the Real Estate Settlement Procedures Act of 1974 (12 U.S.C. 2601 and following), including amendments. Program regulations may be found at 24 CFR Parts 3500 and 3800. RESPA is administered by the Consumer and Regulatory Affairs Department within HUD's office. You may write to the director for RESPA violations at the Office of Consumer and Regulatory Affairs, Room 9146, 451 Seventh Street, SW, Washington, DC 20410.

Occupancy Affidavit and Financial Status

In the **occupancy affidavit** and financial status document, the borrower is attesting that he or she is planning to personally occupy the property. If the loan is for a non-owner-occupied property, no form would be included in the loan package. Also, if the loan is funded and closed with documents in the escrow in which the seller is leasing back the premises for a period after the close of escrow, this document will have to be recompleted. The form has a place available to refer to the case number for the loan type, such as DVA or FHA. If the loan is sold on the secondary money market, such as to FNMA as discussed in Chapter 12, the servicing department will complete this form later. The mortgage loan broker should be reminded that the status of the occupancy will likely be checked on later, and there could be serious consequences if the file is audited and fraud is found. In addition to possible loss of license, penalties, fines, and other consequences, the mortgage loan broker may have to buy the loan back from the investor for the full amount of funds that the investor placed into the loan.

Borrower's Certification and Authorization

Borrower's Certification is the form that authorizes the lender to have the borrower's permission to order another credit report. Although the mortgage loan broker already ran a credit report at the initial stages of prequalification and used this report to submit the loan to the lender for approval, the lender will often want a last-minute report before funding, which is when the instructions to the borrower at the initial stages of the loan process become important. Many borrowers who are using the new loan funds to purchase a home do not wait until after the close of escrow to make purchases on credit for furniture and other household goods. On a refinance, the borrower may not have been instructed to not spend the money until it is actually received. If the refinance is going to be used to remodel, the borrower should not add a lot to charge accounts to pay for the material costs. The investor may even want to run its own credit report to verify the status of the borrower. This form allows written permission for a third party to verify credit.

Borrower's Certification as to Other Loans

This is the form that the lender has the borrower sign to attest that under penalty of perjury the borrower represents that no undisclosed loans are in place. It is used by the lender to disclose to the investor the status of the debtor's loan representations. The primary purpose is to prevent the investor from coming back to the mortgage loan broker at a later date.

Hardship Letter

Hardship letter is used when the loan is funded into the month. The borrowers need to sign that the payment being due in less than 30 days will not create a hardship and that they will be able to make the payment. As an example, should the loan fund on the fifth day of any month (such as June), the first payment would normally not fall before 30 days after the loan is funded. Thus, the due date on the first payment would be the fifth of the following month (such as July 5). However, the parties want the payment to be due on the first day of each month. By waiting the full 30 days (such as July 5), the next first of the month (such as August 1) may fall after the date the loan docs would expire (such as July 10). Thus, all the parties want to have the first payment due on the next first of the month (such as July 1), which falls before a full 30 days after the loan is funded (such as July 5). If the loan docs expire, new docs would have to be drawn, which usually curtails a different loan rate and terms, in addition to additional fees and charge to redraw docs. The letter states that the payment being due on the next first of the month (such as July 1) would not cause a hardship. It is not usual that if the docs had to be redrawn, the borrowers may not qualify for the loan if the rate increased or that they may not have adequate funds to close the loan if the charges increased.

Fair Lending Notice

This part of the loan docs was discussed in Chapter 7.

Document Correction Compliance Agreement

The purpose of this form is to receive written permission from the borrower to make changes when necessary. It is not generally used to make changes on the note and trust deed or mortgage because the lender and investor would want these to be redrawn to result in a correct document. It is used, however, for clerical errors, such as a misspelled name or incorrect legal description found on the other loan documents.

Notice of Availability of Real Estate Appraisal

This document gives written notice that the appraisal report is available for review, if it was paid for by the borrower or if the borrower is willing to pay for a copy. Many lenders today do not charge for the appraisal so that they do not have to furnish a copy to anyone. This makes the appraisal report an inside document that the lender paid for and is exclusively for the lender's own use. Notice that the form specifically does not want the appraisal report to be used for establishing the market value or sales price but is used to determine whether the loan amount can be justified by meeting the reasonable value to support the debt. The notice also does not want anyone to use the information found on the report for determining the dimensions of the property or its improvements. Although the real estate sales agent usually lists the room measurements for purchasers to determine whether their furniture would fit into the rooms, the appraiser rarely shows a diagram of the actual improvement interior. Instead, as shown on the appraisal report found in Chapter 9, the appraiser measures and draws the exterior and merely labels the approximate location of the interior rooms without indicating the actual walls. Also, note that borrowers are required to request the appraisal within 90 days or they will lose the right to obtain a copy, even if they did pay for the report.

Federal Flood Disaster Protection Act of 1973

This protection is now required. The lender usually checks with a company who provides service on this information, much as the lender relies upon the outside title insurance company. For a fee a company checks to see whether the property is within an area that needs to have flood insurance or other flood compliance.

IRS W-9

This form is the signed authorization by the borrower for the loan interest tax deduction. The W-9 form is required by the IRS to report income paid to the lender. The form indicates the loan number, the person who paid the interest to the lender (borrower), plus the address and Social Security number of each borrower. Thus, one W-9 is completed for each borrower.

IRS 4506-T

This form gives the borrower's permission for the lender to request a copy of the debtor's tax forms directly from IRS. The loan number is shown in the upper right-hand corner, and the form is completed with each borrower's name, address, and Social Security number. The notice is usually faxed to the IRS to expedite processing time. Ten working days are allotted for the request to be handled. However, in most cases it takes approximately three days to get the form back from the IRS. This form is used primarily by quality control (QC) (see Chapter 8, Figure 8.7) to guard against loan fraud.

One and the Same Name Affidavit

This affidavit is used to match names of a borrower. For example, a borrower may show last year's tax returns in her maiden name, and to verify that the name on the tax return is the same as that of the borrower, the form is completed. Today, some women remain working under their maiden name long after they are married and do not change their last name to that of their husband. When a woman who has school-age children remarries after changing from her maiden name to her first husband's last name, she may wish to continue using that name while the children have school records. She may continue to file separate tax returns and not file jointly. Today, a man who had a child prior to his first marriage choose to file separate tax returns and not file jointly because he wants to show the separate earnings. Yet the wife may have combined her maiden name with her married name with a hyphen so that their last names are not exactly the same. When seniors marry who have established separate assets, they may choose to own assets that are held separately in their trust for which they are using to qualify. The lender will need to verify that these assets are owned by this borrower, even though the name on the asset is different from the name of the borrower. Further, some U.S. purchasers come from cultures in which people merely add the last name of the current spouse to their own name when they marry. This means that a borrower's full legal name may consist of the first and middle name she has had since birth, her mother's maiden name, her father's name, and the last name of her new husband, for a total of five names.

Loan Servicing Disclosure Statement

This form is used to disclose to the borrower that it is the lender's intent to sell the loan rather than retain the mortgage. On the sample shown, the lender sold 100 percent of all loans it funded in 1992 and in 1993. In 1994, however, it retained 10 percent and sold 90 percent. As borrowers' own portfolios of income grow, they are better able to have funds of their own to loan. In this case, T. J. Financial is having the borrowers sign the loan servicing transfer form before they have the loan. Loan servicing will be discussed in more detail in Chapter 12 (see Figure 12.1).

Authorization for Impound Account

This authorization allows the lender to establish an **impound account** for the borrower, to collect the sums monthly, and to pay from such account as is necessary. For many loans that have a 90 percent LTV, the property taxes, hazard insurance, and mortgage insurance may be impounded. For loans under a 90 percent LTV, it is common that only the mortgage insurance be impounded, and then for only three months.

Assignment of Deed of Trust

These are duplicates of the assignment of the loan. Primera was the mortgage loan broker who originated the loan, whereas T. J. Financial was the lender. The borrowers who are indebted for the loan are Bryan and Betty Byer, and the trustee is a title insurance company, Investors Title Corporation, a California corporation. The second line inside the box on the form states that T. J. Financial "does hereby grant, sell, assign, transfer to," and then a blank line appears before continuing with "all beneficial interest under that certain Deed of Trust...." The name of the investor will be inserted later, probably after the loan is sold on the secondary market, as discussed in Chapter 12.

Request for Change to Insurance Policy

This request is the assignment of the insurance policy. When the loan funds, the insurance will be in the name of the lender, T. J. Financial. After the loan closes, this document shows that the loan will be transferred to Countrywide Home Loans, Inc., by assignment. Countrywide may keep the loan in its own portfolio or they may sell the loan on the secondary money market and retain the servicing, or it may sell both the loan and the servicing. This form changes the payee endorsements directly to Countrywide so that T. J. Financial would not be shown as a loss payee.

Typical provisions found in a mortgage or trust deed would be part of the promissory note, that is, the borrower's promises to repay the loan or part of the security instrument, such as the mortgage or trust deed. The following is a partial list of clauses that affect the borrower and the lender relationship for the real property loan.

- *Acceleration clause.* The term is often referred to as the "due on sale" clause because the lender can call the entire unpaid balance due and payable upon the triggering of an event that is written into the loan terms. The triggering event may be not only transferring the loan payments to a different borrower but also "committing waste" to the property, in which the property becomes dilapidated, thus compromising the physical property that is security for the loan.

- *Alienation clause.* In this type of acceleration clause, a name other than the borrower's is trying to comply with the loan terms. The note may prohibit a subsequent borrower from making payment on the loan given by the lender.

- *Assumption clause.* The loan will specify the terms and conditions for a subsequent borrower to take over the existing loan. Often, a written assumption agreement includes whether the interest rate will remain the same or increase, the cost of assuming the loan (i.e., 1% of the current unpaid balance as a one-point assumption fee), or whether assumption is prohibited. In 1982, the U.S. Supreme Court upheld that a "subject to" may violate the lenders' right to the terms of the assumption agreement of the original loan terms.

- *Foreclosure.* A trust deed typically does not contain a deficiency clause in which the borrower may be personally liable if the property does not resell at a foreclosure for sufficient funds to cover the cost of the foreclosure and the existing loan payoff. A mortgage typically contains a foreclosure clause stating the judicial foreclosure terms with the right of redemption by the debtor. More common in recent times, however, are terms and conditions for nonjudicial foreclosure proceedings, which may or may not include deficient judgment terms.

- *Prepayment clause.* When a loan is paid off prior to maturity, the lender may have a loan term that initiates some penalty. The lender must consent to early payoff. The lender often does not want to have to bear the cost to replace the funds in the loan market prior to the agreed-upon terms given to the investor who gave the lender the funds that the borrower is trying to repay early. Some lenders do not charge a prepayment penalty but have a transaction fee. A typical calculation is the current unpaid loan amount times 80% times the note interest rate divided by two.

- *Transaction fee.* A fee charged by a lender for any change in the contract. An example is on a refinance or loan payoff prior to the note maturity due date. The amount varies but is often the same amount as a prepayment penalty.

- *Subordination clause.* This clause is typically used when an existing loan of record agrees to step into second place and allow the new lender loan to be in first priority. Construction loans typically may use such a clause in the terms of the loan.

11.5 FUNDING

The **funder** advises the mortgage loan broker or the loan officer of the underwriting conditions and advises the escrow of the escrow or title conditions. The loan docs are usually given to escrow to be notarized and signed. When escrow receives the loan docs, the escrow officer notifies the title company to alert the title officer of the wire transfer information and to be in a position for the file to be able to fund and close. The escrow officer notifies the borrowers to obtain the final signatures on all documents, including loan docs and amendments to the escrow, as well as existing loan payoff amounts in the case of a refinance. The escrow officer will be in contact with both the funder and the title company by telephone after all documents have been properly executed by the borrowers. The funder may request specific documents to be faxed for review at the last minute, such as an insurance endorsement or copy of the notarized grant deed prior to recordation.

When everything is in order, the funder will release the funds to the title company after the escrow officer has requested the wire transfer. At this point, the lender is the most vulnerable because the loan has funded and the money is released, but the loan has not yet recorded to secure the loan against the property. Industry refers to this by saying that the loan has funded.

11.6 CLOSING

Novices to the mortgage loan brokerage business believe that at this point the loan is closed and the work is completed. Nothing could be further from the truth. The title company may have recorded the deeds, but it still needs to issue the final title insurance policy, which goes to the escrow company. The escrow company still has to figure the file. The escrow closing statements cannot be issued until all accounting and all documents are in order. Then the documents are delivered to the lender. After the close of escrow, the escrow company issues the loan fee for the mortgage loan broker and commission check for the real estate sales agents, in addition to paying all the bills that were approved and submitted to escrow for payment, such as termite and insurance, if any. Then these individuals are no longer involved in the transaction or with the file. But the lender still has much work to do after the escrow officer delivers the closing documents and statements. The lender puts the file in order with regard to the impound account, loan servicing, insurance policies, final closing statement accounting, and similar items. The next section is about the secondary market, with Chapter 12 discussing the shipping and servicing of the loan after the close of escrow.

SUMMARY

The loan processing final steps for the mortgage loan broker prior to payment for handling the loan consist of work coordinated and completed by the escrow and title officers and the lender's funder. To achieve a closed file after the underwriter and quality control have completed their portion of the process, the doc department draws up the computer-generated loan documents, reviews all forms for accuracy, and then forwards the loan docs to escrow. After the loan docs are verified and forwarded to escrow, the lender is notified to authorize the wire transfer to the title company for the funds necessary to close the escrow. When the loan has been funded and recorded, the file is forwarded to the lender to finish the file before shipping and servicing.

REVIEWING YOUR UNDERSTANDING

1. The loan document audit sheet is an internal document that is usually only seen by the:
   A. Borrower
   B. Mortgage loan broker
   C. Escrow officer
   D. Lender

2. When a loan has been funded, it means:
   A. Funds are released to the title company to close the escrow
   B. The loan is closed and commissions have been paid to the mortgage loan broker and real estate sales agent
   C. Loan docs can be drawn and can be reviewed
   D. The lender is ready to ship and service the loan

3. The loan docs are good until the end of the calendar month or until:
   A. Close of escrow
   B. The interest rate expires
   C. Either buyer or seller decided to withdraw from the transaction
   D. The lender funds the loan

4. The Deed of Trust may be the most important document of the loan file. Prior to recording it must contain:
   A. APN number
   B. Lender's name
   C. Loan broker's signature
   D. Funding date

5. An IRS W-9 form is:
   A. The signed authorization
   B. The loan interest tax deduction
   C. Required by the IRS to report income paid to the lender
   D. All of the above

6. What would an underwriter require if the credit report does not show a mortgage payment record?
   A. A VOE
   B. A VOM indicating no mortgage rates in the last 12 months
   C. A VOD
   D. A & C are correct

7. The closing statements cannot be issued until:
   A. Approved by the lender
   B. Approved by the seller and the buyer/borrower
   C. All accounting and documents are in order
   D. Specified by the appraiser, escrow officer, lender, and investor

8. The loan doc verifier is also referred to as the:
   A. Closer
   B. Funder
   C. Processor
   D. Underwriter

9. Most lenders require at least ____ hours notice prior to funding.
   A. 12 to 24
   B. 24 to 36
   C. 36 to 48
   D. 48 to 72

10. For the borrowers to receive a copy of an appraisal report, they must:
    A. Request a copy from the seller
    B. Have paid the lender for the report
    C. Get a court order release
    D. Write to the appraiser for a copy

ANSWERS TO REVIEWING YOUR UNDERSTANDING

1. D (p. 348)	4. A (p. 350)	7. C (p. 356)	9. D (p. 347)
2. A (p. 356)	5. D (p. 353)	8. B (p. 345)	10. B (p. 353)
3. B (p. 346)	6. B (p. 344)		

PART IV
The Secondary Money Market

Chapter

12

IMPORTANT TERMS

Affordability index

Article 5

Article 6

Article 7

Flow of funds

FRM

Guaranteed note

Housing affordability index

Mortgage-backed securities

NOD

NOS

Pledge

Promotional note

Real property security

Refinance

REIT

Securities dealer

Servicer

Yield

Yield spread premium (YSP)

Shipping and Servicing

PREVIEW

Just as most loan brokers do not perform all functions of processing the loan, so also they do not service the loan after the loan has funded because it is prohibited. However, the loan broker must know all phases of the loan to better understand the entire loan business and to be able to answer any questions the borrower might ask. The borrower may believe that the loan agent has an ongoing relationship and that the monthly payments are made payable to the loan broker, which is normally not the case.

The secondary money market is designed to match borrowers with available lending funds. Demand from one portion of the country is often not matched with the amount of local savings available within the same area. Regulation of funds that move from international investments across state lines and between banks brings most real estate loans under the government's legal umbrella. This chapter discusses protecting the funds of the investor by explaining how the secondary money market works. The **flow of funds** moves from the initial investor by release of capital funds through the primary market, in which the lender makes the original loan, to a consumer-borrower. The borrower makes payments to a loan servicer, who, in turn, forwards the collected funds to the investor. Loan servicing has a national code of behavior for the industry.

This chapter also discusses alternatives and trends in the markets. Real estate loans are traded as securities, similar to the movement of money for bonds and stocks. Real estate economics knowledge helps the loan broker better predict trends. To aid in understanding markets, longterm interest rates, consumer confidence, employment changes, housing affordability, and numbers of loan originations are reviewed.

CHAPTER OBJECTIVES

At the end of this chapter, the student learning outcomes include:

1. Outline the components of loan shipping and servicing.
2. Identify Department of Corporation (DOC) and Department of Real Estate (DRE) securities dealer transactions and regulations.
3. Explain how the general real estate economic market affects loans.
4. Diagram the flow of funds from investor to borrower and from borrower to investor.
5. Describe discounts and yields used by lenders' and investors property loans.
6. Discuss the DRE regulations concerning loan types.
7. Explain the national code of behavior for the loan servicing industry.

12.1 SHIPPING

After the lender receives the closing documents from escrow, subsequent to the loan recording, there is still much work to do before the loan is ready for final turnover to the *investor*. The paperwork in the file must be assimilated in an exact order, similar to the prior discussion about stacking order. Many additional documents are added to the file. The ALTA title insurance policy is now received instead of the file containing only the preliminary title report. The hazard insurance, along with insurance assignment and endorsements, is received. The final escrow closing settlement statement is included. The final compilation of all the last documents is known as reading the file for shipping. Once completed, the file is shipped to either the *servicing* department of the lender, if that lender is retaining the servicing, or to some outside firm that will perform the servicing.

12.2 LOAN SERVICING

Loan servicing includes collecting payments from borrowers, disbursing payments to the holder of the note, mailing appropriate notices, monitoring the status of senior liens and encumbrances, maintaining adequate insurance coverage(s), notifying junior lien holders in the event of default, and coordinating foreclosure proceedings only if instructed to do so by the beneficiary.

Payment

After the loan has been funded and recorded, the escrow is closed. The borrower is notified about making the payments after the close of escrow. The name of the beneficiary on the promissory note is often not the name to whom the payment is made on a regular monthly basis. It is common practice for the beneficiary to have someone else service the loan. The servicing of the loan may have any arrangement between the parties, but the four most common methods are:

1. *Monthly billing.* The lender mails a payment notice, usually a computer printout, prior to the loan payment due date. The borrower mails the payment with the notice or a stub provided on the notice.

2. *Coupon.* The lender sends the borrower a set of twelve coupons once a year. Each month, the borrower tears one coupon out of the book mails the coupon to the lender, along with the payment. The coupon may have a stub to record the check number and date of payment method is decreasing among institutional lenders.

3. *Direct deposit.* The lender automatically debits the amount of the loan payment directly from the borrower's account for a pre-agreed upon amount paid on a specific date each month. Some lenders offer a lower interest rate for the loan if this payment method is used.

4. *On-line debit.* This method of payment is similar to a bank debit card. The borrower dials in and accesses the on-line account to make a bill payment through the computer. The funds are transferred electronically.

Allocation

The **servicer** collects the payment from the borrower and then distributes each portion to the appropriate fund or account. A typical payment comprises the following: It is "A PITI" to have to make the payment. The components are A = association dues, P = principal, I = interest, T = taxes on the property, and I = insurance. The loan payment components are discussed below.

Association Dues

Many properties belong to a group of properties that have homeowner association fees or dues. The association may regulate use of the property, fixtures, and transfer of ownership. The fees may be part of the monthly payment made, such as under a blanket mortgage for a cooperative. In California, it is more common for association dues to be paid directly by the homeowner to the association, such as on a condominium, rather than payment made to the lender.

Principal

The amount applied against the unpaid loan balance is forwarded to the beneficiary or note holder or the account with the servicer. The principal is the last thing taken from a payment. All other fees and items—including *late fees* and impounds—are deducted from the payment first. The servicer pays any principal collected to the beneficiary.

Interest

The amount charged for the use of the borrowed funds is calculated according to the terms of the note. The interest portion of the payment is typically figured against the unpaid loan balance at payment. Interest may accrue and become negative amortization, should the interest portion be greater than the payment. The servicer forwards the interest to the investor.

Property Taxes

Most government property tax payments are made on a fiscal year from July 1 through June 30 of each year. The servicer typically adjusts any future loan payment according to presentation of the tax bill, and the servicer makes the payment. The borrower may not know when the payment was actually made by the servicer. An annual statement for tax purposes is usually furnished by the servicer to the borrower to show the amount paid to the proper tax authority.

Insurance Reserve

Hazard, fire, and disaster (earthquake/flood) insurance policy premiums may be required to be collected, held by, paid by, and accounted for by the servicer. The lender usually requires the collection of one-twelfth of the annual estimated amount, with at least a two-month reserve held in advance for the amount of the last premium. Because the premium amounts vary during subsequent years, the loan payments must be adjusted to reflect the current new billing amount due for such items. The servicer usually pays the premium directly to the insurance company.

Mortgage Insurance

In addition to a two-month reserve, one-twelfth of the annual premium is normally collected and held by the servicer until payment distribution is made. The servicer usually pays the premium directly to the insurance provider.

Late Fees

The amount of any late charge is determined by the note. FHA limits the maximum charge to 2 percent of the monthly payment if not received within 15 days of the due date. DVA has a maximum of 4 percent of the monthly payment if not received within 15 days of the due date. CalVet limits the late fee to $10 if the payment is not received by the 10th of the month. Conventional loans may not exceed 6 percent of the installment of principal and interest, with a $5 minimum for a single-family, owner-occupied dwelling with a minimum of 10 days from the due date. Jumbo, industrial, commercial, business, and other loans do not have these restrictions. The loan servicing agreement will determine whether the late fee is kept by the servicer as part of its charges or whether the late fee is forwarded to the beneficiary. For some home loans, the law allows a late charge of up to 10 percent per installment.

Collection

The loan servicer normally collects the payment from the borrower, records the various portions of the loan payment, and forwards the amount due to the note holder after deducting the loan servicing fees. If the loan servicer protects the security of the note or contract being serviced by making a payment with funds other than those received from the person obligated on the note or contract, other items are required. Within 10 days after making such payment, the loan servicer is responsible for the following and must give written notice to the mortgagee, beneficiary, or owner:

- Record the date the payment is received.
- Show the total amount of the payment received by the servicer.
- Name the person to whom the payment was made.
- State the source of the funds.
- Indicate the reason for making the payment.

Advance Funds

California law does not allow the loan broker to advance funds for payments that otherwise should have been paid by the borrower, unless the licensee receives permission from DRE or DOC as part of an issuer's plan. Thus, a mortgage loan broker may not represent nor imply in any way that he or she will advance funds to the investor, whether or not the borrower has performed, or that advance payments are made to senior lien holders to protect the junior investor. Unless the mortgage loan broker has received a special permit from DRE or DOC, the licensee may not in any way guarantee the investment or imply that the investment is guaranteed.

When a loan is secured by California real property containing one to four residential units, the law requires notice to the borrower when the servicing/collection function is transferred. The notice must be delivered 30 days before the borrower is obligated to redirect the payments. However, transfer of the servicing-collection function to a trustee under a deed of trust, acting either to foreclose or recover the deed of trust pursuant to Civil Code Section 2924 et seq., does not constitute a transfer of loan servicing under this law (CC 2937).

A borrower should receive a written notice from the party to whom the current payment has been sent stating that the loan will no longer be serviced by that entity. This notice should be received before the borrower makes payments to any other party. A mere letter from new servicers that the next payment should be directed to them is not sufficient. Federal regulations have officially stated that notice of the transfer of loan servicing must be disclosed 30 days in advance of the payment due date to the borrower (National Affordability Housing Act Section 941).

Servicer

Lenders and note holders decide whether to handle the loan servicing directly or through a servicing agent such as a loan banker. A loan servicer is compensated for performing services or collecting payments for borrowers, lenders, or note owners in connection with one of the following:

- Loans secured by real property or a business opportunity
- Real property sales contracts.

An agent who is servicing loans on behalf of another or others must be a licensed real estate broker or qualified for a specific exemption from licensing. Under the Residential Mortgage Lending Act, effective January 1, 1996, licensure is required for not only the mortgage lender but also the mortgage loan servicers through the Department of Corporations (DOC). No formal disclosures are required unless the loan servicer arranged the loan, evidenced by the note or real property sales contract, or acted as an agent in the sale of the note or real property sales contract.

A loan servicer must have a written authorization from the borrower, lender, or contract holder for whom the servicer performs servicing before undertaking any activity. The written servicing agreement should provide that payments received be immediately deposited into a client trust account and forwarded to the lender or note holder in accordance with the instruction. The servicing agreement should identify the person who has the authority to instruct the trustee under the deed of trust to proceed with and record a **notice of default (NOD)** or a **notice of trustee's sale (NOS)**. It should further identify whether that authority vests in the servicing agent or is retained by the lender for NOD or NOS. A provision should be included requiring the servicing agent to record requests for notice of delinquency and notes from senior lien holders and notice to the investor.

The agreement should provide that the lender or note holder of 50 percent or more of the beneficiary interest in the note determine and direct the actions to be taken in the event of default or with respect to other matters involving enforcement of the terms of the note. It is important that the original promissory note and security instrument, together with any applicable assignments or endorsements, be delivered first to the investor or an independent custodian on behalf of all the note holders prior to the delivery of the servicing agent documents.

The compensation required by the servicing agent should be described in the servicing agreement. Many mortgage loan brokers who service loans retain a portion of the interest rate being paid by the borrower on promissory notes being serviced. The servicing agreement may permit the mortgage loan broker to retain the late fee charges (as described previously) and prepayment penalties as consideration for loan servicing activities.

The servicing agreement should describe how and under what circumstances the investor/lender and the servicing agent may terminate the loan-servicing agency. Provisions require written notification, a minimum notice period, records storage and availability of data, the signature of all majority note holders, and the payment of a cancellation fee, if any. Figure 12.1 shows a sample of a servicing disclosure that must be given to the borrower when servicing is transferred from the originator to a subsequent entity.

Borrower Dispute

If the borrower has a disagreement with the authorized services about the loan or the application of any payment, the borrower should write a letter to the servicer and keep a copy. The letter should state what the problem is and what the borrower wants the servicer to do about the problem. The item should be specific and as detailed as possible.

If a payment was not credited, the borrower should give the account number, amount of payment, date of payment, and check number. A copy of the front and

FIGURE 12.1   Transfer of servicing disclosure statement.

NOTICE TO FIRST LIEN LOAN APPLICANTS: THE RIGHT TO COLLECT YOUR MORTGAGE LOAN PAYMENTS MAY BE TRANSFERRED. FEDERAL LAW GIVES YOU CERTAIN RELATED RIGHTS. IF YOUR LOAN IS MADE, SAVE THIS STATEMENT WITH YOUR LOAN DOCUMENTS. SIGN THE ACKNOWLEDGMENT AT THE END OF THIS STATEMENT ONLY IF YOU UNDERSTAND ITS CONTENTS.

Because you are applying for a mortgage loan covered by the Real Estate Settlement Procedures Act (RESPA) (12 U.S.C. 2601 et.seq.) you have certain rights under that federal law. This statement tells you about those rights. It also tells you what the chances are that the servicing for this loan may be transferred to a different loan servicer. "Servicing" refers to collecting your principal, interest, and escrow account payments, if any. If your loan servicer changes, there are certain procedures that must be followed. This statement explains those procedures.

Transfer Practices and Requirements

If the servicing of your loan is assigned, sold, or transferred to a new servicer, you must be given notice of that transfer. The present servicer must send you notice in writing of the assignment, sale, or transfer of the servicing not less than 15 days before the effective date of the transfer. The new loan servicer must also send you notice within 15 days after the effective date of the transfer. The present servicer and the new servicer may combine this information in one notice, so long as the notice is sent to you 15 days before the effective date of transfer. The 15-day period is not applicable if a notice of prospective transfer is provided to you at settlement. The law allows a delay in the time (not more than 30 days after a transfer) for servicers to notify you under certain limited circumstances, when your servicer is changed abruptly. The exception applies only if your servicer is fired for cause, is in bankruptcy proceedings, or is involved in a conservatorship or receivership initiated by a federal agency.

Notices must contain certain information. They must contain the effective date of the transfer of the servicing of your loan to the new servicer, and the name, address, and toll-free or collect call telephone number of the new servicer, and toll-free or collect-call telephone numbers of a person or department for both your present servicer and your new servicer to answer your questions about the transfer of servicing. During the 60-day period following the effective date of the transfer of the loan servicing, a loan payment received by your old servicer before its due date may not be treated by the new servicer as late, and a late fee may not be imposed on you.

Complaint Resolution

Section 6 of RESPA (12 U.S.C. 2605) gives you certain consumer rights, *whether or not your loan servicing is transferred*. If you send a "qualified written request" to your loan servicer, your servicer must provide you with a written acknowledgment within 20 business days of receipt of your request. A "qualified written request" is a written correspondence, other than notice on a payment coupon or other payment medium supplied by the servicer, which includes your name and account number, and the information regarding your request. Not later than 60 business days after receiving your request, your servicer must make an appropriate correction to your account, or must provide you with written clarification regarding any dispute. During this 60-day period, your servicer may not provide information to a consumer reporting agency concerning any overdue payment related to such period or qualified written request.

FIGURE 12.1 (*Continued*)

Damages and Costs

Section 6 of RESPA also provides for damages and costs for individuals or classes of individuals in circumstances where services are shown to have violated the requirements of that section.

Servicing Transfer Estimates by Original Lender

1. The following is the best estimate of what will happen to the servicing of your loan: We may assign, sell, or transfer the servicing of your loan while the loan is outstanding. We are able to service your loan, but we have not decided whether to service your loan.
2. For all loans that we make in a 12-month period after your loan is funded, we estimate that the percentage of loans for which we will transfer servicing is between:
   __X__ 0–25% _____ 26–50% _____ 51–75% _____ 76–100%
   This estimate does not include assignments, sales, or transfers to affiliates or subsidiaries. This is only our best estimate and it is not binding. Business conditions or other circumstances may affect our future transferring decisions.
3. We have previously assigned, sold, or transferred the servicing of federally related loans.

Acknowledgment of Loan Applicant

I/We have read this disclosure form, and understand its contents, as evidence by my/our signatures below. I/We understand that this acknowledgment is a required part of the loan application.

_____   _____
Signature   Date   Signature   Date
Lender Representative: _____ Date: _____
Mortgage Servicing Transfer Disclosure

---

back of a canceled check may be helpful, but original documents should not be sent. A confirming telephone conversation should be documented. If no satisfactory response is given within a reasonable amount of time, 30 to 60 days, the borrower should file a complaint with DRE or DOC.

HUD/FHA Insurance Refund

HUD processes FHA mortgage loan premiums that are paid by borrowers either to lenders or servicers. The borrower may be eligible for a refund of a portion of the insurance premium if the party acquired the loan after September 1, 1983, and if the borrower paid an up-front mortgage insurance premium at the close of escrow and did not default on the mortgage payments.

The mortgage loan broker or loan servicer may be asked to determine how much premium is to be refunded by the borrower. A declining scale has been established for MIP insurance, and a borrower should write to the lender and mortgage insurer to obtain additional information. The broker or servicer must refer the party to HUD to make direct contact. HUD refunds are processed when the mortgage company notifies HUD of insurance termination. HUD either requests the Treasury to issue a check for the refund or asks the borrower for additional information.

From the time of refund request, it takes approximately 45 days after loan payoff for the lender to confirm that the request has been sent to HUD to indicate the termination. Thus, the impatient borrower may continue to contact the mortgage loan broker or servicer in hopes of speeding up a possible refund. All inquiries should include the borrower's name, 10-digit FHA case number, paid-in-full date, property address, and daytime telephone number. The borrower should be directed to contact:

U.S. Department of Housing and Urban Development
P.O. Box 23699
Washington, DC 90026-3699
(703) 235-8117 8:30 a.m. to 8:30 p.m. (EST) Monday through Friday

12.3 SECURITIES DEALER

The word *security* has many meanings. To some, it is a technical business transaction for investments. To others, it is a **pledge**, something deposited or given as assurance for the fulfillment of an obligation. For certain people, it means something that gives or assures safety, which does not mean a guarantee of protection against loss, as some members of the public believe when they hear the word *security* used in regard to real estate. A security dealer represents investment opportunities, not safety.

A **securities dealer** is one who undertakes to fulfill the obligation of another and to transact business on behalf of another. When most people hear the term *securities dealer*, they think of a person to go to for information about stocks, bonds, T-bills, and money market investments. Article 6 of the Real Estate Law covered regulation of real property securities dealers and transfer of loan servicing for DRE licensees.

According to the Department of Real Estate (DRE), the term **real property security** has specific meaning (Business & Professions Code 10237.1). First, it means an agreement made in connection with the arranging of a loan, evidenced by a promissory note on real property, including notes that are secured directly or collaterally by a lien. It also includes any loan made in connection with the sale of a promissory note secured by real property. The primary coverage of this part of the code is for **guaranteed notes**. The meaning also covers the arranging of a real property sales contract when the real property securities dealer or his or her principal agrees, expressly or by implication, to do any one of the following:

- Guarantee the note or contract against loss at any time.
- Guarantee that payment of principal or interest will be paid in conformity with the terms of the note or contract.

- Assume any payments necessary to protect the security of the note or contract.
- Accept partial payments for funding the loan or purchasing the note or contract.
- Guarantee a specific yield or return on the note or contract.
- Pay with his or her own funds any interest or premium for a period prior to actual purchase and delivery of the note or contract.
- Repurchase the note or contract.

The second part of the code definition includes the real estate broker who arranges the loan or negotiates the sale of the note or who is servicing the note when a promissory note is secured by a real property lien or sales contract. Payments of principal or interest made in good faith to the owner by a broker must be made from only the funds of the obligor. The emphasis on this part of the code is to cover defaulted notes and advance payments made by the broker. Exemptions include when the loan is a seller carryback and a land sale's contract in which the obligor is the vendee.

The third part of the code definition pertains when a "**promotional note**" is used in conjunction with liens on or sales of real property in a subdivision. This third meaning will not be detailed because the provision does not include a note more than three years before being offered for sale or a note secured by a first trust deed.

Every real property securities dealer must file an annual report with the DRE real estate commissioner (Business & Professions Code 10238.1). The report must contain financial statements that are completed according to generally accepted accounting principles and must be accompanied by an opinion of a certified public accountant (CPA) according to an audit. The report must be filed with the DRE commissioner within 60 days after the close of the report period. The real property security dealer (RPSD) should obtain Form RE281 from the California Department of Real Estate. The report, similar to the data shown in Figure 12.2, includes:

- Receipt of all funds
- Disposition of all funds paid out
- Total number of sales as principal or agent
- Total dollar volume of sales

Article 6 of the DRE Real Estate Law describes registration and regulatory requirements for dealers. It is intended to control bulk transactions in investment plans dealing with real property sales contracts and trust deed. In 1993, however, DRE stopped issuing DRE licensed brokers the special Securities Dealer endorsement. Because of the differences between real estate and other financial securities, such as stocks and bonds, in 1995–96 AB 3343 was proposed. It repealed the former DRE securities regulations effective January 1, 1997. Instead, the Corporate Securities Law (CSL) of 1968 was emphasized (see http://www.leginfo.ca.gov). The CSL is handled by DOC, and virtually all former DRE regulations covering real property securities notes can now be found in California Corporation Codes 25000.

FIGURE 12.2   RSPD application.

Application

General Information

Type or print clearly in ink.

Basic Information

Name of applicant: _____

Business address: _____

Mailing address: _____

Name of attorney or agent for applicant: _____

Business telephone number: _____

Business address: _____

Aggregate value of securities for which permit requested: _____

Fee remitted with appropriate fee: _____

Applicant's status: Corporate General Partnership Individual Other: _____

Permit Information

Are you applying for authority to:

1. sell or exchange real property sales contracts?
2. issue or sell promotional notes?
3. issue or sell guaranteed notes?
4. issue or sell promotional notes and guaranteed notes?
5. optionally cause any payment on the note or contract to be made to the owner, directly or indirectly, with funds other than funds of the obligor while the obligor is delinquent on the note or contract?

If guaranteed notes are to be issued:

1. Will the notes be evidencing loans to be arranged?
2. Will the notes be existing notes?
3. Will the notes be evidencing loans to be arranged and existing notes?
   a. If the guaranteed notes are existing notes, will you be the lender on all the notes?
   b. If the guaranteed notes are existing notes, will you be the lender on some of the notes?
   c. If you will be the lender on any notes, set forth your loan underwriting criteria below including your criteria for qualifying the borrower and the securing real property.
4. If you will not be the lender, set forth the criteria used to qualify an existing note for sale to the public.

List the name(s) and license number(s) of the DOC licensee who will conduct or supervise negotiations with lenders/purchasers under authority of the permit.

Name: _____ License number: _____

Name: _____ License number: _____

FIGURE 12.2   *(Continued)*

If the RPSD is a corporation, list the names of the individual brokers who will conduct negotiations under authority of the permit or who will supervise real estate salespersons conducting such negotiations:

Name: _____   License number: _____

Name: _____   License number: _____

By whom and where will books and records of transactions conducted under authority of the permit be kept?

Custodian name: _____

Business address: _____

Business telephone number: _____

List the location of accounts where trust funds received by the applicant in negotiating and servicing notes and contracts under authority of the permit will be maintained.

Negotiating—Name of Financial Institution: _____

Business address: _____

Name of account: _____

Number of account: _____

Servicing—Name of Financial Institution: _____

Business address: _____

Name of account: _____

Number of account: _____

List the "Exhibits" that are attached to this application:

Certification

I am the applicant or the _____ of the applicant.
(Title of Corporate Officer)

Applicant, its officers, employees and agents intend to transact business under authority of the requested permit, fairly and honestly.

Applicant, its officers, employees and agents who will carry on the business of applicant under authority of the permit are familiar with all applicable provisions of Article 5 of Chapter 3 of the Real Estate Law and Regulations of the Real Estate Commissioner and regulatory sections set form in Corporate Securities Law under California Corporation Code 25000.

I have read the application and the exhibits incorporated by reference. All information in the application and exhibits is true of my own knowledge.

_____

I declare under penalty of perjury that the foregoing is true and correct.

Signature of Applicant: _____   Date: _____

Title of Applicant: _____

(see http://www.leginfo.ca.gov/cgi-bin/displaycode?section=corp&group= 24001-25000&file=25000-25023). The regulations found under these DOC code series require notice periods, disclosures, and similar items as were formerly required.

12.4 TYPES OF SECURITIES

Many types of securities are available. The mortgage loan broker deals with the creation of the original loan that will most likely be sold as a security after the loan has funded; however, the loan broker does not collateralize the loan; the lender does. The lender funds the loan that the loan broker processed. The lender creates the real estate collateralized securities during the normal course of his or her business and then often sells the loan to an investor. More than 80 percent of real estate loan *organizations* go through the secondary money market as securities. Loan originators like to sell newly originated real estate loans immediately to obtain more money to lend again to make a profit. The lender may buy back loans from the **secondary money market** so that the risk of loss is lessened because of the predominance of mortgage insurance. The securities backed by real estate loans are traded to investors and Wall Street dealers. A few of the common kinds are described below.

The Government National Mortgage Association (GNMA) was created in 1968 through an amendment to Title III of the National Housing Act. It falls under the Housing and Urban Development (HUD) Act of l968 and was converted to a private corporation to provide secondary support for the private residential mortgage market. The **Mortgage-Backed Securities** Program increases funds in the secondary mortgage market and attempts to attract new sources of financing for residential loans. GNMA facilitates the use of mortgages as collateral for securities by guaranteeing the mortgage. The mortgage is pledged to GNMA as collateral for the guarantee. GNMA also purchases conventional and government-backed mortgages on an emergency basis under the Emergency Home Purchase Act of 1974. The emergency portion was updated by the Housing and Community Development Action of 1980. GNMA also manages a portfolio of federally owned mortgages under its management and liquidation function.

The Federal National Mortgage Association (FNMA) is commonly called Fannie Mae. As of December 8, 1994, servicers were notified that the agency would not relieve the borrower of a property from the mortgage obligation even if the property is transferred to a third-party company. Thus, the secondary money market tightened its overseeing policies to avert securities losses. Servicers are to report credit information related to any mortgage delinquency to credit bureaus in the borrower's name, not in the name of the company paying the defaulting loan.

The Federal Home Loan Bank Corporation (FHLMC) is known as Freddie Mac. Recent policy indicated that, like FNMA, Freddie Mac must report any default in the name of the original owner who signs the loan obligation, including any deed-in-lieu of foreclosure. As of March 7, 1994, companies must provide a letter to the credit reporting agency in this event.

12.5 REAL ESTATE ECONOMICS

The primary mortgage market is where lender's original real estate mortgages are received directly from borrowers. In the secondary money market, the originated loans are sold to investors. Private investors, lending institutions and governmental agencies, corporate investors, and international investors purchase loans that were originated in the primary money market. From the investor portfolio, loans are bought and sold regularly.

To succeed in the real estate loan business, a mortgage loan broker or banker must keep abreast of current market conditions and trends in real estate and other investment markets. The movement of the stock market, corporate bond yields, the T-bill rate, foreign stock market returns, and taxfree bond investments affect the cost and availability of funds for real estate loans. Studying both college-level accounting or real estate economics is strongly recommended for those who want to understand the indicators that affect both the demand for real estate and the supply of funds to support the movement of assets in real estate transactions.

For example, Figure 3.5 shows the **index** for the adjustable-rate loan indicated for a long-term downward trend on both the rate of return for the investor and the interest rate paid by the borrower for an ARM loan. Because most variable-rate loans are tied to one of the indexes discussed, the mortgage loan broker should know the general direction toward which the index is headed. Similarly, when a variable-rate loan is made on income or investment property, the loan is usually tied to one of these indexes. Should the interest rate in the market be rising, this would affect the borrower's ability to pay after the initial start date of the original loan, which would need to be analyzed to see the effect on the loan repayment. The projected cash flow is part of the loan information represented to the lender and investor, and the loan broker is expected to give reasonably accurate projections. Likewise, on the cash flow of income property, if the index rises, then the loan payment would rise. Assuming that in the short term, or with rent control, the income could not quickly increase to cover the increased payment that is tied to an index, the cash flow for the property owner would decrease, which puts more stress on the loan approval process on calculating the cash flow for an income property and the likelihood of the borrower's ability to repay the debt.

The loan agent needs to have economic data on whether a fixed-rate loan (see Figure 12.3) or a variable-rate loan (see Figure 12.4) is best for the customer. Figure 12.3 shows an almost 30-year period for the 30-year **fixed rate mortgage (FRM)** contract rate. Since the early 1980s, a long-term decline (from the peak of 17 percent in 1981) in interest rates (down to under 7 percent interest rates in 2000–2001) has been the general trend. Interest rates rose from 10 percent to 12 percent in 1982, from 8 percent to 10 percent in 1987, and from 7 percent to almost 9 percent in 1994. Few variable-rate loans were tracked before the early 1980s, and Figure 12.4 shows about 20 years' worth. Since that time, the difference between fixed-rate loans and variable-rate loans has not changed substantially. The two are running at about a 2 percent difference consistently over the long run.

FIGURE 12.3 Thirty-year FRM contract rate chart.

Source: Federal Home Loan Mortgage Corp.

Before 1989, more loans were adjustable than fixed rate, and since 1989 far more loans have fixed rates. The 30-year fixed-rate loans in the early 2000s are at their lowest rate in 25 years. Starting in 2005, the trend is reversing to adjustable-rate loans. As the affordability index shrinks, reducing the number of borrowers

FIGURE 12.4 Consumer confidence chart.

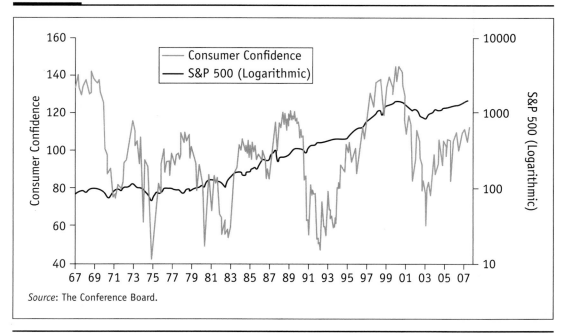

Source: The Conference Board.

who can purchase property under fixed-rate programs, that assumes a 20 percent down payment, and with property values continuing to escalate, borrowers have returned to the adjustable-rate market. Because buyers rely on the mortgage loan broker to decide which loan they should obtain, a review of this information with the applicants may better prepare them to make their own decision. As interest rates increase slightly, borrowers are switching from variable to fixed rate loans in 2006. Today, it is possible for the buyer or the seller to buy down the interest rate on a loan or to obtain a "no-points" loan. A borrower may obtain a no-point loan and obtain a lower interest rate, which has lessened the drastic increases and decreases of market rates for the individual borrower now that the interest rate is negotiated and not dictated.

The loan agent needs to keep abreast of indicators that reflect a changing market. Although many economic indicators may be viewed, few truly reflect the trend for real estate loan activity. For example, a decrease in interest rates may not increase the amount of sales activity. Instead, the number of **refinance** loans may increase. Also, if an area is experiencing a rise in local unemployment, with layoffs and downsizing, home sales may not increase. If homeowners in that area have high equity in their home and local retraining for a new career is available, the individuals may chose to refinance their home to lower the interest rate, use some of their equity to tide them over until they finish the new career training, and keep the property. Another trend to watch is the increase in online providers, which is changing how business is handled.

Some economic indicators should signal an alarm for the mortgage loan broker who keeps abreast of conditions affecting the real estate loan business. One such indicator is shown in Figure 12.4. When consumer confidence is high, people expect things to go well. This is usually a time when people will commit to long-term debt, such as buying a home. When consumer confidence is low, people are afraid of the future. They may think they will be losing their job. They may believe the economy is heading down. A period of low consumer confidence usually means that people will not commit to long-term debt, such as a 30-year loan on real property.

Similarly, Figure 12.5 indicates the U.S. Department of Labor figures for change in payroll employment. The consumer confidence indicator in Figure 12.4 is what people believe may be true and which may or may not occur, whereas Figure 12.5 indicates the reality of employment and unemployment. When people actually do not have jobs, they are not usually able to qualify for a 30-year loan of any kind; thus, higher unemployment means fewer loans processed, no matter how low the interest rate drops.

In contrast to consumer confidence and unemployment rates, there are other reality indicators. Figure 12.6 shows the housing affordability index for about 20 years. The **housing affordability index** assumes that the borrower will place a 20 percent down payment. If people have a job and have confidence in the economy, even if interest rates are low, but the price of the property is too high, people cannot purchase the property. Far fewer new loans are generated when the prices rise drastically. Wages must catch up with home prices before people can afford to make a purchase. The housing affordability uses the median home

FIGURE 12.5   Unemployment, 4-week moving average of initial claims 1967–2009, Federal Reserve Bank of St. Louis (economic resource).

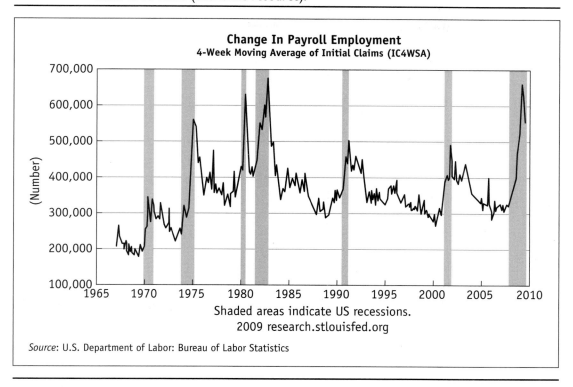

Change In Payroll Employment
4-Week Moving Average of Initial Claims (IC4WSA)

Shaded areas indicate US recessions.
2009 research.stlouisfed.org

Source: U.S. Department of Labor: Bureau of Labor Statistics

FIGURE 12.6   Housing affordability chart.

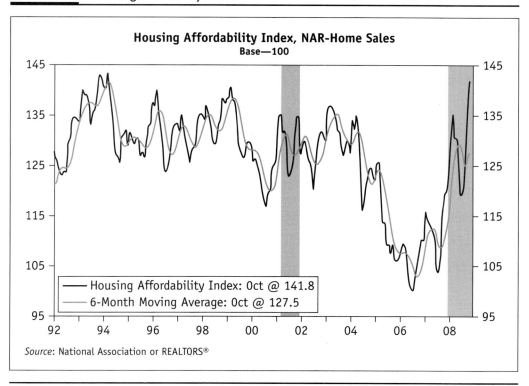

Housing Affordability Index, NAR-Home Sales
Base—100

— Housing Affordability Index: Oct @ 141.8
— 6-Month Moving Average: Oct @ 127.5

Source: National Association or REALTORS®

price in the area and determines the number or percentage of people who can afford (qualify) to purchase a home in the area in which they reside. In high-cost areas, few people can afford to buy. California runs as low as 25 percent up to 33 percent, meaning only one-fourth to one-third of the residents of a particular area can afford to purchase a home in the area in which they live.

The mortgage loan broker should know where the predominant source of their loan business is to position marketing efforts to the proper consumer. For example, the loan broker should know the type of loans consumers are predominantly seeking. In 1983, about 25 percent of all one- to four-family-property loan originations were government FHA or DVA loans, whereas in 1992 less than 10 percent of the same type of originations were government loans. In a 10-year period, 15 percent of the loan brokers who specialized only in government loans would probably be out of the business if they did not learn to handle conventional loans and subprime loans. The ongoing changes in the financial markets require the loan broker to keep abreast of the many types of loans, as described in Chapters 3 and 4, so that when a shift in the market occurs, the loan broker is able to move with the market to service clients and create loans.

For example, in 1998–99, the bulk of the business was in refinance loans rather than loans made with a purchase. Because most FHA and DVA loans are originated from original purchases and generally not from refinancing, the loan broker could see where to position business activities. Figure 12.7 shows the 4.1 percent trend for purchase originations during a 12-year period. The loan agent should constantly seek information on trends in the mortgage loan brokerage business.

Besides reviewing specific areas of real estate economics, the mortgage loan broker should be aware of appraisal and sales (real estate practice) trends. The information could be used to aid the lender and investor in making loan decisions and the broker in making income projections for personal revenue.

FIGURE 12.7   Purchase originations chart.

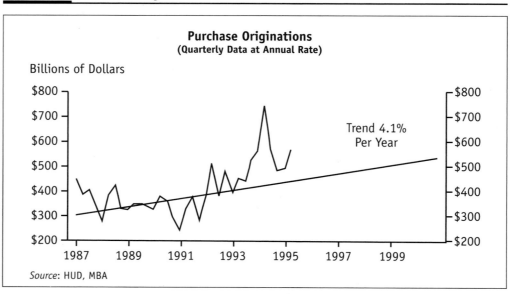

The long-term trend is for California prices to increase due to the demographic increase in population, and for prices to increase. This trend is also national because the median price of a home is only $195,000 nationally. This information would be used by the mortgage loan broker when reviewing the appraisal report for value. It is used to project commissions and fees that the mortgage loan broker will earn. The general real estate business will tie to a long-term growth trend. Figure 12.7 erases the peaks and valleys of short-term changes to show the gradual increase of 4.1 percent per year, which would agree with normal population growth in demand for housing.

In some of the graphs shown below, a dark bar appears in selected areas. This dark area is the denotation of a recessionary period in the U.S.

The Consumer Price Index as shown in Figure 12.8 reflects the change in U.S. monetary policy by removing the tie of money to the gold standard. Prior to 1974 economical growth was artificially limited due to a lack of capital availability. After the change from gold-backed funds to the current "trust-backed" monetary policy, economic expansion has occurred at a rapid growth rate. However, this has come at the price of inflation. The ensuing devaluation of U.S. currency has benefited real estate capital values.

As shown in Figure 12.9, with the exception of World War II, prior to the 1974 elimination of the gold standard, the United States had a relative stable surplus and/or deficit budget condition. The general average is an ever-increasing federal budget deficit. The only exceptions are the short-term inflationary incomes, as shown in 1997–99 with the dot.com bubble, and again in the 2006–07 housing bubble. The move of assets of those markets triggered capital gains income to the

FIGURE 12.8   Consumer Price Index for all urban consumers: all items 1913–2009, Federal Reserve Bank of St. Louis (economic resource).

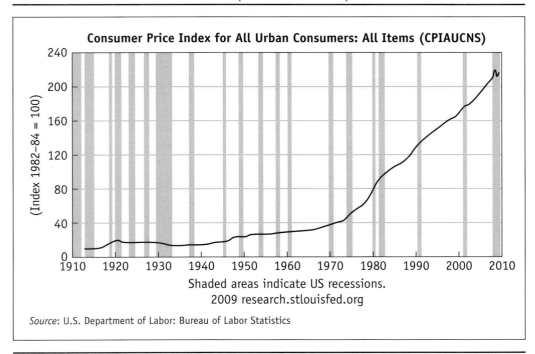

Source: U.S. Department of Labor: Bureau of Labor Statistics

FIGURE 12.9   U.S. Government federal deficit, 1900–2007, Federal Reserve Bank of St. Louis (economic resource).

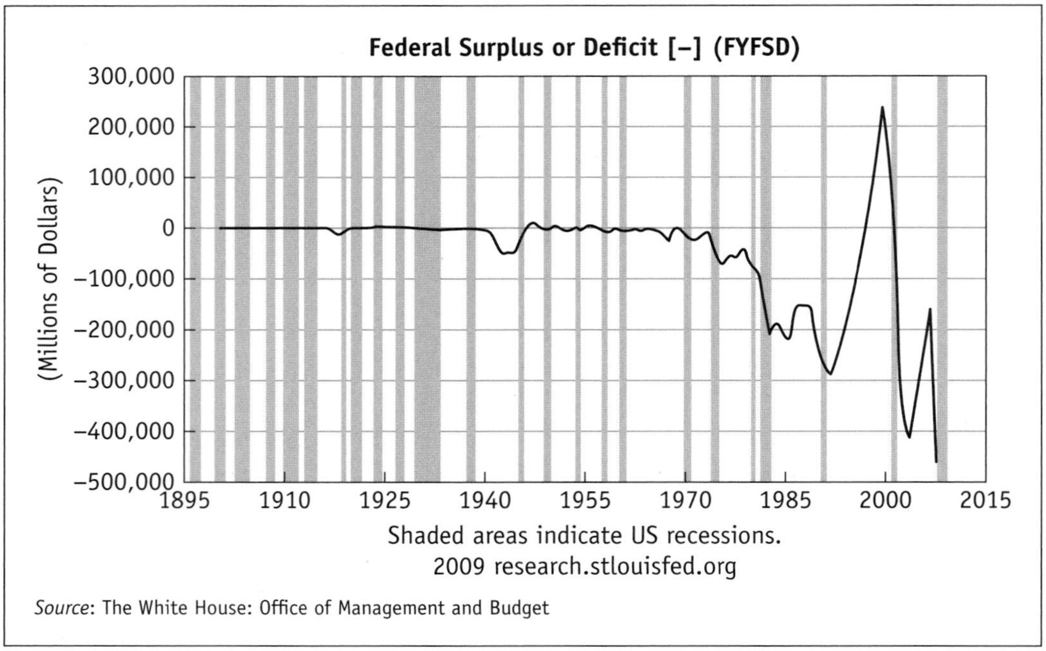

Federal Surplus or Deficit [–] (FYFSD)

Shaded areas indicate US recessions.
2009 research.stlouisfed.org

Source: The White House: Office of Management and Budget

federal government that offset the general trend. These short-term gains are far offset by the overall trend of a continuation decline because of deficit spending.

This long-term deficit presents a structural challenge to the federal government which is highly likely to create either hyper inflation or long-term super inflation. An alternative option is a much higher structural tax rate, which may not occur due to political constraints.

Judging from past action by the federal government, it is more probably that more money will be printed with green ink and thus create inflationary pressure to offset the negative balance. This is likely to devalue the dollar and may have an inverse relationship to "real" property values.

As shown in Figure 12.10, the subsequent economic development after the 1974 removal of the gold standard created a condition where virtually all of the variables of the economy were optimized. From unemployment to inflation, from housing prices to stock values, from new competitive advantage for U.S. corporations to U.S. government influence overseas, the major inputs to structural outcomes were managed efficiently. Unfortunately, as with all systems, the over-leveraging of the financial instruments created fragility and weakness. Sooner or later all systems correct, and the late 2000s are the period where the corrections occurred. All complex systems need redundancy and buffered capacity to assure smooth operations. The economic system simply lost its ability to absorb the shocks of normal cyclical output rate changes.

As shown in Figure 12.11, the recent economic meltdown, and specifically the mortgage loan meltdown and stock market meltdowns, are largely triggered by the current non-cyclical crash. From the late 1950s to 2007 there was a long

FIGURE 12.10   Institutional money funds, 1974–2009, Federal Reserve Bank of St. Louis (economic resource).

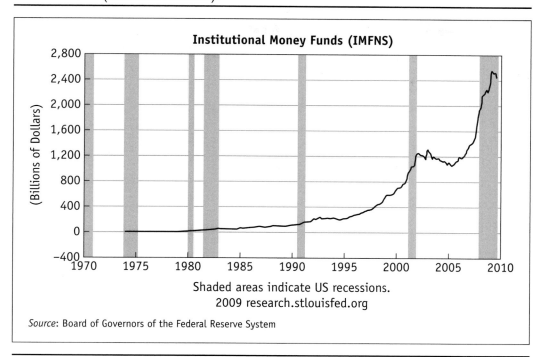

Institutional Money Funds (IMFNS)

Shaded areas indicate US recessions.
2009 research.stlouisfed.org

Source: Board of Governors of the Federal Reserve System

FIGURE 12.11   Discount window borrowings of depository institutions from the federal reserve, 1959–2009, Federal Reserve Bank of St. Louis (economic resource).

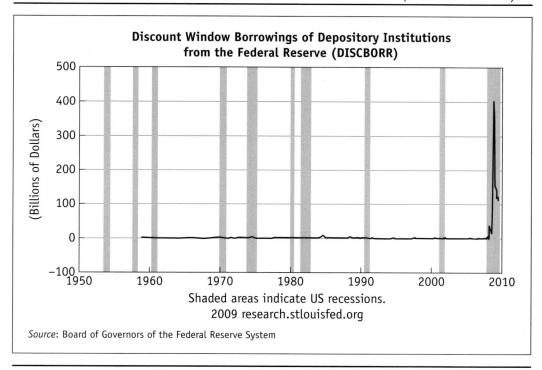

Discount Window Borrowings of Depository Institutions from the Federal Reserve (DISCBORR)

Shaded areas indicate US recessions.
2009 research.stlouisfed.org

Source: Board of Governors of the Federal Reserve System

period of great economic normalcy. The system was self-regulating and self-funding. After the collapse of several large financial entities that were severely over-leveraged, a trickle-down effect of a house of cards fell. This caused additional financial entities to follow suit. This chain reaction created a lock-up in the capital markets.

The federal government was forced to step in and subsidize the capital market with hundreds of billions of dollars as a bailout and to try to avoid a continuing decline. From AIG to General Motors, from Fannie Mae to Freddie Mac, from TARP funding to Lehman Brothers, from Bank of America taking over Countrywide, and Chase Bank taking over Washington Mutual Bank, a deleveraging of the capital markets was forced upon the economy.

The net result of this new capital and leveraging position on the current economy has led to a vastly different mortgage market than the one in which most existing mortgage loan brokers were trained and have previously worked and built their business plans. The employment mix and job availability for all participants have changed. This new structure will likely lead to a more stable and viable staffing and loan-origination market.

There is much more contraction in the sourcing of loans. The loan origination is more tightly controlled and held by the fewer lenders. The restructure of the appraisal process where the mortgage loan broker no longer is able to order an appraisal is but one example. The appraiser must go through an approved pool and the appraisal may not be ordered by the loan broker. The lenders call a pool, and that pool assigns an anonymous appraiser within that pool. Many operations are vastly different, which allows opportunities for those learning the new markets, new structure, and new rules for the new mortgage loan brokerage business. Looking to the federal government's response to the crisis of the 1930s, the future financial markets and mortgage loan structure are likely to be much more regulated and much more restricted for the foreseeable future.

For jobs and employment trends, there is a general shift away from institutional lenders making direct loans to consumers. Instead, mortgage companies have risen steadily to the current 50 percent of all one- to four-family loan originations for several reasons, including marketing and advertising efforts directly at specific market niche consumer groups. The larger institutions are slow to react to consumer demands and are far less flexible to shift with the rapid changes in demographics and market demands. Another reason for the pre-dominating shift is the services provided by the mortgage loan broker. With virtually no difference in rate or costs, the mortgage loan broker provides a great deal of personal service that greatly appeals to today's consumers. There is no reason to believe that the future will not provide even more opportunities for the trained mortgage loan property professional who is dedicated to ongoing educational knowledge of the business and a commitment to the consumer.

A significant change in the loan business is projected because of the decreased costs and availability of online lenders. However, many homeowners with equity will not put confidential information on the Internet to apply for and obtain an online loan. The mortgage loan broker is still sought by those who desire personal service. Some online sources are shown in Figure 12.12.

FIGURE 12.12   Online loan providers.

Feature	GoLoan.com	Loanworks.com	WDLoans.com
Commission to agent:	¾% to 1 ½%	½ %	Whatever "the market will bear"
Parent company:	Delta Home Loans	IndyMac Bank, FSB	Wholesale Direct Mortgage Network
Loans funded through:	Delta Home Loans (investors include Bank of America, Washington Mutual, Citicorp)	IndyMac Mortgage Bank	Dozens of selected lenders
Mortgage banker or broker?	Broker and banker	Banker	Broker
Loan types available:	Refinance, conventional, equity, home improvement	Fixed, adjustable, hybrid, refinance	Every type of financing available including commercial and estate
VA or FHA?	FHA (no fee can be paid to the REALTOR®)	VA & FHA	Call for availability
Phone assistance:	1-800-222-0668	1-888-930-3863	1-800-668-3995
Prequalification letter:			Available 24/7
Normal loan decision made	90 seconds	15 minutes	
Online help	Good for REALTORS®	Good for consumers	Good for REALTORS®
Demo	Order "Live Demo"	Online	Online
Check status online	Yes	Yes	Yes
Information	Extensive help on understanding loans	Three online calculators for determining how much house a client can afford	Market report, 13 calculators available

Other major changes to the field include the decrease in primary lenders. Figure 12.13 shows a partial list of the top 25 bank failures in 2008 and the top 36 U.S. bank failures for 2009. The largest bank in 2009 actually failed in 2008, but the takeover of that bank by the federal government's FDIC did not finalize until 2009. Note that the amount of assets for this one bank is equal to the following two through seventeen banks on the list. Many of these names should be familiar as a bank where you have either had a consumer loan, real estate loan, savings or checking account, for which the bank has either been merged with another bank or has gone out of business. This decrease in primary banks means fewer choices for the mortgage loan broker to use for the consumer, a decrease in types of loans offered, a difference in rates and terms of the few remaining loans, and the massing of the loan business in the hands of the few.

FIGURE 12.13   Bank failures, 2008–2009.

List of bank failures in 2008

1. Douglass National Bank, Kansas City, MO. Failed on January 25, 2008
2. Hume Bank, Hume, MO. Failed on March 7, 2008
3. ANB Financial, NA, Bentonville, AR. Failed on May 9, 2008
4. First Integrity Bank, NA, Staples, MN. Failed on May 30, 2008
5. IndyMac Bank, Pasadena, CA. Failed on July 11, 2008
6. First National Bank of Nevada, Reno, NV. Failed on July 25, 2008
7. First Heritage Bank, NA, Newport Beach, CA. Failed on July 25, 2008
8. First Priority Bank, Bradenton, FL. Failed on August 1, 2008
9. The Columbian Bank and Trust Company, Topeka, KS. Failed on August 22, 2008
10. Integrity Bancshares Inc., Alpharetta, GA. Failed on August 29, 2008
11. Silver State Bank, Henderson, NV. Failed on September 5, 2008
12. Ameribank, Northfork, WV. Failed on September 19, 2008
13. Washington Mutual Bank, Henderson, NV and Washington Mutual Bank FSB, Park City, UT. Failed on September 25, 2008
14. Main Street Bank, Northville, MI. Failed on October 10, 2008
15. Meridian Bank, Eldred, IL. Failed on October 10, 2008
16. Alpha Bank & Trust, Alpharetta, GA. Failed on October 24, 2008
17. Freedom Bank, Bradenton, FL. Failed on October 31, 2008
18. Franklin Bank, Houston, TX. Failed on November 7, 2008
19. Security Pacific Bank, Los Angeles, CA. Failed on November 7, 2008
20. The Community Bank, Loganville, GA. Failed on November 21, 2008
21. Downey Savings and Loan, Newport Beach, CA. Failed on November 21, 2008
22. PFF Bank and Trust, Pomona, CA. Failed on November 21, 2008
23. First Georgia Community Bank, Jackson, GA. Failed on December 5, 2008
24. Haven Trust Bank, Duluth, GA. Failed on December 12, 2008
25. Sanderson State Bank, Sanderson, TX. Failed on December 12, 2008

FIGURE 12.13   (Continued)

Largest U.S. bank failures —2009

1. Washington Mutual, Seattle, WA, (2008), Total assets: $307 billion
2. Continental Illinois National Bank and Trust, Chicago, IL, (1984), Total assets: $40.0 billion
3. First Republic Bank, Dallas, TX, (1988), Total assets: $32.5 billion
4. IndyMac Bank, Pasadena, CA, (2008), Total assets: $32 billion
5. American S&LA, Stockton, CA, (1988), Total assets: $30.2 billion
6. Colonial Bancgroup, Montgomery, AL (2009), Total assets: $25 billion (largest bank failure of 2009, so far)
7. Bank of New England, Boston, MA, (1991), Total assets: $21.7 billion
8. MCorp, Dallas, TX, (1989), Total assets: $18.5 billion
9. Gibraltar Savings and Loan, Simi Valley, CA, (1989), Total assets: $15.1 billion
10. First City National Bank, Houston, TX, (1988), Total assets: $13.0 billion
11. Guaranty Bank, Austin, TX, (1988), Total assets: $13.0 billion
12. Downey Savings and Loan, Newport Beach, CA, (2008), Total assets: $12.8 billion
13. BankUnited FSB, Coral Gables, FL, (2009), Total assets: $12.8 billion
14. HomeFed Bank, San Diego, CA, (1992), Total assets: $12.2 billion
15. Southeast Bank, Miami, FL, (1991), Total assets: $11.0 billion
16. Goldome, Buffalo, NY, (1991), Total assets: $9.9 billion
17. Corus Bank, Chicago, IL, (2009), Total assets: $7.0 billion
18. Franklin Bank, Houston, TX, (2008), Total assets: $5.1 billion
19. Silverton Bank, Atlanta, GA, (2009), Total assets: $4.1 billion
20. PFF Bank & Trust, (Pomona, CA, (2008), Total assets: $3.7 billion
21. First National Bank of Nevada, Reno, NV, (2008), Total assets: $3.4 billion
22. Irwin Union Bank and Trust Co., Columbus, IN, (2009), Total assets: $2.7 billion
23. ANB Financial, Bentonville, AR, (2008), Total assets: $2.1 billion
24. Silver State Bank, Henderson, NV, (2008), Total assets: $2.0 billion
25. New Frontier Bank, Greeley, CO, (2009), Total assets: $2.0 billion
26. Georgian Bank, Atlanta, GA, (2009), Total assets: $2.0 billion
27. Vineyard Bank, Rancho Cucamonga, CA, (2009), Total assets: $1.9 billion
28. County Bank, Merced, CA, (2009), Total assets: $1.7 billion
29. Mutual Bank, Harvey, IL, (2009), Total assets: $1.6 billion
30. Community Bank of Nevada, Las Vegas, NV, (2009), Total assets: $1.5 billion
31. First Bank of Beverly Hills, Calabasas, CA, (2009), Total assets: $1.5 billion
32. Temecula Valley Bank, Temecula, CA, (2009), Total assets: $1.5 billion
33. Security Bank of Bibb County, Macon, GA, (2009), Total assets: $1.2 billion
34. Alliance Bank, Culver City, CA, (2009), Total assets: $1.1 billion
35. Integrity Bank, Alpharetta, GA, (2008), Total assets: $1.1 billion
36. Affinity Bank, Ventura, CA (2009), Total assets: $1.0 billion

12.6 THE SECONDARY MONEY MARKET: INVESTOR PROTECTION

The primary goal of government-related lending programs is to make financing of real estate available for the general public. The guidelines set forth by the regulators are designed to protect the general public making investments while enhancing the availability of affordable housing projects. Mandated disclosures for borrowers in the lending process were discussed in Chapter 5. Additional disclosures are necessary when performing loan acts in California to comply with **Article 5** (loan fee disclosure), **Article 6** (discussed in a later chapter), and **Article 7** (loan origination and servicing) of real estate law.

In addition to protecting the borrower, the investor also needs protection. A diagram of the flow of funds is depicted in Figure 12.14, showing the persons involved.

A loan consists of funds that are collected from myriad sources. The original funds may be a pool of individual bonds sold on the secondary money market, such as the FNMA auction. The funds may be from large investors such as private corporations who make large investments in real estate loan holdings. The profits of the business operation of the bank or lender may be loaned directly to borrowers. Individual investors place their money with the lender so that the lender can oversee making the loan to borrowers, as with persons who place their funds in a savings account or long-term fund offered by a lender.

Each of these types of investors requires the government to oversee the business operations that handle their money to reasonably protect them against

FIGURE 12.14   Flow of funds.

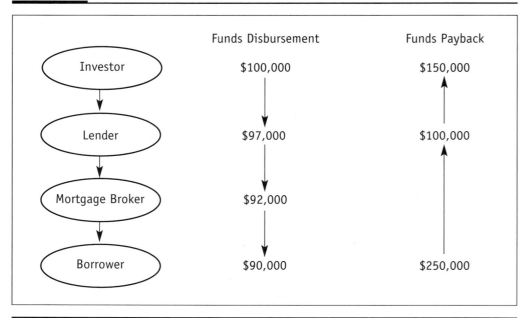

loss. The amount of risk must be disclosed, along with the possibility of loss. In finance terms, the general rule is that the greater the risk, the greater the return. The higher returns have greater possibilities of loss. Laws have been enacted to address the risk issues that each group of investors would want to know. The lender is required to make specific disclosures to the investor about the risks involved.

As an example, shown in Figure 12.14, Grandma receives $100,000 from a life insurance policy that was paid to her after the settlement of Grandpa's estate. She decides to place the funds into her savings bank in a 60-month certificate of deposit account. The bank places this money into its portfolio investment pool of money that becomes available for bank loans for automobiles, furniture, business operations, and real estate. A mortgage broker who works under a wholesale agreement with the bank needs money for a borrower on a real estate loan. In this case, Grandma would expect and demand that certain representations about the safety of her funds be disclosed by the bank to her. Likewise, the lender would require the mortgage broker to protect Grandma's funds by obtaining certain data before releasing the funds to the borrower. From the $100,000 received from Grandma (the investor), the saving bank (the lender) keeps $3,000 for costs and overhead and allows $97,000 to transfer to the mortgage loan broker. The loan broker receives $5,000 in points and loan fees from the funds held by the lender, giving the investor $92,000 cash on a $100,000 note owed. When the loan is repaid, the principal of $100,000 is repaid by the borrower, plus about $150,000 in interest during the life of a 30-year loan. The borrower pays a total of $250,000 of principal and interest back to the lender, who returns about $150,000 principal and interest to the investor on the original $100,000 that the investor invested. The lender keeps the difference as the cost of doing business, the cost of the loan servicing, to pay loan fees and charges, and other costs.

A better way to understand the interaction between the primary and the secondary money markets can be shown in the following example. If a savings bank is paying 3 percent to depositors on savings accounts, this is known as the cost of funds for the lender. The funds in the savings account are the bank's inventory. If a borrower wants a real estate loan, the lender will check the employment, income, and credit history of the individual and the value of the home. When the bank's underwriter approves the loan, the borrower agrees to pay 7 percent interest on the loan. The bank earns money because it obtained the funds it borrowed from its depositors at 3 percent and used those funds to make a 7 percent loan, keeping the 4 percent difference for costs and profit.

The bank makes similar loans to many people in its local community. If the bank kept all these loans in its own portfolio, a point may be reached at which the bank would have to turn away potential borrowers if the bank did not have enough savings deposits to fund the loans being requested. The borrowers could try other banks in the local area. If all the local banks in that area were in the same position, the local real estate market would stagnate because no loan funds are available.

The secondary money market becomes extremely important at this point because it has the ability to give the bank money for the loans that the bank is holding in its portfolio. The ability to liquidate the long-term loans into almost immediate cash is one of the primary functions of the secondary money market. In the case just described, the bank could sell the real estate loans to FNMA, FHLMC, GNMA, or a similar organization. The industry typically holds FNMA or GNMA auctions every two weeks.

FNMA is willing to purchase loans from the bank because the loans comply with the strict guidelines set forth in FNMA underwriting requirements, which means that in checking the borrower's finances, the bank uses the FNMA formulas to determine the financial stability of the borrower to repay the loan. The banks use the loan-to-value (LTV) ratios, which are established to ensure the likelihood that the borrower will not default on the loan. The LTV is also designed to cover the amount of the loan proceeds that would result because of a foreclosure procedure in case of default. FNMA's purchase of the loan from the bank at a *discount* gives the bank money to use to fund more loans so that the bank will not have to turn away other potential borrowers.

FNMA sells securities to private investors, corporate investors, and international investors using the loans that it buys from banks as the collateral for the securities. Investors are willing to accept the FNMA mortgage-backed security loans because the lender's underwriting standards ensure a minimum quality for the loans. The underwriting standards cut down the risk enough so that investors from all over the world do not need to see the specific house that the borrower is obtaining. The investor does not have to meet with the individual borrower and review his or her finances. The sale of the securities gives FNMA money to buy more loans from local institutions such as the bank.

On the other hand, there are times when the local bank has more depositor funds than local demand for loans. The bank has collected funds from depositor's savings account and promised to pay a rate of return to these depositors. Yet, if the bank is not loaning the funds at a higher rate, the bank would suffer great financial loss. The banking industry calls these excess idle funds. In this event, the bank could take these idle funds to the secondary money market. The standardized underwriting criteria on the secondary money market make it reasonably safe for the bank to buy loans for properties located outside the local bank's area. The flow of these funds back and forth across the nation is what makes a more stabilized interest rate and funds availability for the real estate market. Because thousands of loans pass through the secondary money market each year, it is easy to see that this is really big business. Changes in the secondary market due to the subprime meltdown caused the government to take over FNMA and FHLMC in 2008–2009 federal legislation, as was discussed in Chapter 1, section 2.

12.7 PACKAGING AND SELLING LOANS

There is a shift away from institutional lenders making direct loans to consumers. Instead, the number of loans handled by a mortgage loan company has risen steadily to the current 50 percent of all one- to four-family home loan originations. Reasons for this change include marketing and advertising efforts directed to specific market niche consumer groups. The larger institutions are slow to react to and are not flexible enough to shift to rapid changes in demographics and market demands by consumers. Another reason for the shift is the services provided by the loan broker, thus reducing the long-term overhead of the lender. The loan broker provides a great deal of personal service that appeals to today's consumers. The future is expected to provide even more opportunities for the trained loan broker who is knowledgeable about the consumer-oriented business.

The more funds available to a lender to loan, the more loans that the lender will be able to place. Very large lenders are able to use the secondary money market and their own portfolio of funds from private investors because of the large amount of lending funds available to them. Very small lenders must rely solely on other lenders' funds to obtain money for loans. The largest institutional lenders will tend to remain in the top 20 out of hundreds of possible lenders, but their individual position will vary from year to year.

The vast majority of loan funds are from sources that are not individuals, such as the example with Grandma given earlier. These large investors may be pension funds, endowment funds, insurance company investments, foreign investors, mutual funds, and the like. Some of the investor groups receive special tax applications, which allow them to make their funds available at a lower cost to the lender. This procedure allows the lender to offer a lower rate to the borrower or charge lower loan costs, such as fewer points.

For example, a **real estate investment trust (REIT)** pools individual investor funds to develop a nonprofit corporation to use the funds to assist in the development, operation, and preservation of low-income housing for senior citizens. The occupants of the units, once developed, receive subsidized or assisted rental rates that guarantee the developer a specific rent level of income for the project.

The REIT funds may be available at a lower rate. The lower rate could be passed along to the borrower in terms of lower interest rate. However, the lower rate is usually absorbed in the loan placement costs to pay for points, costs, and expenses or to raise yields for the investor. Another use of the lower-cost money is when the lender obtains the funds from the investor, makes the money available to mortgage loan brokers for borrowers at the regular market rate price, and keeps the difference. It may appear that the lender is benefiting from getting the low-cost funds. However, a look at the volatility of the banking industry would show that over many years, lenders are the risk takers in proportion to loans they place on long-term real estate or on short-term, higher-yield consumer loans. The longer the loan funds are tied up, the less the lenders can predict the future cost of doing business and the future rate of return on their money. This is the reason that lenders enforce prepayment penalties and acceleration clauses.

By retaining the lower fund's difference, the lender increases the **yield** on the loan. In other words, the lender obtains the funds at a low interest rate, loans the money to the borrower at the current, competitive rate offered by other lenders, and keeps the difference to increase the yield on the loan. The increased yield is used to offset the lender's cost of doing business. Any remaining funds would be considered the lender's profit. If lenders made loans at the normal market rate, long-term growth trends would then result in predictable returns for the lenders so they could project desired demand. However, the supply and demand of the market varies greatly. Thus, when the lenders can get funds to loan at a lower rate, they have a choice about how to handle the difference between the market rate and the lower rate that is available. As prices in the late 1980s rose, a greater demand for higher loan amounts put pressure on lenders to make larger loans. As prices fell in the early 1990s, fewer new loans were in demand. In addition, many of the existing loan amounts exceeded the current market value, so the borrower merely walked away from the loan, leaving the lender with a foreclosure sale or short pay, increasing the lender's financial insolvency because the lender must bear the loss. This loss must be passed on to the investors, who will ultimately bear the loss of their original investment if no other arrangement is agreed upon.

To protect the investor from bearing the brunt of the loss, investors have required the government and lenders to enact policies and practices to protect their funds. The most common method used is one of many types of insurance pools, such as PMI or MIP. Another is when lenders require the loan to be insured or guaranteed, such as FHA or DVA loans. Some lenders require the borrower to sign a note for the difference between the amount of the short pay and the current loan amount in case the loan is sold below what the borrower owes on the current loan balance, just as some investors require the lender to pay the difference of any short-sale foreclosure action.

Another example of how the lower funds rate may be used by the lender is funds offered under special programs. If a foreign retirement fund pool has $80 million available and is offering the funds at 5 percent, the lender may use ten mortgage brokers to place the loans. Each broker may be offered $8 million. In areas with loan demand and high loan amounts, the funds will be placed within days. In areas with lower demand and lower property values, it would take longer to place the money. So when one lender advertises a lower-than-market-rate offering, the mortgage loan broker should ascertain the source of the lender's funds because the broker may have a borrower who would qualify only at 5 percent and be unable to meet the lender's standards at a 7 percent market rate. If the broker did not inquire about the amount of funds available at 5 percent and the source of these funds, the broker would spend time and effort making borrowers believe they could obtain loan funds at a better than market rate. When the lender's funds at 5 percent are all placed, the lender then would convert the broker's loan to the lender's regular, current loan programs at current market rate. The broker's responsibility is to protect the borrower by disclosing this chain of events.

12.8 YIELD SPREAD PREMIUM

The **yield spread premium (YSP)** is the points, charges, or fees paid by lenders for high-rate loans. Points are an upfront charge, expressed as a percentage of the loan. On low-rate loans, lenders charge points to increase the yield, or return, for tying up their loan funds for a specified yield return. On high-rate loans, the lenders pay points back to the loan broker in exchange for obtaining the higher yield return on the loan.

In many cases, the yield spread premium may be all of the loan broker's compensation on the loan. Two types of YSPs work in the marketplace. The first is when the loan broker receives fees as reasonable compensation for services actually rendered. A YSP may be legally paid to a loan broker if the amount is reasonably related to the value of the services provided to the borrower. However, sometimes the fee paid to the broker is indefensible and is merely the excess fee charged to the unknowledgeable borrower and given back to the loan broker who created the high-fee loan.

As of October 2001, HUD issued a statement of policy to clarify a 1999 policy concerning the disclosure by the lender of the payment to the borrower about the amount received by the mortgage loan broker (called a yield spread premium) under the RESPA Act. Numerous court cases arose because the old policy was unclear and not clearly defined.

HUD wants the disclosure of the yield spread premium to be made as early as possible in the transaction so that the borrower can make an informed choice about obtaining a loan. Consumers tend to be infrequent borrowers and are not usually informed. Thus, the timely disclosure of upfront costs and loan terms permits consumers to shop loan alternatives more intelligently.

Prior to 2001, the lender made this payment to the broker and listed the amount on the good faith estimate (GFE) (as shown in Chapter 5) and again under the "800" series line items on the HUD-1 settlement closing statement. The name of the broker receiving the fee is clearly indicated, along with the name of the fee and the amount of the fee. The new policy seeks better disclosure, which would include a description of the services to be performed by the broker, a statement of whether the broker is acting as an agent for the borrower, the amount of the total compensation to the broker, and the yield spread premium paid by the lender to the broker. For example, a loan applicant may be offered (1) a higher up-front-cost loan that has a lower contract interest rate, or (2) a higher interest rate in return for lower up-front costs. In the case of (2), the loan broker may be receiving a yield spread premium from the lender. The best practice is for the borrower to receive full disclosure as early in the process as possible, with a written acknowledgment by the borrower.

Alternatively, the loan broker may report the value over par for the loan, with a premium rate as a yield spread premium paid to the loan broker and reported in the "200" series line item on the GFE and HUD-1 statement as a credit to the borrower. In this case, the borrower could see that the yield spread premium is a direct reduction in his or her closing costs and see the extent of the reduction.

New RESPA and HUD Settlement Statement federal laws are limiting loan fees and requiring advance disclosure of costs where the initial Estimate of Closing Costs must match the Closing Statement. In the past national average fees, prices and costs for various loan and escrow amounts were used for the initial estimate. It was not required to contact the escrow company or the title company for their actual fees, which was readily available if contact were made between the companies. Therefore, the closing statement in the past never matched the original estimate, which confused the borrower, rather than allowed the borrower to shop transactions, which was the purpose of the law. Now the two are being brought together so that they must match much more closely. The areas that do not have to match the original estimate are such items as additional requirements called out on an appraisal report, such as a roof certification, or an item such as the actual final termite report expenses. All parties must stay abreast of new regulations and changes in this volatile market.

12.9 NATIONAL CODE OF REAL ESTATE LOAN SERVICING INDUSTRY

The federal government has spelled out a national code of behavior for the real estate loan servicing industry as a result of investigations by the Federal Trade Commission (FTC) and the U.S. Department of Housing and Urban Development (HUD) for predatory servicing practices. The code came after a large settlement with the Fairbanks Capital Corp., the largest U.S. servicer of subprime or credit-impaired home loans; from the *Boulware v. Crossland Mortgage Corporation* case; and the class action suit against Freddie Mac.

The new code is intended to prohibit predatory practices by the industry as a whole and includes the following specifics:

- Loan servicing firms must follow detailed requirements designed to properly credit on-time loan payments by homeowners.
- Loan servicers cannot force high-cost hazard insurance policies on homeowners who already have valid coverage.
- Loan companies cannot impose fees on borrowers for services not specifically sanctioned in the loan documents.

Other requirements in the federal code of conduct include prohibitions against:

- Unfair, misleading or deceptive debt collection techniques in connection with real estate loans.
- Using negative monthly reports about false delinquencies as a tool to squeeze money out of borrowers.
- Knowingly providing false credit report data to the national credit bureaus.

- Failing to respond to customer inquiries and complaints within 20 days after receipt of an inquiry and resolving the matter within 60 days.
- Failing to maintain adequate toll-free call center operations specifically dedicated to handling consumer complaints or questions.
- Pyramiding fees and charges to create false delinquencies on customer accounts.
- Taking quick foreclosure action against a homeowner before verifying that the consumer has failed to make full monthly payment for three months.

SUMMARY

The local supply of money often does not match the local demand for money. The secondary money market matches borrowers to funds available for loans from all over the country. The working of the secondary money market is to protect investors while providing funding at local levels. Many layers are involved with this type of financing.

The mystery of the secondary money market for most individuals is two-fold. First, the numbers are so large on so many loans that the totals seem overwhelming to the novice. Second, the business is predominantly divided into many small factions, with little overview of how the pieces all fit into the big financial picture. Investors rarely know what mortgage loan brokers do to gain loan approval. Underwriters rarely deal with discounts and investor yields. Mortgage loan brokers are prohibited from handling the loan servicing process. Each area has diverse regulations administered by various entities. Mortgage loan brokers are often under individual state licensing regulators of either DRE or DOC. The banking industry for institutional lenders predominantly falls under banking codes and federal regulations. The securities laws often oversee the investors dealing with the secondary money market.

Real estate securities transactions are similar to other Wall Street activities. The securities, however, are backed by real estate loans. Several quasigovernment agencies participate to set up uniform guidelines for loans that they will accept, which leads the market to comply so that the loans will be marketable.

After the loan has closed escrow, the final documents are forwarded to the lender, and the loan servicing may be retained or may be shipped to an independent servicing firm. Upon collection of the payment, the loan servicer distributes the funds to the appropriate parties.

In addition, loan brokers may receive not only points up front for the loan but also an amount from the lender after the close of escrow, termed a yield spread premium. Legislation in 2001 requires loan brokers to disclose all compensation received from all sources as soon as possible in the transaction so the borrower may seek choices.

REVIEWING YOUR UNDERSTANDING

1. All other fees and items are deducted from the payment first. The remaining amount is called:
   A. Net profit
   B. Gross profit before taxes
   C. Principal
   D. Principal and interest

2. The servicing agreement should identify the person who has the authority to instruct the trustee under the Deed of Trust to proceed with and record the NOD or NOS:
   A. Notice of deficiency or notice of surrender
   B. Notice of default or notice of trustee's sale
   C. Notice of delinquency or notice of subsequence
   D. Notice of due on sale or notice of suspension

3. Real Property Security is:
   A. Defined in the Business & Professions Code
   B. Agreement made in connection with the arranging of a loan using real property
   C. Promissory note secured by real property
   D. All of the above

4. The yield spread premium allows a loan to be offered with:
   A. A higher up-front cost but lower interest rate
   B. A lower up-front cost but high interest rate
   C. Both a and b
   D. Neither a nor b

5. The yield spread premium is disclosed in:
   A. The 200 series line item on the HUD-1
   B. The 800 series line item on the HUD-1
   C. The good faith estimate
   D. All of the above

6. The acronym NOD stands for:
   A. Notice of default
   B. Notice and default
   C. Notice for default
   D. None of the above

7. The acronym GNMA stands for:
   A. Government National Mortgage Association
   B. Government North Mortgage Association
   C. Secondary Money Market
   D. None of the above

8. The yield spread premium (YSP):
   A. Violates the RESPA Act
   B. Must be disclosed to the seller
   C. Is permitted, if disclosed
   D. All of the above

9. _____ of the Real Estate Law spells out registration and regulatory requirements for dealers.
   A. Article 2
   B. Article 6
   C. Article 10
   D. Article 12

10. What safeguards have been put into place to protect investors in a volatile real estate market?
    A. PMI/MIP
    B. Loan guarantees
    C. Lenders require borrowers to sign a note for the difference in a short sale
    D. All of the above

ANSWERS TO REVIEWING YOUR UNDERSTANDING

1. C (p. 363)   4. B (p. 391)   7. A (p. 373)   9. B (p. 386)

2. B (p. 366)   5. B (p. 391)   8. C (p. 391)   10. D (p. 390)

3. D (p. 369)   6. A (p. 366)

PART V
Regulations and Operations

Chapter

13

IMPORTANT TERMS

Articles of
   incorporation

Business plan

Business structure

Bylaws

Commissioner
   regulations

Compensation

Computer software

CRMLA

DOC commissioner

DRE commissioner

Fictitious business name

FLL

Independent contractor

Loan agent application

Loan flipping

MARIA

Marketing plan

Mortgage banker

Office layout

Packing

Patience and
   persistence

Personal property

Positive mental attitude

Predatory lending

Referral fee

Real property

Small Business
   Administration (SBA)

Time management

Wholesale broker
   agreement

WORK

The Business Operational Practices and Department of Corporations (DOC) Licensing

PREVIEW

All business entities have certain requirements to maintain their operations which are discussed in this chapter. The broker must meet the requirements for standard business operations such as legal business name, office layout and location, and human resources management, including personnel issues, capital constraints, policies, and procedures. Sample documents are shown in Appendixes H-1, H-2, and H-3. The business activities must comply with not only retail regulations, such as predatory lending laws, but also all real estate lending practices. In addition, this chapter covers the Department of Corporations (DOC) licensees for firms that use real and personal property as collateral for loans. The DOC web site is found in Appendix J.

CHAPTER OBJECTIVES

At the end of this chapter, the student learning outcomes include:

1. Discuss the business operations for creating a business plan, ownership of the business, obtaining a legal business name, and determining initial financial capital.

2. List the factors for consideration for an office layout, organizational chart, and a firm's policy and procedures manual.

3. Outline key elements contained in the wholesale broker application, concurrent funding, and wholesale broker agreement.

4. Outline the criteria required to become a mortgage banker.

5. Describe the elements contained in a loan agent "employment" contract.

6. Discuss the steps needed to be successful in the mortgage business.

7. Distinguish between-lender computer applications.

8. Describe predatory lending practices.

9. Describe the characteristics of a loan broker working under the DOC licensing regulations.

10. Distinguish between real and personal property as the collateral for a loan.

13.1 EMPLOYMENT CONSIDERATIONS

The loan broker is a self-employed individual who establishes his or her own business operations under the employment terms. Some loan brokers are salespersons working with an employing broker, yet client lead generating is most often up to the individual loan agent. Most loan agents have never been self-employed and are accustomed to someone else dictating the hours of employment, working conditions, and time off for lunch, and vacation. Upon the broker's entering the real estate profession, the amount of hard work required to establish a self-employment business is often a shock, but the flexibility of the business and the ability to set one's own business plan, hours of operation, and client base is what attracts individuals to the field of loan brokerage to establish his or her new business.

To have a successful career as a mortgage loan broker, it is helpful to develop a network of people in the industry to assist with job opportunities, to establish yourself in affiliated trade associations, and to have certain degree of L-U-C-K! The "L" means you need to learn to be a better Listener. The "U" is to Utilize the talent you were given to really crank up your understanding of your best traits. The "C" is for Communication skills that need to be focused with final goals that can be verbalized into your vision of the future. Last but not least is the "K" that is for Knowledge. People who are able to get a job may often not be able to keep that job if it proved that they really don't have the knowledge needed to perform. Don't oversell what you do not have and figure that you can learn it later. Companies today are struggling with many layers of incompetency and unknowledgeable personnel among the troops. Those who actually have the knowledge of the business will shine among the competition. Where do you shine?

According to the Better Business Bureau, 80 percent of all new businesses fail within the first two years. The two reasons attributed for failure are lack of capital and lack of management. Therefore, to succeed in any business operation, an entrepreneur should have some basic management skills. Several factors should be considered before actual operations are begun:

The Six Steps for Success

1. PMA = **Positive Mental Attitude**

   In the loan business, the loan agent is in the business of sales when trying to obtain new business for loans. The real estate business and all sales jobs are full of a great deal of rejection. As an example, think of the record for sales success as a baseball game. Ball players who hit in the 300s are considered successful hitters. That means for every 10 times that they go to the plate, they successfully hit the ball 3 times. So that means that they "struck out" 7 out of 10 times, or 70 percent. That's a lot of rejection! To overcome depression from being rejected 70 percent of the time, each player must maintain PMA (positive mental attitude). So too must the loan broker set aside a poor mental attitude. One method often used in the real estate community is to use various books, tapes, and motivational seminars to help maintain PMA. Some suggested materials include:

- *Think and Grow Rich*, by Napoleon Hill
- *The Richest Man in Babylon*, by George S. Clason
- *Rich Dad, Poor Dad*, by Robert T. Klyosaki
- *The Power of Attitude*, by Mac Anderson
- *The Nature of Success*, by Mac Anderson
- *The 7 Habits of Highly Effective People* by Stephen R. Covey
- *How to Win Friends and Influence People* by Dale Carnegie
- *How to Lead & Still Have a Life – The 8 Principles of LESS is MORE Leadership* by H. Dale Burke

2. PP = **Patience and Persistence**

In addition to facing rejection, some individuals begin the loan business with the idea that it is a get-rich-quick business. It is unusual for anyone to be an "overnight" success. It takes time to see the benefits, so allow for work results to occur within a reasonably short period but not immediately. It takes patience and persistence to succeed! Individuals who have the patience and persistence to continue working in the face of rejection will reap the rewards of his or her hard work.

Before farmers can reap the rewards of their harvest, they must first till the soil to remove existing weeds, fertilize to amend the existing soil conditions, plant appropriate seeds for specific crops, nurture the crop while it is growing, which requires patience to allow outside conditions such as sun and rain to occur, and then keep having persistence to tend to the crop all the way to harvest. The real estate community refers to licensees having a "farm" because much of the same mental attitude and steps used in farming are used in sales. The loan profession is no different.

A new loan agent must first select the appropriate market and weed out the competition by being available, approachable, and knowledgeable for others who might seek loan services, similar to tilling and weeding the soil. The agent must make contact with the selected target market and firmly establish a market niche, similar to a farmer who would fertilize the soil. The loan agent must plant the appropriate seeds by having the appropriate loan programs and services available to potential clients, for which persistence is required to keep contacting potential clients. A loan agent who wants to specialize in commercial loans would not likely go door to door in a residential neighborhood to explain the services and loan programs available. The highest level of patience is required to wait until the client has the need. With the average person staying in one property for three to twelve years, it sometimes takes years of consistent follow-up to establish a trust relationship so that the client calls the loan agent when a need arises. It takes time to reap the rewards.

3. **Time Management**

It is essential that the loan broker organize his or her time. Most real estate professionals use a day planner, a handheld Palm or Blackberry phone with calendar and reminder functions, or software computer calendar (such as Outlook). This planner should have time slots available from 7:00 AM to at least 10:00 PM seven days a week, because it is common for the loan agent to meet with clients when they are not working, during nights and weekends. The only time to meet with a prospective borrower may be rather late on a weeknight very early in the morning, or during the client's lunch.

The planner should also contain at least a full 12-month calendar and indicate common holidays. The loan agent needs personal time for friends and family, but many times scheduled days off are midweek. The loan agent should plan to attend an open house with a sales agent on a Sunday to prequalify prospective clients. Holiday weekends are often when the client has time to meet and go over extensive loan information, such as gathering all of the loan application documents or the signing loan documents. A new agent usually is not good at scheduling how long an appointment will take, including driving time to and from the location. As agents gain experience, they become better at time management. Several courses are taught that aid in setting up good records, such as Franklin Day Planner sessions, Top Producer software training, or a Microsoft Outlook video.

4. **WORK**

The mortgage loan broker needs to follow a strong "WORK" ethic to succeed.

Wealth: Created by having a PMA, using PP and obtaining skills in time management.

Opportunities: Readily available for those individuals willing to work. In the beginning, working 50 to 60 hours a week should be expected because of poor organization, lack of experience on "closing techniques," poor prequalification skills, and misuse of time.

Rewards: These come naturally when an established client base has been created. The loan agent can then expect a 40-hour workweek and should reap the results from all the prior hard work.

Knowledge: Expect to keep going to school for the rest of your life. Community colleges, private schools, online loan programs, and company training offer courses about new loan programs or modifications to existing loan programs. No other area of real estate changes as much as the loan program criteria and details required to close an escrow on a real property loan. Excellent classes are available for the mortgage and real estate profession. The continuing education includes motivational seminars.

5. **Business Plan**

The loan broker will need to brainstorm with mentors, financial advisors, and others to explain the Who, What, Where, When and How of the loan business. Ongoing operations will require the novice to adjust to the business climate. Interviewing people in the business to determine what can be expected in terms of initial startup costs to operate and maintain a loan business is extremely helpful to the beginner. Establishing a mastermind group with other members who are established loan brokers and with other self-employed individuals can help bring ongoing, new, and creative ideas to the existing business. Sources of information may include the following:

- A community college small business management course entitled Starting Your Own Business.
- **Small business administration (SBA)** seminars on various subjects. Many Internet resources, including http://www.myownbusiness.org, or type in a computer search engine "how to develop a business plan."
- A trip to a local bookstore to browse materials available on the subject.
- The scheduling of an interview with successful, self-employed individuals, such as a tax preparer, insurance agent, contractor, or real estate broker.

A good business plan will outline the target market niche that the operations will cover, the corporate structure of personnel, including referral lead-generating sources and assistants, financial requirements, and legal constraints. The business plan must be written not just for financial backers but also as a constant reminder of what the business wishes to accomplish. Clients, assistants, and coworkers need to see the loan agent's plan, goals, and ideas on future success to obtain feedback and to share in the accomplishments of the loan broker's later success. Those who work around the loan broker need to see the loan agent's vision to support the steps required to accomplish the rewards for a successful business. To achieve short-term and long-term goals for the business plan, the loan broker must develop "*GOALS*":

G = goal-oriented

O = opportunities

A = accomplishments

L = learning

S = success

6. Marketing Plan

A **marketing plan** must also be developed at the beginning of establishing the business plan. It will consist of the types of media that will be used to tell friends and others that the business has been established. Start by using the computer search engine to find the many sites pertaining to how to develop a marketing plan. Some marketing plan items would include:

- Paper media: Stationery, brochures, and business cards that would have contact information, such as office phone number, fax number, cell phone number; the office address; a professional photograph; and professional designations, such as MBA, RECI, GRI, CRS or similar, as discussed in Chapter 1. Note: SB 1361 requires DRE licensees to have their DRE license identification number on their printed materials, and more specifically on all first point of contact marketing materials, including on the purchase agreement, advertising fliers, and solicitation materials. (See Winter 2008 DRE Bulletin).

- Themes media: Neighborhood fliers; special loan seminars for sales agents or the public; free services such as how a potential client could obtain a copy of his or her own credit check; or important information for the reader, such as a newsletter to agents on new loan programs or to the public on how to get on the "do not call" list.

- Advertising media: newspaper, magazine, billboard, or television advertising campaigns and promotions as discussed in Chapter 2.

Employment

An individual is considered an **independent contractor** for IRS tax purposes when acting as a real estate loan broker, unless specifically contracted otherwise. The independent contractor status means that the loan agent is responsible only for the results of the work. Neither lenders nor principals want the broker to act as an employee because of the liability, insurance, and employment laws associated with employer-employee, such as worker's compensation, unemployment, disability, and minimum wage.

Current state real estate laws govern licensees, however, and consider all licensed broker-associates and salespersons working under the broker license to be the employee of that broker. The broker is responsible for supervising these licensees. Yet, for tax purposes, the licensees under the broker are exempt from withholding tax. The loan agent must file timely quarterly estimates to avoid penalties and set up a self-directed retirement plan.

A sample employment application that may be found in the mortgage loan business is shown in Appendix H-1. The employment agreement between salesperson and broker requires a written contract, such as the example found in Appendix H-2. These two sample **loan agent applications** and employment agreement contracts are rarely found in education texts and may be somewhat different for the specific firm with which you may become associated.

Should any individual within the business use an assistant, a separate, written employment contract must be executed to establish the terms of employment with this individual, who may not work for the firm or the broker be employed by only the sales agent. Because the assistant would have access to office files and information, specific information must be contained within the contract. The California Association of REALTORS® has created one form that may be used on the WinForms software program.

Organizational Chart

The size of the organization determines the layout of the organizational chart. The purpose of the chart is to indicate the lines of authority and the avenues of communication. It is the key to the organization's structure. Larger organizations usually are more structured, with positions specialized. Smaller firms are more adaptable, with one person performing many functions.

Office Policy and Procedures Manual

Each business operation usually has an office policy and procedures manual as shown in Appendix H-3, and is required to have such if licensed by the Department of Real Estate (DRE) which is discussed in more detail in Chapter 14, but is applicable to DOC operations in like manner. In larger offices, the manual is often written by the corporate office and given to branch offices to follow. In smaller offices, the manual is usually flexible and is more of an original guideline of how the owner has set up the office. Because of the ever-changing realm of loan processing, office manuals are rarely kept up to date for the manner in which operations are currently administered.

A clear set of guidelines must be differentiated between employees who work for the firm, such as the processor and receptionist, and independent contractors such as the loan officers licensed under DRE or DOC. Under DRE regulations, all agents licensed by the firm are considered to be employees. Yet, for IRS purposes, these same agents may handle income tax under the guidelines of independent contractors. It is important that employment forms be completed by all personnel working with the firm, such as W-9 or 1099 information for tax reporting. Both the IRS and the labor commissioner have made many rulings on such matters; therefore, legal and financial advice on the office setup is critical. As of January 1, 2006, California employers with 50 or more employees must provide two hours every two years of sexual harassment training and education to all supervisory personnel (AB1825.1).

13.2 BUSINESS OFFICE OPERATIONS

Business Structure

A loan brokerage business can operate under the broker license of an individual person who uses his or her name on the broker license. It is more typical in the loan business, however, to operate under the name of a business rather than an individual's name, such as a corporation or partnership. Advantages and disadvantages for each form of business must be considered before embarking on a business venture, including government considerations such as licensing, fees, and taxation matters. A mortgage loan broker has the following options:

1. *Sole ownership.* Easy to start with one person making the decisions but may lack adequate capital, management skills, and multi-level talents.
2. *Partnerships.* Either a general partnership or a limited partnership may be formed. The acts being performed may be conducted by a partnership. The acts for which a real estate broker license is required include regulations that every partner for whom the partnership acts must be a licensed real estate broker. The salesperson may perform acts for, or on behalf of, the partnership

so long as the individual is licensed to work for the partnership under the supervision of a licensed broker. The most important factor is to select the partners carefully.

3. *Corporation.* Several factors must be considered:
   - Double taxation on business earnings may be a factor.
   - Articles of incorporation with regular meeting dates are necessary to meet legal requirements (see Figure 13.1.)

Bylaws of the corporation are required, which show where the principal and branch offices are located, the directors and officers, shareholders' meetings, transfer of shares, records, annual report, corporate seal, and accounting year (see Figure 13.2).

FIGURE 13.1 Articles of incorporation.

```
                                                    ENDORSED
                                                     FILED
                                        In the office of the Secretary of State of
                                                the State of California
                        SAMPLE, INC.              JUNE 22, 2XXX
                                             Bill Jones, Secretary of State
                            NAME                    By L.C. Chen
    One:    The name of the corporation is: SAMPLE, INC.    Deputy

                            PURPOSE
    Two:    The purpose of this corporation is to engage in any lawful act or activity for
    which a corporation may be organized under the General Corporation Law of California
    other than the banking business, the trust company business or the practice of a
    profession permitted to be incorporated by the California Corporations Code.


                        AGENT FOR SERVICE
    Three:  The name and address in the State of California of the corporation's initial agent
    for service of process is:  Mortgage Broker, XXXX Main St., City, CA 900XX.


                        AUTHORIZED SHARES
    Four:   The total number of shares which this corporation is authorized to issue is:
    one hundred thousand (100,000) shares.


                    CLOSE CORPORATION ELECTION
    Five:   This corporation is a close corporation.  All of the corporation's issued shares
    of all classes shall be held of record by not more than ten (10) persons.
                                            Signature of Mortgage Broker
                                            Mortgage Broker (name typed)


    The undersigned declares that he or she is the person who has executed these Articles
    of Incorporation and hereby declares that this instrument is the act and deed of the
    undersigned.
                                            Signature of Mortgage Broker
                                            Mortgage Broker (name typed)
```

FIGURE 13.2   Bylaw of sample, Inc.

BYLAWS OF SAMPLE, INC.,
A CALIFORNIA CORPORATION
ARTICLE I: OFFICES

Section 1.   PRINCIPAL OFFICE
Section 2.   OTHER OFFICES

ARTICLE II: DIRECTORS—MANAGEMENT

Section 1.   RESPONSIBILITY OF BOARD OF DIRECTORS
Section 2.   STANDARD OF CARE
Section 3.   EXCEPTION FOR CLOSE CORPORATION
Section 4.   NUMBER AND QUALIFICATION OF DIRECTORS
Section 5.   ELECTION AND TERM OF OFFICE OF DIRECTORS
Section 6.   VACANCIES
Section 7.   REMOVAL OF DIRECTORS
Section 8.   NOTICE, PLACE AND MANNER OF MEETINGS
Section 9.   ORGANIZATION MEETINGS
Section 10.   OTHER REGULAR MEETINGS
Section 11.   SPECIAL MEETINGS—NOTICES—WAIVERS
Section 12.   SOLE DIRECTOR PROVIDED BY ARTICLES OF INCORPORATION OR BYLAWS
Section 13.   DIRECTORS ACTION BY UNANIMOUS WRITTEN CONSENT
Section 14.   QUORUM
Section 15.   NOTICE OF ADJOURNMENT
Section 16.   COMPENSATION OF DIRECTORS
Section 17.   COMMITTEES
Section 18.   ADVISORY DIRECTORS
Section 19.   RESIGNATIONS

ARTICLE III: OFFICERS

Section 1.   OFFICERS
Section 2.   ELECTION
Section 3.   SUBORDINATE OFFICERS, ETC.
Section 4.   REMOVAL AND RESIGNATION OF OFFICERS
Section 5.   VACANCIES
Section 6.   CHAIRMAN OF THE BOARD
Section 7.   PRESIDENT
Section 8.   VICE PRESIDENT
Section 9.   SECRETARY
Section 10.   CHIEF FINANCIAL OFFICER

ARTICLE III: SHAREHOLDERS' MEETINGS

Section 1.   PLACE OF MEETINGS
Section 2.   ANNUAL MEETINGS
Section 3.   SPECIAL MEETINGS
Section 4.   NOTICE OF MEETINGS—REPORTS
Section 5.   WAIVER OF NOTICE OR CONSENT BY ABSENT SHAREHOLDERS
Section 6.   SHAREHOLDERS ACTING WITHOUT A MEETING—DIRECTORS
Section 7.   OTHER ACTIONS WITHOUT A MEETING
Section 8.   QUORUM
Section 9.   VOTING
Section 10.   PROXIES
Section 11.   ORGANIZATION
Section 12.   INSPECTORS OF ELECTION
Section 13.   (A) SHAREHOLDERS' AGREEMENTS
              (B) EFFECT OF SHAREHOLDERS' AGREEMENTS

ARTICLE V: CERTIFICATES AND TRANSFER OF SHARES

Section 1.   CERTIFICATES FOR SHARES
Section 2.   TRANSFER ON THE BOOKS

FIGURE 13.2 *(Continued)*

CERTIFICATE OF ADOPTION OF BYLAWS
ADOPTION BY INCORPORATOR(S) OR FIRST DIRECTOR(S)

The undersigned person(s) appointed in the Articles of Incorporation to act as the Incorporator(s) or First Director(s) of the above named corporation hereby adopt the same as the ByLaws of said corporation.

Executed this _____ day of _____ , 2XXX. _____
                                                              Name

CERTIFICATE BY SECRETARY
I DO HEREBY CERTIFY AS FOLLOWS:

That I am the duly elected, qualified and acting Secretary of the above named corporation, that the foregoing bylaws were adopted as the bylaws of said corporation on the date set forth above by the person(s) appointed in the Articles of Incorporation to act as the Incorporator(s) or First Director(s) of said corporation.

IN WITNESS WHEREOF, I have hereunto set my hand and affixed the corporate seal the _____ day of _____ , 2XXX. _____
                                                              Secretary

CERTIFICATE BY SECRETARY OF ADOPTION BY SHAREHOLDERS' VOTE.
THIS IS TO CERTIFY:

That I am the duly elected, qualified and acting Secretary of the above named corporation and that the above and foregoing Code of bylaws was submitted to the Shareholders at their first meeting and recorded in the minutes thereof, was ratified by the vote of Shareholders entitled to exercise the majority of the voting power of said corporation.

IN WITNESS THEREOF, I have hereunto set my hand this

_____ day of _____ , 2XXX. _____
                                                              Secretary

Fictitious Business Name

An individual who applies for a license under a business name would need to comply with the requirements to obtain a fictitious name, which is accomplished by filing for a fictitious name in the county where the main office of the business will operate. The fictitious business name is commonly referred to as a "dba" meaning that the owner(s) is doing business under? a specified name other than their legal name. Often, the entire process can be handled by contacting a local newspaper. The dba division of the paper assists the individual applying by having all the necessary forms and procedures explained. The newspaper forwards the paperwork to the county clerk for filing after checking that the exact name is not already in use by another operation and after the proper publishing requirements. Publishing must be in a paper of general circulation to the local area. Figure 13.3 shows a sample fictitious business name application. Most real estate businesses, including loan brokers and loan bankers and banks file with the DOC because they work as a corporation. The DRE requires a certified copy with the dba.

Financial Factors

The initial capital to open an office should cover at least six months' operating expenses in addition to startup costs. Typical opening costs include business formation fees, equipment and furniture, promotions, initial lease rent and deposits, professional services, supplies, utility startup installation and deposits, licenses, and insurance. Ongoing operational costs include advertising, salaries, utilities, rent, and supplies. To fund these costs, a decision must be made on how the initial capital will be raised. Alternatives encompass the way the business formation structure is established. In the case of a corporation, funds can be raised by selling shares to investors or licensees of the company. For a sole proprietor, an SBA or similar loan may fund initial costs.

Location

If the broker is predominantly engaged in single-family, one- to four-unit, DVA, FHA, or conventional loans, it may be necessary to have higher visibility, which will include street location and storefront signage, as well as advertising flyers and marketing.

If the business activity is well established, the physical location becomes less important. Typically, mortgage loan brokers who deal predominantly in larger residential units, such as apartments with 16 to 150 units, or those lending on commercial, industrial, or special-use properties have an established clientele. In this case, a less visible physical office location may be acceptable.

Physical Layout and Equipment

The office furniture should be placed to ease operations. Determine the flow of paperwork from the front door, through each person's hands, to the end of the file processing to establish the best placement of work areas. A sample floor plan is shown in Figure 13.4.

FIGURE 13.3   Fictitious business name.

Mail certified copies to:	Publish in newspaper:

COUNTY OF _____

COUNTY CLERK

FICTITIOUS BUSINESS NAME STATEMENT
FILING FEE IS $35.00

FILE # _____

Mail certified copies to:

Name: _____

Address _____

_____

_____

Publish in newspaper:

Name: _____

Representative _____

Telephone: _____

THE FOLLOWING PERSON(S) IS (ARE) DOING BUSINESS AS: (FICTITIOUS NAME)

_____

ADDRESS OF FICTITIOUS BUSINESS (CITY, STATE, ZIP)

_____

NAME AND ADDRESS (CITY, STATE, ZIP) OF REGISTRANT #1   RESIDENCE ADDRESS

_____

NAME AND ADDRESS (CITY, STATE, ZIP) OF REGISTRANT #2   RESIDENCE ADDRESS

_____

NAME AND ADDRESS (CITY, STATE, ZIP) OF REGISTRANT #3   RESIDENCE ADDRESS

_____

NAME AND ADDRESS (CITY, STATE, ZIP) OF REGISTRANT #4   RESIDENCE ADDRESS

_____

This business is conducted by: Check one

☐ INDIVIDUAL   ☐ GENERAL   ☐ LIMITED PARTNERSHIP

☐ UNINCORPORATED ASSOCIATION OTHER THAN A PARTNERSHIP

☐ CORPORATION   ☐ BUSINESS TRUST
   (if corporation—show state of incorporation)

☐ OTHER (SPECIFY)

DATE: _____   SIGNED: _____

This statement was filed with the County Clerk of _____ County on date
indicated by file stamp above.

CERTIFICATION

I hereby certify that the foregoing is a correct copy of the original on file in my office.

V. S. Garcia, County Clerk

Dated: _____ by _____ , Deputy

This statement expires on: _____.

> REMINDER
> 1. SUBMIT ORIGINAL AND 3 COPIES
> 2. PROVIDE RETURN ENVELOPE, IF MAILED

OFFICIAL
SUPERIOR
COURT
STAMP

FIGURE 13.4   Office layout.

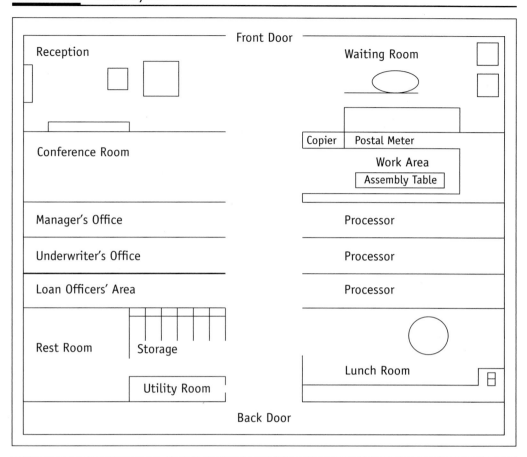

The **office layout** should include consideration of the following. The receptionist should not have to walk to the rear of the office, leaving the front unattended, to make copies of documents. The postage meter and similar equipment should also be placed near the persons performing the act, typically the receptionist and processor. The copier should be located where it is accessible for processors, receptionists, and loan officers, along with loan underwriting and reference materials. The cabinets that hold the closed files should be placed in the rear office storage area, whereas current "open loan" files would be near the processor or loan officer working on that particular file. All paper files should be in a fireproof cabinet, if possible. All computer data files should have backup that is placed at the end of each workday in a fireproof container. Some offices have the office manager take a backup copy off premises daily. Refreshments, including refrigerator and lunch table, are usually located in the lunchroom, but the front work area or waiting room area may have a water cooler or coffeepot. The assembly table is an important work area and is where the processor and others spread out and assemble the documents in the proper stacking order (see Chapter 8), which is required before the file is forwarded to the lender. The manager's office should have some kind of safety in which any funds received from clients, referred to as client trust funds (see Chapter 15), are logged on the proper DRE-approved form (see Chapter 14) and where these funds are placed for safekeeping until banked. For ergonomic considerations, check for adequate lighting, chair design, and desk height. In the loan officer work area, make sure the work surfaces have easy access to the necessary outlets for computer, telephone lines, and similar network tie-in cables.

13.3 WHOLESALE BROKER AGREEMENT

The mortgage loan broker must apply to the lender to be qualified to act as a broker under a **wholesale broker agreement**, as shown in Appendix I-2. The broker would begin by executing a wholesale broker application such as the one shown in Appendix I-1. Note the authorization at the end. Likewise, the agreement between the broker and the principals must also be in writing, as shown in Appendix I.

If the lender approves the individual mortgage loan broker, then a wholesale brokerage agreement is entered into between the individual broker and the lender, as shown in Appendix I. Each lender has its own legal contract, which may vary from the one shown. Most, however, will contain many of the same clauses shown. Typically, these arrangements have contract provisions that limit the authority of the broker to represent the lender's loan programs. Typically, loan servicing, appraisal, and credit report requirements are spelled out, along with agreements on the terms of termination and indemnification. Note that the loan agent is the one who executes and obtains most of the disclosure forms, such as RESPA, Fair Credit, and Truth-in-Lending Act (Reg Z and HOEPA) laws.

It is also common for many mortgage loan brokers to execute a contract with a lender by using a concurrent wholesale funding broker agreement, such as the one shown in Appendix I-3. This agreement is a written contract that differs from the previous wholesale brokerage agreement in that this agreement allows the broker to fund, process, package, and close loans in the loan agent or loan broker's name and to subsequently submit these loans to the lender/investor. The agreement in Appendix I does not allow the broker to fund using the investor's funds. This increased convenience for the loan broker also comes with a higher degree of contract requirements and commitments on the broker's part. One such clause is the specific agreement that the broker will repurchase from the lender any loan submitted to the lender that has already been funded and closed, upon the triggering of certain events. If any warranty made by the broker is found to be untrue, the broker must repurchase the loan within 100 days if instructed by the lender. Thus, the broker wants to ensure that each such loan is found to be in good order by all of the broker's personnel.

13.4 HOW TO BECOME A MORTGAGE BANKER

Once the loan agent has an established clientele and business operation, along with increased levels of education, the next step is usually to become a broker. Most loan agents who become the broker of record for a business begin by becoming the manager of a branch office for a loan brokerage firm. As business and profits grow, then that loan broker may establish his or her own operation. However, all of these operations are conducted so that the loan agent is using the funds of someone else to complete the loan transaction.

The next step is for loan brokers to be able to use their own funds from the profit of their business to make real property loans to clients. Thus, after one becomes a mortgage broker, the logical course of action is to become a **mortgage banker**. To establish the necessary criteria to accomplish this business action, the loan agent should conduct Internet searches to find existing loan brokers who may be able to help with the initial requirements. The Mortgage Brokers' Association (MBA) can help with the various state guidelines and business practices needed to establish a firm or individual as a mortgage banker. However, in California the minimum items include being a mortgage broker for a minimum of two years and having an asset base of at least $250,000.

13.5 COMPUTER APPLICATIONS AND PUBLICATIONS

NMA and FHLMC are moving toward the complete paperless loan. Much of the loan processing is performed by the computer, from the loan application and processing to the underwriting and funding through the closing. Some **computer software** companies that have software programs available are shown below in Figure 13.5. The processor may wish to call other mortgage companies and ask them what computer software system they use and what it will do. If the mortgage loan broker works with one or two particular lenders regularly, it may be helpful for the processor to ask lenders what type of software they use. Electronic transmission of the processor's documents to compatible lender computer formats will become a common practice. Soon, investors will be able to handle their loans by computer, so the mortgage loan broker will need to know what to look for in a loan file before the information is transmitted by the processor to the lender.

In addition to lending software, the business office should have basic computer accounting packages for payroll, office management, day-planner scheduling, and the like.

13.6 ACTS BY THE LOAN AGENT

The loan agent must obey the instructions of both the borrower and the investor. One area in which this problem arises is the applicant's telling the loan agent confidential information, such as a history of bad credit or no established credit. When the loan agent uses the confidential information for purposes of price gouging and taking unfair advantage of the borrower, the agent is following unscrupulous lending practices, which is a violation of the code of ethics and fair lending practices and may even fall under the predatory lending laws.

Predatory lending is the term used to describe unfair and deceptive credit practices in which the loan agent charges excessively high fees and commissions and conceals or misrepresents the loan terms, such as high penalties for early payoff of the loan. Some lenders target vulnerable borrowers who may not be

FIGURE 13.5   Software loan programs.

SOFTWARE PROGRAMS

ELLIE MAE Company
The Loan Handler® Loan
Origination Software
4115 Hopard Rd
Pleasanton, CA 94566
Phone: (877) 355-4362
Fax: (952) 277-9030
http://www.elliemae.com

CALYX SOFTWARE
6475 Camden Avenue, Suite 207
San Jose, CA 95120
Phone: (800) 362-2599
Fax: (408) 323-0715
http://www.calyxsoftware.com

PIPELINE SOLUTIONS-Sensible Software
P. O. Box 81016
Rancho Santa Margarita, CA 92688
Phone: (800) 843-3002
Fax: (949) 305-3274
http://www.pipesoft.com

FNMA's Loan Prospector

FHLMC's Desktop Underwriter

BYTE® Enterprises 11332 NE 122nd Way, Suite 100 Kirkland, WA 98034 (800) 695-1008 www.bytesoftware.com	Document Systems, Inc., 20501 S. Avalon Blvd, Suite B, Carson, CA 90746 (800) 649-1362 (310) 323-1994 http://www.docmagic.com
Calyx® Software 6475 Camden Avenue, Suite 207 San Jose, CA 95120 (800) 362-2599 www.calyxsoftware.com	EllieMae 4155 Hopyard Road Pleasanton, CA 94566 (877) 355-4362 www.elliemae.com

informed about choices in lending, such as low-income borrowers, some women, senior citizens, minorities, or recent immigrant borrowers.

In California, the government has pushed for legislation to protect borrowers from illegal and improper lending practices, such as Assembly Bill (AB 489). The primary emphasis is to educate and inform the public to be careful about the lender they select while making sure that people get the credit they need to obtain a loan on real property. Predatory lending practices include:

- Steering borrowers toward interest rates that far exceed the lender's risks.
- Charging excessively high fees and commissions.
- Persuading a borrower to repeatedly refinance a loan in order for the lender to charge high points and fees each time the loan is due or refinanced, termed **loan flipping**.
- Misrepresenting the terms and conditions of the loan.
- Requiring high-cost credit insurance as a term of the loan, termed **packing.**

Authority, Delegation, Liability, and Limitations

The loan agent must obey the legal instructions of the principal. Thus, the agent should not take advantage of the principal because of the confidence information that has been bestowed. An agent is to avoid even the appearance of a conflict of interest. In addition, the principal is liable for the acts of the agent within the scope of the agent's actual authority, which may occur when borrowers tell the loan agent that they are buying the property for a rental, then apply for an owner-occupied loan. Further, when the loan agent exceeds his or her authority, the agent takes on the liability for his or her actions.

The principal is liable for the acts of the agent because of the laws concerning master-servant and principal-agent. If the principal puts the agent in a position to commit fraud upon an innocent third party, the principal may be subject for the liability of that fraud.

The agent is usually not authorized in the agreement to do certain things regarding the welfare of the principal. Unless expressly authorized, the agent should

- act in the agent's name for property of the principal.
- act on his or her own behalf with the principal, unless indicated on all written documents.
- not encumber the principal's property.
- not enter into a contract to encumber the principal's property.
- collect money or service a loan only on the principal's behalf.

The principal limits the extent of the agent's authority in the written agency to a specific, narrow scope. Thus, the real estate mortgage broker is a "special agent" with limited authority conveyed by the principal for specific acts on specific transactions.

The agent, in turn, has the power to delegate mechanical acts that require no discretion, which could be the execution of an already agreed-on contract. The agent is usually entitled to solicit and negotiate on behalf of the principal, such as trying to sell the principal's note at some discount to obtain cash for the principal. These powers are vested from the principal to the agent according to special trust, confidence, personal ability, or integrity and cannot be delegated by the agent without the principal's consent.

The agent is responsible for communicating knowledge obtained to the principal. Because the authority given is specific, no higher powers are given than those specifically mentioned in the agreement. Naturally, the agent and lender cannot fail to disclose a material fact to the borrower. In addition, the agent cannot fail to disclose a material fact to the intended lender. So the agent is responsible for making sure both directions of the transaction are not fraudulent.

13.7 COMPENSATION AND REFERRAL FEES

All **compensation** agreement for real estate transactions must be in writing according to the Statute of Frauds. If a principal gave an agent exclusive authorization or employment to perform acts on behalf of the principal, then an agreement exists. The agreement must have a definite termination date. The agreement to exclusively negotiate a loan on real property is limited to no more than 45 days.

The act of the agent must be in writing so the actual agency agreement becomes a contract. Agreements to commit or lock in loans must be in writing for any loan in excess of $100,000 for other than one- to four-residential units (CC1624).

Ratification is the adoption or affirming by the principal of the previous unauthorized act of an agent. Ratification rests upon the intentions of the principal to approve prior acts of the agent. If the principal ratified an act of an agent, the agent is entitled to compensation.

Example: A broker has a written contract to obtain a loan and obtains a source through an unauthorized act. Ratification of that unauthorized act by the principal entitles the broker to a commission under the agreement.

In addition to having a written compensation agreement, the agent must set forth in full all the compensation expected to be received, regardless of form, time, or source of payment. A dual agent who does not obtain consent from both principals to the dual agency is not entitled to compensation.

A broker may elect to act as a lender other than the sales agent in a transaction. The licensee may provide services as a sales agent in negotiating, procuring, or arranging the loan. For this service, the broker may receive a commission or the broker may collect a loan origination fee, points, bonuses, or other charges for arranging the loan in lieu of the sales commission. The costs and expenses must be disclosed and would be in addition to the loan fee and points. A broker is prohibited from collecting or charging any fee or charge that has not actually been paid, incurred, or reasonably earned by the loan broker.

Two areas about broker commissions are often misunderstood. The first is the payment to a broker of a commission as a **referral fee** for referring a loan to a loan broker. In this event, a referral fee may be paid only to a person who does real work or substantial service. The mere business acquaintance is not grounds for raising borrowers' costs and fees by charging additional commission or fees to pay another broker.

The second area involves related services. As a full-service broker, a licensee may handle sales, rentals, escrow, and financing of real property. An escrow depository group that handles a loan transaction cannot charge a borrower a fee for the loan brokerage and an escrow fee. The group includes a licensed escrow agent, a title insurance company, a bank, a trust company, or a savings and loan association. If a fee is charged to the borrower by the escrow depository for the escrow function, no additional fee may be charged by the loan broker, those licensed with that broker, or any entity controlled by the broker.

The agent should always obtain direct and clear authority from the principal for compensation to any other licensee. The payment of referral fees should be secured for payment directly from the principal. If not, the subagent may be obligated to seek compensation from the agent rather than the principal.

The real estate industry has a common practice among and between licensees who sell homes to pay a referral fee. In a sale situation, one broker may refer a client to another broker to sell a property, or one broker may refer a customer to purchase real property. This type of referral fee situation, however, is strictly prohibited for mortgage loan brokerage.

Under the **DOC commissioner** finance company lenders law, compensation to any unlicensed person is prohibited, as is any rebate. Any fee paid to another broker must be licensed under the same DOC license. Both DOC and DRE require a referral fee to only be paid to a broker who actually renders service in connection with the transaction.

The primary source of problems for compensation received by any party is found under the federal regulations for disclosure of all fees, commissions and charges under the Real Estate Settlement and Procedures Act (RESPA). The HUD-1 closing statement must put in writing all loan costs or the parties to the transaction may be in violation of federal law.

13.8 EXEMPTIONS FROM LICENSING REQUIREMENTS

Activity by a Principal

A principal is the person who is dealing with his or her own property. A principal who buys, sells, or exchanges promissory notes secured by liens on real property on seven or fewer such transactions in a calendar year is exempt from any licensure. The exemption also applies to the collection of payments for real property sales contracts or promissory notes for liens on real property on seven or fewer in one year. A person who handles eight or more transactions in one calendar year is not considered a modest investor but is defined as being "in the business."

In the Business

The Business and Professions (B & P) Code defines being in the business as related to a principal as including the acquisition for resale to the public of eight or more promissory notes secured directly or collaterally by liens on real property during a calendar year. The entity that meets this level of activity must perform under a broker license.

Institutional Lenders

Abroad groups of persons are exempt from DRE licensing. An officer of a corporation who is performing the regular duties and is not being compensated extra is exempt from DRE licensing. A person or employee doing business relating to banks, trust companies, savings and loan associations, industrial loan companies, pension trusts, credit unions, or insurance companies is exempt from licensure.

Persons who are under the common management, direction, or control in the conduct of their activities are usually considered as one group for the purpose of applying the license requirement or as meeting the exemption criteria.

Employees, agents, authorized agents, loan representatives, and underwriters working for only one institution would be considered acting as an employee of that institution, which applies whether the individual is employed as an independent contractor or receives a salary.

Lending personnel who are exempt from licensing, such as bank or thrift institution personnel must follow specific guidelines. The activities performed must directly relate to their employer. The placement of a loan for the employer would be exempt, as would the handling of a foreclosure property by the employer of the lender.

Exemptions from Licensure

The individual who makes loans collateralized against real property or who combines real and personal property under one loan would need a license to do so from the DOC commissioner, unless under the DOC rules.

One exemption is any loan of the financial code that requires a DRE license, such as a DRE broker. The California Financial Code guidelines divide activities into two groups. One group is the loan correspondent who provides loan documents (notes, trust deeds, mortgages) for more than one institutional lender. The individual who completes loans for multiple savings and loan associations would be required to have a DRE license and discussed later in this chapter. The loan correspondent, however, who has a written agreement to conduct loans for only one savings and loan is viewed more as an employee or branch office of that one institutional lender. This agent is acting on behalf of one particular lender and is *exempt* from DRE licensing (Business and Professions Code 10133.1). If the savings and loan is chartered to business in California, the exemption applies. If the savings and loan is not chartered to do business in California but in another state, then a DRE license would be required.

Many acts are described for which a DRE real estate license is not required. The following are specifically outlined in the law as *exempt* if performed by the person noted.

1. A regular officer or partner in connection with the real property of the corporation or partnership, which is similar to the exemption in which an individual does not need a license to handle his or her own property.
2. A person holding a legal power of attorney (*legal* means one that is properly executed and recorded) to act for another. One person is substituted to act for another, so he or she is acting for his or herself.
3. An attorney handling the normal course of his or her business. The attorney is merely rendering legal services to a client.
4. A receiver in bankruptcy. The receiver is acting under a court order to carry out business for another. A judge has rendered a decision to empower one to act for another.
5. A trustee in a trust deed foreclosure. The trustee is acting for the owner, similar to the power of attorney. The trustee is legally allowed to act for the beneficiary.

6. A person who makes collections on 10 or fewer loans or when the total amounts collected are $40,000 or less in a calendar year [Business and Professions Code 10133.1(b)(1)]. These loan servicing acts are felt to merely accommodate client needs rather than being a business whose volume requires licensing.

The exemptions are specifically not applicable to a person who attempts to use the exclusions to evade the necessary licensing. Any person found in violation would be subject to a $10,000 fine, and a corporation would be subject to penalties up to $50,000.

In general, exemptions from a DRE broker license law exist because the individual or company does work under a different law. Thus, two government agencies would each have its own regulations to oversee business activities. Exemptions include those who fall under:

1. Food and Agricultural Code lending or advancing of money and bank credit under provisions of an act of Congress entitled Agricultural Credits Act of 1923.
2. Any cemetery authority under Section 7018 of the Health and Safety Code.
3. A savings institution agent authorized by Section 652 of the Finance Code or Federal Home Loan Bank Board.
4. An agency acting within the scope of its authority granted by a license in connection with a sale, purchase offer, or exchange as a securities dealer license.

The DOC oversees each DOC broker who conducts transactions under the Finance Lender Law (FFL) or under the California Residential Mortgage Lender Act (**CRMLA**). DOC brokers include those with direct employees and affiliates who negotiate (or service) 20 or more new or existing notes secured on real property within any successive 12-month period whose amounts of unpaid principal balance at sale is $2,000,000 or more. Notes not sold in the real estate transactions are not counted, such as when an owner carries back a loan on the sale of his or her own property.

Another exempt transaction is for a loan with a finance company, provided the exemption activity was not used to evade the law or the rules. Commercial finance lenders licensed under DOC are not subject to a DRE license. Thus, the FFL and CRMLA lender and commercial finance lender are exempt from DRE licensing, but may not need a DOC broker license. Employees of these categories who are acting within the scope and authority of their job are also exempt.

13.9 LICENSE LAW FOR LOAN AGENTS

Two state government agencies oversee loan activities for California licensees. One is the DRE and the other is the DOC. The individual who works as a mortgage loan broker is called a broker: one who is either the DRE real estate agent broker or the DOC broker for loans made under FLL or CRMLA. Two parts of this arrangement are confusing to most people. One is that both the DRE

FIGURE 13.6 License options for loan agents.

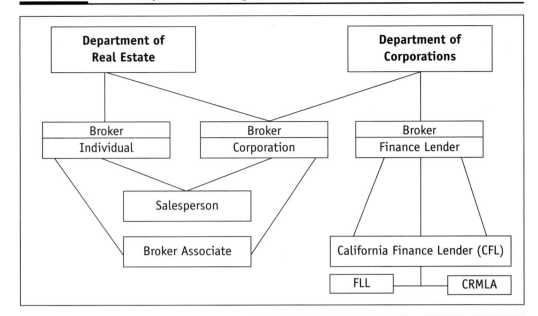

licensed agent and the finance company loan agent can loan on real property. The other confusing fact is that both government agencies call the person working under their regulations a "broker."

As of July 1, 1995, the DOC broker regulations fall under the California Finance Lenders (CFL) Law. The California Finance Code 24000 and 22000 created the FLL. The FLL allows persons or entities to broker, make, and service mortgage loans. The law permits brokering of loans only to other FLL licensees, permits selling loans only to "institutional investors," and permits servicing only for loans under the FLL. Under DOC, a consumer loan means a loan of less than $5,000, the proceeds of which are intended by the borrower for use primarily for other than personal, family, or household purposes. CRMLA licensees under this act are able to make, with their own funds (including warehouse lines of credit), residential mortgage loans. They may also service, but not broker, these loans. An individual could obtain a broker's license from either the DRE or the DOC or have a corporate broker license with either or both agencies. Figure 13.6 diagrams the licensing.

A lender may wish to form a business corporation by getting approval for the corporation by the DOC commissioner. The firm may wish to do business with the DRE by obtaining a corporation real estate license, which requires at least one licensed real estate broker to act as a director or officer for the corporation.

Similarities between Commissioner's Regulations

Both DRE and DOC require notification of any criminal action involving personnel. The commissioners require notice of change of personal address, business address, and branch office activity.

1. If applicant will be doing business under a **fictitious business name** (dba), the following must be provided: a true copy of the certificate filed with the county clerk under the laws of the State of California pertaining to the conduct of business under a fictitious business name (see Figure 13.3).

2. If applicant is a partnership or association, the following must be provided: a copy of the articles of partnership or association and a copy of any certificates filed under the Uniform Limited Partnership Act, together with any changes that have been filed since the inception.

3. If applicant is a corporation, the following must be provided: a copy of the original **articles of incorporation** (see Figure 13.1) showing the date of filing with the secretary of state and any amendment's a copy of the bylaws, and a copy of the minutes of directors' or stockholders' meeting in which the resolution has been adopted to file this application for a DOC license.

Books and records must be maintained at the licensed place of business. Individual loan records are required to be maintained and must include:

- Disclosure statements
- Security agreement/wage assignment promissory note
- Signed loan application
- Payment record
- Escrow instructions and statement insurance policies

  It is also wise to include the following:

- Real property appraisal
- Credit report
- Transfer/servicing agreements
- All broker received commissions, fees, and compensation
- All papers received in connection with the loan

Differences between Commissioner's Regulations

The two California regulatory agencies are run by two parties. The California DRE is headed by the **DRE commissioner**, and the California DOC is headed by the DOC commissioner. The DRE may handle only matters relating to real estate. The Office of Corporations handles matters pertaining to all corporations, whether they are related to real estate or not. The corporation commissioner oversees the activities of real estate corporations, escrow corporations, and lending corporations.

A primary distinction is that a business licensed under the real estate commissioner typically can expect to pay a referral fee or commission to another DRE licensee for some activity relating to the transaction. Lenders under the FLL and CRMLA laws may pay compensation, such as a finder's fee or broker's fee, to anyone who is not licensed as a broker under this same law, except for employees of the specific business. Thus, a DOC broker can pay a DRE broker a referral fee, but DRE cannot pay a DOC licensee. DRE salespersons may never receive compensation directly from anyone except their employing broker.

A broker licensed under the FFL and CRMLA laws may broker loans only to lenders licensed under this same law. The license does not allow brokers to broker loans to nonlicensees, such as banks or savings and loans. A real estate broker under the DRE may package a loan under a wholesale-loan arrangement directly to a bank or savings and loan. This DRE broker may have a separate escrow for the transaction and be providing the service of assisting a borrower in obtaining retail-financing arrangements from various sources. This activity is a commission transaction in which the broker may pay a commission or referral fee to a DRE licensed salesperson or broker.

Another distinction between the operations under the two commissioners is that a DRE brokerage business does not need to maintain any bank account (client trust account) for the client transactions. A business operating under the CFL law, however, must maintain a separate trust account in which fees collected for credit reports and appraisal reports are to be placed. DOC requires a written receipt with license number on the receipt. Both DRE and DOC brokers have specific requirements for handling and record-keeping client trust funds.

Both the DRE brokers and the DOC brokers may offer a variety of loan programs to borrowers, including refinancing, equity lines/loans, purchase money, and property improvement loans. The distinction is that DOC brokers may offer both secured and unsecured consumer loans on real or personal property. A DRE broker may handle only loans secured on real property. DRE has disclosure forms that DOC brokers do not have, but DOC lenders have agreement forms that are similar. A number of licensees possess both DOC and DRE types of licenses in order to maintain the flexibility for both types of loans.

Real Property versus Personal Property

A clear distinction must be made in the lending process to determine what real property is compared to items that are considered personal property. The collateral terms of the loan make it necessary to have a thorough understanding of the differences.

The law states that anything that is not real property is personal property. Things can change from personal property and be considered real property. Real property consists of the land surface (dirt, rock, swamp, river), the underground (substances such as dirt, oil, water, rock) and the airspace (up to the Federal Aviation Administration lower limit). The raw land may include such rights as stock in a water company or an easement. Thus, a loan on real property that consisted of these features only would be considered a land loan.

Most loans, however, are made on the land plus the improvements that are on the land. Improvements are items that become affixed to the land and as such are regarded as a permanent part of the land. Buildings are considered improvements. Things attached by roots, such as trees and vines, may become real property after a specific time, unless the vegetation is severed. Fixtures are also considered real property. Items such as above-ground swimming pools, potted plants, and swing sets are considered personal property.

Personal property can become real property and vice versa. Such is the case with fixtures. The personal property fixture items that become part of the real property do so because the item has become integrated into the real property. Because of the confusion, the courts have set up a test to determine the identity, often referred to as the "**MARIA**" test: (M)ethod of attachment, (A)daptability of ordinary use, the (R)elationship of the parties, (I)ntention of the parties, and the (A)greement between the parties.

The necessity to clarify the real from the personal property as the collateral for the loan is important, especially under foreclosure proceedings. The amount of loan and the terms of the loan will vary according to the amount of **real property** or personal property. The personal property tends to depreciate rather quickly, usually within three to seven years. Real property, however, tends to depreciate slowly over a much longer period, such as 27 1/2 or 31 years. The lender must be careful to clarify all items that are to be used for collateral for the loan.

Trade fixtures, used for business purposes, have different guidelines. The lender who uses trade fixtures for collateral on a loan would include the personal property items as real property that becomes, by law, affixed to the land. These items usually include cash registers, tables, desks, counters, kitchen equipment, machine equipment, and similar items that are used in the ordinary course of the trade in order to operate the business. Many business operations rent, rather than own, the space in which they conduct their business. The trade fixtures may or may not be considered the personal property or the real property of the tenant or of the landlord. The ultimate investor who places funds for the loan would require that the mortgage loan broker clearly distinguish the collateral for the loan.

13.10 CALIFORNIA DOC

A broker under the California DOC laws is one who is engaged in the business of making only consumer loans. A consumer loan is one in which the proceeds are intended for a line of credit, auto, personal, family, or household use. In the normal course of that business, liens may be placed on real property or on personal property.

Consumer finance lenders fall into two groups. One group is for those who make both regulated and unregulated loans. The other group is for those who make only unregulated loans with specific dollar limitations. No specific name for a separate license, such as salesperson or broker, is given. The difference between the two is in the plan of business that is submitted with the application to become licensed. Each business entity must submit a **business plan** describing the business activities that will be performed.

A DOC broker is considered a negotiator. This individual negotiates loans and performs the acts of negotiation in connection with loans made by a lender who is licensed under the FFL or CRMLA laws. Brokers may not make any direct loans by using their own funds under this broker law.

As of July 1, 1995, the DOC commissioner placed the regulations under the CFL law for finance company rules. In order to obtain a license, the California DOC commissioner requires completion of several documents and items:

1. A balance sheet of the applicant as of a date not more than 90 days prior to the date of application, indicating a net worth of at least $250,000 (Financial Code Section 24203), and maintain a surety bond of $50,000 as of 1/1/96.

2. A Statement of Identity and Questionnaire (Figure 13.7), to be completed by all persons named as an officer if the business is a corporation, association, joint stock company, or a trust. Every location where business is conducted requires a separate license.

3. An affidavit from all persons identified in #2 who will be active in the operations, management, or supervision of the business proposed to be licensed stating that they have read and are familiar with the California FLL and CRMLA rules. A statement must also be given naming each partner, officer, and director who will not be active in the proposed business.

4. A detailed statement of how the applicant will conduct the loan business to be licensed. A clear distinction is made between the making of a loan as a lender and the negotiating of a loan as a broker, depending upon the license status being sought. A list of prospective lenders to which the loans will be brokered to must be provided (as per Sections 24002, 24008, 24009, and 24050). A statement must indicate the minimum amount of loan that would be made or brokered (as per Section 24053). A statement of the type of loans that the business will offer to consumers is also required.

5. A statement that a loan register will be maintained, with appropriate details of all loans brokered, including name and address of borrower and of the lender, amount, date, terms, and amount of brokerage fees.

6. Two copies of proposed advertising to be used in connection with the business must be submitted as discussed in Chapter 2.

7. A Customer Authorization of Disclosure of Financial Records form must be completed and signed by an owner or an officer or director.

8. A detailed statement describing any other business not coming within the purview of the DOC Lenders Law, proposed to be conducted on the same premises, or in association or conjunction with the business to be licensed or which is presently engaged in by any affiliate of the applicant.

9. If the applicant is a wholly owned subsidiary, a statement disclosing the parent corporation's name and state where incorporated and copies of licenses obtained or applied for at other locations or affiliates in California operating under a similar plan of business, and a statement disclosing the name, complete business address, and telephone number of applicant's managing officer in California.

10. A letter must be submitted indicating the lenders that the DOC broker/firm will deal with. This list is used to compare finance companies to real estate lenders.

Effective July 1, 1995, the FFL replaced the Consumer FFL (repealed 6/30/95). Under the new law, a finance lender includes any person who is

FIGURE 13.7   DOC identity questionnaire.

Department of Corporations
State of California   File no./License Number
STATEMENT OF IDENTITY AND QUESTIONNAIRE

Print exact full name: _____

Position to be filled in connection with the preparation of this questionnaire (i.e., Officer/Director, Manager, etc.)

Sex _____ Hair _____ Eyes _____ Height _____ Weight _____ Birthdate _____

Social Security or Taxpayer Identification No. _____ Driver's License No. _____

Residence phone no. (____)_____ Business phone no. (____)_____

Hours of employment _____ Place of Birth _____

1. Residence addresses for the last 10 years:

From	To	Number	Street	City	Zip
____	____	_____		_____	_____
____	____	_____		_____	_____

2. Employment for the last 10 years:

From	To	Number	Street	City	Zip
____	____	_____		_____	_____

3. Have you ever been named in any order, judgment or decree of any court or any governmental agency or administrator, temporarily or permanently restraining or enjoining you from engaging in or continuing any conduct, practice or employment? _____ No _____ Yes If Yes, write and attach details.

4. Have you ever been refused a license to engage in any business in this state or any other state, or has any such license ever been suspended or revoked? _____ No _____ Yes If Yes, write and attach details

5. Have you ever been convicted of or pleaded nolo contendere to a misdemeanor or felony other than traffic violations? _____ No _____ Yes If Yes, write and attach details.

6. Have you ever been a defendant in a civil court action other than divorce, condemnation, or personal injury? _____ No _____ Yes If Yes, write and attach details.

7. Have you ever been a subject to a bankruptcy or a petition in bankruptcy? _____ No _____ Yes If Yes, write and attach details.

8. Have you ever been refused a bond, or have you ever had a bond revoked or canceled? _____ No _____ Yes If Yes, write and attach details.

9. Have you ever changed your name or ever been known as any name other than that herein listed? _____ No _____ Yes If Yes, write and attach details.

10. Have you ever done business under a fictitious firm name either as an individual or in the partnership or corporate form? _____ No _____ Yes If Yes, write and attach details.

11. In what capacity will you be employed? _____

12. Do you expect to be a party to, or broker or salesperson in connection with escrows conducted by the escrow company which is employing you? _____ No _____ Yes If Yes, write and attach details.

This statement will be considered confidential information and will be filed and maintained as part of the confidential records not subject to public inspection.

VERIFICATION

I, the undersigned, state that I am the person named in the foregoing Statement of Identity and Questionnaire, that I have read and signed said Statement of Identity and Questionnaire and know the contents thereof, including all exhibits attached thereto, and that the statements made therein, including any exhibits attached thereto, are true.

I certify under penalty of perjury that the foregoing is true and correct.

Executed at _____   _____   _____
                  City   County   State
On this _____ day of _____ , 2xxx

Signature of Declarant _____

engaged in the business of making consumer or commercial loans. Under the new CRML rules, in-house escrows are no longer permitted, such as for refinance, equity, or other loans. The escrow must be a DOC corporation with a fidelity bond.

FIGURE 13.8 DOC corporation commissioner regulations.

Subchapter 1	General Provisions
Subchapter 2	Corporate Securities
	260.105.30 Real Estate Loans: Multiple lender transactions
Article 4	Standards for the exercise of the commissioner's authority
	Subarticle 10 Real estate programs
Subchapter 3	Credit Unions
Article 8	Loans (970–981)
Article 9	Appraisals (985–987)
Subchapter 4	Industrial Loans
Article 6	Loans and obligations receivable (1155–1178)
Article 6.5	Leases (1179)
Article 10	Appraisals (1210–1218)
Article 12	Advertising (1230–1242)
Article 17	Premium finance agencies (1285–1289)
Article 18	Mortgage Bankers (1290)
Subchapter 6	Personal Property Brokers, Consumer Finance Lenders, and Commercial Finance Lenders (Finance Company Rules)
Article 1	General Provisions (1400–1413)
Article 2	Applications (1420)
Article 3	Books, records and examinations (1425–1435)
Article 4	Loans (1445–1460)
Article 5	Charges on scheduled balances (1475–1479)
Article 6	Insurance (1485–1499)
Article 7	Credit insurance (1510–1517)
Article 8	Appraisal (1525–1526)
Article 9	Repossession and sale of personal property (1535–1542)
Article 10	Advertising (1550–1558)
Article 11	Hearings and complaints
Article 12	Exceptions to rules (1570)
Subchapter 9	Escrow agents
Article 1	General provisions (1700–1711)
Article 2	Application (1712–1717)
Article 3	Bonds (1718–1726)
Article 4	Books, records and accounts (1730–1741)
Article 5	Advertising (1742–1744)
Article 6	Accusations and hearings
Article 7	Guarantee of trust obligations (1760–1769)

The DOC requires a residential mortgage loan report showing an annual financial and statistical report to be submitted by March 31 of each year. These mortgage loan lending data are to be collected annually from January 1 to December 31. The form must be filed by lenders that:

1. Make regularly qualified loans on one- to four-unit residential real property that total at least 10 percent of the loans made during the preceding calendar year. Regularly means at least twelve transactions annually during the immediately preceding calendar year that in aggregate total more than $50,000 in value.

2. Have total assets of 10 million and less and do not report to a federal or state regulatory agency (unless exempt under the HMDA of 1975).

The laws that govern California **FLL** law are found in Title 10 (Investment) of the California Code of Regulations under Government Code 11344.6. Chapter 3 pertains to the DOC commissioner which consists of chapters, subchapters, articles, and sections. The DOC **commissioner regulations** are shown in Figure 13.8.

The DOC indicates that each DOC broker who conducts transactions under the FFL or under the CRMLA must file a report with the DOC commissioner showing a review of its trust account activity. Trust accounts are discussed in Chapter 15.

No funds need be cashed by the DRE broker in the real estate purchase loan or refinance. Many DRE brokers choose not to maintain any client funds. However, some DRE brokers do maintain a broker trust account for client funds. The buyer's initial deposit, a tenant's monthly rent, or a lender's fee for a credit report or appraisal may be placed into this account. Subsequently, checks may be written against these funds for each disbursement of client funds.

SUMMARY

The mortgage loan brokerage business is a specialized type of operation within the business community that include six items for success, including PMA, PP, time management skills, WORK (wealth, opportunities, rewards, knowledge), a business that includes GOALS (goal-oriented, opportunities, accomplishments, learning, success), and a marketing plan.

The two areas that the loan broker will need to establish are the people side of the business, including employment issues, and the operational functions for the loan business. Employment issues include the relationship between the loan agent and a coworker, assistant, employing broker or firm, and those who may work for the loan agent, which requires such items as an organizational chart and a office policy and procedures manual.

The business operations includes meeting DRE requirements for this specialized type of business to comply with real estate law, including filing the proper forms for the place of business, branch office disclosure, officers and directors and broker information, and fictitious business name, in addition to compliance with sexual harassment training for supervisory personnel. The office location and layout are critical for operations and workflow to the employees and independent contractors.

The loan broker usually works under the lender through a wholesale broker agreement. Various aspects of the business can be facilitated through use of such computer applications. Both salesperson and broker licensees who work under the designated broker require specific supervision for acts performed for the mortgage business. The regulations for agency relationships may be applicable for the DRE mortgage broker, so a review of the agent, dual agency, and subagency was discussed. The scope, authority, delegation, liability, and limitations for agency were covered in this chapter. A comparison between DOC and DRE license requirements and acts was covered. Financial compensation issues such as referral fees and commission were reviewed as well.

REVIEWING YOUR UNDERSTANDING

1. A real estate licensee is required to place his/her license identification number on all first point of contact marketing materials by:
   A. January 1, 2009
   B. July 1, 2009
   C. January 1, 2010
   D. July 1, 2010

2. The acronym "WORK" stands for:
   A. Wealth, Opportunities, Recompense, Knowledge
   B. Wealth, Open, Richness, Knowledge
   C. Worries, Opportunities, Rewards, Knowledge
   D. Wealth, Opportunities, Rewards, Knowledge

3. According to the Better Business Bureau, 80% of all business fail within the first two years because of a:
   A. Lack of positive mental attitude
   B. Lack of patience and persistence
   C. Lack of capital and lack of management
   D. Lack of time management skills

4. Individuals would be "in the business" if in one year they handled _____ loans.
   A. 3
   B. 6
   C. 8
   D. 10

5. A broker licensed under the DOC must provide a balance sheet as of a date not more than _____ days prior to the date of application, indicating a net worth of at least _____.
   A. 60/$50,000
   B. 90/$50,000
   C. 60/$250,000
   D. 90/$250,000

6. The MARIA test stands for:
   A. Miles, acres, range, inches, altitude
   B. Market, arrangement, rate, imagination, agreement
   C. Method, adaptability, relationship, intention, agreement
   D. Mortgage, agreement, rate, interest, APR

7. Under the DOC Commissioner Finance Company Lenders law, compensation to any unlicensed person is:
   A. Prohibited
   B. Prohibited, as is any rebate
   C. Permitted
   D. Permitted up to $1,000

8. Predatory lending refers to:
   A. Adding high-cost credit insurance to a loan
   B. Adding life insurance to the cost of a loan
   C. Conducting unfair and deceptive credit practices
   D. All of the above

9. The term *loan flipping* refers to:
   A. Persuading a borrower to repeatedly refinance a loan
   B. Adding high-cost insurance to a loan
   C. Conducting unfair and deceptive credit practices
   D. All of the above

10. The initial capital to open an office should cover at least _____ months of operating expenses, in addition to startup cost.
    A. Three
    B. Six
    C. Nine
    D. Twelve

ANSWERS TO REVIEWING YOUR UNDERSTANDING

1. B (pp. 403–404)
2. D (p. 402)
3. C (p. 400)
4. C (p. 417)
5. D (p. 424)
6. C (p. 423)
7. B (p. 417)
8. C (p. 413)
9. A (p. 414)
10. B (p. 409)

Chapter

14

IMPORTANT TERMS

Branch office

Broker

Business and
Professions Code

Continuing education
(C/E)

Corporate broker

DRE

Employee

Independent contractor

License renewal

Real Estate law

Salesperson

California Department of Real Estate (DRE) License Activity for Loan Agents

PREVIEW

Although some activities are exempt from state licensing and some activities fall under the DOC, the majority of loan activity in California falls under the DRE, which regulates licensees who work on real property. This chapter discusses the loan business that requires a DRE state license, including obtaining and maintaining a DRE license.

Both the state of California and the federal government have enacted laws regarding mortgage loan originators (MLO). Under the Federal Safe Act the single license records for each MLO are outlined and discussed.

Of the 10 most common violations found in DRE audits, trust fund handling and record-keeping are the most troublesome. This chapter discusses the legal requirements for receiving and handling of trust funds in a real estate transaction and the requirements for maintaining the paper trail for records.

CHAPTER OBJECTIVES

At the end of this chapter, the student learning outcomes include:

1. Outline the activities that do not require a DRE license.
2. List activities that require a DRE broker license.
3. Describe the DRE license requirements for the salesperson and broker license.
4. Identify topics and differentiate between the B&P Code and the DRE Real Estate Commissioner's Code of Regulations.
5. Discuss the most common DRE violations.

14.1 DRE LICENSE

Activities That Do Not Require a DRE License

The DRE commissioner promotes real estate internship programs that educate trainees. A **DRE** license is not required for many entry-level positions such as starting the business as an assistant to a loan agent. An employing **broker** is given maximum flexibility to design activities for such individuals. However, the *DRE* has specific penalties for those who try to circumvent the license requirement for activities that do require licensure.

The DRE is cooperative when you write and ask in advance about specific details. You may wish to check with the legal council of a professional loan association or your own attorney to see which activities require a license. The following activities do not require a license, according to a list prepared by DRE Managing Deputy Commissioner J. Chris Graves:

1. Participation in market analyses, such as obtaining comparable sales prices or loan amounts recorded against similar properties
2. Review of government reports, such as zoning, coastal commission, or environmental findings, and seeking disclosure, as described in Chapter 5
3. Report on items of interest in trade publications, such as FNMA underwriting guidelines or obtaining blank, current lending forms, such as the loan application (1003) described in Chapter 6
4. Participation in office training sessions on loan processing or servicing.
5. Participation in sales meetings of the loan agents, describing Reg. Z advertising regulations, as described in Chapter 2
6. Keeping records on loans, including principal, interest, taxes, or insurance.
7. Observing certain phases of office management, such as personnel and files and typing rate sheets that are approved by the broker
8. Contact with the title company regarding vesting of a prospective buyer, as described in Chapter 8
9. Contact with the title company about property information that is of public record, such as square footage of land and improvements and tax liens
10. Contact with real estate licensees to obtain recent sales data and financing terms
11. Help in the preparation of advertising copy, such as to place or cancel advertising, as described in Chapter 2
12. Contact with DVA, FHA, FNMA, or FHLMC to obtain underwriting guidelines and instructions
13. Contact with the DRE to obtain license information and forms
14. Telephone answering assignments (cannot quote price or rates) to take messages for loan agents

A loan assistant's job is to free time so the licensee may generate new loans. An assistant might be responsible for screening e-mails, handling mail, creating checklists of tasks the loan agent must do, and maintaining the loan agent's computer database.

The individual or corporation who does not have a real estate license but is performing acts that require the license also may be fined. An individual may be fined up to $10,000 and may receive up to six months' imprisonment. The fine for a corporation may not exceed $50,000. The act of soliciting borrowers or lenders for, or negotiating loans secured directly or collaterally by, liens on real property fall under this part of the real estate law.

Activities That Require a DRE Broker License

The California DRE commissioner's regulations define a real estate broker as a person who actually receives compensation or who expects to receive compensation when acting for another. The broker or the **salesperson** employed to act for the broker acts or negotiates to act for another. The following are duties that do require a license under the California DRE:

1. Soliciting borrowers for loans and soliciting lenders for loans.
2. Negotiating loans.
3. Collecting payments for loans secured on real property or performing loan servicing for borrowers or for lenders in connection with loans on real property.
4. Selling or offering to sell a promissory note secured collaterally by a lien on real property.
5. Buying or offering to buy a promissory note secured by a lien on real property.
6. Exchanging or offering to exchange a promissory note secured directly by real property.
7. Performing services for the promissory note holder secured by a lien on real property.

DRE License Requirements

Current DRE license levels for real estate in California include the real estate salesperson and the real estate broker. For persons working in the areas of mortgage loans who do require a California DRE license, the individual:

1. Must qualify to be licensed.
   a. Successfully pass state examination.
   b. Have reached 18th birthday.
   c. Submit license fee.
   d. Submit a set of live-scan fingerprints; pay fingerprint fee.
   e. Not have a criminal record (a felony) that would warrant denial (see Figure 14.1).
2. Obtain the state license:
   a. California licensed Salesperson:
      1. Complete real estate principles, real estate practice, and one additional course (such as mortgage loan brokerage and lending or real estate finance).
      2. Pass the state Salesperson examination of 150 questions with a minimum of 70 percent or more correct.

FIGURE 14.1   Denial of a DRE license application.

A. All criminal convictions and pending criminal charges must be disclosed on the license application.

B. The crime or act must be substantially related to the qualifications, functions, or duties of the licensee, such as:
   1. Fraudulently taking, obtaining, appropriating or retaining funds or property belonging to another person.
   2. Counterfeiting, forging, or altering an instrument.
   3. Attempting to derive personal financial benefit by not paying government taxes, assessments, or levies.
   4. Employing bribery, fraud, deceit, falsehood or misrepresentation to achieve an end.
   5. Failing to obtain a license before engaging in business.
   6. Doing any unlawful act for financial benefit that injures another person.

   Commissioner's Regulation 2910, Section 480 and 490.

3. California licensed Broker:

   a. Education: Complete 8 approved courses named in legislation

   1. 4 required courses: real estate practice, legal aspects of real estate, real estate finance, and real estate appraisal.

   2. 1 course: choice of college accounting or real estate economics.

   3. 3 elective courses from a list, including: real estate principles, real estate finance, and mortgage loan brokering and lending.

   b. Experience: Show proof of experience, within the past five years of:

   1. Two years as a licensed Salesperson, full-time equivalent, under a licensed Broker; or,

   2. One year of experience and a two-year college degree (with the required educational courses); or,

   3. Four-year college degree with no experience (with the required educational courses).

Real Estate Salesperson

A person who has fulfilled the requirements from the California DRE as a licensed DRE salesperson is identified as the salesperson. The general public typically refers to these individuals as the licensee or agent. The DRE identifies these individuals as employees under the real estate licensed broker. The DRE commissioner oversees the license-issuing agency. The salesperson is required to work under the direct supervision of a licensed real estate broker.

Any individual who fails to meet the legislated educational requirements, including proof of legal presence, being current on child support payments, and "existing licensee" continuing education requirements would not have a current license. If an individual had a license but his or her license expires, he or she would not be licensed and therefore could no longer perform any loan activities that require a license.

To obtain the salesperson license, the licensee must complete real estate principles and real estate practice, plus one additional college-level courses, such as real estate finance or mortgage loan brokering and lending. Thus, a total of three college-level courses must be completed for the salesperson license.

Real Estate Broker

An individual who acts for others for compensation or in expectation of compensation to negotiate the purchase, sale, or leasing of real property must have a real estate broker's license approved by the DRE. Article 5 of the real estate law deals with mortgage loan negotiation and the purchase, sale, and exchange of trust deeds. A broker's license is required for

- Soliciting borrowers or lenders or negotiating loans.
- Collecting payments.
- Performing services for borrowers or lenders or note owners on real property loans.
- Selling or offering to sell a real property secured note or contract.
- Buying or offering to buy a real property secured note or contract.
- Exchanging or offering to exchange a real property secured note or contract.

An individual who engages in the business of selling real property securities to the public must obtain a separate license under the Securities License Law and not under the DRE regulations. When mortgage loan brokers act as principals or agents for a lender, they are considered an employee of the lender and would be subject to a DRE license because they are negotiating real property transactions within the state.

A licensed real estate broker may be an individual or a corporation. As a legal entity, the corporation must have an individual specified as the responsible party for overseeing and supervising the licensees who are named as being under the guidance of that broker. A real estate brokerage company may offer diverse real estate specialty areas, such as property management, sales, and financial loan arranger. The firm may specialize even further by handling residential homes, mobile homes, and commercial or industrial properties.

To obtain a real estate broker license, the individual must complete eight college-level courses, which may include the three taken to qualify for the salesperson license, such as real estate principles, real estate practice, or mortgage loan brokering and lending. To obtain and retain the broker license, the licensee must document experience requirements (one of the following):

1. two years of full-time real estate experience with no college degree.
2. one year of full-time real estate experience with an associate's degree.
3. no experience with a bachelor's or law degree.

DRE Corporation Requirements

If a designated officer applies for a real estate broker license for the corporation, a specific DRE form is required to be completed, including

- A background statement of information on each director, the chief executive officer, the president, first-level vice presidents, secretary, chief financial officer, and subordinate officers.
- Each must sign the background statement of information.
- All parties responsible for forming corporation policy must comply.
- All natural persons owning or controlling more than 10% of the corporation shares must comply.

The designated officer must also notify the DRE within 30 days of each new person's subsequent participation in the corporation. The officer must also notify the DRE of any new person doing corporate business.

The background statement of information form required by DRE would contain data on the following information about the person:

- Full legal name
- Corporation title
- Date of birth
- Residential address for past 5 years
- Employment history for past 5 years
- Fictitious business name activity for past 10 years
- County or government agency orders or judgments for past 10 years
- License denied, revocation, criminal convictions, or cancellation of a bond or license for past 10 years

Excluded lenders are subsidiaries, affiliates, or holding companies of any of the above. Also excluded are self-directed IRAs, Keoghs, and 401Ks because they fall under other regulatory agencies. Naturally, the lender would be subject to liability when a relationship is established with a broker who is a loan correspondent or authorized agent.

License Renewal and Continuing Education

Every four years from each license date, every licensee must complete required **continuing education (C/E)** courses, such as shown in Figure 14.2.

A total of 45 hours of C/E is required for each **license renewal** after the issuance of an original license. The requirements differ for each license according to Section 10170.5 of the B&P Code. The DRE separates C/E courses into several categories, including ethics, consumer protection, and consumer service. A consumer protection course is one that is intended to help the licensee better protect the public in a real property transaction. A consumer service course is one that teaches the licensee how to be a better licensee. A course on how to identify and how to show a client information on the various disclosures would be considered consumer protection. An example of a consumer service course is

FIGURE 14.2   Continuing education C/E.

TYPE OF LICENSE	C/E REQUIREMENTS FOR RENEWAL DATES:		
	Initial Renewal on or after 1/1/96	Second Renewal after 1/1/96 for "A" and "B" Licensees	All Subsequent Renewals for "A" and "B" Licensees
A All licenses, broker and salesperson, except as proviaed in "B" below	☐ 45 hours including 3 hours of agency, ethics, fair housing, and trust fund handling courses *and* at least 18 hours (within the 45 hours) of consumer protection courses	☐ 45 hours including 18 hours of consumer protection courses *and* any two of the four mandated courses (agency, ethics, fair housing, and trust fund handling) *or* a 6-hour survey course that includes all four mandated courses	☐ 45 total hours including 18 hours of consumer protection courses *and* if two of the four mandated courses were submitted for the previous renewal, the two courses not previously taken, *or* a 6-hour survey course, *or,* if the survey course was used in the ethics, previous renewal period, another survey course, *or* two of the four mandated courses.
B Salespersons renewing for the first time after original license	☐ 3 hours each of agency, fair housing, and trust fund handling (12 hours total)		

Note: Licenses expiring on December 31 of any year have a renewal date of the next January 1.

one that instructs agents on keystrokes for various financial calculators or one that teaches detailed math calculations for a HUD closing statement.

First-time renewal for salesperson licensees, because they take college-level courses after taking the salesperson test, is different from the renewal of all other licensees. First-time salesperson renewal requirements include only the four 3-hour courses for a total of only 15 hours of (1) agency, (2) ethics, (3) trust fund handling, (4) fair housing, and (5) risk management in order to qualify for renewal.

The subsequent renewal requirements for all licensees renewing after the first renewal of an original salesperson license, excluding the first-time salespersons, are 45 hours of C/E. The hours include four mandatory 3-hour courses in (1) agency, (2) ethics, (3) trust fund handling, (4) fair housing, and (5) risk management, including a minimum of 18 hours of consumer protection. The balance of the required 45 hours of C/E may be in either the consumer service or consumer protection category.

For the third and all subsequent renewals after January 1, 1996, licensees have a choice. A licensee may take either a six-hour survey course covering all four mandatory subjects or separate three-hour courses in the two mandatory subjects *that were not used to qualify for the previous renewal as* part of the 45 hours.

(Example: If ethics and agency were taken for the third renewal, the licensee could take either (1) fair housing and trust funds for the fourth renewal or (2) the

6-hour survey course covering all four subjects, for any licensee, except first-time salesperson licensees.)

AB 223 amended Section 10170.5 of the B & P that revises the continuing education requirements on July 1, 2007 to include an additional course. A three-hour course in risk management that includes principles, practices, and procedures calculated to avoid errors and omissions in the practice of real estate licensed activities is being added to the mandatory list. Instead of 12 hours of mandated, 18 hours of consumer protection and the balance of the 45 hours in consumer service or consumer protection, the new law will change to 15 mandated hours and 18 hours consumer protection, for a total of 45 hours of continuing education for license renewal.

Employment Agreement

The DRE regulations are specific about the requirements for the relationship between the licensed salespersons and the licensed broker acting as the designated broker of record. Every broker must have a written agreement with each salesperson (see Appendix H). The contract should contain the following:

- Names of parties as shown on their DRE license and full legal name, if different
- Date the contract is signed
- Definition and description of the activities of the licensee requiring broker supervision
- Duties of each party to the contract clearly outlined
- Compensation detailed with method of payment, time period, when earned, when paid, direct fees from broker-salesperson activities, indirect referral fees compensation outstanding upon termination and where payment jurisdiction resides

The contract must be retained by each party for a minimum of three years from the date of termination of the contract. Each party must keep a copy of the contract available for inspection upon request by the DRE commissioner.

The broker must notify the DRE commissioner within five days of beginning employment with the salesperson. A specific DRE form was required and had to be signed by both the broker and the salesperson licensees, as shown in Figures 3.1 and 3.2. Today, however, the broker would go to the DRE Web site at http://www.dre.ca.gov to locate the area needed. The DRE homepage for electronic licensing data shows the following list from which to select:

- Mailing address, changes
- License renewals
- Broker discontinuation of salesperson employment
- Broker certificate of salesperson employment
- Salesperson additions/changes of employing broker

Whether online or with the written form, the notification form contains the following information:

- Name and business address of the broker

- Residence address of the salesperson
- Date employment entered into
- Name and address of last broker
- Date of termination with last broker

In addition, the salesperson is required to complete several additional steps to be in compliance on the hardcopy paper license:

- Certification that the preceding broker has notice of termination of the prior relationship
- Mark out the former address of the prior broker on the face of the license
- Type or write the new main office address in ink on the reverse side
- Date and initial the changes on the license
- An acceptable alternative is to mail notice to the commissioner on the required form within the ten days after termination (see Figure 3.1).

The broker retains the license of each salesperson or broker whom the broker employs. The licenses are kept at the main business office of the broker and must be readily available for inspection by the DRE. Upon termination of employment, the broker must immediately return the license to the salesperson.

The broker is responsible for reviewing the type of license the salesperson was issued. The broker cannot compensate a salesperson who does not have a valid license. Examples of when a license is no longer valid may include:

- Salesperson's failure to complete the required 45 hours of C/E (including the 12 hours just previously described) and submit proof to the commissioner every four years to have salesperson license renewed for another four years.
- Broker who works under the supervision of a broker for employment purposes who fails to complete the required 45 hours of C/E (as described above) to obtain proper renewal license for another four years.
- Persons who had a DRE license that is restricted have special requirements that the commissioner has given as privileges, restrictions, or other.
- Persons who had a DRE license that is suspended or revoked are not licensed under the employing broker.

Business Office

Every broker must have and maintain a definite place of business in the state of California. This location shall serve as the office for the purpose for the transaction of business. This office is where the broker's license is displayed. Personal consultations with clients are often held at the office (Section 10162.2).

For the business to use a fictitious name, referred to as a dba (doing business as), the licensed broker is the holder of that name on the license that bears the fictitious name. A certified copy of the fictitious business name must be filed with the DRE license application (B&P Code 10159.5). The DRE commissioner will not approve a fictitious name license to a broker if the name:

- is misleading.
- would constitute false advertising.

- implies a partnership when such does not exist.
- implies a corporation that is not in legal existence.
- includes any licensed salesperson's name.
- is a name previously used by any entity for which that license was revoked.

Branch Office

The DRE commissioner may determine whether a real estate broker is doing brokerage business at a particular location. If it is determined that the mortgage brokerage is from a location other than the main office, the broker must comply with the **branch office** requirements according to B&P Code 10163 of the California real estate law. An additional license is issued for each branch office. The broker must apply for and procure the additional license or else not do business at that additional location. The application states the name of the person and the places of business. No licensee is authorized to do business from any location that is not stipulated by the commissioner. No licensee may do business except from the location stipulated in the real estate license as issued by the DRE according to Section 10161.8 of the code. Every licensed broker must have a definite place of business in the state of California that serves as the office for the transaction of business, as stipulated by code Section 10162.

Prohibitions and Penalties

A broker is prohibited from compensating a person not licensed by the California DRE who is performing acts that do require a license. Effective after June 30, 2009, any person acting as a licensee without being licensed, or who advertises using words indicating that the person is licensed, may be punished up to $20,000 or by six months imprisonment in the county jail; and, if a corporation, may be punished up to $60,000. These funds, when collected, are put into a Real Estate Fraud Prosecution Trust Fund. As of July 1, 2009, a licensee may not publish, circulate, distribute, or cause to be published in any newspaper or periodical or by mail pertaining any activity that requires a license. All fines collected by the commissioner are credited to the real estate recovery account of the real estate fund.

A real estate licensee is prohibited from offering inducements in real estate loan transactions. The licensee may not give or offer to give a prospective borrower or lender any premium, gift, or other object of value, which applies to making the original loan or purchasing a promissory note. The note may include one that is directly or collaterally a lien on real property. A real property sales contract with possible owner financing is included in the prohibited acts.

The license law does not allow the individual to work for more than one broker or to receive compensation from any licensee other than the employing broker. A salesperson licensee must notify the DRE on the approved form when changing employment to a different sponsoring broker. It is common for the salesperson to be employed under **independent contractor** status for IRS tax purposes, meaning that the salesperson would be expected to be paid on a commission-only basis and that no taxes or other "benefits" deductions would be taken from the gross amount due to the licensee. Some licensees who work for a lending corporation may have other compensation arrangements, such as a level-payment commission in which the salesperson receives advances against future earnings. Some licensees receive a salary when employed by some financial institution.

An individual who is licensed as a broker may work under the license of another broker. A broker may work under the **corporate broker** license for the company. If the broker works for one broker and receives all compensation from that broker, the individual is usually referred to as a broker-associate. When a broker makes a change in operation affecting DRE license data, the proper form must be submitted to the real estate commissioner. Unlike a salesperson, the broker may receive compensation from more than one entity. The broker is under contract law for compensation. Thus, brokers may work as a fee-per-hour consultant to arrange a loan, for a commission-only compensation with a monthly rental fee for their portion of the firm's expenses, or as employees with a flat salary or a salary plus bonus plan. The variety of employment arrangements is unlimited and subject only to contractual arrangements between the parties.

14.2 DRE BROKER SUPERVISION

The DRE licensed broker is required to exercise reasonable supervision over the activities of all licensed DRE salespersons working under that broker's license. The broker may be an individual or may be a person who owns or controls 10% or more of the stock in a real estate corporation. The supervision also applies to an officer designated by a corporate broker license. The broker or officer who fails to exercise reasonable supervision and control over the activities of the salesperson or corporation for which a real estate license is required falls under the DRE commissioner's rules and regulations (Section 10159.2).

Many mortgage loan brokerage firms act under the name of a corporation. A real estate license is then issued to a corporation with an officer designated to act as a real estate broker. It is also not uncommon for the corporation to desire additional officers to act as real estate brokers. In this case, the corporation must procure an additional license to employ each additional officer.

Broker Supervision

There are some basic guidelines for the broker-salesperson relationship. At no time can the corporation perform acts on behalf of or in the name of the corporation under only a real estate salesperson's license. The salesperson who acts singly under his or her license, or with one or more licensed salespersons, is specifically prohibited from acting for the corporation. This action is also prohibited when the salesperson licensee owns or controls a majority of the corporation's shares of stock. The broker may delegate the responsibility and authority for review of the instruments as described above. However, the broker cannot relinquish the overall responsibility for supervision of the acts of the licensed salespersons. Thus, a broker or designated officer who delegates document review and initialing is still responsible for the results. A branch manager, loan officer, or office manager may be the document reviewer by contract with the broker, but the broker would be the DRE employment supervisor for enforcement purposes.

The broker may delegate the review process to another DRE licensee if certain acts are carried out. First, the designated broker may delegate to another licensed broker. The broker must have entered into written agreement specifying the delegation of document review. Second, the designated broker may delegate the authority to a licensed real estate salesperson. However, the salesperson must have accumulated at least two years' full-time experience during the preceding five-year period with the same designated broker. Further, a written agreement must specify the duties with respect to the delegation of responsibility.

A corporate broker license that has procured additional broker licenses for officers may assign supervisory responsibility over the salespersons who are licensed to the corporation under the broker-officers. In order to do so, the corporation must have a corporate resolution signed by the board of directors. A certified copy of any corporate resolution assigning supervisory responsibility over licensed salespersons must be filed with the DRE. Notice to the real estate commissioner must be made within five to ten days after adoption or modification of supervision.

14.3 CALIFORNIA CODES AND REGULATIONS FOR LICENSEES

Real Estate Law References

The real estate commissioner has issued regulations in specific areas that should be reviewed by the licensee and familiar to the loan broker. For general reference, the laws regulating the real estate industry fall into several categories. The articles of the **Business and Professions Code** are commonly known as the **real estate law** and have two parts. Part 1 (Figure 14.3) describes the licensing of persons in sections 10000 through 10580, and Part 2 (Figure 14.4) describes the regulations of transactions in sections 11000 through 11200.

As Agent

Salespersons and broker associates are representatives of the **agent**. They act on behalf of the broker who is the agent of the principal. They do not have authority to act independently of their employing broker.

Under California law, the real estate mortgage broker is the agent of someone in a real property or may be acting in a real property-secured transaction in which the broker is not the go-between or the facilitator. In this case, the DRE regulations require the mortgage broker to complete a notification form for the mortgage loan section, in addition to other licensee reporting.

FIGURE 14.3   Business and Professions Code, real estate law.

Part I   Licensing of Persons

10000	Licensing
10028	Trust Deed
10029	Real Property Sales Contract
10032	Broker-Salesperson Relationship—Independent Contractor or Employer—No Effect on Obligations to Public
10085	Advance Fee—Loan Secured by Lien on Real Property
10130	License Required
10131	Broker Defined
10132	Salesperson Defined
10137	Penalties for Payment of Unlawful Compensation
10140	False Advertising
10145	Handling of Trust Funds
10146	Advance Fees to be Deposited in Trust Account
10158	Corporation License
10159	Fictitious Name, Corporations
10170	Continuing Education
10230–10236	Transactions in Trust Deeds and Real Property Sales Contracts
10240–10248	Real Property Loans
10240	Written disclosure statement
10240.1	Application of Provisions
10240.2	"Dwelling" defined
10241	Statement content
10241.1	Insurance limitations
10241.2	Broker-controlled loan funds—Notice to borrower
10241.3	Appraisal report to be given to borrower and lender
10241.4	Notice regarding balloon payment/extension of loan
10242	Maximum expenses, charges, and interest
10242.5	Late charges
10242.6	Loan prepayment
10243	Borrower liable
10244	Substantially equal payments—loans under three years
10244.1	Loans under six years—owner occupied
10245	Exceptions
10246	Right to recover
10247	Third-party liability
10248	Charges limited by Section 10242
10248.1	Laws governing charges and fees
10248.2	Borrower's rights and remedies—may not waive
10248.3	Limits of article

Excluded lenders are subsidiaries, affiliates, or holding companies of any of the above. Also excluded are self-directed IRAs, Keoghs, and 401Ks because they fall under other regulatory agencies. Naturally, the lender would be subject to liability when a relationship is established with a broker who is a loan correspondent or authorized agent.

FIGURE 14.4   DRE commissioner code of regulations.

List of Pertinent Articles

3	Licensee applications, fees and charges
4	Brokers
5	Licenses under fictitious names
6	Corporate license
7	Salesperson
9	Advertising
15	Trust fund accounts
16	Mortgage loan brokerage
18	Contracts, writings and other documents
19	Escrows: Records and funds handling
21	Advance fee agreements

Table of Pertinent Sections

2725	Broker supervision and review of instruments
2726	Broker-salesperson agreements
2731	Use of fictitious name
2740	Corporate licenses: Broker officers and salespersons
2743	Assignment of supervisory responsibility
2746	Corporate real estate brokers, officers, directors and shareholders
2770	Advertising on the internet, license designation
2830	Trust fund account
2831	Trust fund records: Separate record for each beneficiary; Reconciliation
2835	Commingling
2840	Approved borrower disclosure statement (Good Faith Estimate; HUD-1)
2842	Signing Mortgage Loan Disclosure Statement
2843	Restrictions on chargeable costs and expenses
2846	Approved Lender/Purchaser Disclosure Statement
2847	Submission of proposed advertising
2848	Advertising criteria
2849	Annual report format

14.4 REVIEW OF INSTRUMENTS

Timeline Compliance

The designated broker of record must review every instrument prepared or signed by the licensed salesperson that is connected with any real estate transaction for which a license is required. The broker review of instruments must be performed regularly. The DRE is looking for "broker supervision" with a level of competence by the brokers that they are regularly overseeing the activities of licensees who are working directly for them.

As Agent or Principal

When the real estate mortgage broker acts as a principal, that status must be disclosed to all other principals or parties to the transaction. The broker must ensure that these parties are aware of the broker's acts. The broker must clearly be acting only as a principal and not as a licensee, or the broker must clearly communicate that he or she is acting in the capacity of both an agent and a principal.

As Lender

The real estate mortgage broker may not represent to be a lender or an agent of any particular lender unless that representation is true. A written agreement is required when a broker is an authorized agent of a bank or a savings and loan. These regulations are found both in the B&P code and in the Federal Home Loan Bank Board regulations.

The broker may obtain written status to be a loan correspondent under California law. This status is limited to a lender or an employee or authorized agent of a lender. Typical lenders would include a bank, trust company, pension trust, credit union, or insurance company.

Excluded lenders are subsidiaries, affiliates, or holding companies of any of the above. Also excluded are self-directed IRAs, Keoghs, and 401Ks because they fall under other regulatory agencies. Naturally, the lender would be subject to liability when a relationship is established with a broker who is a loan correspondent or authorized agent.

Documents Requiring Review

The documents that require review include any paper that might have an effect upon the rights or the obligations of a party. If a real estate licensee is involved and completes the necessary documents, the mortgage broker would not need to obtain a duplication of the same documents. It is recommended that you obtain a copy to retain for your file. Some transactions have no sales licensee, as in the case of a refinance, a sale by the owner, or an estate transfer to heirs. In this case, you are the licensed real estate agent who is held responsible for ensuring that the documents are completed. The list below is not intended to be all inclusive but does name documents frequently used in connection with a mortgage loan, which the broker or designee would be required to review. A good rule of thumb is that if the principal or borrower signed the document in conjunction with the transaction, there should be a document review. (See Appendix G for a full set of loan documents that include most of these forms.)

- Mortgage loan disclosure statement (borrower)—Chapter 5
- Mortgage loan disclosure statement/good faith estimate—Chapter 5
- Real estate settlement procedures act (RESPA)—Chapter 5
- Truth-in-lending (T-I-L)—Chapter 5
- Residential loan application (1003)—Appendix A
- Credit authorization—Chapter 7

- Lead-based paint, termite report, if applicable—Chapter 5
- Equal credit opportunity act (ECOA) and credit explanation letter
- Appraisal copy signed by and given to borrower—Chapter 7
- Adjustable rate mortgage (ARM), Federal Housing Administration (FHA), or Department of Veterans Administration (DVA) disclosures, if applicable—Chapter 4
- Transfer disclosure statement (TDS)—Chapter 5
- Preliminary title report—Appendix F
- Gift letter—Chapter 8

The slightest misrepresentation, concealment, or adverse pressure of any kind may be considered a breach of good faith toward the principal. The mortgage loan agent must keep communications with many parties, including not only the principals but also the processor, escrow agent, underwriter, and investor. Ongoing dialogue by the loan agent is sought. A log of paperwork is transferred between these parties. A telephone conversation log and file check list were shown in Chapter 8. However, the person who reviews the file should also devise some type of summary log to ensure supervision of each file. Any form may be used, but it is recommended that the employing broker keep some kind of record on the activity of the licensee and the file, such as the loan information sheet. The agent employed by the broker must also keep the employing broker and the principal informed of his or her acts. Too often the loan agent does not remember to keep communications as a vital activity.

In addition, the real estate commissioner is empowered to enforce regulations that have been adopted. The regulations are contained in Title 10 and referred to as the California Code of Regulations, having the force and authority of the law since March 1945. The commissioner's regulations are arranged in two parts. The first part contains articles 2 through 26 that cover various aspects pertaining to real estate. The second part consists of the section numbers that are found within the articles, beginning with section 2705 through 3109. A summary of pertinent DRE articles and sections is shown in Figure 14.4.

The Administrative Procedure Act comes from the Government Code, Title 2, with 11503 through 11528 covering the rights of persons holding a license. The areas of real estate law and the commissioner's regulations both refer to hearings conducted according to certain legal requirements, which is covered by the Administrative Procedure Act. In addition, many other California codes pertain to real estate transactions. Knowledge of the B&P Code, Civil Code, Corporations Code, Financial Code, Government Code, Insurance Code, Labor Code, and Revenue and Taxation Code may all relate to the activities within the mortgage loan brokerage activities; for example, each broker is required to complete an annual residential mortgage loan report under the Health and Safety Code (Sections 35815 and 35816) and submit the report to the DRE as the enforcement agency.

No funds need be cashed by the DRE broker in the real estate purchase loan or refinance. Many DRE brokers choose not to maintain any client funds. However, other DRE brokers do maintain a broker trust account for client funds. The buyer's initial deposit, a tenant's monthly rent, or a lender's fee for a credit

FIGURE 14.5 Ten most common DRE violations.

1. Retention of records (B&P, Section 10148)
2. Use of false or fictitious name (Regulation 2731)
3. Trust fund records to be maintained (Regulation 2831)
4. Separate record for each beneficiary or transaction (Regulation 2831.1)
5. Trust account reconciliation (Regulation 2831.2)
6. Trust fund handling for multiple beneficiary—Trust fund shortage (2832.1)
7. Trust fund handling (Regulation 2832)
8. Trust account withdrawals (Regulation 2834)
9. Commingling (B&P, Section 10145/Regulation 2835)
10. Written disclosure statement (B&P, Section 10240)

report or appraisal may be placed into this account. Subsequently, checks may be written against these funds for each individual disbursement of client funds. Compensation earned must be taken out of the client trust fund within 30 days.

Common DRE Violations

The DRE audits licensees on a regular, ongoing basis, in addition to audits requested by some judicial body or investigation. A review of the most common DRE violations and deficiencies is shown in Figure 14.5. The licensee must ensure compliance with these laws and regulations.

14.5 CALIFORNIA FINANCIAL CODE

National legislative issues have been brought to the forefront in recent years because banking financial institutions have come to be allowed into various areas real estate activities that require either a DRE or DOC license. If the institutions are allowed to proceed, the industry would drastically change.

At the federal level, the passage of the Gramm-Leach-Bliley Act (GLBA) in 1999 was the first step in the process that granted banks the authority to operate insurance and securities businesses but not real estate licensee activities. In 2005, the full House Financial Services Committee held hearings on the issue of allowing banks in real estate. The National Association of REALTORS® is pushing to pass the Community Choice in Real Estate Act to clarify that real estate brokerage, leasing, and property management are commercial activities. The act states that it permanently excludes and would make illegal mixing banking and commerce for financial holding companies and national bank subsidiaries with real estate activity without the proper real estate license, H.R. 111. Opposing this restriction is H.R. 2660, the Fair Choice and Competition in Real Estate Act, which would allow national banks to handle real estate brokerage, leasing, and management.

Although the issue is clearly not decided either way, the discussion of whether banking institutions or their subsidiaries are involved in the real estate business will affect how business will be conducted. The mortgage loan broker should review the codes listed in Figure 14.6 that outline the headings for the

FIGURE 14.6 California financial code.

Division 1.	Banks	
Division 1.1	The setting of fees in consumer credit agreements and related consumer protections	
Division 1.2	California Financial Information Privacy Act	
Division 1.5	Depository corporations—wale, merger, and conversion	
Division 1.6	General provisions and enforcement	
Division 1.7	Securities sales	
Division 1.8	Persons connected with financial institutions	
Division 2	Savings association law	
Division 2.5	Other authorized investment in bonds and securities	
Division 3	Check sellers, bill payers, and proraters	
Division 4	Automated teller machines: user safety	
Division 4.5	Automated teller machine surcharge disclosure	
Division 5	Credit unions	
Division 6	Escrow agents	
Division 7	Industrial loan companies	
	Chapter 1	General provisions
	Article 3	Real property held
	Article 4	Advertising
	Chapter 2	Formation and organization
	Chapter 3	Loans and purchased obligations
	Article 3	Disclosure and loan documents
	Article 5	Limitations and regulations on loans and purchased obligations
	Article 6	Insurance sold with loans
	Article 6.5	Open-end loans
Division 8	Pawnbrokers	
Division 9	California finance lenders law	
	Chapter 1	General provisions
	Chapter 2	Consumer loans
	Article 1	Definitions
	Article 2	Exemptions
	Article 3	Loan regulations
	Article 4	Charges on scheduled balances
	Article 5	Open-end loan programs
	Article 6	Disclosure of loan applications
Division 10	California deferred deposit transaction law	
Division 11.5	National housing act loans	
Division 15	Business and industrial development corporations	
Division 15.5	State assistance fund for enterprise, business, and industrial development corporation	
Division 16	Payment instruments	
Division 19	Release of demand deposit funds	
Division 20	California residential mortgage lending act	
	Chapter 1	General
	Chapter 2	Licensing: Residential mortgage lender
	Chapter 3	Licensing: Residential mortgage loan servicer
	Chapter 4	Financial condition, transaction and bond requirements
	Chapter 5	Administration and powers of the commissioner
	Chapter 6	Assessments
	Chapter 7	Prohibited practices and penalties
	Chapter 8	Operation of division
	Chapter 9	Brokerage services for borrowers

California Financial Code. Several sections of the law pertain directly to those who place loans on real property. The close ties to the mortgage loan brokerage business and the banking community, unlike real estate sales, leasing, and property management activities, will be ongoing no matter which regulations the loan broker works under because the lender who has the funds used for the loan is often a banking financial institution.

In 2005, the DRE commissioner had legislation change the form for the annual loan and trust deed report and amended Section 2849.01 to read: 2849.01, Annual Report Format.

For reports submitted to the Department, the following format shall be used by a real estate broker who meets the criteria of section 10232 and/or 10238 of the Code for the annual report required by section 10232.2(c) and 10238(p). For the most current up-to-date list of forms to use, please visit, http://www.dre.ca.gov/frm_forms.html and search by function or number for the form you have interest in using.

If reporting broker is an individual licensee, he/she must sign this report. If reporting broker is a corporate licensee, the corporation's designated licensed officer must sign this report.

14.6 S.A.F.E. ACT - LICENSE LAW

As discussed elsewhere in this text, Senate Bill 36 (SC36) was signed into law in October 2009. The purpose of the law was to enable the identification of any and all real estate licensees who conduct mortgage activities so that California can comply with the federal **S**ecure **A**nd **F**air **E**nforcement (SAFE) Act, which is part of the Housing and Economic Recovery Act of 2009 (Public Law 110-289).

The SAFE Act requires all states to adhere to minimum requirements for residential mortgage loan broker licensees. Many agencies were involved in the compilation of the requirements to set up safeguards against future mortgage meltdowns as happened between 2005 and 2009 throughout the nation. The meltdown triggered national and international changes in financial markets. Investors required regulators to put into place some system to monitor the activity of those who work within the loan business. This new act monitors the activities of each individual. Among the various entities involved, the following lists the main groups:

- Conference of State Bank Supervisors (CSBS)
- American Association of Residential Mortgage Regulators (AARMR)
- Nationwide Mortgage Licensing System and Registry (NMLS&R)
- Mortgage Loan Originator (MLO)
- Department of Real Estate (DRE)
- National Association of Mortgage Brokers (NAMB)
- California Mortgage Loan Broker Association (CAMB)

The NMLS&R will contain a single license record for each mortgage loan lender, broker, branch and mortgage loan originator (MLO) that can be used to apply for, amend, and renew a license in any state. The Resource Center is found at www.mortgage.nationwidelicensingsystem.org.

SB36 requires all DRE real estate licensees who conduct residential MLO activities, as outlined in the SAFE Act, to meet the following requirements to qualify for the MLO real estate license endorsement. Qualification processing fees are non-refundable. The criteria for endorsement approval include the following items:

1. The individual must take and pass both the National and the California Unique State component of the SAFE written examination, administered by a NMLS&R vendor. The National exam is available as of January 1, 2010, and the California state component is available by March 2010. The Professional Requirements tab on the NMLS&R Web site gives additional details.

2. The individual must complete 20 hours of pre-license education. Current DRE licensees may already have satisfied this requirement, and CSBS is pending approval for such. The DRE Web site will maintain the information for the education component.

3. As of March 2010, the individual must file an online MLO license endorsement application and pay the license endorsement fee to NMLS&R.

4. The individual must submit a new set of live scaned fingerprints using a NMLS&R-approved vendor. The information will be provided during the license endorsement application process.

5. The individual will be required to authorize NMLS&R to obtain a credit report from a consumer reporting agency as part of the online application process.

The SAFE Act prohibits the licensing of individuals for the MLO endorsement if an applicant has:

1. Ever been convicted of a felony involving an act of fraud, dishonesty, breach of trust, money laundering, or if convicted of any felony in the past seven years before filing.

2a. Ever had a loan originator license revoked in any governmental jurisdiction, or

2b. Demonstrated a lack of financial responsibility by showing disregard in the management of his or her own financial condition.

The SAFE Act requires that within 30 days of any residential loan activity from January 31, 2010, the DRE licensed broker must report to the California DRE any and all activity in the making, arranging or servicing of any loan secured by real property, for both residential and commercial property. DRE form # RE 866, *Mortgage Loan Activity Notification*, must be completed online at www.dre.ca.gov.

In addition, in order to comply with the California statutes and regulations, as opposed to how other states are implementing the national SAFE ACT, if the loan broker must:

1. Conduct activities for which a DRE license is required as a residential mortgage loan originator (MLO), then a special endorsement given by the California DRE is required for the individual real estate licensee.

2. Register with the National Mortgage Licensing System and Registry (NMLS&R). The NMLS&R will contain a single license record of each mortgage loan lender, broker, branch and mortgage loan originator (MLO).

3. Satisfy the federal requirements for MLO licensure. Requirements include new qualification assessments, federal and state examinations, and a background check. There are no exceptions for complying with this law.

4. Obtain a MLO endorsement on the individual real estate license by January 1, 2011 in order to conduct business. The initial MLO license endorsements will expire on December 31, 2011. MLO endorsements are issued annually and expire December 31st each year. The endorsement will carry a nationwide identification number known as a "unique identifier" which will be assigned by the NMLS&R.

Failure to submit the required DRE RE866 Report when due results in a $50 per day assessment penalty for the first 30 days that the report is not filed, and failure to obtain the required MLO endorsement results in a $100 per day penalty for every day thereafter for a maximum of $10,000.

To learn more, visit the DRE web page and for specific information about these new requirements, go to: http://dre.ca.gov/lic_sb36_safe.html

14.7 LICENSE LAWS

Each state directs its own set of license laws for the department of real estate salespersons and brokers, for loan originators, for property managers and other segments of the real estate industry. The following information is a partial list of information for various states. Many licensees do business between various states on a semi-regular basis and become multi-state licensed and need to comply with the regulations for each state. For example, New York and New Jersey agents may work both states. Many California agents do regular business with Nevada and Arizona persons or property. The states are listed in alphabetic order for easier referencing. Figure 14.7 is a summary.

Arizona

Who is required to have the Arizona Mortgage Loan Originator License? Any natural person who in expectation or for compensation or gain who takes a residential loan application, or offers/negotiates terms of a residential loan, or, on behalf of a borrower, negotiates with a lender for a loan modification.

Exempt are registered loan originators, individuals who offer/negotiate terms of residential loans secured by the individual's residence, a responsible person who does not act as a loan originator, an employee of a licensed commercial loan banker or broker, a seller of real property who receives one or more loans as security for a purchase money obligation, a licensed attorney, an individual acting for an immediate family member, a manufactured home retailer and its employees who act only in clerical or support duties, or a person involved in loss mitigation efforts for a loan modification.

FIGURE 14.7 State requirements for brokers.

State	License Type	State Fee	Net Worth	Surety Bond	Audited Financial Statement?	Physical Office?	Test Required?	Loan Officer License Required?	Experience	Branch Licensing?	Renewal Period
Alabama	Broker	600	25,000	0	No	Yes	No	No	none- 12 hrs of CE	Yes	Dec 31st every year
Arizona	Broker	1050	N/A	10-15,000	No	Yes	Yes	No	3 years & resident or RI	Yes	Sept 30th every year
Arkansas	Broker	250	25,000	50,000	No	No	No	Yes	3 years	Yes	every year
California	Finance Broker/ Lender	300	25,000	25,000	No	No	No	No	No	Yes	1 year
Colorado	Mortgage Broker	250	N/A	25,000 and 100,000 E&O Policy	No	No	No	Yes	No	No	3 years
Connecticut	1st Broker	200	25,000	40,000 per location	No	No	No	Yes	3 years in the last 5 years	Yes	Sept 30th of even years
Connecticut	2nd Broker	200	0	0	No	No	No	Yes	3 years in the last 5 years	Yes	Sept 30th of even years
Delaware	Broker	500	40,000	25,000	No	No	No	No	No	Yes	Dec 31st every year
FHA - HUD	Loan Corresponde-nt (Mini Eagle)	1000	63,000	0	Yes	No	No	No	3 yrs	Yes	Annual Report
FHA - HUD	Non-Supervised Lender (Full Eagle)	1000	250,000	0	Yes	No	No	No	5 yrs	Yes	Annual Report
Florida	Broker and Broker Business	625	0	0	No	No	Yes	Yes	1 year	Yes	every 2 years
Georgia	Broker	750	0	50,000	No	No	No	No	2 Years or 40 Hrs of Education	Yes	June 30th every year

FIGURE 14.7 (Continued)

State	License Type	State Fee	Net Worth	Surety Bond	Audited Financial Statement?	Physical Office?	Test Required?	Loan Officer License Required?	Experience	Branch Licensing?	Renewal Period
Hawaii	Broker	100	N/A	15,000	No	Yes	No	Yes	2 yrs	Yes	Dec 31st every even numbered year
Idaho	Broker	350	10,000	25,000 plus 10,000k each branch	No	No	No	Yes	3 years for each branch mgr	Yes	Oct 31st every year
Illinois	Residential Loan	2700	50,000 or 100,000 with no in state office	20,000 and 100,000 Fidelity Bond with no office in IL	Yes	No	Yes	Yes	3 years	No, unless in IL	Dec 31st every year
Indiana	Loan Broker	200	N/A	50,000	No	No	No	Yes	3 years	No, must list	Dec 1st every 2 years
Iowa	Broker	500	N/A	50,000	No	No	No	Yes	No	Yes	June 30th every year
Kansas	1st Broker	250	N/A	50,000 with an in-state office. 100,000 without	No	No	No	Yes	None	Yes	Aug 30th of odd numbered years
Kansas	2nd Broker	400	N/A	100,000	No	No	No	Yes	None	Yes	Dec 1st every 2 years
Kentucky	Broker	300	none	50,000	No	No	No	Yes	3 years	Yes	Dec 1st every year
Louisiana	Broker	446	$50,000 or Surety Bond for $50K	$50,000 or Audited Fin of $50K	Yes or $50k Bond	No	Yes if less than 2 years exp. PSIexams.com	Yes	No	Yes	
Maine	Credit Services	400	0	25,000 plus 25,000k for each branch	No	No	No	Yes	No	Yes	Jan 31 on even numbered years (2008, 2010, etc)

FIGURE 14.7 (*Continued*)

State	License Type	State Fee	Net Worth	Surety Bond	Audited Financial Statement?	Physical Office?	Test Required?	Loan Officer License Required?	Experience	Branch Licensing?	Renewal Period
Maryland	Broker	1100	0	Based on Loan Volumes. $15k to $75k	No	No, unless home state requires it	No	Yes	3 years	Yes	2 years
Massachusetts	Broker	1115	25,000	75,000	Yes	No	No	No	3 years	Yes	
Michigan	1st SBroker	800	25,000	N/A if you don't collect fees prior to closing	No	No	No	No	1 to 3 yrs reviewed	No	June 1st every year
Michigan	2nd Broker	350	0	N/A if you don't collect fees prior to closing	No	No	No	No		No	June 1st every year
Minnesota	Originator	2125 for 2 years	25,000	$50,000 or FHA license or $250,000 audited net worth	No	No	No	No		No	2 years
Mississippi	Broker	300	0	25,000	No	No	No	Yes	2 yrs in past 4	Yes	every year
Missouri	Broker	800	25,000	25,000	No	Yes	No	No	1yr	No	every 2 years
Montana	1st Broker	500	0	25,000	No	Yes	Yes	Yes	3 yrs	Yes	May 30th each year
Montana	2nd Broker	250			No	Yes	Yes	Yes			
Nebraska	Broker	300	0	100,000	No	No	No	No	No	Yes	Nov 30th every year
Nevada	Broker	2600	N/A	0	No	Yes	No	Yes	2yr	Yes	Dec 31st each year
New Hampshire	Broker	500	0	20,000	No	No	No	Yes	3yr out of 5yr	Yes	Nov 31st every year
New Jersey	1ST Broker	1000	50,000	100,000	Yes	Yes	Yes	Yes	none	Yes	every 2 years
New Jersey	2nd Broker	600	50,000	50,000	Yes	Yes	Yes	Yes	none	Yes	every 2 years

FIGURE 14.7 (Continued)

State	License Type	State Fee	Net Worth	Surety Bond	Audited Financial Statement?	Physical Office?	Test Required?	Loan Officer License Required?	Experience	Branch Licensing?	Renewal Period
New Mexico	Loan Company	400	0	25,000	No	No	No	No	none	free to register & will issue a lic.	1 year
New York	Broker	1500	0	10,000	No	No	No	Yes	2 years	Yes	March 1st every year
North Carolina	Broker/Lender	1850	25,000 (Broker), 100,000 (Lender)	50,000 (Broker), 150,000 (Lender)	No	Yes Broker, No Lender	Yes	Yes	3 years	Yes	Dec 31st every year
North Dakota	Money Broker	500	0	25,000	No	No	No	No		No	
Ohio	1st	350	N/A	50,000	No	Yes	Yes	Yes	3 in 5	Yes	Dec 31st each year
Oklahoma	Broker	300	N/A	0	No	Yes	Yes	Yes	3 years	Yes	
Oklahoma	Supervised Lender	350	25,000	5,000	No	No	No	No		Yes	
Oregon	Broker	825	N/A	$25,000 plus $5000 per branch	No	No	Yes	Yes	3 years in past 5	Yes	every 2 years
Pennsylvania	1st Broker	500		0	No	Yes	No	No	none but reviewed	Yes	July 1st each year
Pennsylvania	2nd Broker	500	0	0	No	Yes	No	No		Yes	
Rhode Island	Broker	550	10,000	10,000 plus 5,000 per branch	No	No	No	No	5	Yes	Mar 31 / sub to change
South Carolina	Broker	750	N/A	10,000	No	Yes	No	Yes	2yr with exeptions	Yes	Sept 30th each year
South Dakota	Broker	365	N/A	25,000	No	No	No	No	2yr	No	Nov 1st every year
Tennessee	Broker	600	25,000 plus 25k per branch	90,000	Reviewed	No	No	Yes	1 to 3 yrs reviewed	Yes	1yr Nov 1 $500

FIGURE 14.7 *(Continued)*

State	License Type	State Fee	Net Worth	Surety Bond	Audited Financial Statement?	Physical Office?	Test Required?	Loan Officer License Required?	Experience	Branch Licensing?	Renewal Period
Texas	Broker	434	25,000	Only if net worth isn't $25k	No	Yes	Yes	Yes	3 years	Yes	1 year
Utah	1st broker	276	N/A	0	No	No	Yes	Yes	3years	Yes	2yr from issue. 6 wks. prior to exp date
Utah	2nd Notification	100	0	0	No	No	Yes	Yes	3 years	Yes	
Vermont	Broker	500	0	10,000 plus 25k per branch	No	No	No	No	reviewed	Yes	Dec 1st every year
Virginia	Broker	500	0	25,000	No	No	No	No	reviewed	Yes	Annual Report, no renewal
Washington	Broker	372	N/A	20k-60k depending on L/O's	No	No	Yes	Yes	2 years	Yes	1 year from issue
Washington D.C.	Broker	1100	10,000	Based on Loan Volumes; $12,500 to $50,000	No	No	No	No	No	Yes	1 year
West Virginia	Broker	350	10,000	50,000 in-state or 100,000 out of state	No	No	No	Yes	2yr	Yes	Oct 1st every year
Wisconsin	Broker	1000	250,000	120,000 (unless located in WI)	No	No	No	Yes	one but reviewed	No	2 years from issue
Wyoming	Broker	500	N/A	25,000	No	No	No	No		Yes	

The prerequisites for registration application include 20 units of pre-licensing education that include 3 units of federal law, 3 units of ethics, 2 hours of nontraditional mortgage products, 4 units of Arizona loan related law (title, appraisal, real estate, etc., as it relates to the loan industry), and 8 units of other loan-related courses (FHA, VA, appraisal, etc.). The state license also requires 75% or higher on the national and state test. Each applicant may not have been convicted of a felony during the past 7 years or of any crime of breach of trust or dishonesty, fraud, or money laundering at any time. Every mortgage loan originator must be covered under a surety bond or recovery fund by either paying $100 to the recovery fund at the time of application, or having their employer provide evidence of a surety bond of not less than $200,000. The employer must have a loan broker or banker license.

Iowa

Who is required to have the Iowa Mortgage Loan Originator License? Any individual who in expectation of or for compensation takes a residential loan application or offers or negotiates terms for a residential loan.

Exempt is an individual who is not an independent contractor loan processor or underwriter, who solely is involved in extensions of credit relating to timeshare plans, and who is employed as a loan servicer and involved in loss mitigation efforts. A "registered" loan originator who is an employee of a depository institution regulated by a farm credit administration and regulated by a federal banking agency is exempt. Also exempt is an individual who only performs real estate brokerage activities and is licensed with the state and is not compensated for any part of a loan.

The prerequisites for registration application include a national criminal background check, an authorized independent credit report, education and passing the National and state exams with at least 75%. Education requirements are 20 hours of approved pre-license that include 3 hours of federal law and regulations pertaining to residential loan origination, 3 hours of ethics that include fraud, consumer protection and fair lending issues, and 2 hours related to lending standards for the nontraditional loan product market.

Idaho

Who is required to have an Idaho Mortgage Loan Originator License? Any person who, for expectation of compensation or gain, directly or indirectly takes a residential loan application or modification, or offers/negotiates terms for a residential loan or loan modification. Exempt is a licensed attorney or a registered loan originator who acts on behalf of a depository institution regulated by a federal banking agency or by the farm credit administration.

The prerequisites for license application include $100 paid to the recovery fund and may not be sponsored by or perform loan acts for more than one Idaho broker/lender. Education requirements include 10 hours of pre-license course instruction, consisting of a minimum of 3 hours of federal law and regulation, 3 hours of ethics (including fraud, consumer protection and fair lending), 2 hours of lending standards for nontraditional mortgages, 2 hours directly related to Idaho residential mortgage practices, and 10 hours of additional approved courses. The individual must pass the National and Idaho State Component test with a minimum score of 75%.

Mississippi

Who is required to have the Mississippi Loan Originator Registration? An individual **employee** of a licensed mortgage broker/lender whose conduct of the loan business is the responsibility of the company, and whose job responsibilities include direct contact with borrowers during the loan origination process (including soliciting, negotiating, acquiring, arranging or making loans for others, assisting in preparation of the loan application or other documents, quoting loan rates or terms, or providing required disclosures). Exempt is a person acting as a loan processor, doing clerical duties in connection with a residential loan transaction.

The prerequisites for registration application include a criminal background and fingerprint check. Experience requirements include documentation of a minimum of one year of experience directly in lending in Mississippi within the past two years of date of the application. If the applicant does not meet that criteria, the individual must complete a minimum of 24 hours of pre-license education. If the person has one year of experience, but not in the state, the individual must complete four hours of Mississippi loan Consumer Protection Law.

New Hampshire

Who is required to have the New Hampshire Mortgage Loan Originator License? Any individual who in expectation of or for direct or indirect compensation or gain takes a loan application or offers, negotiates, solicits, arranges or finds a loan, or who assists a consumer in obtaining or applying to obtain a loan, or advising on loan terms (including rates, fees and other costs), preparing loan packages or collecting information on behalf of the loan. A sole proprietor licensed as a loan broker, servicer, or loan banker shall also obtain a license. A loan processor or underwriter who is an independent contractor requires a license. No individual may act as an originator for more than one licensee.

Exempt is a person who performs clerical or support duties as an employee of a licensed originator, a person solely involved in extensions of credit relating to timeshare plans, and loan originators who are employees of a depository institution regulated by the Farm Credit Administration AND regulated by a federal banking agency. Also exempt is a person who only performs real estate brokerage activities and is licensed or registered in accordance with applicable state law, unless compensated by a lender, loan broker, servicer, or other loan originator.

The prerequisites for license applications include the following list:

- Net worth—No
- Bond amount— No
- Criminal background check—Yes, as of 7/31/09 through the NMLS
- Credit check—Yes, as of 7/31/09 through the NMLS
- Experience—No

- Testing—Yes, as of 7/31/09 through the NMLS
- Education—Yes, as of 7/31/09 through the NMLS
- Home state licensing or registration

New Mexico

Any natural person in expectation or for compensation or gain, directly or indirectly takes a loan application, negotiates or offers to negotiate the terms of a loan; and is employed or associated with not more than one loan company licensee regulated by the Division.

Any processor or underwriter who is an independent contractor.

Exempt is a registered loan originator who acts for an entity that meets the definition of loan originator and when the individual is an employee of a depository institution, a subsidiary that is owned and controlled by a depository institution and regulated by a federal banking agency, or an institution regulated by the farm credit administration; an individual who offers or negotiates terms of a residential loan with or on behalf of an immediate family member of the individual; an individual who offers or negotiates terms of a real property sale financed in whole or in part by the seller and secured by the seller's real property; a licensed attorney; a clerical or support loan processor employee under supervision of a licensed person.

The prerequisites for license applications include the following:

- Education—20 hours of pre-licensing education, including 3 hours of New Mexico specific education.
- Testing—at least 75% on both the national and state exam
- Background check with fingerprints
- Credit report
- Surety bond. A bond in the amount of $50,000 is required for the first year licensed as a loan originator. After the first year, it is based on:
  - $0 – $3,000,000 = $50,000 surety bond
  - > $3,000,000, < $10,000,000 = $100,000 surety bond
  - > $10,000,000 = $150,000 surety bond

North Carolina

Who is required to have the North Carolina Mortgage Loan Originator License? An individual in expectation or for compensation or gain whether through contact by telephone, by electronic means, by mail, or in person with prospective borrowers, either takes a loan application, offers to negotiate terms for a residential loan, accepts or offers to accept a loan application, solicits or offers to solicit a loan, negotiates the terms or conditions of a loan, or issues loan commitments or interest rate guarantee agreements to prospective borrowers.

Exempt is an individual engaged solely as a loan processor or underwriter, a person who performs real estate brokerage activities and is licensed by the state who does not do loans, a person who extends credit or sells time share plans, and an individual who is a salesperson for a licensed manufactured housing retailer.

Also exempt is a person who only informs a prospective borrower of the availability of persons engaged in the loan business, does not take or assist in the completion of a loan application, and does not discuss specific terms or conditions of a loan.

The prequalifications for license application include 24 hours of pre-license education of which 20 hours must be live classroom, must pass the national and state exams, submit valid fingerprint card, and submit an Authorization for Release of Information form.

Pennsylvania

Who is required to have the Pennsylvania Mortgage Originator License? Partners with 10% or more equity ownership, or directors of a licensed mortgage loan business who originate loans, individuals originating loans secured by manufactured or mobile homes, individual originating residential construction loans, loan originators who are employees of affiliates of banking institutions or credit unions, agents, as independent contractors, who originate loans for banking institutions or credit unions, individuals who originate fewer than three loans in a calendar year, originators employed by an agency of the federal government or a corporation created by an act of Congress, originators employed by an agency of a state or local government, including the Pennsylvania Housing Finance Agency, originators of nonprofit corporations who hold themselves out to the public as engaged in the loan business, independent loan processors or underwriters, an individual who re-negotiates an existing loan, including loan modifications and an originator who is an employee of a single mortgage broker, lender, or loan correspondent who is licensed by the Pennsylvania department.

Exempt are federal government agencies, banking institutions, credit unions, consumer discount companies, and non-profit corporations who do fewer than 12 loans in a calendar year with its own funds.

The prequalifications for license application include a criminal background check, credit check, tax certification, education, and the state and federal exam with at least 75% correct. Education requires 20 hours of pre-license education to include:

- 3 hours of federal law and regulation
- 3 hours of ethics, consumer protection and fair lending
- 2 hours of lending standards for the nontraditional mortgage marketplace
- 3 hours of Pennsylvania law and regulations
- 9 hours of elective courses related to the mortgage industry

Virginia

Who is required to have the Virginia Mortgage Loan Originator License? Individuals who take a loan application or offer or negotiate the terms of a residential loan containing 1 to 4 units, including a condominium unit, cooperative unit, mobile home, or trailer that is used as a residence. Individuals acting as loan originators who are employees or exclusive agents of licensed loan lender/brokers and whose employees or exclusive agents of persons exempt from licensure, and those who are not employees or exclusive agents of persons licensed or exempt from the licensing law.

Exempt are individuals who perform administrative or clerical tasks on behalf of a licensed lender or broker who is a loan originator, licensed real estate brokers, if they do not do loan originations, persons solely involved in extensions of credit relating to timeshare plans, an individual who negotiates with or on behalf of an immediate family member, a licensed attorney, and an individual performing activities as an employee of a loan servicer. Also exempt is a registered mortgage loan originator, who meets the definition of loan originator and is an employee of a depository institution, a subsidiary of a depository institution and regulated by a federal banking agency, or an institution regulated by the Farm Credit Administration.

The prequalifications for license application include a surety bond, fingerprint cards and criminal background check, pre-license education, passing the national and state exam, and a finding of financial responsibility, and character and general fitness, including a satisfactory credit report. The surety bond amount requirements are based upon loan volume for the bond amount.

Loan Volume	Bond Amount
$0–$5,000,000	$ 25,000
$5,000,000–$20,000,000	$ 50,000
$20,000,000–$50,000,000	$ 75,000
$50,000,000–$100,000,000	$100,000
Over–$100,000,000	$150,000

Washington

Who is required to have the Washington Loan Originator License? An individual who offers loans to Washington State citizens or for property in Washington State, including employees and independent contractors; an individual who represents a Washington State licensed consumer loan company; or, an individual who represents a credit union service organization.

Exempt is a designed broker for a Washington licensed mortgage broker, an employee of a Washington State-licensed consumer loan company or if the individual represents a depository institution (bank or credit union).

The prerequisite for the license includes:

- Net worth—not unique to the loan originator (LO)
- Bond amount—not unique to the loan originator (LO)
- Criminal background check—yes (completed by the Department of Financial Institutions)
- Credit check—yes (completed by the Department of Financial Institutions)
- Experience—no
- Testing—yes
- Education—yes

SUMMARY

The California Department of Real Estate (DRE) regulates the actions of the non-licensed individual who performs acts that do not require a license and for those individuals that do perform acts for which a license is required. A review of the salesperson and broker license requirements, along with the DRE Corporation license, license renewal, and continuing education are? covered in this chapter. The employment agreement, business office and branch office information, along with the prohibitions and penalties for violation of the laws are reviewed, as well as required broker supervision.

The California Codes and Regulations for licensees gave data on real estate law references when the person is acting as an agent, as a principal, and as a lender. The timeline compliance and document review requirements are outlined, along with the most common DRE violations.

The last part of this chapter is a review of the new federal SAFE ACT for residential mortgage loan originators (MLO) effective January 1, 2010. The license requirements for various U.S. states and licensing agencies is discussed with some information for individual states, because loan brokers often work multi-state.

REVIEWING YOUR UNDERSTANDING

1. Which one of the following does not require a Real Estate Broker's license:
   A. Soliciting borrowers for loans and soliciting lenders for loans.
   B. Buying or offering to buy a promissory note secured by a lien on real property.
   C. Performing services for the promissory note holder secured by a lien on real property.
   D. Contacting a title insurance company for a property profile.

2. To obtain a real estate broker license, the individual must complete _____ college level courses:
   A. 3
   B. 5
   C. 6
   D. 8

3. The most common DRE violations is in the area of:
   A. Business & Profession code
   B. False or Fictitious name
   C. Commingling of funds
   D. Trust funds violations

4. The Secure And Fair Enforcement Act (SAFE) is part of:
   A. Housing and Economic Recovery Act
   B. National Housing Act
   C. Conference of State Bank Supervisors Act
   D. Nationwide Mortgage Licensing System and Registry Act

5. The DRE licensee regulations for the mortgage loan broker would be found in the:
   A. Business and Professions Code
   B. Health and Safety Code
   C. Loan Service Regulations
   D. IRS and Franchise Board regulations

6. Every broker must have a written agreement with each salesperson and each party must keep a copy of the agreement for:
   A. 1 year
   B. 2 years
   C. 3 years
   D. 4 years

7. A broker must have and maintain a definite place of business. It may be located in:
   A. Any office building
   B. In a mobile home or personal residence
   C. In the broker's personal residence, mobile home or office building
   D. Can never be in the brokers personal residence

8. A broker may delegate the review process to a licensed salesperson if they have accumulated at least _____ years full-time experience during the preceding five-year period with the same designated broker.
   A. Two
   B. Three
   C. Four
   D. Salesperson does not need any more than one year of experience to be able to review documents.

9. Activities that do not require a DRE license include:
   A. Participation in office training sessions on loan processing or servicing.
   B. Keeping records on loans, including principal, interest, taxes, or insurance.
   C. Contact with real estate licensees to obtain recent sales data and financing terms.
   D. Any of the above items do not require a license to perform.

10. A broker is prohibited from compensating a person not licensed by the California DRE who is performing act that do require a license. The broker may be fined up to _____ by the real estate commissioner, as assessed after a hearing has been held.
    A. $15,000
    B. $20,000
    C. $30,000
    D. $60,000

ANSWERS TO REVIEWING YOUR UNDERSTANDING

1. D (p. 433)   4. A (p. 449)   7. C (p. 439)   10. B (p. 440)
2. D (p. 435)   5. A (p. 442)   8. D (p. 442)
3. D (p. 447)   6. C (p. 438)   9. D (p. 432)

Chapter

15

Math and Trust Funds for the Loan Agent

PREVIEW

Many facets of the loan business include using various math computations. Many real estate students begin in the loan business and find that they need to become more proficient in math. This chapter covers the common areas of real estate mathematics used by loan agents, including the use of a financial calculator, loan-to-value (LTV) ratio, debt ratio, amount of interest paid throughout the life of a loan, reading a payment factor chart, loan comparison, and legal requirements for handling of trust fund accounting records.

CHAPTER OBJECTIVES

At the end of this chapter, the student learning outcomes include:

1. Determine maximum loan amount and sales price, including LTV ratio.
2. Calculate the buyer qualifying ratios: front-end ratio and back-end ratio.
3. Read a payment factor chart to determine the total monthly payment.
4. Compare different loan amortization schedules for alternative loans.
5. Contrast alternative financing programs, including second and third trust deeds, and private-party carryback financing.
6. Use a financial calculator to obtain annual percentage rate (APR).
7. Determine the investor's rate of return for a real estate loan.
8. Maintain DRE trust fund account record logs of client funds.
9. Differentiate between trust funds and non-trust funds.
10. Outline trust fund bank account requirements for record-keeping.

15.1 INTRODUCTION

The loan agent is expected to use mathematic calculations daily for loan purposes. Many sales agents rely on the loan agent to do the math for their client. This chapter shows keystrokes for various financial calculators in addition to reading manual payment factor and amortization charts. As the market changes, so do the loan programs offered. This chapter examines many alternative ways to do a loan.

The first half of this chapter will calculate various typical loan computations encountered by the loan agent in the normal course of business, such as LTV ratio and loan payment. For calculation purposes, the primary example used throughout the sample problems that follow are based on the escrow instructions as found in Appendix D and other appendix documents, with a sales price based upon the appraised value of $425,500.

Several different types of loan programs are represented so that amortization comparison may be made between required total cash to close escrow and monthly loan payments for the first several years of the loan and for the ending years of the loan. The examples used are (1) 15-year, fully amortized loan at 7¼ percent interest; (2) 30-year, fully amortized loan at 7½ percent interest; (3) 30-year, fully amortized loan, adding one extra payment per year, payable with an extra one-twelfth per month increase in the monthly payment (equal to 13 payments per year instead of 12 payments per year, but paid in 12 payments); (4) 30-year, fully amortized loan at 7½ percent, but at the end of each year calculating an increased monthly payment by 4½ percent, so that the first 12 months' payments remain the original contract monthly payment but each subsequent year begins with a once-a-year increase in the monthly payment at month 13, month 25, month 37, month 49, month 61, etc.; (5) 30-year, fully amortized interest only for the first five years and then fully amortized for the remaining 25 years; (6) comparison of two conventional loans in which the buyer places 10 percent cash down payment and obtains either a 90 percent first trust deed with required PMI or an 80 percent conventional first trust deed with a 10 percent second trust deed without PMI; (7) private party carryback financing; and (8) two-step mortgage.

The California DRE and DOC licensing agencies audit files to determine whether disclosure of the correct mathematical numbers has been represented to the principal/borrower—the public. Basic debit and credit accounting for the handling of client funds is not only expected but also required. The occurrence of a trust fund violation is the most common government agency citation against licensees.

15.2 LTV RATIO

The **LTV Ratio** is the amount of the loan in relationship to the value of the property, expressed as a percentage. For example, the LTV for the $425,500 appraised value for a property for which the buyer puts a 20 percent cash down payment would be:

$425,500	=	the appraised value of the property
−85,100	=	down payment of 20%
$340,400	=	amount of new loan

$340,400 divided by $425,500 = 80% LTV

15.3 BORROWER QUALIFYING INCOME

The monthly payment used to qualify a borrower consists of adding the association dues (A), principal (P), interest (I), property taxes (P), insurance (I), and mortgage insurance (MI) together. The borrower usually pays the association dues separately. The property taxes and insurance may be paid by the lender and collected with the monthly payment, or the borrower may pay it separately. The mortgage loan broker must qualify the applicant according to the total expenses, regardless of how the payments are made or by whom. A common learning tool is the saying, "PITI MI," pronounced pity me. Other payments may be required according to specific loan criteria (CalVet life insurance premium) or property location (land lease payment, flood insurance, earthquake insurance).

Front-End Ratio

The front-end ratio consists of the total housing expense in relationship to the borrower's gross income. For example, using the $425,500 value, with a 20% down payment, the loan amount would be $340,400. For a 30-year loan at 7.5%, the principal and interest payment is $2,380.13.

Front-End Ratio
2,380.13 PI (340,400 × [6.992145 7.5%, 30-yr.]) see (Figure 15.1)
443.23 T (425,500 × 1.25%), 12 =
99.28 I (340,400 × 0.35%), 12 =
$2,922.64 PITI (Total Housing Expense)

The next step is to divide the housing expense by the borrower's total gross income. Using the information in Figure 6.3, the example shows the gross monthly income is $10,852. To determine front-end ratio, divide $2,922.64 PITI by $10,852, which equals 27 percent. For conventional financing, using the ratios shown in Figure 6.12, the borrower would qualify for an 80 percent loan because the ratio is 27 percent. FNMA indicates that the front-end ratio for a borrower may not have more than 32 percent total housing debt for 80 percent loan. However, for the 90 percent LTV, the investor would use the lower ratio of 28/36, as shown in Figure 6.13. For FHA financing, the maximum front-end ratio, as shown in Figure 6.10, should not exceed 29 percent. For a VA-approved financing program, as shown in Figure 6.7, no front-end ratio is used. This borrower is qualified because the ratio is lower and does not exceed the maximum debt ratio.

FIGURE 15.1   Principal and interest payment factors for a 15- and a 30-year loan.

RATE	15-YEAR P&I FACTOR	30-YEAR P&I FACTOR	RATE	15-YEAR P&I FACTOR	30-YEAR P&I FACTOR
4.000	7.396879	4.7744153	8.500	9.847396	7.689135
4.125	7.459676	4.846497	8.625	9.920804	7.777897
4.250	7.522784	4.919399	8.750	9.994487	7.867004
4.375	7.586204	4.992853	8.875	10.068441	7.956449
4.500	7.649933	5.066853	9.000	10.142666	8.046226
4.625	7.713972	5.141395	9.125	10.217160	8.136330
4.750	7.778320	5.216474	9.250	10.291923	8.226754
4.875	7.842974	5.292082	9.375	10.366952	8.317494
5.000	7.907937	5.368216	9.500	10.442247	8.408542
5.125	7.973204	5.444870	9.625	10.517805	8.499894
5.250	8.038777	5.522037	9.750	10.593627	8.591544
5.375	8.104655	5.599713	9.875	10.669709	8.683486
5.500	8.170835	5.677890	10.000	10.746051	8.775716
5.625	8.237317	5.756564	10.125	10.822652	8.868226
5.750	8.304101	5.835729	10.250	10.899509	8.961013
5.875	8.371185	5.915378	10.375	10.976622	9.054070
6.000	8.438568	5.995505	10.500	11.053989	9.147393
6.125	8.506250	6.076105	10.625	11.131609	9.240976
6.250	8.574229	6.157172	10.750	11.209480	9.334814
6.500	8.711074	6.320680	10.875	11.287600	9.428901
6.625	8.779938	6.403110	11.000	11.365969	9.523234
6.750	8.849095	6.485981	11.125	11.444585	9.617806
6.875	8.918543	6.569288	11.250	11.523446	9.712614
7.000	8.988283	6.653025	11.375	11.602551	9.807651
7.125	9.058312	6.737185	11.500	11.681898	9.902914
7.250	9.128629	6.821763	11.625	11.761486	9.998398
7.375	9.199233	6.906751	11.750	11.841314	10.094097
7.500	9.270124	6.992145	11.875	11.921379	10.190008
7.625	9.341299	7.077937	12.000	12.001681	10.286126
7.750	9.412758	7.164122	12.125	12.082217	10.382446
7.875	9.484499	7.250694	12.250	12.162987	10.478964
8.000	9.556521	7.337646	12.375	12.243989	10.575676
8.125	9.628823	7.424972	12.500	12.325221	10.672578
8.250	9.701404	7.512666	12.675	12.406682	10.769664
8.375	9.774262	7.600722	12.750	12.488370	10.866932
			12.875	12.570284	10.964377

Back-End Ratio

The **back-end ratio** consists of the total housing expense plus long-term install-ment and revolving debt, usually with payments of at least six or nine months remaining. The Martinez family has $389 monthly car payment with their credit union and a car payment of $106 to ABC Car Sales and total credit card debt of

$3,500 total unpaid balance with a minimum of 5 percent monthly payment, $150 per month. This results in $645 per month for long-term, nonhousing debt.

To obtain the back-end ratio, add the total housing expense ($2,922.64 PITI) and the total long-term debt of $645 together, for a total that equals $3,567.64. Next divide the $3,567.64 total debt by the $10,852 gross monthly income, which results in a 33.0 percent back-end ratio. For conventional financing, the maximum allowable debt ratio for an 80 percent loan is 38 percent, and therefore the Martinez family would qualify for this loan because their 33 percent is less than the 38 percent maximum allowed.

15.4 PAYMENT FACTOR CHART

The mortgage loan broker may have to read a **payment factor** chart, as is shown in Figure 15.1, the principal and interest factors chart. The chart shows both 15-year and 30-year amortization periods for a loan amount of $1,000, showing interest rates from 4 percent to 12.875 percent. To read this chart, the loan broker would read down the column to locate the interest rate in question, which is located on the left side of the chart under header labeled Rate; then, read across to either the 15-year or 30-year P&I Factor. The loan amount is then multiplied by the payment Rate factor. The resulting answer will then need to be changed to reflect the actual loan payment by moving the decimal point three places to the left, or by dividing the answer by 1,000. This payment factor chart is beneficial when a financial calculator is not available or when a visual-learner borrower wants to "see" how to obtain the payment. Also, to obtain a copy of a payment factor amortization book you may search several online sources or contact your local title insurance company, which may furnish you with a copy of the tables and charts.

For example, using the $425,500 sales price for the Martinez family, with an 80% loan, the loan amount would be $340,400 at 7.5 percent interest. The payment factor for 15 years would be 9.270124, and for 30 years it would be 6.992145.

For the 15-year loan, multiply the $340,400 × 9.270124 (factor for 15 years) = 3,155,550.21. Move the decimal three places to the left or divide by 1,000. The monthly PI payment would be $3,155.55.

For the 30-year loan, multiply the $340,400 × 6.992145 (factor for 30 years) = 2,380,126.16. Move the decimal three places to the left or divide by 1,000. The monthly PI payment would be $2,380.13.

The difference between the $3,155.55 and the $2,380.13 is $775.42 per month, or $9,305.04 per year. During the life of the loan, the extra $775 a month payment generates savings to the borrower of just under $300,000, as shown below:

Payment		Months		Annual		Term		
$2,380.13	×	12	=	$28,561.56	×	30	=	$856,846.80
$3,155.55	×	12	=	$37,866.60	×	15	=	$567,999.00
				Savings difference				$288,847.80

15.5 AMORTIZATION COMPARISON

This section compares many different types of amortization schedules for the same borrower, using the same 20 percent cash down payment and obtaining an 80 percent new conventional loan. This example is shown so that the learner may compare and contrast the results for a borrower so the loan broker may be better able to comprehend and explain the options available. Many examples are shown individually, with an explanation of the differences between the various loans describing the conclusions. In addition, one example shows a comparison between two conventional loans when the buyer has only 10 percent cash for a down payment and the effects on the buyer if mortgage insurance is required for the loan.

A summary of the examples listed below is for a loan with an original principal unpaid loan amount of $340,400, followed by a more detailed explanation and math chart for each type of loan. Example 1 is a 15-year, fully amortized loan at 7¼ percent interest, as shown in Figure 15.2, because a 15-year loan is normally offered at a lower interest rate to the borrower. All of the other examples (Figures 15.3–15.6) are at 7½ percent interest because they are 30-year loans, except when a second and third trust deed is involved. The higher the risk, the higher the rate of interest charged.

Figure 15.2 Example 1: (Term: 15-year, fully amortized) (Rate: fixed, 7¼% interest).

Figure 15.3 Example 2: (Term: 30-year, fully amortized) (Rate: fixed, 7½% interest).

Figure 15.4 Example 3: (Term: 30-year, fully amortized) (Rate: fixed, 7½% interest) paying one extra payment per year.

Figure 15.5 Example 4: (Term: 30-year, fully amortized) (Rate 7½% interest) paying an extra 4½% per year beginning in year 2.

Figure 15.6 Example 5: (Term: 30-year, fully amortized) (Rate 7½% interest) paying interest only for the first five years.

Example 6: (Term: 30-year, fully amortized) (Rate 7½% interest).

Comparing a 90 percent LTV first trust deed loan with mortgage insurance to a loan with an 80 percent LTV first at 7½ percent and a 10 percent LTV second trust deed at 9½ percent with no mortgage insurance.

Example 7: Private-party carryback financing, with three loans (Term: 30-year, fully amortized first trust deed) (Rate 7¾%), plus (second trust deed amortized over 30 years, but due in 15 years) (Rate 9%) plus (third trust deed, interest only/straight note, due in 5 years) (Rate 11%).

Example 8: Two-step mortgage, private party carryback (Term: existing fully amortized first trust deed, 25 years remaining, paid off in one year upon re-financing) (Rate: 7½ percent interest), plus (Term: new second trust deed, straight note, due in one year) (Rate: 10%).

FIGURE 15.2   Example 1: $340,400 principal at 7 1/4% for a 15-year loan.

15 Year

Compound Period:	Monthly	Nominal Annual Rate:	7.250
Effective Annual Rate:	7.496	Periodic Rate:	0.6042
Daily Rate:	0.01986		

Event	Start Date	Amount	Number	Period	End Date
1 Loan	10/1/2005	340,400.00	1		
Points 1.500		5,106.00			
Prorate Days 16 @ 68.55		1,096.84			
Other Charges		0.00			
2 Payment	01/31/2005	3,107.39	180	Monthly	10/01/2020

Amortization Schedule—Normal Amortization

Loan	10/01/2005				340,400.00
2005 Totals		**0.00**	**0.00**	**0.00**	
	Date	Payment	Interest	Principal	Balance
1	11/01/2005	3,107.39	2,056.58	1,050.81	339,349.19
2	12/01/2005	3,107.39	2,050.23	1,057.16	338,292.03
2005 Totals		**6,214.78**	**4,106.81**	**2,107.97**	
3	01/1/2006	3,107.39	2,043.85	1,063.54	337,228.49
4	02/1/2006	3,107.39	2,037.42	1,069.97	336,158.52
5	03/1/2006	3,107.39	2,030.96	1,076.43	335,082.09
6	04/1/2006	3,107.39	2,024.45	1,082.94	333,999.15
7	05/1/2006	3,107.39	2,017.91	1,089.48	332,909.67
8	06/1/2006	3,107.39	2,011.33	1,096.06	331,813.61
9	07/1/2006	3,107.39	2,004.71	1,102.68	330,710.93
10	08/1/2006	3,107.39	1,998.05	1,109.34	329,601.59
11	09/1/2006	3,107.39	1,991.34	1,116.05	328,485.54
12	10/1/2006	3,107.39	1,984.60	1,122.79	327,362.75
2006 Totals		**37,288.68**	**24,093.43**	**13,195.25**	
171	01/1/2020	3,107.39	181.64	2,925.75	27,138.50
172	02/1/2020	3,107.39	163.96	2,943.43	24,195.07
173	03/1/2020	3,107.39	146.18	2,961.21	21,233.86
174	04/1/2020	3,107.39	128.29	2,979.10	18,254.76
175	05/1/2020	3,107.39	110.29	2,997.10	15,257.66
176	06/1/2020	3,107.39	92.18	3,015.21	12,242.45
177	07/1/2020	3,107.39	73.96	3,033.43	9,209.02
178	08/1/2020	3,107.39	55.64	3,051.75	6,157.27
179	09/1/2020	3,107.39	37.20	3,070.19	3,087.08
180	10/1/2020	3,107.39	20.31	3,087.08	0.00
2020 Totals		**31,073.90**	**1,009.65**	**30,064.25**	
Grand Totals	**After 2020**	**559,330.20**	**218,930.20**	**340,400**	

FIGURE 15.3   Example 2: Fully amortized loan at $340,400 principal, 7½% interest, 30-year loan.

Compound Period:	Monthly	Nominal Annual Rate:	7.500
Effective Annual Rate:	7.763	Periodic Rate:	0.6250
Daily Rate:	0.02055		

Cash Flow Data:

Event	Start Date	Amount	Number	Period	End Date
1 Loan	10/1/2005	340,400.00	1		
Points 1.500		5,106.00			
Prepaid Days 30 @ 35.42					
Other Charges		0.00			
2 Payment	11/1/2005	2,380.13	360	Monthly	10/1/2035

Amortization Schedule—Normal Amortization

Loan	10/1/2005				340,400.00
2005 Totals		0.00	0.00	0.00	
	Date	Payment	Interest	Principal	Balance
1	11/1/2005	2,380.13	2,127.50	252.63	340,147.37
2	12/1/2005	2,380.13	2,125.92	254.21	339,893.16
2005 Totals		**4,760.26**	**4,253.42**	**506.84**	
3	01/1/2006	2,380.13	2,124.33	255.80	339,637.36
4	02/1/2006	2,380.13	2,122.73	257.40	339,379.96
5	03/1/2006	2,380.13	2,121.12	259.01	339,120.95
6	04/1/2006	2,380.13	2,119.51	260.62	338,860.33
7	05/1/2006	2,380.13	2,117.88	262.25	338,598.08
8	06/1/2006	2,380.13	2,116.24	263.89	338,334.19
9	07/1/2006	2,380.13	2,114.59	265.54	338,068.65
10	08/1/2006	2,380.13	2,112.93	267.20	337,801.45
11	09/1/2006	2,380.13	2,111.26	268.87	337,532.58
12	10/1/2006	2,380.13	2,109.58	270.55	337,262.03
2006 Totals		**28,561.56**	**25,384.25**	**3,177.31**	
171	01/1/2020	2,380.13	1,651.53	728.60	263,516.87
172	02/1/2020	2,380.13	1,646.98	733.15	262,783.72
173	03/1/2020	2,380.13	1,642.40	737.73	262,045.99
174	04/1/2020	2,380.13	1,637.79	742.34	261,303.65
175	05/1/2020	2,380.13	1,633.15	746.98	260,556.67
176	06/1/2020	2,380.13	1,628.48	751.65	259,805.02
177	07/1/2020	2,380.13	1,623.78	756.35	259,048.67
178	08/1/2020	2,380.13	1,619.05	761.08	258,287.59
179	09/1/2020	2,380.13	1,614.30	765.83	257,521.76
180	10/1/2020	2,380.13	1,609.51	770.62	256,751.14
181	11/1/2020	2,380.13	1,604.69	775.44	255,975.70
182	12/1/2020	2,380.13	1,599.85	780.28	255,195.42
2020 Totals		**28,561.56**	**19,511.51**	**9,050.05**	
Grand Totals	**After 2020**	**856,846.80**	**516,446.80**	**340,400.00**	

FIGURE 15.4 Example 3: $340,400 principal at 7.5% for a 30-year loan paying one extra payment per year.

30 Year

Compound Period:	Monthly	Nominal Annual Rate:	7.500
Effective Annual Rate:	7.763	Periodic Rate:	0.6250
Daily Rate:	0.02055		

Cash Flow Data:

Event	Start Date	Amount	Number	Period	End Date
1 Loan	10/1/2005	340,400.00	1		
Points 1.500		5,106.00			
Prepaid Days 30 @ 35.42					
Other Charges		0.00			
2 Payment	11/1/2005	2,578.47	279	Monthly	01/01/2029
3 Payment	02/1/2029	2,164.44	1		

Amortization Schedule

Loan	10/1/2005				340,400.00
2005 Totals		0.00	0.00	0.00	
	Date	Payment	Interest	Principal	Balance
1	11/1/2005	2,578.47	2,127.50	450.97	339,949.03
2	12/1/2005	2,578.47	2,124.68	453.79	339,495.24
2005 Totals		5,156.94	4,252.18	904.76	
3	01/1/2006	2,578.47	2,121.85	456.62	339,038.62
4	02/1/2006	2,578.47	2,118.99	459.48	338,579.14
5	03/1/2006	2,578.47	2,116.12	462.35	338,116.79
6	04/1/2006	2,578.47	2,113.23	465.24	337,651.55
7	05/1/2006	2,578.47	2,110.32	468.15	337,183.40
8	06/1/2006	2,578.47	2,107.40	471.07	336,712.33
9	07/1/2006	2,578.47	2,104.45	474.02	336,238.31
10	08/1/2006	2,578.47	2,101.49	476.98	335,761.33
11	09/1/2006	2,578.47	2,098.51	479.96	335,281.37
12	10/1/2006	2,578.47	2,095.51	482.96	334,798.41
2006 Totals		30,941.64	25,269.81	5,671.83	
171	01/1/2020	2,578.47	1,277.85	1,300.62	203,155.86
172	02/1/2020	2,578.47	1,269.72	1,308.75	201,847.11
173	03/1/2020	2,578.47	1,261.54	1,316.93	200,530.18
174	04/1/2020	2,578.47	1,253.31	1,325.16	199,205.02
175	05/1/2020	2,578.47	1,245.03	1,333.44	197,871.58
176	06/1/2020	2,578.47	1,236.70	1,341.77	196,529.81
177	07/1/2020	2,578.47	1,228.31	1,350.16	195,179.65
178	08/1/2020	2,578.47	1,219.87	1,358.60	193,821.05
179	09/1/2020	2,578.47	1,211.38	1,367.09	192,453.96
180	10/1/2020	2,578.47	1,202.84	1,375.63	191,078.33
181	11/1/2020	2,578.47	1,194.24	1,384.23	189,694.10
182	12/1/2020	2,578.47	1,185.59	1,392.88	188,301.22
2020 Totals		30,941.64	14,786.38	16,155.26	
Grand Totals	After 2020	721,557.57	381,157.57	340,400.00	

FIGURE 15.5 Example 4: $340,400 principal at 7.5% for a 30-year loan paying an extra $4\frac{1}{2}$% per year beginning in year 2.

30 Year

Compound Period:	Monthly		Nominal Annual Rate:	7.500
Effective Annual Rate:	7.763		Periodic Rate:	0.6250
Daily Rate:	0.02055			

Cash Flow Data:

Event	Start Date	Amount	Number	Period	End Date
1 Loan	10/1/2005	340,400.00	1		
Points 1.500		5,106.00			
Prepaid Days 30 @ 35.42					
Other Charges		0.00			
2 Payment	11/1/2005	2,380.13	12	Monthly	10/1/2006
3 Payment	11/1/2006	2,487.24	12	Monthly	10/1/2007

Amortization Schedule

Loan	10/01/2005				340,400.00
2005 Totals		**0.00**	**0.00**	**0.00**	
	Date	**Payment**	**Interest**	**Principal**	**Balance**
1	11/1/2005	2,380.13	2,127.50	252.63	340,147.37
2	12/1/2005	2,380.13	2,125.92	254.21	339,893.16
2005 Totals		**4,760.26**	**4,253.42**	**506.84**	
3	01/1/2006	2,380.13	2,124.33	255.80	339,637.36
4	02/1/2006	2,380.13	2,122.73	257.40	339,379.96
5	03/1/2006	2,380.13	2,121.12	259.01	339,120.95
6	04/1/2006	2,380.13	2,119.51	260.62	338,860.33
7	05/1/2006	2,380.13	2,117.88	262.25	338,598.08
8	06/1/2006	2,380.13	2,116.24	263.89	338,334.19
9	07/1/2006	2,380.13	2,114.59	265.54	338,068.65
10	08/1/2006	2,380.13	2,112.93	267.20	337,801.45
11	09/1/2006	2,380.13	2,111.26	268.87	337,532.58
12	10/1/2006	2,380.13	2,109.58	270.55	337,262.03
13	11/1/2006	2,487.24	2,107.89	379.35	336,882.68
14	12/1/2006	2,487.24	2,105.52	381.72	336,500.96
2006 Totals		**28,775.78**	**25,383.58**	**3,392.20**	
171	01/1/2020	4,407.89	367.94	4,039.95	54,830.67
172	02/1/2020	4,407.89	342.69	4,065.20	50,765.47
173	03/1/2020	4,407.89	317.28	4,090.61	46,674.86
174	04/1/2020	4,407.89	291.72	4,116.17	42,558.69
175	05/1/2020	4,407.89	265.99	4,141.90	38,416.79
176	06/1/2020	4,407.89	240.10	4,167.79	34,249.00
177	07/1/2020	4,407.89	214.06	4,193.83	30,055.17
178	08/1/2020	4,407.89	187.84	4,220.05	25,835.12
179	09/1/2020	4,407.89	161.47	4,246.42	21,588.70
180	10/1/2020	4,407.89	134.93	4,272.96	17,315.74
181	11/1/2020	4,606.25	108.22	4,498.03	12,817.71
182	12/1/2020	4,606.25	80.11	4,526.14	8,291.57
2020 Totals		**53,291.40**	**2,712.35**	**50,579.05**	
Grand Totals	**After 2020**	**610,347.30**	**269,947.30**	**340,400.00**	

FIGURE 15.6 Example 5: $340,400 principal at 7.5% for a 30-year loan paying interest only for the first five years.

30 Year

Compound Period:	Monthly	Nominal Annual Rate:	7.500
Effective Annual Rate:	7.763	Periodic Rate:	0.6250
Daily Rate:	0.02055		

Cash Flow Data:

Event	Start Date	Amount	Number	Period	End Date
1 Loan	10/1/2005	340,400.00	1		
Points 1.500		5,106.00			
Prepaid Days 30 @ 35.42					
Other Charges		0.00			
2 Payment	11/1/2005	Interest Only	60	Monthly	10/1/2010
3 Payment	11/1/2010	2,515.53	300	Monthly	10/1/2035

Amortization Schedule

Loan	10/1/2005				340,400.00
2005 Totals		0.00	0.00	0.00	
	Date	Payment	Interest	Principal	Balance
1	11/1/2005	2,127.50	2,127.50	0.00	340,400.00
2	12/1/2005	2,127.50	2,127.50	0.00	340,400.00
2005 Totals		4,255.00	4,255.00	0.00	
3	01/1/2006	2,127.50	2,127.50	0.00	340,400.00
4	02/1/2006	2,127.50	2,127.50	0.00	340,400.00
5	03/1/2006	2,127.50	2,127.50	0.00	340,400.00
6	04/1/2006	2,127.50	2,127.50	0.00	340,400.00
7	05/1/2006	2,127.50	2,127.50	0.00	340,400.00
8	06/1/2006	2,127.50	2,127.50	0.00	340,400.00
9	07/1/2006	2,127.50	2,127.50	0.00	340,400.00
10	08/1/2006	2,127.50	2,127.50	0.00	340,400.00
11	09/1/2006	2,127.50	2,127.50	0.00	340,400.00
12	10/1/2006	2,127.50	2,127.50	0.00	340,400.00
2006 Totals		25,530.00	25,530.00	0.00	
171	01/1/2020	2,515.53	1,745.49	770.04	278,508.18
172	02/1/2020	2,515.53	1,740.68	774.85	277,733.33
173	03/1/2020	2,515.53	1,735.83	779.70	276,953.63
174	04/1/2020	2,515.53	1,730.96	784.57	276,169.06
175	05/1/2020	2,515.53	1,726.06	789.47	275,379.59
176	06/1/2020	2,515.53	1,271.12	794.41	274,585.18
177	07/1/2020	2,515.53	1,716.16	799.37	273,785.81
178	08/1/2020	2,515.53	1,711.16	804.37	272,981.44
179	09/1/2020	2,515.53	1,706.13	809.40	272,172.04
180	10/1/2020	2,515.53	1,701.08	814.45	271,357.59
181	11/1/2020	2,515.53	1,695.98	819.55	270,538.04
182	12/1/2020	2,515.53	1,690.86	824.67	269,713.37
2020 Totals		30,186.36	20,621.51	9,564.85	
Grand Totals	After 2020	882,309.00	541,909.00	340,400.00	

Example 3: A 30-year, fully amortized at 7½ percent interest, shown in Figure 15.4, adding one extra payment per year, payable with an extra one-twelfth per month increase in the monthly payment (equal to 13 payments per year instead of 12 payments per year, but paid in 12 payments).

Example 4: A 30-year loan, fully amortized at 7½ percent is shown in Figure 15.5, in which at the end of each year an increased monthly payment by 4½ percent is calculated, so that the first 12 months' payments remain the original contract monthly payment, but each subsequent year begins with a once-a-year increase in the monthly payment at month 13, month 25, month 37, month 49, month 61, etc.

Example 5: A 30-year, fully amortized loan at 7.5 percent interest, shown in Figure 15.6, with interest-only payments for the first five years and then fully amortized for the remaining 25 years.

Example 6: Comparing a First Trust Deed with Private Mortgage Insurance (PMI) to a First with a Second Trust Deed

This is an example of a comparison of two conventional loans. For one loan, the buyer places 10 percent cash down payment and obtains a 90 percent first trust deed with required **private mortgage insurance (PMI)**, called a 90-10. For the second loan, the buyer obtains an 80 percent conventional first trust deed with a 10 percent second trust deed without PMI, often referred to in the business as an 80-10-10.

Whenever a loan amount exceeds the current maximum FNMA loan limits, it is referred to as a jumbo loan or nonconforming loan. When this occurs, the interest rate is often slightly higher than the rate offered for conforming loan limits. Using the example loan with a sales price equal to the appraised value of $425,500, with interest at 7½ percent and amortized over 30 years, the loan amount would be calculated as follows:

$425,500 × 90% = $382,950 × the interest rate factor of 7.164122, as shown in Figure 15.1. This equals a monthly principal and interest payment of $2,743.50. Because the loan amount is greater than 80%, the lender requires mortgage insurance. The monthly payment, without property taxes or insurance, would be $2,743.50, as shown below.

$2,743.50 PI
165.95 PMI (382,950 × .52% ÷ 12 = $165.95)
$2,909.45(P) + (I) + (MI)

Note that no repayment of the principal amount is tax deductible because it is paying back the original amount borrowed. Thus, the extra $165.95 payment each month is also not tax deductible. Only the interest portion of the payment is deductible for income tax purposes.

In comparison, if the buyer obtains an 80 percent LTV no PMI is required, which lowers the cost by a large amount. The buyer obtains a new 80 percent conforming conventional loan after placing a 10 percent cash down payment and obtains a second trust deed for the 10 percent gap.

The calculation would be

$425,500 × 80% = $340,400 @ 7.5% int. 30/30
$425,500 × 10% = $ 42,550 @ 9.5% int. 30/15

$340,400 the payment would be	$2,380.13 PI
$ 42,550 the payment would be	$357.78 PI
	$2,737.91 PI

In this case, the difference between the payment for the 90-10 and the payment for the 80-10-10 loan amounts to $171.54 per month. The savings for one year would amount to $2,058.48, and over a 30-year loan the borrower would save more than $61,754.40 in interest.

Example 7: Private-Party Carryback Financing

Borrower and Loan Information

On occasion, a borrower who makes sufficient income to be able to make a loan payment does not have an adequate (or any) down payment that would be required by a conventional lender for a new loan. Therefore, the borrower would not qualify under normal income-to-debt ratios for down payment requirements. In this case, the borrower could obtain a loan only through a private-party lender, such as the seller of the property. The most common private-party loan is with the seller but can be with any noninstitutional lender, which includes the pool of investors in the marketplace.

Licensees should understand how this type of financing works when considering private-party carryback financing. For example, whereas the price was $425,500 for conventional financing, it is not unusual for the purchase price to be increased $10,000 higher to $435,500 because of the additional risk that is inherent in private-party carryback financing terms. The offset to the buyer for the higher loan amount is similar to the buyer financing closing costs above the sales price that were described in earlier chapters. The savings to the borrower is the reduced closing costs because on this type of loan there are often no loan origination fee, points, or other costs affiliated with traditional loan financing. Thus, the additional $10,000 in price is less than the total loan costs that the borrower would have paid through escrow, above the purchase price, as part of the closing costs.

Although the examples have been at 7½ percent, when a borrower cannot obtain a conventional loan and seeks financing from a private party, the interest rate charged for the loan is usually at a higher rate. The increase from 7½ percent to 7¾ percent increases the yield for the investor to cover the additional risk.

In the example below, the first trust deed is amortized over a 30-year period and due in 30 years, the second trust deed is amortized over 30 years and due in 15 years, and the third trust deed is an interest-only loan with a balloon payment that is due in 5 years. The financing would look like this:

New 1st trust deed of $235,000 @ 7.75%, 30/30   (54% LTV)
New 2nd trust deed of $125,000 @ 9.0%, 30/15   (29% LTV)

New 3rd trust deed of $ 75,500 @ 11.0%   interest only for   (17% LTV)
5 yrs

$435,500	Total loan amount	(100% CLTV)
-0-	Down payment	
$435,500	Sales Price	

The payments would be:

1st TD	$1,684.29	PI (principal, interest)
2nd TD	$1,005.78	PI
3rd TD	$692.08	I
	$3,382.15	PI

The difference between the 90 percent loan with PMI and the private-party carryback finance is $472.70, or $15.76 per day. When borrowers are in a position in which they are able to pay a higher payment, the privateparty carryback loan may be more advantageous than the traditional 90-10 with PMI. With no cash for a down payment, the borrower needs to finance the closing costs and the loan amount, which enables a borrower to purchase a home rather than rent and to save cash for a future purchase. An additional savings to the borrower is that after five years, when a borrower's income typically has increased, the third trust deed would be paid off, which could lower the monthly payment by $692.08. Beginning the sixth year, the monthly payment would include only the first and second trust deeds. In another ten years, the second trust deed would likewise terminate.

The above loan scenario has many benefits for both the buyer and the seller. Advantages for the buyer:

- No qualifying with an institutional lender
- No qualifying with the private mortgage insurance company
- No cash needed for down payment
- No cash needed for closing costs
- Reduced closing costs, such as loan fees, appraisal, and origination fee
- Ability to own a home that otherwise may not have been possible
- Interest expense tax write-off because of effective interest rate instead of rent receipts
- With a purchase price of $435,500, and if the buyer placed only 10 percent down payment ($43,550), because the loan amount would then be $391,950, which exceeds the maximum FNMA loan amount of $359,650, this loan would be considered a nonconforming jumbo loan, which warrants a higher interest rate, such as the 7¾ percent shown in the example, instead of the 7½ percent used in examples 2 through 6.
- Calculations for the effective rate of return on the combined first, second, and third trust deeds, which amounts to 8.67 percent, as is described below.

Computing the Rate of Return

To compute the rate of return for the investor who makes the loan for the above example, the calculation would be as follows:

1st TD of $235,000 @ 7.75%	=	$18,212.50
2nd TD of $125,000 @ 9.0%	=	$11,250.00
3rd TD of $75,500 @ 11.0%	=	$8,305.00
		$37,767.50

To compute the effective interest rate for the borrower, the calculation takes the total interest paid and divides it by total loans: $37,767.50 ÷ $435,500 = 8.67 percent rate of return. If a borrower only had one new loan at 7.5 percent, the rate would be less interest; however, the advantage to the borrower is that there is no qualifying, no down payment, no appraisal fee, no loan fee, and no PMI, which may save the borrower more than the difference between 8.67 percent and 7.5 percent. The three loans enable the borrower to obtain the property, whereas trying to obtain one new loan may not be possible because the borrower cannot be approved by the lender.

Advantages for the seller:

- Seller is able to transfer ownership of the property at a higher value.
- By offering to carry the financing, the seller would open up the market to more potential buyers.
- Sellers would receive a higher rate of return for their money. Example: If the property is free and clear of all encumbrances except property taxes and the seller could either receive cash at the close of escrow with a conventional loan or could reap additional benefits at higher yields

  - A conventional sale would net the seller about $387,205.00 consisting of a sales price of $425,500, less about 9 percent in closing cost, or $38,295 in costs. If this amount were placed into a certificate of deposit (CD) account earning a rate of 2.37 percent, the principal would earn $9,176.76 a year, or $764.73 a month. If the seller carries the financing, the income would be $3,382.15 per month, that is, $2,617.42 more per month than what would have been earned on the CD.

- The seller, or private-party lender, is virtually prohibiting the buyer from placing any other financing on the property until the private-party carryback loan is paid off because the property would already be encumbered with a first, second, and third trust deed. It would be very difficult for the buyer to obtain any additional financing on this property.
- The seller, or private-party lender, would always know whether the buyer was delinquent on the monthly payment because the seller collects all the loan payments. Such private-party carryback loans may require the buyer to place a reserve of three months' loan payments into an interest-bearing bank account, with the seller and buyer as cosignatories. This is part of the written escrow and loan note that would state that if the buyer is late on a payment,

the seller would be authorized to make a payment from the reserve account and may begin foreclosure procedures.

Example 8: Two-Step Mortgage

Borrower and Loan Information

For property value for $425,500 the loan broker discovered after the loan interview with the borrower and obtaining the loan application and credit report that the:

- Borrower has been on the job for only nine months and earns $13.50 for 40 hours a week. FICO score is in the mid-500 range. The property is a single-family home with air conditioning and built in 1971. The borrower was born in 1940.
- Current financing consists of a first trust deed of $96,000 at 6.75 percent, with PI payments of $660 a month. Property taxes are $102.48 a month, and the association dues are $176.00 a month.
- Long-term debts consist of a car payment of $299.00, with a balance of $10,974. A balance of $3,341.00 shows on a credit card account. (Use 5% of the balance for a monthly payment, or $167.05.)

The loan broker would do the following calculations: Total current house payment is $938.48, and current total debts are $1,404.53. The borrower's total current monthly gross income is $2,340 ($13.50 × 40 hrs a wk. = $540.00 a wk. × 52 weeks = $28,080 ÷ 12 = $2,340.00 in monthly gross income). The income-to-debt ratio is 40.10/60.02. This debt ratio would not be acceptable to either a primary lender or a subprime lender because the back-end ratio is more than 55 percent.

However, the mortgage broker would need to look at the total picture, in that (1) the prospective borrower has a large equity position; and (2) the borrower may be receiving additional income within the near future. In this case, the borrower will soon be receiving Social Security income. When the mortgage broker looks at just these two factors, an alternative to merely rejecting the loan applicant is to consider obtaining a private-party second trust deed on the property under the terms of a straight note, in which no payment is due until maturity.

One consideration for the loan broker would be to review the predatory lending guidelines to establish prior to closing the loan that there is a reasonable and highly likely chance that the borrower can make the loan payment(s), based upon current and projected income. Since the back-end ratio exceeds the normally accepted guidelines, documentation should be placed into the file with the justification and statement of explanation. However, it is common to charge an investment fee, such as $1,000, for the second step, the refinance—establishing the borrower's ability to qualify for a conforming, new FNMA loan.

As an example, when using the information from above, the loan broker is able to secure a second mortgage for $25,000 at 10 percent interest for one year with no payments due until maturity. The scenario may look like this:

Step 1:

- Value: $425,500
- 489
- Total loans would be $121,000 ($96,000 first amortized for 30 years + $25,000 second due in one year) or a new combined loan to value (CLTV) of 28 percent.
- Pay off all debts, the car, and credit cards ($10,974 + $3,341 = $14,315) Because of the age of the property, the private-party lender may require items that enhance the value of the property, such as replacing the carpet and air conditioner.
- Funds available for closing costs (investor fee, broker fee, credit report, escrow, title insurance, recording fee, etc.)

Step 2:

The loan broker may be wise to consider the above scenario to generate future business. By having five to six private individuals with $10,000 to $50,000 who would like to invest in trust deeds, the loan broker would be able to help a borrower at the current time on this loan and be in a position to do a refinance in one year, when the second trust deed becomes due. This would allow the borrower to reduce current debts and provide time to improve the FICO score. By the end of the first year, the borrower could show proof of making the payments on the first trust deed on time, with no late payments during the past 12 months. In addition, the borrower would have established a longer period on the job, with 21 months instead of 9 months.

At the end of the one-year period, the loan broker could assist the borrower in obtaining a refinance loan that would demonstrate 21 months on the job, a credit score in the mid-600 range, with increased income—the $2,340 base pay, plus the $1,340 Social Security income, for a total of $3,680. The new loan would include the current unpaid balance on the existing first trust deed of approximately $96,000 plus $27,500 that includes the current unpaid balance on the second plus the closing costs needed to close the loan. This new loan of $128,000 at 7½ percent interest, amortized over 30 years, would have a monthly payment as follows:

$894.99	principal and interest
102.48	property taxes
176.00	homeowner association dues
$1,173.47	a PITI

$1,173.47 ÷ 3,680 = 31.88% front-end and back-end ratio

The borrower would end up with no debt. The new loan would confirm to FNMA guidelines with very conservative new LTV of 30% ($128,000 ÷ $425, 500).

Computing the Rate of Return

What would be the rate of return for the investor? The investor would realize $2,500 interest income earned on the $25,000 at 10 percent plus $1,000 investment fee, or a total of $3,500. Take the $3,500 amount earned and divide by $25,000 amount loaned to equal a 14 percent return on investment.

The mortgage broker may have five to six private individuals with as little as $10,000 or more who wish to invest in real estate. These individuals often do not have enough funds or do not desire to make a purchase of a single property. By pooling together smaller sums, the loan broker may have a group of individuals who can assist in private financing. In the above example, the advantages for the borrower are (1) elimination of their current debts; (2) future improvement of their FICO score; (3) proof of on-time payment record for the first TD, which shows no late payments in the past 12 months; and (4) longer time on the job. In fact, at refinance under the normal terms of the loan, the borrower would show 21 months on the job.

How would the loan look for the borrower when the loan is due after one year? The loan broker would most likely be able to obtain a new loan for the borrower and pay off all existing loans because the borrower has met the payment obligation for one year. The loan broker could do a full refinance loan on the existing loans because the borrower now has 21 months on the job, the credit score would increase to the mid-600 range if no additional debt or late fees occur during that year, and the income would have gone up. The base pay of $2,340, plus the new Social Security income of $1,340, means that the borrower would then have a total new income of $3,680. When the loan broker obtains a new loan for $128,000 that would consist of a new first loan of $96,000 and a second for $27,500, plus adding the closing costs, the payment would be based upon $128,000 at 7.5 percent, 30 years fully amortized = $894.99 principal and interest, plus $102.48 for property taxes and $176.00 association dues. The new housing payment ratio would be 31.88 percent ($1,173.47 ÷ $3,680), which is within FNMA guidelines. The new LTV would be 47 percent ($128,000 ÷ $270,000 = 47%), which is a very conservative loan. Remember that when the mortgage broker is considering doing the above-referenced loan, he or she must consider "predatory lending." Always remember that the broker must be able to show that the borrower has the ability to repay the debt.

15.6 FINANCIAL CALCULATORS

The mortgage loan broker makes use of calculations as a daily ongoing process. The DRE allows applicants for the real estate licensee examination to use a calculator that they are comfortable using, but they must also become proficient in the keystrokes for the required daily applications. The majority of real estate licensees use one of three calculators. They are:

1. Hewlett-Packard (www.hp.com/country/us/en/prodserv/calculator. html)

2. Texas Instruments (http://education.ti.com/educationportal/sites/US/ productCategory/us_financial.html)

3. Calculated Industries (www.calculated.com/cat11/Real+Estate+ Calculators.html)

The Hewlett-Packard series of calculators has been predominantly used by those working in financial institutions, including stock and brokerage house and advanced appraisal techniques. Today, nonresidential real estate persons tend to stay with the HP calculator. The Texas Instruments Business Analysis (BA II) has been predominantly used at four-year universities with finance majors. Many individuals who buy and sell discounted notes still use the TI regularly. In more recent years, for the residential sales agents, the Real Estate Master series has been the dominant calculator of preference. The Calculated Industries series calculators, such as the Real Estate Master II or the Qualifier Plus III fx Real Estate Qualifying with Cash Flow Model 3430, are also preferred by many loan agents today. The authors and publisher have no preference or recommendation about which calculator is easier, faster, better, or more reliable because people's preferences vary. It is strongly recommended, however, that loan agents obtain a manual on the calculator they plan to use and thoroughly review all keystrokes regularly needed to perform their job.

Figure 15.7 shows keystrokes for each of the three calculators to determine the APR for a small $10,000 loan in which the only difference between the two loans is the choice of either a 15 percent or a 25 percent amount used for the loan fees, including points and discounts. Each keystroke is shown for each calculator. In this example, a loan that has a stated rate of 10 percent per annum has an APR of 21.56 percent that must be disclosed to the borrower.

15.7 TRUST FUND ACCOUNTING

Trust funds are deemed as anything of value not belonging to the broker, who maintains the item that must be segregated and kept separate, distinct, and apart for each principal for which the item is held in trust. Every broker shall keep a record of all trust funds received, including uncashed checks held pursuant to instruction of his or her principal (Article 15, Code 2831), including any advance fee received, authorized interest earned on the funds held, and promissory notes and trust deeds secured on real property.

DRE Brokers Requirements

When a broker maintains a trust account, certain records must be kept. Brokers are instructed to maintain generally accepted accounting principles to be in compliance with DRE Article 15 Regulation 2830 regarding trust fund accounts in the handling of a client's funds. The record should set forth in chronological order and columnar form the following information:

- Date funds were received
- Name of party from whom funds were received
- Amount of funds received
- Date of deposit of the trust funds
- Check number of any check deposited
- Date of trust fund disbursement

FIGURE 15.7 APR financial calculator keystrokes.

Loan information:

	Loan A	Loan B
Original unpaid loan balance	$10,000	$10,000
Interest rate on face of the note	10%	10%
Term of the loan	36 months	36 months
Loan fees—points and discounts	15%	25%
Holding period	3 years	3 years

HP Calculator Strokes

1.	3 g	12x	36
2.	10 g	12 divide	0.83
3.	10000	PV	10,000
4.	0	FV	0
5.	PMT		-322.67-
6.	RCL	PV	10,000
7.	Loan A	15 % −	8,500
	Loan B	25 % −	7,500
8.	PV		8,500
9.	i		1.80 2.59
10.	12 ×		21.56

To clear calculator registers: ON CLX g END f FIN.

TI BAII strokes

1.	36	□ 3 × 12 = N	
2.	0.83	10 / 12 = %i	
3.	10,000	10,000 PV	
4.	0		
5.	322.67	2nd PMT 322.67	
6.	10,000	10,000 PV	
7.		− 15 % =	
		− 25 % =	
8.	7,500	PV	
9.		2nd %i	
10.	31.04	× 12 =	

To clear calculator memory: ON/C 2nd CMR FIX 2 2nd Mode (until "FIN" displays).

Real Estate Master II ® Strokes

Clear calculator	[On/C] [On/C]
Enter loan amount	10000 [L/A]
Enter interest	10 [Int]
Enter term	3 [Term]
Find monthly payment	[Pmt] "run"
Find total points and fees	10000 [x] 15 [%] = 1500
Subtract from "stated" L/A	10000 [-] 1500 [=]
Reenter as loan amount	[L/A]
Find APR	[Int] "run"

- Name of entity to whom trust funds were disbursed
- Daily balance for each separate principal's funds
- Daily balance of trust account

The mortgage loan broker may receive funds that are not deposited into the broker trust account, such as funds collected and received by the loan broker that are made payable to an appraiser or to a credit reporting bureau or to pay off the debt of a borrower or to a title insurance company or escrow holder. In this case, the loan broker must show the identity of such funds to indicate:

- Date funds were received
- Name of party from whom funds were received
- Amount of funds received
- Check number of any check
- Name of entity to whom trust funds were disbursed

In addition to keeping records for all funds received, the broker must keep a separate record for each beneficiary and transaction. The broker must account for all funds that have been deposited into the broker's trust account and any interest earned on the trust funds on deposit. Information for each record must be sufficient to identify both the parties to the transaction and the specific transaction. One party may have several transactions with the broker, and each must have an individual accounting. One transaction may have several principals, so individual account records must be accounted for to each principal. Each accounting record should contain the following information in columnar form in chronological order:

- Date deposit received
- Amount of deposit received
- Date of each disbursement
- Check number of each disbursement
- Amount of each disbursement
- Dates and amount of interest earned and credited to the account
- Balance after posting each transaction

Documents routinely involved in a brokerage transaction include all those involving the funds of a principal. The broker should have available for inspection by the DRE such documents as a purchase contract, deposit receipt, and advance funds, which must show when the deposit was received by the broker, as well as collection receipts from rental income or note collections. Bank deposit slips with the bank stamp and date, along with escrow receipts, must be documented. Canceled trust fund account checks and itemized check stubs are proper record-keeping documents. Bank statements must be available with **reconciliation** data. The real estate commission Regulation 2831.2 indicates that the balance of all separate beneficiary or transaction records maintained by the broker must be reconciled with the record of all trust funds received and disbursed at least once a month. A record of the reconciliation must be maintained. This record must identify the bank account name and number, the date of the reconciliation, the account number and name of the principal(s) or beneficiary(ies) or transaction(s), and the trust fund liability(ies) of the broker to each.

As an example using the John and Mary Martinez transaction, as shown in Appendix D, the loan broker would handle the trust records as shown in Figure 15.8 for funds received but not placed into the broker trust account. The real estate selling office received a $5,000 check, #2104, from the prospective purchasers on June 15, 2005. Their check was never deposited into the broker trust

FIGURE 15.8   Record of trust funds.

NOT PLACED IN BROKERS TRUST ACCOUNT
PURCHASE
RECORD OF ALL TRUST FUNDS RECEIVED—NOT PLACED IN BROKER'S TRUST ACCOUNT
(Include Notes and Uncashed Checks Taken as Deposits)

2005 Date Received	Form of Receipt (Cash, note, etc.)	Amount	Received From	Description of Property or Other Identification	Disposition of Funds (to escrow, principal trust account, or returned)	Date of Disposition
7/15	#2104 Check	$5,000	From: John G & Mary S. Martinez	7711 Pleasant Drive Anytown	Uncashed Trust Funds	
7/15		$5,000	To: Grover Escrow, Inc.	Escrow #678B	To Escrow	7/15

Reproduced with permission of California Department of Real Estate.

account. Rather, it was forwarded directly to the escrow company, uncashed, after escrow was opened after being endorsed by the sales licensee or authorized office manager directly to the specific escrow company. The check was originally made payable to the broker and received by a DRE licensed salesperson, the agent handling the Martinez transaction. This check was endorsed on the back of the check as follows:

> Donna Grogan, Broker by F. Smith,
> WITHOUT RECOURSE, to:
> Grover Escrow, Inc. #678-B

The mortgage loan broker who is a DRE licensee met with the Martinez family for a prequalification before their real estate agent placed an offer to purchase. On June 15, 2005, the mortgage loan broker received a check for $20 to cover the cost of the credit report. Figure 15.9 indicates the trust fund record required by DRE to identify and segregate the Martinez trust funds. Note that the funds were received when the original loan application was obtained, but the broker did not pay out the fee to the credit company until the monthly billing cycle for office expense payments, payable on the first of each month. The July 1 payment would include all credit fees billed from June 1 to June 30 handled by the loan broker firm. Figure 15.10 shows all trust account income and expenses for the month from June 1 through July, with a daily balance for the entire account. The $20 credit report fee collected for the Martinez transaction is included, along with other activities of the business.

FIGURE 15.9 Separate record for each beneficiary.

IDENTIFICATION OF TRANSACTION (names, addresses, account numbers, etc.)

John G. and Mary S. Martinez
Refinance of 7711 Pleasant Drive, Anytown

DESCRIPTION	DISCHARGE OF TRUST ACCOUNTABILITY FOR FUNDS PAID OUT			TRUST ACCOUNTABILITY FOR FUNDS RECEIVED		ACCOUNT BALANCE
	Date of Check	Check Number	Amount	Date of Deposit	Amount	
Credit Report Fee				6/15	$20	$20.00
Impact Credit Corp	7/1	612	$20.00			$0

Reproduced with permission of California Department of Real Estate.

In the event that this transaction was a refinance instead of a purchase, the credit report fee would typically be collected up front when the loan application is taken. The appraisal fee is paid directly to the appraiser by the property owner "at the door" when the appraiser arrives to perform the appraisal. For example; if the appraisal fee is $350 and the credit report fee is $20, no DRE form would be used for the appraisal amount, but the credit report fee would still need to be posted on the appropriate DRE form.

Commingling is described in Section 10176 (e) of the Business and Professions Code and states that the word means the illegal act of mixing one client's funds with the funds of a different principal and also the mixing of client funds with the funds of the broker or business firm. However, special rules apply that are indicated in Section 2835 of the regulations of the real estate commission, stating that the following does not constitute the act of commingling:

- A trust account balance not to exceed $200 of the broker's own funds or the business funds, specifically to pay for any service charges or fees levied or assessed against the trust account by the financial institution where the account is maintained.

- Funds in the trust account belonging in part to the broker's principal and in part to the broker, such as a commission paid from the client funds to the broker. Such funds must be disbursed no later than 25 days after deposit of the client funds into the trust account.

- Funds deposited into the trust account that are broker-owned funds in connection with activities of making, collecting payment, or servicing a loan, provided:
  - All funds in the account that are owned by the broker are identified at all times in a separate record that is distinct from any separate record maintained for a beneficiary.
  - All broker-owned funds deposited into the account are disbursed from the account not later than 25 days after their deposit.

FIGURE 15.10 Columnar record of all trust funds.

2005 Date Received	From Whom Received or to Whom Paid	Description	Received				Paid Out				Daily Balance of Trust Bank Account
			Amount Received	Reference	Date of Deposit	XX	Amount Paid Out	Check Number	Date of Check	XX	
6/1	Juan & Margo Lopez	603 Elm	$20	113	6/2						
6/5	Gisela & Max Cunningham	10312 Bridge	$20	201	6/15						$20
6/7	Lois Griffith	6140 Weston	$20	78	6/10						$40
6/9	Gayle Brown	9335 Layton	$20	132	6/10						$60
6/15	John & Mary Martinez	7711 Pleasant Dr Anytown	$20	2101	6/16						$80
6/18	Fred Hamner	#4 8112 Condo Ave	$20	604	6/20						$100
6/25	Betty & Al Sanchez	21640 Popular	$20	1642	6/25						$120
6/27	Butch & Marlene Harris	413 Beach	$20	1107	6/29						$140
6/28	Jim & Sally Morris	5561 Manzanar	$20	32	6/29						$160
7/1	Impact Credit Corp	7711 Pleasant Dr Anytown					$160	1612	7/1		$0

Table title (top of table): COLUMNAR RECORD OF ALL TRUST FUNDS RECEIVED AND PAID OUT / TRUST FUND BANK ACCOUNT

Reproduced with permission of California Department of Real Estate.

Advance Fees

Any real estate broker who contracts for or collects an advance fee from any other person (the principal) must deposit such an amount(s), when collected, into a trust account with a recognized depository, which are not the funds of the broker. Amounts may be withdrawn for the benefit of the agent only when actually expended for the benefit of the principal, or five days after the verified accounts have been mailed to the principal. The principal may recover treble damages for amounts misapplied, in addition to reasonable attorney fees for any action brought to recover from a violation of this procedure.

Reconciliation of Accounting Records

Each verified accounting to a principal or to the commissioner must include the following information (B&P Code 10146):

- Name of the agent
- Name of the principal
- Description of the services rendered or to be rendered
- Identification of the trust fund account into which the advance fee has been deposited
- The amount of the advance fee collected
- A list of the names and addresses of persons to whom information pertaining to the principal's loan requirements were submitted and the dates of submittal when an advance fee arranged is used
- The amount allocated or disbursed from the advance fee for
  (1) services rendered
  (2) commissions paid to field agents and representatives
  (3) overhead costs and profit

The DRE requires a broker to review the account and reconcile the trust account at least once per month (B&P Section 10145) (Commissioner Regulation 2831) (Figure 15.11). One commissioner regulation, Section 2833, was adopted August 11, 1991, and deals with trust fund bank account overages. Entitled *Unexplained Trust Account Overages*, it defines the amount as those funds that exceed the aggregate trust fund liability of such accounts in which the broker is unable to determine the ownership of such excess funds. The following are conditions for such funds:

1. Unless the broker can establish the ownership of such funds, the overage must be maintained in the broker's trust fund account or may be placed in a separate trust fund account established to hold such funds.

2. Overages may not be used to offset or cover shortages that may exist otherwise in the trust account.

3. A separate record of unexplained trust overages, including a separate subsidiary ledger to record the potential trust fund liability, must be maintained. The record must include the date of recording such funds as they are discovered as unexplained overage, and the broker must perform a monthly reconciliation of such funds.

Threshold Reporting Requirements

A broker meets the "threshold of business activity" when one of the following occurs: (1) 20 or more loans aggregating $2 million, or (2) loan collections aggregating $500,000 on behalf of nonexempt lenders (B&P Section 10232). A threshold broker must file the following reports:

- Quarterly trust fund status report (B&P Code 10232.25) (Commissioner Regulation 2846.8) (see Figure 15.5).
- Annual trust fund report (B&P Code 10232.2) (Commission Regulation) (see Figure 15.6). The annual report of a review of trust fund financial

FIGURE 15.11   Trust fund bank account reconciliation.

STATE OF CALIFORNIA	DEPARTMENT OF REAL ESTATE
	MORTGAGE LENDING

TRUST FUND BANK ACCOUNT RECONCILIATION

REPORT DATE *(DATE QUARTER ENDED)*

RE 856 (Rev. 2/90)

GENERAL INFORMATION

- Complete *one* form for *each* trust fund bank account.
- Attach this form and copy of the corresponding bank statement to Trust Fund Status Report (RE 855).
- Refer to mailing instructions on RE 855.

NAME OF BROKER

REAL ESTATE ID#

NAME OF BANK

ACCOUNT NAME

ACCOUNT NUMBER

BANK BUSINESS ADDRESS (STREET, CITY, STATE, ZIP CODE)

REPORT PERIOD

☐ FIRST QUARTER   ☐ SECOND QUARTER   ☐ THIRD QUARTER

DATE QUARTER ENDED (MM/DD/YY)

BANK ACCOUNT RECONCILIATION

1. **Account Balance** as of _____ *(per appended bank statement)*..................... $ _____

   Plus: Deposits in transit (deposits made through end of fiscal quarter not reflected in bank statement). .... + _____

   Number of deposits in transit: .... _____

   Less: Outstanding (uncleared) checks (checks issued through end of fiscal quarter not reflected in bank statement).. – _____

   Number of outstanding checks:.............................. _____

2. *SubTotal:* .... _____

3. *Other Adjustments (describe)*

   _____   _____

   _____

   _____   _____

4. *Adjusted Trust Fund Bank Account Balance (as of end of the report quarter)*............... $ _____

5. The balance on line #4 ☐ *agreed* ☐ *did not agree* with the balance reflected in the broker's records. Attach explanation if different.

statements requires confirmation by an independent accountant that (1) the broker maintains the records and reconciles the records; (2) each trust fund bank account is maintained by the broker in compliance with real estate law; (3) the accountant has reviewed the balances, receipts, and disbursements of trust fund accounts as of the last day of the year; (4) the accountant is not aware of any material modifications that should be made to the trust fund financial statements in order for them to conform with general accounting principles;

(5) the adjusted balance of the trust accounts shown in financial statements is on deposit as of the financial statement date; (6) the trust fund bank account receipts, disbursements, and balances agree with the amounts on the cash records; and (7) the trust fund liability balance for each open account shown on financial statements agrees with the amounts shown on the separate beneficiary records.

Audits and Examinations

Upon request of the DRE commissioner, a broker shall furnish an authorization for examination of financial records of the trust account (Government Code, Section 7473). The commissioner may issue rules and regulations regulating the method of accounting of trust funds to accomplish the purpose of the advance fees code.

Effective January 1, 1989, DRE is required to charge a broker for the cost of an audit if a final desist and refrain order or if a final decision after a disciplinary hearing is awarded that the broker has been found in violation of real estate law. The commissioner may maintain an action for the recovery of the cost of an audit in any court of competent jurisdiction. The commissioner may use the estimated average hourly cost for all persons performing audits of real estate brokers to determine the cost incurred by the commissioner for the audit.

Trust Fund Violations: Standard Terms and Conditions for a Restricted License: Pursuant to Section 10148 of the Business and Professions Code, Respondent shall pay the DRE Commissioner's reasonable cost for: a) the audit which led to disciplinary action and, b) a subsequent audit to determine if Respondent has corrected the trust fund violation(s) found in the Determination of Issues. In calculating the amount of the Commissioner's reasonable cost, the DRE Commissioner may use the estimated average hourly salary for all persons performing audits of real estate brokers, and shall include an allocation for travel time to and from the auditor's place of work. Respondent shall pay such cost within 60 days of receiving an invoice from the DRE Commissioner detailing the activities performed during the audit and the amount of time spent performing those activities. The DRE Commissioner may suspend the restricted license issued to the Respondent pending a hearing held in accordance with Section 11500, et seq., of the Government Code, if payment is not timely made as provided for herein, or as provided for in a subsequent agreement between the Respondent and the DRE Commissioner. The suspension shall remain in effect until payment is made in full or until Respondent enters into an agreement satisfactory to the DRE Commissioner to provide for payment, or until a decision providing otherwise is adopted following a hearing held pursuant to this condition.

SUMMARY

The mortgage broker often needs to offer a prospective borrower several loan program options. The more loan programs that are available in the marketplace for an applicant to select from, the higher the chance of obtaining the best financing for the borrower. The total amount of interest that may be charged will depend on the loan terms. The loan broker needs to look at "compensating" factors that may offset underwriting concerns and not just use only the standard income-to-debt ratio for the loan program. Be sure to look into having private investors available to do short-term loans.

REVIEWING YOUR UNDERSTANDING

1. Which one of the following does not require a Real Estate Broker's license:
   A. Soliciting borrowers for loans and soliciting lenders for loans
   B. Buying or offering to buy a promissory note secured by a lien on real property.
   C. Performing services for the promissory note holder secured by a lien on real property.
   D. Contacting a title insurance company for a property profile.

2. Using the information in question #8, what is the unpaid balance on the loan after the first payment is made?
   A. $99,989.91
   B. $99,988.91
   C. $99,971.39
   D. $99,917.93

3. Using the information in question #8, how much total interest would be paid if the borrower paid all payments amortized over a 30-year period?
   A. $269,392.40
   B. $270,299.60
   C. $270,929.60
   D. $270,992.60

4. A borrower purchases a home for $157,250 with a 20% down payment. How much is the down payment?
   A. $15,725
   B. $23,587
   C. $28,540
   D. $31,450

5. Using the information in question #11, how much is the PI if the interest rate is 7.875% with a payment factor of 7.250694 when amortized over 30 years?
   A. $912.14
   B. $912.31
   C. $921.13
   D. $921.41

6. Using the information in question #11, if the property tax rate is 1.25%, what is the approximate amount of the first year's annual property taxes?
   A. $1,386
   B. $1,639
   C. $1,893
   D. $1,965

7. Using the information in question #11, what is the approximate amount of the monthly property insurance at a rate of 0.35%?
   A. $45.86
   B. $36.69
   C. $63.96
   D. $ 54.68

8. How much is the first month's payment on a $188,215 purchase price after putting a 15% down payment, with a 7.125% interest rate for 15 years (payment factor 9.058312)?
   A. $1,077
   B. $1,449
   C. $1,770
   D. $1,944

9. Using the information in question #15, how much is the down payment?
   A. $42,400
   B. $36,360
   C. $28,232
   D. $10,600

10. Using the information in question #15, if the rate is 1.275%, the monthly property tax payment would be
   A. $199.89.
   B. $199.98.
   C. $230.77.
   D. $244.92.

ANSWERS TO REVIEWING YOUR UNDERSTANDING

1. A	4. D	7. B	10. B
2. C	5. A	8. B	
3. B	6. D	9. C	

Please see the Instructor's Manual for the answers.

Appendix A

Loan Application FNMA Form 1003: English and Spanish

Uniform Residential Loan Application

This application is designed to be completed by the applicant(s) with the Lender's assistance. Applicants should complete this form as "Borrower" or "Co-Borrower," as applicable. Co-Borrower information must also be provided (and the appropriate box checked) when ☐ the income or assets of a person other than the Borrower (including the Borrower's spouse) will be used as a basis for loan qualification or ☐ the income or assets of the Borrower's spouse or other person who has community property rights pursuant to state law will not be used as a basis for loan qualification, but his or her liabilities must be considered because the spouse or other person has community property rights pursuant to applicable law and Borrower resides in a community property state, the security property is located in a community property state, or the Borrower is relying on other property located in a community property state as a basis for repayment of the loan.

If this is an application for joint credit, Borrower and Co-Borrower each agree that we intend to apply for joint credit (sign below):

_____   _____
Borrower   Co-Borrower

I. TYPE OF MORTGAGE AND TERMS OF LOAN

Mortgage Applied for:	☐ VA ☐ FHA	☐ Conventional ☐ USDA/Rural Housing Service	☐ Other (explain):	Agency Case Number	Lender Case Number

Amount	Interest Rate	No. of Months	Amortization Type:		
$	%		☐ Fixed Rate ☐ GPM	☐ Other (explain): ☐ ARM (type):	

II. PROPERTY INFORMATION AND PURPOSE OF LOAN

Subject Property Address (street, city, state & ZIP)	No. of Units

Legal Description of Subject Property (attach description if necessary)	Year Built

Purpose of Loan	☐ Purchase ☐ Construction ☐ Other (explain): ☐ Refinance ☐ Construction-Permanent	Property will be: ☐ Primary Residence ☐ Secondary Residence ☐ Investment

Complete this line if construction or construction-permanent loan.

Year Lot Acquired	Original Cost	Amount Existing Liens	(a) Present Value of Lot	(b) Cost of Improvements	Total (a + b)
	$	$	$	$	$

Complete this line if this is a refinance loan.

Year Acquired	Original Cost	Amount Existing Liens	Purpose of Refinance	Describe Improvements ☐ made ☐ to be made
	$	$		Cost: $

Title will be held in what Name(s)	Manner in which Title will be held	Estate will be held in: ☐ Fee Simple ☐ Leasehold (show expiration date)

Source of Down Payment, Settlement Charges, and/or Subordinate Financing (explain)

III. BORROWER INFORMATION

Borrower	Co-Borrower
Borrower's Name (include Jr. or Sr. if applicable)	Co-Borrower's Name (include Jr. or Sr. if applicable)

Social Security Number	Home Phone (incl. area code)	DOB (mm/dd/yyyy)	Yrs. School	Social Security Number	Home Phone (incl. area code)	DOB (mm/dd/yyyy)	Yrs. School

☐ Married ☐ Unmarried (include ☐ Separated single, divorced, widowed)	Dependents (not listed by Co-Borrower) no. ages	☐ Married ☐ Unmarried (include ☐ Separated single, divorced, widowed)	Dependents (not listed by Borrower) no. ages

Present Address (street, city, state, ZIP) ☐ Own ☐ Rent ___ No. Yrs.	Present Address (street, city, state, ZIP) ☐ Own ☐ Rent ___ No. Yrs.

Mailing Address, if different from Present Address	Mailing Address, if different from Present Address

If residing at present address for less than two years, complete the following:

Former Address (street, city, state, ZIP) ☐ Own ☐ Rent ___ No. Yrs.	Former Address (street, city, state, ZIP) ☐ Own ☐ Rent ___ No. Yrs.

IV. EMPLOYMENT INFORMATION

Borrower	Co-Borrower
Name & Address of Employer ☐ Self Employed	Yrs. on this job Yrs. employed in this line of work/profession	Name & Address of Employer ☐ Self Employed	Yrs. on this job Yrs. employed in this line of work/profession

Position/Title/Type of Business	Business Phone (incl. area code)	Position/Title/Type of Business	Business Phone (incl. area code)

If employed in current position for less than two years or if currently employed in more than one position, complete the following:

Borrower				IV. EMPLOYMENT INFORMATION (cont'd)		Co-Borrower		
Name & Address of Employer		☐ Self Employed	Dates (from – to)	Name & Address of Employer	☐ Self Employed		Dates (from – to)	
			Monthly Income $				Monthly Income $	
Position/Title/Type of Business			Business Phone (incl. area code)	Position/Title/Type of Business			Business Phone (incl. area code)	
Name & Address of Employer		☐ Self Employed	Dates (from – to)	Name & Address of Employer	☐ Self Employed		Dates (from – to)	
			Monthly Income $				Monthly Income $	
Position/Title/Type of Business			Business Phone (incl. area code)	Position/Title/Type of Business			Business Phone (incl. area code)	

V. MONTHLY INCOME AND COMBINED HOUSING EXPENSE INFORMATION

Gross Monthly Income	Borrower	Co-Borrower	Total	Combined Monthly Housing Expense	Present	Proposed
Base Empl. Income*	$	$	$	Rent	$	
Overtime				First Mortgage (P&I)		$
Bonuses				Other Financing (P&I)		
Commissions				Hazard Insurance		
Dividends/Interest				Real Estate Taxes		
Net Rental Income				Mortgage Insurance		
Other (before completing, see the notice in "describe other income," below)				Homeowner Assn. Dues		
				Other:		
Total	$	$	$	Total	$	$

*   Self Employed Borrower(s) may be required to provide additional documentation such as tax returns and financial statements.

Describe Other Income   *Notice:* **Alimony, child support, or separate maintenance income need not be revealed if the Borrower (B) or Co-Borrower (C) does not choose to have it considered for repaying this loan.**

B/C		Monthly Amount
		$

VI. ASSETS AND LIABILITIES

This Statement and any applicable supporting schedules may be completed jointly by both married and unmarried Co-Borrowers if their assets and liabilities are sufficiently joined so that the Statement can be meaningfully and fairly presented on a combined basis; otherwise, separate Statements and Schedules are required. If the Co-Borrower section was completed about a non-applicant spouse or other person, this Statement and supporting schedules must be completed about that spouse or other person also.

Completed ☐ Jointly ☐ Not Jointly

ASSETS Description	Cash or Market Value	Liabilities and Pledged Assets. List the creditor's name, address, and account number for all outstanding debts, including automobile loans, revolving charge accounts, real estate loans, alimony, child support, stock pledges, etc. Use continuation sheet, if necessary. Indicate by (*) those liabilities, which will be satisfied upon sale of real estate owned or upon refinancing of the subject property.		
Cash deposit toward purchase held by:	$			
List checking and savings accounts below		**LIABILITIES**	**Monthly Payment & Months Left to Pay**	**Unpaid Balance**
Name and address of Bank, S&L, or Credit Union		Name and address of Company	$ Payment/Months	$
Acct. no.	$	Acct. no.		
Name and address of Bank, S&L, or Credit Union		Name and address of Company	$ Payment/Months	$
Acct. no.	$	Acct. no.		
Name and address of Bank, S&L, or Credit Union		Name and address of Company	$ Payment/Months	$
Acct. no.	$	Acct. no.		

VI. ASSETS AND LIABILITIES (cont'd)			
Name and address of Bank, S&L, or Credit Union		Name and address of Company	$ Payment/Months	$
Acct. no.	$	Acct. no.		
Stocks & Bonds (Company name/ number & description)	$	Name and address of Company	$ Payment/Months	$
		Acct. no.		
Life insurance net cash value	$	Name and address of Company	$ Payment/Months	$
Face amount: $				
Subtotal Liquid Assets	$			
Real estate owned (enter market value from schedule of real estate owned)	$			
Vested interest in retirement fund	$			
Net worth of business(es) owned (attach financial statement)	$	Acct. no.		
Automobiles owned (make and year)	$	Alimony/Child Support/Separate Maintenance Payments Owed to:	$	
Other Assets (itemize)	$	Job-Related Expense (child care, union dues, etc.)	$	
		Total Monthly Payments	$	
Total Assets a.	$	**Net Worth** (a minus b) ► $	**Total Liabilities b.**	$

Schedule of Real Estate Owned (If additional properties are owned, use continuation sheet.)

Property Address (enter S if sold, PS if pending sale or R if rental being held for income) ▼	Type of Property	Present Market Value	Amount of Mortgages & Liens	Gross Rental Income	Mortgage Payments	Insurance, Maintenance, Taxes & Misc.	Net Rental Income
		$	$	$	$	$	$
Totals		$	$	$	$	$	$

List any additional names under which credit has previously been received and indicate appropriate creditor name(s) and account number(s):

Alternate Name	Creditor Name	Account Number

VII. DETAILS OF TRANSACTION		VIII. DECLARATIONS				
a.	Purchase price	$	If you answer "Yes" to any questions a through i, please use continuation sheet for explanation.	Borrower		Co-Borrower	
				Yes No		Yes No	
b.	Alterations, improvements, repairs		a. Are there any outstanding judgments against you?	☐ ☐		☐ ☐	
c.	Land (if acquired separately)		b. Have you been declared bankrupt within the past 7 years?	☐ ☐		☐ ☐	
d.	Refinance (incl. debts to be paid off)		c. Have you had property foreclosed upon or given title or deed in lieu thereof in the last 7 years?	☐ ☐		☐ ☐	
e.	Estimated prepaid items		d. Are you a party to a lawsuit?	☐ ☐		☐ ☐	
f.	Estimated closing costs		e. Have you directly or indirectly been obligated on any loan which resulted in foreclosure, transfer of title in lieu of foreclosure, or judgment?	☐ ☐		☐ ☐	
g.	PMI, MIP, Funding Fee		(This would include such loans as home mortgage loans, SBA loans, home improvement loans, educational loans, manufactured (mobile) home loans, any mortgage, financial obligation, bond, or loan guarantee. If "Yes," provide details, including date, name, and address of Lender, FHA or VA case number, if any, and reasons for the action.)				
h.	Discount (if Borrower will pay)						
i.	Total costs (add items a through h)						

Uniform Residential Loan Application
Freddie Mac Form 65   7/05 (rev.6/09)

Fannie Mae Form 1003   7/05 (rev.6/09)

VII. DETAILS OF TRANSACTION		VIII. DECLARATIONS				

			Borrower		Co-Borrower	
		If you answer "Yes" to any questions a through i, please use continuation sheet for explanation.	Yes	No	Yes	No
j. Subordinate financing		f. Are you presently delinquent or in default on any Federal debt or any other loan, mortgage, financial obligation, bond, or loan guarantee?	☐	☐	☐	☐
k. Borrower's closing costs paid by Seller		g. Are you obligated to pay alimony, child support, or separate maintenance?	☐	☐	☐	☐
l. Other Credits (explain)		h. Is any part of the down payment borrowed?	☐	☐	☐	☐
		i. Are you a co-maker or endorser on a note?	☐	☐	☐	☐
m. Loan amount (exclude PMI, MIP, Funding Fee financed)		j. Are you a U.S. citizen?	☐	☐	☐	☐
n. PMI, MIP, Funding Fee financed		k. Are you a permanent resident alien?	☐	☐	☐	☐
o. Loan amount (add m & n)		l. Do you intend to occupy the property as your primary residence? If Yes," complete question m below.	☐	☐	☐	☐
p. Cash from/to Borrower (subtract j, k, l & o from i)		m. Have you had an ownership interest in a property in the last three years?	☐	☐	☐	☐
		(1) What type of property did you own—principal residence (PR), second home (SH), or investment property (IP)?	———		———	
		(2) How did you hold title to the home— by yourself (S), jointly with your spouse (SP), or jointly with another person (O)?	———		———	

IX. ACKNOWLEDGEMENT AND AGREEMENT

Each of the undersigned specifically represents to Lender and to Lender's actual or potential agents, brokers, processors, attorneys, insurers, servicers, successors and assigns and agrees and acknowledges that: (1) the information provided in this application is true and correct as of the date set forth opposite my signature and that any intentional or negligent misrepresentation of this information contained in this application may result in civil liability, including monetary damages, to any person who may suffer any loss due to reliance upon any misrepresentation that I have made on this application, and/or in criminal penalties including, but not limited to, fine or imprisonment or both under the provisions of Title 18, United States Code, Sec. 1001, et seq.; (2) the loan requested pursuant to this application (the "Loan") will be secured by a mortgage or deed of trust on the property described in this application; (3) the property will not be used for any illegal or prohibited purpose or use; (4) all statements made in this application are made for the purpose of obtaining a residential mortgage loan; (5) the property will be occupied as indicated in this application; (6) the Lender, its servicers, successors or assigns may retain the original and/or an electronic record of this application, whether or not the Loan is approved; (7) the Lender and its agents, brokers, insurers, servicers, successors, and assigns may continuously rely on the information contained in the application, and I am obligated to amend and/or supplement the information provided in this application if any of the material facts that I have represented herein should change prior to closing of the Loan; (8) in the event that my payments on the Loan become delinquent, the Lender, its servicers, successors or assigns may, in addition to any other rights and remedies that it may have relating to such delinquency, report my name and account information to one or more consumer reporting agencies; (9) ownership of the Loan and/or administration of the Loan account may be transferred with such notice as may be required by law; (10) neither Lender nor its agents, brokers, insurers, servicers, successors or assigns has made any representation or warranty, express or implied, to me regarding the property or the condition or value of the property; and (11) my transmission of this application as an "electronic record" containing my "electronic signature," as those terms are defined in applicable federal and/or state laws (excluding audio and video recordings), or my facsimile transmission of this application containing a facsimile of my signature, shall be as effective, enforceable and valid as if a paper version of this application were delivered containing my original written signature.

Acknowledgement. Each of the undersigned hereby acknowledges that any owner of the Loan, its servicers, successors and assigns, may verify or reverify any information contained in this application or obtain any information or data relating to the Loan, for any legitimate business purpose through any source, including a source named in this application or a consumer reporting agency.

Borrower's Signature X	Date	Co-Borrower's Signature X	Date

X. INFORMATION FOR GOVERNMENT MONITORING PURPOSES

The following information is requested by the Federal Government for certain types of loans related to a dwelling in order to monitor the lender's compliance with equal credit opportunity, fair housing and home mortgage disclosure laws. You are not required to furnish this information, but are encouraged to do so. The law provides that a lender may not discriminate either on the basis of this information, or on whether you choose to furnish it. If you furnish the information, please provide both ethnicity and race. For race, you may check more than one designation. If you do not furnish ethnicity, race, or sex, under Federal regulations, this lender is required to note the information on the basis of visual observation and surname if you have made this application in person. If you do not wish to furnish the information, please check the box below. (Lender must review the above material to assure that the disclosures satisfy all requirements to which the lender is subject under applicable state law for the particular type of loan applied for.)

BORROWER ☐ I do not wish to furnish this information	CO-BORROWER ☐ I do not wish to furnish this information
Ethnicity: ☐ Hispanic or Latino ☐ Not Hispanic or Latino	Ethnicity: ☐ Hispanic or Latino ☐ Not Hispanic or Latino
Race: ☐ American Indian or Alaska Native ☐ Asian ☐ Black or African American ☐ Native Hawaiian or Other Pacific Islander ☐ White	Race: ☐ American Indian or Alaska Native ☐ Asian ☐ Black or African American ☐ Native Hawaiian or Other Pacific Islander ☐ White
Sex: ☐ Female ☐ Male	Sex: ☐ Female ☐ Male

To be Completed by Loan Originator:
This information was provided:
☐ In a face-to-face interview
☐ In a telephone interview
☐ By the applicant and submitted by fax or mail
☐ By the applicant and submitted via e-mail or the Internet

Loan Originator's Signature X		Date
Loan Originator's Name (print or type)	Loan Originator Identifier	Loan Originator's Phone Number (including area code)
Loan Origination Company's Name	Loan Origination Company Identifier	Loan Origination Company's Address

CONTINUATION SHEET/RESIDENTIAL LOAN APPLICATION		
Use this continuation sheet if you need more space to complete the Residential Loan Application. Mark **B** f or Borrower or **C** for Co-Borrower.	Borrower:	Agency Case Number:
	Co-Borrower:	Lender Case Number:

I/We fully understand that it is a Federal crime punishable by fine or imprisonment, or both, to knowingly make any false statements concerning any of the above facts as applicable under the provisions of Title 18, United States Code, Section 1001, et seq.

Borrower's Signature	Date	Co-Borrower's Signature	Date
X		X	

FannieMae

Uniform Residential Loan Application/*Solicitud Uniforme para Préstamo Hipotecario Residencial*

This application is designed to be completed by the applicant(s) with the Lender's assistance. Applicants should complete this form as "Borrower" or "Co-Borrower," as applicable. Co-Borrower information must also be provided (and the appropriate box checked) when ☐ the income or assets of a person other than the Borrower (including the Borrower's spouse) will be used as a basis for loan qualification or ☐ the income or assets of the Borrower's spouse or other person who has community property rights pursuant to state law will not be used as a basis for loan qualification, but his or her liabilities must be considered because the spouse or other person has community property rights pursuant to applicable law and Borrower resides in a community property state, the security property is located in a community property state, or the Borrower is relying on other property located in a community property state as a basis for repayment of the loan.

Esta solicitud se diseñó para ser completada por el solicitante o solicitantes con la ayuda del prestador. Los solicitantes deben completar esta solicitud como "Prestatario" o "Co-Prestatario", según corresponda. La información sobre el Co-Prestatario también debe proporcionarse (marque el cuadro correspondiente) ☐ si el ingreso o los bienes de una persona que no sea el "Prestatario" (incluyendo el cónyuge del prestatario) se emplearán como base para calificar para el préstamo o ☐ los bienes e ingresos del cónyuge del prestatario o de otra persona con derechos de comunidad conyugal de conformidad con la ley estatal no se usarán como base para calificar para el préstamo, pero las deudas de dichas personas tienen que considerarse debido a que el cónyuge u otra persona tienen derechos de comunidad conyugal de conformidad con la ley aplicable y a que el Prestatario reside en un estado en el que rige el régimen de comunidad conyugal, la propiedad que se ofrece como garantía se encuentra en un estado en el que rige el régimen de comunidad conyugal, o el Prestatario depende de otra propiedad que se encuentra en un estado en el que rige el régimen de comunidad conyugal para el pago total del préstamo.

If this is an application for joint credit, Borrower and Co-Borrower each agree that we intend to apply for joint credit (sign below):

Si se trata de una solicitud de crédito conjunto, el Prestatario y Co-Prestatario acuerdan que pretenden solicitar un crédito conjunto (firmar a continuación):

Borrower / *Prestatario* _____   Co-Borrower / *Co-Prestatario* _____

I. TYPE OF MORTGAGE AND TERMS OF LOAN/*TIPO DE HIPOTECA Y CONDICIONES DEL PRÉSTAMO*

Mortgage Applied for/ *Préstamo Hipotecario Solicitado:*	☐ VA/*VA* ☐ FHA/*FHA*	☐ Conventional/*Convencional* ☐ USDA/Rural Housing Service *USDA/Servicio Rural de Vivienda*	☐ Other (explain)/ *Otro (explique):*	Agency Case Number/ *N° de Préstamo de la Agencia*	Lender Case Number/ *N° de Préstamo del Prestador*

Amount/*Cantidad Total del Préstamo* $	Interest Rate/ *Tasa de Interés* ____ %	No. of Months/ *Plazo (Meses)*	Amortization Type/ *Tipo de Amortización:*	☐ Fixed Rate/ *Tasa Fija* ☐ GPM/*GPM*	☐ Other (explain)/ *Otro (explique):* ☐ ARM (type)/ *ARM (tipo):*

II. PROPERTY INFORMATION AND PURPOSE OF LOAN/*INFORMACIÓN SOBRE LA PROPIEDAD Y PROPÓSITO DEL PRÉSTAMO*

Subject Property Address (street, city, state & ZIP)/ *Dirección de la Propiedad (calle, ciudad, estado y código postal)*	No. of Units/ *N° de Unidades*

Legal Description of Subject Property (attach description if necessary)/ *Descripción Legal de la Propiedad (adjunte descripción si es necesario)*	Year Built/ *Año de Construcción*

Purpose of Loan/ *Propósito del Préstamo*	☐ Purchase/*Compra* ☐ Refinance/ *Refinanciamiento*	☐ Construction/*Construcción* ☐ Construction-Permanent/ *Financiamiento Permanente de Construcción*	☐ Other (explain): *Otro (explique)*	Property will be/*La propiedad será:* ☐ Primary Residence/ *Residencia Principal* ☐ Secondary Residence/ *Residencia Secundaria*	☐ Investment/ *Inversión*

Complete this line if construction or construction-permanent loan./ Complete esta línea si es un préstamo para construcción o financiamiento permanente de construcción.

Year Lot Acquired/ *Año en que se Adquirió el Lote*	Original Cost/ *Costo Original* $	Amount Existing Liens/ *Monto de los Gravámenes Actuales* $	(a) Present Value of Lot/ *Valor Actual del Lote* $	(b) Cost of Improvements/ *Costo de las Mejoras* $	Total (a + b)/ *Total (a + b)* $

Complete this line if this is a refinance loan./Complete esta línea si es un préstamo de refinanciamiento.

Year Acquired/ *Año en que se Adquirió*	Original Cost/ *Costo Original* $	Amount Existing Liens/ *Monto de los Gravámenes Actuales* $	Purpose of Refinance/ *Propósito del Refinanciamiento*	Describe Improvements/ *Descripción de las Mejoras* Cost/*Costo:* $	☐ made/ *realizadas* ☐ to be made/ *por realizarse*

Title will be held in what Name(s) /*Nombre(s) que se Registrará(n) en el Título*	Manner in which Title will be held/ *Manera en que se Registrará el Título*	Estate will be held in/ *La propiedad se mantendrá en:* ☐ Fee Simple/ *Pleno Dominio* ☐ Leasehold (show expiration date)/ *Arrendamiento (indique fecha de vencimiento)*
Source of Down Payment, Settlement Charges, and/or Subordinate Financing (explain)/ *Origen de Pago Inicial, Costos de Cierre y/o Financiamiento Subordinado (explique)*		

Borrower/*Prestatario*	III. BORROWER INFORMATION/ *INFORMACIÓN SOBRE EL PRESTATARIO*	Co-Borrower/*Co-Prestatario*

Borrower's Name (include Jr. or Sr. if applicable)/
Nombre del Prestatario (indique Jr., o Sr. si aplica)

Co-Borrower's Name (include Jr. or Sr. if applicable)/
Nombre del Co-Prestatario (indique Jr., o Sr. si aplica)

Social Security Number/ *Número de Seguro Social*	Home Phone (incl. area code)/ *Teléfono de la Casa (incluya código de área)*	DOB (mm/dd/yyyy)/ *Fecha de nacimiento (mm/dd/aaaa)*	Yrs. School/ *Años de Educación*	Social Security Number/ *Número de Seguro Social*	Home Phone (incl. area code)/ *Teléfono de la Casa (incluya código de área)*	DOB (mm/dd/yyyy)/ *Fecha de nacimiento (mm/dd/aaaa)*	Yrs. School/ *Años de Educación*

☐ Married *Casado* ☐ Unmarried (include single, divorced, widowed)/ *No está casado (incluye soltero, divorciado, viudo)*
☐ Separated *Separado*

Dependents (not listed by Co-Borrower)/ *Dependientes (no incluidos por el Co-Prestatario)*
No./*N°*   Ages/*Edades*

☐ Married *Casado* ☐ Unmarried (include single, divorced, widowed)/ *No está casado (incluye soltero, divorciado, viudo)*
☐ Separated *Separado*

Dependents (not listed by Borrower)/ *Dependientes (no incluidos por el Prestatario)*
No./*N°*   Ages/*Edades*

Present Address (street, city, state, ZIP)/ *Dirección Actual (calle, ciudad, estado, código postal)*   ☐ Own/ *Propietario* ☐ Rent *Inquilino* ____ No. Yrs./ *N° de Años*

Present Address (street, city, state, ZIP)/ *Dirección Actual (calle, ciudad, estado, código postal)*   ☐ Own/ *Propietario* ☐ Rent *Inquilino* ____ No. Yrs./ *N° de Años*

Mailing Address, if different from Present Address/ *Dirección donde recibe su correspondencia, si es diferente de su dirección actual*

Mailing Address, if different from Present Address/ *Dirección donde recibe su correspondencia, si es diferente de su dirección actual*

If residing at present address for less than two years, complete the following:/Si habita en dicha dirección hace menos de dos años, por favor complete:

Former Address (street, city, state, ZIP) Yrs./ *Dirección Anterior (calle, ciudad, estado, código postal)*   ☐ Own *Propietario* ☐ Rent *Inquilino* ____ No. *N° de Años*

Former Address (street, city, state, ZIP)/ *Dirección Anterior (calle, ciudad, estado, código postal)*   ☐ Own *Propietario* ☐ Rent *Inquilino* ____ No. Yrs. *N° de Años*

Borrower/*Prestatario*	IV. EMPLOYMENT INFORMATION/ *INFORMACIÓN SOBRE EL EMPLEO*	Co-Borrower/*Co-Prestatario*

Name & Address of Employer/ *Nombre y Dirección del Empleador*   ☐ Self Employed/ *Empleado por Cuenta Propia*

Yrs. on this job/ *Años en este trabajo*
Yrs. employed in this line of work/profession/ *Años de empleo en este tipo de trabajo/profesión*

Name & Address of Employer/ *Nombre y Dirección del Empleador*   ☐ Self Employed/ *Empleado por Cuenta Propia*

Yrs. on this job/ *Años en este trabajo*
Yrs. employed in this line of work/profession/ *Años de empleo en este tipo de trabajo/profesión*

Position/Title/Type of Business/ *Posición/Título/Tipo de Negocio*

Business Phone (incl. area code)/*Teléfono en el lugar de trabajo (incluya código de área)*

Position/Title/Type of Business/ *Posición/Título/Tipo de Negocio*

Business Phone (incl. area code)/*Teléfono en el lugar de trabajo (incluya código de área)*

If employed in current position for less than two years or if currently employed in more than one position, complete the following:/
Si ha estado trabajando en la posición actual menos de dos años o si actualmente está empleado en más de una posición, complete lo siguiente:

Name & Address of Employer/ *Nombre y Dirección del Empleador*   ☐ Self Employed/ *Empleado por Cuenta Propia*

Dates (from – to)/ *Fechas de empleo (desde – hasta)*
Monthly Income/ *Ingreso Mensual*
$

Name & Address of Employer/ *Nombre y Dirección del Empleador*   ☐ Self Employed/ *Empleado por Cuenta Propia*

Dates (from – to)/ *Fechas de empleo (desde – hasta)*
Monthly Income/ *Ingreso Mensual*
$

Position/Title/Type of Business/ *Posición/Título/Tipo de Negocio*

Business Phone (incl. area code)/ *Teléfono en el lugar de trabajo (incluya código de área)*

Position/Title/Type of Business/ *Posición/Título/Tipo de Negocio*

Business Phone (incl. area code)/ *Teléfono en el lugar de trabajo (incluya código de área)*

Name & Address of Employer/ *Nombre y Dirección del Empleador*   ☐ Self Employed/ *Empleado por Cuenta Propia*

Dates (from – to)/ *Fechas de empleo (desde – hasta)*
Monthly Income/ *Ingreso Mensual*
$

Name & Address of Employer/ *Nombre y Dirección del Empleador*   ☐ Self Employed/ *Empleado por Cuenta Propia*

Dates (from – to)/ *Fechas de empleo (desde – hasta)*
Monthly Income/ *Ingreso Mensual*
$

	IV. EMPLOYMENT INFORMATION/		
Borrower/*Prestatario*	***INFORMACIÓN SOBRE EL EMPLEO* (cont'd)**		**Co-Borrower/***Co-Prestatario*
Position/Title/Type of Business/ *Posición/Título/Tipo de Negocio*	Business Phone (incl. area code)/ *Teléfono en el lugar de trabajo (incluya código de área)*	Position/Title/Type of Business/ *Posición/Título/Tipo de Negocio*	Business Phone (incl. area code)/ *Teléfono en el lugar de trabajo (incluya código de área)*

V. MONTHLY INCOME AND COMBINED HOUSING EXPENSE INFORMATION/
INFORMACIÓN SOBRE EL INGRESO Y LOS GASTOS MENSUALES COMBINADOS DE VIVIENDA

Gross Monthly Income *Ingreso Bruto Mensual*	Borrower *Prestatario*	Co-Borrower *Co-Prestatario*	Total	Combined Monthly Housing Expense/*Gastos Mensuales Combinados de Vivienda*	Present *Actual*	Proposed *Propuesto*
Base Empl. Income* *Ingreso Básico del Empleado**	$	$	$	Rent *Alquiler*	$	
Overtime *Horas extra*				First Mortgage (P&I) *Hipoteca Principal (Principal e Interés)*		$
Bonuses *Pagas Extras*				Other Financing (P&I) *Otro Financiamiento (Principal e Interés)*		
Commissions *Comisiones*				Hazard Insurance *Seguro Contra Riesgos*		
Dividends/Interest *Dividendos/Intereses*				Real Estate Taxes *Impuestos Sobre Bienes Raíces*		
Net Rental Income *Ingreso Neto por Alquiler*				Mortgage Insurance *Seguro de Hipoteca*		
Other (before completing, see the notice in "describe other income", below) *Otros (antes de llenar, vea el aviso en "describa otros ingresos", a continuación)*				Homeowner Assn. Dues *Cuotas de la Asociación de Propietarios* Other: *Otro:*		
Total	$	$	$	Total	$	$

      *   **Self Employed Borrower(s) may be required to provide additional documentation such as tax returns and financial statements.**

      *   *Se podrá requerir al Prestatario o Prestatarios que trabajan por cuenta propia que proporcionen documentos adicionales, tales como declaraciones y planillas de impuestos y estados financieros.*

Describe Other Income/ *Describa Otros Ingresos*

Notice: **Alimony, child support, or separate maintenance income need not be revealed if the Borrower (B) or Co-Borrower (C) does not choose to have it considered for repaying this loan.**
Aviso: La pensión conyugal, pensión para el sustento de los hijos o ingreso de mantenimiento por separación, no tienen que declararse si el Prestatario (B) o Co-Prestatario (C) no desea que se considere para el pago de este Préstamo.

B/C		Monthly Amount *Cantidad Mensual*
		$

VI. ASSETS AND LIABILITIES/*BIENES Y PASIVOS*

This Statement and any applicable supporting schedules may be completed jointly by both married and unmarried Co-Borrowers if their assets and liabilities are sufficiently joined so that the Statement can be meaningfully and fairly presented on a combined basis; otherwise, separate Statements and Schedules are required. If the Co-Borrower section was completed about a non-applicant spouse or other person, this Statement and supporting schedules must be completed about that spouse or other person also.
Esta Declaración y cualquier anexo respaldatorio pertinente pueden llenarse conjuntamente tanto por Co-Prestatarios casados como no casados si sus bienes y deudas están suficientemente unidos de manera que la Declaración pueda presentarse con sentido sobre una base combinada y de una forma fiel; o de lo contrario, se requieren Declaraciones y Anexos por separado. Si en la sección del Co-Prestatario se completó la parte sobre el cónyuge, no solicitante u otra persona, esta Declaración y los anexos respaldatorios también deben completarse para dicho cónyuge u otra persona.

Completed/*Se completó* ☐ Jointly/*En Conjunto* ☐ Not Jointly/*Por Separado*

ASSETS/*BIENES* Description/*Descripción*	Cash or Market Value/ *Valor en Efectivo o Valor en el Mercado*	Liabilities and Pledged Assets. List the creditor's name, address, and account number for all outstanding debts, including automobile loans, revolving charge accounts, real estate loans, alimony, child support, stock pledges, etc. Use continuation sheet, if necessary. Indicate by (*) those liabilities, which will be satisfied upon sale of real estate owned or upon refinancing of the subject property. *Deudas y Bienes Gravados. Indique el nombre, la dirección y el número de cuenta de todas las deudas pendientes, incluyendo préstamos para autos, cuentas de poder de: crédito rotativo, préstamos de bienes raíces, pensión conyugal, pensión para el sustento de hijos, valores gravados, etc. Si es necesario, use una hoja adicional. Indique con un (*) aquellas deudas que se satisfarán al venderse o refinanciarse la propiedad inmobiliaria en cuestión.*
Cash deposit toward purchase held by:/ *Depósito en efectivo para la compra en poder de:*	$	

Uniform Residential Loan Application
Freddie Mac Form 65   7/05 (rev.6/09)   Page 3 of 8
Página 3 de 8   Fannie Mae Form 1003s   7/05 (rev.6/09)

		VI. ASSETS AND LIABILITIES/*BIENES Y PASIVOS* (cont'd)		
		LIABILITIES/*PASIVOS*	Monthly Payment & Months Left to Pay/ *Pago Mensual y N° de Pagos Mensuales que quedan por pagar*	Unpaid Balance/ *Balance Pendiente*
List checking and savings accounts below/ *Indique abajo las cuentas de cheques y de ahorros*		Name and address of Company/ *Nombre y dirección de la Compañía*	$ Payment/Months *$ Pagos/Meses*	$
Name and address of Bank, S&L, or Credit Union/ *Nombre y dirección del Banco, Asociación de Ahorro y Préstamo o Cooperativa de Crédito*				
		Acct. no./*N° de Cuenta*		
Acct. no./*N° de Cuenta*	$	Name and address of Company/ *Nombre y dirección de la Compañía*	$ Payment/Months *$ Pagos/Meses*	$
Name and address of Bank, S&L, or Credit Union/ *Nombre y dirección del Banco, Asociación de Ahorro y Préstamo o Cooperativa de Crédito*				
		Acct. no./*N° de Cuenta*		
Acct. no./*N° de Cuenta*	$	Name and address of Company/ *Nombre y dirección de la Compañía*	$ Payment/Months *$ Pagos/Meses*	$
Name and address of Bank, S&L, or Credit Union/ *Nombre y dirección del Banco, Asociación de Ahorro y Préstamo o Cooperativa de Crédito*				
		Acct. no./*N° de Cuenta*		
Acct. no./*N° de Cuenta*	$	Name and address of Company/ *Nombre y dirección de la Compañía*	$ Payment/Months *$ Pagos/Meses*	$
Name and address of Bank, S&L, or Credit Union/ *Nombre y dirección del Banco, Asociación de Ahorro y Préstamo o Cooperativa de Crédito*				
		Acct. no./*N° de Cuenta*		
Acct. no./*N° de Cuenta*	$	Name and address of Company/ *Nombre y dirección de la Compañía*	$ Payment/Months *$ Pagos/Meses*	$
Stocks & Bonds (Company name/number and description)/ *Acciones y Bonos (Nombre de la compañía/número y descripción de los valores y bonos)*	$			
		Acct. no./*N° de Cuenta*		
Life insurance net cash value/ *Valor en efectivo neto del seguro de vida*	$	Name and address of Company/ *Nombre y dirección de la Compañía*	$ Payment/Months *$ Pagos/Meses*	$
Face amount: *Monto de la póliza:* $				
Subtotal Liquid Assets/ *Subtotal de los Bienes Líquidos*	$			
Real estate owned (enter market value from schedule of real estate owned)/ *Propiedad inmobiliaria de la cual es dueño (indique el valor en el mercado según el anexo de la propiedad inmobiliaria)*	$			
Vested interest in retirement fund/ *Intereses adquiridos en el fondo de retiro*	$			
Net worth of business(es) owned (attach financial statement)/ *Valor neto de negocio(s) propio(s) (incluya estados financieros)*	$	Acct. no./*N° de Cuenta*		
Automobiles owned (make and year) / *Automóviles de los cuales es dueño (marca y año)*	$	Alimony/Child Support/Separate Maintenance Payments Owed to:/ *Pensión Alimenticia/Pensión Para el Sustento de los Hijos/Manutención por Separación:*	$	
Other Assets (itemize)/ *Otros Bienes (detalle)*	$	Job-Related Expense (child care, union dues, etc.)/ *Gastos Relacionados con el Empleo(cuidado de los hijos, cuotas de sindicatos, etc.)*	$	
		Total Monthly Payments/ *Total de Pagos Mensuales*	$	
Total Assets a./ *Total de Bienes a.*	$	Net Worth ► (a minus b) Valor Neto (a menos b) $	**Total Liabilities b.** *Total de Pasivos b.* $	

VI. ASSETS AND LIABILITIES//*BIENES Y PASIVOS* (cont'd)

Schedule of Real Estate Owned (If additional properties are owned, use continuation sheet.)
Anexo de Propiedades Inmobiliarias *(Si es dueño de más propiedades, use la hoja a continuación.)*

Property Address (enter S if sold, PS if pending sale or R if rental being held for income)/ *Dirección de la Propiedad (ponga una S por vendida, una PS por venta pendiente o una R si recibe ingreso por alquiler)* ▼	Type of Property/ *Tipo de Propiedad*	Present Market Value/ *Valor Actual en el Mercado*	Amount of Mortgages & Liens/ *Cantidad de Hipotecas y Gravámenes*	Gross Rental Income/ *Ingreso Bruto por Alquiler*	Mortgage Payments/ *Pagos Hipotecarios*	Insurance, Maintenance, Taxes & Misc./ *Seguro, Mantenimiento, Impuestos y Otros*	Net Rental Income/ *Ingreso Neto por Alquiler*
		$	$	$	$	$	$
Totals/ *Totales*		$	$	$	$	$	$

List any additional names under which credit has previously been received and indicate appropriate creditor name(s) and account number(s):/
Indique otros nombres bajo los cuales ha recibido crédito anteriormente, así como los nombres de los acreedores y el número de las cuentas.

Alternate Name/*Otro Nombre*	Creditor Name/*Nombre del Acreedor*	Account Number/*Número de Cuenta*

VII. DETAILS OF TRANSACTION/ *DETALLES DE LA TRANSACCIÓN*

a.	Purchase price/*Precio de compra*	$
b.	Alterations, improvements, repairs/ *Remodelaciones, mejoras, reparaciones*	
c.	Land (if acquired separately)/ *Terreno (si fue adquirido por separado)*	
d.	Refinance (incl. debts to be paid off)/ *Refinanciamiento (incluya deudas que se pagarán)*	
e.	Estimated prepaid items/ *Estimado de partidas prepagadas*	
f.	Estimated closing costs/ *Estimado de los costos de cierre*	
g.	PMI, MIP, Funding Fee/ *Seguro de hipoteca privado (PMI), Primas de seguro de hipoteca (MIP), Costos de Financiamiento*	
h.	Discount (if Borrower will pay)/ *Descuento (si el Prestatario lo pagará)*	
i.	Total costs (add items a through h)/ ***Total d e costos (s ume la s l íneas " a" hasta la "h")***	
j.	Subordinate financing/ *Financiamiento subordinado*	
k.	Borrower's closing costs paid by Seller/ *Costos de cierre del Prestatario pagados por el Vendedor*	
l.	Other Credits (explain)/ *Otros Créditos (explique)*	

VIII. DECLARATIONS/ *DECLARACIONES*

If you answer "Yes" to any questions a through i, please use continuation sheet for explanation. /
Si responde "Sí" a cualquier de las preguntas de la "a" a la "i", debe utilizar una hoja adicional para dar una explicación.

	Borrower/ *Prestatario* Yes/*Sí* No	Co-Borrower/ *Co-Prestatario* Yes/*Sí* No
a. Are there any outstanding judgments against you? *¿Existe alguna sentencia o fallo judicial pendiente en contra suya?*	☐ ☐	☐ ☐
b. Have you been declared bankrupt within the past 7 years? *¿Se ha declarado en bancarrota durante los últimos 7 años?*	☐ ☐	☐ ☐
c. Have you had property foreclosed upon or given title or deed in lieu thereof in the last 7 years? *¿Se le ha entablado una ejecución hipotecaria o ha transferido el título de propiedad en sustitución de una ejecución hipotecaria en los últimos 7 años?*	☐ ☐	☐ ☐
d. Are you a party to a lawsuit? *¿Es usted parte en una demanda judicial?*	☐ ☐	☐ ☐
e. Have you directly or indirectly been obligated on any loan which resulted in foreclosure, transfer of title in lieu of foreclosure, or judgment? *¿Ha estado usted obligado, directa o indirectamente, en algún préstamo que provocó una ejecución hipotecaria, transferencia de título en sustitución de una ejecución hipotecaria, o alguna sentencia, o fallo en su contra?*	☐ ☐	☐ ☐

(This would include such loans as home mortgage loans, SBA loans, home improvement loans, educational loans, manufactured (mobile) home loans, any mortgage, financial obligation, bond, or loan guarantee. If "Yes," provide details, including date, name, and address of Lender, FHA or VA case number, if any, and reasons for the action.)
(Esto incluye préstamos tales como préstamos hipotecarios para vivienda, préstamos SBA, préstamos para mejoras en la casa, préstamos educacionales, préstamos para casa móviles, cualquier hipoteca, obligación financiera, bono o préstamo garantizado. Si la respuesta es "Sí", incluya la fecha, el nombre y la dirección del Prestador, o el número de caso de FHA o VA, si lo hubiera, y las razones de la acción.)

	Borrower Yes/*Sí* No	Co-Borrower Yes/*Sí* No
f. Are you presently delinquent or in default on any Federal debt or any other loan, mortgage, financial obligation, bond, or loan guarantee? If "Yes," give details as described in the preceding question. *¿Se encuentra atrasado, moroso o en incumplimiento con alguna deuda federal o cualquier otro préstamos, hipoteca, obligación financiera, bono o garantía de préstamos? Si la respuesta es "Sí", provea detalles según se describe en la pregunta anterior.*	☐ ☐	☐ ☐
g. Are you obligated to pay alimony, child support, or separate maintenance? *¿Está obligado a pagar por pensión alimenticia, pensión para el sustento de los hijos, o manutención por separación?*	☐ ☐	☐ ☐
h. Is any part of the down payment borrowed? *¿Le prestaron alguna parte del pago inicial?*	☐ ☐	☐ ☐

VII. DETAILS OF TRANSACTION/ *DETALLES DE LA TRANSACCIÓN*		VIII. DECLARATIONS/ *DECLARACIONES*				
m.	Loan amount (exclude PMI, MIP, Funding Fee financed)/ *Cantidad del Préstamo (excluya PMI, MIP, Costos de Financiamiento financiados)*	i. Are you a co-maker or endorser on a note? *¿Es usted co-prestatario o fiador de un pagaré?*	☐	☐	☐	☐
		j. Are you a U.S. citizen? *¿Es usted ciudadano de los Estados Unidos?*	☐	☐	☐	☐
n.	PMI, MIP, Funding Fee financed/ *Seguro de hipoteca privado (PMI), Primas de seguro de hipoteca (MIP), Costos de Financiamiento financiados*	k. Are you a permanent resident alien? *¿Es usted un residente extranjero permanente de los Estados Unidos?*	☐	☐	☐	☐
o.	Loan amount (add m & n) / *Cantidad del Préstamo (sume líneas "m" y "n")*	l. Do you intend to occupy the property as your primary residence? If "Yes," complete question m below. *¿Tiene usted la intención de ocupar la propiedad como su residencia principal? Si la respuesta es "Sí" conteste la pregunta "m".*	☐	☐	☐	☐
p.	Cash from/to Borrower (subtract j, k, l & o from i)/ *Dinero del / para el Prestatario (reste j, k, l & o de i)*	m. Have you had an ownership interest in a property in the last three years? *¿Ha tenido usted participación como dueño en una propiedad en los últimos 3 años?* (1) What type of property did you own—principal residence (PR), second home (SH), or investment property (IP)? *¿De qué tipo de propiedad era usted dueño–residencia principal (PR), reisdencia secundaria (SH) o propiedad de inversion (IP)?* (2) How did you hold title to the home—solely by yourself (S), jointly with your spouse (SP), or jointly with another person (O)? *¿Cómo estaba registrado el título–a nombre suyo solamente (S), conjuntamente con su cónyuge (SP), o conjuntamente con otra persona (O)?*	☐ ____ ____	☐ ____ ____	☐ ____ ____	☐ ____ ____

IX. ACKNOWLEDGEMENT AND AGREEMENT/*RECONOCIMIENTO Y ACUERDO*

Each of the undersigned specifically represents to Lender and to Lender's actual or potential agents, brokers, processors, attorneys, insurers, servicers, successors and assigns and agrees and acknowledges that: (1) the information provided in this application is true and correct as of the date set forth opposite my signature and that any intentional or negligent misrepresentation of this information contained in this application may result in civil liability, including monetary damages, to any person who may suffer any loss due to reliance upon any misrepresentation that I have made on this application, and/or in criminal penalties including, but not limited to, fine or imprisonment or both under the provisions of Title 18, United States Code, Sec. 1001, et seq.; (2) the loan requested pursuant to this application (the "Loan") will be secured by a mortgage or deed of trust on the property described in this application; (3) the property will not be used for any illegal or prohibited purpose or use; (4) all statements made in this application are made for the purpose of obtaining a residential mortgage loan; (5) the property will be occupied as indicated in this application; (6) the Lender, its servicers, successors or assigns may retain the original and/or an electronic record of this application, whether or not the Loan is approved; (7) the Lender and its agents, brokers, insurers, servicers, successors, and assigns may continuously rely on the information contained in the application, and I am obligated to amend and/or supplement the information provided in this application if any of the material facts that I have represented herein should change prior to closing of the Loan; (8) in the event that my payments on the Loan become delinquent, the Lender, its servicers, successors or assigns may, in addition to any other rights and remedies that it may have relating to such delinquency, report my name and account information to one or more consumer reporting agencies; (9) ownership of the Loan and/or administration of the Loan account may be transferred with such notice as may be required by law; (10) neither Lender nor its agents, brokers, insurers, servicers, successors or assigns has made any representation or warranty, express or implied, to me regarding the property or the condition or value of the property; and (11) my transmission of this application as an "electronic record" containing my "electronic signature," as those terms are defined in applicable federal and/or state laws (excluding audio and video recordings), or my facsimile transmission of this application containing a facsimile of my signature, shall be as effective, enforceable and valid as if a paper version of this application were delivered containing my original written signature.

Cada uno de los suscritos representa específicamente al Prestamista y a los verdaderos o posibles agentes, corredores, procesadores, abogados, aseguradores, administradores, sucesores y cesionarios del Prestamista, y está de acuerdo y acepta que: (1) la información se proporciona en esta solicitud es exacta y correcta a partir de la fecha expuesta en la línea opuesta a mi firma, y que toda distorsión, intencional o negligente, de esta información contenida en esta solicitud pudiera resultar en una penalidad civil, incluyendo daños monetarios, hacia cualquier persona que sufra alguna pérdida debido a la toma de decisiones hecha en base a cualquier declaración falsa que yo haya hecho en esta solicitud, o en castigos penales, incluyendo, pero sin limitar a, multa o arresto o ambos, de acuerdo con las disposiciones del Título 18, del Código de los Estados Unidos, Sec. 1001, et seq.; (2) el préstamo solicitado de acuerdo a esta solicitud (el "Préstamo") estará asegurado por una hipoteca o escritura de fideicomiso sobre la propiedad descrita en la presente solicitud; (3) la propiedad no se utilizará para ningún propósito o uso ilegal o prohibido; (4) todas las declaraciones realizadas en esta solicitud se hacen con el fin de obtener un préstamo hipotecario residencial; (5) la propiedad se ocupará de acuerdo con lo indicado en la presente solicitud; (6) el Prestamista, sus administradores, sucesores o cesionarios pudieran retener los registros originales o electrónicos contenidos en esta solicitud, se apruebe o no el Préstamo; (7) el Prestamista y sus agentes, corredores, aseguradores, administradores, sucesores y cesionarios, pueden tomar decisiones constantemente en base a la información contenida en esta solicitud, y yo estoy obligado a corregir y complementar la información proporcionada en esta solicitud si alguno de los hechos significativos que he declarado en la presente cambia antes del cierre del Préstamo; (8) en el caso de que mis pagos al Préstamo se atrasen, el Prestamista, sus administradores, sucesores o cesionarios pudiera, además de cualquier otro derecho y recurso que pueda tener relacionado a dicho atraso, reportar mi nombre e información de cuenta a una o más agencias de información de crédito del consumidor; (9) la propiedad del Préstamo o la administración de la cuenta del Préstamo pudiera transferirse otorgando la notificación que requiera la ley; (10) ningún Prestamista ní sus agentes, corredores, aseguradores, administradores, sucesores o cesionarios me han hecho alguna manifestación o garantía, expresa o implícita, respecto a la propiedad, o la condición o el valor de la propiedad; (11) mi transmisión de esta solicitud como un "registro electrónico" que contenga mi "firma electrónica", como se definen esos términos en las leyes federales y estatales correspondientes (excluyendo grabaciones de audio y video), o mi transmisión de facsímil de esta solicitud que contenga un facsímil de mi firma, deberá ser tan eficaz, acatable y válida como si se hubiera entregado una versión en papel de esta solicitud que contenga mi firma escrita original.

Acknowledgement. Each of the undersigned hereby acknowledges that any owner of the Loan, its servicers, successors and assigns, may verify or reverify any information contained in this application or obtain any information or data relating to the Loan, for any legitimate business purpose through any source, including a source named in this application or a consumer reporting agency.

Reconocimiento. Cada uno de los abajo firmantes reconocen por la presente que el titular del Préstamo, sus administradores, sucesores y cesionarios pueden verificar y reverificar cualquier información incluida en esta solicitud u obtener cualquier información o datos relacionados con el Préstamo, para cualquier propósito comercial legítimo, a través de cualquier fuente, incluida una fuente mencionada en esta solicitud o una agencia de crédito del consumidor.

THE SPANISH TRANSLATION IS FOR CONVENIENCE PURPOSES ONLY. IN THE EVENT OF AN INCONSISTENCY BETWEEN THE ENGLISH AND SPANISH LANGUAGE VERSIONS OF THIS FORM, THE ENGLISH LANGUAGE VERSION SHALL PREVAIL.
LA TRADUCCIÓN AL ESPAÑOL ES PARA SU CONVENIENCIA ÚNICAMENTE. EN CASO DE QUE EXISTA UNA INCONSISTENCIA ENTRE LA VERSIÓN EN INGLÉS Y LA VERSIÓN EN ESPAÑOL DE ESTE FORMULARIO, PREVALECERÁ LA VERSIÓN EN INGLÉS.

LEA ESTO PRIMERO: Este documento contiene una traducción al español de su texto en inglés.

Borrower's Signature/*Firma del Prestatario*	Date/*Fecha*	Co-Borrower's Signature/*Firma del Co-Prestatario*	Date/*Fecha*
X		X	

X. INFORMATION FOR GOVERNMENT MONITORING PURPOSES/*INFORMACIÓN PARA FINES DE VERIFICACIÓN POR EL GOBIERNO*

The following information is requested by the Federal Government for certain types of loans related to a dwelling in order to monitor the lender's compliance with equal credit opportunity, fair housing and home mortgage disclosure laws. You are not required to furnish this information, but are encouraged to do so. The law provides that a lender may not discriminate either on the basis of this information, or on whether you choose to furnish it. If you furnish the information, please provide both ethnicity and race. For race, you may check more than one designation. If you do not furnish ethnicity, race, or sex, under Federal regulations, this lender is required to note the information on the basis of visual observation and surname if you have made this application in person. If you do not wish to furnish the information, please check the box below. (Lender must review the above material to assure that the disclosures satisfy all requirements to which the lender is subject under applicable state law for the particular type of loan applied for.)

La siguiente información la solicita el gobierno Federal para ciertos tipos de préstamos relacionados con una vivienda, con el fin de verificar el cumplimiento del Prestador con las leyes de igualdad de Oportunidades de Crédito, "fair housing" y las leyes de divulgación de hipotecas para viviendas. Usted no está obligado a proporcionar esta información, pero le instamos a hacerlo. La ley dispone que un Prestador no puede discriminar en base a esta información ni por el hecho de que decida o no proporcionarla. Si usted decide proporcionarla debe indicar grupo étnico y raza. Usted puede indicar más de una raza. Si usted no desea suministrar la información, de acuerdo a las reglamentaciones federales el Prestador debe anotar la raza y el sexo basado en una observación visual y de acuerdo a su apellido si usted preparó esta solicitud en persona. Si usted no desea proporcionar la información, sírvase marcar en el cuadro ubicado en la parte inferior. (El Prestador debe evaluar el material arriba mencionado para asegurarse de que la información proporcionada cumple con todos los requisitos a los que está sujeto el Prestador bajo la ley estatal pertinente para el tipo de préstamo en particular que se ha solicitado.)

BORROWER/*PRESTATARIO* ☐ I do not wish to furnish this information *No deseo proporcionar esta información*	CO-BORROWER/*CO-PRESTATARIO* ☐ I do not wish to furnish this information *No deseo proporcionar esta información*
Ethnicity: ☐ Hispanic or Latino/ ☐ Not Hispanic or Latino/ *Grupo étnico* *Hispano o Latino* *No Hispano o Latino*	**Ethnicity:** ☐ Hispanic or Latino/ ☐ Not Hispanic or Latino/ *Grupo étnico* *Hispano o Latino* *No Hispano o Latino*
Race/*Raza*: ☐ American Indian or ☐ Asian/ ☐ Black or African American/ Alaska Native/ *Asiático* *Negro o Afroamericano* *Indio Americano o* *Nativo de Alaska* ☐ Native Hawaiian or ☐ White/*Blanco* Other Pacific Islander/ *Nativo de Hawaí o de* *otra isla del Pacífico*	**Race/*Raza*:** ☐ American Indian or ☐ Asian/ ☐ Black or African American/ Alaska Native/ *Asiático* *Negro o Afroamericano* *Indio Americano o* *Nativo de Alaska* ☐ Native Hawaiian or ☐ White/*Blanco* Other Pacific Islander/ *Nativo de Hawaí o de* *otra isla del Pacífico*
Sex/*Sexo*: ☐ Female/*Femenino* ☐ Male/*Masculino*	**Sex/*Sexo*:** ☐ Female/*Femenino* ☐ Male/*Masculino*

To be Completed by Loan Originator:
A COMPLETARSE POR EL ORIGINADOR DEL PRÉSTAMO
This information was provided:
Esta informacion fue proporcionada a través de:
☐ In a face-to-face interview /*Entrevista en persona*
☐ In a telephone interview/*Entrevista por teléfono*
☐ By the applicant and submitted by fax or mail/*El solicitante y enviado por fax o por correo*
☐ By the applicant and submitted via e-mail or the Internet/*El solicitante y enviado por correo electrónico o por el Internet*

Loan Originator's Signature *Firma del Originador del Préstamo* **X**	Date/ *Fecha*

Loan Originator's Name (print or type) *Nombre del Originador del Préstamo (use en letra de imprenta o a máquina)*	Loan Originator Identifier *Identificación del Originador del Préstamo*	Loan Originator's Phone Number (including area code) *Nº de Teléfono del Originador del Préstamo (incl. código de área)*
Loan Origination Company's Name *Nombre de la Compañía Originadora del Préstamo*	Loan Origination Company Identifier *Identificación de la Compañía Originadora del Préstamo*	Loan Origination Company's Address *Dirección de la Compañía Originadora del Préstamo*

CONTINUATION SHEET/RESIDENTIAL LOAN APPLICATION/*HOJA DE CONTINUACIÓN/SOLICITUD PARA PRÉSTAMO HIPOTECARIO RESIDENCIAL*		
Use this continuation sheet if you need more space to complete the Residential Loan Application. Mark **B** f or Borrower or **C** for Co-Borrower. *Utilice esta hoja si necesita más espacio para completar la aplicación para hipoteca residencial. Escriba* **"B"** *para Prestatario y* **"C"** *para Co–Prestatario.*	Borrower/*Prestatario*:	Agency Case Number/ *Número de Préstamo de la Agencia:*
	Co-Borrower/*Co-Prestatario*:	Lender Case Number/ *Número de Préstamo del Prestador:*

I/We fully understand that it is a Federal crime punishable by fine or imprisonment, or both, to knowingly make any false statements concerning any of the above facts as applicable under the provisions of Title 18, United States Code, Section 1001, et seq.
Entiendo/Entendemos que es un crimen federal penado con multa o encarcelamiento, o ambos, el hacer declaraciones falsas con respecto a cualquiera de los hechos arriba declarados, según sea pertinente de acuerdo con las disposiciones del Título 18 del Código de los Estados Unidos, Artículo 1001, et seq.

Borrower's Signature/*Firma del Prestatario*	Date/*Fecha*	Co-Borrower's Signature/*Firma del Co-Prestatario*	Date/*Fecha*
X		X	

Uniform Residential Loan Application
Freddie Mac Form 65   7/05 (rev.6/09)   **Page 8 of 8**
                                                             Página 8 de 8   Fannie Mae Form 1003s   7/05 (rev. 6/09)

Appendix B
Credit Report

1
P.O. Box 6029

MORTGAGE FAX INC.
A LENDING INFORMATION COMPANY

Garden Grove, CA 92846
www.mortgagefaxinc.com

Tel: (714) 899-2656
Fax: (714) 899-9027

MORTGAGE FAX, INC.
PREPARED FOR:

2 **MORTGAGE LENDER COMPANY**
12792 VALLEY VIEW ST #AB-1, GARDEN GROVE, CA 92845

3 Attention:	JOANNE	9 Prepared By:	JOANNE	13 Report Type:	1INFILE 3 BUR 3
4 Reference #:	AFCPN-5608084	10 Request Date:	7/16/2005	14 Sources:	TU, EFX and XPN
5 Password:	yyi486ZA3m	11 Completed Date:	7/16/2005	15 Loan Type:	CONV
6 Client Loan #:	ADM-230	12 Client #:	4000	16 ECOA Type:	JOINT
7 Fannie Mae #:				17 Price: $0.00 Tax: $0.00 Total:$0.00	
8 Loan Officer:	MIKE A.				

ACCOUNT BASICS/HEADER

1. **Contact Information**
   Our company name, mailing address and phone numbers.

2. **Company Name**
   This section displays your company name.

3. **Attention**
   The person's name that accessed this report.

4. **Reference #**
   Reference number automatically assigned to the report once credit has been accessed. Refer to this # when contacting our Customer Service, Technical Support or Billing Dept.

5. **Password**
   A security feature built into the report. This number is used by underwriters or security personnel to authenticate the accuracy of the report.

6. **Client Loan #**
   Number used by some lenders for internal tracking.

7. **Fannie Mae #**
   A number assigned when the loan is logged into the Fannie Mae engine.

8. **Loan Officer**
   Identifies the name of the loan officer.

9. **Prepared By**
   The Customer Service Specialist who last worked on your consumer's file.

10. **Request Date**
    Indicates the date the report was requested.

11. **Completed Date**
    Indicates the date the report was completed.

12. **Client #**
    Indicates your account number.

13. **Report type**
    Indicates the type of report you ordered.

14. **Sources**
    Identifies the repositories used to access credit data.

15. **Loan Type**
    Conventional, FHA, VA.

16. **ECOA Type**
    Individual or Joint...Equal Credit Opportunity Act Compliance.

17. **Price**
    Total cost for this credit report.

Applicant/Co-Applicant Information

1	Applicant:	MARTINEZ, JOHN G	DOB: 03/17/57	SSN#: 548-60-3388
2	Co-Applicant	MARTINEZ, MARY S	DOB: 05/02/60	SSN#: 111-22-5678
3	Street Address:	49 LONGGONE LN	6 Marital Status:	MARRIED
4	City, State, Zip:	ANYTOWN, CA 91502	7 Own/Rent:	OWN
	Length of Time:		8 Dependents:	2
5	Property	623 HAPPY ST., ANYTOWN, CA 91502		

APPLICANT/CO-APPLICANT INFORMATION

1. **Applicant**
    Applicant's name, date of birth and Social Security number; always enter the borrower's full name when accessing credit. Middle initial and generation identity (Sr., Jr., 3rd) are extremely important if you wish to minimize mixed credit files with other family members or similarly named individuals.

2. **Co-Applicant**
    Co-applicant's name, date of birth and Social Security number.

3. **Address**
    The current address of the applicant as it appears on the application.

4. **Length of Time**
    The length of time the applicant/s have been residing at their current address.

5. **Property**
    The property address being considered for this loan.

6. **Martial Status**
    Identifies the applicant/s marital status.

7. **Own/Rent**
    Indicates whether they own or rent at their given residence.

8   **Dependents**
    Total number of dependents.

Score Information

EFX FACTA BEACON 5.0   **658**   Range 300 to 850   FOR: MARTINEZ, JOHN G
Score Date: 7/16/2005

14 LENGTH OF TIME ACCOUNTS HAVE BEEN ESTABLISHED
10 PROPORTION OF BALANCES TO CREDIT LIMITS IS TOO HIGH ON BANK REVOLVING OR OTHER REVOLVING ACCOUNTS
05 TOO MANY ACCOUNTS WITH BALANCES
12 LENGTH OF TIME REVOLVING ACCOUNTS HAVE BEEN ESTABLISHED

TU EMPIRICA SCORE   **625**   Range 336 to 843   FOR: MARTINEZ, JOHN G
Score Date: 7/16/2005

40 DEROGATORY PUBLIC RECORD OR COLLECTION FILED
10 PROPORTION OF BALANCES TO CREDIT LIMITS IS TOO HIGH ON BANK REVOLVING OR OTHER REVOLVING ACCOUNTS
14 LENGTH OF TIME ACCOUNTS HAVE BEEN ESTABLISHED
20 LENGTH OF TIME SINCE DEROGATORY PUBLIC RECORD OR COLLECTION IS TOO SHORT

XPN/FAIR, ISAAC MODEL II **613**   Range 300 to 850   FOR: MARTINEZ, JOHN G
Score Date: 7/16/2005

40 DEROGATORY PUBLIC RECORD OR COLLECTION FILED
14 LENGTH OF ACCOUNTS HAS BEEN ESTABLISHED
10 PROPORTION OF BALANCE TO HIGH CREDIT ON BANK REVOLVING OR ALL REVOLVING ACCOUNT
12 LENGTH OF TIME REVOLVING ACCOUNTS HAVE BEEN ESTABLISHED

SCORE INFORMATION

1. *CREDIT SCORES*

Lenders use credit scores to determine the level of risk they are taking by lending you money. You will have 3 credit scores, one from each of the major credit bureaus. FICO scores are the most common scores used by the lending industry. Some common facts about credit scores:

- Higher scores are better

- Scores range from 300 to 850.

- Scores are determined at the time the credit is accessed; they may change each time your profile is updated.

- Scores can govern the amount of money you wish to borrow, affect your interest rates for home loans, auto loans and insurance rates.

- Each credit bureau has a different name for their score; **Experian** = Fair Isaac Model II...**Trans Union** = Empirica 4...**Equifax** = Beacon 5.0; these models are primarily used for real estate loans.

- There are approximately 25+ different types of risk score models in use within the various credit markets eg. automotive, mortgage loans, bank cards, retail cards, and generic (used by online credit monitoring companies).

- Credit scores can vary from credit bureau to credit bureau depending on the data being reported in the file. Many creditors do not report their information to all three credit bureaus, either by error or selectively, this causes disparity between the credit scores.

- Credit scores are not influenced by age, sex, race, religion, occupation or marital status.

HOW A SCORE IS EVALUATED

The five main categories used in the development of a score.

- Payment History   35%
- Amounts Owed   30%
- Length of Credit History   15%
- Types of Credit in Use   10%
- New Credit/Inquiries   10%

2. *For*

The name associated with the score. Some consumers may have two scores for the same credit bureau; this occurs if the consumer has maintained credit in additional names or social security #'s.

3.   *Score Narratives*

The four lines of remarks following each score are called score factors or reason codes. These narratives are very important because they tell you why your score is not an 850. They are listed in the order of importance as to how they affect your score and vary from person to person. A good understanding of this section can help you to raise a credit score from 1 to 100 points by making strategic changes to a line of credit.
 The numbers listed to the left of each reason code have no value. They are simply the number assigned to the code. All repositories utilize the same list of reason codes for their Mortgage Scores.

4.   *Inability to Score*

Some people do not have scores; when this occurs you may need to consider a Non-Traditional Borrower Credit Report (NTBC). There are five reasons a borrower may not have a score:

- The borrower has no credit for evaluation

- The borrower has credit, but there has been no activity for the past 6 months or more

- The borrower's history has too much credit and a risk model has not been developed to evaluate their level of risk

- One or more of the creditor's indicate the borrower is deceased

- The credit file is *locked* for security reasons and can only be *unlocked* by the consumer

Trades / Derogatory Trades									
Creditor Name	Date Reported	Date Opened	High Credit	Balance Owing	Terms	Current Status	Historical Status # Mo — Times Past Due 30 / 60 / 90		Past Due
Account Number	DLA		Credit Limit		Acct. Type	ECOA			Last Past Due
[1]MOUNTAIN BK	[2] 07/05	03/00	[5] 43225	19330 [7]	[8]956	30 SLOW [10]	39 1	[12] 0 0	956 [13]
3562A0197325346R12345	[3] 06/05	[4]	[6]		[9] INST	J [11]		XPN-1 [15]	06/05 [14]
[16]Loan Term: 60M									
[17]Late Dates: 30 SLOW – 06/05									
HOME COMING FUNDING [18]	11/01	17/00	108750	108337	1223	30 SLOW 10	9 0 0		1278
23802654388		09/01			MTG	J XPN-1, XPN-2,TU-1,TU-2 EFX-1			
Loan Term: 360M						EFX-2			11/01

TRADES/DEROGATRORY TRADES/COLLECTION INFORMATION

1. **Creditor Name/Account Number** – The creditor's name and account number is listed for each trade line.

2. **Date Reported**
   The date the "payment history" was last updated to the repository.

3. **DLA**
   Date of last activity – The last date a payment was made on this account.

4. **Date Opened**
   Date account opened.

5. **High Credit**
   The highest amount charged on this account since it opened.

6. **Credit Limit**
   Amount of credit extended to the consumer.

7. **Balance Owing**
   The balance owing as of the last reported date.

8. **Terms**
   Monthly payment.

9. **Acct Type**
   Designates the type of account as reported by the creditor.

10. **Current Status**
    Present payment status of the account.

11. **ECOA (Equal Credit Opportunity Act)**
    A code that indicates whether the account is held individually or jointly.

12. **Historical Status**
    Indicates how many times and to what degree the account has been late.

13. **Past Due**
    The payment amount past due as of the last reported date.

14. **Last Past Due**
    The date the account was last past due

15. **File Segment**
    Indicates which bureaus reported the account and specifies which identity the account is held under. These codes correlate with the last page of the credit report (see Source Information).

16. **Loan Term**
    Designates the length of time (in months) the consumer has to pay the debt.

17. **Late Dates**
    Dates the account was previously past due

Collection Information

Account Name	Date Reported	Date Opened	High Credit	Balance	Acct. Type	Account Status	Past Due
Account Number	Client				Credit Limit	ECOA	Last Past Due

CHAMBERS COLLECTIONS	07/05	09/04	500	650	R	CHG OFF	
98E543182136	CITIBANK					J XPN-1	

DATE OF LAST ACTIVITY WITH ORIGINAL CREDITOR: 09/01/2004
PREVIOUS STATUS 09
PREVIOUSLY IN COLLECTION

Inquiry Information

MORTGAGE FAX		7-07-05	TU-1, TU-2
ODPT/CBUSA		6-20-05	XPN-2

Public Record Information

Public Record Type	Date Reported	Date Filed	Original Amount	Balance	Current Status	Amount Past Due
Case/Court Number	Name					Segment

OBTAINED THROUGH TU, EFX and XPN

Judgment			1200			
B1234P50987 / 3019999	ALLIED COMPANY					XPN-1
COURT NAME: COUNTY SPR CT SANTA ANA						
BANKRUPTCY CH-13			*LIAB*	*ASSET EXEMPT*		*XPN-1*
35054539906234561 / 3009999			*100000*	*8500*		*Filed 02/10/2003*
COURT NAME: U S BANKRUPTCY COURT						
COUNTY TAX LIEN	02/00		12450		Released 07/01/2004	
B476P2109 / 3051111						XPN-1
COURT NAME: SO CALIF DISTRICT COURT						

1. **Collection Information**
   This section reports open and closed collections, charge offs, repos, foreclosures, and accounts settled for less than the full amount.

2. **Inquiries**
   Names and dates of creditors that have inquired into a consumer's credit profile. Inquiries are listed in date order and will be reported for the previous 90 days.

3. **Public Records**
   Indicates the type of public record being reported and the court location where the public record was recorded. The most common types of public records are: judgments, foreclosures (in some states), tax liens, and bankruptcies. Criminal Records are not a part of your credit profile.

The Following AKA(s) Were Reported

AKA Name	AKA SSN#
MARTINEZ, JON	XPN-1
MARTINEZ, MARY SANCHEZ	XPN-2

Bureau Addresses

Equifax, PO BOX 105873, ATLANTA, GA 30348   (800) 685-1111
Trans Union, 2 BALDWIN PLACE, PO BOX 1000, CHESTER, PA 19022   (800) 888-4213
EXPERIAN, 701 EXPERIAN PARKWAY PO BOX 949, ALLEN, TX 75013   (800) 682-7654

Source(s) of Information

File Segment	File Holder Name	Social Security #	Address
EFX-1	MARTINEZ, JOHN G	548-60-3388	49 LONGGONE LN. ANYTOWN, CA 91502
XPN-1	MARTINEZ, JOHN G	548-60-3388	49 LONGGONE LN. ANYTOWN, CA 91502
TU-1	MARTINEZ, JOHN G	548-60-3388	49 LONGGONE LN ANYTOWN, CA 91502
EFX-2	MARTINEZ, MARY S	111-22-5678	49 LONGGONE LN. ANYTOWN, CA 91502
TU-2	MARTINEZ, MARY S	111-22-5678	49 LONGGONE LN. ANYTOWN, CA 91502
TU-3	SANCHEZ, MARY S	111-22-5678	49 LONGGONE LN. ANYTOWN, CA 91502
XPN-2	MARTINEZ, MARY S	111-22-5678	49 LONGGONE LN. ANYTOWN, CA 91502

1. **AKA Section**
   "Also Known As" – The names and social security numbers listed in this section are additional identities the consumer/s may have used to apply for credit. This information is reported by the creditor.

2. **Bureau Addresses**
   Addresses and phone numbers to the three major credit bureaus.

3. **File Segments**
   Identifies the source of the data; the applicant's segments will be referenced by #1 after each bureau abbreviation. A #2 segment refers to the co-applicant; additional numbers refer to AKA names or AKA social security numbers that have been used to obtain credit.

4. **File Holder Name**
   Identifies the name on record; reported by creditors or inquiring entities.

5. **Social Security #**
   Identifies the social security # on record; reported by creditors or inquiring entities.

6. **Address**
   Identifies the consumer/s current address on record; reported by creditors or inquiring entities.

Employment Information

Applicant	Co-Applicant
Employer: Ace, Inc.	Employer: St. Joseph's Hospital
Position Held:	Position Held:
Start/Stop Dates:	Start/Stop Dates:
Income:	Income:
Verified By/Date:	Verified By/Date:

See Additional Employment section for more information.

Creditor Information List

Company	Phone	Address	City,State,Zip
STATE BANK	(800) 628-0679	140 W INDUSTRIAL DR	EL, IL 60126
BAY COMPANY	(BYM) AIL-ONLY	PO BOX 1990	TE, AZ 85280

1. **Employment Information**
   Employment information is stored by the repositories and is obtained from your creditors, insurance companies, tenant screening firms, employment screening companies, promotional offers, and inquiries for new credit.

2. **Creditor Information List**
   Directory of addresses and phone numbers for the creditors and inquiries contained in the report.

CURRENT STATUS CODES

Current	Current or paid according to terms
30 Slow	Account is 30-59 days past due
60 Slow	Account is 60-89 days past due
90 Slow	Account is 90-119 days past due
120 Slow	Account is 120+ days past due
Chg Off	Charge off account. Charged off by creditor to profit & loss
Coll	Collection account
Repo	Repossession
Incl	Account included in Bankruptcy
Unrated	Account or loan has not been rated

LATE DATE CODES

01	Current or paid according to terms
02	Account is 30-59 days past due
03	Account is 60-89 days past due
04	Account is 90-119 days past due
05	Account is 120+ days past due
07	Making regular payments under a wage earner plan or similar arrangement
08	Repossession
09	Bad debt placed for collection, charge off or skip account
00	Not used, too new to rate, or account has not been rated

ECOA (Equal Credit Opportunity Act) Code Key

A	Authorized User:	This individual is authorized to charge on another individual's credit card but has no contractual responsibility to pay the debt.
B	Borrower:	Individual account in borrower's name only
C	Co-Borrower:	Individual account in co-borrower's name only
D	Deceased:	Consumer deceased
G	Co-Signer:	This individual has guaranteed this account and assumes responsibility should the signer default
J	Joint:	Account for which both the borrower and co-borrower are contractually liable
K	Co-Maker:	This individual has guaranteed this account and assumes responsibility should maker default.
M	Maker:	This individual is responsible for this account, which is guaranteed by a co-maker
O	On Behalf Of:	This individual has signed an application for the purpose of securing credit for another individual, other than spouse.
P	Participant:	Participant on account
S	Signer:	Account for which borrower/co-borrower is guarantor, and assumes responsibility should maker default
T	Terminated:	A previously active joint account which a separated or divorced spouse is no longer associated with.
U	Undesignated:	Account has not been specified

CREDIT FACTS

A **Credit Report** is a record of your financial behavior. Your accounts are updated and reported every 30 days by your creditor's to the three national credit agencies known as Experian, Equifax and Trans Union. They are also referred to as credit repositories or credit bureaus. These three agencies report the following information on your credit profile.

You're Identification: Your name, social security number, present and past employers, present and past addresses, date of birth and sometimes current and past phone numbers.

You're Credit History: Contains details when you opened an account, the type and terms of the account, monthly payments and how you pay or paid your account. Accounts stay on your credit report for 10 years from the date of last activity. Delinquencies, collections and charge-offs remain on your credit for 7 years from date of your last payment.

Inquiries: A creditor who has been authorized by yourself, to look at your credit history for the purpose of extending credit. Some creditors will access credit to monitor current paying habits with other debtors, extend higher credit limits and/or to pre-qualify you for promotional offerings.

Public Records: Recorded items of public record are reported on your credit history. Items containing criminal charges are not reported to the repositories.

Items of public record will remain on your credit report for the following periods:

    Judgments: 7 years from the date of filing whether paid or unpaid

    Tax Lien: 7years from the date the lien was paid; <u>or up to 15 years</u>, should the lien not be reported paid.

    Bankruptcies: Chapter 7 Bankruptcy –10 years from the date of filing.
                      Chapter 11 and 12 Bankruptcy –10 years from the date of filing.
                      Chapter 13 Bankruptcy or Wage Earner –7 years from the date of filing.

Credit Score: A credit score is a numeric indication of how likely you will repay your debts based upon your current payment habits.

Credit scores are continually changing as the data in your file is updated. Much like a snap shot, scores are generated at the time the credit is accessed.

Score Factors: The reason codes explain why the score is not an 850. Factors are listed in the order of importance as to how they affect the score. Understanding these narratives is critical to improving the score.

The following are a list of facts and tips for improving your scores:

- We utilize the *"mortgage score model"* for our credit reports. There are a minimum of 25+ different score models used by different industries. The repositories utilize a *generic score* for their consumer reports. The most current and commonly used scores by the lending industry are:

- Equifax...Beacon 5.0
- Experian...Fair Isaac Risk Model (FICO II)
- Trans Union... Empirica Risk Score (Classic 04)

    FICO scores were formulated from the following 5categories for the general population:

35%	Payment History-How you pay your debts
30%	Amounts Owed
15%	Length of time credit has been established.
10%	New Credit-Inquiries are a sub-set of this category
10%	Types of Credit in Use...Mixture of bank cards, retail, mortgages, and installment (finance co. /banks).

- Search the credit report for trade lines that are reported currently past due. Making these accounts current can improve your score. Scores reflect credit payment patterns over time; however, more emphasis is placed on recent activity.

- Identify revolving accounts with balances more than 40% of the credit limit.

- Always enter your buyer's full name when accessing credit. Middle initials and generation identity (Sr., Jr., 3rd) are extremely important if you wish to minimize joining other family members credit, or similarly named individuals with your buyer's file.

- Scan your report for errors. Look at the last reported dates to make sure that balances are current and that past due accounts have been properly updated to reflect a current status. Search for creditors that do not belong to your buyer, duplicates on the same repository or lates that have been incorrectly reported.

- Identify all trade lines that report an " A " under the ECOA section of the report. This code means that your buyer is an authorized user on the account. Should there be any lates or a derogatory status associated with this account your buyer can request the trade to be deleted from his/her credit report. Authorized users may legally charge on the account but are not required by law to pay the debt.

- Inquiries remain on your credit report for a period of 24 months. Scores may start to decline after 6 inquiries have been accessed within a 12-month period. Multiple inquiries, due to rate shopping, for auto and /or mortgage loans have special considerations. When the Risk score is calculated, the model will ignore all auto and mortgage related inquiries within the prior 30 days. In addition, all auto and/or mortgage related inquiries within any 14-day period are grouped together and counted as a single inquiry.

TYPES OF CREDIT REPORTS

3 Bureau In-Files: Also known as a tri-merge, this report is a compilation of the three national credit repositories (Experian, Equifax, Trans Union) merged into one report with most duplicates removed.

Merge Plus: A three bureau merged report plus any three of the following items updated manually: Manual Tradeline Update, Employment Verification or Rental Verification.

RMCR: A three bureau merged report plus the following: employment verifications, residence history stated for a 2 year period and tradelines manually updated within a 60-90 days from last reported date.

Supplements: An addendum to the credit report usually updating or clarifying information reported on the report.

Non-Traditional Credit Report:

This report is manually prepared by compiling credit data from non-traditional sources such as utility companies, storage facilities, schools (tuition) or any other institution that extends credit to your buyer. New technology, through a company called "PRBC", makes FICO Scores available for this type of report.

7181 Garfield Ave

Huntington Beach, CA 92648

www.mortgagefaxinc.com

Tel: (714) 899-2656

Fax: (714) 899-9027

MORTGAGE FAX, INC.

PREPARED FOR:

MORTGAGE BROKERING & LENDING

7181 Garfield Ave, Huntington Beach, CA 92648

Attention:	JOANNE	**Prepared By:**	JOANNE	**Report Type:**	INFILE 3 BUR 3
Reference #:	AFCPN-5608084	**Request Date:**	7/16/2009	**Sources:**	TU, EFX and XPN
Password:	yyi486ZA3m	**Completed Date:**	7/16/2009	**Loan Type:**	CONV
Client Loan #:	ADM-230	**Client #:**	4000	**ECOA Type:**	JOINT
Fannie Mae #:				Price: $14.00 Tax: $0.00	**Total:**$14.00
Loan Officer:	MIKE A.				

Applicant/Co-Applicant Information

Applicant:	MARTINEZ, JOHN G	DOB: 03/17/57	SSN#: 000-00-0000
Co-Applicant	MARTINEZ, MARY S	DOB: 05/02/60	SSN#: 111-11-1111
Street Address:	49 LONGGONE LN	Marital Status:	MARRIED
City, State, Zip:	ANYTOWN, CA 91502	Own/Rent:	OWN
Length of Time:		Dependents:	2
Property	623 HAPPY ST., ANYTOWN, CA 91502		

Score Information

EFX FACTA BEACON 5.0   658   Range 300 to 850 FOR: MARTINEZ, JOHN G
Score Date: 7/16/2009

14 LENGTH OF TIME ACCOUNTS HAVE BEEN ESTABLISHED
10 PROPORTION OF BALANCES TO CREDIT LIMITS IS TOO HIGH ON BANK REVOLVING OR OTHER REVOLVING ACCOUNTS
05 TOO MANY ACCOUNTS WITH BALANCES
12 LENGTH OF TIME REVOLVING ACCOUNTS HAVE BEEN ESTABLISHED

TU EMPIRICA SCORE   625   Range 336 to 843 FOR: MARTINEZ, JOHN G
Score Date: 7/16/2009

40 DEROGATORY PUBLIC RECORD OR COLLECTION FILED
10 PROPORTION OF BALANCES TO CREDIT LIMITS IS TOO HIGH ON BANK REVOLVING OR OTHER REVOLVING ACCOUNTS
14 LENGTH OF TIME ACCOUNTS HAVE BEEN ESTABLISHED
20 LENGTH OF TIME SINCE DEROGATORY PUBLIC RECORD OR COLLECTION IS TOO SHORT

XPN/FAIR ISAAC MODEL II 613   Range 300 to 850 FOR: MARTINEZ, JOHN G
Score Date: 7/16/2009

40 DEROGATORY PUBLIC RECORD OR COLLECTION FILED
14 LENGTH OF ACCOUNTS HAS BEEN ESTABLISHED
10 PROPORTION OF BALANCE TO HIGH CREDIT ON BANK REVOLVING OR ALL REVOLVING ACCOUNT
12 LENGTH OF TIME REVOLVING ACCOUNTS HAVE BEEN ESTABLISHED

Score Information (continued)

EFX FACTA BEACON 5.0   **779**   Range not given   FOR: MARTINEZ, MARY S
Score Date: 7/16/2009

30 TIME SINCE MOST RECENT ACCOUNT OPENING IS SHORT
14 LENGTH OF TIME ACCOUNTS HAVE BEEN ESTABLISHED
05 TOO MANY ACCOUNTS WITH BALANCES
08 TOO MANY INQUIRIE S IN LAST 12 MONTHS

TU EMPIRICA SCORE   **704**   Range 336 to 843   FOR: MARTINEZ, MARY S
Score Date: 7/16/2009

39 SERIOUS DELINQUINCY
13 TIME SINCE DELINQUINCY IS TOO RECENT OR UNKNOWN
05 TOO MANY ACCOUNTS WITH BALANCES
14 LENGTH OF TIME ACCOUNTS HAVE BEEN ESTABLISHED

XPN/FAIR ISAAC II   **745**   Range 300 to 850   FOR: MARTINEZ, MARY S
Score Date: 7/16/2009

39 SERIOUS DELINQUINCY
14 LENGTH OF TIME ACCOUNTS HAVE BEEN ESTABLISHED
08 NUMBER OF RECENT INQUIRIES
33 PROPORTION OF CURRENT LOAN BALANCE TO ORIGINAL

Trades

Creditor Name	Date Reported	Date Opened	High Credit	Balance Owing	Terms	Current Status	Historical Status			Past Due
							# Mo	Times Past Due		
Account Number	DLA		Credit Limit		Acct. Type	ECOA		30	60	90	Last Past Due
HOME FINANCIAL	06/09	05/90	400000	234000	3128	CURR	92	0	0	0	
24000098500012	06/09				MTG	J			XPN-1, XPN-2	
Loan Term: 360M								TU-1, TU-2, EFX-1, EFX-2		
STATE BANK	06/09	01/90	9612	8628	255	CURR	77	0	0	0	
4271008232	06/09		10000		REV	C			XPN-2, TU-2,	
Loan Term: REV								EFX-2		
ISLAND SAVINGS	06/09	05/00	5700	6800		CURR	17	0	0	0	
405855254820	06/09		7000		REV	A			XPN-2, TU-2,	
Loan Term: REV								EFX-2		
EMPLOYEES CREDIT UNION	06/09	02/85	7108	6029	180	CURR	99	0	0	0	
525556601	06/09		10000		REV	J			XPN-1, XPN-2	
Loan Term: REV								TU-1, TU-2, EFX-1, EFX-2		
BAY COMPANY	06/09	01/02		0		CURR	99	0	0	0	
525556601	05/09		1400		REV	J			XPN-2, TU-3	
Loan Term: REV										
TRAVEL CHARGE USA	06/09	03/99	3612	0		CURR	33	0	0	0	
4271008232	04/07		4000		REV	B			XPN-1	
Loan Term: 1M										

AFCPN-5608084

Bureau Addresses

Equifax, PO BOX 105873, ATLANTA, GA 30348   (800) 685-1111
Trans Union, 2 BALDWIN PLACE, PO BOX 1000, CHESTER, PA 19022   (800) 888-4213
EXPERIAN, 701 EXPERIAN PARKWAY PO BOX 949, ALLEN, TX 75013   (800) 682-7654

Notice: This is a Merged report containing information supplied by the sources shown. The merge process is automated and the report may include some duplications and/or omissions.

SCORE(S) DISCLOSURE

NOTICE TO THE HOME LOAN APPLICANT

In connection with your application for a home loan, the lender must disclose to you the score that a consumer reporting agency (credit bureau) distributed to users and the lender used in connection with your home loan, and the key factors affecting your credit scores.

The credit score is a computer generated summary calculated at the time of the request and based on information a consumer reporting agency (credit bureau) or lender has on file. The scores are based on data about your credit history and payment patterns. Credit scores are important because they are used to assist the lender in determining whether you will obtain a loan. They may also be used to determine what interest rate you may be offered on the mortgage. Credit scores can change over time, depending on your conduct, how your credit history and payment patterns change, and how credit scoring technologies change.

Because the score is based on information in your credit history, it is very important that you review the credit related information that is being furnished to make sure it is accurate. Credit records may vary from one company to another.

If you have questions about your credit score or the credit information that is furnished to you, contact the consumer reporting agency (credit bureau) at the address and telephone number provided with this notice, or contact the lender, if the lender developed or generated the credit score. The consumer reporting agency (credit bureau) plays no part in the decision to take any action on the loan application and is unable to provide you with specific reasons for the decision on a loan application.

If you have questions concerning the terms of the loan, contact the lender

The credit reporting agency (CRA) is allowed to charge a reasonable fee for this disclosure

Equifax, PO BOX 105873, ATLANTA, GA 30348   (800) 685-1111
Trans Union, 2 BALDWIN PLACE, PO BOX 1000, CHESTER, PA 19022   (800) 888-4213
EXPERIAN, 701 EXPERIAN PARKWAY PO BOX 949, ALLEN, TX 75013   (800) 682-7654

Source(s) of Information

File Segment	File Holder Name	Social Security #	Address
EFX-1	MARTINEZ, JOHN G	000-00-0000	49 LONGGONE LN. ANYTOWN, CA 91502
XPN-1	MARTINEZ, JOHN G	000-00-0000	49 LONGGONE LN. ANYTOWN, CA 91502
TU-1	MARTINEZ, JOHN G	000-00-0000	49 LONGGONE LN ANYTOWN, CA 91502
EFX-2	MARTINEZ, MARY S	111-11-1111	49 LONGGONE LN. ANYTOWN, CA 91502
TU-2	MARTINEZ, MARY S	111-11-1111	49 LONGGONE LN. ANYTOWN, CA 91502
TU-3	SANCHEZ, MARY S	111-11-1111	49 LONGGONE LN. ANYTOWN, CA 91502
XPN-2	MARTINEZ, MARY S	111-11-1111	49 LONGGONE LN. ANYTOWN, CA 91502

*** END OF REPORT - 4/26/2005 2:44:34 PM ***

AFCPN-5608084

Appendix C

Verifications

Request for Verification of Employment

Privacy Act Notice: This information is to be used by the agency collecting it or its assignees in determining whether you qualify as a prospective mortgagor under its program. It will not be disclosed outside the agency except as required and permitted by law. You do not have to provide this information, but if you do not your application for approval as a prospective mortgagor or borrower may be delayed or rejected. The information requested in this form is authorized by Title 38, USC, Chapter 37 (if VA); by 12 USC, Section 1701 et. seq. (if HUD/FHA); by 42 USC, Section 1452b (if HUD/CPD); and Title 42 USC, 1471 et. seq., or 7 USC, 1921 et. seq. (if USDA/FmHA).

Instructions: Lender - Complete items 1 through 7. Have applicant complete item 8. Forward directly to employer, named in item 1.
Employer - Please complete either Part II or Part III as applicable. Complete Part IV and return directly to lender named in item 2.
The form is to be transmitted directly to the lender and is not to be transmitted through the applicant or any other party.

Part I - Request

1. To (Name and address of employer)	2. From (Name and address of lender)

I certify that this verification has been sent directly to the employer and has not passed through the hands of the applicant or any other interested party.

3. Signature of Lender	4. Title	5. Date	6. Lender's No. (Optional)

I have applied for a mortgage loan and stated that I am now or was formerly employed by you. My signature below authorizes verification of this information.

7. Name and Address of Applicant (include employee or badge number)	8. Signature of Applicant

Part II - Verification of Present Employment

9. Applicant's Date of Employment	10. Present Position	11. Probability of Continued Employment

12A. Current **Gross**Base Pay (Enter Amount and Check Period)

☐ Annual ☐ Hourly
☐ Monthly ☐ Other (Specify)
$ _____ ☐ Weekly

12B. Gross Earnings

Type	Year To Date	Past Year 19	Past Year 19
Base Pay	Thru 19 $	$	$
Overtime	$	$	$
Commissions	$	$	$
Bonus	$	$	$
Total	$	$	$

13. For Military Personnel Only	
Pay Grade	
Type	Monthly Amount
Base Pay	$
Rations	$
Flight or Hazard	$
Clothing	$
Quarters	$
Pro Pay	$
Overseas or Combat	$
Variable Housing Allowance	$

14. If Overtime or Bonus is Applicable, Is Its Continuance Likely?
Overtime   Yes ☐   No ☐
Bonus   Yes ☐   No ☐

15. If paid hourly-average hours per week

16. Date of applicant's next pay increase

17. Projected amount of next pay increase

18. Date of applicant's last pay increase

19. Amount of last pay increase

20. Remarks (if employee was off work for any length of time, please indicate time period and reason)

Part III - Verification of Previous Employments

21. Date Hired	23. Salary/Wage at Termination Per (Year)(Month)(Week)			
22. Date Terminated	Base	Overtime	Commissions	Bonus
24. Reason for Leaving	25. Position Held			

Part IV - Authorized Signature

Federal statutes provide severe penalties for any fraud, intentional misrepresentation, or criminal connivance or conspiracy purposed to influence the issuance of any guaranty or insurance by the VA Secretary, the U.S.D.A., FmHA/FHA Commissioner, or the HUD/CPD Assistant Secretary.

26. Signature of Employer	27. Title (Please print or type)	28. Date
29. Print or type name signed in Item 26	30. Phone No.	

Fannie Mae
Form 1005   July 96

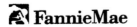

Request for Verification of Deposit

Privacy Act Notice: This information is to be used by the agency collecting it or its assignees in determining whether you qualify as a prospective mortgagor under its program. It will not be disclosed outside the agency except as required and permitted by law. You do not have to provide this information, but if you do not your application for approval as a prospective mortgagor or borrower may be delayed or rejected. The information requested in this form is authorized by Title 38, USC, Chapter 37 (If VA); by 12 USC, Section 1701 et.seq. (If HUD/FHA); by 42 USC, Section 1452b (if HUD/CPD); and Title 42 USC, 1471 et.seq. or 7 USC, 1921 et.seq. (If USDA/FmHA).

Instructions: Lender — Complete Items 1 through 8. Have applicant(s) complete Item 9. Forward directly to depository named in Item 1.
Depository — Please complete Items 10 through 18 and return DIRECTLY to lender named in Item 2.
The form is to be transmitted directly to the lender and is not to be transmitted through the applicant(s) or any other party.

Part I — Request

1. To (Name and address of depository)	2. From (Name and address of lender)

I certify that this verification has been sent directly to the bank or depository and has not passed through the hands of the applicant or any other party.

3. Signature of lender	4. Title	5. Date	6. Lender's No. (Optional)

7. Information To Be Verified

Type of Account	Account in Name of	Account Number	Balance
			$
			$
			$

To Depository: I/We have applied for a mortgage loan and stated in my financial statement that the balance on deposit with you is as shown above. You are authorized to verify this information and to supply the lender identified above with the information requested in Items 10 through 13. Your response is solely a matter of courtesy for which no responsibility is attached to your institution or any of your officers.

8. Name and Address of Applicant(s)	9. Signature of Applicant(s)

To Be Completed by Depository
Part II — Verification of Depository

10. Deposit Accounts of Applicant(s)

Type of Account	Account Number	Current Balance	Average Balance For Previous Two Months	Date Opened
		$	$	
		$	$	
		$	$	

11. Loans Outstanding To Applicant(s)

Loan Number	Date of Loan	Original Amount	Current Balance	Installments (Monthly/Quarterly)		Secured By	Number of Late Payments
		$	$	$	per		
		$	$	$	per		
		$	$	$	per		

12. Please include any additional information which may be of assistance in determination of credit worthiness. (Please include information on loans paid-in-full in Item 11 above.)

13. If the name(s) on the account(s) differ from those listed in Item 7, please supply the name(s) on the account(s) as reflected by your records.

Part III — Authorized Signature - Federal statutes provide severe penalties for any fraud, intentional misrepresentation, or criminal connivance or conspiracy purposed to influence the issuance of any guaranty or insurance by the VA Secretary, the U.S.D.A., FmHA/FHA Commissioner, or the HUD/CPD Assistant Secretary.

14. Signature of Depository Representative	15. Title (Please print or type)	16. Date
17. Please print or type name signed in item 14	18. Phone No.	

Fannie Mae
Form 1006   July 96

Appendix D
Sale Escrow Instructions

Grover Escrow Corporation
P.O. Box 190, 111 South Illinois Street
Anaheim, CA 92815-0190
P: (714) 533-1311 • F: (714) 533-1661

John G Martinez and Mary S Martinez

2972 Happy Street
Any Town, CA 12345-6000

Date: August 12, 2009
Escrow No.:

RE: Property Address: **7711 Pleasant Drive, Any Town, CA 12345-6000**

Dear **Mr. and Mrs. John G Martinez**:

Thank you for selecting **Grover Escrow Corporation** to process your escrow. We appreciate the opportunity to be of service to you in this transaction. Enclosed please find the following:

SIGN AND RETURN the enclosed items, retain the copy for your records:
    Escrow Instructions

COMPLETE IN FULL, SIGN AND RETURN the enclosed items:
    Statement of Information
    Preliminary Change of Ownership Report
    Insurance Information Request

    SPECIAL NOTE: Please have your insurance agent contact this office well in advance of the anticipated closing date. If you are obtaining a new loan please be advised that all lenders require your insurance policy be in their possession and in effect before they will release loan funds.

All documents should be signed EXACTLY as your names(s) appear. Should you name(s) be misspelled, sign them correctly and advise us in writing when you return these papers.

Should you have any questions or need any further assistance, please do not hesitate to contact the undersigned. Thank you.

Grover Escrow Corporation

Escrow Officer

Grover Escrow Corporation

P.O. Box 190, 111 South Illinois Street
Anaheim, CA 92815-0190
P: (714) 533-1311 • F: (714) 533-1661

Charles D Lee and Elizabeth C Lee

7711 Pleasant Drive
Any Town, CA, 12345-6000

Date: August 12, 2009
Escrow No.:

Property: **7711 Pleasant Drive, Any Town, CA 12345-6000**

* * * SELLER'S CERTIFICATION FOR REAL ESTATE REPORTING REQUIREMENTS * * *

In connection with the above numbered escrow that has been opened with us, we request the following tax information be completed and returned to this office prior to the close of escrow. This information is required by the Internal Revenue Service under the 1986 Tax Reform Act. Any failure to complete this form fully and promptly return to escrow may result in delaying the close of your escrow.

PLEASE NOTE: IF TAXPAYERS ARE HUSBAND AND WIFE, FILING A JOINT 1040 TAX RETURN, INSERT 100% IN ITEM 1C BELOW. A VALID TRUST, ESTATE, OR PARTNERSHIP ENTITY MUST DESIGNATE THEIR TIN/FEIN NUMBER IN ITEM 1B BELOW....IF A SOCIAL SECURITY NUMBER IS USED, WE WILL HAVE TO REPORT TAXPAYER AS AN INDIVIDUAL AT CLOSING FOR THE PURPOSE OF THIS IRS REPORTING REQUIREMENT ONLY.

1. Taxpayer Name Line 1: _____

1b. Social Security/TIN/FEIN #: _____ 1c. % of Ownership: _____

2. Taxpayer Name Line 2: _____

2b. Social Security/TIN/FEIN #: _____ 2c. % of Ownership: _____

3. Forwarding Street Address: _____
4. City, State, Zip: _____
5. Contract Sales Price: $ _____
6. Is this an Exchange? Yes ☐   No ☐
7. Taxpayer Type: ☐ Individual   ☐ Trust   ☐ Estate   ☐ Partnership   ☐ Other

NOTE: The information on this form is being furnished to the Internal Revenue Service.

Under penalty of perjury, I/We certify that the taxpayer I.D. number shown on this form is my/our correct Social Security or Federal Employer Identification Number. I/We understand that I/We am/are required by law to provide my/our correct taxpayer identification number and I/We may be subject to civil or criminal penalties if I/We provide incorrect information.

Date_____   Date _____

_____   _____
Charles D Lee   Elizabeth C Lee

Grover Escrow Corporation

P.O. Box 190, 111 South Illinois Street
Anaheim, CA 92815-0190
P: (714) 533-1311 • F: (714) 533-1661

FIRE INSURANCE INFORMATION FORM

Date: August 12, 2009

Escrow No:
Officer:

Re: **7711 Pleasant Drive, Any Town, CA 12345-6000**

The following information is needed to process your escrow. Please complete this form and return as soon as possible to our offices.

INSURANCE AGENCY   _____

AGENT   _____

POLICY NUMBER   _____

ADDRESS   _____

CITY, STATE, ZIP   _____

PHONE NUMBER   _____

FAX NUMBER   _____

PLEASE:

1. Contact your agency and discuss the coverages you desire.

2 Have your agent contact our office in order that we may provide additional information which may be required.

PLEASE COMPLETE AND RETURN

We hereby authorize you as Escrow Holder to discuss my file with the above named agent with reference to insurance necessary to process this escrow.

_____   _____
John G Martinez   Mary S Martinez

SMS StreamLine - Fire Insurance Information Form January 5, 2005

Grover Escrow Corporation
P.O. Box 190, 111 South Illinois Street
Anaheim, CA 92815-0190
P: (714) 533-1311 • F: (714) 533-1661

Date: August 12, 2009

Escrow No.:

RE: **7711 Pleasant Drive, Any Town, CA 12345-6000**

Escrow Officer: ,

INSTRUCTIONS TO PAY COMMISSION

Upon close of escrow, from funds received and/or held by you on my behalf you are instructed to pay:

A B C Realty
a licensed real estate broker, the sum of $ 12,750.00

and also pay **X Y Z Realty**
a licensed real estate broker, the sum of $ 12,750.00

The employment of said broker(s) to effect the sale-mortgage-exchange of the property described in said escrow is acknowledged by the undersigned, who agreed to pay said sum to said broker(s) as a commission for services rendered pursuant to said employment.

This is an IRREVOCABLE COMMISSION ORDER and cannot be amended or revoked, insofar as it relates to payment of commission, without the prior written consent of broker(s) named herein, who shall be deemed a party to the escrow for the sole and exclusive purpose of receiving said commission.

Charles D Lee   Elizabeth C Lee

Please mail payment(s) to address(es) below, unless payment is called for on the day the above escrow is closed.

Bob Smith   **George Smith**
A B C Realty   **X Y Z Realty**

By: _____   By: _____
License No.:   License No.:
Address: **9876 Realty Rd**   Address: **123 Realty Street**
            Any Town, CA 12356   **Any Town, CA 12345**
Telephone   Telephone:

RECORDING REQUESTED BY:
Grover Escrow Corporation

AND WHEN RECORDED MAIL TO:

John G Martinez
7711 Pleasant Drive
Any Town, CA 12345-6000

Order No. **12345678**
Escrow No.
Parcel No. **123-456-789**

SPACE ABOVE THIS LINE FOR RECORDER'S USE

GRANT DEED

THE UNDERSIGNED   THAT DOCUMENTARY TRANSFER TAX IS **$467.50** and CITY $
☐   computed on full value of property conveyed, or
☐   computed on full value less liens or encumbrances remaining at the time of sale.
☐   unincorporated area: ☐   **Any Town**, and

FOR A VALUABLE CONSIDERATION, receipt of which is hereby acknowledged,
Charles D Lee and Elizabeth C Lee, Husband and Wife as Joint Tenants

hereby GRANTS to **John G Martinez and Mary S Martinez, Husband and Wife as Joint Tenants**

the following described real property in the County of **Orange**, State of California:

Lot 1 of Tract No. 12456   in the City of Any Town, County of Orange, State of California, as per map recorded in Book 78 Page(s) 910 of Miscellaneous Maps in the Office of the County Recorder of Orange County.

Date   August 12, 2009

_____   _____
Charles D Lee   Elizabeth C Lee

STATE OF CALIFORNIA   }
                                                              }S.S.
COUNTY OF _____   }

On _____, before me, _____,
personally appeared **Charles D Lee and Elizabeth C Lee** who proved to me on the basis of satisfactory evidence to be the person(s) whose name(s) is/are subscribed to the within instrument and acknowledged to me that he/she/they executed the same in his/her/their authorized capacity(ies), and that by his/her/their signature(s) on the instrument the person(s), or the entity upon behalf of which the person(s) acted, executed the instrument.

I certify under PENALTY OF PERJURY under the laws of the State of California that the foregoing paragraph is true and correct.

WITNESS my hand and official seal.

Signature _____   (Seal)

Mail Tax Statement to: SAME AS ABOVE or Address Noted Below

Grover Escrow Corporation
P.O. Box 190, 111 South Illinois Street
Anaheim, CA 92815-0190
P: (714) 533-1311 • F: (714) 533-1661

Charles D Lee and Elizabeth C Lee

7711 Pleasant Drive
Any Town, CA 12345-6000

Date: August 12, 2009
Escrow No.:

RE: Property Address: **7711 Pleasant Drive, Any Town, CA 12345-6000**

Dear **Mr. and Mrs. Charles D Lee**:

Thank you for selecting **Grover Escrow Corporation** to process your escrow. We appreciate the opportunity to be of service to you in this transaction. Enclosed please find the following:

SIGN AND RETURN the enclosed items, retain the copy for your records:
   Escrow Instructions
   Commission Instructions

COMPLETE IN FULL, SIGN AND RETURN the enclosed items:
   CAL-FIRTPA 593B Form and/or Certificate
   Statement of Information
   Loan Information Sheet
   IRS 1099 Reporting Form

SIGN AND ACKNOWLEDGE BEFORE A NOTARY PUBLIC Exactly as your name(s) appear on the enclosed items:
   Grant Deed

All documents should be signed EXACTLY as your names(s) appear. Should you name(s) be misspelled, sign them correctly and advise us in writing when you return these papers.

Should you have any questions or need any further assistance, please do not hesitate to contact the undersigned. Thank you.

Grover Escrow Corporation

Escrow Officer

CALIFORNIA
FORM

YEAR

2009   Real Estate Withholding Certificate

593-C

Part I – Seller's Information   Return this form to your escrow company.

Name Charles D Lee	SSN or ITIN 123-45-6789
Spouse/RDP Name (if jointly owned) Elizabeth C Lee	Spouse's/RDP SSN or ITIN 987-65-4321
Address (including suite, room, PO Box, or PMB no.) 4892 Happy Street	☐ FEIN or ☐ CA Corp no.

City Any Town	State CA	Zip Code 12345-6000	Ownership Percentage %

Property address (if no street address, provide parcel number and county)
7711 Pleasant Drive, Any Town, CA 12345-6000

To determine whether you qualify for a full or partial withholding exemption, check all boxes that apply to the property being sold or transferred. (See line-by-notes in the Instructions)

Part II – Certifications which fully exempt the sale from withholding:

1. • ☐ The property qualifies as the seller's (or decedent's, if being sold by the decedent's estate) principal residence within the meaning of Internal Revenue Code (IRC) Section 12.

2. • ☐ The seller (or decedent, if being sold by the decedent's estate) last used the property as the seller's (decedent's) principal residence within the meaning of IRC Section 121 without regard to the two-year time period.

3. • ☐ The seller has a loss or zero gain for California income tax purposes on this sale. To check this box you must complete Form 593-E, Real Estate Withholding-Computation of Estimated Gain or Loss, and have a loss or zero gain on line 16.

4. • ☐ The property is being compulsorily or involuntarily converted and the seller intends to acquire property that is similar or related in service or use to qualify for nonrecognition of gain for California income tax purposes under IRC Section 1033.

5. • ☐ The transfer qualifies for nonrecognition treatment under IRC Section 351 (transfer to a corporation controlled by the transferor) or IRC Section 721 (contribution to a partnership in exchange for a partnership interest).

6. • ☐ The seller is a corporation (or a limited liability company (LLC) classified as a corporation for federal and California income tax purposes) that is either qualified through the California Secretary of State or has a permanent place of business in California.

7. • ☐ The seller is a California partnership, or qualified to do business in California (or an LLC that is classified as a partnership for federal and California income tax purposes and is not a single member LLC) that is not disregarded for federal and California income tax purposes. If this box is checked, the partnership or LLC must withhold on nonresident partners or members.

8. • ☐ The seller is a tax-exempt entity under California or federal law.

9. • ☐ The seller is an insurance company, individual retirement account, qualified pension/profit sharing plan, or charitable remainder trust.

Part III – Certifications that may partially or fully exempt the sale from withholding:

Real Estate Escrow Person (REEP): See instructions for amounts to withhold.

10. • ☐ The transfer qualifies as a simultaneous like-kind exchange within the meaning of IRC Section 1031.
11. • ☐ The transfer qualifies as a deferred like-kind exchange within the meaning of IRC Section 1031.
12. • ☐ The transfer of this property is an installment sale where the buyer is required to withhold on the principal portion of each installment payment. Copies of Form 593-I, Real Estate Withholding Acknowledgement, and the promissory note are attached.

Part IV – Seller's Signature

Under penalties of perjury, I hereby certify that the information provided above is, to the best of my knowledge, true and correct. If conditions change, I will promptly inform the withholding agent. I understand that the Franchise Tax Board may review relevant escrow documents to ensure withholding compliance and that completing this form does **not** exempt me from filing a California income or franchise tax return to report this sale.

Seller's Name and Title _Charles D Lee_____ Seller's Signature_____ Date: _____

Spouse's/RDP's Name _Elizabeth C Lee_____ Spouse's/RDP's Signature _____ Date: _____

Please verify that the SSN or ITIN listed above in Part 1 of this form is correct.

Seller: If you checked any box in Part II, you are exempt from real estate withholding.

If you checked any box in Part III, you may qualify for a partial or complete withholding exemption.

If you did not check any box in Part II or Part III, the withholding will be 3 1/3% (.0333) of the total sales price or the optional gain on sale withholding amount certified by seller on Form 593, Real Estate Withholding Tax Statement.

If you are withheld upon, the withholding agent should give you one copy of Form 593. Attach a copy to the lower front of your California income tax return and make a copy for your records.

Keep Form 593-C for five years following the close of the transaction. You must furnish the form to the FTB upon request.

Instructions for Form 593-C
Real Estate Withholding Certificate

References in these instructions are to the Internal Revenue Code (IRC) as of **January 1, 2005**, and to the California Revenue and Taxation Code (R&TC).

Purpose

Use Form 593-C, Real Estate Withholding Certificate, to determine whether you qualify for a full or partial withholding exemption

> Qualifying for an exemption from withholding or being withheld upon does not relieve you of your obligation to file a California tax return and pay any tax due on the sale of California real estate
>
> The seller must submit this form before the close of escrow to prevent withholding on the transaction After escrow has closed, amounts withheld may be recovered only by claiming the withholding as a credit on the appropriate year's tax return

Part I Seller's Information

Name, Address, and Taxpayer Identification Number Enter the name, address, and tax identification number of the seller or other transferor If the seller does not provide a tax identification number, then Form 593-C is void, and withholding is required

If the seller is an **individual**, enter the social security number (SSN) or individual taxpayer identification number (ITIN) If the sellers are spouses/registered domestic partners (RDPs) and plan to file a joint return, enter the name and SSN or ITIN for each spouse/RDP Otherwise, do not enter information for more than one seller Instead, complete a separate Form 593-C for each seller.

If you do not have a SSN because you are a nonresident or a resident alien for federal tax purposes, and the Internal Revenue Service (IRS) issued you an ITIN, enter the ITIN in the space provided for the SSN.

An ITIN is a tax processing number issued by the IRS to individuals who have a federal tax filing requirement and do not qualify for a SSN It is a nine-digit number that always starts with the number 9.

If the seller is a **grantor trust**, enter the grantor's individual name and SSN For tax purposes, the grantor trust is disregarded for tax purposes and the individual seller must report the sale and claim the withholding on their individual tax return If the trust was a grantor trust that became irrevocable upon the grantor's death, enter the name of the trust and the trust's federal employer identification number (FEIN) **Do not enter the decedent's or trustee's name or SSN.**

If the seller is a **non-grantor trust**, enter the name of the trust and the trust's FEIN **Do not enter trustee information.**

If the seller is a **single member disregarded LLC**, enter the name and tax identification number of the single member

Real Estate Escrow Person (REEP): If you choose to provide a copy of Form 593-C to the buyer, delete the seller's tax identification number on the buyer's copy.

Ownership Percentage

Enter your ownership percentage rounded to two decimal places (e g 66 67%) If you are on the title for incidental purposes and you have no financial ownership, enter 0 00 and skip to Part IV You will not be withheld upon

Examples of sellers who are on title for incidental purposes are:

- Co-signors on title (e g , parents co-signed to help their child qualify for the loan)
- Family members on title to receive property upon the owner's death

Part II Certifications That Fully Exempt Withholding

Line 1 – Principal Residence

To qualify as your principal residence under Internal Revenue Code (IRC) Section 121, you (or the decedent) generally must have owned and lived in the property as your main home for at least two years during the five-year period ending on the date of sale Military and Foreign Service, get FTB Pub 1032, Tax Information for Military Personnel.

You can have only one main home at a time If you have two homes and live in both of them, the main home is the one you lived in most of the time.

There are exceptions to the two-year rule if the primary reason you are selling the home is for a change in the place of employment, health, or unforeseen circumstances such as death, divorce or termination of registered domestic partnership, or loss of job, etc For more information about what qualifies as your principal residence or exceptions to the two-year rule, get federal Publication 523, Selling Your Home. You can get this publication by accessing the IRS website at **irs.gov**, or by calling the IRS at 800 829 3676.

If only a portion of the property qualifies as your principal residence, insert the percentage allocated to the principal residence in the space above line 1 and inform the REEP.

The allocation method should be the same as the seller used to determine depreciation

Line 2 – Property last used as your principal residence

If the property was last used as the seller's or decedent's principal residence within the meaning of IRC Section 121 without regard to the two-year time period, no withholding is required If the last use of the property was as a vacation home, second home, or rental, you do not qualify You must have lived in the property as your main home.

If you have two homes and live in both of them, the main home is the one you lived in most of the time

Line 3 – Loss or Zero Gain

You have a loss or zero gain for California income tax purposes when the amount realized is less than or equal to your adjusted basis You must complete Form 593-E, Real Estate Withholding — Computation of Estimated Gain or Loss, and have a loss or zero gain on line 16 to certify that the transaction is fully exempt from withholding.

You may not certify that you have a net loss or zero gain just because you do not receive any proceeds from the sale or because you feel you are selling the property for less than what it is worth

Line 4 – Involuntary Conversion

The property is being involuntarily or compulsorily converted when both of the following apply:

- The California real property is transferred because it was (or threatened to be) seized, destroyed, or condemned within the meaning of IRC Section 1033.

- The transferor (seller) intends to acquire property that is similar or related in service or use in order to be eligible for nonrecognition of gain for California income tax purposes.

Get federal Publication 544, Sales and Other Dispositions of Assets, for more information about involuntary conversions

Line 5 – Non-recognition Under IRC Section 351 or 71

The transfer must qualify for nonrecognition treatment under IRC Section 351 (transferring to a corporation controlled by transferor) or IRC Section 721 (contributing to a partnership in exchange for a partnership interest) **Real Estate Escrow Person:** If, during the escrow, an individual seller transfers title to a corporation or partnership and then the corporation or partnership transfers title to the buyer, then there are two transfers for withholding purposes Accordingly, two separate Forms 593-C should be completed for withholding purposes The individual must complete one form for the transfer to the corporation or partnership The corporation or partnership must complete the other form for the transfer to the buyer

Line 6 – Corporation

A corporation has a permanent place of business in California if any of the following apply:

- It is organized and existing under the laws of California
- It is qualified to transact business in California through the California Secretary of State
- It will maintain and staff a permanent office in California

S corporations must withhold on nonresident S corporation shareholders Get FTB Pub 1017, Resident and Nonresident Withholding Guidelines, for more information.

Line 7 – Partnership or Limited Liability Company (LLC)

Withholding is not required if the title to the property transferred is recorded in the name of a partnership.

However, partnerships are required to withhold on nonresident partners. For more information, get FTB Pub. 1017.

Withholding is not required if the title to the property transferred is in the name of an LLC, and the LLC meets both of the following requirements:

- The LLC is classified as a partnership for federal and California income tax purposes.
- The LLC is **not** a single member LLC that is disregarded for federal and California income tax purposes.

If the LLC meets these conditions, the LLC must still withhold on nonresident members. Get FTB Pub. 1017 for more information.

If the single member LLC (SMLLC) is classified as a corporation for federal and California income tax purposes, then the seller is considered a corporation for withholding purposes. Refer to Line 6.

If the LLC is a SMLLC that is disregarded for federal and California income tax purposes, then that single member is considered the seller and title to the property is considered to be in the name of the single member for withholding purposes.

When completing Form 593-C as the single member of a disregarded LLC, write on the bottom of the form that the information on the form is for the single member of the LLC, so the REEP will understand why it is different from the recorded title holder.

- If the single member is an individual, Form 593-C should be completed using the individual's information.
- If the single member is a corporation, Form 593-C should be completed using the corporation's information.
- If the single member is a partnership, Form 593-C should be completed using the partnership's information.
- If the single member is an LLC, Form 593-C should be completed using the single member's information.

Line 8 – Tax-Exempt Entity

Withholding is not required if the seller is tax-exempt under either California or federal law (e.g., religious, charitable, educational, not for profit organizations, etc.).

Line 9 – Insurance Company, Individual Retirement Account, Qualified Pension or Profit-Sharing Plan, or Charitable Remainder Trust

Withholding is not required when the seller is an insurance company, individual retirement account, qualified pension or profit-sharing plan, or a charitable remainder trust.

Part III Certifications That May Partially or Fully Exempt the Sale From Withholding

Complete Part III only if you did not meet any of the exemptions in Part II. If you met an exemption in Part II skip to Part IV.

Line 10 – Simultaneous Exchange

If the California real property is part of a simultaneous like-kind exchange within the meaning of IRC Section 1031, the transfer is exempt from withholding. However, if the seller receives taxable proceeds (boot) exceeding $1,500 from the sale, the withholding agent must withhold on the boot.

Line 11 – Deferred Exchange

If the California real property is part of a deferred like-kind exchange within the meaning of IRC Section 1031, the sale is exempt from withholding at the time of the initial transfer. However, if the seller receives taxable proceeds (boot) exceeding $1,500 from the sale, the withholding agent must withhold on the boot.

The intermediary or accommodator must withhold on all cash or cash equivalent (boot) it distributes to the seller if the amount exceeds $1,500.

If the exchange does not take place or if the exchange does not qualify for nonrecognition treatment, the intermediary or accommodator must withhold 3 1/3% of the total sales price.

Line 12 – Installment Sale

Beginning January 1, 2009, the buyer is required to withhold on the principal portion of each installment payment if the sale is structured as an installment sale. The buyer must complete and sign Form 593-I, Real Estate Withholding Sale Acknowledgement, and attach a copy of the promissory note with the first installment payment.

When the withholding amount on the first installment principal payment is sent to the FTB, the FTB must also receive a completed Form 593-I, Real Estate Withholding Sale Acknowledgement, a completed Form 593, Real Estate Withholding Tax Statement, and a copy of the promissory note.

Part IV Seller's Signature

You must sign this form and return it to your REEP by the close of escrow for it to be valid. Otherwise, the withholding agent must withhold the full 31/3% of the total sales price or the optional gain on sale withholding amount from line 5 of Form 593 that is certified by the seller.

Any transferor (seller) who, for the purpose of avoiding the withholding requirements, knowingly executes a false certificate is liable for a penalty of $1,000 or 20% of the required withholding amount, whichever is greater

CONFIDENTIAL INFORMATION STATEMENT

Grover Escrow Corporation

Escrow No.:
Order No.:

In order to expedite the completion of your transaction, we are requesting that you complete the following "Statement of Information" form. We are not unnecessarily interested in your personal affairs, however, we have been asked to insure the title to real property in which you are interested and that requires a title search.

Party 1	Party 2
FIRST MIDDLE LAST	FIRST MIDDLE LAST
FORMER LAST NAME(S), IF ANY	FORMER LAST NAME(S), IF ANY
BIRTHPLACE BIRTH DATE	BIRTHPLACE BIRTH DATE
SOCIAL SECURITY NUMBER DRIVER'S LICENSE NUMBER	SOCIAL SECURITY NUMBER DRIVER'S LICENSE NUMBER
I ☐ AM SINGLE ☐ AM MARRIED ☐ HAVE A DOMESTIC PARTNER	I ☐ AM SINGLE ☐ AM MARRIED ☐ HAVE A DOMESTIC PARTNER
NAME OF CURRENT SPOUSE OR DOMESTIC PARTNER (if different from Party 2)	NAME OF CURRENT SPOUSE OR DOMESTIC PARTNER (if different from Party 1)
NAME OF FORMER SPOUSE OR DOMESTIC PARTNER (IF NONE, WRITE "NONE")	NAME OF FORMER SPOUSE OR DOMESTIC PARTNER (IF NONE, WRITE "NONE")

RESIDENCES LAST 10 YEARS

Party One
Number and Street   City, State, Zip Code   From (Date)   To (Date)
Number and Street   City, State, Zip Code   From (Date)   To (Date)

Party Two
Number and Street   City, State, Zip Code   From (Date)   To (Date)
Number and Street   City, State, Zip Code   From (Date)   To (Date)

OCCUPATIONS LAST 10 YEARS

Party One
Occupation   Firm Name   Address   No. Years
Occupation   Firm Name   Address   No. Years

Party Two
Occupation   Firm Name   Address   No. Years
Occupation   Firm Name   Address   No. Years

Party One

Signature:
Date:
Home Phone:
Business Phone:

Party Two

Signature:
Date:
Home Phone:
Business Phone:

Grover Escrow Corporation
P.O. Box 190, 111 South Illinois Street
Anaheim, CA 92815-0190
P: (714) 533-1311 • F: (714) 533-1661

A B C Realty
9876 Realty Rd
Any Town, CA 12356

Date: August 12, 2009
Escrow No.:

Attn: Bob   Smith

RE: Property Address: **7711 Pleasant Drive, Any Town, CA 12345-6000**

Thank you for selecting **Grover Escrow Corporation** to process your client's escrow. We appreciate the opportunity to be of service to you, and your client. Enclosed please find the following:

SIGN AND RETURN the enclosed items, retain the copy for your records:
Commission Instructions

The following is ENCLOSED for your records:
Escrow Instructions
Commission Instructions

Should you have any questions or need any further assistance, please do not hesitate to contact the undersigned. Thank you.

Grover Escrow Corporation

Escrow Officer

Grover Escrow Corporation

P.O. Box 190, 111 South Illinois Street
Anaheim, CA 92815-0190
P: (714) 533-1311 • F: (714) 533-1661

X Y Z Realty
123 Realty Street
Any Town, CA 12345

Date: August 12, 2009
Escrow No.:

Attn: George Smith

RE: Property Address: **7711 Pleasant Drive, Any Town, CA 12345-6000**

Thank you for selecting **Grover Escrow Corporation** to process your client's escrow. We appreciate the opportunity to be of service to you, and your client. Enclosed please find the following:

SIGN AND RETURN the enclosed items, retain the copy for your records:
> Commission Instructions

The following is ENCLOSED for your records:
> Escrow Instructions
> Commission Instructions

Should you have any questions or need any further assistance, please do not hesitate to contact the undersigned. Thank you.

Grover Escrow Corporation

Escrow Officer

Grover Escrow Corporation
P.O. Box 190, 111 South Illinois Street
Anaheim, CA 92815-0190
P: (714) 533-1311 • F: (714) 533-1661

Good Time Lending   Date: August 12, 2009
100 S South Street   Escrow No.:
Your Town , CA 12345   Your Loan No.: **123456**

Attn: Mr Lender

RE: Borrower: **John G Martinez and Mary S Martinez**
      Property Address: **7711 Pleasant Drive, Any Town, CA 12345-6000**

In connection with the above referenced escrow, we enclose the following documents and/or papers:
    Certified Copy of Escrow Instructions
    Preliminary Report to follow issued by **Big Time Title**, Order Number **12345678**.

A title order has been opened with:
                Big Time Title
                100 N North Street, Your Town, Ca 12345
                Title Officer:
                ,   **Sammy   Title** Phone No714-123-4567

If you do not receive your preliminary report and other requested items shortly, please call them direct for faster delivery…….thank you.

We appreciate the opportunity to be of service to you in this transaction. Should you have any questions, please call us at the telephone number(s) referenced above.

Grover Escrow Corporation

Escrow Officer

Escrow No.: _____

PRELIMINARY CHANGE OF OWNERSHIP

(To be completed by transferee (buyer) prior t transfer of subject property in accordance with Section 480.3 of the Revenue and Taxation Code.) This report is not a public document.

A preliminary Change in Ownership Report must be filed with each conveyance in the County Recorder's office for the county where the property is located: this particular form may be used in all 58 counties of California	

SELLER/TRANSFEROR: **Charles D Lee and Elizabeth C Lee**

BUYER/TRANSFEREE: **John G Martinez and Mary S Martinez**

ASSESSOR'S PARCEL NUMBER(S): **123-456-789**

PROPERTY ADDRESS OR LOCATION: **7711 Pleasant Drive, Any Town, CA 12345-6000**

Mail Tax Information to: (Name): **John G Martinez**

Mary S Martinez

(Address): **7711 Pleasant Drive**

Any Town, CA 12345-6000

PHONE NUMBER (8 a.m. to 5 p.m.): _____

NV-O	NV-T
CSH	PP
AREA	

NOTICE: A lien for property taxes applies to your property on January 1 of each year for the taxes owing in the following fiscal year, July 1 through June 30. One-half of these taxes is due November 1, and one-half is due February 1. The first installment becomes delinquent on December 10, and the second installment becomes delinquent on April 10. One tax bill is mailed before November 1 to the owner of record.

IF THIS TRANSFER OCCURS AFTER JANUARY 1 AND ON OR BEFORE DECEMBER 31, YOU MAY BE RESPONSIBLE FOR THE SECOND INSTALLMENT OF TAXES DUE FEBRUARY 1.

The property which you acquired may be subject to supplemental assessment in an amount to be determined by the **Orange** County Assessor. For further information on your supplemental roll obligation, please call the Assessor Realty Division at _____ . For information about this form, please call the Change of Ownership Section at _____ .

PART I: TRANSFER INFORMATION   *Please answer all questions*

YES NO

☐ ☑ A. Is this transfer solely between husband and wife (Addition of a spouse, death of a spouse, divorce settlement, etc.)?

☐ ☑ B. Is this transaction only a correction of the name(s) of the person(s) holding title to the property (For example, a name change upon marriage)?

☐ ☑ C. Is this document recorded to create, terminate, or reconvey a lender's interest in the property?

☐ ☑ D. Is this transaction recorded only as a requirement for financing purposes or to create, terminate, or reconvey a security interest (e.g. consigner)?

☐ ☑ E. Is this document recorded to substitute a trustee under a deed of trust, mortgage, or other similar document?

☐ ☑ F. Did this transfer result in the creation of a joint tenancy in which the seller (transferor) remains as one of the joint tenants?

☐ ☑ G. Does this transfer return property to the person who created the joint tenancy (original transferor)?

☐ ☑ H. Is this transfer of property:

 1. to a trust for the benefit of the grantor, or grantor's spouse?

 2. to a trust revocable by the transferor?

 3. to a trust from which the property reverts to the grantor within 12 years?

☐ ☑ I. If this property is subject to a lease, is the remaining lease term 35 years or more including written options?

☐ ☑ *J. Is this a transfer between parent(s) and child(ren) ☐ or from grandparent(s) to grandchild(ren)? ☐

☐ ☑ *K. Is this a transaction to replace a principal residence by a person 55 years of age or older?
 Within the same county? ☐ Yes ☐ No

☐ ☑ *L. Is this a transaction to replace a principal residence by a person who is severely disabled as defined by Revenue and Taxation Code Section 69.5? Within the same county? ☐ Yes ☐ No

*If you checked yes to J, K, or L, you may qualify for a property tax reassessment exclusion, which may result in lower taxes on your property. Failure to file a claim results in the reassessment of the property.

Please provide any other information that would help the Assessor to understand the nature of the transfer _____

IF YOU HAVE ANSWERED "YES" TO ANY OF THE ABOVE QUESTIONS EXCEPT J, K, OR L, PLEASE SIGN AND DATE, OTHERWISE COMPLETE BALANCE OF THE FORM.

PART II: OTHER TRANSFER INFORMATION

A. Date of transfer if other than recording date: _____

B. Type of transfer. Please check appropriate box.

☑ Purchase ☐ Foreclosure ☐ Gift ☐ Trade or Exchange ☐ Merger, Stock, or Partnership Acquisition

☐ Contract of Sale – Date of Contract _____

☐ Inheritance – Date of Death _____ ☐ Other (please explain): _____

☐ Creation of a Lease ☐ Assignment of a Lease ☐ Termination of a Lease ☐ Sale/Leaseback

☐ Date lease began _____

☐ Original term in years (including written options) _____

☐ Remaining term in years (including written options) _____

C. Was only a partial interest in the property transferred? ☐ Yes ☑ No

If 'Yes' indicate the percentage transferred: __100__ %.

AS-SV 25 SBE-ASD AH 502-A BACK (Revised 2/29/00)

PRELIMINARY CHANGE OF OWNERSHIP
Please answer, to the best of your knowledge, all applicable questions, sign and date. If a question does not apply, indicate with "N/A".

PART III: PURCHASE PRICE & TERMS OF SALE

A.   CASH DOWN PAYMENT OR Value of Trade or Exchange (excluding closing costs)   Amount $ 85,100.00

B.   FIRST DEED OF TRUST @ 5.5 %   Interest for 30 years.   Payments/Mo. = $_____ (Prin. & Int. only) $ 340,400 α
Amount

☐ FHA (_____ Discount Points)   ☐ Fixed Rate   ☑ New Loan
☑ Conventional   ☐ Variable Rate   ☐ Assumed Existing Loan Balance
☐ VA (_____ Discount Points)   ☐ All Inclusive D.T. ($_____ Wrapped)   ☐ Bank or Savings & Loan
☐ Cal-Vet   ☐ Loan Carried by Seller   ☐ Finance Company
Balloon Payment   ☐ Yes   ☐ No   Due Date   Amount
                                                                       $_____

C.   SECOND DEED OF TRUST @ _____%   Interest for _____ years.   Payments/Mo. = $_____ (Prin. & Int. only)
Amount $_____

☐ Bank or Savings & Loan   ☐ Fixed Rate   ☐ New Loan
☐ Loan Carried by Seller   ☐ Variable Rate   ☐ Assumed Existing Loan Balance
Balloon Payment   ☐ Yes   ☐ No   Due Date   Amount
                                                                       $_____

D.   OTHER FINANCING – Is other financing involved not covered in (B) and (C) above?   ☐ Yes   ☐ No   Amount
                                                                       $_____

Type _____ @ _____%   Interest for _____ years.   Payments/Mo. = $_____ (Prin. & Int. only)

☐ Bank or Savings & Loan   ☐ Fixed Rate   ☐ New Loan
☐ Loan Carried by Seller   ☐ Variable Rate   ☐ Assumed Existing Loan Balance
Balloon Payment   ☐ Yes   ☐ No   Due Date   Amount
                                                                       $_____

E.   WAS AN IMPROVEMENT BOND ASSUMED BY THE BUYER?   ☐ Yes   ☐ No   Outstanding Balance: Amount
                                                                       $_____

F.   TOTAL PURCHASE PRICE (or acquisition price, if traded or exchanged, include real estate commission if paid).
Total Items A through E | $425,000.00 |

G.   PROPERTY PURCHASED: ☐ Through a broker: ☐ Direct from seller: ☐ From a Family member   ☐ Other (explain)

Bob Smith
If purchased through a broker, provide broker's name and phone no.: _____

Please explain any special terms, seller concessions, or financing and any other information that would help the Assessor understand the purchase price

and terms of sale. _____

PART IV: PURCHASE PRICE & TERMS OF SALE

A.   TYPE OF PROPERTY TRANSFERRED:
☑ Single-family residence   ☐ Agricultural   ☐ Timeshare
☐ Multiple-family residence (no. of units: _____)   ☐ Co-op / Own-your-own   ☐ Manufactured Home
☐ Commercial / Industrial   ☐ Condominium   ☐ Unimproved lot
☐ Other (Description: _____

B.   IS THIS PROPERTY INTENDED AS YOUR PRINCIPAL RESIDENCE?   ☑ Yes   ☐ No
If 'Yes', enter date of occupancy _____/_____, _____ or intended occupancy _____/_____, _____
Month   Day   Month   Day

C.   Is Personal Property included in the Purchase Price (i.e. furniture, farm equipment, machinery, etc.
(other than a manufactured home subject to local property tax?)   ☐ Yes   ☑ No
If yes, enter the value of the personal property included in the purchase price $_____   (Attach itemized list of personal property)

D.   IS A MANUFACTURED HOME included in the purchase price?   ☐ Yes   ☐ No
If yes, how much of the purchase price is allocated to the manufactured home? $_____
Is the manufactured home subject to local property tax?   ☐ Yes   ☐ No   What is the Decal Number? _____

E.   DOES THE PROPERTY PRODUCE INCOME?   ☐ Yes   ☑ No   If yes, the income from:
☐ Lease / Rent   ☐ Contract   ☐ Mineral Rights   ☐ Other – Explain: _____

F.   WHAT WAS THE CONDITION OF THE PROPERTY AT THE TIME OF SALE?
☐ Good   ☐ Average   ☐ Fair   ☐ Poor
Please explain the physical condition of the property and provide any other information (such as restrictions, etc) that would assist the Assessor in
determining the value of the property. _____

I certify that the foregoing is true, correct and complete to the best of my knowledge and belief.
Signed _____   Date _____
NEW OWNER/CORPORATE OFFICER
Please Print Name of New Owner / Corporate Officer _____
(NOTE: The Assessor may contact you for further information)

If a document evidencing a change of ownership is presented to the recorder for recordation without the concurrent filing of a Preliminary
Change of Ownership Report, the recorder may charge an additional recording fee for twenty dollars ($20).

Appendix E
Appraisal Report

APPRAISAL REPORT OF

Martinez

7711 Pleasant Dr

Anytown, CA 92841

AS OF

08/20/2009

PREPARED FOR

Savings & Loans
1600 Imperial Blvd, Suite 110
Anytown, CA 92841

PREPARED BY

Nicolae Gavrilas
On Time Appraisal
5642 Oak Meadow Dr
Yorba Linda, CA 92886

On Time Appraisal

File No. 0108/20/2009
Case No.

Uniform Residential Appraisal Report

The purpose of this summary appraisal report is to provide the lender/client with an accurate, and adequately supported, opinion of the market value of the subject property.

SUBJECT

Property Address 7711 Pleasant Dr	City Anytown	State CA Zip Code 92841
Borrower Martinez	Owner of Public Record WELLS FARGO BANK NA 2007	County Orange

Legal Description TRACT 9938 LOT NO 35

Assessor's Parcel # 1051-401-73   Tax Year 2008   R.E. Taxes $ 4,207.38

Neighborhood Name N/A   Map Reference 642-C5   Census Tract 0018.02

Occupant [X] Owner [ ] Tenant [ ] Vacant   Special Assessments $ 0   [ ] PUD   HOA $ N/A   [ ] per year [ ] per month

Property Rights Appraised [X] Fee Simple [ ] Leasehold [ ] Other (describe)

Assignment Type [X] Purchase Transaction [ ] Refinance Transaction [ ] Other (describe)

Lender/Client Savings & Loans   Address 1600 Imperial Blvd, Suite 110, Anytown, CA 92841

Is the subject property currently offered for sale or has it been offered for sale in the twelve months prior to the effective date of this appraisal? [X] Yes [ ] No

Report data source(s) used, offerings price(s), and date(s). MLS# I08167071, $435,900., List Date:06/19/2009.

CONTRACT

I [X] did [ ] did not analyze the contract for sale for the subject purchase transaction. Explain the results of the analysis of the contract for sale or why the analysis was not performed.   Typical terms and conditions apply. Seller to credit buyer a total of 3% of purchase price towards closing costs & prepaids.

Contract Price $ 425,000   Date of Contract 08/07/2009   Is the property seller the owner of public record? [X] Yes [ ] No   Data Source(s) RealQuest

Is there any financial assistance (loan charges, sale concessions, gift or downpayment assistance, etc.) to be paid by any party on behalf of the borrower? [X] Yes [ ] No

If Yes, report the total dollar amount and describe the items to be paid. Seller to credit buyer a total of 3% of purchase price towards closing costs & prepaids.

NEIGHBORHOOD

Note: Race and the racial composition of the neighborhood are not appraisal factors.

Neighborhood Characteristics			One-Unit Housing Trends			One-Unit Housing		Present Land Use %	
Location [ ] Urban [X] Suburban [ ] Rural			Property Values [ ] Increasing [X] Stable [ ] Declining			PRICE	AGE	One-Unit	85 %
Built-Up [X] Over 75% [ ] 25-75% [ ] Under 25%			Demand/Supply [ ] Shortage [X] In Balance [ ] Over Supply			$ (000)	(yrs)	2-4 Unit	5 %
Growth [ ] Rapid [X] Stable [ ] Slow			Marketing Time [ ] Under 3 mths [X] 3-6 mths [ ] Over 6 mths			350 Low	14	Multi-Family	5 %
Neighborhood Boundaries Pomona Fwy 60 to the North, Vineyard Ave to the East, Chino Ave to the South						580 High	42	Commercial	5 %
and Mountain Ave to the West.						425 Pred.	30	Other	%

Neighborhood Description   The subject is conforming to the neighborhood in quality of construction, curb appeal, functional utilities and overall amenities. Subject is located in an area of SFR's of average quality. All schools, shopping, parks and other necessary facilities and services are within a reasonable distance.

Market Conditions (including support for the above conclusions) The market is generally stable. Some sellers paying closing costs on a one time basis. Government insured loans are typical for the area. Property values appear to be stable based on 1004 MC form, sales activity and marketing time on MLS.

SITE

Dimensions 64Ft x 125Ft   Area 8,000 SqFt   Shape Rectangular   View Residential

Specific Zoning Classification R-1   Zoning Description Residential

Zoning Compliance [X] Legal [ ] Legal Nonconforming (Grandfathered Use) [ ] No Zoning [ ] Illegal (describe)

Is the highest and best use of subject property as improved (or as proposed per plans and specifications) the present use? [X] Yes [ ] No If No, describe.

Utilities	Public	Other (describe)		Public	Other (describe)	Off-site Improvements--Type	Public	Private
Electricity	[X]		Water	[X]		Street Asphalt	[X]	
Gas	[X]		Sanitary Sewer	[X]		Alley None		

FEMA Special Flood Hazard Area [ ] Yes [X] No   FEMA Flood Zone X   FEMA Map # 0602788620F   FEMA Map Date 03/18/1996

Are the utilities and/or off-site improvements typical for the market area? [X] Yes [ ] No If No, describe.

Are there any adverse site conditions or external factors (easements, encroachments, environmental conditions, land uses, etc.)? [ ] Yes [X] No If Yes, describe.

The subject is not located in a special flood hazard area. No adverse conditions noted. Soils and preliminary title report was not provided or reviewed.

IMPROVEMENTS

General Description		Foundation		Exterior Description materials/condition	Interior materials/condition
Units [X] One [ ] One with Accessory Unit		[X] Concrete Slab [ ] Crawl Space		Foundation Walls Concrete/Avg.	Floors Carpet/Wood/Avg.
# of Stories 1 Story		[ ] Full Basement [ ] Partial Basement		Exterior Walls Stucco/Wood/Avg.	Walls Drywall/Avg.
Type [X] Det. [ ] Att. [ ] S-Det./End Unit		Basement Area N/A sq. ft.		Roof Surface Comp-Singles/Avg.	Trim/Finish Paint/Avg.
[X] Existing [ ] Proposed [ ] Under Const.		Basement Finish N/A %		Gutters & Downspouts Adequate	Bath Floor Vinyl/Tile/Avg.
Design (Style) Conventional		[ ] Outside Entry/Exit [ ] Sump Pump		Window Type Aluminum/Avg.	Bath Wainscot Ceramic/Tile/Avg.
Year Built 1979		Evidence of [ ] Infestation None Noted		Storm Sash/Insulated Yes	Car Storage [ ] None
Effective Age (Yrs) 22-24		[ ] Dampness [ ] Settlement		Screens Yes/Partial	[X] Driveway # of Cars 2
Attic [ ] None		Heating [X] FWA [ ] HWBB [ ] Radiant		Amenities [ ] Woodstove(s) #	Driveway Surface Concrete
[ ] Drop Stair [ ] Stairs		[ ] Other Fuel Gas		[X] Fireplace(s) # 1 [X] Fence Wood/Block	[X] Garage # of Cars 2
[ ] Floor [X] Scuttle		Cooling [X] Central Air Conditioning		[X] Patio/Deck [X] Porch	[ ] Carport # of Cars
[ ] Finished [ ] Heated		[ ] Individual [ ] Other Fans		[ ] Pool [ ] Other	[X] Att. [ ] Det. [ ] Built-in
Appliances [ ] Refrigerator [X] Range/Oven [X] Dishwasher [X] Disposal [X] Microwave [ ] Washer/Dryer [ ] Other (describe)					

Finished area **above** grade contains: 7 Rooms   4 Bedrooms   2.50 Bath(s)   1,726 Square Feet of Gross Living Area Above Grade

Additional features (special energy efficient items, etc.) No special energy efficient items were found.

Describe the condition of the property (including needed repairs, deterioration, renovations, remodeling, etc.).   Subject improvements are judged to be in average condition. Quality of construction appear to be average. The subject property does not appear to have any roof damage. There is no apparent structural damage to the subject. The appraiser did notice the exterior-interior paint have been applied within the last ten years therefore it has been determined that this is not a lead base paint. No apparent adverse conditions to the subject property. No need of repairs were noted.

Are there any physical deficiencies or adverse conditions that affect the livability, soundness, or structural integrity of the property? [ ] Yes [X] No If Yes, describe

No adverse environmental conditions that would affect the subject, site, improvements or immediate vicinity noted or disclosed to appraiser at the time of the inspection. See Limiting Condition # 5.

Does the property generally conform to the neighborhood (functional utility, style, condition, use, construction, etc.)? [X] Yes [ ] No If No, describe   The subject is conforming to the neighborhood in quality of construction, curb appeal, functional utilities and overall amenities. Subject is located in an area of SFR's of average quality.

Freddie Mac Form 70 March 2005

ClickFORMS Appraisal Software 800-622-8727

Fannie Mae Form 1004 March 2005

Page 1 of 18

On Time Appraisal

File No.   0108/20/2009
Case No.

Uniform Residential Appraisal Report

There are 7 comparable properties currently offered for sale in the subject neighborhood ranging in price from $ 405,000 to $ 485,000 .			
There are 54 comparable sales in the subject neighborhood within the past twelve months ranging in sale price from $ 375,000 to $ 490,000 .			

FEATURE	SUBJECT	COMPARABLE SALE # 1	+(-) $ Adjustment	COMPARABLE SALE # 2	+(-) $ Adjustment	COMPARABLE SALE # 3	+(-) $ Adjustment
Address	7711 Pleasant Dr	2528 N. Sultana Ave		2439 Caldwell St		625 W. Tam Shanter St	
	Anytown, CA 92841	Anytown, CA 92841		Anytown, CA 92841		Anytown, CA 92841	
Proximity to Subject		0.11 miles SW		0.31 miles E		0.28 miles SE	
Sale Price	$ 425,000	$ 425,000		$ 427,500		$ 470,000	
Sale Price/Gross Liv. Area	$ 246.23 sq. ft.	$ 276.33 sq. ft.		$ 259.88 sq. ft.		$ 247.63 sq. ft.	
Data Source(s)		RealQuest, MLS		RealQuest, MLS		RealQuest, MLS	
Verification Source(s)		APN# 1053-285-68		APN# 1051-192-12		APN# 1051-491-68	
VALUE ADJUSTMENTS	DESCRIPTION	DESCRIPTION	+(-) $ Adjustment	DESCRIPTION	+(-) $ Adjustment	DESCRIPTION	+(-) $ Adjustment
Sale or Financing		FHA		FHA		Conv.	
Concessions		None Noted		None Noted		None Noted	
Date of Sale/Time		06/27/2009		07/20/2009		07/29/2009	
Location	Suburban	Suburban		Suburban		Suburban	
Leasehold/Fee Simple	Fee Simple	Fee Simple		Fee Simple		Fee Simple	
Site	8,000 SqFt	7,150 SqFt	0	7,800 SqFt	0	7,226 SqFt	0
View	Residential	Residential		Residential		Residential	
Design (Style)	Conventional	Conventional		Conventional		Conventional	
Quality of Construction	Average	Average		Average		Average	
Actual Age	30 years	31 years		30 years		14 years	-5,000
Condition	Average	Average		Average		Superior	-25,000
Above Grade	Total / Bdrms. / Baths	Total / Bdrms. / Baths		Total / Bdrms. / Baths		Total / Bdrms. / Baths	0
Room Count	7 / 4 / 2.50	6 / 4 / 2.00	+2,000	7 / 4 / 2.00	+2,000	6 / 3 / 2.50	0
Gross Living Area	1,726 sq. ft.	1,538 sq. ft.	+3,760	1,645 sq. ft.	0	1,898 sq. ft.	-3,540
Basement & Finished							
Rooms Below Grade	N/A	N/A		N/A		N/A	
Functional Utility	Average	Average		Average		Average	
Heating/Cooling	FWA/CAC	FWA/CAC		FWA/CAC		FWA/CAC	
Energy Efficient Items	None Noted	None Noted		None Noted		None Noted	
Garage/Carport	2 Car Garage	2 Car Garage	0	2 Car Garage	0	3 Car Garage	-5,000
Porch/Patio/Deck	Porch,Patio	Porch,Patio		Porch,Patio		Porch,Patio	
Fireplaces	1 Fireplace	1 Fireplace	0	1 Fireplace	0	1 Fireplace	0
Pool/Spa							
Net Adjustment (Total)		X + ☐ -	$ 5,760	X + ☐	$ 2,000	☐ + X -	$ -38,540
Adjusted Sale Price		Net Adj: 1%		Net Adj: 0%		Net Adj: -8%	
of Comparables		Gross Adj: 1%	$ 430,760	Gross Adj: 0%	$ 429,500	Gross Adj: 8%	$ 431,460

I X did ☐ did not research the sale or transfer history of the subject property and comparable sales. If not, explain

My research X did ☐ did not reveal any prior sales or transfers of the subject property for the three years prior to the effective date of this appraisal.
Data source(s) RealQuest, MLS.
My research X did ☐ did not reveal any prior sales or transfers of the comparable sales for the year prior to the date of sale of the comparable sale.
Data source(s) RealQuest, MLS.
Report the results of the research and analysis of the prior sale or transfer history of the subject property and comparable sales (report additional prior sales on page 3).

ITEM	SUBJECT	COMPARABLE SALE # 1	COMPARABLE SALE # 2	COMPARABLE SALE # 3
Date of Prior Sale/Transfer	03/27/2009	No other transfer	No other transfer	No other transfer
Price of Prior Sale/Transfer	$1,000	N/A	N/A	N/A
Data Source(s)	RealQuest	RealQuest/MLS	RealQuest/MLS	RealQuest/MLS
Effective Date of Data Source(s)	08/09/2009	08/09/2009	08/09/2009	08/09/2009

Analysis of prior sale or transfer history of the subject property and comparable sales   The subject's previous owner transfer information was a foreclosure transaction. No other sale in the last 36 months. Currently the subject property is listed for sale.

Summary of Sales Comparison Approach   All sales were given equal consideration. The subject and comparable sales are conforming to the neighborhood. The value of the subject property, as indicated by the sale comparison approach, was estimated after careful comparison with four sold similar properties. The comparable sales selected are the most similar to subject with regard to lot size, livable area, age, quality of construction and overall general amenities. Subject falls within the indicated value range as reflected by the market data analysis prior and after adjustments. This information is compiled from RealQuest, MLS and public records and is not guaranteed.
Adjustments for the differences in location, lot size, building size, room count, garage parking are made accordingly.
Bath adjusted at $4,000, Site adjusted at $2.0 per SqFt.

Indicated Value by Sales Comparison Approach $ 425,000

Indicated Value by: Sales Comparison Approach $ 425,000   Cost Approach (if developed) $ 425,584   Income Approach (if developed) $ N/A
The market data approach, the principle of substitution was given more consideration in the estimate of value. Cost approach is merely supportive. Income approach was inapplicable in this evaluation.

This appraisal is made X "as is," ☐ subject to completion per plans and specifications on the basis of a hypothetical condition that the improvements have been completed, ☐ subject to the following repairs or alterations on the basis of a hypothetical condition that the repairs or alterations have been completed, or ☐ subject to the following required inspection based on the extraordinary assumption that the condition or deficiency does not require alteration or repair: This is a Complete Summary Report, prepared for use by lender/client and/or assigns - Savings & Loans.
Based on a complete visual inspection of the interior and exterior areas of the subject property, defined scope of work, statement of assumptions and limiting conditions, and appraiser's certification, my (our) opinion of the market value, as defined, of the real property that is the subject of this report is
$ 425,000   , as of   08/20/2009   , which is the date of inspection and the effective date of this appraisal.

Freddie Mac Form 70   March 2005

ClickFORMS Appraisal Software 800-622-8727

Fannie Mae Form 1004   March 2005

Page   2 of 18

On Time Appraisal

File No. 0108/20/2009
Case No.

Uniform Residential Appraisal Report

The purpose of this appraisal is to estimate the market value of the property described in the body of this appraisal report.
An inspection of the property and a study of pertinent factors, including valuation trends and an analysis of neighborhood data, led the appraiser to the conclusion that the market value, as of 08/20/2009 is: $425,000.
The opinion of value expressed in this report is contingent upon the limiting conditions attached to this report.

Environmental Conditions:
The appraisal is not a home inspection report and should not be relied upon to report the condition of the subject property being appraised.
The appraiser is unaware of any hazardous wastes, toxic substances, or other adverse environmental conditions on the subject property, or the immediate vicinity, which would negatively impact the value of the subject. There was no evidence of mold at the time of inspection, however the appraiser is not an expert in this field and offers no opinions or warranties concerning mold.

Final Reconciliation:
Greatest emphasis has been placed on the sales comparison approach as it best reflects the fluctuations of the marketplace and the interaction between typically informed buyers and sellers.

Sale and Listing History:
A title report was not provided or reviewed to determine the sales history of the subject property. The basis for the sales history is from abstract of public records data.

Clarification of Intended Use and Intended User:
The Intended User of this appraisal report is the Lender/Client. The Intended Use is to evaluate the property that is the subject of this appraisal for a mortgage finance transaction, subject to the stated Scope of Work, purpose of the appraisal, reporting requirements of this appraisal report form, and Definition of Market Value. No additional Intended Users are identified by the appraiser.

COST APPROACH TO VALUE (not required by Fannie Mae.)

Provide adequate information for the lender/client to replicate your cost figures and calculations.
Support for the opinion of site value (summary of comparable land sales or other methods for estimating site value) The subject's site value was based on research via county auditors, public data sources and appraisal data, including, but not limited to sales and or active/pending offerings. When sales of vacant land were not available the appraiser employed the extraction method to the improved sales for verify site values in the immediate area.

ESTIMATED ☐ REPRODUCTION OR ☒ REPLACEMENT COST NEW	OPINION OF SITE VALUE			=$	263,000
Source of cost data Marshall & Swift	Dwelling 1,726 Sq. Ft. @ $	110	=$		190,260
Quality rating from cost service Avg. Effective date of cost data July -2009	Bsmt. Sq. Ft. @ $		=$		
Comments on Cost Approach (gross living area calculations, depreciation, etc.)					
The land value to improvement value ratio is typical for the area.	Garage/Carport 441 Sq. Ft. @ $	35	=$		15,935
Marshall & Swift handbook used in cost approach. Depreciation based	Total Estimate of Cost-new		=$		206,195
on observed physical deterioration and age of property. Estimated	Less Physical 26 Functional 0 External 0				
remaining economic life is 40-45 years.	Depreciation 53,611		=$ (		53,611)
	Depreciated Cost of Improvements		=$		152,584
	"As-is" Value of Site Improvements		=$		10,000
Estimated Remaining Economic Life (HUD and VA only) 40 Years	Indicated Value By Cost Approach		=$		425,584

INCOME APPROACH TO VALUE (not required by Fannie Mae.)
Estimated Monthly Market Rent $ N/A X Gross Multiplier N/A =$ N/A Indicated Value by Income Approach
Summary of Income Approach (including support for market rent and GRM) N/A

PROJECT INFORMATION FOR PUDs (if applicable)
Is the developer/builder in control of the Homeowner's Association (HOA)? ☐ Yes ☐ No Unit type(s) ☐ Detached ☐ Attached
Provide the following information for PUDs ONLY if the developer/builder is in control of the HOA and the subject property is an attached dwelling unit.
Legal Name of Project
Total number of phases Total number of units Total number of units sold
Total number of units rented Total number of units for sale Data source(s)
Was the project created by the conversion of existing building(s) into a PUD? ☐ Yes ☐ No If Yes, date of conversion.
Does the project contain any multi-dwelling units? ☐ Yes ☐ No Data source.
Are the units, common elements, and recreation facilities complete? ☐ Yes ☐ No If No, describe the status of completion.

Are the common elements leased to or by the Homeowner's Association? ☐ Yes ☐ No If Yes, describe the rental terms and options.

Describe common elements and recreational facilities.

Freddie Mac Form 70 March 2005
ClickFORMS Appraisal Software 800-622-8727
Fannie Mae Form 1004 March 2005
Page 3 of 18

On Time Appraisal
EXTRA COMPARABLES 4-5-6

File No.   0108/20/2009
Case No.

Borrower   Martinez
Property Address   7711 Pleasant Dr
City   Anytown   County   Orange   State   CA   Zip Code   92841
Lender/Client   Savings & Loans   Address   1600 Imperial Blvd, Suite 110, Anytown, CA 92841

FEATURE	SUBJECT	COMPARABLE SALE # 4		COMPARABLE SALE # 5		COMPARABLE SALE # 6	
Address	7711 Pleasant Dr	1002 W. Bermuda Dunes St		958 W. Bermuda Dunes St		2411 S. Phoenix Ct	
	Anytown, CA 92841	Anytown, CA 92841		Anytown, CA 92841		Anytown, CA 92841	
Proximity to Subject		0.63 miles E		0.65 miles E		0.24 miles E	
Sale Price	$ 425,000	$ 440,000		$ 440,000		$ 427,500	
Sale Price/Gross Liv. Area	$ 246.23 sq. ft.	$ 254.92 sq. ft.		$ 223.46 sq. ft.		$ 259.88 sq. ft.	
Data Source(s)		RealQuest, MLS		RealQuest, MLS		RealQuest, MLS	
Verification Source(s)		APN# 1051-361-70		APN# 1051-391-89		APN# 1051-191-23	
VALUE ADJUSTMENTS	DESCRIPTION	DESCRIPTION	+(-) $ Adjustment	DESCRIPTION	+(-) $ Adjustment	DESCRIPTION	+(-) $ Adjustment
Sale or Financing		FHA		LP/SP		LP/SP	
Concessions		None Noted		MLS# C09159754		MLS# C09266876	
Date of Sale/Time		06/23/2009		Active:05/31/2009		Active:06/03/2009	
Location	Suburban	Suburban		Suburban		Suburban	
Leasehold/Fee Simple	Fee Simple	Fee Simple		Fee Simple		Fee Simple	
Site	8,000 SqFt	7,200 SqFt	0	7,200 SqFt	0	8,800 SqFt	0
View	Residential	Residential		Residential		Residential	
Design (Style)	Conventional	Conventional		Conventional		Conventional	
Quality of Construction	Average	Average		Average		Average	
Actual Age	30 years	31 years		31 years		30 years	
Condition	Average	Superior	-20,000	Average		Average	
Above Grade	Total Bdrms. Baths	Total Bdrms. Baths	0	Total Bdrms. Baths	0	Total Bdrms. Baths	0
Room Count	7 4 2.50	6 3 2.50	0	7 4 3.00	-2,000	6 4 2.00	+2,000
Gross Living Area	1,726 sq. ft.	1,726 sq. ft.	0	1,969 sq. ft.	-4,860	1,645 sq. ft.	0
Basement & Finished							
Rooms Below Grade	N/A	N/A		N/A		N/A	
Functional Utility	Average	Average		Average		Average	
Heating/Cooling	FWA/CAC	FWA/CAC		FWA/CAC		FWA/CAC	
Energy Efficient Items	None Noted	None Noted		None Noted		None Noted	
Garage/Carport	2 Car Garage	2 Car Garage	0	2 Car Garage	0	2 Car Garage	0
Porch/Patio/Deck	Porch,Patio	Porch,Patio		Porch,Patio		Porch,Patio	
Fireplaces	1 Fireplace	1 Fireplace	0	1 Fireplace	0	1 Fireplace	0
Pool/Spa							
Net Adjustment (Total)		+ X -	$ -20,000	+ X -	$ -6,860	X + -	$ 2,000
Adjusted Sale Price		Net Adj: -5%		Net Adj: -2%		Net Adj: 0%	
of Comparables		Gross Adj : 5%	$ 420,000	Gross Adj: 2%	$ 433,140	Gross Adj: 0%	$ 429,500

Report the results of the research and analysis of the prior sale or transfer history of the subject property and comparable sales

ITEM	SUBJECT	COMPARABLE SALE # 4	COMPARABLE SALE # 5	COMPARABLE SALE # 6
Date of Prior Sale/Transfer	03/27/2009	No other transfer	No other transfer	04/27/2009
Price of Prior Sale/Transfer	$1,000	N/A	N/A	$270,000
Data Source(s)	RealQuest	RealQuest	RealQuest/MLS	RealQuest
Effective Date of Data Source(s)	08/09/2009	08/09/2009	08/09/2009	08/09/2009

Analysis of prior sale or transfer history of the subject property and comparable sales   Comp# 1 title shows 4 bedrooms, currently being used as 5 bedrooms and in need of some repairs according to the MLS, DOM= 71. Comp# 2 was bank owned, similar condition, DOM= 97. Comp# 3 was corporate owned, superior condition/upgrades (granite kitchen countertops, one bath remodeled) according to the MLS, 3 car garage, DOM=117. Comp# 4 was bank owned, superior condition/upgrades according to the MLS, DOM= 131. Comp# 5 active and is a short sale subject to lender approval. Comp# 6 active and is bank owned, similar condition according to the MLS, previous owner transfer information was a foreclosure transaction.

As shown on the 1004MC form, the list price to sale price ratio is currently over 100%, so no adjustment was made for LP/SP.

Summary of Sales Comparison Approach

ClickFORMS Appraisal Software 800-622-8727   Page   4   of   18

On Time Appraisal

Market Conditions Addendum to the Appraisal Report

File No. 0108/20/2009
Case No.

The purpose of this addendum is to provide the lender/client with a clear and accurate understanding of the market trends and conditions prevalent in the subject neighborhood. This is a required addendum for all appraisal reports with an effective date on or after April 1, 2009.

Property Address	7711 Pleasant Dr	City	Anytown	State	CA	ZIP Code	92841

Borrower   Martinez

Instructions: The appraiser must use the information required on this form as the basis for his/her conclusions and must provide support for those conclusions, regarding housing trends and overall market conditions as reported in the Neighborhood section of the appraisal report form. The appraiser must fill in all the information to the extent it is available and reliable and must provide analysis as indicated below. If any required data is unavailable or is considered unreliable, the appraiser must provide an explanation. It is recognized that not all data sources will be able to provide data for the shaded areas below; if it is available, however, the appraiser must include that data in the analysis. If data sources provide all the required information as an average instead of the median, the appraiser should report the available figure and identify it as an average. Sales and listings must be properties that compete with the subject property, determined by applying the criteria that would be used by a prospective buyer of the subject property. The appraiser must explain any anomalies in the data, such as seasonal markets, new construction, foreclosures, etc.

Inventory Analysis	Prior 7-12 Months	Prior 4-6 Months	Current - 3 Months	Overall Trend				
Total # of Comparable Sales (Settled)	26	12	16	X	Increasing		Stable		Declining
Absorption Rate (Total Sales/Months)	4.33	4.00	5.33	X	Increasing		Stable		Declining
Total # of Comparable Active Listings	80	48	40	X	Declining		Stable		Increasing
Months of Housing Supply (Total Listings/Ab. Rate)	18.48	12.00	7.50	X	Declining		Stable		Increasing

Median Sales & List Price, DOM, Sale/List %	Prior 7-12 Months	Prior 4-6 Months	Current - 3 Months	Overall Trend				
Median Comparable Sales Price	$440,500	$430,500	$425,500		Increasing	X	Stable		Declining
Median Comparable Sales Days on Market	27	41	24	X	Increasing		Stable		Increasing
Median Comparable List Price	$450,950	$430,450	$420,750		Increasing	X	Stable		Declining
Median Comparable Listing Days on Market	145	87	42	X	Declining		Stable		Increasing
Median Sale Price as % of List Price	102.61%	104.67%	103.52%		Increasing	X	Stable		Declining
Seller-(developer, builder, etc,) paid financial assistance prevalent?	X Yes		No		Declining	X	Stable		Increasing

Explain in detail seller concessions trends for the past 12 months (e.g. seller contributions increased from 3% to 5%, increasing use of buydowns, closing costs condo fees, options, etc.)

Seller concessions for the subject's area do appear to be prevalent. Most concessions are credit towards buyers closing cost at a rate ranging from 1.5% - 4% of the purchase contract.

Are foreclosure sales (REO sales) a factor in the market? X Yes No If yes, explain (including the trends in listings and sales of foreclosed properties).
In the market area considered there is a significant number of short and foreclosed sales and this has a negative effect on property values. Nearly 80% of all properties listed for sale are either bank owned or short sale listings. Foreclosure sales were included as comparables within the appraisal report because the market is currently being dominated by foreclosure activity. Sale of existing foreclosure appears to be on the rise due to low prices and investors buying property for rental purposes.

Cite data sources for above information.
Multiple Listing Service -Tempo, RealQuest Data.

Summarize the above information as support for your conclusions in the Neighborhood section of the appraisal report form. If you used any additional information, such as an analysis of pending sales, and/or expired and withdrawn listings, to formulate your conclusions, provide both an explanation and support for your conclusions.
Market research and analysis shows the number of closed sales and absorption rate is increasing. The number of comparable listings is declining and the months of housing supply is declining which might indicate a slight recovery in the market. The comparable median sales price and list price remained fairly stable. The listing days on market is declining and the list to sale price ratio appear to be stable. Pending sales and withdrawn listings were used in the research and are considered to have similar results as the data above.

If the subject is a unit in a condominium or cooperative project, complete the following: Project Name:

Subject Project Data	Prior 7-12 Months	Prior 4-6 Months	Current - 3 Months	Overall Trend		
Total # of Comparable Sales (Settled)				Increasing	Stable	Declining
Absorption Rate (Total Sales/Months)				Increasing	Stable	Declining
Total # of Active Comparable Listings				Declining	Stable	Increasing
Months of Unit Supply (Total Listings/Ab. Rate)				Declining	Stable	Increasing

Are foreclosures sales (REO sales) a factor in the project? Yes No If yes, indicate the number of REO listings and explain the trends in listings and sales of foreclosed properties.

Summarize the above trends and address the impact on the subject unit and project.

Signature	Nick Gavin	Signature	
Appraiser Name	Nicolae Gavrilas	Supervisor Name	
Company Name	On Time Appraisal	Company Name	
Company Address	5642 Oak Meadow Dr, Yorba Linda, CA 92886	Company Address	
State License/Certification #	AR035745 State CA	State License/Certification #	State
Email Address	ngavrilas@sbcglobal.net	Email Address	

Freddie Mac Form 71 March 2009   ClickFORMS Appraisal Software 800-622-8727   Fannie Mae Form 1004MC March 2009
Page 5 of 18

On Time Appraisal

Uniform Residential Appraisal Report

File No.   0108/20/2009
Case No.

This report form is designed to report an appraisal of a one-unit property or a one-unit property with an accessory unit; including a unit in a planned unit development (PUD). This report form is not designed to report an appraisal of a manufactured home or a unit in a condominium or cooperative project.

This appraisal report is subject to the following scope of work, intended use, intended user, definition of market value, statement of assumptions and limiting conditions, and certifications. Modifications, additions, or deletions to the intended use, intended user, definition of market value, or assumptions and limiting conditions are not permitted. The appraiser may expand the scope of work to include any additional research or analysis necessary based on the complexity of this appraisal assignment. Modifications or deletions to the certifications are also not permitted. However, additional certifications that do not constitute material alterations to this appraisal report, such as those required by law or those related to the appraiser's continuing education or membership in an appraisal organization, are permitted.

SCOPE OF WORK: The scope of work for this appraisal is defined by the complexity of this appraisal assignment and the reporting requirements of this appraisal report form, including the following definition of market value, statement of assumptions and limiting conditions, and certifications. The appraiser must, at a minimum: (1) perform a complete visual inspection of the interior and exterior areas of the subject property, (2) inspect the neighborhood, (3) inspect each of the comparable sales from at least the street, (4) research, verify, and analyze data from reliable public and/or private sources, and (5) report his or her analysis, opinions, and conclusions in this appraisal report.

INTENDED USE: The intended use of this appraisal report is for the lender/client to evaluate the property that is the subject of this appraisal for a mortgage finance transaction.

INTENDED USER: The intended user of this appraisal report is the lender/client.

DEFINITION OF MARKET VALUE: The most probable price which a property should bring in a competitive and open market under all conditions requisite to a fair sale, the buyer and seller, each acting prudently, knowledgeably and assuming the price is not affected by undue stimulus. Implicit in this definition is the consummation of a sale as of a specified date and the passing of title from seller to buyer under conditions whereby: (1) buyer and seller are typically motivated; (2) both parties are well informed or well advised, and each acting in what he or she considers his or her own best interest; (3) a reasonable time is allowed for exposure in the open market; (4) payment is made in terms of cash in U. S. dollars or in terms of financial arrangements comparable thereto; and (5) the price represents the normal consideration for the property sold unaffected by special or creative financing or sales concessions* granted by anyone associated with the sale.

*Adjustments to the comparables must be made for special or creative financing or sales concessions. No adjustments are necessary for those costs which are normally paid by sellers as a result of tradition or law in a market area; these costs are readily identifiable since the seller pays these costs in virtually all sales transactions. Special or creative financing adjustments can be made to the comparable property by comparisons to financing terms offered by a third party institutional lender that is not already involved in the property or transaction. Any adjustment should not be calculated on a mechanical dollar for dollar cost of the financing or concession but the dollar amount of any adjustment should approximate the market's reaction to the financing or concessions based on the appraiser's judgment.

STATEMENT OF ASSUMPTIONS AND LIMITING CONDITIONS: The appraiser's certification in this report is subject to the following assumptions and limiting conditions:

1. The appraiser will not be responsible for matters of a legal nature that affect either the property being appraised or the title to it, except for information that he or she became aware of during the research involved in performing this appraisal. The appraiser assumes that the title is good and marketable and will not render any opinions about the title.

2. The appraiser has provided a sketch in this appraisal report to show the approximate dimensions of the improvements. The sketch is included only to assist the reader in visualizing the property and understanding the appraiser's determination of its size.

3. The appraiser has examined the available flood maps that are provided by the Federal Emergency Management Agency (or other data sources) and has noted in this appraisal report whether any portion of the subject site is located in an identified Special Flood Hazard Area. Because the appraiser is not a surveyor, he or she makes no guarantees, express or implied, regarding this determination.

4. The appraiser will not give testimony or appear in court because he or she made an appraisal of the property in question, unless specific arrangements to do so have been made beforehand, or as otherwise required by law.

5. The appraiser has noted in this appraisal report any adverse conditions (such as needed repairs, deterioration, the presence of hazardous wastes, toxic substances, etc.) observed during the inspection of the subject property or that he or she became aware of during the research involved in performing this appraisal. Unless otherwise stated in this appraisal report, the appraiser has no knowledge of any hidden or unapparent physical deficiencies or adverse conditions of the property (such as, but not limited to, needed repairs, deterioration, the presence of hazardous wastes, toxic substances, adverse environmental conditions, etc.) that would make the property less valuable, and has assumed that there are no such conditions and makes no guarantees or warranties, express or implied. The appraiser will not be responsible for any such conditions that do exist or for any engineering or testing that might be required to discover whether such conditions exist. Because the appraiser is not an expert in the field of environmental hazards, this appraisal report must not be considered as an environmental assessment of the property.

6. The appraiser has based his or her appraisal report and valuation conclusion for an appraisal that is subject to satisfactory completion, repairs, or alterations on the assumption that the completion, repairs, or alterations of the subject property will be performed in a professional manner.

On Time Appraisal
Uniform Residential Appraisal Report

File No.   0108/20/2009
Case No.

APPRAISER'S CERTIFICATION: The Appraiser certifies and agrees that:

1. I have, at a minimum, developed and reported this appraisal in accordance with the scope of work requirements stated in this appraisal report.

2. I performed a complete visual inspection of the interior and exterior areas of the subject property. I reported the condition of the improvements in factual, specific terms. I identified and reported the physical deficiencies that could affect the livability, soundness, or structural integrity of the property.

3. I performed this appraisal in accordance with the requirements of the Uniform Standards of Professional Appraisal Practice that were adopted and promulgated by the Appraisal Standards Board of The Appraisal Foundation and that were in place at the time this appraisal report was prepared.

4. I developed my opinion of the market value of the real property that is the subject of this report based on the sales comparison approach to value. I have adequate comparable market data to develop a reliable sales comparison approach for this appraisal assignment. I further certify that I considered the cost and income approaches to value but did not develop them, unless otherwise indicated in this report.

5. I researched, verified, analyzed, and reported on any current agreement for sale for the subject property, any offering for sale of the subject property in the twelve months prior to the effective date of this appraisal, and the prior sales of the subject property for a minimum of three years prior to the effective date of this appraisal, unless otherwise indicated in this report.

6. I researched, verified, analyzed, and reported on the prior sales of the comparable sales for a minimum of one year prior to the date of sale of the comparable sale, unless otherwise indicated in this report.

7. I selected and used comparable sales that are locationally, physically, and functionally the most similar to the subject property.

8. I have not used comparable sales that were the result of combining a land sale with the contract purchase price of a home that has been built or will be built on the land.

9. I have reported adjustments to the comparable sales that reflect the market's reaction to the differences between the subject property and the comparable sales.

10. I verified, from a disinterested source, all information in this report that was provided by parties who have a financial interest in the sale or financing of the subject property.

11. I have knowledge and experience in appraising this type of property in this market area.

12. I am aware of, and have access to, the necessary and appropriate public and private data sources, such as multiple listing services, tax assessment records, public land records and other such data sources for the area in which the property is located.

13. I obtained the information, estimates, and opinions furnished by other parties and expressed in this appraisal report from reliable sources that I believe to be true and correct.

14. I have taken into consideration the factors that have an impact on value with respect to the subject neighborhood, subject property, and the proximity of the subject property to adverse influences in the development of my opinion of market value. I have noted in this appraisal report any adverse conditions (such as, but not limited to, needed repairs, deterioration, the presence of hazardous wastes, toxic substances, adverse environmental conditions, etc.) observed during the inspection of the subject property or that I became aware of during the research involved in performing this appraisal. I have considered these adverse conditions in my analysis of the property value, and have reported on the effect of the conditions on the value and marketability of the subject property.

15. I have not knowingly withheld any significant information from this appraisal report and, to the best of my knowledge, all statements and information in this appraisal report are true and correct.

16. I stated in this appraisal report my own personal, unbiased, and professional analysis, opinions, and conclusions, which are subject only to the assumptions and limiting conditions in this appraisal report.

17. I have no present or prospective interest in the property that is the subject of this report, and I have no present or prospective personal interest or bias with respect to the participants in the transaction. I did not base, either partially or completely, my analysis and/or opinion of market value in this appraisal report on the race, color, religion, sex, age, marital status, handicap, familial status, or national origin of either the prospective owners or occupants of the subject property or of the present owners or occupants of the properties in the vicinity of the subject property or on any other basis prohibited by law.

18. My employment and/or compensation for performing this appraisal or any future or anticipated appraisals was not conditioned on any agreement or understanding, written or otherwise, that I would report (or present analysis supporting) a predetermined specific value, a predetermined minimum value, a range or direction in value, a value that favors the cause of any party, or the attainment of a specific result or occurrence of a specific subsequent event (such as approval of a pending mortgage loan application).

19. I personally prepared all conclusions and opinions about the real estate that were set forth in this appraisal report. If I relied on significant real property appraisal assistance from any individual or individuals in the performance of this appraisal or the preparation of this appraisal report, I have named such individual(s) and disclosed the specific tasks performed in this appraisal report. I certify that any individual so named is qualified to perform the tasks. I have not authorized anyone to make a change to any item in this appraisal report; therefore, any change made to this appraisal is unauthorized and I will take no responsibility for it.

20. I identified the lender/client in this appraisal report who is the individual, organization, or agent for the organization that ordered and will receive this appraisal report.

On Time Appraisal

File No.   0108/20/2009
Case No.

Uniform Residential Appraisal Report

21. The lender/client may disclose or distribute this appraisal report to: the borrower; another lender at the request of the borrower; the mortgagee or its successors and assigns; mortgage insurers; government sponsored enterprises; other secondary market participants; data collection or reporting services; professional appraisal organizations; any department, agency, or instrumentality of the United States; and any state, the District of Columbia, or other jurisdictions; without having to obtain the appraiser's or supervisory appraiser's (if applicable) consent. Such consent must be obtained before this appraisal report may be disclosed or distributed to any other party (including, but not limited to, the public through advertising, public relations, news, sales, or other media).

22. I am aware that any disclosure or distribution of this appraisal report by me or the lender/client may be subject to certain laws and regulations. Further, I am also subject to the provisions of the Uniform Standards of Professional Appraisal Practice that pertain to disclosure or distribution by me.

23. The borrower, another lender at the request of the borrower, the mortgagee or its successors and assigns, mortgage insurers, government sponsored enterprises, and other secondary market participants may rely on this appraisal report as part of any mortgage finance transaction that involves any one or more of these parties.

24. If this appraisal report was transmitted as an "electronic record" containing my "electronic signature," as those terms are defined in applicable federal and/or state laws (excluding audio and video recordings), or a facsimile transmission of this appraisal report containing a copy or representation of my signature, the appraisal report shall be as effective, enforceable and valid as if a paper version of this appraisal report were delivered containing my original hand written signature.

25. Any intentional or negligent misrepresentation(s) contained in this appraisal report may result in civil liability and/or criminal penalties including, but not limited to, fine or imprisonment or both under the provisions of Title 18, United States Code, Section 1001, et seq., or similar state laws.

SUPERVISORY APPRAISER'S CERTIFICATION: The Supervisory Appraiser certifies and agrees that:

1. I directly supervised the appraiser for this appraisal assignment, have read the appraisal report, and agree with the appraiser's analysis, opinions, statements, conclusions, and the appraiser's certification.

2. I accept full responsibility for the contents of this appraisal report including, but not limited to, the appraiser's analysis, opinions, statements, conclusions, and the appraiser's certification.

3. The appraiser identified in this appraisal report is either a sub-contractor or an employee of the supervisory appraiser (or the appraisal firm), is qualified to perform this appraisal, and is acceptable to perform this appraisal under the applicable state law.

4. This appraisal report complies with the Uniform Standards of Professional Appraisal Practice that were adopted and promulgated by the Appraisal Standards Board of The Appraisal Foundation and that were in place at the time this appraisal report was prepared.

5. If this appraisal report was transmitted as an "electronic record" containing my "electronic signature," as those terms are defined in applicable federal and/or state laws (excluding audio and video recordings), or a facsimile transmission of this appraisal report containing a copy or representation of my signature, the appraisal report shall be as effective, enforceable and valid as if a paper version of this appraisal report were delivered containing my original hand written signature.

APPRAISER	SUPERVISORY APPRAISER (ONLY IF REQUIRED)
Signature _Nick Gavril_	Signature _____
Name _Nicolae Gavrilas_	Name _____
Company Name _On Time Appraisal_	Company Name _____
Company Address _5642 Oak Meadow Dr_	Company Address _____
Yorba Linda, CA 92886	
Telephone Number _(714) 728-5934_	Telephone Number _____
Email Address _ngavrilas@sbcglobal.net_	Email Address _____
Date of Signature and Report _08/24/2009_	Date of Signature _____
Effective Date of Appraisal _08/20/2009_	State Certification # _____
State Certification # _____	or State License # _____
or State License # _AR035745_	State _____
or Other (describe) _____ State # _____	Expiration Date of Certification or License _____
State _CA_	
Expiration Date of Certification or License _11/30/2010_	

ADDRESS OF PROPERTY APPRAISED

7711 Pleasant Dr

Anytown, CA 92841

APPRAISED VALUE OF SUBJECT PROPERTY $ _425,000_

LENDER/CLIENT

Name _____

Company Name _Savings & Loans_

Company Address _1600 Imperial Blvd, Suite 110_

Anytown, CA 92841

Email Address _____

SUBJECT PROPERTY

☐ Did not inspect subject property
☐ Did inspect exterior of subject property from street
    Date of Inspection _____
☐ Did inspect interior and exterior of subject property
    Date of Inspection _____

COMPARABLE SALES

☐ Did not inspect exterior of comparable sales from street
☐ Did inspect exterior of comparable sales from street
    Date of Inspection _____

On Time Appraisal

DIGITAL SIGNATURE AUTHENTICATION

File No.   0108/20/2009
Case No.

Borrower Martinez
Property Address 7711 Pleasant Dr

City Anytown	County	Orange	State	CA	Zip Code	92841

Lender/Client Savings & Loans   Address 1600 Imperial Blvd, Suite 110, Anytown, CA 92841

This report contains an electronic digital signature(s) affixed by the appraiser(s). This advanced technology has been authorized by the Appraisal Standards Board of the Appraisal Foundation as compliant under specific reporting guidelines of the Uniform Standards of Professional Appraisal Practice (USPAP). The process not only acknowledges the authenticity of a printed paper copy of the report but also the file in its state of electronic storage.

The technology encompasses transmission integrity, signature security, and record keeping for each individual appraiser that affixes the signature. The appraiser has sole personal control of affixing a signature certifying its authenticity and accepting reponsibility for content analysis, and conclusions in the report.

Signature *Nick Gavus*   Date 08/24/2009
Nicolae Gavrilas

ClickFORMS Appraisal Software 800-622-8727   Page 9 of 18

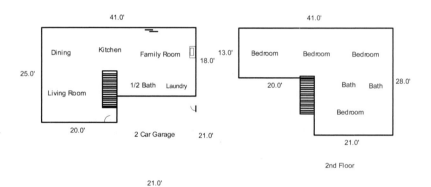

On Time Appraisal
SKETCH ADDENDUM

File No.   0108/20/2009
Case No.

Borrower	Martinez					
Property Address	7711 Pleasant Dr					
City Anytown		County	Orange	State	CA	Zip Code	92841
Lender/Client	Savings & Loans			Address	1600 Imperial Blvd, Suite 110, Anytown, CA 92841	

2nd Floor

SKETCH CALCULATIONS	Perimeter	Area
Living Area		
First Floor		878.0
Second Floor		848.0
Total Living Area		**1726.0**
Garage Area		
Attached Garage		441.0
Total Garage Area		**441.0**

ClickFORMS Appraisal Software 800-622-8727

Page   10   of   18

On Time Appraisal
LOCATION MAP ADDENDUM

File No.   0108/20/2009
Case No.

Borrower	Martinez		
Property Address	7711 Pleasant Dr		
City Anytown	County	Orange	State CA Zip Code 92841
Lender/Client Savings & Loans		Address 1600 Imperial Blvd, Suite 110, Anytown, CA 92841	

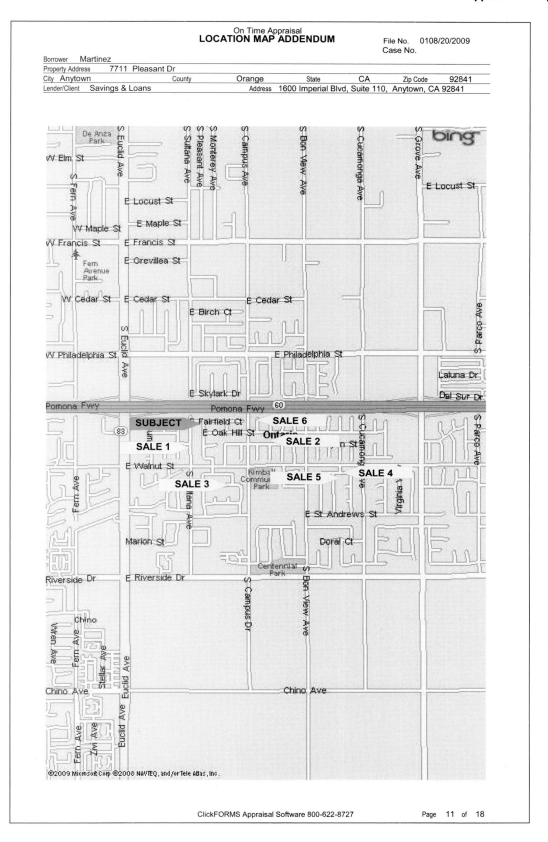

On Time Appraisal
PLAT MAP

File No.   0108/20/2009
Case No.

Borrower   Martinez
Property Address   7711 Pleasant Dr
City Anytown   County   Orange   State   CA   Zip Code   92841
Lender/Client   Savings & Loans   Address   1600 Imperial Blvd, Suite 110, Anytown, CA 92841

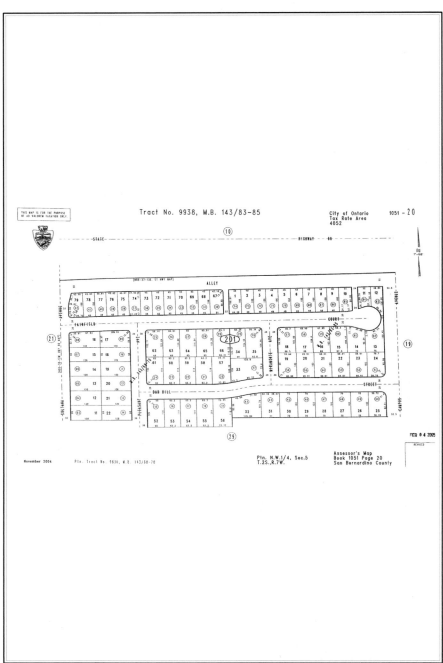

On Time Appraisal
SUBJECT PHOTO ADDENDUM

File No.   0108/20/2009
Case No.

Borrower   Martinez
Property Address   7711 Pleasant Dr
City Anytown   County   Orange   State   CA   Zip Code   92841
Lender/Client   Savings & Loans   Address   1600 Imperial Blvd, Suite 110, Anytown, CA 92841

**FRONT OF
SUBJECT PROPERTY**
7711 Pleasant Dr
Anytown, CA 92841

**REAR OF
SUBJECT PROPERTY**

STREET SCENE

ClickFORMS Appraisal Software 800-622-8727   Page   13   of   18

SUBJECT PHOTO ADDENDUM

File No.   0108/20/2009
Case No.

Borrower	Martinez					
Property Address	7711 Pleasant Dr					
City Anytown		County	Orange	State	CA	Zip Code 92841
Lender/Client	Savings & Loans		Address	1600 Imperial Blvd, Suite 110, Anytown, CA 92841		

Family Room

Bath

Kitchen

ClickFORMS Appraisal Software 800-622-8727   Page 14 of 18

On Time Appraisal
SUBJECT PHOTO ADDENDUM   File No.   0108/20/2009
Case No.

Borrower	Martinez						
Property Address	7711 Pleasant Dr						
City Anytown		County		Orange	State	CA	Zip Code 92841
Lender/Client	Savings & Loans			Address	1600 Imperial Blvd, Suite 110, Anytown, CA 92841		

Bedroom

Bedroom

Bedroom

ClickFORMS Appraisal Software 800-622-8727   Page   15   of   18

On Time Appraisal
SUBJECT PHOTO ADDENDUM

File No.   0108/20/2009
Case No.

Borrower	Martinez						
Property Address	7711 Pleasant Dr						
City Anytown		County	Orange	State	CA	Zip Code	92841
Lender/Client	Savings & Loans		Address	1600 Imperial Blvd, Suite 110, Anytown, CA 92841			

Bath

Right Side of Subject Property

Left Side of Subject Property

ClickFORMS Appraisal Software 800-622-8727   Page 16 of 18

On Time Appraisal
COMPARABLES 1-2-3

File No.   0108/20/2009
Case No.

Borrower   Martinez
Property Address   7711 Pleasant Dr
City Anytown   County   State   CA   Zip Code   92841
Lender/Client   Savings & Loans   Address   1600 Imperial Blvd, Suite 110, Anytown, CA 92841

COMPARABLE SALE #   1
2528 N. Sultana Ave
Anytown, CA 92841

COMPARABLE SALE #   2
2439 Caldwell St
Anytown, CA 92841

COMPARABLE SALE #   3
625 W. Tam Shanter St
Anytown, CA 92841

On Time Appraisal
COMPARABLES 4-5-6

File No.   0108/20/2009
Case No.

Borrower   Martinez
Property Address   7711 Pleasant Dr
City Anytown   County   Orange   State   CA   Zip Code   92841
Lender/Client   Savings & Loans   Address   1600 Imperial Blvd, Suite 110, Anytown, CA 92841

COMPARABLE SALE #   4
1002 W. Bermuda Dunes St
Anytown, CA 92841

COMPARABLE SALE #   5
958 W. Bermuda Dunes St
Anytown, CA 92841

COMPARABLE SALE #   6
2411 S. Phoenix Ct
Anytown, CA 92841

File No.   0108/20/2009
Case No.

INVOICE

Company	On Time Appraisal
Appraiser	Nicolae Gavrilas
Address	5642 Oak Meadow Dr
City, State, Zip	Yorba Linda, CA 92886

Contract Information

**** Invoices not paid within 30 days of receipt will incur a late charge of $25.00. ***

BILL TO
Savings & Loans
1600 Imperial Blvd, Suite 110
Anytown, CA 92841

PROPERTY
Martinez   Unit No. _____
7711 Pleasant Dr
Anytown, CA 92841

LENDER NO.	LOAN NO.	LOAN OFFICER	INVOICE DATE	INVOICE NO.
			08/24/2009	

DESCRIPTION	PRICE INFO.	MISC INFO.	INVOICE AMOUNT
Full Appraisal Report Paid COD			375.00

Comments/Notes
_____
_____
_____

Subtotal	$	375.00
Shipping & Handling	$	
Sales Tax @ %	$	
Total	$	375.00

(Office Copy - Clients Copy - Lenders Copy)

- -

LENDER. NO.	LOAN NO.	LOAN OFFICER	INVOICE DATE	INVOICE NO.
			08/24/2009	

Borrower: Martinez   Property Address: 7711 Pleasant Dr, Anytown, CA 92841

Billed To:	Savings & Loans 1600 Imperial Blvd, Suite 110 Anytown, CA 92841	Amount Due	$ 375.00
		Amount Paid	$

Mail To: On Time Appraisal   Contact: Nicolae Gavrilas
5642 Oak Meadow Dr
Yorba Linda, CA 92886   Phone #: (714) 728-5934

ClickFORMS Appraisal Software 800-622-8727

Appendix F
Preliminary Title Report

Loan Broker, Processor, Underwriter

Review of Sample Preliminary Title Report[1]

1. Under Schedule A Item C. The Trace No. is incorrect. It should be Tract 56, not 53.

2. Under Notes and Requirements Item 4. Homeowners Exemption: Shows NONE. This may not be an error. If you are doing an owner occupied Refinance with cash out, why has the owner not taken the exemption for tax purposes? This may be a "Red Flag".

3. Under Schedule B Item 5. Under Trustor: Charles C. & Elizabeth D. Lee. This should be Charles D. & Elizabeth C. Lee, husband and wife.

4. This is the wrong plat map.

---

[1] Are the first four items corrections to be made? If not, please explain.

SAMPLE PRELIMINARY TITLE REPORT
First United Title Insurance
2379 Escrow Avenue
City and State Zip Code

Client's Name (Usually the escrow or title company): Park Lane Escrow

Client's Address: 1234 Any Street

City and State with Zip Code: Anytown, USA 00000

Attention: Contact person at the escrow Ruth Marion

Your No.: Escrow number 00012-09-RM

Our No.: Preliminary title report number

Dated as of: Date of the report at: time of day. (Usually 7:30 AM)

IN RESPONSE TO THE ABOVE-REFERENCED APPLICATION FOR A POLICY OF TITLE INSURANCE, TITLE INSURANCE COMPANY'S NAME, a California Corporation, hereby reports that it is prepared to issue, or cause to be issued, as of the date hereof, a (Title Insurance Company's name) policy or policies of title insurance describing the land and the estate or interest therein hereinafter set forth, insuring against loss that may be sustained by reason of any defect, lien, or encumbrance not shown or referred to as an exception in Schedule B or not excluded from coverage pursuant to the printed schedules, conditions and stipulations of said forms.

The printed exceptions and exclusions from the coverage of said policy or policies are set forth in the attached cover sheet. Copies of the policy forms should be read. They are available from the office that issued this report.

Please read the exceptions shown or referred to in Schedule B of this report and the exceptions and exclusions set forth in the cover sheet attached to this report carefully. The exceptions and exclusions are meant to provide you with notice of matters that are not covered under the terms of the title insurance policy and should be carefully considered.

It is important to note that this preliminary report is not a written representation as to the conditions of title and may not list all liens, defects, and encumbrances affecting title to the land.

THIS REPORT, (AND ANY SUPPLEMENTS OR AMENDMENTS HERETO) IS ISSUED SOLELY FOR THE PURPOSE OF FACILITATING THE ISSUANCE OF A POLICY OF TITLE INSURANCE, AND NO LIABILITY IS ASSUMED HEREBY. IF IT IS DESIRED THAT LIABILITY BE ASSUMED PRIOR TO THE ISSUANCE OF A POLICY OF TITLE INSURANCE, A BINDER OR COMMITMENT SHOULD BE REQUESTED.

The form of policy of title insurance contemplated by this report is:

1. Land Title Association Standard Coverage Policy   ( )
2. American Land Title Association Owner's Policy   ( )
3. American Land Title Association Residential Title Insurance Policy   ( )
4. American Land Title Association Loan Policy   ( )

Title Officer:
Direct Telephone Line:
FAX Line:

ORDER NO.: 0000

SCHEDULE A

The estate or interest in the land hereinafter described or referred to covered by this report is:

A.   A FEE

Title to said estate or interest at the date hereof is vested in:

B.   Charles D. Lee and Elizabeth C. Lee, husband and wife, as joint tenants

The land referred to in this report is situated in the state of California, County of Anywhere, and is described as follows:

C.   Lot 17, Tract 53, in the city of Anytown, county of Anywhere, state of USA, as per map recorded in Book 789, Page 12 and 13, inclusive of miscellaneous maps, in the office of the county recorder of said county.

D.   EXCEPT all oil, gas, and hydrocarbon substances and other mineral rights, without, however, the right to enter the surface of said land down to a distance of 500 feet from the surface thereof, as reserved in the deed recorded October 11, 1975, in Book 5654, page 140, of official records.

ORDER NO.: 0000

SCHEDULE A-1

NOTES AND REQUIREMENTS

NOTE NO. 1:

California Insurance Code Section 12413.1, which was enacted by Chapter 598 of the laws of 1989 (AB 512) effective January 1, 1990, regulates the disbursement of escrow funds by title companies. Funds received by (Title Insurance Company's name) via wire transfer may be disbursed upon receipt. Funds received by this company via cashier's check or teller's check may be disbursed on the next business day after the day of deposit. IF ESCROW FUNDS (INCLUDING SHORTAGE CHECKS) ARE DISBURSED TO THIS COMPANY OTHER THAN BY WIRE TRANSFER OR CASHIER'S CHECK OR TELLER'S CHECK, DISBURSEMENT OR CLOSING WILL BE DELAYED 3 TO 7 BUSINESS DAYS. Questions concerning deposit or disbursement of escrow and sub escrow funds and recording should be directed to your title officer, escrow officer, or loan payoff officer.

1. Outgoing wire transfers will not be authorized until we have confirmation of our recording and one of the following:

    A.   We have received confirmation of the respective incoming wire.

    B.   Collection of a deposited check.

Wires directed to this office of (Title Insurance Company's name) must be directed to:

Title Wire Bank
123 ABC Street
Anytown, CA 90505
Acct. #: 55555
ABA #: 2222
FOR: 4321-5

NOTE NO. 2:

Please be advised that this company will require that the beneficiary or beneficiaries sign an estimated settlement statement any time we are presented for payoff

2.   A.   a *net proceeds* demand; or

         B.   a *short payoff* demand in which the beneficiary or beneficiaries are accepting for payoff an amount that is less than the total amount owed.

NOTE NO. 3:

We will require a statement of information from the parties named below in order to complete this report, based on the effect of documents, proceedings, liens, decrees, or other matters that do not specifically describe said land but which, if any do exist, may affect the title or impose liens or encumbrances thereon.

Parties: All Parties

3. *Note:* The statement of information is necessary to complete the search and examination of title under this order. Any title search includes matters that are indexed by name only, and having a completed statement of information assists the company in the elimination of certain matters that appear to involve the parties but in fact affect another party with the same or similar name. Be assured that the statement of information is essential and will be kept strictly confidential to this file.

NOTE NO. 4:
Property taxes, including general and special taxes, personal property taxes, if any, and any assessments collected with taxes for the fiscal year shown below are paid. For proration purposes, the amounts are:

Fiscal year 2003–2004

4. | 1st Installment: | $982.57 |
    | 2nd Installment: | $982.56 |
    | | |
    | Homeowners Exemption: | NONE |
    | | |
    | Code Area: | 01-003 |
    | Assessment No.: | 123-456-78 |

NOTE NO. 5:
5. There are no conveyances affecting said land, recorded with six months of the date of this report.

NOTE NO. 6:
6. None of the items shown in this report will cause the company to decline to attach CLTA endorsement Form 100 to an ALTA loan policy, when issued.

NOTE NO. 7:
7. There is located on said land a single-family residence known as 7711 Pleasant Drive, in the city of Anytown, county of Anywhere, state of California.

NOTE NO. 8:
8. The charge for a policy of title insurance, when issued through this title order, will be based on the short-term rate (if this applies; usually requires less than two years of ownership).

ORDER NO.: 0000

SCHEDULE B

AT THE DATE HEREOF, EXCEPTIONS TO COVERAGE IN ADDITION TO THE PRINTED EXCEPTIONS AND EXCLUSIONS IN THE POLICY FORM DESIGNATED ON THE FACE PAGE OF THIS REPORT WOULD BE AS FOLLOWS:

A. Property taxes, including general and special taxes, personal property taxes, if any, and any assessments collected with taxes, to be levied for the fiscal year 2004–2005, which are a lien not yet payable.

B. Supplemental or escaped assessments of property taxes, if any, assessed pursuant to the Revenue and Taxation Code of the state of _____ of the USA.

1. An easement for the purposes shown below and rights incidental thereto as shown or as offered for dedication on the recorded map shown below.

    Map of: Tract 56
    Purpose: Pipeline
    Affects: The southerly 10 feet of said land

2. An easement for the purpose shown below and rights incidental thereto as set forth in a document

    Granted to: Southern California Edison Company
    Purpose: Public utilities
    Recorded: March 6, 1975 in Book 4798, Page 368 of official records
    Affects: The northerly 6 feet of said land

3. An easement for the purpose shown below and rights incidental thereto as set forth in a document

    Granted to: General Telephone Company
    Purpose: Pole lines
    Recorded: June 15, 1975 in Book 4850, Page 114 of official records
    Affects: The exact location and extent of said easement is not disclosed of record

Note: If a CLTA Form 103.3 endorsement with respect to said easement is desired, please advise so that a determination can be made whether such endorsement can be issued.

4. Covenants, conditions, and restrictions (deleting there from any restrictions based on race, color, or creed) as set forth in the document.

    Recorded: July 15, 1975 in Book 4855, Page 112 of official records

Said covenants, conditions, and restrictions provide that a violation thereof shall not defeat the lien of any mortgage or deed of trust made in good faith and for value.

    Modification(s) of said covenants, conditions, and restrictions
    Recorded: October 10, 1976 in Book 4901, Page 110 of official records

5. A Deed of trust to secure an indebtedness in the amount shown below and any other obligations secured thereby

Amount:	$400,000.00
Dated:	October 10, 1991
Trustor:	Charles D Lee and Elizabeth C Lee, husband and wife
Trustee	Title Insurance Company, a California Corporation
Beneficiary:	Fly-by-Night Savings and Loan Association, a California corporation
Recorded:	October 20, 1991 as instrument No. 91-611311 of official records

An assignment of the beneficial interest under said deed of trust which names

As Assignee:	Good Deed Savings and Loan Association, a corporation
Recorded:	January 5, 1992 as instrument No. 92-0003546 of official records

6. A deed of trust to secure an indebtedness in the amount shown below and any other obligations secured thereby

Amount:	$40,000.00
Dated:	October 10, 1999
Trustor:	Charles D. Lee and Elizabeth C. Lee, husband and wife
Trustee:	Title Insurance Company, a California corporation
Beneficiary:	Your Friendly Credit Union
Recorded:	October 20, 1999 as instrument No. 91-611312 of official records

A notice of default under the terms of said deed of trust

Executed by:	Your Friendly Credit Union
Recorded:	April 15, 2001 as instrument No. 93-0112456 of official records

A substitution of trustee under said deed of trust which names as the substituted trustee, the following

Trustee:	Title Insurance Company, a California corporation
Recorded:	April 15, 2001 as instrument No. 93-0112457 of official records

7. An abstract of judgment for the amount shown below and any other amounts due.

Debtor:	Charles D. Lee and Elizabeth C. Lee
Creditor:	Cool Pool Inc., a state corporation
Dated entered:	May 5, 2003
County:	Los Angeles
Court:	Central Court of Anytown
Case No.:	AO3914
Amount:	$2,365.30, Plus interest and costs
Recorded:	June 17, 2003 as instrument No. 92-214567 of official records

8. A tax lien for the amount shown and any other amounts due in favor of the United States of America, assessed by the district director of internal revenue.

> Federal Serial No.: 93641
>
> Taxpayer: Charles D. Lee and Elizabeth C. Lee
>
> Amount: 936.40
>
> Recorded: July 15, 2002 as instrument No. 93-21568

9. A tax lien for the amount shown and any other amounts due, in favor of the state of California.

> Amount: $320.45
>
> Filed by: State Board of Equalization
>
> Taxpayer: Charles D. Lee and Elizabeth C. Lee
>
> Certification No.: 73492
>
> Recorded: August 1, 2002 as instrument No. 93-216789

10. A lien for unsecured property taxes filed by the tax collector of the county shown, for the amount set forth, and any other amounts due.

> County: Any County
>
> Fiscal Year: 2001
>
> Taxpayer: Charles D. Lee and Elizabeth C. Lee
>
> County Identification No.: 513456
>
> Amount: $193.60
>
> Recorded: August 15, 2001 as instrument No. 93-217890 of official records

11. A judgment lien for child support.

> Debtor: John G. Martinez
>
> Recorded: June 1, 1999 as instrument No. 86-771320
>
> Case No.: 86-220-971
>
> Filed by: County of Greenville
>
> Amount: None given

END OF SCHEDULE B

IMPORTANT INFORMATION: PLEASE REFER TO THE "NOTES AND REQUIREMENTS" SECTION FOR ANY INFORMATION NECESSARY TO COMPLETE THIS TRANSACTION.

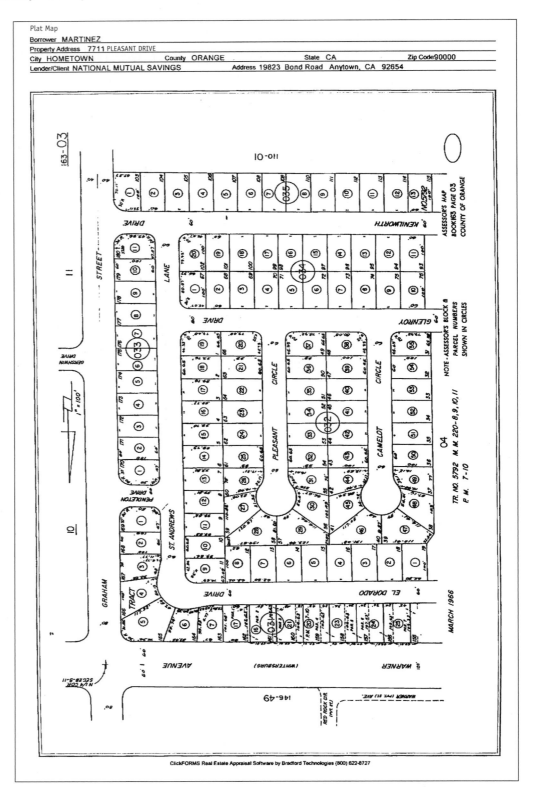

Plat Map
Borrower MARTINEZ
Property Address 7711 PLEASANT DRIVE
City HOMETOWN   County ORANGE   State CA   Zip Code 90000
Lender/Client NATIONAL MUTUAL SAVINGS   Address 19823 Bond Road Anytown, CA 92654

ClickFORMS Real Estate Appraisal Software by Bradford Technologies (800) 622-8727

Appendix G
Loan Documents

Loan Number:

Borrower Name:

Create Date:

LOAN NAME: VANDER HORCK   LOAN NO.: 2109053817

CLOSING INSTRUCTIONS

Lender

PLAZA HOME MORTGAGE, INC.

3633 INLAND EMPIRE BLVD #250
ONTARIO , CA 91764

PHONE: (909)890-9999   FAX: (909) 890-9444

ALL DOCUMENTS MUST BE IN OUR OFFICE

48   HOURS

PRIOR TO DISBURSEMENT OF LOAN FUNDS

Settlement Company

PERFORMANCE PLUS MORTGAGE
9 AZALEA
IRVINE, CA 92620-
SYLVIA CISNEROS
PHONE: (714) 502-4632   FAX: (714) 491-8636
ORDER NO: 72101

Important Dates

DOCUMENT DATE: AUGUST 10, 2009
CLOSING DATE:
FUNDING DATE:
RESCISSION DATE:
DOCUMENTS EXPIRE: AUGUST 31, 2009

Title Company

FIDELITY NATIONAL TITLE
7595 IRVINE CENTER DRIVE, SUITE 250
IRVINE, CA 92616-
JEFF ALLEN
PHONE: (949) 788-2800   FAX: (949) 341-0250
ORDER NO: 30162529

Monthly Payment

P & I	$	582.13
TAX	$	122.45
INSURANCE	$	40.00
PMI/MMI	$	0
OTHER IMPOUNDS	$	0
TOTAL	$	744.58

- We enclose the following documents necessary to complete the above-captioned loan.
- Return all documents completed as shown   24 hours after closing.
- Deliver to Borrower one (1) copy of each document signed by Borrower.
- Each Borrower must receive (2) copies of the "Notice of Right to Cancel".

[X] **Deed of Trust or Mortgage**:   *Conform and Certify copies. Deliver original to Title Company along with other originals to be recorded.*
[X] **Note**:   *Conform and Certify copies.*

ADD. TO CLOSING INSTR.	SECOND HOME RIDER	FEDERAL TIL DISC STMT
ITEMIZATION OF AMOUNT FINANCED	PAYMENT LETTER TO BORROWER	MORTGAGE FRAUD NOTICE
RESPA SERVICING DISCLOSURE	HAZARD INSURANCE AUTHORIZATION	W-9(s)
Form 4506-T REQ FOR TRANSCRIPT	SIGNATURE AFFIDAVIT AND AKA	IMPORTANT APPLICANT INFORMATION
ERROR & OMISSIONS/COMPLIANCE A	BORROWER'S CERT. & AUTHORIZATION	LIMITED POWER OF ATTORNEY
EQUAL CREDIT OPPORTUNITY ACT	FLOOD INSURANCE CERTIFICATION	OCCUPANCY STATEMENT
BORROWER CONTACT INFORMATION	INITIAL ESCROW ACCOUNT DISCLOSURE	IMPOUND ACCOUNT DISC AGREEMENT
YOUR RIGHT TO PRIVACY	DISCLOSURE OF CREDIT SCORE INFO	NOTICE FURNISHING OF NEGATIVE INFO
CALIFORNIA INSURANCE DISCLOSURE	INTERIM INTEREST PAYMENT DISCLOSURE	BORROWER'S LACK. OF DISCLOSURES
CALIFORNIA CREDIT SCORE NOTICE		

[   ] FHA 2900 or VA 1876/1820 - Borrower to execute and return all copies.   **DO NOT DATE.**
IN ADDITION TO THE ABOVE, FURNISH US THE FOLLOWING WHEN REQUESTING FUNDS:
[   ] Termite Report.
[xx] Certified copy of your original Closing Instructions.

SEE ATTACHED "ADDENDUM TO CLOSING INSTRUCTIONS - FUNDING CONDITIONS".

PRIOR TO CLOSING WE WILL OBTAIN:
[   ] Final Compliance Inspection Report.
   ALTA POLICY must contain Endorsements   8.1,100,116,100.12,103.1,100.29
   with liability in the amount of our loan on property described herein.
   LIABILITY SUBJECT ONLY TO: (Gen. & Spec. taxes) Fiscal Year   08/09   ALL PAID
      Funds may be used for account of the vestees, and you will record all instruments when you comply with
      the following:
      1. Issue said form of Policy showing title vested as shown on page 2.
      2. Issue said form of Policy free from encumbrances except items   1-3,4A-4D,6-8
          of preliminary Title Report dated   07/27/2009
          Secondary financing in the amount of $ -0-   has been approved.

LOAN NAME: VANDER HORCK LOAN NO.: 2109053817

CLOSING INSTRUCTIONS

Borrowers:
JOHN C. VANDER HORCK AND JOANN VANDER HORCK, HUSBAND AND WIFE, AS JOINT TENANTS

Property Address: 39566 BARBARA LEE LANE, FAWNSKIN, CA 92333-

Mailing Address: 5131 CARITA STREET, LONG BEACH, CA 90808-

| Property County: SAN BERNARDINO | Case Number: N/A |
| First Payment Date: OCTOBER 01, 2009 | Last Payment Date: SEPTEMBER 01, 2039 |

| Loan Amount: $ 110,000.00 | Interest Rate: 4.875 % Term: 360 months | Investor: |
| Sales Price: $ N/A | Loan Type: LEVEL | Program: FX ALL TERMS - 1ST LIEN |

FEES:

	Lender	Broker	Borrower Due	Seller Due	Borrower POC	Pay To
LOAN ORIGINATION FEE	$	$ 1,650.00	$ 1,650.00	$	$	PERFORMANCE PLUS MORTGAGE
DISCOUNT FEE	$ 138.60	$	$ 138.60	$	$	PLAZA HOME MORTGAGE, INC.
SETTLEMENT/CLOSING FEE	$ 650.00	$	$ 650.00	$	$	PERFORMANCE PLUS MORTGAGE
PROCESSING FEE	$	$ 495.00	$ 495.00	$	$	PERFORMANCE PLUS MORTGAGE
UNDERWRITING FEE	$ 830.00	$	$ 830.00	$	$	PLAZA HOME MORTGAGE, INC.
APPRAISAL REVIEW FEE TO L	$ 75.00	$	$ 75.00	$	$	PLAZA HOME MORTGAGE, INC.
WIRE FEE (ESCROW)	$ 50.00	$	$ 50.00	$	$	PERFORMANCE PLUS MORTGAGE
NOTARY FEES	$ 80.00	$	$ 80.00	$	$	PERFORMANCE PLUS MORTGAGE
WIRE FEE (TITLE)	$ 50.00	$	$ 50.00	$	$	FIDELITY NATIONAL TITLE
MERS FEE	$ 6.95	$	$ 6.95	$	$	PLAZA HOME MORTGAGE, INC.
SUB ESCROW FEE	$ 125.00	$	$ 125.00	$	$	FIDELITY NATIONAL TITLE
RECORDING FEE	$ 170.00	$	$ 170.00	$	$	FIDELITY NATIONAL TITLE
CREDIT REPORT FEE	$	$ 20.00	$ 20.00	$	$	PERFORMANCE PLUS MORTGAGE
TITLE INSURANCE FEE	$ 440.00	$	$ 440.00	$	$	FIDELITY NATIONAL TITLE
ENDORSEMENT FEE	$ 100.00	$	$ 100.00	$	$	FIDELITY NATIONAL TITLE
18 DAYS @ $ 14.692	$	$	$	$	$	
TOTALS:	$ 2,715.55	$ 2,165.00	$ 4,880.55	$	$	DEDUCTION SUBTOTAL $ 3,481.95

PAYOFFS:

[x] Closing Agent to pay directly to creditor.

[ ] Lender to pay. Will be deducted from check/wire.

WELLS FARGO	$ 75,320.00
	$
	$
	$
	$
	$
	$
	$
	$
TOTAL PAYOFFS	$ 75,320.00

IMPOUNDS:

7	MOS. COUNTY TAX	@ $ 122.45 = $	857.15
6	MOS. HAZ. INS.	@ $ 40.00 = $	240.00
	AGGREGATE ADJUSTMENT	(122.46)	

| TOTAL IMPOUNDS | $ | 974.69 |

PER DIEM INTEREST:

$ 14.692 PER DIEM INTEREST
FROM 08/14/2009 TO 09/01/2009 = $ 264.46

These are FEES NOT paid by the Borrower

	% = $
	% = $
	% = $
	% = $

CHECK / WIRE TO THE TITLE COMPANY CHECK / WIRE NO.

| | | | $ |
| | | | $ |

**IF YOU HAVE QUESTIONS ON THE ABOVE CHARGES PLEASE
NOTIFY THIS OFFICE PRIOR TO CLOSING.**

LOAN NAME: VANDER HORCK

LOAN NO.: 2109053817

CLOSING INSTRUCTIONS

-Lender must review and approve the Estimated HUD-1. Final HUD-1 and Estimated HUD-1 must match exactly. No disbursements or changes in fees are authorized unless the changes are approved by Lender prior to closing.

-Disbursements to non-lien third parties on Purchase or Refinance transactions are prohibited unless approved, in writing, by Lender.

-For recording and certified copies, the property's legal description must be attached to the Deed of Trust.

-Closing package is due within 72 hours after closing and must be sent to the closing branch listed on the Closing Instructions.

-Closing shall be said to occur only after Closing Agent has disbursed all proceeds regardless of when the Deed of Trust is recorded.

-Two certified copies of Borrower's & Seller's Settlement Statement (Final HUD-1) must be forwarded to lender within 72 hours after closing.

-If for any reason this loan does not close, please return all documents to lender.

-Lender intends to sell this loan on the secondary mortgage market after closing. If the loan is unmarketable or diminished in value as the result of a breach of these Closing Instructions by the Closing Agent, Lender's financial loss will be deemed a form of damages consequent to the breach.

I have read, understood, and have complied with all requirements listed on these instructions.

ACKNOWLEDGED AND ACCEPTED:

_____		_____	
JOHN C. VANDER HORCK	(Date)	JOANN VANDER HORCK	(Date)
_____		_____	
	(Date)		(Date)
_____		_____	
	(Date)		(Date)
_____		_____	
	(Date)		(Date)

By my signature hereon, I acknowledge that I have read, understand, and have complied with all requirements listed on these instructions any Addendums hereto, and with all requirements relating to settlement agent responsibilities under the 1986 Tax Reform Act.

PLAZA HOME MORTGAGE, INC.

_____		_____	
Closing Agent	Date	Lender's Authorized Signature	Date

LOAN NAME: VANDER HORCK   LOAN NO.: 2109053817

ADDENDUM TO CLOSING INSTRUCTIONS
FUNDING CONDITIONS

The following conditions must be met prior to funding. Please include all necessary documentation with the funding package.

1) PRIOR TO: FUNDING - CURRENT PAYOFF DEMAND FOR WELLS FARGO TO SHOW NO LATES

2) PRIOR TO: FUNDING - PHM TO COMPLETE DEMAND CHECKLIST

3) PRIOR TO: FUNDING - PAYOFF: WELLS FARGO $75,320

4) PRIOR TO: FUNDING - SIGNED & DATED FINAL TYPED 1003

5) PRIOR TO: FUNDING - 1040S TO BE SIGNED IN ESCROW

6) PRIOR TO: FUNDING - HAZARD INSURANCE

7) PRIOR TO: FUNDING - GRANT DEED OUT OF TRUST

8) PRIOR TO: FUNDING - QC W/VERBAL VOE

9) PRIOR TO: FUNDING - ESCROW AMEND RE; LENDER; RATE; TERMS

10) PRIOR TO: FUNDING - CASH OUT NOT TO EXCEED $200,000

11) PRIOR TO: FUNDING - CLOSING PROTECTION LETTER

12) PRIOR TO: FUNDING - AKA: JOHN C VANDER; JOHN C MCCARLEY; JOANN MCCARLEY

13) PRIOR TO: FUNDING - CREDIT INVOICE FOR $20

14) PRIOR TO: FUNDING - INSURANCE COVERAGE MUST = $183,520

15) PRIOR TO: FUNDING - APPRAISER TO CORRECT STREET NAME TO "BARBARA LEE LANE" (PER TITLE)

16) PRIOR TO: - BORROWER(S) TO EXECUTE IRS FORM 4506

17) PRIOR TO: - ALL FUNDS RECEIVED FOR CLOSING MUST BE RECEIVED DIRECTLY FROM THE BORROWER(S) ACCOUNTS AS LISTED ON THE LOAN APPLICATION UNLESS OTHERWISE APPROVED BY PLAZA MORTGAGE.

18) PRIOR TO: - ALL SIGNATURES IN BLUE INK

19) PRIOR TO: - BORROWER(S) TO SIGN/DATE TYPED LOAN APPLICATION

20) PRIOR TO: - CHANGES IN FEES AFTER PLAZA'S APPROVAL OF THE ESTIMATED HUD-1 MAY RESULT IN NEW TIL DISCLOSURE AND IF APPLICABLE, RE-OPENING RESCISSION.

21) PRIOR TO: - CLOSING AGENT TO NOTIFY LENDER IN WRITING IF THE NEW MORTGAGE REPRESENTS AN INCREASE OF OVER 25% OF A PREVIOUS MORTGAGE AMOUNT MADE WITHIN THE PAST 180 DAYS.

22) PRIOR TO: - CLOSING AGENT TO NOTIFY LENDER IN WRITING PRIOR TO CLOSING IF TITLE TO THE SUBJECT PROPERTY HAS CHANGED HANDS WITHIN THE PAST 180 DAYS .

23) PRIOR TO: - CLOSING AGENT TO NOTIFY THE LENDER IN WRITING IF THE AGENT IS AWARE OF ANY CONCURRENT OR SUBSEQUENT TRANSACTIONS INVOLVING THE BORROWER(S) OR THE SUBJECT PROPERTY.

24) PRIOR TO: - CLOSING PACKAGE AND FINAL HUD-1 IS DUE WITHIN 72 HOURS OF CLOSING AND MUST BE SENT TO THE CLOSING BRANCH LISTED ON THE LENDERS INSTRUCTIONS.

25) PRIOR TO: - COPY OF BORROWER(S) DRIVERS LICENSE(S)

26) PRIOR TO: - COPY OF DEMANDS AND PAYOFF STATEMENTS ARE REQUIRED TO BE ATTACHED TO THE ESTIMATED HUD-1 SUBMITTED TO PLAZA FOR APPROVAL.

27) PRIOR TO: - DISBURSEMENTS TO NON-LIEN THIRD PARTIES ON PURCHASE OR REFINANCE TRANSACTIONS ARE PROHIBITED UNLESS APPROVED, IN WRITING, BY PLAZA HOME MORTGAGE.

28) PRIOR TO: - E&O/FIDELITY BOND COVERAGE WITH PER INCIDENT COVERAGE OF AT LEAST THE LOAN AMOUNT AND $1 MILLION TOTAL IN LIEU OF CLOSING PROTECTION LETTER IS ACCEPTABLE IN IA, NY AND WA (IF ATTORNEY OR ESCROW CLOSING)

LENDER SUPPORT SYSTEMS, INC. GEN-159.XDP

Loan Name: VANDER HORCK   LOAN NO.: 2109053817

ADDENDUM TO CLOSING INSTRUCTIONS

Attention Settlement Agents:

Plaza Home Mortgage will <u>not</u> disburse funds to cover borrower fees that either do <u>not</u> appear on the Estimated HUD-1 or fees that were <u>not</u> verified by a Closer employed by Plaza Home Mortgage.

Lenders are required to accurately disclose fees to our borrowers. Any increase or decrease greater than <u>$35</u> for borrower paid fees will require the redraw and resigning of the TIL, Itemization, Closing Instructions, and Right to Cancel (if applicable) documents.

Please thoroughly review the fees listed on our Truth-in-Lending Itemization and verify that these fees match those on the final HUD-1 Settlement Statement. The settlement agent <u>cannot</u> change fee amounts, after the final documents have been signed by the borrower. **Note: An additional redraw fee of $150 may be charged to the broker and/or settlement agent.**

In the event Settlement Company or its agent(s) fails to follow these Closing Instructions, Lender reserves the right: (1) to file a complaint with the appropriate licensing, governing and/or policing agency; and (2) to file a civil lawsuit against the Settlement Company for damages. If suit is filed as a result of any alleged breach or failure of Settlement Company to follow these Closing Instructions, then the prevailing party obtaining final judgment in such action or proceeding shall be entitled to receive from the other its reasonable attorneys' fees incurred by reason of such action or proceeding and all costs associated with such action or proceeding.

The settlement agent is <u>required</u> to sign & date below.

By signing, the settlement agent certifies that there are no additional payoffs or fees that were not disclosed to the lender either verbally or on an Estimated HUD-1.

Acknowledged and agreed:

BY: _____

    Settlement Agent's Signature   Date

LENDER SUPPORT SYSTEMS, INC. PHM-001.PHM

NOTE

LOAN NO.: 2109053817

MIN: 100109800001173955
MERS Phone: 1-888-679-6377

AUGUST 10, 2009
[Date]

IRVINE
[City]

CALIFORNIA
[State]

39566 BARBARA LEE LANE, FAWNSKIN, CA 92333
[Property Address]

1. BORROWER'S PROMISE TO PAY

In return for a loan that I have received, I promise to pay U.S. $ 110,000.00 (this amount is called "Principal"), plus interest, to the order of the Lender. The Lender is

PLAZA HOME MORTGAGE, INC.

I will make all payments under this Note in the form of cash, check or money order.

I understand that the Lender may transfer this Note. The Lender or anyone who takes this Note by transfer and who is entitled to receive payments under this Note is called the "Note Holder."

2. INTEREST

Interest will be charged on unpaid Principal until the full amount of Principal has been paid. I will pay interest at a yearly rate of 4.875%.

The interest rate required by this Section 2 is the rate I will pay both before and after any default described in Section 6(B) of this Note.

3. PAYMENTS

(A) Time and Place of Payments

I will pay Principal and interest by making a payment every month.

I will make my monthly payment on the 1st day of each month beginning on **OCTOBER 2009**. I will make these payments every month until I have paid all of the Principal and interest and any other charges described below that I may owe under this Note. Each monthly payment will be applied as of its scheduled due date and will be applied to interest before Principal. If, on **SEPTEMBER 01, 2039**, I still owe amounts under this Note, I will pay those amounts in full on that date, which is called the "Maturity Date."

I will make my monthly payments at

PLAZA HOME MORTGAGE, INC.
5090 SHOREHAM PLACE #206, SAN DIEGO, CA 92122
or at a different place if required by the Note Holder.

(B) Amount of Monthly Payments

My monthly payment will be in the amount of U.S. $582.13.

4. BORROWER'S RIGHT TO PREPAY

I have the right to make payments of Principal at any time before they are due. A payment of Principal only is known as a "Prepayment." When I make a Prepayment, I will tell the Note Holder in writing that I am doing so. I may not designate a payment as a Prepayment if I have not made all the monthly payments due under the Note.

I may make a full Prepayment or partial Prepayments without paying a Prepayment charge. The Note Holder will use my Prepayments to reduce the amount of Principal that I owe under this Note. However, the Note Holder may apply my Prepayment to the accrued and unpaid interest on the Prepayment amount, before applying my Prepayment to reduce the Principal amount of the Note. If I make a partial Prepayment, there will be no changes in the due date or in the amount of my monthly payment unless the Note Holder agrees in writing to those changes.

MULTISTATE fixed RATE NOTE - Single Family - Fannie Mae/Freddie Mac UNIFORM INSTRUMENT

Form 3200   1/01

VMP5N (0803).00

Page 1 of 3

LENDER SUPPORT SYSTEMS, INC. 5N.NEW (05/08)

5. LOAN CHARGES

If a law, which applies to this loan and which sets maximum loan charges, is finally interpreted so that the interest or other loan charges collected or to be collected in connection with this loan exceed the permitted limits, then: (a) any such loan charge shall be reduced by the amount necessary to reduce the charge to the permitted limit; and (b) any sums already collected from me which exceeded permitted limits will be refunded to me. The Note Holder may choose to make this refund by reducing the Principal I owe under this Note or by making a direct payment to me. If a refund reduces Principal, the reduction will be treated as a partial Prepayment.

6. BORROWER'S FAILURE TO PAY AS REQUIRED

(A) Late Charge for Overdue Payments

If the Note Holder has not received the full amount of any monthly payment by the end of **15** calendar days after the date it is due, I will pay a late charge to the Note Holder. The amount of the charge will be **5.000**% of my overdue payment of Principal and interest. I will pay this late charge promptly but only once on each late payment.

(B) Default

If I do not pay the full amount of each monthly payment on the date it is due, I will be in default.

(C) Notice of Default

If I am in default, the Note Holder may send me a written notice telling me that if I do not pay the overdue amount by a certain date, the Note Holder may require me to pay immediately the full amount of Principal which has not been paid and all the interest that I owe on that amount. That date must be at least 30 days after the date on which the notice is mailed to me or delivered by other means.

(D) No Waiver By Note Holder

Even if, at a time when I am in default, the Note Holder does not require me to pay immediately in full as described above, the Note Holder will still have the right to do so if I am in default at a later time.

(E) Payment of Note Holder's Costs and Expenses

If the Note Holder has required me to pay immediately in full as described above, the Note Holder will have the right to be paid back by me for all of its costs and expenses in enforcing this Note to the extent not prohibited by applicable law. Those expenses include, for example, reasonable attorneys' fees.

7. GIVING OF NOTICES

Unless applicable law requires a different method, any notice that must be given to me under this Note will be given by delivering it or by mailing it by first class mail to me at the Property Address above or at a different address if I give the Note Holder a notice of my different address.

Any notice that must be given to the Note Holder under this Note will be given by delivering it or by mailing it by first class mail to the Note Holder at the address stated in Section 3(A) above or at a different address if I am given a notice of that different address.

8. OBLIGATIONS OF PERSONS UNDER THIS NOTE

If more than one person signs this Note, each person is fully and personally obligated to keep all of the promises made in this Note, including the promise to pay the full amount owed. Any person who is a guarantor, surety or endorser of this Note is also obligated to do these things. Any person who takes over these obligations, including the obligations of a guarantor, surety or endorser of this Note, is also obligated to keep all of the promises made in this Note. The Note Holder may enforce its rights under this Note against each person individually or against all of us together. This means that any one of us may be required to pay all of the amounts owed under this Note.

9. WAIVERS

I and any other person who has obligations under this Note waive the rights of Presentment and Notice of Dishonor. "Presentment" means the right to require the Note Holder to demand payment of amounts due. "Notice of Dishonor" means the right to require the Note Holder to give notice to other persons that amounts due have not been paid.

MULTISTATE fixed RATE NOTE - Single Family - Fannie Mae/Freddie Mac UNIFORM INSTRUMENT

10. UNIFORM SECURED NOTE

This Note is a uniform instrument with limited variations in some jurisdictions. In addition to the protections given to the Note Holder under this Note, a Mortgage, Deed of Trust, or Security Deed (the "Security Instrument"), dated the same date as this Note, protects the Note Holder from possible losses which might result if I do not keep the promises which I make in this Note. That Security Instrument describes how and under what conditions I may be required to make immediate payment in full of all amounts I owe under this Note. Some of those conditions are described as follows:

If all or any part of the Property or any Interest in the Property is sold or transferred (or if Borrower is not a natural person and a beneficial interest in Borrower is sold or transferred) without Lender's prior written consent, Lender may require immediate payment in full of all sums secured by this Security Instrument. However, this option shall not be exercised by Lender if such exercise is prohibited by Applicable Law.

If Lender exercises this option, Lender shall give Borrower notice of acceleration. The notice shall provide a period of not less than 30 days from the date the notice is given in accordance with Section 15 within which Borrower must pay all sums secured by this Security Instrument. If Borrower fails to pay these sums prior to the expiration of this period, Lender may invoke any remedies permitted by this Security Instrument without further notice or demand on Borrower.

WITNESS THE HAND(S) AND SEAL(S) OF THE UNDERSIGNED.

_____ (Seal)		_____ (Seal)	
JOHN C. VANDER HORCK -Borrower		**JOANN VANDER HORCK** -Borrower	
_____ (Seal) -Borrower		_____ (Seal) -Borrower	
_____ (Seal) -Borrower		_____ (Seal) -Borrower	
_____ (Seal) -Borrower		_____ (Seal) -Borrower	

MULTISTATE fixed RATE NOTE - Single Family - Fannie Mae/Freddie Mac UNIFORM INSTRUMENT

Recording Requested By:
PLAZA HOME MORTGAGE, INC.

Return To:
PLAZA HOME MORTGAGE, INC.
5090 SHOREHAM PLACE #206
SAN DIEGO, CA 92122

Prepared By:
PLAZA HOME MORTGAGE, INC.
5090 SHOREHAM PLACE #206
SAN DIEGO, CA 92122

_____ [Space Above This Line For Recording Data] _____

DEED OF TRUST

LOAN NO.: 2109053817
ESCROW NO.: 72101

MIN: 100109800001173955
MERS Phone: 1-888-679-6377

DEFINITIONS

Words used in multiple sections of this document are defined below and other words are defined in Sections 3, 11, 13, 18, 20 and 21. Certain rules regarding the usage of words used in this document are also provided in Section 16.

(A) "Security Instrument" means this document, which is dated **AUGUST 10, 2009**, together with all Riders to this document.

(B) "Borrower" is

JOHN C. VANDER HORCK AND JOANN VANDER HORCK, HUSBAND AND WIFE, AS JOINT TENANTS.

Borrower's address is **5131 CARITA STREET, LONG BEACH, CA 90808-**
Borrower is the trustor under this Security Instrument.

(C) "Lender" is

PLAZA HOME MORTGAGE, INC.

Lender is a **CORPORATION**
organized and existing under the laws of **CALIFORNIA**.

Lender's address is

5090 SHOREHAM PLACE #206, SAN DIEGO, CA 92122.

(D) "Trustee" is

FIDELITY NATIONAL TITLE

(E) "MERS" is Mortgage Electronic Registration Systems, Inc. MERS is a separate corporation that is acting solely as a nominee for Lender and Lender's successors and assigns. **MERS is the beneficiary under this Security Instrument**. MERS is organized and existing under the laws of Delaware, and has an address and telephone number of P.O. Box 2026, Flint, MI 48501-2026, tel. (888) 679-MERS.

CALIFORNIA-Single Family-**Fannie Mae/Freddie Mac UNIFORM INSTRUMENT WITH MERS**   Form 3005 1/01

VMP-6A(CA) (0711)   Page 1 of 15   LENDER SUPPORT SYSTEMS, INC. MERS6ACA.NEW (01/08)

(F) "Note" means the promissory note signed by Borrower and dated **AUGUST 10, 2009**
The Note states that Borrower owes Lender **ONE HUNDRED TEN THOUSAND AND NO/100 X X X X X X X X X X X X X X X X X X X X X X** Dollars (U.S. **$110,000.00**) plus interest. Borrower has promised to pay this debt in regular Periodic Payments and to pay the debt in full not later than **SEPTEMBER 01, 2039.**

(G) "Property" means the property that is described below under the heading "Transfer of Rights in the Property."

(H) "Loan" means the debt evidenced by the Note, plus interest, any prepayment charges and late charges due under the Note, and all sums due under this Security Instrument, plus interest.

(I) "Riders" means all Riders to this Security Instrument that are executed by Borrower. The following Riders are to be executed by Borrower [check box as applicable]:

☐ Adjustable Rate Rider	☐ Condominium Rider	☐ 1-4 Family Rider
☐ Graduated Payment Rider	☐ Planned Unit Development Rider	☐ Biweekly Payment Rider
☐ Balloon Rider	☐ Rate Improvement Rider	☒ Second Home Rider
☐ Other(s) [specify]		

(J) "Applicable Law" means all controlling applicable federal, state and local statutes, regulations, ordinances and administrative rules and orders (that have the effect of law) as well as all applicable final, non-appealable judicial opinions.

(K) "Community Association Dues, Fees, and Assessments" means all dues, fees, assessments, and other charges that are imposed on Borrower or the Property by a condominium association, homeowners association or similar organization.

(L) "Electronic Funds Transfer" means any transfer of funds, other than a transaction originated by check, draft, or similar paper instrument, which is initiated through an electronic terminal, telephonic instrument, computer, or magnetic tape so as to order, instruct, or authorize a financial institution to debit or credit an account. Such term includes, but is not limited to, point-of-sale transfers, automated teller machine transactions, transfers initiated by telephone, wire transfers, and automated clearinghouse transfers.

(M) "Escrow Items" means those items that are described in Section 3.

(N) "Miscellaneous Proceeds" means any compensation, settlement, award of damages, or proceeds paid by any third party (other than insurance proceeds paid under the coverages described in Section 5) for: (i) damage to, or destruction of, the Property; (ii) condemnation or other taking of all or any part of the Property; (iii) conveyance in lieu of condemnation; or (iv) misrepresentations of, or omissions as to, the value and/or condition of the Property.

(O) "Mortgage Insurance" means insurance protecting Lender against the nonpayment of, or default on, the Loan.

(P) "Periodic Payment" means the regularly scheduled amount due for (i) principal and interest under the Note, plus (ii) any amounts under Section 3 of this Security Instrument.

(Q) "RESPA" means the Real Estate Settlement Procedures Act (12 U.S.C. Section 2601 et seq.) and its implementing regulation, Regulation X (24 C.F.R. Part 3500), as they might be amended from time to time, or any additional or successor legislation or regulation that governs the same subject matter. As used in this Security Instrument, "RESPA" refers to all requirements and restrictions that are imposed in regard to a "federally related mortgage loan" even if the Loan does not qualify as a "federally related mortgage loan" under RESPA.

(R) "Successor in Interest of Borrower" means any party that has taken title to the Property, whether or not that party has assumed Borrower's obligations under the Note and/or this Security Instrument.

CALIFORNIA-Single Family-**Fannie Mae/Freddie Mac UNIFORM INSTRUMENT WITH MERS**

TRANSFER OF RIGHTS IN THE PROPERTY

The beneficiary of this Security Instrument is MERS (solely as nominee for Lender and Lender's successors and assigns) and the successors and assigns of MERS. This Security Instrument secures to Lender: (i) the repayment of the Loan, and all renewals, extensions, and modifications of the Note; and (ii) the performance of Borrower's covenants and agreements under this Security Instrument and the Note. For this purpose, Borrower irrevocably grants and conveys to Trustee, in trust, with power of sale, the following described property located in the

COUNTY	of	**SAN BERNARDINO**
[Type of Recording Jurisdiction]		[Name of Recording Jurisdiction]

LEGAL DESCRIPTION ATTACHED HERETO AND MADE A PART HEREOF

Parcel ID Number: **0304-205-10-0-000**   which currently has the address of

39566 BARBARA LEE LANE   [Street]

FAWNSKIN   [City], California   **92333**   [Zip Code]

("Property Address"):

TOGETHER WITH all the improvements now or hereafter erected on the property, and all easements, appurtenances, and fixtures now or hereafter a part of the property. All replacements and additions shall also be covered by this Security Instrument. All of the foregoing is referred to in this Security Instrument as the "Property." Borrower understands and agrees that MERS holds only legal title to the interests granted by Borrower in this Security Instrument, but, if necessary to comply with law or custom, MERS (as nominee for Lender and Lender's successors and assigns) has the right: to exercise any or all of those interests, including, but not limited to, the right to foreclose and sell the Property; and to take any action required of Lender including, but not limited to, releasing and canceling this Security Instrument.

BORROWER COVENANTS that Borrower is lawfully seized of the estate hereby conveyed and has the right to grant and convey the Property and that the Property is unencumbered, except for encumbrances of record. Borrower warrants and will defend generally the title to the Property against all claims and demands, subject to any encumbrances of record.

THIS SECURITY INSTRUMENT combines uniform covenants for national use and non-uniform covenants with limited variations by jurisdiction to constitute a uniform security instrument covering real property.

UNIFORM COVENANTS. Borrower and Lender covenant and agree as follows:

1. Payment of Principal, Interest, Escrow Items, Prepayment Charges, and Late Charges. Borrower shall pay when due the principal of, and interest on, the debt evidenced by the Note and any prepayment charges and late charges due under the Note. Borrower shall also pay funds for Escrow Items pursuant to Section 3. Payments due under the Note and this Security Instrument shall be made in U.S. currency. However, if any check or other instrument received by Lender as payment under the Note or this Security Instrument is returned to Lender unpaid, Lender may require that any or all subsequent payments due under the Note and this Security Instrument be made in one or more of the following forms, as selected by Lender: (a) cash; (b) money order; (c) certified check, bank check, treasurer's check, or cashier's check, provided any such check is drawn upon an institution whose deposits are insured by a federal agency, instrumentality, or entity; or (d) Electronic Funds Transfer.

Payments are deemed received by Lender when received at the location designated in the Note or at such other location as may be designated by Lender in accordance with the notice provisions in Section 15. Lender may return any payment or partial payment if the payment or partial payments are insufficient to bring the Loan current. Lender may accept any payment or partial payment insufficient to bring the Loan current, without waiver of any rights hereunder

CALIFORNIA-Single Family-**Fannie Mae/Freddie Mac UNIFORM INSTRUMENT WITH MERS**

or prejudice to its rights to refuse such payment or partial payments in the future, but Lender is not obligated to apply such payments at the time such payments are accepted. If each Periodic Payment is applied as of its scheduled due date, then Lender need not pay interest on unapplied funds. Lender may hold such unapplied funds until Borrower makes payment to bring the Loan current. If Borrower does not do so within a reasonable period of time, Lender shall either apply such funds or return them to Borrower. If not applied earlier, such funds will be applied to the outstanding principal balance under the Note immediately prior to foreclosure. No offset or claim which Borrower might have now or in the future against Lender shall relieve Borrower from making payments due under the Note and this Security Instrument or performing the covenants and agreements secured by this Security Instrument.

2. Application of Payments or Proceeds. Except as otherwise described in this Section 2, all payments accepted and applied by Lender shall be applied in the following order of priority: (a) interest due under the Note; (b) principal due under the Note; (c) amounts due under Section 3. Such payments shall be applied to each Periodic Payment in the order in which it became due. Any remaining amounts shall be applied first to late charges, second to any other amounts due under this Security Instrument, and then to reduce the principal balance of the Note.

If Lender receives a payment from Borrower for a delinquent Periodic Payment which includes a sufficient amount to pay any late charge due, the payment may be applied to the delinquent payment and the late charge. If more than one Periodic Payment is outstanding, Lender may apply any payment received from Borrower to the repayment of the Periodic Payments if, and to the extent that, each payment can be paid in full. To the extent that any excess exists after the payment is applied to the full payment of one or more Periodic Payments, such excess may be applied to any late charges due. Voluntary prepayments shall be applied first to any prepayment charges and then as described in the Note.

Any application of payments, insurance proceeds, or Miscellaneous Proceeds to principal due under the Note shall not extend or postpone the due date, or change the amount, of the Periodic Payments.

3. Funds for Escrow Items. Borrower shall pay to Lender on the day Periodic Payments are due under the Note, until the Note is paid in full, a sum (the "Funds") to provide for payment of amounts due for: (a) taxes and assessments and other items which can attain priority over this Security Instrument as a lien or encumbrance on the Property; (b) leasehold payments or ground rents on the Property, if any; (c) premiums for any and all insurance required by Lender under Section 5; and (d) Mortgage Insurance premiums, if any, or any sums payable by Borrower to Lender in lieu of the payment of Mortgage Insurance premiums in accordance with the provisions of Section 10. These items are called "Escrow Items." At origination or at any time during the term of the Loan, Lender may require that Community Association Dues, Fees, and Assessments, if any, be escrowed by Borrower, and such dues, fees and assessments shall be an Escrow Item. Borrower shall promptly furnish to Lender all notices of amounts to be paid under this Section. Borrower shall pay Lender the Funds for Escrow Items unless Lender waives Borrower's obligation to pay the Funds for any or all Escrow Items. Lender may waive Borrower's obligation to pay to Lender Funds for any or all Escrow Items at any time. Any such waiver may only be in writing. In the event of such waiver, Borrower shall pay directly, when and where payable, the amounts due for any Escrow Items for which payment of Funds has been waived by Lender and, if Lender requires, shall furnish to Lender receipts evidencing such payment within such time period as Lender may require. Borrower's obligation to make such payments and to provide receipts shall for all purposes be deemed to be a covenant and agreement contained in this Security Instrument, as the phrase "covenant and agreement" is used in Section 9. If Borrower is obligated to pay Escrow Items directly, pursuant to a waiver, and Borrower fails to pay the amount due for an Escrow Item, Lender may exercise its rights under Section 9 and pay such amount and Borrower shall then be obligated under Section 9 to repay to Lender any such amount. Lender may revoke the waiver as to any or all Escrow Items at any time by a notice given in accordance with Section 15 and, upon such revocation, Borrower shall pay to Lender all Funds, and in such amounts, that are then required under this Section 3.

Lender may, at any time, collect and hold Funds in an amount (a) sufficient to permit Lender to apply the Funds at the time specified under RESPA, and (b) not to exceed the maximum amount a lender can require under RESPA. Lender shall estimate the amount of Funds due on the basis of current data and reasonable estimates of expenditures of future Escrow Items or otherwise in accordance with Applicable Law.

The Funds shall be held in an institution whose deposits are insured by a federal agency, instrumentality, or entity (including Lender, if Lender is an institution whose deposits are so insured) or in any Federal Home Loan Bank. Lender shall apply the Funds to pay the Escrow Items no later than the time specified under RESPA. Lender shall not charge Borrower for holding and applying the Funds, annually analyzing the escrow account, or verifying the Escrow Items, unless Lender pays Borrower interest on the Funds and Applicable Law permits Lender to make such a charge. Unless an agreement is made in writing or Applicable Law requires interest to be paid on the Funds, Lender shall not be required to pay Borrower any interest or earnings on the Funds. Borrower and Lender can agree in writing, however, that interest shall be paid on the Funds. Lender shall give to Borrower, without charge, an annual accounting of the Funds as required by RESPA.

If there is a surplus of Funds held in escrow, as defined under RESPA, Lender shall account to Borrower for the excess funds in accordance with RESPA. If there is a shortage of Funds held in escrow, as defined under RESPA, Lender shall notify Borrower as required by RESPA, and Borrower shall pay to Lender the amount necessary to make up the shortage in accordance with RESPA, but in no more than 12 monthly payments. If there is a deficiency of Funds held in escrow, as defined under RESPA, Lender shall notify Borrower as required by RESPA, and Borrower shall pay to Lender the amount necessary to make up the deficiency in accordance with RESPA, but in no more than 12 monthly payments.

Upon payment in full of all sums secured by this Security Instrument, Lender shall promptly refund to Borrower any Funds held by Lender.

4. Charges; Liens. Borrower shall pay all taxes, assessments, charges, fines, and impositions attributable to the Property which can attain priority over this Security Instrument, leasehold payments or ground rents on the Property, if any, and Community Association Dues, Fees, and Assessments, if any. To the extent that these items are Escrow Items, Borrower shall pay them in the manner provided in Section 3.

Borrower shall promptly discharge any lien which has priority over this Security Instrument unless Borrower: (a) agrees in writing to the payment of the obligation secured by the lien in a manner acceptable to Lender, but only so long as Borrower is performing such agreement; (b) contests the lien in good faith by, or defends against enforcement of the lien in, legal proceedings which in Lender's opinion operate to prevent the enforcement of the lien while those proceedings are pending, but only until such proceedings are concluded; or (c) secures from the holder of the lien an agreement satisfactory to Lender subordinating the lien to this Security Instrument. If Lender determines that any part of the Property is subject to a lien which can attain priority over this Security Instrument, Lender may give Borrower a notice identifying the lien. Within 10 days of the date on which that notice is given, Borrower shall satisfy the lien or take one or more of the actions set forth above in this Section 4.

Lender may require Borrower to pay a one-time charge for a real estate tax verification and/or reporting service used by Lender in connection with this Loan.

5. Property Insurance. Borrower shall keep the improvements now existing or hereafter erected on the Property insured against loss by fire, hazards included within the term "extended coverage," and any other hazards including, but not limited to, earthquakes and floods, for which Lender requires insurance. This insurance shall be maintained in the amounts (including deductible levels) and for the periods that Lender requires. What Lender requires pursuant to the preceding sentences can change during the term of the Loan. The insurance carrier providing the insurance shall be chosen by Borrower subject to Lender's right to disapprove Borrower's choice, which right shall not be exercised unreasonably. Lender may require Borrower to pay, in connection with this Loan, either: (a) a one-time charge for flood zone determination, certification and tracking services; or (b) a one-time charge for flood zone determination and certification services and subsequent charges each time remappings or similar changes occur which reasonably might affect such determination or certification. Borrower shall also be responsible for the payment of any fees imposed by the Federal Emergency Management Agency in connection with the review of any flood zone determination resulting from an objection by Borrower.

If Borrower fails to maintain any of the coverages described above, Lender may obtain insurance coverage, at Lender's option and Borrower's expense. Lender is under no obligation to purchase any particular type or amount of coverage. Therefore, such coverage shall cover Lender, but might or might not protect Borrower, Borrower's equity in the Property, or the contents of the Property, against any risk, hazard or liability and might provide greater or lesser coverage than was previously in effect. Borrower acknowledges that the cost of the insurance coverage so obtained might significantly exceed the cost of insurance that Borrower could have obtained. Any amounts disbursed by Lender under this Section 5 shall become additional debt of Borrower secured by this Security Instrument. These amounts shall bear interest at the Note rate from the date of disbursement and shall be payable, with such interest, upon notice from Lender to Borrower requesting payment.

All insurance policies required by Lender and renewals of such policies shall be subject to Lender's right to disapprove such policies, shall include a standard mortgage clause, and shall name Lender as mortgagee and/or as an additional loss payee and Borrower further agrees to generally assign rights to insurance proceeds to the holder of the Note up to the amount of the outstanding loan balance. Lender shall have the right to hold the policies and renewal certificates. If Lender requires, Borrower shall promptly give to Lender all receipts of paid premiums and renewal notices. If Borrower obtains any form of insurance coverage, not otherwise required by Lender, for damage to, or destruction of, the Property, such policy shall include a standard mortgage clause and shall name Lender as mortgagee and/or as an additional loss payee and Borrower further agrees to generally assign rights to insurance proceeds to the holder of the Note up to the amount of the outstanding loan balance.

In the event of loss, Borrower shall give prompt notice to the insurance carrier and Lender. Lender may make proof of loss if not made promptly by Borrower. Unless Lender and Borrower otherwise agree in writing, any insurance proceeds, whether or not the underlying insurance was required by Lender, shall be applied to restoration or repair of the Property, if the restoration or repair is economically feasible and Lender's security is not lessened. During such repair and restoration period, Lender shall have the right to hold such insurance proceeds until Lender has had an opportunity to inspect such Property to ensure the work has been completed to Lender's satisfaction, provided that such inspection shall be undertaken promptly. Lender may disburse proceeds for the repairs and restoration in a single payment or in a series of progress payments as the work is completed. Unless an agreement is made in writing or Applicable Law requires interest to be paid on such insurance proceeds, Lender shall not be required to pay Borrower any interest or earnings on such proceeds. Fees for public adjusters, or other third parties, retained by Borrower shall not be paid out of the insurance proceeds and shall be the sole obligation of Borrower. If the restoration or repair is not economically feasible or Lender's security would be lessened, the insurance proceeds shall be applied to the sums secured by this Security Instrument, whether or not then due, with the excess, if any, paid to Borrower. Such insurance proceeds shall be applied in the order provided for in Section 2.

If Borrower abandons the Property, Lender may file, negotiate and settle any available insurance claim and related matters. If Borrower does not respond within 30 days to a notice from Lender that the insurance carrier has offered to settle a claim, then Lender may negotiate and settle the claim. The 30-day period will begin when the notice is given. In either event, or if Lender acquires the Property under Section 22 or otherwise, Borrower hereby assigns to Lender (a) Borrower's rights to any insurance proceeds in an amount not to exceed the amounts unpaid under the Note or this Security Instrument, and (b) any other of Borrower's rights (other than the right to any refund of unearned premiums paid by Borrower) under all insurance policies covering the Property, insofar as such rights are applicable to the coverage of the Property. Lender may use the insurance proceeds either to repair or restore the Property or to pay amounts unpaid under the Note or this Security Instrument, whether or not then due.

6. Occupancy. Borrower shall occupy, establish, and use the Property as Borrower's principal residence within 60 days after the execution of this Security Instrument and shall continue to occupy the Property as Borrower's principal residence for at least one year after the date of occupancy, unless Lender otherwise agrees in writing, which consent shall not be unreasonably withheld, or unless extenuating circumstances exist which are beyond Borrower's control.

7. Preservation, Maintenance and Protection of the Property; Inspections. Borrower shall not destroy, damage or impair the Property, allow the Property to deteriorate or commit waste on the Property. Whether or not Borrower is residing in the Property, Borrower shall maintain the Property in order to prevent the Property from deteriorating or decreasing in value due to its condition. Unless it is determined pursuant to Section 5 that repair or restoration is not economically feasible, Borrower shall promptly repair the Property if damaged to avoid further deterioration or damage. If insurance or condemnation proceeds are paid in connection with damage to, or the taking of, the Property, Borrower shall be responsible for repairing or restoring the Property only if Lender has released proceeds for such purposes. Lender may disburse proceeds for the repairs and restoration in a single payment or in a series of progress payments as the work is completed. If the insurance or condemnation proceeds are not sufficient to repair or restore the Property, Borrower is not relieved of Borrower's obligation for the completion of such repair or restoration.

Lender or its agent may make reasonable entries upon and inspections of the Property. If it has reasonable cause, Lender may inspect the interior of the improvements on the Property. Lender shall give Borrower notice at the time of or prior to such an interior inspection specifying such reasonable cause.

8. Borrower's Loan Application. Borrower shall be in default if, during the Loan application process, Borrower or any persons or entities acting at the direction of Borrower or with Borrower's knowledge or consent gave materially false, misleading, or inaccurate information or statements to Lender (or failed to provide Lender with material information) in connection with the Loan. Material representations include, but are not limited to, representations concerning Borrower's occupancy of the Property as Borrower's principal residence.

CALIFORNIA-Single Family-**Fannie Mae/Freddie Mac UNIFORM INSTRUMENT WITH MERS**

9. Protection of Lender's Interest in the Property and Rights Under this Security Instrument. If (a) Borrower fails to perform the covenants and agreements contained in this Security Instrument, (b) there is a legal proceeding that might significantly affect Lender's interest in the Property and/or rights under this Security Instrument (such as a proceeding in bankruptcy, probate, for condemnation or forfeiture, for enforcement of a lien which may attain priority over this Security Instrument or to enforce laws or regulations), or (c) Borrower has abandoned the Property, then Lender may do and pay for whatever is reasonable or appropriate to protect Lender's interest in the Property and rights under this Security Instrument, including protecting and/or assessing the value of the Property, and securing and/or repairing the Property. Lender's actions can include, but are not limited to: (a) paying any sums secured by a lien which has priority over this Security Instrument; (b) appearing in court; and (c) paying reasonable attorneys' fees to protect its interest in the Property and/or rights under this Security Instrument, including its secured position in a bankruptcy proceeding. Securing the Property includes, but is not limited to, entering the Property to make repairs, change locks, replace or board up doors and windows, drain water from pipes, eliminate building or other code violations or dangerous conditions, and have utilities turned on or off. Although Lender may take action under this Section 9, Lender does not have to do so and is not under any duty or obligation to do so. It is agreed that Lender incurs no liability for not taking any or all actions authorized under this Section 9.

Any amounts disbursed by Lender under this Section 9 shall become additional debt of Borrower secured by this Security Instrument. These amounts shall bear interest at the Note rate from the date of disbursement and shall be payable, with such interest, upon notice from Lender to Borrower requesting payment.

If this Security Instrument is on a leasehold, Borrower shall comply with all the provisions of the lease. If Borrower acquires fee title to the Property, the leasehold and the fee title shall not merge unless Lender agrees to the merger in writing.

10. Mortgage Insurance. If Lender required Mortgage Insurance as a condition of making the Loan, Borrower shall pay the premiums required to maintain the Mortgage Insurance in effect. If, for any reason, the Mortgage Insurance coverage required by Lender ceases to be available from the mortgage insurer that previously provided such insurance and Borrower was required to make separately designated payments toward the premiums for Mortgage Insurance, Borrower shall pay the premiums required to obtain coverage substantially equivalent to the Mortgage Insurance previously in effect, at a cost substantially equivalent to the cost to Borrower of the Mortgage Insurance previously in effect, from an alternate mortgage insurer selected by Lender. If substantially equivalent Mortgage Insurance coverage is not available, Borrower shall continue to pay to Lender the amount of the separately designated payments that were due when the insurance coverage ceased to be in effect. Lender will accept, use and retain these payments as a non-refundable loss reserve in lieu of Mortgage Insurance. Such loss reserve shall be non-refundable, notwithstanding the fact that the Loan is ultimately paid in full, and Lender shall not be required to pay Borrower any interest or earnings on such loss reserve. Lender can no longer require loss reserve payments if Mortgage Insurance coverage (in the amount and for the period that Lender requires) provided by an insurer selected by Lender again becomes available, is obtained, and Lender requires separately designated payments toward the premiums for Mortgage Insurance. If Lender required Mortgage Insurance as a condition of making the Loan and Borrower was required to make separately designated payments toward the premiums for Mortgage Insurance, Borrower shall pay the premiums required to maintain Mortgage Insurance in effect, or to provide a non-refundable loss reserve, until Lender's requirement for Mortgage Insurance ends in accordance with any written agreement between Borrower and Lender providing for such termination or until termination is required by Applicable Law. Nothing in this Section 10 affects Borrower's obligation to pay interest at the rate provided in the Note.

Mortgage Insurance reimburses Lender (or any entity that purchases the Note) for certain losses it may incur if Borrower does not repay the Loan as agreed. Borrower is not a party to the Mortgage Insurance.

Mortgage insurers evaluate their total risk on all such insurance in force from time to time, and may enter into agreements with other parties that share or modify their risk, or reduce losses. These agreements are on terms and conditions that are satisfactory to the mortgage insurer and the other party (or parties) to these agreements. These agreements may require the mortgage insurer to make payments using any source of funds that the mortgage insurer may have available (which may include funds obtained from Mortgage Insurance premiums).

As a result of these agreements, Lender, any purchaser of the Note, another insurer, any reinsurer, any other entity, or any affiliate of any of the foregoing, may receive (directly or indirectly) amounts that derive from (or might be characterized as) a portion of Borrower's payments for Mortgage Insurance, in exchange for sharing or modifying the

CALIFORNIA-Single Family-**Fannie Mae/Freddie Mac UNIFORM INSTRUMENT WITH MERS**

VMP-6A(CA) (0711)   Page 7 of 15   Form 3005 1/01

mortgage insurer's risk, or reducing losses. If such agreement provides that an affiliate of Lender takes a share of the insurer's risk in exchange for a share of the premiums paid to the insurer, the arrangement is often termed "captive reinsurance." Further:

(a) Any such agreements will not affect the amounts that Borrower has agreed to pay for Mortgage Insurance, or any other terms of the Loan. Such agreements will not increase the amount Borrower will owe for Mortgage Insurance, and they will not entitle Borrower to any refund.

(b) Any such agreements will not affect the rights Borrower has - if any - with respect to the Mortgage Insurance under the Homeowners Protection Act of 1998 or any other law. These rights may include the right to receive certain disclosures, to request and obtain cancellation of the Mortgage Insurance, to have the Mortgage Insurance terminated automatically, and/or to receive a refund of any Mortgage Insurance premiums that were unearned at the time of such cancellation or termination.

11. Assignment of Miscellaneous Proceeds; Forfeiture. All Miscellaneous Proceeds are hereby assigned to and shall be paid to Lender.

If the Property is damaged, such Miscellaneous Proceeds shall be applied to restoration or repair of the Property, if the restoration or repair is economically feasible and Lender's security is not lessened. During such repair and restoration period, Lender shall have the right to hold such Miscellaneous Proceeds until Lender has had an opportunity to inspect such Property to ensure the work has been completed to Lender's satisfaction, provided that such inspection shall be undertaken promptly. Lender may pay for the repairs and restoration in a single disbursement or in a series of progress payments as the work is completed. Unless an agreement is made in writing or Applicable Law requires interest to be paid on such Miscellaneous Proceeds, Lender shall not be required to pay Borrower any interest or earnings on such Miscellaneous Proceeds. If the restoration or repair is not economically feasible or Lender's security would be lessened, the Miscellaneous Proceeds shall be applied to the sums secured by this Security Instrument, whether or not then due, with the excess, if any, paid to Borrower. Such Miscellaneous Proceeds shall be applied in the order provided for in Section 2.

In the event of a total taking, destruction, or loss in value of the Property, the Miscellaneous Proceeds shall be applied to the sums secured by this Security Instrument, whether or not then due, with the excess, if any, paid to Borrower.

In the event of a partial taking, destruction, or loss in value of the Property in which the fair market value of the Property immediately before the partial taking, destruction, or loss in value is equal to or greater than the amount of the sums secured by this Security Instrument immediately before the partial taking, destruction, or loss in value, unless Borrower and Lender otherwise agree in writing, the sums secured by this Security Instrument shall be reduced by the amount of the Miscellaneous Proceeds multiplied by the following fraction: (a) the total amount of the sums secured immediately before the partial taking, destruction, or loss in value divided by (b) the fair market value of the Property immediately before the partial taking, destruction, or loss in value. Any balance shall be paid to Borrower.

In the event of a partial taking, destruction, or loss in value of the Property in which the fair market value of the Property immediately before the partial taking, destruction, or loss in value is less than the amount of the sums secured immediately before the partial taking, destruction, or loss in value, unless Borrower and Lender otherwise agree in writing, the Miscellaneous Proceeds shall be applied to the sums secured by this Security Instrument whether or not the sums are then due.

If the Property is abandoned by Borrower, or if, after notice by Lender to Borrower that the Opposing Party (as defined in the next sentence) offers to make an award to settle a claim for damages, Borrower fails to respond to Lender within 30 days after the date the notice is given, Lender is authorized to collect and apply the Miscellaneous Proceeds either to restoration or repair of the Property or to the sums secured by this Security Instrument, whether or not then due. "Opposing Party" means the third party that owes Borrower Miscellaneous Proceeds or the party against whom Borrower has a right of action in regard to Miscellaneous Proceeds.

Borrower shall be in default if any action or proceeding, whether civil or criminal, is begun that, in Lender's judgment, could result in forfeiture of the Property or other material impairment of Lender's interest in the Property or rights under this Security Instrument. Borrower can cure such a default and, if acceleration has occurred, reinstate as provided in Section 19, by causing the action or proceeding to be dismissed with a ruling that, in Lender's judgment, precludes forfeiture of the Property or other material impairment of Lender's interest in the Property or rights under this security instrument. To proceeds of any award or claim for damages that are attributable to the impairment of Lender's interest in the Property are hereby assigned and shall be paid to Lender.

All Miscellaneous Proceeds that are not applied to restoration or repair of the Property shall be applied in the order provided for in Section 2.

12. Borrower Not Released; Forbearance By Lender Not a Waiver. Extension of the time for payment or modification of amortization of the sums secured by this Security Instrument granted by Lender to Borrower or any Successor in Interest of Borrower shall not operate to release the liability of Borrower or any Successors in Interest of Borrower. Lender shall not be required to commence proceedings against any Successor in Interest of Borrower or to refuse to extend time for payment or otherwise modify amortization of the sums secured by this Security Instrument by reason of any demand made by the original Borrower or any Successors in Interest of Borrower. Any forbearance by Lender in exercising any right or remedy including, without limitation, Lender's acceptance of payments from third persons, entities or Successors in Interest of Borrower or in amounts less than the amount then due, shall not be a waiver of or preclude the exercise of any right or remedy.

13. Joint and Several Liability; Co-signers; Successors and Assigns Bound. Borrower covenants and agrees that Borrower's obligations and liability shall be joint and several. However, any Borrower who co-signs this Security Instrument but does not execute the Note (a "co-signer"): (a) is co-signing this Security Instrument only to mortgage, grant and convey the co-signer's interest in the Property under the terms of this Security Instrument; (b) is not personally obligated to pay the sums secured by this Security Instrument; and (c) agrees that Lender and any other Borrower can agree to extend, modify, forbear or make any accommodations with regard to the terms of this Security Instrument or the Note without the co-signer's consent.

Subject to the provisions of Section 18, any Successor in Interest of Borrower who assumes Borrower's obligations under this Security Instrument in writing, and is approved by Lender, shall obtain all of Borrower's rights and benefits under this Security Instrument. Borrower shall not be released from Borrower's obligations and liability under this Security Instrument unless Lender agrees to such release in writing. The covenants and agreements of this Security Instrument shall bind (except as provided in Section 20) and benefit the successors and assigns of Lender.

14. Loan Charges. Lender may charge Borrower fees for services performed in connection with Borrower's default, for the purpose of protecting Lender's interest in the Property and rights under this Security Instrument, including, but not limited to, attorneys' fees, property inspection and valuation fees. In regard to any other fees, the absence of express authority in this Security Instrument to charge a specific fee to Borrower shall not be construed as a prohibition on the charging of such fee. Lender may not charge fees that are expressly prohibited by this Security Instrument or by Applicable Law.

If the Loan is subject to a law which sets maximum loan charges, and that law is finally interpreted so that the interest or other loan charges collected or to be collected in connection with the Loan exceed the permitted limits, then: (a) any such loan charge shall be reduced by the amount necessary to reduce the charge to the permitted limit; and (b) any sums already collected from Borrower which exceeded permitted limits will be refunded to Borrower. Lender may choose to make this refund by reducing the principal owed under the Note or by making a direct payment to Borrower. If a refund reduces principal, the reduction will be treated as a partial prepayment without any prepayment charge (whether or not a prepayment charge is provided for under the Note). Borrower's acceptance of any such refund made by direct payment to Borrower will constitute a waiver of any right of action Borrower might have arising out of such overcharge.

15. Notices. All notices given by Borrower or Lender in connection with this Security Instrument must be in writing. Any notice to Borrower in connection with this Security Instrument shall be deemed to have been given to Borrower when mailed by first class mail or when actually delivered to Borrower's notice address if sent by other means. Notice to any one Borrower shall constitute notice to all Borrowers unless Applicable Law expressly requires otherwise. The notice address shall be the Property Address unless Borrower has designated a substitute notice address by notice to Lender. Borrower shall promptly notify Lender of Borrower's change of address. If Lender specifies a procedure for reporting Borrower's change of address, then Borrower shall only report a change of address through that specified procedure. There may be only one designated notice address under this Security Instrument at any one time. Any notice to Lender shall be given by delivering it or by mailing it by first class mail to Lender's address stated herein unless Lender has designated another address by notice to Borrower. Any notice in connection with this Security Instrument shall not be deemed to have been given to Lender until actually received by Lender. If any notice required by this

CALIFORNIA-Single Family-**Fannie Mae/Freddie Mac UNIFORM INSTRUMENT WITH MERS**

Security Instrument is also required under Applicable Law, the Applicable Law requirement will satisfy the corresponding requirement under this Security Instrument.

16. Governing Law; Severability; Rules of Construction. This Security Instrument shall be governed by federal law and the law of the jurisdiction in which the Property is located. All rights and obligations contained in this Security Instrument are subject to any requirements and limitations of Applicable Law. Applicable Law might explicitly or implicitly allow the parties to agree by contract or it might be silent, but such silence shall not be construed as a prohibition against agreement by contract. In the event that any provision or clause of this Security Instrument or the Note conflicts with Applicable Law, such conflict shall not affect other provisions of this Security Instrument or the Note which can be given effect without the conflicting provision.

As used in this Security Instrument: (a) words of the masculine gender shall mean and include corresponding neuter words or words of the feminine gender; (b) words in the singular shall mean and include the plural and vice versa; and (c) the word "may" gives sole discretion without any obligation to take any action.

17. Borrower's Copy. Borrower shall be given one copy of the Note and of this Security Instrument.

18. Transfer of the Property or a Beneficial Interest in Borrower. As used in this Section 18, "Interest in the Property" means any legal or beneficial interest in the Property, including, but not limited to, those beneficial interests transferred in a bond for deed, contract for deed, installment sales contract or escrow agreement, the intent of which is the transfer of title by Borrower at a future date to a purchaser.

If all or any part of the Property or any Interest in the Property is sold or transferred (or if Borrower is not a natural person and a beneficial interest in Borrower is sold or transferred) without Lender's prior written consent, Lender may require immediate payment in full of all sums secured by this Security Instrument. However, this option shall not be exercised by Lender if such exercise is prohibited by Applicable Law.

If Lender exercises this option, Lender shall give Borrower notice of acceleration. The notice shall provide a period of not less than 30 days from the date the notice is given in accordance with Section 15 within which Borrower must pay all sums secured by this Security Instrument. If Borrower fails to pay these sums prior to the expiration of this period, Lender may invoke any remedies permitted by this Security Instrument without further notice or demand on Borrower.

19. Borrower's Right to Reinstate After Acceleration. If Borrower meets certain conditions, Borrower shall have the right to have enforcement of this Security Instrument discontinued at any time prior to the earliest of: (a) five days before sale of the Property pursuant to any power of sale contained in this Security Instrument; (b) such other period as Applicable Law might specify for the termination of Borrower's right to reinstate; or (c) entry of a judgment enforcing this Security Instrument. Those conditions are that Borrower: (a) pays Lender all sums which then would be due under this Security Instrument and the Note as if no acceleration had occurred; (b) cures any default of any other covenants or agreements; (c) pays all expenses incurred in enforcing this Security Instrument, including, but not limited to, reasonable attorneys' fees, property inspection and valuation fees, and other fees incurred for the purpose of protecting Lender's interest in the Property and rights under this Security Instrument; and (d) takes such action as Lender may reasonably require to assure that Lender's interest in the Property and rights under this Security Instrument, and Borrower's obligation to pay the sums secured by this Security Instrument, shall continue unchanged. Lender may require that Borrower pay such reinstatement sums and expenses in one or more of the following forms, as selected by Lender: (a) cash; (b) money order; (c) certified check, bank check, treasurer's check or cashier's check, provided any such check is drawn upon an institution whose deposits are insured by a federal agency, instrumentality or entity; or (d) Electronic Funds Transfer. Upon reinstatement by Borrower, this Security Instrument and obligations secured hereby shall remain fully effective as if no acceleration had occurred. However, this right to reinstate shall not apply in the case of acceleration under Section 18.

20. Sale of Note; Change of Loan Servicer; Notice of Grievance. The Note or a partial interest in the Note (together with this Security Instrument) can be sold one or more times without prior notice to Borrower. A sale might result in a change in the entity (known as the "Loan Servicer") that collects Periodic Payments due under the Note and this Security Instrument and performs other mortgage loan servicing obligations under the Note, this Security Instrument, and Applicable Law. There also might be one or more changes of the Loan Servicer unrelated to a sale of the Note. If there is a change of the Loan Servicer, Borrower will be given written notice of the change which will state the name and address of the new Loan Servicer, the address to which payments should be made and any other information RESPA requires in connection with a notice of transfer of servicing. If the Note is sold and thereafter the Loan is serviced by a Loan Servicer other than the purchaser of the Note, the mortgage loan servicing obligations to Borrower will remain with the Loan Servicer or be transferred to a successor Loan Servicer and are not assumed by the Note purchaser unless otherwise provided by the Note purchaser.

Neither Borrower nor Lender may commence, join, or be joined to any judicial action (as either an individual litigant or the member of a class) that arises from the other party's actions pursuant to this Security Instrument or that alleges that the other party has breached any provision of, or any duty owed by reason of, this Security Instrument, until such Borrower or Lender has notified the other party (with such notice given in compliance with the requirements of Section 15) of such alleged breach and afforded the other party hereto a reasonable period after the giving of such notice to take corrective action. If Applicable Law provides a time period which must elapse before certain action can be taken, that time period will be deemed to be reasonable for purposes of this paragraph. The notice of acceleration and opportunity to cure given to Borrower pursuant to Section 22 and the notice of acceleration given to Borrower pursuant to Section 18 shall be deemed to satisfy the notice and opportunity to take corrective action provisions of this Section 20.

21. Hazardous Substances. As used in this Section 21: (a) "Hazardous Substances" are those substances defined as toxic or hazardous substances, pollutants, or wastes by Environmental Law and the following substances: gasoline, kerosene, other flammable or toxic petroleum products, toxic pesticides and herbicides, volatile solvents, materials containing asbestos or formaldehyde, and radioactive materials; (b) "Environmental Law" means federal laws and laws of the jurisdiction where the Property is located that relate to health, safety or environmental protection; (c) "Environmental Cleanup" includes any response action, remedial action, or removal action, as defined in Environmental Law; and (d) an "Environmental Condition" means a condition that can cause, contribute to, or otherwise trigger an Environmental Cleanup.

Borrower shall not cause or permit the presence, use, disposal, storage, or release of any Hazardous Substances, or threaten to release any Hazardous Substances, on or in the Property. Borrower shall not do, nor allow anyone else to do, anything affecting the Property (a) that is in violation of any Environmental Law, (b) which creates an Environmental Condition, or (c) which, due to the presence, use, or release of a Hazardous Substance, creates a condition that adversely affects the value of the Property. The preceding two sentences shall not apply to the presence, use, or storage on the Property of small quantities of Hazardous Substances that are generally recognized to be appropriate to normal residential uses and to maintenance of the Property (including, but not limited to, hazardous substances in consumer products).

Borrower shall promptly give Lender written notice of (a) any investigation, claim, demand, lawsuit or other action by any governmental or regulatory agency or private party involving the Property and any Hazardous Substance or Environmental Law of which Borrower has actual knowledge, (b) any Environmental Condition, including but not limited to, any spilling, leaking, discharge, release or threat of release of any Hazardous Substance, and (c) any condition caused by the presence, use or release of a Hazardous Substance which adversely affects the value of the Property. If Borrower learns, or is notified by any governmental or regulatory authority, or any private party, that any removal or other remediation of any Hazardous Substance affecting the Property is necessary, Borrower shall promptly take all necessary remedial actions in accordance with Environmental Law. Nothing herein shall create any obligation on Lender for an Environmental Cleanup.

NON-UNIFORM COVENANTS. Borrower and Lender further covenant and agree as follows:

22. Acceleration; Remedies. Lender shall give notice to Borrower prior to acceleration following Borrower's breach of any covenant or agreement in this Security Instrument (but not prior to acceleration under Section 18 unless Applicable Law provides otherwise). The notice shall specify: (a) the default; (b) the action required to cure the default; (c) a date, not less than 30 days from the date the notice is given to Borrower, by which the default must be cured; and (d) that failure to cure the default on or before the date specified in the notice may result in acceleration of the sums secured by this Security Instrument and sale of the Property. The notice shall further inform Borrower of the right to reinstate after acceleration and the right to bring a court action to assert the non-existence of a default or any other defense of Borrower to acceleration and sale. If the default is not cured on or before the

CALIFORNIA-Single Family-**Fannie Mae/Freddie Mac UNIFORM INSTRUMENT WITH MERS** date specified in the notice, Lender at its option may require immediate payment in full of all sums secured by this Security Instrument without further demand and may invoke the power of sale and any other remedies permitted by Applicable Law. Lender shall be entitled to collect all expenses incurred in pursuing the remedies provided in this Section 22, including, but not limited to, reasonable attorneys' fees and costs of title evidence.

If Lender invokes the power of sale, Lender shall execute or cause Trustee to execute a written notice of the occurrence of an event of default and of Lender's election to cause the Property to be sold. Trustee shall cause this notice to be recorded in each county in which any part of the Property is located. Lender or Trustee shall mail copies of the notice as prescribed by Applicable Law to Borrower and to the other persons prescribed by Applicable Law. Trustee shall give public notice of sale to the persons and in the manner prescribed by Applicable Law. After the time required by Applicable Law, Trustee, without demand on Borrower, shall sell the Property at public auction to the highest bidder at the time and place and under the terms designated in the notice of sale in one or more parcels and in any order Trustee determines. Trustee may postpone sale of all or any parcel of the Property by public announcement at the time and place of any previously scheduled sale. Lender or its designee may purchase the Property at any sale.

Trustee shall deliver to the purchaser Trustee's deed conveying the Property without any covenant or warranty, expressed or implied. The recitals in the Trustee's deed shall be prima facie evidence of the truth of the statements made therein. Trustee shall apply the proceeds of the sale in the following order: (a) to all expenses of the sale, including, but not limited to, reasonable Trustee's and attorneys' fees; (b) to all sums secured by this Security Instrument; and (c) any excess to the person or persons legally entitled to it.

23. Reconveyance. Upon payment of all sums secured by this Security Instrument, Lender shall request Trustee to reconvey the Property and shall surrender this Security Instrument and all notes evidencing debt secured by this Security Instrument to Trustee. Trustee shall reconvey the Property without warranty to the person or persons legally entitled to it. Lender may charge such person or persons a reasonable fee for reconveying the Property, but only if the fee is paid to a third party (such as the Trustee) for services rendered and the charging of the fee is permitted under Applicable Law. If the fee charged does not exceed the fee set by Applicable Law, the fee is conclusively presumed to be reasonable.

24. Substitute Trustee. Lender, at its option, may from time to time appoint a successor trustee to any Trustee appointed hereunder by an instrument executed and acknowledged by Lender and recorded in the office of the Recorder of the county in which the Property is located. The instrument shall contain the name of the original Lender, Trustee and Borrower, the book and page where this Security Instrument is recorded and the name and address of the successor trustee. Without conveyance of the Property, the successor trustee shall succeed to all the title, powers and duties conferred upon the Trustee herein and by Applicable Law. This procedure for substitution of trustee shall govern to the exclusion of all other provisions for substitution.

25. Statement of Obligation Fee. Lender may collect a fee not to exceed the maximum amount permitted by Applicable Law for furnishing the statement of obligation as provided by Section 2943 of the Civil Code of California.

The undersigned Borrower requests that a copy of any Notice of Default and any Notice of Sale under this Security Instrument be mailed to the Borrower at the address set forth above. A copy of any Notice of Default and any Notice of Sale will be sent only to the address contained in this recorded request. If the Borrower's address changes, a new request must be recorded.

BY SIGNING BELOW, Borrower accepts and agrees to the terms and covenants contained in this Security Instrument and in any Rider executed by Borrower and recorded with it.

-Witnesses:

_____

-Witness

_____

-Witness

CALIFORNIA-Single Family-**Fannie Mae/Freddie Mac UNIFORM INSTRUMENT WITH MERS**

_____ (Seal)   _____ (Seal)

JOHN C. VANDER HORCK   -Borrower   **JOANN VANDER HORCK**   -Borrower

_____ (Seal)   _____ (Seal)

-Borrower   -Borrower

_____ (Seal)   _____ (Seal)

-Borrower   -Borrower

_____ (Seal)   _____ (Seal)

-Borrower   -Borrower

SAMPLE

CALIFORNIA-Single Family-**Fannie Mae/Freddie Mac UNIFORM INSTRUMENT WITH MERS**

State of _____ **CALIFORNIA** _____)

County of _____)

On _____ before me,

_____, personally appeared

(here insert name and title of the officer)

<u>JOHN C. VANDER HORCK AND JOANN VANDER HORCK</u> _____

_____ ,

who proved to me on the basis of satisfactory evidence to be the person(s) whose name(s) is/are subscribed to the within instrument and acknowledged to me that he/she/they executed the same in his/her/their authorized capacity (ies), and that by his/her/their signature(s) on the instrument the person(s), or the entity upon behalf of which the person(s) acted, executed the instrument.

I certify under PENALTY OF PERJURY under the laws of the State of California that the foregoing paragraph is true and correct.

WITNESS my hand and official seal.

Signature _____ (Seal)

CALIFORNIA-Single Family-**Fannie Mae/Freddie Mac UNIFORM INSTRUMENT WITH MERS**

SECOND HOME RIDER

LOAN NO.: 2109053817

MIN: 100109800001173955
MERS Phone: 1-888-679-6377

THIS SECOND HOME RIDER is made this 10th day of AUGUST, 2009, and is incorporated into and shall be deemed to amend and supplement the Mortgage, Deed of Trust, or Security Deed (the "Security Instrument") of the same date given by the undersigned (the "Borrower" whether there are one or more persons undersigned) to secure Borrower's Note to
PLAZA HOME MORTGAGE, INC.

(the "Lender") of the same date and covering the Property described in the Security Instrument (the "Property"), which is located at:

39566 BARBARA LEE LANE, FAWNSKIN, CA 92333-
[Property Address]

In addition to the covenants and agreements made in the Security Instrument, Borrower and Lender further covenant and agree that Sections 6 and 8 of the Security Instrument are deleted and are replaced by the following:

6. Occupancy. Borrower shall occupy, and shall only use, the Property as Borrower's second home. Borrower shall keep the Property available for Borrower's exclusive use and enjoyment at all times, and shall not subject the Property to any timesharing or other shared ownership arrangement or to any rental pool or agreement that requires Borrower either to rent the Property or give a management firm or any other person any control over the occupancy or use of the Property.

8. Borrower's Loan Application. Borrower shall be in default if, during the Loan application process, Borrower or any persons or entities acting at the direction of Borrower or with Borrower's knowledge or consent gave materially false, misleading, or inaccurate information or statements to Lender (or failed to provide Lender with material information) in connection with the Loan. Material representations include, but are not limited to, representations concerning Borrower's occupancy of the Property as Borrower's second home.

BY SIGNING BELOW, Borrower accepts and agrees to the terms and covenants contained in this Second Home Rider.

_____ (Seal)
JOHN C. VANDER HORCK   -Borrower

_____ (Seal)
                               -Borrower

_____ (Seal)
                               -Borrower

_____ (Seal)
                               -Borrower

_____ (Seal)
JOANN VANDER HORCK   -Borrower

_____ (Seal)
                               -Borrower

_____ (Seal)
                               -Borrower

_____ (Seal)
                               -Borrower

MULTISTATE SECOND HOME RIDER - Single Family - **Fannie Mae/Freddie Mac UNIFORM INSTRUMENT**   Form 3890   1/01

VMP-365R (0811)   Page 1 of 1   LENDER SUPPORT SYSTEMS, INC. 365R.NEW (12/08)

FEDERAL TRUTH - IN - LENDING DISCLOSURE STATEMENT
(THIS IS NEITHER A CONTRACT NOR A COMMITMENT TO LEND)

Creditor:

PLAZA HOME MORTGAGE, INC.

3633 INLAND EMPIRE BLVD #250
ONTARIO, CA 91764

Date: AUGUST 10, 2009
Check box if applicable:

Borrower:

JOHN C. VANDER HORCK AND JOANN VANDER HORCK

5131 CARITA STREET
LONG BEACH, CA 90808-
Loan Number: 2109053817

ANNUAL PERCENTAGE RATE The cost of your credit as a yearly rate.	FINANCE CHARGE The dollar amount the credit will cost you.	Amount Financed The amount of credit provided to you or on your behalf.	Total of Payments The amount you will have paid after you have made all payments as scheduled.	[ ] Total Sale Price The total cost of your purchase on credit including your down-payment of $ N/A
5.236 %	$ 103,981.81	$ 105,584.99	$ 209,566.80	$ N/A

[ ] REQUIRED DEPOSIT: The annual percentage rate does not take into account your required deposit.
PAYMENTS: Your payment schedule will be:

Number of Payments	Amount of Payments	When Payments Are Due Monthly Beginning:	Number of Payments	Amount of Payments	When Payments Are Due Monthly Beginning:	Number of Payments	Amount of Payments	When Payments Are Due Monthly Beginning:
360	582.13	10/01/2009						

[ ] DEMAND FEATURE: This obligation has a demand feature.
[ ] VARIABLE RATE: Your loan contains variable rate features.
   [ ] Information regarding the variable rate features of your loan have been provided to you earlier in a separate document.
   [ ] Information regarding the variable rate features of your loan are provided hereinafter. The annual percentage rate may increase or
     decrease during the term of this transaction with increases or decreases in the value of the "Index" (or "Reference Rate"). The
     rate that you will pay may not be changed more often than every _____ commencing _____
      [ ] Rate Change Limits: The rate may not **increase or decrease by more than** _____ %
      [ ] The rate will never be greater than _____ %
      [ ] Any increase in the rate will result in a corresponding increase in the payment.
      [ ] Rate increases may occur without immediate and/or corresponding payment increases.
      [ ] Unpaid interest will be added to the principal.
      The "Index" (or "Reference Rate") is the:

INSURANCE: The following insurance is required to obtain credit:
[ ] Credit life insurance and credit disability   [XX] Property insurance   [ ] Flood insurance
You may obtain the insurance from anyone you want that is acceptable to creditor.
[ ] If you purchase   [ ] property   [ ] flood insurance from creditor you will pay $ _____ for one year term.
SECURITY: You are giving a security interest in:
  39566 BARBARA LEE LANE, FAWNSKIN, CA 92333-
[ ] The goods or property being purchased   XX [ ] Real property you already own.
FILING FEES: $ 170.00
LATE CHARGE: If a payment is more than 15 days late, you will be charged 5.00 % of the Principal & Interest payment.
PREPAYMENT: If you pay off early, you
[ ] may   X X] will not   have to pay a penalty.
[ ] may   X X] will not   be entitled to a refund of part of the finance charge.
ASSUMPTION: Someone buying your property
[ ] may   [ ] may, subject to conditions   [XX] may not assume the remainder of your loan on the original terms.
See your contract documents for any additional information about nonpayment, default, any required repayment in full before the scheduled
date and prepayment refunds and penalties.
[ ] "e" means an estimate   [ ] all dates and numerical disclosures except the late payment disclosures are estimates.

The undersigned acknowledge receiving and reading a completed copy of this disclosure.
You are not required to complete this agreement merely because you have received these disclosures or signed a loan application.

[ ] I/We have received the Variable Rate Disclosure for the loan program for which I/We have applied.

_____   (Date)   _____   (Date)
JOHN C. VANDER HORCK   JOANN VANDER HORCK

_____   (Date)   _____   (Date)

Prepared by: **PLAZA HOME MORTGAGE, INC.**
Contact Phone #:

PLAZA HOME MORTGAGE, INC.

3633 INLAND EMPIRE BLVD #250
ONTARIO , CA 91764
(909)890-9999

TAX INFORMATION SHEET
NEW LOAN TAX INFORMATION FOR _____ CALIFORNIA _____
(State)

Loan Number: 2109053817
Date of Closing:
Purchaser: JOHN C. VANDER HORCK AND JOANN VANDER HORCK

Seller:

Property Address: 39566 BARBARA LEE LANE, FAWNSKIN, CA 92333-

Impounded/Escrowed:	[X] YES	[ ] NO
Refinance:	[X] YES	[ ] NO
New Construction:	[ ] YES	[ ] NO
Parcel to be Segregated:	[ ] YES	[ ] NO

Taxing Authority and Name if Applicable	Mailing Address and Phone Number		Type Tax
Parcel/Folio/Acct #	**Tax Installment Due Dates**	**Date of 1st Tax Payment Lender Must Pay**	**Amount of Last Tax Installment Paid**
	1st _____ 2nd _____ 3rd _____ 4th _____	1st _____ 2nd _____ 3rd _____ 4th _____	1st _____ 2nd _____ 3rd _____ 4th _____
Taxing Authority and Name if Applicable	Mailing Address and Phone Number		Type Tax
Parcel/Folio/Acct #	**Tax Installment Due Dates**	**Date of 1st Tax Payment Lender Must Pay**	**Amount of Last Tax Installment Paid**
	1st _____ 2nd _____ 3rd _____ 4th _____	1st _____ 2nd _____ 3rd _____ 4th _____	1st _____ 2nd _____ 3rd _____ 4th _____
Taxing Authority and Name if Applicable	Mailing Address and Phone Number		Type Tax
Parcel/Folio/Acct #	**Tax Installment Due Dates**	**Date of 1st Tax Payment Lender Must Pay**	**Amount of Last Tax Installment Paid**
	1st _____ 2nd _____ 3rd _____ 4th _____	1st _____ 2nd _____ 3rd _____ 4th _____	1st _____ 2nd _____ 3rd _____ 4th _____
Taxing Authority and Name if Applicable	Mailing Address and Phone Number		Type Tax
Parcel/Folio/Acct #	**Tax Installment Due Dates**	**Date of 1st Tax Payment Lender Must Pay**	**Amount of Last Tax Installment Paid**
	1st _____ 2nd _____ 3rd _____ 4th _____	1st _____ 2nd _____ 3rd _____ 4th _____	1st _____ 2nd _____ 3rd _____ 4th _____

CLOSING AGENT INSTRUCTIONS
1. Form must be completed accurately. If information is not available state why.
2. Attach any applicable documentation you may have to this form.
3. Call Branch if you have questions.
This form has been completed by:

_____   _____   _____
NAME   COMPANY   DATE

FHA/VA/CONV

• Tax Information Sheet
2C103-US (04/02)(d)

LENDER SUPPORT SYSTEMS INC. COU-15.COU (12/03)

"FEDERAL TRUTH-IN-LENDING DISCLOSURE STATEMENT" - PAGE 2
"ITEMIZATION OF AMOUNT FINANCED"

Creditor:
PLAZA HOME MORTGAGE, INC.

3633 INLAND EMPIRE BLVD #250
ONTARIO, CA 91764

Re:
JOHN C. VANDER HORCK AND JOANN VANDER HORCK

5131 CARITA STREET
LONG BEACH, CA 90808-

Date: AUGUST 10, 2009
Interest Rate: 4.875 %
BROKER'S LICENSE #: 01272296
DEPT. OF REAL ESTATE LICENSE INFO LINE: (916) 227-0931

Loan Number: 2109053817

Loan Amount: 110,000.00

Ref HUD-1 Statement		** Amount Paid on your Account	* Broker = B Other = O	
			PAID	FINANCED	*
	WELLS FARGO		$	75,320.00 E	
			$		
			$		
Amount Paid To Others on your Behalf:					
804	CREDIT REPORT FEE TO PERFORMANCE PLUS MORTGAGE		$	20.00	B
1001	HAZARD INSURANCE 6 MONTHS @ $ 40.00 PER MO.		$	240.00	
1004	COUNTY PROPERTY TAXES 7 MONTHS @ $ 122.45 PER MO.		$	857.15	
1108	TITLE INSURANCE FEE TO FIDELITY NATIONAL TITLE		$	440.00	
1201	RECORDING FEE TO FIDELITY NATIONAL TITLE		$	170.00	
	ENDORSEMENT FEE TO FIDELITY NATIONAL TITLE		$	100.00	
	AGGREGATE ADJUSTMENT		$	(122.46)	
			$		
			$		
			$		
			$		
LOAN PROCEEDS PAID TO:	FIDELITY NATIONAL TITLE		$	28,560.30	

AMOUNT FINANCED $ 105,584.99

Prepaid Finance Charge:			PAID	FINANCED	*
801	LOAN ORIGINATION FEE (pd to broker)		$	1,650.00	B
802	LOAN DISCOUNT (pd to lender) 0.126 %		$	138.60	
808	PROCESSING FEE TO PERFORMANCE PLUS MORTGAGE		$	495.00	B
1101	SETTLEMENT/CLOSING FEE TO PERFORMANCE PLUS MORTGAGE		$	650.00	
901	INTEREST 18 DAYS @ $ 14.692 /DAY		$	264.46	
	UNDERWRITING FEE TO PLAZA HOME MORTGAGE, INC.		$	830.00	
	APPRAISAL REVIEW FEE TO L TO PLAZA HOME MORTGAGE, INC.		$	75.00	
	WIRE FEE (ESCROW) TO PERFORMANCE PLUS MORTGAGE		$	50.00	
1106	NOTARY FEES TO PERFORMANCE PLUS MORTGAGE		$	80.00	
	WIRE FEE (TITLE) TO FIDELITY NATIONAL TITLE		$	50.00	
	MERS FEE TO PLAZA HOME MORTGAGE, INC.		$	6.95	
1112	SUB ESCROW FEE TO FIDELITY NATIONAL TITLE		$	125.00	
			$		
			$		
			$		

Total Prepaid Finance Charge: $ 4,415.01

These are FEES NOT paid by the Borrower	
	$
	$
	$

Total Estimated Funds needed to close		**Total Estimated Monthly Payment**	
Down Payment	$	Principal & Interest	$ 582.13
Estimated Closing Costs	$ 4,880.55	Total Real Estate Taxes	122.45
Estimated Prepaid Items/Reserves	$ 1,239.15	Flood & Hazard Insurance	$ 40.00
Other: TOTAL PAYOFFS	$ 75,320.00	Mortgage Insurance	$
TOTAL EST. FUNDS NEEDED TO CLOSE $	81,439.70	Total Other Impounds	$
		TOTAL MONTHLY PAYMENT	$ 744.58

This form does not cover all items you will be required to pay in cash at settlement; for example, deposits in escrow for real estate taxes and insurance may be different. You may wish to inquire as to the amounts of such other items. You may be required to pay other additional amounts at settlement.
Neither you nor the lender previously has become obligated to make or accept this loan, nor is any such obligation made by the delivery or signing of this disclosure. Each of the Undersigned acknowledge receiving and reading a completed copy of this disclosure.

_____
JOHN C. VANDER HORCK   (Date)

_____
JOANN VANDER HORCK   (Date)

_____
(Date)

_____
(Date)

LENDER SUPPORT SYSTEMS, INC. GEN-002D.GEN (08/02)

PAYMENT LETTER TO BORROWER

FROM: **PLAZA HOME MORTGAGE, INC.**

3633 INLAND EMPIRE BLVD #250, ONTARIO, CA 91764

TO: **JOHN C. VANDER HORCK AND JOANN VANDER HORCK**

Property Address: **39566 BARBARA LEE LANE, FAWNSKIN, CA 92333-**

Loan Number: **2109053817**

Dear Borrower:

Disclosed below is an estimate of the amount of your initial monthly payment for the loan referred to above.

Payments are scheduled to begin **OCTOBER 01, 2009**, with the final payment due on **SEPTEMBER 01, 2039.**

A.   [XX]   The interest rate and payment amount are scheduled to remain level throughout the loan term.

B.   [ ]   This is a Graduated Payment loan which means that even though the interest rate will not change, the payments will increase in the second year and each year thereafter for the next _____ years. A schedule of the subsequent monthly payment amounts is provided to you on the Federal Truth In Lending Disclosure Statement.

C.   [ ]   This is an Adjustable Rate loan which means that the monthly payment amounts may vary from time to time in conjunction with adjustments in the interest rate. Review the Federal Truth In Lending Disclosure Statement and your Promissory Note for more information concerning future payment amounts.

Your initial monthly payment amount will consist of the following:

PRINCIPAL AND INTEREST	$ 582.13*
MMI/PMI Monthly Premium	$ 0.00*
County Property Taxes Reserve	$ 122.45*
Hazard Insurance Reserve	$ 40.00*
Flood Insurance Reserve	$ 0.00*
City Property Taxes Reserve	$ 0.00*
Annual Assessment Reserve	$ 0.00*
Other	$ *
Other	$ *
Other	$
Total Initial Monthly Payment	$ 744.58

These items are estimates at this time; you will be given notice of the actual amount of your monthly payment upon closing of this transaction. Also, understand that these amounts may vary slightly from year to year requiring adjustments in the amount of your payment.

IT IS POSSIBLE THAT YOU WILL NOT RECEIVE YOUR FIRST "NOTICE OF PAYMENT DUE" BEFORE THE DUE DATE OF YOUR FIRST PAYMENT. Unless notified otherwise, please remit your first payment and all future payments to the following address:

PLAZA HOME MORTGAGE, INC.

5090 SHOREHAM PLACE #206

SAN DIEGO, CA 92122

During any correspondence or phone calls in connection with this loan, please give the loan number shown above for the lender's reference.

BY SIGNING BELOW, Borrower acknowledges reading this Payment Letter and receiving a copy of the same.

JOHN C. VANDER HORCK	Date	**JOANN VANDER HORCK**	Date
	Date		Date

MORTGAGE FRAUD IS
INVESTIGATED BY THE FBI

Mortgage Fraud is investigated by the Federal Bureau of Investigation and is punishable by up to 30 years in federal prison or $1,000,000 fine, or both. It is illegal for a person to make any false statement regarding income, assets, debt, or matters of identification, or to willfully overvalue any land or property, in a loan and credit application for the purpose of influencing in any way the action of a financial institution.

Some of the applicable Federal criminal statutes which may be charged in connection with Mortgage Fraud include:

18 U.S.C. ½ 1001 - Statements or entries generally
18 U.S.C. ½ 1010 - HUD and Federal Housing Administration Transactions 18
U.S.C. ½ 1014 - Loan and credit applications generally
18 U.S.C. ½ 1028 - Fraud and related activity in connection with identification documents 18
U.S.C. ½ 1341 - Frauds and swindles by Mail
18 U.S.C. ½ 1342 - Fictitious name or address
18 U.S.C. ½ 1343 - Fraud by wire
18 U.S.C. ½ 1344 - Bank Fraud
42 U.S.C. ½ 408(a) - False Social Security Number

Unauthorized use of the FBI seal, name, and initials is subject to prosecution under Sections 701, 709, and 712 of Title 18 of the United States Code. This advisement may not be changed or altered without the specific written consent of the Federal Bureau of Investigation, and is not an endorsement of any product or service.

JOHN C. VANDER HORCK	(Date)	JOANN VANDER HORCK	(Date)
	(Date)		(Date)

V-**554** (0706)

LENDER SUPPORT SYSTEMS, INC. V-554.XDP (08/07)

SERVICING DISCLOSURE STATEMENT

Lender	Borrower	Date
PLAZA HOME MORTGAGE, INC.	JOHN C. VANDER HORCK AND JOANN VANDER HORCK	AUGUST 10, 2009

Lender
PLAZA HOME MORTGAGE, INC.

3633 INLAND EMPIRE BLVD #250 ONTARIO, CA 91764

Borrower
JOHN C. VANDER HORCK AND JOANN VANDER HORCK

Date
AUGUST 10, 2009

Loan Number
LOAN NO.: 2109053817

Property Address
39566 BARBARA LEE LANE, FAWNSKIN, CA 92333-

NOTICE TO FIRST LIEN MORTGAGE LOAN APPLICANTS: THE RIGHT TO COLLECT YOUR MORTGAGE LOAN PAYMENTS MAY BE TRANSFERRED.

You are applying for a mortgage loan covered by the Real Estate Settlement Procedures Act (RESPA) (12 U.S.C. 2601 et seq.). RESPA gives you certain rights under Federal law. This statement describes whether the servicing for this loan may be transferred to a different loan servicer. "Servicing" refers to collecting your principal, interest, and escrow payments, if any, as well as sending any monthly or annual statements, tracking account balances, and handling other aspects of your loan. You will be given advance notice before a transfer occurs.

Servicing Transfer Information

☐ We may assign, sell, or transfer the servicing of your loan while the loan is outstanding.

☐ We do not service mortgage loans of the type for which you applied. We intend to assign, sell, or transfer the servicing of your mortgage loan before the first payment is due.

☐ The loan for which you have applied will be serviced at this financial institution and we do not intend to sell, transfer, or assign the servicing of the loan.

By signing below, I/we acknowledge receiving a copy of this disclosure.

JOHN C. VANDER HORCK	Date	JOANN VANDER HORCK	Date
	Date		Date

Servicing Disclosure Statement

VMP-552R (0812).00   Page 1 of 1   LENDER SUPPORT SYSTEMS, INC. 552R.NEW (12/08)

HAZARD INSURANCE AUTHORIZATION & REQUIREMENTS

Lender: **PLAZA HOME MORTGAGE, INC.**
      3633 INLAND EMPIRE BLVD #250
      ONTARIO, CA 91764

Date: **AUGUST 10, 2009**
Loan No.: **2109053817**
Escrow No.: **72101**

Escrow Co.: **PERFORMANCE PLUS MORTGAGE**
         9 AZALEA
         IRVINE, CA 92620

Borrower's Name(s): **JOHN C. VANDER HORCK AND JOANN VANDER HORCK**

Property Address: **39566 BARBARA LEE LANE, FAWNSKIN, CA 92333**

AN ACCEPTABLE HAZARD INSURANCE POLICY, WITH ENDORSEMENTS AND/OR ASSIGNMENTS, MUST BE IN LENDER'S OFFICE BEFORE THIS LOAN CAN BE FUNDED; OTHERWISE, LENDER MAY BE FORCED TO PLACE INTERIM COVERAGE ON THE PROPERTY AT AN ADDITIONAL COST TO THE BORROWER(S).

Your Lender may require that you or your Insurance Agency provide the "ORIGINAL POLICY", but generally, a "Binder" or a "Certificate of Evidence of Insurance" is acceptable. Ask your Lender which they will accept. Please forward all policies, assignments, and/or endorsements to Lender at the above address,

"ATTENTION: LOAN PROCESSING."

Listed below are your Lender's policies and procedures, and minimum requirements, for Hazard Insurance coverage.

1. The amount of coverage provided by the policy must be no less than the lesser of: 1) the replacement value of the improvements on the above referenced property as established by the insurance company providing coverage, or 2) an amount equal to the sum of this loan amount plus the balances of all other existing liens.

2. The insurance company providing coverage must have a **"B"** rating or better in the latest edition of "Best's Insurance Guide," must be licensed to do business in the State in which the property is located, and must be licensed to transact the lines of insurance required.

3. The Policy must provide at least "Broad Form" coverage on properties of one to four units, and at least "Vandalism & Malicious Mischief" on properties with over four units, **WITH NO DEVIATION.** Homeowners policies must provide coverage equal to "HO3" form.

4. Deductibles may not exceed five percent (5.0%) of the coverage amount as determined using the guidelines in Requirement #1 above (This limit applies for loans secured by residential properties of 1 to 4 units which may be sold to or originated for either: Federal National Mortgage Association, Federal Home Loan Mortgage Corporation, FHA or VA). Your Lender's deductible requirements may be more stringent; if so, you will be notified of your Lender's requirements prior to funding.

5. The policy must provide coverage for a term of at least one year. Premiums may be paid on an annual installment basis only if the policy provides that the Lender will be notified in writing of cancellation 30 days prior to expiration of coverage, for any cause.

6. If a Policy of coverage is already "in force" (typical in refinance transactions) which expires within **4** months from the date of the recording of this loan, Lender may require renewal of said policy for a term as required in #5 above.

7. All forms and endorsements pertaining to the Lender's requirements must appear on the "Declaration Page" of policy.

8. For loans which have Hazard Insurance premiums impounded by the Lender, when notifying Lender of any new policy or changes of Insurance Carrier, said notification must be accompanied by a signed "Broker of Record Authorization. "

9. Verification of renewal of insurance policies must be in Lender's office at least thirty days prior to the expiration date of the policy. If this requirement is not met, LENDER OR ITS SUCCESSORS AND/OR ASSIGNS MAY AT THEIR OPTION, BUT WITHOUT THE OBLIGATION TO DO SO, PROVIDE COVERAGE TO REPLACE ANY

EXPIRING POLICIES WHICH HAVE NOT BEEN PROPERLY RENEWED. Premiums for such coverage shall be remitted promptly by the undersigned, or Lender may charge borrower's account for the cost thereof.

10. Lender's Loss Payable Endorsement 438 BFU to be affixed to policy in favor of:

PLAZA HOME MORTGAGE, INC.

WITH FIRST MORTGAGEE ENDORSEMENT

ITS SUCCESSORS AND/OR ASSIGNS
5090 SHOREHAM PLACE #206
SAN DIEGO, CA 92122
RE: Loan No.: 2109053817

11. The property address and the insured's names must be designated on the policy exactly as on the ALTA Title Policy.

12. The Lender's loan number must appear on the policy and on any subsequent endorsements.

13. The effective date of new policies, endorsements, and/or assignments shall be as of, or prior to, the date of recording of this loan.

14. Please notify your agent to forward future premium notices directly to you.

15. If the security property is a Condominium, the Master Policy must contain a minimum of $1,000,000.00 liability coverage for "Directors & Officers" liability. A copy of the Master Policy, or a certificate showing proof of coverage for both the Homeowners Association and the Condominium unit owner, must be submitted to the Lender prior to funding.

Certain loan programs require evidence of walls-in coverage in the Master or Blanket policy. If the coverage is not provided under the Master Policy a separate HO-6 policy, providing no less than 20% of the condominium unit's appraised value, is required.

BY SIGNING BELOW, each of the undersigned acknowledges that he or she has read, understands and accepts the foregoing provisions and insurance requirements. This authorization shall remain irrevocable for the undersigned as owner(s) of the property, and for any assignee(s), for as long as this loan remains on the subject property.

_____   _____
JOHN C. VANDER HORCK   JOANN VANDER HORCK

_____   _____

LENDER SUPPORT SYSTEMS, INC. GEN-011.GEN (09/03)

Form **W-9** (Rev. October 2007) Department of the Treasury Internal Revenue Service	**Request for Taxpayer Identification Number and Certification**	Give form to the requester. Do not send to the IRS.

Name (as shown on your income tax return)
JOHN C. VANDER HORCK

Business name, if different from above

Check appropriate box: ☐ Individual/Sole proprietor ☐ Corporation ☐ Partnership
☐ Limited liability company. Enter the tax classification (D=disregarded entity, C=corporation, P=partnership) ▶ _____
☐ Other (see instructions) ▶

☐ Exempt payee

Address (number, street, and apt. or suite no.)
5131 CARITA STREET

Requester's name and address (optional)

City, state, and ZIP code
LONG BEACH, CA 90808-

List account number(s) here (optional)

Print or type
See Specific Instructions on page 2.

Part I   Taxpayer Identification Number (TIN)

Enter your TIN in the appropriate box. The TIN provided must match the name given on Line 1 to avoid backup withholding. For individuals, this is your social security number (SSN). However, for a resident alien, sole proprietor, or disregarded entity, see the Part I instructions on page 3. For other entities, it is your employer identification number (EIN). If you do not have a number, see *How to get a TIN* on page 3.

Note. If the account is in more than one name, see the chart on page 4 for guidelines on whose number to enter.

Social security number
558 : 58 : 8901

or

Employer identification number

Part II   Certification

Under penalties of perjury, I certify that:

1. The number shown on this form is my correct taxpayer identification number (or I am waiting for a number to be issued to me), and

2. I am not subject to backup withholding because: (a) I am exempt from backup withholding, or (b) I have not been notified by the Internal Revenue Service (IRS) that I am subject to backup withholding as a result of a failure to report all interest or dividends, or (c) the IRS has notified me that I am no longer subject to backup withholding, and

3. I am a U.S. citizen or other U.S. person (defined below).

Certification instructions. You must cross out item 2 above if you have been notified by the IRS that you are currently subject to backup withholding because you have failed to report all interest and dividends on your tax return. For real estate transactions, item 2 does not apply. For mortgage interest paid, acquisition or abandonment of secured property, cancellation of debt, contributions to an individual retirement arrangement (IRA), and generally, payments other than interest and dividends, you are not required to sign the Certification, but you must provide your correct TIN. See the instructions on page 4.

Sign Here	Signature of U.S. person ▶	Date ▶

General Instructions

Section references are to the Internal Revenue Code unless otherwise noted.

Purpose of Form

A person who is required to file an information return with the IRS must obtain your correct taxpayer identification number (TIN) to report, for example, income paid to you, real estate transactions, mortgage interest you paid, acquisition or abandonment of secured property, cancellation of debt, or contributions you made to an IRA.

Use Form W-9 only if you are a U.S. person (including a resident alien), to provide your correct TIN to the person requesting it (the requester) and, when applicable, to:

1. Certify that the TIN you are giving is correct (or you are waiting for a number to be issued),

2. Certify that you are not subject to backup withholding, or

3. Claim exemption from backup withholding if you are a U.S. exempt payee. If applicable, you are also certifying that as a U.S. person, your allocable share of any partnership income from a U.S. trade or business is not subject to the withholding tax on foreign partners' share of effectively connected income.

Note. If a requester gives you a form other than Form W-9 to request your TIN, you must use the requester's form if it is substantially similar to this Form W-9.

Definition of a U.S. person. For federal tax purposes, you are considered a U.S. person if you are:

● An individual who is a U.S. citizen or U.S. resident alien,

● A partnership, corporation, company, or association created or organized in the United States or under the laws of the United States,

● An estate (other than a foreign estate), or

● A domestic trust (as defined in Regulations section 301.7701-7).

Special rules for partnerships. Partnerships that conduct a trade or business in the United States are generally required to pay a withholding tax on any foreign partners' share of income from such business. Further, in certain cases where a Form W-9 has not been received, a partnership is required to presume that a partner is a foreign person, and pay the withholding tax. Therefore, if you are a U.S. person that is a partner in a partnership conducting a trade or business in the United States, provide Form W-9 to the partnership to establish your U.S. status and avoid withholding on your share of partnership income.

The person who gives Form W-9 to the partnership for purposes of establishing its U.S. status and avoiding withholding on its allocable share of net income from the partnership conducting a trade or business in the United States is in the following cases:

● The U.S. owner of a disregarded entity and not the entity,

Cat. No. 10231X

Form **W-9** (Rev. 10-2007)

- The U.S. grantor or other owner of a grantor trust and not the trust, and

- The U.S. trust (other than a grantor trust) and not the beneficiaries of the trust.

Foreign person. If you are a foreign person, do not use Form W-9. Instead, use the appropriate Form W-8 (see Publication 515, Withholding of Tax on Nonresident Aliens and Foreign Entities).

Nonresident alien who becomes a resident alien. Generally, only a nonresident alien individual may use the terms of a tax treaty to reduce or eliminate U.S. tax on certain types of income. However, most tax treaties contain a provision known as a "saving clause." Exceptions specified in the saving clause may permit an exemption from tax to continue for certain types of income even after the payee has otherwise become a U.S. resident alien for tax purposes.

If you are a U.S. resident alien who is relying on an exception contained in the saving clause of a tax treaty to claim an exemption from U.S. tax on certain types of income, you must attach a statement to Form W-9 that specifies the following five items:

1. The treaty country. Generally, this must be the same treaty under which you claimed exemption from tax as a nonresident alien.

2. The treaty article addressing the income.

3. The article number (or location) in the tax treaty that contains the saving clause and its exceptions.

4. The type and amount of income that qualifies for the exemption from tax.

5. Sufficient facts to justify the exemption from tax under the terms of the treaty article.

Example. Article 20 of the U.S.-China income tax treaty allows an exemption from tax for scholarship income received by a Chinese student temporarily present in the United States. Under U.S. law, this student will become a resident alien for tax purposes if his or her stay in the United States exceeds 5 calendar years. However, paragraph 2 of the first Protocol to the U.S.-China treaty (dated April 30, 1984) allows the provisions of Article 20 to continue to apply even after the Chinese student becomes a resident alien of the United States. A Chinese student who qualifies for this exception (under paragraph 2 of the first protocol) and is relying on this exception to claim an exemption from tax on his or her scholarship or fellowship income would attach to Form W-9 a statement that includes the information described above to support that exemption.

If you are a nonresident alien or a foreign entity not subject to backup withholding, give the requester the appropriate completed Form W-8.

What is backup withholding? Persons making certain payments to you must under certain conditions withhold and pay to the IRS 28% of such payments. This is called "backup withholding." Payments that may be subject to backup withholding include interest, tax-exempt interest, dividends, broker and barter exchange transactions, rents, royalties, nonemployee pay, and certain payments from fishing boat operators. Real estate transactions are not subject to backup withholding.

You will not be subject to backup withholding on payments you receive if you give the requester your correct TIN, make the proper certifications, and report all your taxable interest and dividends on your tax return.

Payments you receive will be subject to backup withholding if:

1. You do not furnish your TIN to the requester,

2. You do not certify your TIN when required (see the Part II instructions on page 3 for details),

3. The IRS tells the requester that you furnished an incorrect TIN,

4. The IRS tells you that you are subject to backup withholding because you did not report all your interest and dividends on your tax return (for reportable interest and dividends only), or

5. You do not certify to the requester that you are not subject to backup withholding under 4 above (for reportable interest and dividend accounts opened after 1983 only).

Certain payees and payments are exempt from backup withholding. See the instructions below and the separate Instructions for the Requester of Form W-9.

Also see *Special rules for partnerships* on page 1.

Penalties

Failure to furnish TIN. If you fail to furnish your correct TIN to a requester, you are subject to a penalty of $50 for each such failure unless your failure is due to reasonable cause and not to willful neglect.

Civil penalty for false information with respect to withholding. If you make a false statement with no reasonable basis that results in no backup withholding, you are subject to a $500 penalty.

Criminal penalty for falsifying information. Willfully falsifying certifications or affirmations may subject you to criminal penalties including fines and/or imprisonment.

Misuse of TINs. If the requester discloses or uses TINs in violation of federal law, the requester may be subject to civil and criminal penalties.

Specific Instructions

Name

If you are an individual, you must generally enter the name shown on your income tax return. However, if you have changed your last name, for instance, due to marriage without informing the Social Security Administration of the name change, enter your first name, the last name shown on your social security card, and your new last name.

If the account is in joint names, list first, and then circle, the name of the person or entity whose number you entered in Part I of the form.

Sole proprietor. Enter your individual name as shown on your income tax return on the "Name" line. You may enter your business, trade, or "doing business as (DBA)" name on the "Business name" line.

Limited liability company (LLC). Check the "Limited liability company" box only and enter the appropriate code for the tax classification ("D" for disregarded entity, "C" for corporation, "P" for partnership) in the space provided.

For a single-member LLC (including a foreign LLC with a domestic owner) that is disregarded as an entity separate from its owner under Regulations section 301.7701-3, enter the owner's name on the "Name" line. Enter the LLC's name on the "Business name" line.

For an LLC classified as a partnership or a corporation, enter the LLC's name on the "Name" line and any business, trade, or DBA name on the "Business name" line.

Other entities. Enter your business name as shown on required federal tax documents on the "Name" line. This name should match the name shown on the charter or other legal document creating the entity. You may enter any business, trade, or DBA name on the "Business name" line.

Note. You are requested to check the appropriate box for your status (individual/sole proprietor, corporation, etc.).

Exempt Payee

If you are exempt from backup withholding, enter your name as described above and check the appropriate box for your status, then check the "Exempt payee" box in the line following the business name, sign and date the form.

Form W-9 (Rev. 10-2007)   Page **3**

Generally, individuals (including sole proprietors) are not exempt from backup withholding. Corporations are exempt from backup withholding for certain payments, such as interest and dividends.

Note. If you are exempt from backup withholding, you should still complete this form to avoid possible erroneous backup withholding.

The following payees are exempt from backup withholding:

1. An organization exempt from tax under section 501(a), any IRA, or a custodial account under section 403(b)(7) if the account satisfies the requirements of section 401(f)(2),

2. The United States or any of its agencies or instrumentalities,

3. A state, the District of Columbia, a possession of the United States, or any of their political subdivisions or instrumentalities,

4. A foreign government or any of its political subdivisions, agencies, or instrumentalities, or

5. An international organization or any of its agencies or instrumentalities.

Other payees that may be exempt from backup withholding include:

6. A corporation,

7. A foreign central bank of issue,

8. A dealer in securities or commodities required to register in the United States, the District of Columbia, or a possession of the United States,

9. A futures commission merchant registered with the Commodity Futures Trading Commission,

10. A real estate investment trust,

11. An entity registered at all times during the tax year under the Investment Company Act of 1940,

12. A common trust fund operated by a bank under section 584(a),

13. A financial institution,

14. A middleman known in the investment community as a nominee or custodian, or

15. A trust exempt from tax under section 664 or described in section 4947.

The chart below shows types of payments that may be exempt from backup withholding. The chart applies to the exempt payees listed above, 1 through 15.

IF the payment is for . . .	THEN the payment is exempt for . . .
Interest and dividend payments	All exempt payees except for 9
Broker transactions	Exempt payees 1 through 13. Also, a person registered under the Investment Advisers Act of 1940 who regularly acts as a broker
Barter exchange transactions and patronage dividends	Exempt payees 1 through 5
Payments over $600 required to be reported and direct sales over $5,000 [1]	Generally, exempt payees 1 through 7 [2]

[1] See Form 1099-MISC, Miscellaneous Income, and its instructions.
[2] However, the following payments made to a corporation (including gross proceeds paid to an attorney under section 6045(f), even if the attorney is a corporation) and reportable on Form 1099-MISC are not exempt from backup withholding: medical and health care payments, attorneys' fees, and payments for services paid by a federal executive agency.

Part I. Taxpayer Identification Number (TIN)

Enter your TIN in the appropriate box. If you are a resident alien and you do not have and are not eligible to get an SSN, your TIN is your IRS individual taxpayer identification number (ITIN). Enter it in the social security number box. If you do not have an ITIN, see *How to get a TIN* below.

If you are a sole proprietor and you have an EIN, you may enter either your SSN or EIN. However, the IRS prefers that you use your SSN.

If you are a single-member LLC that is disregarded as an entity separate from its owner (see *Limited liability company (LLC)* on page 2), enter the owner's SSN (or EIN, if the owner has one). Do not enter the disregarded entity's EIN. If the LLC is classified as a corporation or partnership, enter the entity's EIN.

Note. See the chart on page 4 for further clarification of name and TIN combinations.

How to get a TIN. If you do not have a TIN, apply for one immediately. To apply for an SSN, get Form SS-5, Application for a Social Security Card, from your local Social Security Administration office or get this form online at *www.ssa.gov*. You may also get this form by calling 1-800-772-1213. Use Form W-7, Application for IRS Individual Taxpayer Identification Number, to apply for an ITIN, or Form SS-4, Application for Employer Identification Number, to apply for an EIN. You can apply for an EIN online by accessing the IRS website at *www.irs.gov/businesses* and clicking on Employer Identification Number (EIN) under Starting a Business. You can get Forms W-7 and SS-4 from the IRS by visiting *www.irs.gov* or by calling 1-800-TAX-FORM (1-800-829-3676).

If you are asked to complete Form W-9 but do not have a TIN, write "Applied For" in the space for the TIN, sign and date the form, and give it to the requester. For interest and dividend payments, and certain payments made with respect to readily tradable instruments, generally you will have 60 days to get a TIN and give it to the requester before you are subject to backup withholding on payments. The 60-day rule does not apply to other types of payments. You will be subject to backup withholding on all such payments until you provide your TIN to the requester.

Note. Entering "Applied For" means that you have already applied for a TIN or that you intend to apply for one soon.

Caution: *A disregarded domestic entity that has a foreign owner must use the appropriate Form W-8.*

Part II. Certification

To establish to the withholding agent that you are a U.S. person, or resident alien, sign Form W-9. You may be requested to sign by the withholding agent even if items 1, 4, and 5 below indicate otherwise.

For a joint account, only the person whose TIN is shown in Part I should sign (when required). Exempt payees, see *Exempt Payee* on page 2.

Signature requirements. Complete the certification as indicated in 1 through 5 below.

1. Interest, dividend, and barter exchange accounts opened before 1984 and broker accounts considered active during 1983. You must give your correct TIN, but you do not have to sign the certification.

2. Interest, dividend, broker, and barter exchange accounts opened after 1983 and broker accounts considered inactive during 1983. You must sign the certification or backup withholding will apply. If you are subject to backup withholding and you are merely providing your correct TIN to the requester, you must cross out item 2 in the certification before signing the form.

3. Real estate transactions. You must sign the certification. You may cross out item 2 of the certification.

4. Other payments. You must give your correct TIN, but you do not have to sign the certification unless you have been notified that you have previously given an incorrect TIN. "Other payments" include payments made in the course of the requester's trade or business for rents, royalties, goods (other than bills for merchandise), medical and health care services (including payments to corporations), payments to a nonemployee for services, payments to certain fishing boat crew members and fishermen, and gross proceeds paid to attorneys (including payments to corporations).

5. Mortgage interest paid by you, acquisition or abandonment of secured property, cancellation of debt, qualified tuition program payments (under section 529), IRA, Coverdell ESA, Archer MSA or HSA contributions or distributions, and pension distributions. You must give your correct TIN, but you do not have to sign the certification.

What Name and Number To Give the Requester

For this type of account:	Give name and SSN of:
1. Individual	The individual
2. Two or more individuals (joint account)	The actual owner of the account or, if combined funds, the first individual on the account [1]
3. Custodian account of a minor (Uniform Gift to Minors Act)	The minor [2]
4. a. The usual revocable savings trust (grantor is also trustee)	The grantor-trustee [1]
b. So-called trust account that is not a legal or valid trust under state law	The actual owner [1]
5. Sole proprietorship or disregarded entity owned by an individual	The owner [3]

For this type of account:	Give name and EIN of:
6. Disregarded entity not owned by an individual	The owner
7. A valid trust, estate, or pension trust	Legal entity [4]
8. Corporate or LLC electing corporate status on Form 8832	The corporation
9. Association, club, religious, charitable, educational, or other tax-exempt organization	The organization
10. Partnership or multi-member LLC	The partnership
11. A broker or registered nominee	The broker or nominee
12. Account with the Department of Agriculture in the name of a public entity (such as a state or local government, school district, or prison) that receives agricultural program payments	The public entity

[1] List first and circle the name of the person whose number you furnish. If only one person on a joint account has an SSN, that person's number must be furnished.

[2] Circle the minor's name and furnish the minor's SSN.

[3] You must show your individual name and you may also enter your business or "DBA" name on the second name line. You may use either your SSN or EIN (if you have one), but the IRS encourages you to use your SSN.

[4] List first and circle the name of the trust, estate, or pension trust. (Do not furnish the TIN of the personal representative or trustee unless the legal entity itself is not designated in the account title.) Also see *Special rules for partnerships* on page 1.

Note. If no name is circled when more than one name is listed, the number will be considered to be that of the first name listed.

Secure Your Tax Records from Identity Theft

Identity theft occurs when someone uses your personal information such as your name, social security number (SSN), or other identifying information, without your permission, to commit fraud or other crimes. An identity thief may use your SSN to get a job or may file a tax return using your SSN to receive a refund.

To reduce your risk:
- Protect your SSN,
- Ensure your employer is protecting your SSN, and
- Be careful when choosing a tax preparer.

Call the IRS at 1-800-829-1040 if you think your identity has been used inappropriately for tax purposes.

Victims of identity theft who are experiencing economic harm or a system problem, or are seeking help in resolving tax problems that have not been resolved through normal channels, may be eligible for Taxpayer Advocate Service (TAS) assistance. You can reach TAS by calling the TAS toll-free case intake line at 1-877-777-4778 or TTY/TDD 1-800-829-4059.

Protect yourself from suspicious emails or phishing schemes. Phishing is the creation and use of email and websites designed to mimic legitimate business emails and websites. The most common act is sending an email to a user falsely claiming to be an established legitimate enterprise in an attempt to scam the user into surrendering private information that will be used for identity theft.

The IRS does not initiate contacts with taxpayers via emails. Also, the IRS does not request personal detailed information through email or ask taxpayers for the PIN numbers, passwords, or similar secret access information for their credit card, bank, or other financial accounts.

If you receive an unsolicited email claiming to be from the IRS, forward this message to *phishing@irs.gov*. You may also report misuse of the IRS name, logo, or other IRS personal property to the Treasury Inspector General for Tax Administration at 1-800-366-4484. You can forward suspicious emails to the Federal Trade Commission at: *spam@uce.gov* or contact them at *www.consumer.gov/idtheft* or 1-877-IDTHEFT(438-4338).

Visit the IRS website at *www.irs.gov* to learn more about identity theft and how to reduce your risk.

Privacy Act Notice

Section 6109 of the Internal Revenue Code requires you to provide your correct TIN to persons who must file information returns with the IRS to report interest, dividends, and certain other income paid to you, mortgage interest you paid, the acquisition or abandonment of secured property, cancellation of debt, or contributions you made to an IRA, or Archer MSA or HSA. The IRS uses the numbers for identification purposes and to help verify the accuracy of your tax return. The IRS may also provide this information to the Department of Justice for civil and criminal litigation, and to cities, states, the District of Columbia, and U.S. possessions to carry out their tax laws. We may also disclose this information to other countries under a tax treaty, to federal and state agencies to enforce federal nontax criminal laws, or to federal law enforcement and intelligence agencies to combat terrorism.

You must provide your TIN whether or not you are required to file a tax return. Payers must generally withhold 28% of taxable interest, dividend, and certain other payments to a payee who does not give a TIN to a payer. Certain penalties may also apply.

| Form **W-9**
(Rev. October 2007)
Department of the Treasury
Internal Revenue Service | **Request for Taxpayer**
Identification Number and Certification | **Give form to the**
requester. Do not
send to the IRS. |

Print or type See Specific Instructions on page 2.

Name (as shown on your income tax return)
JOANN VANDER HORCK

Business name, if different from above

Check appropriate box: ☐ Individual/Sole proprietor ☐ Corporation ☐ Partnership
☐ Limited liability company. Enter the tax classification (D=disregarded entity, C=corporation, P=partnership) ▶ ....
☐ Other (see instructions) ▶
☐ Exempt payee

Address (number, street, and apt. or suite no.)
5131 CARITA STREET

Requester's name and address (optional)

City, state, and ZIP code
LONG BEACH, CA 90808-

List account number(s) here (optional)

Part I   Taxpayer Identification Number (TIN)

Enter your TIN in the appropriate box. The TIN provided must match the name given on Line 1 to avoid backup withholding. For individuals, this is your social security number (SSN). However, for a resident alien, sole proprietor, or disregarded entity, see the Part I instructions on page 3. For other entities, it is your employer identification number (EIN). If you do not have a number, see *How to get a TIN* on page 3.

Note. If the account is in more than one name, see the chart on page 4 for guidelines on whose number to enter.

Social security number
556 : 68 : 3262

or

Employer identification number

Part II   Certification

Under penalties of perjury, I certify that:

1. The number shown on this form is my correct taxpayer identification number (or I am waiting for a number to be issued to me), and

2. I am not subject to backup withholding because: (a) I am exempt from backup withholding, or (b) I have not been notified by the Internal Revenue Service (IRS) that I am subject to backup withholding as a result of a failure to report all interest or dividends, or (c) the IRS has notified me that I am no longer subject to backup withholding, and

3. I am a U.S. citizen or other U.S. person (defined below).

Certification instructions. You must cross out item 2 above if you have been notified by the IRS that you are currently subject to backup withholding because you have failed to report all interest and dividends on your tax return. For real estate transactions, item 2 does not apply. For mortgage interest paid, acquisition or abandonment of secured property, cancellation of debt, contributions to an individual retirement arrangement (IRA), and generally, payments other than interest and dividends, you are not required to sign the Certification, but you must provide your correct TIN. See the instructions on page 4.

Sign Here   Signature of U.S. person ▶   Date ▶

General Instructions

Section references are to the Internal Revenue Code unless otherwise noted.

Purpose of Form

A person who is required to file an information return with the IRS must obtain your correct taxpayer identification number (TIN) to report, for example, income paid to you, real estate transactions, mortgage interest you paid, acquisition or abandonment of secured property, cancellation of debt, or contributions you made to an IRA.

Use Form W-9 only if you are a U.S. person (including a resident alien), to provide your correct TIN to the person requesting it (the requester) and, when applicable, to:

1. Certify that the TIN you are giving is correct (or you are waiting for a number to be issued),

2. Certify that you are not subject to backup withholding, or

3. Claim exemption from backup withholding if you are a U.S. exempt payee. If applicable, you are also certifying that as a U.S. person, your allocable share of any partnership income from a U.S. trade or business is not subject to the withholding tax on foreign partners' share of effectively connected income.

Note. If a requester gives you a form other than Form W-9 to request your TIN, you must use the requester's form if it is substantially similar to this Form W-9.

Definition of a U.S. person. For federal tax purposes, you are considered a U.S. person if you are:

● An individual who is a U.S. citizen or U.S. resident alien,

● A partnership, corporation, company, or association created or organized in the United States or under the laws of the United States,

● An estate (other than a foreign estate), or

● A domestic trust (as defined in Regulations section 301.7701-7).

Special rules for partnerships. Partnerships that conduct a trade or business in the United States are generally required to pay a withholding tax on any foreign partners' share of income from such business. Further, in certain cases where a Form W-9 has not been received, a partnership is required to presume that a partner is a foreign person, and pay the withholding tax. Therefore, if you are a U.S. person that is a partner in a partnership conducting a trade or business in the United States, provide Form W-9 to the partnership to establish your U.S. status and avoid withholding on your share of partnership income.

The person who gives Form W-9 to the partnership for purposes of establishing its U.S. status and avoiding withholding on its allocable share of net income from the partnership conducting a trade or business in the United States is in the following cases:

● The U.S. owner of a disregarded entity and not the entity,

Cat. No. 10231X   Form **W-9** (Rev. 10-2007)

● The U.S. grantor or other owner of a grantor trust and not the trust, and

● The U.S. trust (other than a grantor trust) and not the beneficiaries of the trust.

Foreign person. If you are a foreign person, do not use Form W-9. Instead, use the appropriate Form W-8 (see Publication 515, Withholding of Tax on Nonresident Aliens and Foreign Entities).

Nonresident alien who becomes a resident alien. Generally, only a nonresident alien individual may use the terms of a tax treaty to reduce or eliminate U.S. tax on certain types of income. However, most tax treaties contain a provision known as a "saving clause." Exceptions specified in the saving clause may permit an exemption from tax to continue for certain types of income even after the payee has otherwise become a U.S. resident alien for tax purposes.

If you are a U.S. resident alien who is relying on an exception contained in the saving clause of a tax treaty to claim an exemption from U.S. tax on certain types of income, you must attach a statement to Form W-9 that specifies the following five items:

1. The treaty country. Generally, this must be the same treaty under which you claimed exemption from tax as a nonresident alien.

2. The treaty article addressing the income.

3. The article number (or location) in the tax treaty that contains the saving clause and its exceptions.

4. The type and amount of income that qualifies for the exemption from tax.

5. Sufficient facts to justify the exemption from tax under the terms of the treaty article.

Example. Article 20 of the U.S.-China income tax treaty allows an exemption from tax for scholarship income received by a Chinese student temporarily present in the United States. Under U.S. law, this student will become a resident alien for tax purposes if his or her stay in the United States exceeds 5 calendar years. However, paragraph 2 of the first Protocol to the U.S.-China treaty (dated April 30, 1984) allows the provisions of Article 20 to continue to apply even after the Chinese student becomes a resident alien of the United States. A Chinese student who qualifies for this exception (under paragraph 2 of the first protocol) and is relying on this exception to claim an exemption from tax on his or her scholarship or fellowship income would attach to Form W-9 a statement that includes the information described above to support that exemption.

If you are a nonresident alien or a foreign entity not subject to backup withholding, give the requester the appropriate completed Form W-8.

What is backup withholding? Persons making certain payments to you must under certain conditions withhold and pay to the IRS 28% of such payments. This is called "backup withholding." Payments that may be subject to backup withholding include interest, tax-exempt interest, dividends, broker and barter exchange transactions, rents, royalties, nonemployee pay, and certain payments from fishing boat operators. Real estate transactions are not subject to backup withholding.

You will not be subject to backup withholding on payments you receive if you give the requester your correct TIN, make the proper certifications, and report all your taxable interest and dividends on your tax return.

Payments you receive will be subject to backup withholding if:

1. You do not furnish your TIN to the requester,

2. You do not certify your TIN when required (see the Part II instructions on page 3 for details),

3. The IRS tells the requester that you furnished an incorrect TIN,

4. The IRS tells you that you are subject to backup withholding because you did not report all your interest and dividends on your tax return (for reportable interest and dividends only), or

5. You do not certify to the requester that you are not subject to backup withholding under 4 above (for reportable interest and dividend accounts opened after 1983 only).

Certain payees and payments are exempt from backup withholding. See the instructions below and the separate Instructions for the Requester of Form W-9.

Also see *Special rules for partnerships* on page 1.

Penalties

Failure to furnish TIN. If you fail to furnish your correct TIN to a requester, you are subject to a penalty of $50 for each such failure unless your failure is due to reasonable cause and not to willful neglect.

Civil penalty for false information with respect to withholding. If you make a false statement with no reasonable basis that results in no backup withholding, you are subject to a $500 penalty.

Criminal penalty for falsifying information. Willfully falsifying certifications or affirmations may subject you to criminal penalties including fines and/or imprisonment.

Misuse of TINs. If the requester discloses or uses TINs in violation of federal law, the requester may be subject to civil and criminal penalties.

Specific Instructions

Name

If you are an individual, you must generally enter the name shown on your income tax return. However, if you have changed your last name, for instance, due to marriage without informing the Social Security Administration of the name change, enter your first name, the last name shown on your social security card, and your new last name.

If the account is in joint names, list first, and then circle, the name of the person or entity whose number you entered in Part I of the form.

Sole proprietor. Enter your individual name as shown on your income tax return on the "Name" line. You may enter your business, trade, or "doing business as (DBA)" name on the "Business name" line.

Limited liability company (LLC). Check the "Limited liability company" box only and enter the appropriate code for the tax classification ("D" for disregarded entity, "C" for corporation, "P" for partnership) in the space provided.

For a single-member LLC (including a foreign LLC with a domestic owner) that is disregarded as an entity separate from its owner under Regulations section 301.7701-3, enter the owner's name on the "Name" line. Enter the LLC's name on the "Business name" line.

For an LLC classified as a partnership or a corporation, enter the LLC's name on the "Name" line and any business, trade, or DBA name on the "Business name" line.

Other entities. Enter your business name as shown on required federal tax documents on the "Name" line. This name should match the name shown on the charter or other legal document creating the entity. You may enter any business, trade, or DBA name on the "Business name" line.

Note. You are requested to check the appropriate box for your status (individual/sole proprietor, corporation, etc.).

Exempt Payee

If you are exempt from backup withholding, enter your name as described above and check the appropriate box for your status, then check the "Exempt payee" box in the line following the business name, sign and date the form.

Generally, individuals (including sole proprietors) are not exempt from backup withholding. Corporations are exempt from backup withholding for certain payments, such as interest and dividends.

Note. If you are exempt from backup withholding, you should still complete this form to avoid possible erroneous backup withholding.

The following payees are exempt from backup withholding:

1. An organization exempt from tax under section 501(a), any IRA, or a custodial account under section 403(b)(7) if the account satisfies the requirements of section 401(f)(2),

2. The United States or any of its agencies or instrumentalities,

3. A state, the District of Columbia, a possession of the United States, or any of their political subdivisions or instrumentalities,

4. A foreign government or any of its political subdivisions, agencies, or instrumentalities, or

5. An international organization or any of its agencies or instrumentalities.

Other payees that may be exempt from backup withholding include:

6. A corporation,

7. A foreign central bank of issue,

8. A dealer in securities or commodities required to register in the United States, the District of Columbia, or a possession of the United States,

9. A futures commission merchant registered with the Commodity Futures Trading Commission,

10. A real estate investment trust,

11. An entity registered at all times during the tax year under the Investment Company Act of 1940,

12. A common trust fund operated by a bank under section 584(a),

13. A financial institution,

14. A middleman known in the investment community as a nominee or custodian, or

15. A trust exempt from tax under section 664 or described in section 4947.

The chart below shows types of payments that may be exempt from backup withholding. The chart applies to the exempt payees listed above, 1 through 15.

IF the payment is for . . .	THEN the payment is exempt for . . .
Interest and dividend payments	All exempt payees except for 9
Broker transactions	Exempt payees 1 through 13. Also, a person registered under the Investment Advisers Act of 1940 who regularly acts as a broker
Barter exchange transactions and patronage dividends	Exempt payees 1 through 5
Payments over $600 required to be reported and direct sales over $5,000 [1]	Generally, exempt payees 1 through 7 [2]

[1] See Form 1099-MISC, Miscellaneous Income, and its instructions.

[2] However, the following payments made to a corporation (including gross proceeds paid to an attorney under section 6045(f), even if the attorney is a corporation) and reportable on Form 1099-MISC are not exempt from backup withholding: medical and health care payments, attorneys' fees, and payments for services paid by a federal executive agency.

Part I. Taxpayer Identification Number (TIN)

Enter your TIN in the appropriate box. If you are a resident alien and you do not have and are not eligible to get an SSN, your TIN is your IRS individual taxpayer identification number (ITIN). Enter it in the social security number box. If you do not have an ITIN, see *How to get a TIN* below.

If you are a sole proprietor and you have an EIN, you may enter either your SSN or EIN. However, the IRS prefers that you use your SSN.

If you are a single-member LLC that is disregarded as an entity separate from its owner (see *Limited liability company (LLC)* on page 2), enter the owner's SSN (or EIN, if the owner has one). Do not enter the disregarded entity's EIN. If the LLC is classified as a corporation or partnership, enter the entity's EIN.

Note. See the chart on page 4 for further clarification of name and TIN combinations.

How to get a TIN. If you do not have a TIN, apply for one immediately. To apply for an SSN, get Form SS-5, Application for a Social Security Card, from your local Social Security Administration office or get this form online at *www.ssa.gov*. You may also get this form by calling 1-800-772-1213. Use Form W-7, Application for IRS Individual Taxpayer Identification Number, to apply for an ITIN, or Form SS-4, Application for Employer Identification Number, to apply for an EIN. You can apply for an EIN online by accessing the IRS website at *www.irs.gov/businesses* and clicking on Employer Identification Number (EIN) under Starting a Business. You can get Forms W-7 and SS-4 from the IRS by visiting *www.irs.gov* or by calling 1-800-TAX-FORM (1-800-829-3676).

If you are asked to complete Form W-9 but do not have a TIN, write "Applied For" in the space for the TIN, sign and date the form, and give it to the requester. For interest and dividend payments, and certain payments made with respect to readily tradable instruments, generally you will have 60 days to get a TIN and give it to the requester before you are subject to backup withholding on payments. The 60-day rule does not apply to other types of payments. You will be subject to backup withholding on all such payments until you provide your TIN to the requester.

Note. Entering "Applied For" means that you have already applied for a TIN or that you intend to apply for one soon.

Caution: *A disregarded domestic entity that has a foreign owner must use the appropriate Form W-8.*

Part II. Certification

To establish to the withholding agent that you are a U.S. person, or resident alien, sign Form W-9. You may be requested to sign by the withholding agent even if items 1, 4, and 5 below indicate otherwise.

For a joint account, only the person whose TIN is shown in Part I should sign (when required). Exempt payees, see *Exempt Payee* on page 2.

Signature requirements. Complete the certification as indicated in 1 through 5 below.

1. Interest, dividend, and barter exchange accounts opened before 1984 and broker accounts considered active during 1983. You must give your correct TIN, but you do not have to sign the certification.

2. Interest, dividend, broker, and barter exchange accounts opened after 1983 and broker accounts considered inactive during 1983. You must sign the certification or backup withholding will apply. If you are subject to backup withholding and you are merely providing your correct TIN to the requester, you must cross out item 2 in the certification before signing the form.

3. Real estate transactions. You must sign the certification. You may cross out item 2 of the certification.

4. Other payments. You must give your correct TIN, but you do not have to sign the certification unless you have been notified that you have previously given an incorrect TIN. "Other payments" include payments made in the course of the requester's trade or business for rents, royalties, goods (other than bills for merchandise), medical and health care services (including payments to corporations), payments to a nonemployee for services, payments to certain fishing boat crew members and fishermen, and gross proceeds paid to attorneys (including payments to corporations).

5. Mortgage interest paid by you, acquisition or abandonment of secured property, cancellation of debt, qualified tuition program payments (under section 529), IRA, Coverdell ESA, Archer MSA or HSA contributions or distributions, and pension distributions. You must give your correct TIN, but you do not have to sign the certification.

What Name and Number To Give the Requester

For this type of account:	Give name and SSN of:
1. Individual	The individual
2. Two or more individuals (joint account)	The actual owner of the account or, if combined funds, the first individual on the account [1]
3. Custodian account of a minor (Uniform Gift to Minors Act)	The minor [2]
4. a. The usual revocable savings trust (grantor is also trustee)	The grantor-trustee [1]
b. So-called trust account that is not a legal or valid trust under state law	The actual owner [1]
5. Sole proprietorship or disregarded entity owned by an individual	The owner [3]

For this type of account:	Give name and EIN of:
6. Disregarded entity not owned by an individual	The owner
7. A valid trust, estate, or pension trust	Legal entity [4]
8. Corporate or LLC electing corporate status on Form 8832	The corporation
9. Association, club, religious, charitable, educational, or other tax-exempt organization	The organization
10. Partnership or multi-member LLC	The partnership
11. A broker or registered nominee	The broker or nominee
12. Account with the Department of Agriculture in the name of a public entity (such as a state or local government, school district, or prison) that receives agricultural program payments	The public entity

[1] List first and circle the name of the person whose number you furnish. If only one person on a joint account has an SSN, that person's number must be furnished.

[2] Circle the minor's name and furnish the minor's SSN.

[3] You must show your individual name and you may also enter your business or "DBA" name on the second name line. You may use either your SSN or EIN (if you have one), but the IRS encourages you to use your SSN.

[4] List first and circle the name of the trust, estate, or pension trust. (Do not furnish the TIN of the personal representative or trustee unless the legal entity itself is not designated in the account title.) Also see *Special rules for partnerships* on page 1.

Note. If no name is circled when more than one name is listed, the number will be considered to be that of the first name listed.

Secure Your Tax Records from Identity Theft

Identity theft occurs when someone uses your personal information such as your name, social security number (SSN), or other identifying information, without your permission, to commit fraud or other crimes. An identity thief may use your SSN to get a job or may file a tax return using your SSN to receive a refund.

To reduce your risk:
● Protect your SSN,
● Ensure your employer is protecting your SSN, and
● Be careful when choosing a tax preparer.

Call the IRS at 1-800-829-1040 if you think your identity has been used inappropriately for tax purposes.

Victims of identity theft who are experiencing economic harm or a system problem, or are seeking help in resolving tax problems that have not been resolved through normal channels, may be eligible for Taxpayer Advocate Service (TAS) assistance. You can reach TAS by calling the TAS toll-free case intake line at 1-877-777-4778 or TTY/TDD 1-800-829-4059.

Protect yourself from suspicious emails or phishing schemes. Phishing is the creation and use of email and websites designed to mimic legitimate business emails and websites. The most common act is sending an email to a user falsely claiming to be an established legitimate enterprise in an attempt to scam the user into surrendering private information that will be used for identity theft.

The IRS does not initiate contacts with taxpayers via emails. Also, the IRS does not request personal detailed information through email or ask taxpayers for the PIN numbers, passwords, or similar secret access information for their credit card, bank, or other financial accounts.

If you receive an unsolicited email claiming to be from the IRS, forward this message to *phishing@irs.gov.* You may also report misuse of the IRS name, logo, or other IRS personal property to the Treasury Inspector General for Tax Administration at 1-800-366-4484. You can forward suspicious emails to the Federal Trade Commission at: *spam@uce.gov* or contact them at *www.consumer.gov/idtheft* or 1-877-IDTHEFT(438-4338).

Visit the IRS website at *www.irs.gov* to learn more about identity theft and how to reduce your risk.

Privacy Act Notice

Section 6109 of the Internal Revenue Code requires you to provide your correct TIN to persons who must file information returns with the IRS to report interest, dividends, and certain other income paid to you, mortgage interest you paid, the acquisition or abandonment of secured property, cancellation of debt, or contributions you made to an IRA, or Archer MSA or HSA. The IRS uses the numbers for identification purposes and to help verify the accuracy of your tax return. The IRS may also provide this information to the Department of Justice for civil and criminal litigation, and to cities, states, the District of Columbia, and U.S. possessions to carry out their tax laws. We may also disclose this information to other countries under a tax treaty, to federal and state agencies to enforce federal nontax criminal laws, or to federal law enforcement and intelligence agencies to combat terrorism.

You must provide your TIN whether or not you are required to file a tax return. Payers must generally withhold 28% of taxable interest, dividend, and certain other payments to a payee who does not give a TIN to a payer. Certain penalties may also apply.

Form 4506-T

(Rev. January 2010)

Department of the Treasury
Internal Revenue Service

Request for Transcript of Tax Return

► **Request may be rejected if the form is incomplete or illegible.**

OMB No. 1545-1872

Tip. Use Form 4506-T to order a transcript or other return information free of charge. See the product list below. You can also call 1-800-829-1040 to order a transcript. If you need a copy of your return, use **Form 4506, Request for Copy of Tax Return.** There is a fee to get a copy of your return.

1a Name shown on tax return. If a joint return, enter the name shown first.

JOHN C. VANDER HORCK

1b First social security number on tax return or employer identification number (see instructions)

558-58-8901

2a If a joint return, enter spouse's name shown on tax return.

2b Second social security number if joint tax return

3 Current name, address (including apt., room, or suite no.), city, state, and ZIP code

JOHN C. VANDER HORCK
5131 CARITA STREET, LONG BEACH, CA 90808-

4 Previous address shown on the last return filed if different from line 3

5 If the transcript or tax information is to be mailed to a third party (such as a mortgage company), enter the third party's name, address, and telephone number. The IRS has no control over what the third party does with the tax information.

Caution. *If the transcript is being mailed to a third party, ensure that you have filled in line 6 and line 9 before signing. Sign and date the form once you have filled in these lines. Completing these steps helps to protect your privacy.*

6 **Transcript requested.** Enter the tax form number here (1040, 1065, 1120, etc.) and check the appropriate box below. Enter only one tax form number per request. ►

a **Return Transcript,** which includes most of the line items of a tax return as filed with the IRS. A tax return transcript does not reflect changes made to the account after the return is processed. Transcripts are only available for the following returns: Form 1040 series, Form 1065, Form 1120, Form 1120A, Form 1120H, Form 1120L, and Form 1120S. Return transcripts are available for the current year and returns processed during the prior 3 processing years. Most requests will be processed within 10 business days . . . . . . ☐

b **Account Transcript,** which contains information on the financial status of the account, such as payments made on the account, penalty assessments, and adjustments made by you or the IRS after the return was filed. Return information is limited to items such as tax liability and estimated tax payments. Account transcripts are available for most returns. Most requests will be processed within 30 calendar days. . ☐

c **Record of Account,** which is a combination of line item information and later adjustments to the account. Available for current year and 3 prior tax years. Most requests will be processed within 30 calendar days . . . . ☐

7 **Verification of Nonfiling,** which is proof from the IRS that you **did not** file a return for the year. Current year requests are only available after June 15th. There are no availability restrictions on prior year requests. Most requests will be processed within 10 business days . ☐

8 **Form W-2, Form 1099 series, Form 1098 series, or Form 5498 series transcript.** The IRS can provide a transcript that includes data from these information returns. State or local information is not included with the Form W-2 information. The IRS may be able to provide this transcript information for up to 10 years. Information for the current year is generally not available until the year after it is filed with the IRS. For example, W-2 information for 2007, filed in 2008, will not be available from the IRS until 2009. If you need W-2 information for retirement purposes, you should contact the Social Security Administration at 1-800-772-1213. Most requests will be processed within 45 days . . . ☐

Caution. *If you need a copy of Form W-2 or Form 1099, you should first contact the payer. To get a copy of the Form W-2 or Form 1099 filed with your return, you must use Form 4506 and request a copy of your return, which includes all attachments.*

9 **Year or period requested.** Enter the ending date of the year or period, using the mm/dd/yyyy format. If you are requesting more than four years or periods, you must attach another Form 4506-T. For requests relating to quarterly tax returns, such as Form 941, you must enter each quarter or tax period separately.

Signature of taxpayer(s). I declare that I am either the taxpayer whose name is shown on line 1a or 2a, or a person authorized to obtain the tax information requested. If the request applies to a joint return, **either** husband or wife must sign. If signed by a corporate officer, partner, guardian, tax matters partner, executor, receiver, administrator, trustee, or party other than the taxpayer, I certify that I have the authority to execute Form 4506-T on behalf of the taxpayer. **Note.** *For transcripts being sent to a third party, this form must be received within 120 days of signature date.*

Telephone number of taxpayer on line 1a or 2a

Sign Here

► Signature (see instructions)   Date

► Title (if line 1a above is a corporation, partnership, estate, or trust)

► Spouse's signature   Date

For Privacy Act and Paperwork Reduction Act Notice, see page 2.   Cat. No. 37667N   Form **4506-T** (Rev. 1-2010)

General Instructions

Purpose of form. Use Form 4506-T to request tax return information. You can also designate a third party to receive the information. See line 5.

Tip. Use Form 4506, Request for Copy of Tax Return, to request copies of tax returns.

Where to file. Mail or fax Form 4506-T to the address below for the state you lived in, or the state your business was in, when that return was filed. There are two address charts: one for individual transcripts (Form 1040 series and Form W-2) and one for all other transcripts.

If you are requesting more than one transcript or other product and the chart below shows two different RAIVS teams, send your request to the team based on the address of your most recent return.

Automated transcript request. You can call 1-800-829-1040 to order a transcript through the automated self-help system. Follow prompts for "questions about your tax account" to order a tax return transcript.

Chart for individual transcripts (Form 1040 series and Form W-2)

If you filed an individual return and lived in:	Mail or fax to the "Internal Revenue Service" at:
Florida, Georgia, North Carolina, South Carolina	RAIVS Team P.O. Box 47-421 Stop 91 Doraville, GA 30362
	770-455-2335
Alabama, Kentucky, Louisiana, Mississippi, Tennessee, Texas, a foreign country, or A.P.O. or F.P.O. address	RAIVS Team Stop 6716 AUSC Austin, TX 73301
	512-460-2272
Alaska, Arizona, California, Colorado, Hawaii, Idaho, Illinois, Indiana, Iowa, Kansas, Michigan, Minnesota, Montana, Nebraska, Nevada, New Mexico, North Dakota, Oklahoma, Oregon, South Dakota, Utah, Washington, Wisconsin, Wyoming	RAIVS Team Stop 37106 Fresno, CA 93888
	559-456-5876
Arkansas, Connecticut, Delaware, District of Columbia, Maine, Maryland, Massachusetts, Missouri, New Hampshire, New Jersey, New York, Ohio, Pennsylvania, Rhode Island, Vermont, Virginia, West Virginia	RAIVS Team Stop 6705 P-6 Kansas City, MO 64999
	816-292-6102

Chart for all other transcripts

If you lived in or your business was in:	Mail or fax to the "Internal Revenue Service" at:
Alabama, Alaska, Arizona, Arkansas, California, Colorado, Florida, Hawaii, Idaho, Iowa, Kansas, Louisiana, Minnesota, Mississippi, Missouri, Montana, Nebraska, Nevada, New Mexico, North Dakota, Oklahoma, Oregon, South Dakota, Tennessee, Texas, Utah, Washington, Wyoming, a foreign country, or A.P.O. or F.P.O. address	RAIVS Team P.O. Box 9941 Mail Stop 6734 Ogden, UT 84409
	801-620-6922
Connecticut, Delaware, District of Columbia, Georgia, Illinois, Indiana, Kentucky, Maine, Maryland, Massachusetts, Michigan, New Hampshire, New Jersey, New York, North Carolina, Ohio, Pennsylvania, Rhode Island, South Carolina, Vermont, Virginia, West Virginia, Wisconsin	RAIVS Team P.O. Box 145500 Stop 2800 F Cincinnati, OH 45250
	859-669-3592

Line 1b. Enter your employer identification number (EIN) if your request relates to a business return. Otherwise, enter the first social security number (SSN) shown on the return. For example, if you are requesting Form 1040 that includes Schedule C (Form 1040), enter your SSN.

Line 6. Enter only one tax form number per request.

Signature and date. Form 4506-T must be signed and dated by the taxpayer listed on line 1a or 2a. If you completed line 5 requesting the information be sent to a third party, the IRS must receive Form 4506-T within 120 days of the date signed by the taxpayer or it will be rejected.

Individuals. Transcripts of jointly filed tax returns may be furnished to either spouse. Only one signature is required. Sign Form 4506-T exactly as your name appeared on the original return. If you changed your name, also sign your current name.

Corporations. Generally, Form 4506-T can be signed by: (1) an officer having legal authority to bind the corporation, (2) any person designated by the board of directors or other governing body, or (3) any officer or employee on written request by any principal officer and attested to by the secretary or other officer.

Partnerships. Generally, Form 4506-T can be signed by any person who was a member of the partnership during any part of the tax period requested on line 9.

All others. See Internal Revenue Code section 6103(e) if the taxpayer has died, is insolvent, is a dissolved corporation, or if a trustee, guardian, executor, receiver, or administrator is acting for the taxpayer.

Documentation. For entities other than individuals, you must attach the authorization document. For example, this could be the letter from the principal officer authorizing an employee of the corporation or the Letters Testamentary authorizing an individual to act for an estate.

Privacy Act and Paperwork Reduction Act Notice. We ask for the information on this form to establish your right to gain access to the requested tax information under the Internal Revenue Code. We need this information to properly identify the tax information and respond to your request. You are not required to request any transcript; if you do request a transcript, sections 6103 and 6109 and their regulations require you to provide this information, including your SSN or EIN. If you do not provide this information, we may not be able to process your request. Providing false or fraudulent information may subject you to penalties.

Routine uses of this information include giving it to the Department of Justice for civil and criminal litigation, and cities, states, and the District of Columbia for use in administering their tax laws. We may also disclose this information to other countries under a tax treaty, to federal and state agencies to enforce federal nontax criminal laws, or to federal law enforcement and intelligence agencies to combat terrorism.

You are not required to provide the information requested on a form that is subject to the Paperwork Reduction Act unless the form displays a valid OMB control number. Books or records relating to a form or its instructions must be retained as long as their contents may become material in the administration of any Internal Revenue law. Generally, tax returns and return information are confidential, as required by section 6103.

The time needed to complete and file Form 4506-T will vary depending on individual circumstances. The estimated average time is: **Learning about the law or the form,** 10 min.; **Preparing the form,** 12 min.; and **Copying, assembling, and sending the form to the IRS,** 20 min.

If you have comments concerning the accuracy of these time estimates or suggestions for making Form 4506-T simpler, we would be happy to hear from you. You can write to the Internal Revenue Service, Tax Products Coordinating Committee, SE:W:CAR:MP:T:T:SP, 1111 Constitution Ave. NW, IR-6526, Washington, DC 20224. Do not send the form to this address. Instead, see *Where to file* on this page.

Form **4506-T**
(Rev. January 2010)
Department of the Treasury
Internal Revenue Service

Request for Transcript of Tax Return

► Request may be rejected if the form is incomplete or illegible.

OMB No. 1545-1872

Tip. Use Form 4506-T to order a transcript or other return information free of charge. See the product list below. You can also call 1-800-829-1040 to order a transcript. If you need a copy of your return, use **Form 4506, Request for Copy of Tax Return.** There is a fee to get a copy of your return.

1a Name shown on tax return. If a joint return, enter the name shown first.

JOHN C. VANDER HORCK

1b First social security number on tax return or employer identification number (see instructions)

558-58-8901

2a If a joint return, enter spouse's name shown on tax return.

2b Second social security number if joint tax return

3 Current name, address (including apt., room, or suite no.), city, state, and ZIP code

JOHN C. VANDER HORCK
5131 CARITA STREET, LONG BEACH, CA 90808-

4 Previous address shown on the last return filed if different from line 3

5 If the transcript or tax information is to be mailed to a third party (such as a mortgage company), enter the third party's name, address, and telephone number. The IRS has no control over what the third party does with the tax information.

Caution. *If the transcript is being mailed to a third party, ensure that you have filled in line 6 and line 9 before signing. Sign and date the form once you have filled in these lines. Completing these steps helps to protect your privacy.*

6 **Transcript requested.** Enter the tax form number here (1040, 1065, 1120, etc.) and check the appropriate box below. Enter only one tax form number per request. ►

a **Return Transcript,** which includes most of the line items of a tax return as filed with the IRS. A tax return transcript does not reflect changes made to the account after the return is processed. Transcripts are only available for the following returns: Form 1040 series, Form 1065, Form 1120, Form 1120A, Form 1120H, Form 1120L, and Form 1120S. Return transcripts are available for the current year and returns processed during the prior 3 processing years. Most requests will be processed within 10 business days . . . . ☐

b **Account Transcript,** which contains information on the financial status of the account, such as payments made on the account, penalty assessments, and adjustments made by you or the IRS after the return was filed. Return information is limited to items such as tax liability and estimated tax payments. Account transcripts are available for most returns. Most requests will be processed within 30 calendar days. . ☐

c **Record of Account,** which is a combination of line item information and later adjustments to the account. Available for current year and 3 prior tax years. Most requests will be processed within 30 calendar days . . . . ☐

7 **Verification of Nonfiling,** which is proof from the IRS that you **did not** file a return for the year. Current year requests are only available after June 15th. There are no availability restrictions on prior year requests. Most requests will be processed within 10 business days . . ☐

8 **Form W-2, Form 1099 series, Form 1098 series, or Form 5498 series transcript.** The IRS can provide a transcript that includes data from these information returns. State or local information is not included with the Form W-2 information. The IRS may be able to provide this transcript information for up to 10 years. Information for the current year is generally not available until the year after it is filed with the IRS. For example, W-2 information for 2007, filed in 2008, will not be available from the IRS until 2009. If you need W-2 information for retirement purposes, you should contact the Social Security Administration at 1-800-772-1213. Most requests will be processed within 45 days . . . ☐

Caution. *If you need a copy of Form W-2 or Form 1099, you should first contact the payer. To get a copy of the Form W-2 or Form 1099 filed with your return, you must use Form 4506 and request a copy of your return, which includes all attachments.*

9 **Year or period requested.** Enter the ending date of the year or period, using the mm/dd/yyyy format. If you are requesting more than four years or periods, you must attach another Form 4506-T. For requests relating to quarterly tax returns, such as Form 941, you must enter each quarter or tax period separately.

Signature of taxpayer(s). I declare that I am either the taxpayer whose name is shown on line 1a or 2a, or a person authorized to obtain the tax information requested. If the request applies to a joint return, **either** husband or wife must sign. If signed by a corporate officer, partner, guardian, tax matters partner, executor, receiver, administrator, trustee, or party other than the taxpayer, I certify that I have the authority to execute Form 4506-T on behalf of the taxpayer. **Note.** *For transcripts being sent to a third party, this form must be received within 120 days of signature date.*

Telephone number of taxpayer on line 1a or 2a

Sign Here

► **Signature** (see instructions)   Date

► **Title** (if line 1a above is a corporation, partnership, estate, or trust)

► **Spouse's signature**   Date

For Privacy Act and Paperwork Reduction Act Notice, see page 2.   Cat. No. 37667N   Form **4506-T** (Rev. 1-2010)

Form 4506-T (Rev. 1-2010)   Page **2**

General Instructions

Purpose of form. Use Form 4506-T to request tax return information. You can also designate a third party to receive the information. See line 5.

Tip. Use Form 4506, Request for Copy of Tax Return, to request copies of tax returns.

Where to file. Mail or fax Form 4506-T to the address below for the state you lived in, or the state your business was in, when that return was filed. There are two address charts: one for individual transcripts (Form 1040 series and Form W-2) and one for all other transcripts.

If you are requesting more than one transcript or other product and the chart below shows two different RAIVS teams, send your request to the team based on the address of your most recent return.

Automated transcript request. You can call 1-800-829-1040 to order a transcript through the automated self-help system. Follow prompts for "questions about your tax account" to order a tax return transcript.

Chart for individual transcripts (Form 1040 series and Form W-2)

If you filed an individual return and lived in:	Mail or fax to the "Internal Revenue Service" at:
Florida, Georgia, North Carolina, South Carolina	RAIVS Team P.O. Box 47-421 Stop 91 Doraville, GA 30362
	770-455-2335
Alabama, Kentucky, Louisiana, Mississippi, Tennessee, Texas, a foreign country, or A.P.O. or F.P.O. address	RAIVS Team Stop 6716 AUSC Austin, TX 73301
	512-460-2272
Alaska, Arizona, California, Colorado, Hawaii, Idaho, Illinois, Indiana, Iowa, Kansas, Michigan, Minnesota, Montana, Nebraska, Nevada, New Mexico, North Dakota, Oklahoma, Oregon, South Dakota, Utah, Washington, Wisconsin, Wyoming	RAIVS Team Stop 37106 Fresno, CA 93888
	559-456-5876
Arkansas, Connecticut, Delaware, District of Columbia, Maine, Maryland, Massachusetts, Missouri, New Hampshire, New Jersey, New York, Ohio, Pennsylvania, Rhode Island, Vermont, Virginia, West Virginia	RAIVS Team Stop 6705 P-6 Kansas City, MO 64999
	816-292-6102

Chart for all other transcripts

If you lived in or your business was in:	Mail or fax to the "Internal Revenue Service" at:
Alabama, Alaska, Arizona, Arkansas, California, Colorado, Florida, Hawaii, Idaho, Iowa, Kansas, Louisiana, Minnesota, Mississippi, Missouri, Montana, Nebraska, Nevada, New Mexico, North Dakota, Oklahoma, Oregon, South Dakota, Tennessee, Texas, Utah, Washington, Wyoming, a foreign country, or A.P.O. or F.P.O. address	RAIVS Team P.O. Box 9941 Mail Stop 6734 Ogden, UT 84409
	801-620-6922
Connecticut, Delaware, District of Columbia, Georgia, Illinois, Indiana, Kentucky, Maine, Maryland, Massachusetts, Michigan, New Hampshire, New Jersey, New York, North Carolina, Ohio, Pennsylvania, Rhode Island, South Carolina, Vermont, Virginia, West Virginia, Wisconsin	RAIVS Team P.O. Box 145500 Stop 2800 F Cincinnati, OH 45250
	859-669-3592

Line 1b. Enter your employer identification number (EIN) if your request relates to a business return. Otherwise, enter the first social security number (SSN) shown on the return. For example, if you are requesting Form 1040 that includes Schedule C (Form 1040), enter your SSN.

Line 6. Enter only one tax form number per request.

Signature and date. Form 4506-T must be signed and dated by the taxpayer listed on line 1a or 2a. If you completed line 5 requesting the information be sent to a third party, the IRS must receive Form 4506-T within 120 days of the date signed by the taxpayer or it will be rejected.

Individuals. Transcripts of jointly filed tax returns may be furnished to either spouse. Only one signature is required. Sign Form 4506-T exactly as your name appeared on the original return. If you changed your name, also sign your current name.

Corporations. Generally, Form 4506-T can be signed by: (1) an officer having legal authority to bind the corporation, (2) any person designated by the board of directors or other governing body, or (3) any officer or employee on written request by any principal officer and attested to by the secretary or other officer.

Partnerships. Generally, Form 4506-T can be signed by any person who was a member of the partnership during any part of the tax period requested on line 9.

All others. See Internal Revenue Code section 6103(e) if the taxpayer has died, is insolvent, is a dissolved corporation, or if a trustee, guardian, executor, receiver, or administrator is acting for the taxpayer.

Documentation. For entities other than individuals, you must attach the authorization document. For example, this could be the letter from the principal officer authorizing an employee of the corporation or the Letters Testamentary authorizing an individual to act for an estate.

Privacy Act and Paperwork Reduction Act Notice. We ask for the information on this form to establish your right to gain access to the requested tax information under the Internal Revenue Code. We need this information to properly identify the tax information and respond to your request. You are not required to request any transcript; if you do request a transcript, sections 6103 and 6109 and their regulations require you to provide this information, including your SSN or EIN. If you do not provide this information, we may not be able to process your request. Providing false or fraudulent information may subject you to penalties.

Routine uses of this information include giving it to the Department of Justice for civil and criminal litigation, and cities, states, and the District of Columbia for use in administering their tax laws. We may also disclose this information to other countries under a tax treaty, to federal and state agencies to enforce federal nontax criminal laws, or to federal law enforcement and intelligence agencies to combat terrorism.

You are not required to provide the information requested on a form that is subject to the Paperwork Reduction Act unless the form displays a valid OMB control number. Books or records relating to a form or its instructions must be retained as long as their contents may become material in the administration of any Internal Revenue law. Generally, tax returns and return information are confidential, as required by section 6103.

The time needed to complete and file Form 4506-T will vary depending on individual circumstances. The estimated average time is: **Learning about the law or the form,** 10 min.; **Preparing the form,** 12 min.; and **Copying, assembling, and sending the form to the IRS,** 20 min.

If you have comments concerning the accuracy of these time estimates or suggestions for making Form 4506-T simpler, we would be happy to hear from you. You can write to the Internal Revenue Service, Tax Products Coordinating Committee, SE:W:CAR:MP:T:T:SP, 1111 Constitution Ave. NW, IR-6526, Washington, DC 20224. Do not send the form to this address. Instead, see *Where to file* on this page.

LOAN NO.: 2109053817

SIGNATURE AFFIDAVIT AND AKA STATEMENT

SIGNATURE STATEMENT

I __JOHN C. VANDER HORCK__ _____
certify that this my true and correct signature

__JOHN C. VANDER HORCK_____   ._____
Borrower   Sample Signature

AKA STATEMENT

I __JOHN C. VANDER HORCK_____   further certify that I am also known as:

__J. VANDER HORCK_____   _____
Name Variation (Print)   Sample Signature (Variation)

__JOHN C. VANDER_____   _____
Name Variation (Print)   Sample Signature (Variation)

__JOHN C. MCCARLEY_____   _____
Name Variation (Print)   Sample Signature (Variation)

_____   _____
Name Variation (Print)   Sample Signature (Variation)

_____   _____
Name Variation (Print)   Sample Signature (Variation)

State of __CALIFORNIA_____
County of __SAN BERNARDINO_____

On _____ , before me, _____ , Notary Public,
personally appeared   __JOHN C. VANDER HORCK_____

who proved to me on the basis of satisfactory evidence to be the person(s) whose name(s) is/are subscribed to the within instrument and acknowledged to me that he/she/they executed the same in his/her/their authorized capacity(ies), and that by his/her/their signature(s) on the instrument the person(s), or the entity upon behalf of which the person(s) acted, executed the instrument.

I certify under PENALTY OF PERJURY under the laws of the State of California that the foregoing paragraph is true and correct.

WITNESS my hand and official seal.

Signature _____

LOAN NO.: 2109053817

SIGNATURE AFFIDAVIT AND AKA STATEMENT

SIGNATURE STATEMENT

I   **JOANN VANDER HORCK** _____

certify that this my true and correct signature

_____   _____

JOANN VANDER HORCK

Borrower   Sample Signature

AKA STATEMENT

I   **JOANN VANDER HORCK** _____ further certify that I am also known as:

J. VANDER HORCK _____   _____

Name Variation (Print)   Sample Signature (Variation)

JOANN MCCARLEY _____   _____

Name Variation (Print)   Sample Signature (Variation)

JOANN HORCK _____   _____

Name Variation (Print)   Sample Signature (Variation)

_____   _____

Name Variation (Print)   Sample Signature (Variation)

_____   _____

Name Variation (Print)   Sample Signature (Variation)

State of   **CALIFORNIA** _____

County of   **SAN BERNARDINO** _____

On _____ , before me, _____ , Notary Public,

personally appeared   **JOANN VANDER HORCK** _____

who proved to me on the basis of satisfactory evidence to be the person(s) whose name(s) is/are subscribed to the within instrument and acknowledged to me that he/she/they executed the same in his/her/their authorized capacity(ies), and that by his/her/their signature(s) on the instrument the person(s), or the entity upon behalf of which the person(s) acted, executed the instrument.

I certify under PENALTY OF PERJURY under the laws of the State of California that the foregoing paragraph is true and correct.

WITNESS my hand and official seal.

Signature _____

LOAN NO.:   2109053817

IMPORTANT APPLICANT INFORMATION

Borrower Name(s): JOHN C. VANDER HORCK AND JOANN VANDER HORCK	Lender: PLAZA HOME MORTGAGE, INC. 3633 INLAND EMPIRE BLVD #250 ONTARIO, CA 91764
Property Address: 39566 BARBARA LEE LANE FAWNSKIN, CA 92333-	Date: AUGUST 10, 2009

IMPORTANT INFORMATION ABOUT PROCEDURES FOR OPENING A NEW ACCOUNT OR REQUESTING A LOAN

To help the government fight the funding of terrorism and money laundering activities, Federal law requires all financial institutions to obtain, verify, and record information that identifies each person who opens an account or requests a loan.

What this means for you: When you open an account, we will ask for your name, address, date of birth, and other information that will allow us to identify you. We may also ask to see your driver's license or other identifying documents.

JOHN C. VANDER HORCK _____ Date	JOANN VANDER HORCK _____ Date
_____ Date	_____ Date
_____ Date	_____ Date
_____ Date	_____ Date

08/03

VMP-128 (0308)

LENDER SUPPORT SYSTEMS INC. V-128.GEN   (09/03)

Customer Identification

To help the government fight the funding of terrorism and money laundering activities, federal law requires all financial institutions to obtain, verify and record information that identifies each person who opens an account.

Please advise your customer: When they open an account with any financial institution, they will be asked for their name, address, date of birth, and other information that will allow the financial institution to identify them. The financial institution may also ask to see their driver's license or other identifying documents. Your customer's information will be protected by our Privacy Policy and federal law.

JOHN C. VANDER HORCK
Borrower's Name

2109053817
Loan Number

03/25/1943
Date of Birth

558-58-8901
Taxpayer Identification Number (SSN/TIN)*

5131 CARITA STREET
Residential Street Address [For customers who do not have a residential street address, an AFO/FPO (military) or Next of Kin/Contact Individual address is acceptable.]

LONG BEACH, CA 90808-
City, State, ZIP

*For persons without a SSN/TIN, the ID number must be from one of the following: passport, alien ID card, or any other government issued document evidencing nationality or residence and bearing a photograph or similar safeguard.

At least two forms of identification must be reviewed and documented. For applications taken in person, at least one "Primary" form of ID must be used. For all other applications, any combination of Primary and Secondary IDs may be used. Complete a separate form for each Borrower.

IMPORTANT - Information listed below must be exactly as indicated on the document.

Primary Forms of Identification-must display Borrower's name

Document	Country/State of Origin	ID Number	Date of Birth	Expiration Date
☐ State Issued Driver License				
☐ State Issued ID Card				
☐ Military ID Card				
☐ Passport				
☐ US Alien Registration Card				
☐ Canadian Driver License				

Secondary Forms of Identification-must display Borrower's name

Document	Name of Issuer on Form	ID Number	Issuance Date	Expiration Date
☐ Social Security Card	U.S. Govt.			
☐ Government Issued Visa				
☐ Birth Certificate				
☐ Non-US/Canadian Driver License				
☐ Most Recent Signed Tax Returns [1]	☐ Fed ☐ State	TIN:		
☐ Property Tax Bill		APN:		
☐ Voter Registration Card				
☐ Organizational Membership Card				
☐ Bank/Investment/Loan Statements [1]				
☐ Paycheck stub with name [1]				
☐ Most Recent W-2 [1]				
☐ Home/car/renter insurance papers				
☐ Recent utility bill				

[1] Do not verify identity with documents that illustrate income and/or assets, if the documentation type precludes collection of such documentation.

Comments: _____

I certify that I have personally viewed and accurately recorded the information from the documents identified above, and have reasonably confirmed the identity of the applicant.

Signed _____   Date _____

Printed Name _____

Customer Identification

To help the government fight the funding of terrorism and money laundering activities, federal law requires all financial institutions to obtain, verify and record information that identifies each person who opens an account.

Please advise your customer: When they open an account with any financial institution, they will be asked for their name, address, date of birth, and other information that will allow the financial institution to identify them. The financial institution may also ask to see their driver's license or other identifying documents. Your customer's information will be protected by our Privacy Policy and federal law.

JOANN VANDER HORCK
Borrower's Name

2109053817
Loan Number

03/11/1945
Date of Birth

556-68-3262
Taxpayer Identification Number (SSN/TIN)*

5131 CARITA STREET
Residential Street Address [For customers who do not have a residential street address, an AFO/FPO (military) or Next of Kin/Contact Individual address is acceptable.]

LONG BEACH, CA 90808-
City, State, ZIP

*For persons without a SSN/TIN, the ID number must be from one of the following: passport, alien ID card, or any other government issued document evidencing nationality or residence and bearing a photograph or similar safeguard.

At least two forms of identification must be reviewed and documented. For applications taken in person, at least one "Primary" form of ID must be used. For all other applications, any combination of Primary and Secondary IDs may be used. Complete a separate form for each Borrower.

IMPORTANT - Information listed below must be exactly as indicated on the document.

Primary Forms of Identification-must display Borrower's name

Document	Country/State of Origin	ID Number	Date of Birth	Expiration Date
☐ State Issued Driver License				
☐ State Issued ID Card				
☐ Military ID Card				
☐ Passport				
☐ US Alien Registration Card				
☐ Canadian Driver License				

Secondary Forms of Identification-must display Borrower's name

Document	Name of Issuer on Form	ID Number	Issuance Date	Expiration Date
☐ Social Security Card	U.S. Govt.			
☐ Government Issued Visa				
☐ Birth Certificate				
☐ Non-US/Canadian Driver License				
☐ Most Recent Signed Tax Returns [1]	☐ Fed ☐ State	TIN:		
☐ Property Tax Bill		APN:		
☐ Voter Registration Card				
☐ Organizational Membership Card				
☐ Bank/Investment/Loan Statements [1]				
☐ Paycheck stub with name [1]				
☐ Most Recent W-2 [1]				
☐ Home/car/renter insurance papers				
☐ Recent utility bill				

[1] Do not verify identity with documents that illustrate income and/or assets, if the documentation type precludes collection of such documentation.

Comments: _____

I certify that I have personally viewed and accurately recorded the information from the documents identified above, and have reasonably confirmed the identity of the applicant.

Signed _____   Date _____

Printed Name _____

LENDER: **PLAZA HOME MORTGAGE, INC.**

BORROWER(S): **JOHN C. VANDER HORCK AND JOANN VANDER HORCK**

PROPERTY ADDRESS: **39566 BARBARA LEE LANE, FAWNSKIN, CA 92333-**

LOAN NO.: **2109053817**

ERROR AND OMISSIONS / COMPLIANCE AGREEMENT

The undersigned borrower(s) for and in consideration of the above-referenced Lender funding the closing of this loan agrees, if requested by Lender or Closing Agent for Lender, to fully cooperate and adjust for clerical errors, any or all loan closing documentation if deemed necessary or desirable in the reasonable discretion of Lender to enable Lender to sell, convey, seek guaranty or market said loan to any entity, including but not limited to an investor, Federal National Mortgage Association, Federal Home Loan Mortgage Corporation, Government National Mortgage Association, Federal Housing Authority or the Department of Veterans Affairs, or any Municipal Bonding Authority.

The undersigned borrower(s) agree(s) to comply with all above noted requests by the above-referenced Lender within 30 days from date of mailing of said requests. Borrower(s) agree(s) to assume all costs including, by way of illustration and not limitation, actual expenses, legal fees and marketing losses for failing to comply with correction requests in the above noted time period.

The undersigned borrower(s) do hereby so agree and covenant in order to assure that this loan documentation executed this date will conform and be acceptable in the marketplace in the instance of transfer, sale or conveyance by Lender of its interest in and to said loan documentation, and to assure marketable title in the said borrower(s).

DATED effective this **10th** day of **AUGUST, 2009**

_____
JOHN C. VANDER HORCK

_____
JOANN VANDER HORCK

_____

_____

State of **CALIFORNIA**_____
County of _____
On _____before me, _____,
personally appeared
JOHN C. VANDER HORCK AND JOANN VANDER HORCK
_____
_____,
who proved to me on the basis of satisfactory evidence to be the person(s) whose name(s) is/are subscribed to the within instrument and acknowledged to me that he/she/they executed the same in his/her/their authorized capacity(ies), and that by his/her/their signature(s) on the instrument the person(s), or the entity upon behalf of which the person(s) acted, executed the instrument. I certify under PENALTY OF PERJURY under the laws of the State of California that the foregoing paragraph is true and correct.

WITNESS my hand and official seal.   Signature _____ (Seal)

11/07

VMP-14(CA) (0711)   LENDER SUPPORT SYSTEMS, INC. CA-14.CA (01/08)

Borrower's Certification & Authorization

Certification

LOAN NO.:   2109053817

The undersigned certify the following:

1. I/We have applied for a mortgage loan from
   PLAZA HOME MORTGAGE, INC.
   (lender). In applying for the loan, I/we completed a loan application containing various information on the purpose of the loan, the amount and source of the down payment, employment and income information, and assets and liabilities. I/We certify that all of the information is true and complete. I/We made no misrepresentations in the loan application or other documents, nor did I/we omit any pertinent information.

2. I/We understand and agree that
   PLAZA HOME MORTGAGE, INC.
   (lender) reserves the right to change the mortgage loan review process to a full documentation program. This may include verifying the information provided on the application with the employer and/or the financial institution.

3. I/We fully understand that it is a Federal crime punishable by fine or imprisonment, or both, to knowingly make any false statements when applying for this mortgage, as applicable under the provisions of Title 18, United States Code, Section 1014.

Authorization to Release Information

To Whom It May Concern:

1. I/We have applied for a mortgage loan from
   PLAZA HOME MORTGAGE, INC.
   (lender). As part of the application process,
   PLAZA HOME MORTGAGE, INC.
   (lender) may verify information contained in my/our loan application and in other documents required in connection with the loan, either before the loan is closed or as part of its quality control program.

2. I/We authorize you to provide to
   PLAZA HOME MORTGAGE, INC.
   (lender), and to any investor to whom
   PLAZA HOME MORTGAGE, INC.
   (lender) may sell my/our mortgage, any and all information and documentation that they request. Such information includes, but is not limited to, employment history and income; bank, money market, and similar account balances; credit history; and copies of income tax returns.

3. **PLAZA HOME MORTGAGE, INC.**
   (lender) or any investor that purchases the mortgage may address this authorization to any party named in the loan application or disclosed by any consumer credit reporting agency or similar source.

4. A copy of this authorization may be accepted as an original.

5. Your prompt reply to
   PLAZA HOME MORTGAGE, INC.
   (lender) or the investor that purchased the mortgage is appreciated.

NOTICE TO BORROWERS: This is notice to you as required by the Right to Financial Privacy Act of 1978 that HUD/FHA has a right of access to financial records held by financial institutions in connection with the consideration or administration of assistance to you. Financial records involving your transaction will be available to HUD/FHA without further notice or authorization but will not be disclosed or released by this institution to another Government Agency or Department without your consent except as required or permitted by law.

JOHN C. VANDER HORCK   (Date)

JOANN VANDER HORCK   (Date)

Limited Power of Attorney To Correct Documents

On   **AUGUST 10, 2009**   the undersigned borrower(s), for and in consideration of the approval, closing and funding of the undersigned loan (#   **2109053817**   ) in the amount of $ **110,000.00**   , hereby grant(s) any authorized representative of Plaza Home Mortgage, Inc., its successors and/or assigns, as lender, limited power of attorney to correct and/or execute or initial all typographical or clerical errors discovered in any or all of the loan documentation required to be executed by the undersigned at settlement. In the event this Limited Power of Attorney is exercised, the undersigned will be notified and will receive a copy of the document initialed on their behalf.

THIS LIMITED POWER OF ATTORNEY MAY NOT BE USED TO INCREASE THE INTEREST RATE THE UNDERSIGNED IS PAYING, EXTEND THE TERM OF THE UNDERSIGNED'S LOAN, INCREASE THE UNDERSIGNED'S OUTSTANDING PRINCIPAL BALANCE OR INCREASE THE UNDERSIGNED'S MONTHLY PRINCIPAL AND INTEREST PAYMENT.

Any of these specified changes must be executed directly by the undersigned.

This Limited Power of Attorney shall automatically terminate 180 days from the closing date of the undersigned's mortgage loan.

IN WITNESS WHEREOF, this Limited Power of Attorney has been executed by the undersigned as of the date and year first above referenced.

JOHN C. VANDER HORCK	Borrower	**JOANN VANDER HORCK**	Borrower
	Borrower		Borrower

State of   )
County of   )ss

        On this   day of   , personally came
JOHN C. VANDER HORCK AND JOANN VANDER HORCK

And I have made known to them the contents of this agreement and having personally satisfied myself on the basis of sufficient evidence that he/she/they are the persons signing above executed the same as his/her/their voluntary act and deed.

WITNESS my hand and official seal

_____
Notary Public

My commission expires: _____

                                                                        (seal)

Limited Power of Attorney To Correct Documents   LENDER SUPPORT SYSTEMS, INC. IMM-03.IMM (02/07)

PLAZA HOME MORTGAGE, INC.
3633 INLAND EMPIRE BLVD #250
ONTARIO, CA   91764

LOAN NO.:   2109053817

THE FEDERAL EQUAL CREDIT OPPORTUNITY ACT

ECOA NOTICE

THE FEDERAL EQUAL CREDIT OPPORTUNITY ACT PROHIBITS CREDITORS FROM DISCRIMINATING AGAINST CREDIT APPLICANTS ON THE BASIS OF RACE, COLOR, RELIGION, NATIONAL ORIGIN, SEX, MARITAL STATUS, AGE (PROVIDED THAT THE APPLICANT HAS THE CAPACITY TO ENTER INTO A BINDING CONTRACT); BECAUSE ALL OR PART OF THE APPLICANT'S INCOME DERIVES FROM ANY PUBLIC ASSISTANCE PROGRAM; OR BECAUSE THE APPLICANT HAS IN GOOD FAITH EXERCISED ANY RIGHT UNDER THE CONSUMER CREDIT PROTECTION ACT. THE FEDERAL AGENCY THAT ADMINISTERS COMPLIANCE WITH THIS LAW CONCERNING THIS CREDITOR IS:

**MORTGAGE COMPANIES
FEDERAL TRADE COMMISSION
EQUAL CREDIT OPPORTUNITY
ROOM 4037
WASHINGTON, D.C. 20580**

**MORTGAGE COMPANIES
FEDERAL TRADE COMMISSION
EQUAL CREDIT OPPORTUNITY
ROOM 4037
WASHINGTON, D.C.   20580**

ACKNOWLEDGMENT OF RECEIPT
I/We have received a copy of this notice.

JOHN C. VANDER HORCK	(Date)	JOANN VANDER HORCK	(Date)
	(Date)		(Date)

FLOOD INSURANCE

Lender: **PLAZA HOME MORTGAGE, INC.**
　　　　3633 INLAND EMPIRE BLVD #250
　　　　ONTARIO, CA　91764

Account Number	Loan Number	Disbursement Date	Due Date	Principal Amount	Call Code	Officer No. & Int.	Map No.
	2109053817		10/01/2009	110,000.00			

(TO BE USED WITH ALL LOANS SECURED BY IMPROVED REAL PROPERTY OR BY A MOBILE HOME LOCATED ON REAL PROPERTY)

Dear Customer:

The Lender is currently considering a loan that will be secured either by improved real property or by a mobile home located on real property. Pursuant to federal regulations, we must evaluate whether the property is in an area that is particularly subject to flood risk. We have done so, and we are providing you with notice as follows: Only one of the following three sections applies. The section that applies to your property is:

[xx] Section 1　　　　[ ] Section 2　　　　[ ] Section 3

Section 1.　(Not in flood hazard area)

The property that will secure the loan is not located in an area that has been identified by the Director of the Federal Emergency Management Agency as a area having special flood hazards. Therefore, no special flood hazard insurance is necessary.

Section 2.　(Participating Community)

The property is or will be located in an area designated by the Director of the Federal Emergency Management Agency as a special flood hazard area. This area is delineated on

Flood Insurance Rate Map or, if the Flood Insurance Rate Map is unavailable, on the Flood Hazard Boundary Map. This area has at least a one percent change of being flooded within any given year. The risk of exceeding the one percent change increases with time periods longer than one year. For example, during the life of a 30-year mortgage, a structure located in a special flood hazard area has a 26 percent change of being flooded.

The improved real estate or mobile home securing your loan is or will be located in a community that is now participating in the National Flood Insurance Program. If the property is damaged by flooding in a federally declared disaster, Federal disaster relief assistance may be available. However, such assistance will be unavailable if your community has been identified as a flood-prone area for one year or longer and is not participating in the National Flood Insurance Program when the assistance is approved. This assistance, usually in the form of a loan with a favorable interest rate, may be available for damaged incurred in excess of your flood insurance.

Section 3.　(Non-Participating Community)

(i) The property is or will be located in an area designated by the Director of the Federal Emergency Management Agency as a special flood hazard area. This area is delineated on

Flood Insurance Rate Map, or if the Flood Insurance Rate Map is unavailable, on the Flood Hazard Boundary Map. This area has at least a one percent change of being flooded within any given year. The risk of exceeding the one percent change increases with time periods longer than one year. For example, during the life of a 30-year mortgage, a structure located in a special flood hazard area has a 26 percent chance of being flooded.

(ii) The improved real estate securing your loan is or will be located in a community which is not participating in the National Flood Insurance Program. This means you are not eligible for Federal Flood Insurance. If the property is damaged by flooding in a federally declared disaster, Federal disaster relief assistance for the property will be unavailable if your community has been identified as a flood-prone area for one year or longer. Such assistance may be available only if, at the time the assistance would be approved, your community is participating in the National Flood Insurance Program or has been identified as a flood-prone area for less than one year.

By signing below, you are acknowledging that you received this form at least 10 days before the closing of the transaction, or at least as of the date of Lenders commitment, if any, if the period between Lender's commitment and closing was less than 10 days.

In addition, by signing below you are agreeing to obtain Federal Flood Insurance to the extent such insurance is required and is available for the term of the loan and the full unpaid principal balance of the loan.

ACKNOWLEDGED AND AGREED:

JOHN C. VANDER HORCK　　　　Date　　　　JOANN VANDER HORCK　　　　Date

　　　　Date　　　　Date

　　　　Date　　　　Date

　　　　Date　　　　Date

PREPARED BY:

(Lender/Officer)

LENDER SUPPORT SYSTEMS, INC. HFS-05.HFS (12/00)

PLAZA HOME MORTGAGE, INC.
3633 INLAND EMPIRE BLVD #250, ONTARIO, CA   91764

OCCUPANCY STATEMENT

LOAN NUMBER: 2109053817

DATE: AUGUST 10, 2009

BORROWERS: JOHN C. VANDER HORCK AND JOANN VANDER HORCK

PROPERTY ADDRESS: 39566 BARBARA LEE LANE, FAWNSKIN, CA   92333-

Borrower hereby declares, under penalty of perjury, as follows:

☐   **Owner Occupied**
I/We will occupy the subject property as my/our principal residence as required by, and in compliance with, the terms of the Deed of Trust/Mortgage relating to the subject property;

☒   **Occupied as a Second Home**
I/We will occupy the subject property as my/our second residence as required by, and in compliance with, the terms of the Deed of Trust/Mortgage relating to the subject property;

☐   **Investment Property - Will Not Occupy**
I/We will not occupy the subject property.

I/We are aware of and understand that if at any time it is determined that the foregoing statement is untrue, I/We will be subject to prosecution for fraud under applicable state laws.

I certify under penalty of Chapter 18, U.S.C. 1010 to 1014 that the statement contained herein is true and correct.

JOHN C. VANDER HORCK	Date	**JOANN VANDER HORCK**	Date
	Date		Date
	Date		Date
	Date		Date

PLAZA HOME MORTGAGE, INC.
Borrower Contact Information

DATE: **AUGUST 10, 2009**   LOAN NUMBER: **2109053817**

BORROWER(S): **JOHN C. VANDER HORCK AND JOANN VANDER HORCK**

PROPERTY ADDRESS: **39566 BARBARA LEE LANE, FAWNSKIN, CA 92333-**

Plaza Home Mortgage, Inc. requires the following contact information from each borrower prior to closing. The contact information should be current for after closing (i.e., moving to new home with new phone number)

Borrower 1
Mailing Address: _____
City/State/ZIP: _____
Night/Home Number: _____
Day/Work Number: _____
Mobile Phone/Pager Number: _____
E-mail Address: _____

Borrower 2
Mailing Address: _____
City/State/ZIP: _____
Night/Home Number: _____
Day/Work Number: _____
Mobile Phone/Pager Number: _____
E-mail Address: _____

Borrower 3
Mailing Address: _____
City/State/ZIP: _____
Night/Home Number: _____
Day/Work Number: _____
Mobile Phone/Pager Number: _____
E-mail Address: _____

Borrower 4
Mailing Address: _____
City/State/ZIP: _____
Night/Home Number: _____
Day/Work Number: _____
Mobile Phone/Pager Number: _____
E-mail Address: _____

I CERTIFY THAT THE   ABOVE INFORMATION IS TRUE, ACCURATE AND COMPLETE. I UNDERSTAND THAT THE INFORMATION WILL BE RE-VERIFIED PRIOR TO CLOSING MY TRANSACTION.

_____   _____
JOHN C. VANDER HORCK   (Date)   JOANN VANDER HORCK   (Date)

_____   _____
(Date)   (Date)

Borrower Contact Information   Page 1 of 1   PLAZA HOME MORTGAGE, INC.
                                                                               LENDER SUPPORT SYSTEMS INC. PHM-11.PHM (05/07)

Initial Escrow Account Disclosure Statement

Date: **AUGUST 10, 2009**   Loan Number: **2109053817**   Case Number:

Servicer's Name and Address:

PLAZA HOME MORTGAGE, INC.

3633 INLAND EMPIRE BLVD #250, ONTARIO, CA 91764

Toll Free Number: **858-346-1208**

Borrowers: Property Address:

JOHN C. VANDER HORCK AND JOANN VANDER HORCK   **39566 BARBARA LEE LANE, FAWNSKIN, CA 92333-**

Mailing Address:

5131 CARITA STREET, LONG BEACH, CA 90808-

This is an estimate of activity in your escrow account during the coming year based on payments anticipated to be made from your account.

Month (or Period)	Payments to Escrow Account	Payments from Escrow Account	Description	Escrow Account Balance
Initial Deposit:				$ 974.69
OCTOBER	162.45	0.00		1,137.14
NOVEMBER	162.45	734.70	COUNTY PROPERTY TAX	564.89
DECEMBER	162.45	0.00		727.34
JANUARY	162.45	0.00		889.79
FEBRUARY	162.45	0.00		1,052.24
MARCH	162.45	480.00	HAZARD INSURANCE	734.69
APRIL	162.45	0.00		897.14
MAY	162.45	734.69	COUNTY PROPERTY TAX	324.90
JUNE	162.45	0.00		487.35
JULY	162.45	0.00		649.80
AUGUST	162.45	0.00		812.25
SEPTEMBER	162.45	0.00		974.70

(PLEASE KEEP THIS STATEMENT FOR COMPARISON WITH THE ACTUAL ACTIVITY IN YOUR ACCOUNT AT THE END OF THE ESCROW ACCOUNTING COMPUTATION YEAR.)

Cushion selected by servicer: $ __324.90__

[XX] Your **MONTHLY** mortgage payment for the coming year will be $ 744.58   of which $ 162.45   will go into your escrow account and $ 582.13   will be for principal and interest.

[ ] Your first _____ mortgage payment for the coming year will be $ _____ of which $ _____ will go into your escrow account and $ _____ will be for principal and interest.   The terms of your loan may result in changes to the monthly principal and interest payments during the year.

2/95

VMP-503R (9502).01   LENDER SUPPORT SYSTEMS INC. GEN-040.GEN (08/04)

LENDER: **PLAZA HOME MORTGAGE, INC.**

LOAN NO.: **2109053817**

**3633 INLAND EMPIRE BLVD #250
ONTARIO, CA 91764**

DATE: **AUGUST 10, 2009**

NOTICE TO BORROWER - IMPOUND / ESCROW ACCOUNT

WHAT ARE "IMPOUNDS"?
Funds for the payment of Taxes and Insurance,
collected monthly in with the monthly loan payment.

As the Lender receives borrower's monthly loan payments, Lender deposits these funds into borrower's trust account (commonly known as an "Impound" or "Escrow" Account); the funds are then said to be "impounded". The Lender then pays borrower's property taxes and the annual insurance premium from these funds when such become due and payable.

The monthly impound amount is collected at a rate of 1/12th the estimated annual tax and insurance cost, considering the prior year's actual tax bill and current insurance cost.

The amounts required to pay taxes and insurance may vary from year to year. To assure that sufficient funds are available to pay these costs when due, the Lender may find it necessary to adjust your monthly payment from year to year. You will be notified when such adjustments are necessary.

IMPORTANT -   Please Read Carefully !

You are hereby advised that State law, as it relates to single-family, owner-occupied dwellings only, may prohibit the lender from requiring an impound or escrow account for the payment of taxes, insurance premiums, or other purposes as a condition of the loan except in certain instances.   These instances include:

(1)   Where required by a State or Federal regulatory authority; or

(2)   Where a loan is made, guaranteed, or insured by a State or Federal governmental lending or insuring agency; or

(3)   Upon a failure of the borrower to pay two consecutive tax installments on the property prior to the delinquency date for such payments; or

(4)   Where the original principal amount of such a loan is   90%   or more of the sale price, if the property involved is sold, or is   90%   or more of the appraised value of the property securing the loan; or

(5)   Where the combined principal balances of all loans (first, second, etc.) exceed   80%   of the appraised value of the property securing the loan.

The Deed of Trust or Mortgage provides for the establishment of an impound/escrow account if Lender so requests. However, notwithstanding said provisions, Lender will not require an impound/escrow account as a condition of Lender making a loan where such requirement is prohibited by law.

The law does provide for the establishment of an impound/escrow account for any loan if both parties agree. If you desire voluntarily to establish such an account, you may so indicate in the space provided below.

Whether the establishment of an impound/escrow account is required by Lender or is voluntarily requested by you, all funds received by Lender for such an account will only be accepted on the understanding that as and when required or provided for by law, the Lender will:

(1)   Pay interest on any impound/escrow account funds at the rate required by applicable State law (for example,

(2)   Report said interest earned to the Franchise Tax Board and Internal Revenue Service.

(3)   Have the right to commingle the impound/escrow account funds with other monies.

PLEASE COMPLETE THE FOLLOWING:

[   ]   I/We desire voluntarily to establish an impound/escrow account.

[   ]   I/We desire not to establish an impound/escrow account.

[   ]   An impound/escrow account is required on this loan.

In the event an impound/escrow account is established, whether at the request of the undersigned or otherwise, it is agreed that I/we assume the tax liability, if any, for the earned interest on such account. This agreement shall apply to all loans and is not limited to loans on single-family, owner-occupied dwellings.

EXECUTED this _____ day of _____ .

_____   _____

_____   _____

JOHN C. VANDER HORCK   Date   **JOANN VANDER HORCK**   Date

Date   Date

Borrower Acknowledgement of Appraisal Delivery

Date: **AUGUST 10, 2009**

Applicant: **JOHN C. VANDER HORCK AND JOANN VANDER HORCK**

Case No:

Loan No: **2109053817**

Property: **39566 BARBARA LEE LANE**
            FAWNSKIN, CA 92333-

As earlier disclosed in the Appraisal Report Delivery Disclosure, I understand that I am entitled to receive a copy of any appraisal concerning the subject property at least three business days prior to signing my loan documents (also called the loan closing) and that I may waive this three-day requirement.

By signing below, I either (i) acknowledge receipt of any appraisal concerning the subject property at least three (3) business days prior to closing, or (ii) acknowledge that I have waived the three (3) business days' advance receipt of any appraisal concerning the subject property and have agreed to receive a copy of any appraisal no later than at the time of the loan closing.

If there are multiple borrowers on this loan application, only one borrower is required to sign below.

_____	Date	_____	Date
JOHN C. VANDER HORCK		JOANN VANDER HORCK	
_____	Date	_____	Date

LENDER SUPPORT SYSTEMS, INC. BOA-09.XDP (07/09)

LOAN NO.: 2109053817

YOUR RIGHT TO PRIVACY
IMPORTANT INFORMATION TO KNOW

SECURITY: We restrict access to the information we have about you to those employees who need to know that information to provide products or services to you. We maintain physical, electronic, and procedural safeguards to guard your nonpublic personal information. (We are required to do so by federal regulations.)

CHANGE: We can change this policy, but we will tell you in advance if we do, and we will explain any further rights you might have at that time.

WHO *WE* ARE: In this disclosure, *we* means
PLAZA HOME MORTGAGE, INC.
3633 INLAND EMPIRE BLVD #250
ONTARIO, CA 91764

OUR PRIVACY POLICY

WHAT THIS IS: This is a disclosure required by federal law which is intended to tell you (among other things):
- Where we get information about you (our sources);
- What we do to protect the information we have about you; and
- What our policy is about sharing information about you with others.

WHO *YOU* ARE: This policy applies to *you* if you are a customer of ours.

A "customer" is a natural person (not a corporation) who-for personal, family, or household purposes-has or recently had a financial product with us, such as a mortgage loan.

DEFINITIONS: Here are other terms we will use in this disclosure:

Information means nonpublic personal information, a technical term that generally means

1. information that can identify you;
2. that is not available publicly; and
3. that we collect in connection with providing a financial product or service to you.

We will use the word *information* to mean nonpublic personal information.

Affiliates are companies that are related to one another by ownership, common ownership, or control. For example, if one company owns or controls another company, they are affiliates of each other.

Nonaffiliate means a company that is not an affiliate of another company, and it also means a person who is not an employee of a company.

Opt out means a choice a person can make (in certain cases) to prevent a financial institution from sharing information about that person with others. **(You do not have a right to opt out because we do not share information about you for marketing purposes).**

JOINT ACCOUNTS: If you have a joint account with us (for example, you are, or you have, a co-borrower on a loan), you should share this notice with the person who shares your account. He or she may not get a separate notice.

SOURCES FOR INFORMATION: We collect information about you from the following sources:
- Information you might provide us on applications and other forms;
- Information about transactions we might conduct for you;
- Information about your transactions with nonaffiliated third parties; and
- Information from consumer reporting agencies.

OUR PRIVACY POLICY

WE DO NOT SHARE NONPUBLIC INFORMATION ABOUT YOU WITH ANYONE EXCEPT AS REQUIRED OR PERMITTED BY LAW.

FORMER CUSTOMERS: We have the same policy against disclosing information about former customers as we do about current customers.

JOHN C. VANDER HORCK	(Date)	JOANN VANDER HORCK	(Date)
	(Date)		(Date)

LENDER SUPPORT SYSTEMS INC. GEN-68.GEN (10/02)

LOAN NO.: 2109053817

DISCLOSURE OF CREDIT SCORE INFORMATION

Borrower Name: JOHN C. VANDER HORCK	Lender: PLAZA HOME MORTGAGE, INC.
Property Address: 39566 BARBARA LEE LANE FAWNSKIN, CA 92333-	3633 INLAND EMPIRE BLVD #250 ONTARIO, CA 91764
	Date: AUGUST 10, 2009

We are providing the following credit score information in connection with your loan application.

Credit Score Provider	EQUIFAX INFORMATION SERVICES, LLC	MORTGAGE RATING	EXPERIAN
Current/Most Recent Credit Score	812	812	817
Range of Possible Credit Scores	–	–	375 – -900
Date of Credit Score	MAY 22, 2009	MAY 22, 2009	MAY 22, 2009
Key Factors Adversely Affecting Score			

V-139 (0501)   1/05

LENDER SUPPORT SYSTEMS INC. PHM-30.XDP (08/09)   Page 1 of 2

CREDIT BUREAU RISK SCORE REASONS	EQUIFAX	TRANS UNION	EXPERIAN
Amount owed on accounts is too high	1	1	1
Level of delinquency on accounts	2	2	2
Too few bank revolving accounts	3	N/A	3
Too many bank or national revolving accounts	4	N/A	4
Too many accounts with balances	5	5	5
Too many consumer finance company accounts	6	6	6
Account payment history is too new to rate	7	7	7
Too many recent inquiries last 12 months	8	8	8
Too many accounts recently opened	9	9	9
Proportion of balances to credit limits is too high on bank revolving or other revolving accounts	10	10	10
Amount owed on revolving accounts is too high	11	11	11
Length of time revolving accounts have been established	12	12	12
Time since delinquency is too recent or unknown	13	13	13
Length of time accounts have been established	14	14	14
Lack of recent bank revolving information	15	15	15
Lack of recent revolving account information	16	16	16
No recent non-mortgage balance information	17	17	17
Number of accounts with delinquency	18	18	18
Date of last inquiry too recent	N/A	19	N/A
Too few accounts currently paid as agreed	19	27	19
Length of time since derogatory public record or collection is too short	20	20	20
Amount past due on accounts	21	21	21
Serious delinquency, derogatory public record or collection filed	22	22	22
Number of bank or national revolving accounts with balances	23	N/A	23
No recent revolving balances	24	24	24
Number of revolving accounts	26	N/A	26
Number of established accounts	28	28	28
No recent bankcard balances	N/A	29	29
Time since most recent account opening too short	30	30	30
Too few accounts with recent payment information	31	N/A	31
Lack of recent installment loan information	32	4	32
Proportion of loan balances to loan amounts is too high	33	3	33
Amount owed on delinquent accounts	34	31	34
Serious delinquency and public record or collection filed	38	38	38
Serious delinquency	39	39	39
Derogatory public record or collection filed	40	40	40

Page 2 of 2

LOAN NO.:   2109053817

DISCLOSURE OF CREDIT SCORE INFORMATION

Borrower Name: JOANN VANDER HORCK	Lender: PLAZA HOME MORTGAGE, INC.
Property Address: 39566 BARBARA LEE LANE FAWNSKIN, CA 92333-	3633 INLAND EMPIRE BLVD #250 ONTARIO, CA 91764
	Date: AUGUST 10, 2009

We are providing the following credit score information in connection with your loan application.

Credit Score Provider	EQUIFAX INFORMATION SERVICES, LLC	MORTGAGE RATING	EXPERIAN
Current/Most Recent Credit Score	724	805	818
Range of Possible Credit Scores	–	–	375 — -900
Date of Credit Score	MAY 22, 2009	MAY 22, 2009	MAY 22, 2009
Key Factors Adversely Affecting Score			

V-139 (0501)

LENDER SUPPORT SYSTEMS INC. PHM-30.XDP (08/09)   Page 1 of 2

1/05

CREDIT BUREAU RISK SCORE REASONS	EQUIFAX	TRANS UNION	EXPERIAN
Amount owed on accounts is too high	1	1	1
Level of delinquency on accounts	2	2	2
Too few bank revolving accounts	3	N/A	3
Too many bank or national revolving accounts	4	N/A	4
Too many accounts with balances	5	5	5
Too many consumer finance company accounts	6	6	6
Account payment history is too new to rate	7	7	7
Too many recent inquiries last 12 months	8	8	8
Too many accounts recently opened	9	9	9
Proportion of balances to credit limits is too high on bank revolving or other revolving accounts	10	10	10
Amount owed on revolving accounts is too high	11	11	11
Length of time revolving accounts have been established	12	12	12
Time since delinquency is too recent or unknown	13	13	13
Length of time accounts have been established	14	14	14
Lack of recent bank revolving information	15	15	15
Lack of recent revolving account information	16	16	16
No recent non-mortgage balance information	17	17	17
Number of accounts with delinquency	18	18	18
Date of last inquiry too recent	N/A	19	N/A
Too few accounts currently paid as agreed	19	27	19
Length of time since derogatory public record or collection is too short	20	20	20
Amount past due on accounts	21	21	21
Serious delinquency, derogatory public record or collection filed	22	22	22
Number of bank or national revolving accounts with balances	23	N/A	23
No recent revolving balances	24	24	24
Number of revolving accounts	26	N/A	26
Number of established accounts	28	28	28
No recent bankcard balances	N/A	29	29
Time since most recent account opening too short	30	30	30
Too few accounts with recent payment information	31	N/A	31
Lack of recent installment loan information	32	4	32
Proportion of loan balances to loan amounts is too high	33	3	33
Amount owed on delinquent accounts	34	31	34
Serious delinquency and public record or collection filed	38	38	38
Serious delinquency	39	39	39
Derogatory public record or collection filed	40	40	40

NOTICE REGARDING FURNISHING OF NEGATIVE INFORMATION

Borrower(s):

JOHN C. VANDER HORCK AND JOANN VANDER HORCK

Lender:

PLAZA HOME MORTGAGE, INC.

**3633 INLAND EMPIRE BLVD #250
ONTARIO, CA 91764**

Property Address:

**39566 BARBARA LEE LANE
FAWNSKIN, CA 92333-**

Date: **AUGUST 10, 2009**

Loan Number: **2109053817**

We may report information about your account to credit bureaus.

Late payments, missed payments, or other defaults on your account may be reflected in your credit report.

JOHN C. VANDER HORCK	Date	JOANN VANDER HORCK	Date
	Date		Date
	Date		Date
	Date		Date

FACT Act/Regulation V - Model B-1

V-136 (0406)
LENDER SUPPORT SYSTEMS, INC. V-136.GEN (10/04)

6/04

CALIFORNIA
Insurance Disclosure

Loan Number   **2109053817**

Borrower
JOHN C. VANDER HORCK AND JOANN VANDER HORCK

Property Address

39566 BARBARA LEE LANE, FAWNSKIN, CA   92333-

California Civil Code Section 2955.5(a) states:

"No lender shall require a borrower, as a condition of receiving or maintaining a loan secured by real property, to provide hazard insurance coverage against risks to the improvements on that real property in an amount exceeding the replacement value of the improvements on the property."

Your acknowledgment below signifies that this written notice was provided to you pursuant to the state statute.

JOHN C. VANDER HORCK	Date	**JOANN VANDER HORCK**	Date
	Date		Date
	Date		Date
	Date		Date

1/00

VMP-1039(CA) (0001).01   LENDER SUPPORT SYSTEMS INC. CA-1039.CA (03/05)

INTERIM INTEREST PAYMENT DISCLOSURE

Borrower Name(s): JOHN C. VANDER HORCK AND JOANN VANDER HORCK	Licensee: **PLAZA HOME MORTGAGE, INC.** **3633 INLAND EMPIRE BLVD #250** **ONTARIO, CA 91764**
	Date: AUGUST 10, 2009
	Loan Number: 2109053817

☐ I request that the loan proceeds be disbursed on a Monday (or on a day immediately following a bank holiday, if applicable). I understand that interest will commence accruing on the business day immediately preceding the closing date.
The amount of additional per diem interest I will be charged is: $ 14.69
I also understand that I may avoid the additional per diem interest charge by disbursing the loan proceeds on a day immediately following a business day.

☐ An escrow closing is involved for this loan and I will not pay interest on the loan more than one day prior to the date that the loan proceeds are disbursed from escrow.

☐ An escrow closing is not involved for this loan and I have made a request for recording in connection with the disbursement. I will not pay interest on the loan more than one day prior to the date the loan proceeds are disbursed to me, or to a third party on my behalf, or to the lender to satisfy an existing obligation.

☐ An escrow closing is not involved for this loan and I have not made a request for recording in connection with the disbursement, and I will not pay interest on the loan prior to the date funds are disbursed to me, or to a third party on my behalf, or to the lender to satisfy an existing obligation.

By signing below, borrower(s) acknowledges the additional interest charge, if any, as described above.

JOHN C. VANDER HORCK	Date	JOANN VANDER HORCK	Date
	Date		Date
	Date		Date
	Date		Date

LICENSEE'S CERTIFICATE OF COMPLIANCE

PLAZA HOME MORTGAGE, INC.
have reviewed loan number   2109053817   made by
JOHN C. VANDER HORCK AND JOANN VANDER HORCK

and I have reviewed information in the loan records, including the date of disbursement of the loan proceeds; and I am authorized by the licensee to sign this form on its behalf; and, I make the following statement:

The borrower(s) of this loan was charged per diem interest, if any, in accordance with Civil Code Section 2948.5 as described above. I, the undersigned, state that I am the person named in this Certificate of Compliance; that I have read and signed this Certificate of Compliance and know the contents of it, including any exhibits attached to this certificate; and that based on my review of the information contained in the loan records, the statements made in this document, including any exhibits attached to it, are true and correct to the best of my knowledge.

I certify under penalty of perjury that the foregoing is true and correct.

Licensee:

_____
                                    Date

MUST RETURN WITH FINAL HUD-1 PER D.O.C.

Escrow Agent Certification Of Disbursement Of Funds - Attachment to Final HUD-1

To: **PERFORMANCE PLUS MORTGAGE**

Phone: **(714) 502-4632**   Fax: **(714) 491-8636**

Attention: **SYLVIA CISNEROS**

Section 2948.5 of the CA Civil Code, as amended and effective January 1, 2004, states a borrower shall not be required to pay interest on a principal obligation under a promissory note secured by a mortgage or deed of trust on real property improved with between one to four residential dwelling units for any period that is in excess of one day prior to the date the loan proceeds are disbursed from escrow.

Loan No: **2109053817**   Borrower(s): **JOHN C. VANDER HORCK AND JOANN VANDER HORCK**

Plaza Home Mortgage Funder: **CUSTOMER SERVICE**

Plaza Home Mortgage Funder Fax No.: **858-677-6741**

Plaza Home Mortgage Funder Phone No.: **858-346-1208**

Property Address: **39566 BARBARA LEE LANE, FAWNSKIN, CA 92333-**

Escrow/File No.: **72101**

I certify that subject to the receipt of Lender's funds on _____ , the loan proceeds will be
                                                                                             (Escrow Agent to Enter Date)

disbursed on _____ .
                    (Escrow Agent to Enter Date)*

In the event disbursement of loan proceeds from escrow does not occur on the date entered above, I will contact the Plaza Home Mortgage Funder shown above with the corrected disbursement date and obtain per diem interest adjustment figures.

Date:_____

_____
Signature

_____
Printed Name

---

*RE-CERTIFICATION OF DISBURSEMENT OF FUNDS

To be completed by Escrow Agent when **disbursement** of funds from escrow does not occur on the date first entered above.

Loan proceeds **disbursed** from escrow on _____

Signature   Date

_____
Printed Name

INSTRUCTIONS TO ESCROW AGENT: Insert date of anticipated date of receipt of lender's funds, disbursement date, sign, date, and print name. Fax to Plaza Home Mortgage Funder shown above.

Reviewed by: _____   **Date:** _____

MFCD6182 (09/2006) / 047-162126-8
CERTIFICATION OF DISBURSEMENT   LENDER SUPPORT SYSTEMS, INC. PHM-16.PHM (05/09)

BORROWER'S ACKNOWLEDGMENT OF DISCLOSURES

Borrower Name(s):	Lender:
JOHN C. VANDER HORCK AND JOANN VANDER HORCK	PLAZA HOME MORTGAGE, INC.

	Date:
	AUGUST 10, 2009

Property Address:

39566 BARBARA LEE LANE, FAWNSKIN, CA 92333-

By signing below, I acknowledge that I have received a "Good Faith Estimate" and all applicable disclosures required by the Truth in Lending Act.

_____	(Date)	_____	(Date)
JOHN C. VANDER HORCK		JOANN VANDER HORCK	

_____	(Date)	_____	(Date)

_____	(Date)	_____	(Date)

_____	(Date)	_____	(Date)

10/01

VMP-1069(CA) (0110).01

LENDER SUPPORT SYSTEMS INC. CA-1069.XDP (05/08)

LOAN NO.:   2109053817

CALIFORNIA CREDIT SCORE NOTICE

Borrower Name(s): JOHN C. VANDER HORCK AND JOANN VANDER HORCK	Lender: PLAZA HOME MORTGAGE, INC. 3633 INLAND EMPIRE BLVD #250 ONTARIO, CA 91764
	Date: AUGUST 10, 2009

NOTICE TO THE HOME LOAN APPLICANT

In connection with your application for a home loan, the lender must disclose to you the score that a credit bureau distributed to users and the lender used in connection with your home loan, and the key factors affecting your credit scores.

The credit score is a computer generated summary calculated at the time of the request and based on information a credit bureau or lender has on file. The scores are based on data about your credit history and payment patterns. Credit scores are important because they are used to assist the lender in determining whether you will obtain a loan. They may also be used to determine what interest rate you may be offered on the mortgage. Credit scores can change over time, depending on your conduct, how your credit history and payment patterns change, and how credit scoring technologies change.

Because the score is based on information in your credit history, it is very important that you review the credit-related information that is being furnished to make sure it is accurate. Credit records may vary from one company to another.

If you have questions about your credit score or the credit information that is furnished to you, contact the credit bureau at the address and telephone number provided with this notice, or contact the lender, if the lender developed or generated the credit score. The credit bureau plays no part in the decision to take any action on the loan application and is unable to provide you with specific reasons for the decision on a loan application.

If you have questions concerning the terms of the loan, contact the lender.

One or more of the following credit bureaus will provide the credit score:

Experian	**Equifax Credit Information Services**	**Trans Union**
701 Experian Parkway	P.O. Box 740241	P.O. Box 2000
P.O. Box 2002	Atlanta, GA 30374	Chester, PA 19022
Allen, TX 75013	1-800-685-1111	1-800-916-8800
1-888-397-3742	www.equifax.com	www.transunion.com
www.experian.com/		
reportacess		

Your acknowledgment below signifies that this written notice was provided to you.

JOHN C. VANDER HORCK	Date	JOANN VANDER HORCK	Date
	Date		Date
	Date		Date
	Date		Date

8/06

LOAN NO.: 2109053817

CREDIT SCORE DISCLOSURE

Borrower Name(s):	Lender:
JOHN C. VANDER HORCK AND JOANN VANDER HORCK	PLAZA HOME MORTGAGE, INC.
	3633 INLAND EMPIRE BLVD #250
	ONTARIO, CA 91764

Date:

AUGUST 10, 2009

Property Address: 39566 BARBARA LEE LANE, FAWNSKIN, CA 92333-

Your current Credit Score(s) or most recent Credit Score(s) and the key factors that adversely affect your Credit Score(s) in the model used is/are attached.

The range of possible Credit Scores under the model used is from a low of 250 to a high of 950.

Your Credit Score was created on the same date noted at the top of your Credit Score report.

The information and credit scoring model may be different than the Credit Score that may be used by the lender.

6/01

VMP-139(CA) (0106).01

LENDER SUPPORT SYSTEMS INC. CA-139.XDP (05/03)

Appendix H
Employment Forms

APPENDIX H-1

EMPLOYMENT APPLICATION

APPENDIX H-2

INDEPENDENT CONTRACTOR AGREEMENT

APPENDIX H-3

POLICY AND PROCEDURES MANUAL

Appendix H-1
Employment Application

LOAN AGENT APPLICATION

Today's Date: _____

Name: _____

Address: _____ Apartment #: _____

City: _____ State: _____ Zip: _____

Phone: (   )_____

Cell Phone: (   )_____

E-mail Address: _____

Social Security No: _____ Date Available: _____

Date of Birth: _____ / _____

Position Applying for:

Loan Agent _____ Processor _____ Jr. Processor _____

Funder _____ Document Drawer _____ Receptionist _____

Are you a citizen of the United States? Yes _____ No _____

If no, are you authorized to work in the United States? Yes _____ No _____

Have you ever worked for this company before? Yes _____ No _____ If yes, when?

_____

Have you ever been convicted of a felony? Yes _____ No _____

If yes, explain:

_____

_____

Do you currently hold a valid real estate license? Yes _____ No _____

If yes, what is your license number and expiration date of license: _____

Describe your duties in your current position.

_____

_____

_____

Why are you leaving your current position?

_____

_____

_____

May we contact your current employer? Yes _____ No _____

If yes, what is their name and contact information? _____

EMPLOYMENT HISTORY

Company Name: _____ Phone: (   )_____

Address: _____ Supervisor: _____

City: _____ State: _____ Job Title: _____

Salary: _____ OR Commission _____ per month.

Describe your duties: _____

_____

From: _____ To: _____ Reason for leaving: _____

May we contact your previous employer for a reference? Yes _____ No _____

_____

Employment *continued.*

Company Name: _____ Phone: (   ) _____

Address: _____ Supervisor: _____

City: _____ State: _____ Job Title: _____

Salary: _____ OR Commission _____ per month.

Describe your duties: _____

_____

From: _____ To: _____ Reason for leaving: _____

May we contact your previous employer for a reference? Yes _____ No _____

_____

Company Name: _____ Phone: (   ) _____

Address: _____ Supervisor: _____

City: _____ State: _____ Job Title: _____

Salary: _____ OR Commission _____ per month.

Describe your duties: _____

_____

From: _____ To: _____ Reason for leaving: _____

May we contact your previous employer for a reference? Yes _____ No _____

_____

EDUCATION

High school: _____ Did you graduate? Yes _____ No _____

College: _____ Did you graduate? Yes _____ No _____

Degree: _____

Trade school: _____ Did you graduate? Yes _____ No _____

MILITARY SERVICE

Branch: _____ From: _____ To: _____

Rank at discharge: _____ Type of discharge: _____

If other than honorable, explain: _____

<u>DISCLAIMER AND SIGNATURE</u>

I certify that my answers are true and complete to the best of my knowledge.

If this application leads to employment, I understand that false or misleading information in my application or interview may result in my release.

Signature: _____ Date: _____

Appendix H-2

Independent Contractor Agreement

Zip Code

Web page address

INDEPENDENT CONTRACTOR AGREEMENT

This agreement is made and entered into this _____ day of _____ year of _____, by and between <u>Your Company Name (YCN)</u>, having its principal place of business at 1234 Any Street, Hometown, USA Zip Code and _____ _____, the independent contractor, ("IC").

NOW, THEREFORE, in consideration of the premises and of the mutual covenants made herein, and of other good and valuable consideration, the receipt and adequacy of which are hereby acknowledged, the parties hereto agree as follows:

1. **<u>Term of Agreement.</u>** YCN hereby contracts with the IC, and IC hereby accepts contract with YCN for an indefinite period, which may be terminated by either party upon to the other.

2. **<u>License Requirement.</u>** Regulated by the Department of Real Estate in the state of California, YCN must require that IC have an active real estate salesman license or a real estate broker license, valid in the state of California or in the state that the IC is representing YCN in an IC capacity. This license must be maintained in good standing at all times, in addition to the required continuing classes of education to re-new the license. The IC's license will be registered with the Department of Real Estate under the respective broker license of YCN. The IC's original license will be held at the principal place of business.

3. **<u>Guidelines of Independent Contractor.</u>**

   A. The IC is contracted as an agent to solicit FHA-insured loans and conventional loans eligible for purchase by the Federal Home Loan Mortgage Corporation and by the Federal National Mortgage Association, as well as other conventional loans for other investors, as announced from time to time by YCN. The IC agrees to devote his or her time, attention, and energy as such agent and shall to the best of his or her ability make every effort to solicit loans for YCN.

   B. YCN reserves the right to change the territory assigned to IC at any time in any manner whatsoever in its sole discretion. Changes are to be mutually agreed upon and signified in writing.

   C. The IC at all times during the performance of this contract shall strictly adhere to all the guidelines and regulations now in effective or as subsequently modified governing the relationship between IC and YCN.

   D. This agreement with IC shall continue only as long as the services rendered by IC are satisfactory to YCN, regardless of any other provisions contained in this agreement. YCN shall be the sole judge as to whether the services of IC are satisfactory.

   E. IC shall, at his or her own cost and expense, procure an automobile for use in traveling about his or her designed territory and making calls on customers and prospective customers. IC agrees to indemnify and hold YCN harmless and blameless from any claims out of operation of such automobile by IC.

F. IC shall be obligated for all monies expended for travel, entertainment of customers, car phones, flyers, and similar business expenses, as well as all credits reports and appraisal fees. Said sums may be withdrawn from that compensation due to IC from YCN, i.e., reducing the commission on the next succeeding date after the expenditure.

4. **Compensation for Independent Contractors.** YCN agrees to pay IC commissions for services rendered based on the below formula, providing YCN has collected their commissions (broker's fee) from the assigned lender:

A. **Real Estate Brokerage Fee.** If the IC is a new real estate agent, the brokerage fee split will be as follows: _____ % of the total brokerage fee received by YCN to the IC.

B. **When YCN furnishes the leads.** When Your Company Name furnishes the "leads," mortgages or real estate, to the IC, the compensation will be _____% to the IC, including rebates and _____% to YCN. Any leads developed from the initial lead furnish by YCN will be split 50/50 with the agent.

C. **When Loan Agent Generates the Lead.** When the loan agent generates the lead, then the brokerage fee will be split 50/50 with the loan agent.

D. **Overage (Mortgage Rebates).** _____% Of the overage/rebate between discount schedule established by the lender and discount points charged to the buyer, seller, buyer/seller. Overage commissions shall be paid only on loan applications taken by IC and funded while IC is still associated and actively working with YCN.

E. **Incentive Program.** If a loan agent closes _____ loans in a calendar month, he or she will receive a bonus of up to _____% fee, retroactive to the first of the month This program will start at the first of each month.

F. **Profit Sharing.** Management is working on a profit-sharing program for all personnel.

G. **Loans/Real Estate Sales Made to Agents.** All licensed agents are entitled to do one loan a calendar year for themselves. Any loan(s) made to a family member will be charged loan fees and costs. A processing fee will be charged on all loans. (See management for cost and fees.)

All real estate sales will have a brokerage fee charged. (See management for this charge.)

H. During the term of this contract, IC shall not solicit, sell, process, or in any manner divert loans to or on behalf of any lender other than YCN. In the event that IC does so, IC shall hereby waive all rights to any and all compensations due to or to become due from YCN.

A. In no event shall any compensation due to or to become due exceed that allowable by appropriate _____ regulations.

B. In the event that YCN establishes a pension and profit-sharing plan or similar plan authorized by the Internal Revenue Code, it may from time to time make contributions to said plan but shall govern the exact responsibilities and duties of YCN relative to IC under said plan.

C. IC is hereby duly notified that all compensation from YCN is subject to IC's respective federal, state, and social security income tax bracket per the current code of the Internal Revenue Service. YCN are not responsible for the income tax of IC. However, YCN does strongly suggest to IC that he or she contact an accountant or CPA for advice on estimated taxes for the current year applicable.

D. YCN hereby notifies IC that health benefits, medical benefits, and dental benefits are not provided with this agreement. In the event that such named benefits are made available to IC, YCN will take the necessary steps toward proper notification and explanation of said benefits.

5. **Rights of YCN and IC.** The authority of IC is limited to soliciting loan applications and submitting such applications to YCN for consideration. IC has no authority to make any commitment on behalf of YCN in any manner whatsoever, except to commit YCN to that day's discount points. It is understood and agreed that all loan decisions, including whether to make the loan and, if so, in what amount and on what terms, are retained in their entirety by YCN.

6. **Termination of Employment.**

   A. **Events Causing Termination.** This contract shall terminate immediately and without notice on the occurrence of any of the following events:

   1. The occurrence of circumstances that make it impossible or impracticable for the business of YCN to be continued.
   2. The death of IC.
   3. The loss of legal capacity.
   4. The willful breach/violation of the guidelines, regulations, and terms of the agreement by IC or YCN.
   5. The habitual neglect by IC of the obligation as independent contractor.
   6. The continued incapacity on the part of IC to meet contractual responsibilities.
   7. The reduction from full active capacity of IC's real estate license, including but not limited to revocation, suspension, or restricted status as determined by the Department of Real Estate (DRE).

   B. **Effect of Termination on Compensation.** In the event of a termination by IC, IC shall receive commissions on the loans originated and left by IC in the following manner (compensation will always be paid upon the proper funding of the loan application in question):

   1. One hundred percent of the earned commissions if the loan is approved, all interested parties are notified, and the loan is ready to close.
   2. Fifty percent of the earned commissions if the loan is approved but submitted for underwriting.
   3. Twenty-five percent of the earned commission if the loan is in normal processing and has not been submitted to underwriting and has not been approved.
   4. Credit report fees and appraisal fees remaining unpaid upon the termination of IC shall be deducted from the first commission due to IC after termination, except in those cases in which collection of said fees was not within IC's power.

5. If the termination results from IC's having solicited, sold, processed, or in any manner, directly or indirectly, diverted loans to or on behalf of any lender other than YCN, IC loses all rights toward compensation, except for those loans that have been already closed and funded.

6. In no event shall commissions be paid on overages to an individual not actively employed by YCN.

C. **Time Limit for Claiming Commissions.** All claims of IC for commissions on loans and sales, whether IC or others make the loans/sales, are waived by IC if the loans are not funded within ninety days of the date of the termination of the agreement with YCN.

7. **General Provisions.**

A. **Notices.** Any notices to be given hereunder by either party to the other be in writing and may be effected either by personal delivery or by mail, registered or certified post-age prepaid with return receipt requested. Any notice may be mailed as follows:

YCN: Your Company Name
1234 Any Street
Hometown, USA Zip

IC:

Name _____

Address _____

City, State, Zip _____

Social Security Number _____

Each party may change its respective address by written notice in accordance with this paragraph. Notices delivered personally shall be deemed communicated as of two days after mailing.

B. **Complete Agreement.** This contract supersedes any and all other contracts, either oral or in writing, between the party hereto. Each party to this contract acknowledges that no representations, inducements, promises, or agreements, orally or otherwise, have been made by any party, or anyone acting on behalf of any parties, which are not contained in this contract shall be valid or binding. Any modification of this contract will be effective only if it is in writing.

C. **Severability.** If any provision in this contract is held by a court of competent jurisdiction to be invalid, void, or unenforceable, the remaining provisions shall nevertheless continue in full force without being impaired or invalidated in any way.

D. **Governing Law.** This contract shall be governed by and construed in accordance with the laws of the state of California.

E. **Uncontrollable Events.** Neither party will be responsible for either delays or failures in performance resulting from acts beyond the control of such party. Such acts include, but are not limited to, acts of God, strikes, riots, earthquakes, fire, power failures and communication line failures, or other disasters.

F. **Dispute Resolution.** Any dispute concerning this agreement will be submitted in _____, California, to binding arbitration exclusively. The prevailing party of such action will be entitled to its costs of arbitration and reasonable attorneys' fees.

G. **Auto Insurance.** IC shall furnish a copy of his or her auto insurance policy or a copy of the endorsement page to the policy to YCN.

H. **Business Cards.** YCN will order all business cards, but it is the responsibility of each agent to pay for his or her business cards.

8. **Statement of Policy.**

Your Company Name requires its independent contractors to perform loan origination and servicing according to company policies and procedures. Every independent contract must conform to company, investor, and governmental regulatory requirements, as well as accepted lending practices. In connection with these requirements, a quality-control plan has been implemented. This plan includes quality-control standards and procedures describing the steps in processing and servicing loans.

Another element of the quality plan is the internal compliance review program. Under his program, the quality control reviewer is charged with the responsibility of reviewing the compliance of employees or independent contractor with loan processing and servicing requirements.

The job of the control reviewer is an essential part of our quality-control plan. The reviewer has complete access to all departments and records of this company for use on quality-control reviewing. Each employee or independent contractor must cooperate fully with the reviewer in the performance of quality-control review work. Any misrepresentations made to the reviewer or any falsification of records or the information that tends to mislead the reviewer is cause for immediate dismissal.

Any employee or independent contractor who has knowledge that any of the policies and procedures of this company or requirements of any of our investors or mortgage insurers or government agencies or of any provision of the law has been violated should notify the management immediately.

If anyone who provides this company with business suggests improprieties or exerts pressure to have loans approved, the employee(s) or independent contractors(s) should inform him or her at once of this company's dedication to proper business conduct. Strong and quick reactions to any suggestion to perform a wrongful act will create respect and generate future business from those firms whose business we want to encourage.

There are certain special loan origination problems. These problems appear frequently in mortgage loan origination and require special attention. They include the following; however, they are not exclusive to others not mentioned at this time:

1. **Kickbacks.** Kickbacks to anyone for referral of business are improper and in violation of RESPA, DRE, and DOC regulations. YCN does not make such payments.

2. **Abuse of Rate and Fee Quotes.** YCN does not permit independent contractors to quote interest rates or administration fees solely to get the loan application. Besides the loan product itself,

YCN is also selling its services of knowledge and processing to meet the client's need and objectives. If there is to be an exception, it is to be discussed with the president or the vice-president of loan operations of YCN prior to the quote.

3. **Signing Credit Documents in Blank.** There is an absolute rule that YCN does not permit a loan application or any other document to be signed before being properly completed, either by the independent contractor or the loan processor.

4. **Handling Verifications.** Verification of employment, deposits, consumer loans, and mortgage is a major source of loan origination problems. Verifications that have been hand-carried to employers, banks, etc., but, mailed back without approval from senior management will be cause for dismissal.

5. **Discrepancies in Credit Information.** YCN must resolve any and all material conflicts in the credit information supporting the loan application before approving a loan.

6. **Straw-Buyer Transactions.** YCN does not apply or participate in any transaction in which the applicant is standing in for another party.

7. **Acknowledgments and Release.** IC acknowledged that he or she is not an employee of Your Company Name and that he or she has full control over the details, means, and ways of fulfilling his or her obligations as such. As an IC, he or she assumes all responsibility for federal withholding taxes, social security, city taxes, and worker's compensation insurance.

IC hereby releases, discharges, and agrees to hold harmless and blameless Your Company Name representatives, assigns, employees, or any persons or corporation acting under Your Company Name's authority or permission, as well as any persons or corporation for whom Your Company Name may be acting, including any company, manufacturer, or distributor from and against any liability as a result of any personal physical impairment or loss during the contractual agreement. IC fully understands that Your Company Name assumes no responsibility for any medical expenses during or after the terms of any agreement made through Your Company Name.

This contract is subject to change at management's discretion. All IC and employees will receive a thirty-day notice to any changes to this contract.

Your Company Name ("YCN") and IC have read, acknowledged, accepted, agreed to the foregoing, and received a copy of it.

Your Company Name	**Independent Contractor**
_____	_____
Signature	Signature
_____	_____
Print Name	Print Name
_____	_____
Title	Title
_____	_____
Date	Date
_____	_____
Street Address	Street Address
_____	_____
City, State, Zip	City, State, Zip

Phone: (800) 555-1212; Fax: (800) 555-1213

Home Phone Number

Cell Phone Number

Home E-Mail Address

Birthday (Month and Day)

Appendix H-3
Policy and Procedures Manual

Mission Statement

The mission of Your Company Name (YCN) is to furnish our clients with a fair product at a reasonable price in an expedient manner.

Company Slogan

YCN's company slogan is "Service…Not Just What We Do but Who We Are." This slogan should be used in all advertising material.

Officers of the Corporation

President's Name, President, Broker of Record, Major Stockholder Person's Name, VP of Operations, Stockholder

Organizational Chart

See Page 6 of this manual for YCN's organizational chart.

Equal Opportunity Employer

YCN is an equal opportunity employer and does not discriminate against any race, color, creed, sex, or national origin.

Hours of Operations

YCN hours of operations are:

Monday–to Friday 8:00 AM to 6:00 PM
Saturday   10:00 AM to 5:00 PM
Sunday by appointment
Closed on all major holidays—New
Year's Day, President's Day, Memorial
Day, Independence Day, Labor Day,
Thanksgiving, and Christmas.

Personal and Items Furnished by YCN

YCN will furnish full-time processor, full-time junior processor and receptionist, full-time marketing director, high-tech phone system that allows you to transfer your calls to your home, cell phone, etc., access to a PC or laptop computer, basic office supplies, work station for you to conduct your business. Two shirts with YCN name on it (after your first loan closing).

Hot Leads

YCN purchases "Hot Leads." The leads will be distributed to the full-time loan agents, as we receive them, on a rotating basis.

Floor Schedule

Floor schedule is on a first-come, first-served basis and is also on a voluntary basis.

Full-Time Loan Agent

YCN considers a full-time loan agent anyone who works a minimum of forty hours per week.

Part-Time to Full-Time Loan Agent

YCN considers a part-time to fulltime loan agent as anyone that works from twenty to forty hours a week. This type of loan agent has the understanding that YCN is looking for you to become a full-time loan agent within six months of joining YCN.

Part-Time Loan Agent

YCN considers a part-time loan agent as anyone who works less than twenty hours a week.

Loan Agent Sales Training

Each Wednesday from 4:00 PM to 6:00 PM, YCN offers sales training for the loan agents. A variety of subjects is covered at these sessions, including prospecting, computer training (Encompass, Point), marketing, how to fill out the URLA, farming, and time management.

New Loan Agent Training

The sales manager conducts new loan agent training on the second and fourth Thursday of the month from 4:00 PM to 6:00 PM. Senior management strongly suggests that all new loan agents attend this training.

Independent Contractor Review

Each loan agent will receive a personal review every 90 days by the sales manager. Items such as production objectives, goals, and overall concerns that the loan agent may have will be covered at these meetings.

Brokerage Compensation (Commission)

All loan agents are considered independent contractors and will be paid within 24 hours of receiving the brokerage check from either escrow or the lender. Also, all income is reported to the appropriate agencies via a 1099 form. Each loan agent is responsible to pay his or her quarterly taxes.

Keys to the Office

Keys to the office will be issued by the VP of operations, and each individual will sign for the key. Please report any loss or misplaced keys to management immediately.

Loan Package

Each loan agent can either go into Encompass or Point or go to the copy machine to pull a full copy of a loan package. Review this manual for information on how to retrieve a copy of a loan package from the copy machine.

Emergency Alarm System

YCN is equipped with a fully operational alarm system, including motion detectors.

Arbitration

Any disputes that you may have as a loan agent will be submitted to the following people, in the following order:

a. sales manager

b. VP operations

In the event that the above people are not able to settle the dispute, the sales manager and the VP of operations will take it to the president for review and the final decision.

Marketing/Advertising

All loan agents will meet with our marketing director to develop advertising material that will be designed for their personal use.

All marketing and advertising material, post cards, flyers, newsletters, etc., will be cleared by the marketing director and VP of operations before being placed into use.

Personal Appearance (Dress Code)

Policy

It is the policy of YCN that each independent contractor's and employee's dress, grooming, and personal hygiene be appropriate to the work situation and environment. Always remember that first impressions are lasting impressions, and many times, fair or not, we're initially judged by our outward appearance.

1. Everyone at YCN is expected at all times to present a professional, businesslike image to customers, prospects, and the general public. Acceptable personal appearance is an ongoing requirement of everyone with YCN.

2. All personnel at YCN who have regular contact with the public must comply with the following personal appearance standards:

    a. Everyone at YCN is expected to dress in a manner that is normally acceptable in similar business establishments. Independent contractors and all other employees should not wear suggestive attire, jeans, athletic clothing, shorts, T-shirts, novelty buttons, base-ball hats, and similar items of casual attire that do not present a businesslike appearance.

    b. Hair should be clean, combed, and neatly trimmed or arranged. Shaggy, unkempt hair is not permissible, regardless of length.

    c. Sideburns, moustaches, and beards should be neatly trimmed.

    d. Tattoos and body piercing (other than earrings) should not be visible.

3. We do not have a "casual Friday" dress.

You should always make sure you look presentable, professional, and like someone you would want to do business with.

Office Behavior

YCN employees are expected to conduct themselves in a professional manner at all times.

Sexual Harassment

YCN has a strict policy against any type of sexual harassment, which is grounds for immediate dismissal. [From: Department of Fair Employment and Housing Act, specifically Government Code sections 12940(a), (j), and (k). Prospective employee(s) acknowledges a receipt of the "Sexual Harassment Is Forbidden by Law" handbook.]

Drugs, Narcotics, and Alcohol Use

It is the policy of YCN to maintain a workplace that is free from the effects of drug, narcotics, and alcohol abuse.

Minimum Brokerage Fee

To remain in business, YCN policy for charging a brokerage fee/commission is to receive a minimum of $_____ gross fee per loan. This can be arrived from up-front fees and rebates.

Loan Files

All loan and real estate files are the property of YCN and are to remain in the office at all times.

Education

YCN feels that education is important, and we encourage everyone to continue education, regardless of the number of years in the business, in addition to taking the classes necessary to maintain a real estate license.

Licensing Policy

YCN is licensed under the Department of Real Estate (DRE) and pending license under the Department of Corporations (DOC). When we become approved under the DOC, senior management highly encourages all loan agents to obtain a real estate license within six months of joining YCN.

Business Cards

It is the responsibility of each agent to pay for his or her business cards up front; the independent contractor may choose between quantities of 500 or 1,000 cards. The payment should be in the form of either a personal check or money order, and it should be made out to YCN.

Photographs/Pictures

Each independent contractor and employee will have a photo taken by our professional photographer. All independent contractors will pay for their photo. YCN will reimburse the independent contractor for the expense upon the closing of their first loan.

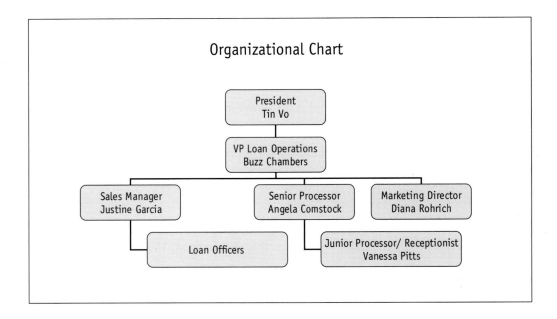

Appendix I
Wholesale Brokerage Agreements

Appendix I-1
Wholesale Broker Application

1. Company Name: _____
   Start Date of Business: _____ Date Incorporated: _____
   Business Address: _____
   Phone No: (_____)_____ Fax No: (_____)_____

2. Principal Officers: Titles: % Of Equity Owned

   _____   _____   _____

   _____   _____   _____

3. Contact Person: _____

4. Production Data: Total # of Loans Funded   Total Loan Amounts

   Projection for this year (2XXX)   _____ $_____
   This year's production (as of 2XXX)   _____ $_____
   Prior Year (2XXX) Volume   _____ $_____
   Two years ago (2XXX) Volume   _____ $_____

5. **Product Mix ($):**

(Volume)	Conventional Conforming	Jumbo	FHA	DVA	Total Amount
This year	_____	_____	_____	_____	_____
Prior year	_____	_____	_____	_____	_____
Two years ago	_____	_____	_____	_____	_____

6. **Primary Markets:**

Cities	Counties	States	%
_____	_____	_____	_____

7. Are you presently insured or approved by:

   ( ) DVA#_____   ( ) FHA#_____
   ( ) Automatic Date:_____   ( ) FHLMC#_____
   ( ) FNMA#_____   ( ) GNMA Issuer#_____
   ( ) FNMA Delegated Program_____   ( ) Other_____

8. Is your company a wholly owned subsidiary or does it have ownership interests in another institution, such as escrow, appraisal, or Credit Bureau? ( ) YES ( ) NO
   If yes, please provide the name(s) of the company: _____
   _____

9. Describe your company's quality control plan that ensures that loan information and documentation are accurate and complete prior to submission to lender:
   _____

10. Has your company ever been terminated or suspended from selling by an investor or a government agency?
    ( ) YES ( ) NO
    If yes, please explain: _____

11. Has any principal or employee ever been excluded from selling or servicing mortgages by an investor, been barred from loan activity by a government agency, or had a business license suspended, revoked, or restricted? ( ) YES ( ) NO
    If yes, please explain: _____

12. Please furnish the following documents:

    A. Most recent P & L, balance sheet (year to date), and financial statements (under 6 mo old).

    B. Resumes of principal officers, supervisors, and lead processor.

    C. Signed copy of wholesale broker agreement.

    D. Copies of license to conduct business in each state of activity.

    E. Executed authorization to release information.

    F. Executed W-9 form.

    G. List of appraisers to be approved by lender, copy of appraisal license.

    H. Articles of incorporation or other organizational documents.

    I. Corporate resolution giving authority to contract with lender.

13. Please provide five funding references:

	Firm	Contact Person	Phone Number
1.	_____	_____	(____)_____
2.	_____	_____	(____)_____
3.	_____	_____	(____)_____
4.	_____	_____	(____)_____
5.	_____	_____	(____)_____

AUTHORIZATION TO RELEASE INFORMATION

    I hereby authorize you to release to _____(Lender), its assigns or affiliate lenders, information that is requested as verification from any source named in the application. By submission of this request for approval to participate in _____ (Lender's) broker program, I represent and warrant that all statements and information contained herein are true and correct. I authorize credit information, business information and other financial matters to be released to _____ (Lender).

Authorized Broker of Record Name (Please Print)

_____

Authorized Broker of Record	Social Security No.	Date
(Signature)		

_____

Authorized Owner/Officer Name (Please Print)

_____

Authorized Owner/Officer	Social Security No.	Date
Name (Signature)		

Appendix I-2
Wholesale Brokerage Agreement

This wholesale brokerage agreement is entered into as of _____, XXX by and between _____ ("Lender"), and _____ ("Broker") with reference to the following facts:

A. Lender is engaged in, among other things, mortgage lending, and desires to approve, close, and fund loans secured by lien on residential real property that are submitted to lender by third-party originators.

B. This agreement is entered into by the parties in order to establish the terms and conditions for the origination and funding of residential mortgage loans and the relationship and responsibility of lender and broker with respect thereto.

NOW THEREFORE, in consideration of the foregoing matters and the mutual covenants hereinafter set forth, the parties hereto agree as follows:

1. Approval of Broker: Subject to the terms, conditions, and limitations hereinafter set forth, lender hereby approves broker as a residential loan broker and agrees to review applications for residential mortgage loans ("Loans") submitted to lender by broker.

2. Broker's Submission Responsibilities: Broker shall use its best efforts to solicit and complete loan application packages, including credit verifications, appraisal, and all other information and documentation required by lender (each, a "loan application package") for submission to the lender. Each loan application package and broker's activities hereunder shall be subject to and shall comply with the terms and conditions of this agreement and lender's loan submission guidelines (the "Guidelines"), as the same may be amended from time to time.

3. Loan Programs: All loan application packages submitted by broker to lender hereunder shall be submitted only for those types of residential loan programs as are offered by lender under this agreement from time to time. Lender will publish a list of program guidelines from time to time, which may include provisions for eligible property types, loan limits, LTV ratios, interest rates, points, and fees. Notwithstanding the foregoing provisions, broker acknowledges that the interest rate, points, fees, and other terms of such loan programs are subject to change and that lender reserves the right to modify, add, or discontinue loan programs subject to this agreement.

4. Appraisal, Credit Report: Broker shall provide an appraisal for each loan application package, which appraisal shall be performed by an appraiser (a) whose qualifications are approved by lender in writing; (b) who holds a valid certification, registration, or license from the applicant state authority with oversight of appraiser's activities; (c) who has no interest, direct or indirect, in the real property subject to the appraisal; and (d) who will not receive compensation that is affected by the approval or declination of the applicable loan. All credit reports submitted in connection with loan application packages must be provided by a credit bureau approved in writing by lender. The cost of all appraisals and credit reports submitted in connection with any loan application package shall be borne by broker, and lender shall have no responsibility for such cost.

5. Funding Service Release: All loans shall be closed in the name of, and shall be funded by, lender. Broker hereby releases all interest in the loans, including without limitation all servicing rights, to lender.

6. Nonexclusive Relationship: In its sole discretion, lender may use other loan brokers, and broker may submit loan applications to other lenders. Nothing contained herein shall be construed as granting to broker any exclusive right, whether with respect to time, territory, or subject matter.

7. Underwriting: Notwithstanding any other provision of this agreement to the contrary, the decision whether any loan shall be approved for funding and the terms of such loan shall be the sole responsibility and at the sole discretion of the lender. Lender will, by written notification, approve or decline each loan application submitted in accordance with lender's then-current lending and underwriting policies. Each loan application package shall be underwritten in accordance with the then-current secondary market standards as they pertain to the loan program requested. Lender shall have no obligation, express or implied, to fund any loan that is not approved in writing by lender. Broker shall be responsible for informing each loan applicant of the matter set forth in this paragraph.

8. Independent Contractor: In the performance of its obligations under this agreement, broker shall be deemed to be acting as an independent contractor and representative of the loan applicant and not of the lender. There shall be no partnership, franchise, joint venture, or any other association between lender and broker arising hereunder.

9. Limitations on Broker's Authority: Broker's authority pursuant to this agreement shall consist solely of offering lender's approved residential mortgage loan programs and processing loan application packages pursuant to this agreement at its own expense and risk. Broker has no authority, express or implied, to bind lender in any manner whatsoever. No statement or representation of broker shall be binding upon lender unless such statement or representation is in writing and signed, printed, or published by an authorized employee of lender.

10. Broker's Compliance Obligations: Broker shall maintain at all times in good standing any and all required business and professional licenses and shall comply with all business, tax requirements, and all state and federal laws, rules and regulations that apply to broker because of broker's activities as a mortgage broker for its loan applicant clients, including but not limited to the Fair Credit Reporting Act, the Equal Credit Opportunity Act, the Truth-in-Lending Act, the Real Estate Settlement Procedures Act, the Home Mortgage Disclosure Act, state licensing laws, all regulations promulgated in connection there-with, and government monitoring regulations and disclosure laws in connection with broker's solicitation of broker's loan application packages.

11. Termination: Except as otherwise provided herein, this agreement may be terminated at any time by either lender or broker. Such termination shall be effective upon receipt of written notice of termination but in no event later than five days after the issuance of written notice. The obligations of the parties with respect to loan application packages that have been registered with lender prior to receipt of such written notice of termination shall survive the termination of this agreement. Lender may terminate this agreement affective immediately without notice to broker in the event of breach by broker of any of broker's obligations, representation, or warranties contained in this agreement or the guidelines.

12. No Third-Party Beneficiaries: This agreement is made for the sole protection and benefit of the parties hereto, and no other person shall have any right of action under this agreement as a third-party beneficiary or otherwise.

13. Indemnification: Broker agrees to indemnify, defend, and hold harmless lender and its directors, officers, agents, and employees from any liability or loss whatsoever (including but not limited to damages, penalties, fines, costs, expenses, and attorney fees) arising out of or connected with (a) any material breach of any representation, warranty, or obligation of broker contained in this agreement, the guidelines, or any other documentation delivered in connection with this agreement; (b) any material negligent or willful act or omission by broker in the performance of broker's obligations under this

agreement; and (c) any violation by broker of any federal, state, or local law or regulation pertaining to the activities contemplated by this agreement. All rights and remedies provided in this agreement to lender shall inure to the benefit of lender, its successors and assignees, and any assignee of or participant in any loan and shall survive the termination of this agreement or the repurchase of any loan by broker.

IN WITNESS WHEREOF, the parties hereto have caused this wholesale brokerage agreement to be executed by their duly authorized representatives as of the date set forth above:

Broker:

_____

Lender:

_____

Name of Company

Name of Company

By: _____

By: _____

Mailing Address:

Mailing Address:

_____

_____

Appendix I-3

Concurrent Wholesale Funding Broker Agreement

This concurrent wholesale funding broker agreement (the "agreement") is entered into this _____ day of _____, 2xxx, between CD Financial Group Funding Corporation, a Delaware Corporation ("DC"), and _____, a California licensed real estate broker corporation ("Broker").

This agreement is intended to set forth the entire understanding between the parties in which DC agrees to fund loans processed, packaged, and closed by broker in broker's name and submitted to DC for funding from time to time, subject to the terms, conditions, and warranties as described.

1. <u>Nonexclusive Relationship:</u> Nothing contained herein shall obligate broker to submit all loan funding requests that it brokers to DC, it being understood that this shall be a nonexclusive agreement.

2. <u>Underwriting:</u> Nothing contained herein shall obligate DC to fund loans submitted by broker without DC's prior review and written approval at DC's sole discretion.

3. <u>Loan Package:</u>

   (a) Broker shall be responsible for the accurate preparation and execution of a complete property and credit loan application package on each loan request submitted, including but not limited to those items listed below, all as may be required by DC and in conformance with DC's policies and procedures as established and as may be modified from time to time. Original loan application and processor-prepared application both signed by borrower.

   (b) Supporting credit information, credit report, and verification of credit.

   (c) Supporting verification of employment, deposits, and mortgage payment history.

   (d) Copies of all government-required disclosures.

   (e) Original appraisal report of the property to be financed.

   (f) All supporting information necessary to substantiate borrower's qualifications for the loan.

4. <u>Loan Approval:</u> DC shall notify broker by telephone of the acceptance or rejection of each completed loan package with 5 days of DC's receipt of the completed loan package. For each accepted loan, DC will fund such loan approximately 48 hours after acceptance, provided that all required documentation accompanies the loan package, including the following:

   a. Properly completed and executed deed of trust.

   b. Unrecorded but recordable assignment of the deed of trust.

   c. The borrower's note endorsed to DC.

   d. All required property and casualty insurance policies naming DC as loss payee.

   e. All required copies of disclosure documents.

   All loans shall be closed on loan documentation and in a manner approved by DC. The property that is the security for such a loan shall be appraised only by an FHA appraiser, who shall submit an appraisal acceptable in form and content.

5. <u>Broker Compliance:</u> Broker agrees at all times to comply with applicable federal, state, and local laws about the processing and origination of such loans, including but not limited to state usury laws, state licensing laws, the Real Estate Settlement Procedures Act, the Equal Opportunity Act, the Truth-in-Lending Act, the Federal Consumer Credit Protection Act, the Fair Credit Reporting Act, and the Equal Credit Opportunity Act.

6. <u>Indemnification:</u> Broker agrees to indemnify and hold DC harmless from and against any and all claims, demands, liabilities, causes of action, and expenses, including attorney's fees actually incurred, relating to, arising out of, or in connection with broker's gross negligence, willful misconduct, or bad faith with regard to any action or inaction of broker hereunder.

7. <u>Broker Warranty:</u> With respect to each loan package submitted to DC for funding, broker hereby represents and warrants that:

   a. It has the authority to sell, transfer, and assign to DC each loan, the right to assign the payments owing, and the right to transfer to DC its security interest and the collateral securing each loan.

   b. This agreement and all actions provided for herein have been duly authorized by the board of directors of broker, if broker is a corporation, or by such individual or individuals empowered and authorized to bind broker, and broker shall, upon execution of this agreement, provide DC with evidence reasonably satisfactory to DC of such authorization.

   c. Each loan is entered into for fair consideration in the ordinary course of business and has been made in compliance with all applicable federal, state, and local statutes and regulations governing fraud, lack of consideration, or unconscionability.

   d. No prior sale, pledge, assignment, or hypothecation of any loan or any portion thereof has been made to any other person or entity.

   e. Broker does not know of any suit, action, arbitration, or legal administrative or other proceeding pending or threatened against broker that would affect its ability to perform its obligations under this agreement.

   f. The borrower has no setoffs, counterclaims, or defenses to the promissory note or the deed of trust or mortgage securing the promissory note arising from the acts or omissions of broker in the origination of borrower's loan, and all signatures on said promissory note and deed of trust or mortgage are the true signatures of the borrower.

   g. Broker has not modified any loan in any material respect; satisfied, canceled, or subordinated any loan in whole or in part; released the mortgaged property in whole or in part from the lien of any loan; or executed any instrument of release, cancellation, modification shall be deemed not to have been made with respect to any matter brought to the attention of DC prior to disbursement of the purchase price, and acknowledged and approved by DC in writing or by express mention in the related title insurance policy.

   h. To the best of broker's knowledge and belief, all documents submitted by broker in connection with loan packages submitted to DC are in every respect valid and genuine, being what on their face they purport to be, and all information (credit or otherwise) submitted in connection with such loan packages is true and accurate.

   i. Broker has no knowledge of any circumstances or conditions with respect to any loan, mortgaged property, mortgagor, or mortgagor's credit standing that can be reasonably expected to cause private institutional investors to regard any loan as an unacceptable investment, cause any loan to become delinquent, or adversely affect the value or marketability of any loan.

   j. To the best of broker's knowledge and belief, no fraudulent information has been provided to DC with respect to a loan submitted to DC for funding. For purposes hereof, the term information shall mean any and all information obtained from the borrower or any reference source that would, according to standard practices and procedures in the mortgage lending industry, be within the control or knowledge of broker, as well as any appraisal-related information that is a result of, or is communicated because of, any relationship or transaction between the appraiser and broker.

8. <u>Repurchase:</u> DC may require broker to repurchase any loan submitted by Broker pursuant to this agreement if any warranty made by the broker is untrue. DC may also enforce any other available remedy at law or in equity. Broker must pay DC the repurchase price within 100 days of receipt of demand therefore from DC. The purchase price shall be equal to the purchase price originally paid by

DC for such loan, with adjustment for principal payments received by DC prior to the time of repurchase. Broker will also indemnify DC and hold DC harmless against any related losses, damages, judgments, or legal expenses for any breach of warranty under this agreement.

9. Independent Contractor: Nothing contained herein shall constitute a partnership or joint venture between DC and broker, and the parties acknowledge that at all times they are operating as independent contractors. Broker shall at no time hold itself to be DC's agent or employee.

10. Broker Fee: Broker may charge the borrower an amount not to exceed _____% of the principal amount of the loan.

11. Termination: DC reserves the right to terminate this agreement at any time and for any reason, which termination shall be effective immediately upon broker's receipt of written notice thereof. Thereafter, DC shall have no further obligations whatsoever under this agreement.

12. Mutual Agreement: This agreement shall be null and void and of no further force or effect unless countersigned by DC, indicating approval and acceptance of the below-listed broker.

Broker: _____

By: _____

Address: _____

DC: _____

Funding Corporation

By: _____

Address: _____

Appendix J
Internet Web Sites

WEB SITES

Please note that any of the following Internet sites are subject to change without notice, and the authors, publishers, and editors represent that every effort has been made to ensure that the following Web sites are accurate.

All Regulations for Mortgage Brokers—www.allregs.com

American Association of Residential Mortgage Regulators, or (AARMR)—http://www.aarmr.org

Apartment Financing Today—www.housingfinance.com

Appraisal Foundation—http://www.appraisalfoundation.org

Bank Owned—www.RealtyTrac.com

Board of Governors of the Federal Reserve System—http://www.federalreserve.gov

Broker Outpost Lender Loan Finder—www.brokeroutpost.com

Building Cost Manual/Building Cost—http://www.building-cost.net

Bureau of Economic Analysis—www.bea.gov

Bureau of Labor Statistics—www.bls.gov/data

Bureau of the Census—www.census.gov

California Association of Mortgage Brokers—http://www.caamb.org

California Business and Professions code—http://www.leginfo.ca.gov/.html/bpc table of contents.html

California Department of Veterans Affairs—http://www.cdva.ca.gov

California Environmental Protection Agency—www.calepa.ca.gov

California Financial Information Privacy Act—http://www.leginfo.ca.gov

California Law, The 29 codes—http://www.leginfo.ca.gov/calaw.html

California legislation—http://www.leginfo.ca.gov/pub/bill/sen

California Office of Real Estate Appraisers—http://www.orea.ca.gov

City Information—http://www.city-data.com

City Informtion—www.usacitiesonline.com

City Information—www.VillagePR.file.com

Comparables—http://www.domania.com

Community Reinvestment Act (CRA)—http://www.ffiec.gov/cra/default.html

Complete Real Estate Software Catalog—http://mmink.com/re/cover

Condominium Information search on national basis—http://www. condo-certs.com

Contractor's State License Board (CSLB) to verify Contractor's License status and insurance coverage and legal actions—www.cslb.ca.gov

County Records—www.CountyRecordsResearch.com

Credit Card-Opt Out—https://www.optoutprescreen.com/?rf=t

Credit Information and FICO score—http://www.myfico.com

Credit: Equifax—http://www.equifax.com

Credit: Experian—http://www.experian.com/consumer/index.html

Credit: Trans Union—http://www.transunion.com

Credit Report Information (First American Title Co.)—http://www. credco.com

Credit Report (annual)—https://www.annualcreditreport.com/cra/index.jsp

Demographics—www.AmericanFactFinder.census.gov

Demographics by Postal Zip Code—www.zipskinny.com

Department of Real Estate (DRE)—www.dre.ca.gov

Department of Real Estate (DRE) Publications and Forms—http://www. dre.ca.gov/pub_home.html

Federal Deposit Insurance Corporation (FDIC)—http://www.fdic.gov/ regulations

Federal Financial Institutions Examination Council (FFIEC)—http:// www.ffiec.gov

Federal Home Loan Bank Act (FHLB)—http://www.fhlb.gov

Federal National Mortgage Association (FNMA)—www.efanniemae.com

Federal Reserve System—http://www.countyrecordsresearch.com/

Foreclosures—http://www.countyrecordsresearch.com/

Foreclosures—www.RealtyTrac.com

Department of Corporations—http://www.corp.ca.gov/

Department of Corporations Financial Services Division—http://www. corp.ca.gov/FSD/

Department of Corporations Financial Services—California Finance Lenders Law—http://www.corp.ca.gov/FDS/lender.asp

Department of Corporations—Financial Services—California Residential Mortgage Lending Act—http://www.corp.ca.gov/FSD/mortgage.asp

Department of Veterans Administration (DVA)—http://www.va.gov

Disclosures—http://www.creia.org/press/index.htm

Fair Credit Reporting Act (FCRA)—http://www.ftc.gov/os/statutes/ fcra.htm#604

Federal National Mortgage Association (FNMA)—http://www.fanniemae.com

Federal Home Loan Mortgage Corporation (FHLMC)—http://www.freddiemac.com/home

Federal Housing Administration—http://www.hud.gov or http://www.hud.gov/fha/sfh or www.fhaloan.com/faq.cfm

Federal Trade Commission—http://www.ftc.gov/credit for credit

Federal Trade Commission—www.ftc.gov or the consumer groups—www.privacyrights.org or www.idtheftcenter.org

Freddie Mac (FHLMC)—http://www.freddiemac.com

Freddie Mac Underwriting Comparison Guidelines—http://www.principal.com/partners/correspondent/sg/forms/uw_collateral.pdf

Free Credit Report—http://www.annualcreditreport.com (877) 322-8228

Freedom of Information Act (FOIA)—http://www.usdoj.gov/index.html

General information on loans—http://www.mortgage101.com

General information on loans from the consumers side—http://www.stepstomortgageloans.com

Glossary of real estate terms (per Department of Real Estate)—http://www.dre.ca.gov/pdf_docs/ref29.pdf

Good Faith Estimate From—www.all-forms.com

Government National Mortgage Association, Ginnie Mae (GNMA)—http:// www.ginniemae.com

Homeowners Association Information—http://www.hoacerts.com

Homes for Sale—www.RedFin.com

Housing Financial Discrimination Act—http://www.leginfo.ca.gov

Housing and Urban Development—http://www.hud.gov

Housing and Urban Development—information on loan limits, by state & county—http://www.hudclips.org/

Identity Theft information: Office of Privacy Protection—www.privacy.ca.gov

Indexes—www. http://mortgage-x.com/general/indexes/mta_history.asp

Insurance News Network—www.insure.com

Lenders—www.lenderlab.com

Loan Modification—www.efanniemae.com

Loan Origination—www.ScotsmanGuide.com

Locate Lenders and Loan Programs—www.lenderlab.com

Locate items on a variety of subjects—www.mentoronline.com

Locate lenders for jumbo loans, nationwide—http://www.noredtape.com

Maps—www.Maps.Google.com

Mortgage Bankers Association of America—http://www.mbaa.org

Mortgage Insurance (MGIC)—www.mgic.com

National Association of Housing and Redevelopment Officials—www.nahro.org

National Association of Mortgage Brokers—http://www.namb.org

National Association of Mortgage Processors—www.namp.com

Newsletter—www.originationnews.com

Notice of Default (NOD)/Notice of Sale(NOS)—www.redloc.com

Office of Real Estate Appraisers (OREA)—www.orea.ca.gov

Office of the Comptroller of the Currency (OCC)—http://www.occ.treas.gov

Office of Thrift Supervision (OTS)—http://www.ots.treas.gov/

Property Information—www.QuickFacts.census.com

Property for Sale—www.Realtor.com

Property Value—www.Zillow.com

Radian Mortgage Insurance—http://www.radiangroupinc.com/index.aspx

Real Estate Agents—www.Realtor.com

Real Estate Agents—www.nareb.com

Reverse Mortgage—www.nrmla.org

Right-To-Know—http://www.rtk.net

Salary—Salary.com

Scholarship—California Real Estate Education Center/Chancellor's Office—http://www.ccsf.edu/reec

Scholarship—California Association of REALTORS—http://www.car.org/index.php?id=MjMw

Site Selection—www.siteselection.com

United States Code—http://www.law.cornell.edu/uscode

United States Housing Market Conditions HUD User—www.huduser.org

VA Mortgage Center—http://www.vamortgagecenter.com/

Appendix K
Glossary of Terms

A

Abstract of judgment Imposes a lien on all real property owned or subsequently acquired by the debtor until satisfaction or expiration of the lien.

Abstract of title A written history of the title on the designated real property. An abstract of title covers the period from the original source of title to the present and summarizes all subsequent instruments of public record by setting forth their material parts.

Acceleration clause A common provision of a mortgage, trust deed, and note providing that the entire principal shall become immediately due and payable upon a certain event.

Acknowledgment A formal declaration, attached to or a part of an instrument made before a duly authorized officer (usually a notary public) by the person who has executed the instrument, declaring the execution to be a free act and deed and that the signature is genuine.

Acquisition cost The FHA-appraised value or purchase price (whichever is less) plus some closing costs.

Acre Equal to 43,560 square feet.

Actual authority Authority expressly given by the principal or given by the law and not denied by the principal.

Adjustable-rate mortgages (ARM) A type of alternative loan instrument in which the interest rate adjusts periodically according to a predetermined index and margin. This adjustment results in the loan payment's either increasing or decreasing. In some situations, the adjustment is made to the outstanding principal.

Adjustment date The date for periodic interest rate adjustments for an adjustable-rate mortgage loan.

Ad valorem tax A tax based on the value of the item being taxed.

Advances Money advanced by the beneficiary under a trust deed to pay real estate taxes or other items to protect the lender's interest under the trust deed. Also refers to additional funds loaned under an open-end trust deed or mortgage.

Advance fee A fee paid in advance of any services rendered. The practice of obtaining a fee in advance for the advertising of property or businesses for sale. Said fees can be incorrectly obtained, thereby becoming a violation of real estate laws and regulations.

Affidavit A sworn statement in writing before a proper official, usually a notary. See *Acknowledgment*.

Affiliation media sometimes referred to as tie-ins because they tie-in to or connect with other business operations. Chapter 2 under "Types of Media"

Affordability Index An index used to determine the number of buyers/borrowers that are on the market, presuming a 20% down payment.

After-funding conditions After a loan has funded and before recording of all pertinent documents, the underwriter may ask for additional conditions to close the loan.

Agent One who legally represents another, called a principal, from whom authority has been derived.

Agreement An exchange of promises, a mutual understanding or arrangement; a contract.

Alienation Transference of some or all of the title/ownership to property from one person to another.

Alienation clause A clause that gives the lender the right to call a loan upon sale of real estate. See *Due-on-sale clause*.

ALTA title policy American Land Title Association. A type of title insurance policy issued by a title insurance company that expands the risks normally insured against under the standard policy to include unrecorded mechanic's liens; unrecorded physical easements; facts a physical survey would show; water and mineral rights; and rights of parties in possession, such as tenants and buyers under unrecorded instruments. Required by the lender for both a new loan and a refinance.

Alternative mortgage instrument Any one of various loans that is different from a traditional mortgage because the monthly payment, interest rate, term, or other provisions are changed in an agreed-upon manner.

American Land Title Association (ALTA) A national association of title insurance companies, abstractors, and attorneys specializing in real property law. The association speaks for the title insurance and abstracting industry and establishes standard procedures and title policy forms.

Amortization Repayment of a debt in equal installments of principal and interest during an equal period of time.

Amortization schedule A table showing the amount of principal and interest due at regular intervals and the unpaid balance of the loan after each payment is made.

Amortized loan A loan that is completely paid off, interest and principal, by a series of regular payments that are equal or nearly equal.

Annual percentage rate (APR) A rate that represents the relationship of the total finance charge (interest, loan fees, points) to the amount of the loan.

Annual statement An annual statement sent to borrowers detailing all activity in their mortgage loan account, including all escrow activity.

Annuity A series of assured equal or nearly equal payments to be made during a period of time or a lump-sum payment to be made in the future. The series of installment payments due to the landlord under a lease or due to a lender under a note.

Application A form used to apply for a loan and to record pertinent information concerning a prospective borrower and the proposed security.

Appraisal A report by a qualified person setting forth an opinion or estimate of value. Also, the process by which this estimate is obtained.

Appraisal methods Major methods of an appraisal: (1) comparable market value, (2) cost approach, and (3) income approach.

Appraisal report (URAR) A written report by an appraiser containing his or her opinion as to the value of a property, including the factual supporting data, such as comparables and qualifications of the appraiser.

Appraised value An opinion of value reached by an appraiser based upon knowledge, experience, and a study of pertinent data as of a particular date.

Appraiser A person qualified by education, training, and experience to estimate the value of real and personal property.

Appreciation An increase in value from outside source. Example: Your home is valued at $315,000 and your neighbors market their home for $330,000. Your home's value should also increase because your neighbor's home sold for more.

Approval with conditions The underwriter gives loan approval with conditions. The underwriter may need additional documentation for the loan file before calling for loan documents.

ARM margin The spread (or difference) between the index rate and the interest rate of an adjustable-rate loan.

Arm's length transaction A transaction in which the borrower has no affiliation with the seller, lender, realtor, or appraiser.

Article 5 Applies to real estate licensees who engage as principals in buying from, selling to, or exchanging deeds of trust with the public and to brokers who make agreements with the public for the collection of payments or the performance of services in connection with deeds of trust.

Article 7 A statutory code enacted to curb abuses of inflated costs and expenses, short-term loans with large balloon payments, misrepresentation, or concealment of material facts. See *Mortgage loan disclosure statement.*

Articles of incorporation An instrument setting forth the basic rules and purposes under which a private corporation is formed.

Assess To determine a value; commonly used in connection with property taxes.

Assessment The process of placing a value on property for the strict purpose of taxation. May also refer to a levy against property for a special purpose, such as a sewer assessment.

Assets Everything owned by a person or corporation that can be used for the payment of debts.

Assignee The person to whom property or a right is assigned or transferred.

Assignment A transfer to another of any property in possession or in action, or of any estate or right therein; transfer by a person of that person's rights under a contract.

Assignor A person who transfers or assigns a right or property.

Assigns, Assignees Those to whom property or interests therein are transferred.

Assumable Loan A loan that allows a new substitute payee or purchaser to take ownership to real estate encumbered by an existing mortgage and assume liability and responsibility for the unpaid balance of the mortgage.

Assumption A written agreement by one party to pay an obligation originally incurred by another.

Assumption fee The fee paid to a lender (usually by the purchaser of real property) resulting from the assumption of an existing loan.

Attachment A seizure of defendant's property by court order as security for any judgment a plaintiff may recover in a legal action.

Audit An examination of records documents that must be retained by a broker, such as listings, deposit receipts, canceled checks, and trust records; a review by a government agency of financial records regulated by DRE and DOC laws.

Auditing Sometimes called "quality control." This is the step taken by a lender to double check a file for its accuracy.

Auditor A person who conducts an audit on a loan file.

Automatic funding A lender has the authority to fund a loan without going to the Department of Veterans Affairs for approval. If it was under direct endorsement, then it would be an FHA loan.

B

B paper See *Subprime loan.*

Back-end ratio Total housing payment plus all long-term debts divided by borrower's monthly gross income. All payments, housing and other, are referred to as back-end ratio.

Balance sheet A financial statement showing assets, liabilities, and the net worth as of a specific date.

Balloon payment The unpaid principal amount of a loan due at a certain date in the future; a lump sum amount due at the end of the term; when any one payment due is greater than twice the normal stated payment.

Balloon payment notice Prior written notice, as required by law, given to inform a borrower that a balloon payment will soon be due; the notice must include to whom the payment is made, the due date, refinance terms, and the amount of all interest principal and charges due.

Bankrupt A person, firm, or corporation who, through a court proceeding, is relieved from the payment of all debts after the surrender of all assets to a court-appointed trustee.

Bankruptcy Proceedings under federal law to relieve a debtor from insurmountable debt. The bankrupt's property is distributed by the court to the creditors as full satisfaction of the debts, in accordance with certain priorities and exemptions. Voluntary bankruptcy is petitioned by the debtor; involuntary, by the creditors.

Beneficiary (1) One for whose benefit a trust is created. (2) In states in which a deed of trusts is commonly used, the lender is called the beneficiary. In states that use a mortgage, the mortgagee is the party who benefits from the loan.

Bill of sale A document in writing that transfers title to personal property.

Binder policy A written evidence of temporary hazard or title insurance coverage that runs for only a limited time and must be replaced by a permanent policy.

biweekly fixed-rate loan A loan with payments due every two weeks, totaling 26 payments a year.

Blanket mortgage or blanket deed of trust A lien on more than one parcel or unit of land frequently incurred by subdividers or developers who have purchased a single tract of land for the purpose of dividing it into smaller parcels for sale or development.

Bona fide In good faith, without fraud.

Bond Written evidence of an obligation given by a corporation or government entity; a surety instrument.

Borrower One who receives funds with the expressed or implied intention of repaying the loan in full. One who borrows with a mortgage is a mortgagor. One who borrows with a trust deed is a trustor.

Borrower certification A form signed by a borrower attesting that he or she has no undisclosed loans.

Breach Violation of a legal obligation.

Broker The person who, for a commission or a fee, brings parties together and assists in negotiating contracts between them.

Business and Professions Code The regulations of California real estate statutes that govern the DOC and DRE commissioner's jurisdiction over real estate law, subdivisions, and licensees. Sections 10000 through 10581 comprise the real estate law, and Sections 11000 through 11200 regulate subdivisions.

Business structure The form of ownership of a business. Sole proprietorship, partnership, corporation, ECT.

Buy-down A loan made by a lender with a below-market interest rate in return for an interest rate subsidy in the form of money received from some source (builder, buyer, seller); may be temporary or permanent; often is a lump sum paid at the beginning of the loan; used to increase the yield on the loan for the investor.

Bylaws Rules and regulations, adopted by an association or corporation, that govern its activities.

C

California Housing Finance Agency (CHFA) Assists low- and moderate-income, first-time homebuyers in obtaining below-average interest rates favoring minority, women, and disabled veteran borrowers.

Cal Vet loans Real estate loans available by the California Department of Veterans Affairs to armed forces veterans at low interest rates.

Cap A limitation on the interest rate increase of the periodic rate, the lifetime rate, or both for an adjustable-rate mortgage.

Capital gains tax The tax on the taxable profit derived from the sale of a capital asset. The capital gain is the difference between the sale price and the basis of the property, after appropriate adjustments are made for closing costs, repair expenses, capital improvements, and allowable depreciation.

Capitalization The process of converting into present value a series of anticipated future installments of net income by discounting them into a present worth, using a specific desired rate of earnings.

Capitalization rate The rate that is believed to represent the proper relationship between the property value and the net income it produces.

Carryback financing Financing in which the seller of real property accepts a note or contract secured by the same real property as a part of his or her equity.

Cash flow The income from an investment after gross income is subtracted from all operating expenses, loan payments, and the allowance for the income tax attributed to the income.

Cash out (1) To take equity in cash; (2) paying off anyone who has an interest in property to end that person's interest; (3) to obtain a new loan on real property, giving the borrower cash above the amount of the loan payoff and the closing costs.

CC&Rs (covenants, conditions, and restrictions) A term used in some areas to describe limitations sometimes put on the use and enjoyment of real property, such as limiting the property to a single family or to a one-story dwelling.

Certificate of deposit (CD) A specific sum of money deposited into a savings institution for a specified period, usually bearing a higher rate of interest than a regular passbook account if left to maturity. Withdrawal privileges are restrictive, with higher costs.

Certificate of eligibility A document used by the DVA to certify a veteran's eligibility for a DVA loan. The veteran also needs a DD-214.

Certificate of reasonable value (CRV) A qualified appraisal report approved by the DVA, establishing maximum value for a DVA-guaranteed loan.

Certified copy A true copy, attested to be true by the officer holding the original.

Certified general appraiser An appraiser who has completed 3,000 hours of acceptable appraisal experience, of which 1,500 hours must be nonresidential and 2½ years (30 months) of experience plus specific educational requirements.

Certified residential appraiser An appraiser who has completed 2,500 hours of acceptable appraisal residential-property experience and 2½ years (30 months) of experience plus specific educational requirements.

Chain of title The history of all the documents transferring title to a parcel or real property, starting with the earliest existing document and ending with the most recent.

Child care statement Statement from the borrower(s) about who will take care of the underage children while the parents are at work.

Clear funds SB1550, passed in 1985, requires that escrow receive "clear funds" from the borrower and lender; that is, the funds must be cleared by the California bank handling the escrow settlement.

Close of escrow (C.O.E.) The conclusion or consummation of a transaction. In real estate closing, includes the delivery of a deed and documents, financial adjustments, the signing of notes, and the disbursement of funds necessary to the sale or loan transaction.

Closing The act of closing an escrow on a real estate transaction, which includes recording the transfer document (deed), preparing the settlement statements for the parties, and issuing the proceeds disbursements to various parties.

Closing costs Expenses incurred in the closing of a real estate transaction. Purchaser's expenses normally include cost of title examination, premiums for title policies, survey, attorney's fees, lender's service fees, and recording charges. In addition, the purchaser may have to place in escrow a sum of money to cover accrued real estate taxes and insurance.

Closing statement A financial disclosure accounting for all funds received and disbursed; includes the impound account, prorations, loans, and fees.

CLTA (California Land Title Association) A type of title insurance policy issued by a title insurance company for standard risk for the transfer of title ownership on real property; usually between a seller and a buyer.

Coborrower A person who signs a note in addition to the borrower to give extra security to the loan. The coborrower is jointly liable for the repayment of the loan.

Code of ethics A set of rules and principles expressing a standard of accepted conduct for a professional group and governing the relationship of members to each other and to the organization.

Coinsurance A sharing of insurance risk between insurer and insured, depending on the relation of the amount of the policy and a specified percentage of the actual value of the property insured at the time of the loss.

Collateral Any property pledged as security for a debt; the hypothecating of property.

Collection Procedure followed to bring the loan account current and to file the necessary notices to proceed with foreclosure when necessary.

Columnar records Prescribed by DRE Commissioner's Regulations 2831 and 2831.1, the trust fund escrow depository funds either (1) received and paid out or (2) received but not placed in a broker's trust account; in either case, a separate record for each beneficiary or transaction must be maintained by the broker.

Commercial bank A financial institution chartered by a state or the federal government to receive, lend, and safeguard money and other items of value.

Commercial loan A loan on property that is zoned for commercial use.

Commingling Mixing deposits or monies belonging to a principal with those of the broker or firm.

Commission An agent's fee for services provided on a real estate or loan transaction.

Commitment A written promise to make or insure a loan for a specified amount and on specified terms.

Common area The entire common-interest development except the separate interest therein.

Community property In some western and southwestern states, a form of ownership under which property acquired during a marriage is presumed to be owned jointly unless acquired in such manner as to be legally considered the separate property of either spouse.

Community reinvestment act Federal law requiring financial institutions to lend in communities served.

Comparables Also called comps; when comparable properties are used for comparative purposes in the appraisal process; facilities of approximately the same size and location with similar amenities; recently sold properties that have characteristics similar to the subject property under consideration, thereby indicating the approximate fair market value of the subject property.

Comparison approach A real estate appraisal method comparing a given property with similar or comparable surrounding properties; also called market comparison approach (CMA).

Compensation Income received for the performance of a service related to a mortgage loan.

Computer An electronic machine that performs high-speed mathematical or logical calculations or assembles, stores, correlates, or otherwise processes and prints information.

Computer software Software that is specifically designed to perform functions in association with a computer.

COMSTAR Allowable closing costs that a buyer may pay for an FHA loan; credit report, origination fee, mortgage insurance, settlement/escrow, title insurance, appraisal fee, recording fee.

Condition In contracts, a future and uncertain event that must happen to create an obligation or that extinguishes an existing obligation. In conveyances of real property, conditions in the conveyance may cause an interest to be vested or defeated.

Conditions prior to docs Items requested by the underwriter (lender/investor) for review prior to drawing the loan documents.

Conditions prior to funding Additional items needed by the lender/investor prior to funding the loan but after "prior to docs" conditions.

Condominium A form of ownership of real property. The owner receives title to a particular unit and a proportionate interest in certain common areas. A condominium generally defines each unit as a separately owned space to the interior surfaces.

Consideration Anything of value given to induce entering into a contract; it may be money, personal services, or even love and affection.

Constant The percentage of the original loan paid in equal annual payments that provide interest and principal reduction throughout the life of the loan.

Construction loan A short-term, interim loan for financing the cost of construction. The lender makes payments to the builder periodically as the work progresses.

Constructive notice Notice given by the public records.

Consumer Credit Protection Act A federal law created to protect consumers when credit reports are run.

Consumer finance lender (CFL) Consumer finance lenders fall into two groups. One group is for those who make both regulated and unregulated loans. The second group is for those who make only unregulated loans with specific dollar loan limitations.

Contingency The dependence upon a stated event that must occur before a contract is binding; in a purchase of a house, for example, contingent upon the buyer obtaining financing.

Continuing education To renew a state license pertaining to real estate, such as salesperson, broker, or appraisal licenses, an individual must complete specific hours of education within the license period.

Contract An oral or written agreement to do or not do a certain thing.

Conversion (1) Change from one legal form or use to another, as in converting an apartment building to condominium use; (2) the unlawful appropriation of another's property, as in the conversion of trust funds.

Convertible loan An adjustable-rate loan whereby the borrower can convert the loan to a fixed-rate loan during a predetermined period.

Conveyance An instrument in writing used to transfer (convey) title property from one person to another, such as a deed or a trust deed.

Cooperative A form of multiple ownership of real estate in which a corporation or business trust entity holds title to a property and grants the occupancy rights to particular apartments or units to shareholders by means of proprietary leases or similar arrangements.

Corporate broker A business entity acting under a corporation that performs real estate acts, in which at least one corporate officer is a licensed real estate broker.

Corporation An artificial person created by law with certain rights, privileges, and duties of natural persons.

Correspondent A mortgage banker who services real estate loans as a representative for the investor or owner of the loan or investor. Also applies to the mortgage banker's role as originator of mortgage loans.

Cosigner A person who signs a legal instrument and therefore becomes individually and jointly liable for repayment or performance of an obligation.

Cost approach An appraisal technique used to establish value by estimating the cost to reproduce the improvement, allowing for depreciation, and then adding in the fair market value of the land.

Covenant A legally enforceable promise or restriction in a contract, such as maintaining insurance. The breach of a covenant usually creates a default and can be the basis for foreclosure.

Cover letter A one-page document that should accompany all loan files at submission to a lender, describing what program they are submitting under and the positive features of the loan request.

Credit agencies Credit depositories that report their findings to credit agencies, which in turn compile the information to be furnished to banks, savings and loans, and mortgage loan bankers or brokers.

Credit authorization Document signed by the borrowers allowing the lender to check into their credit rating and payment history.

Credit rating score A credit rating score developed by the Fair, Isaac Company of San Rafael, California, to determine the risk of the borrower when making a loan. (See *FICO*.)

Credit report A report to a prospective lender on the creditworthiness of a prospective borrower or tenant.

CRV Certificate of reasonable value; appraisal report approved by the DVA.

Custodian An entity that holds for safekeeping loans and related documents backing a mortgage-backed security. A custodian may be required to examine and certify documents.

D

Damages The indemnity recoverable by a person who has sustained an injury, either in his or her person, property, or relative rights, through the act or default of another; loss sustained or harm done to a person or property.

DBA An acronym us to identify the term "doing business as."

DD214 The Department of Veterans affairs form DD214 is the request pertaining to military records, DVA standard form 180, printed by Government Printing Office, which is necessary to determine an individual's record of military service.

Dealer A seller, contractor, or supplier of goods or services in the case of property improvement loans or someone who engages in the business.

Debtor A person who is in debt; the one owing money to another.

Debt service The periodic payment of principal and interest earned on real property loans.

Deed A written legal document that transfers ownership of land from one party to another.

Deed in lieu of foreclosure A deed given by a borrower to a lender to satisfy a debt and avoid foreclosure.

Deed of reconveyance The transfer of legal title from the trustee to the trustor (borrower) after the trust deed debt is paid in full.

Deed of trust A recordable real property loan document. A type of security instrument conveying title in trust to a third party (trustee) for a particular piece of property; used to secure the payment of a trust note; a conveyance of the title to a trustee as collateral security for the payment of a debt, with the condition that the trustee will reconvey the title upon the payment of the debt, and with power of the trustee to sell the land and pay the debt in the event of a default on the part of the debtor.

Default Breach or nonperformance of a clause in either a note or mortgage that, if not cured, could lead to foreclosure.

Deferred interest When interest earned is not fully paid with the current payment and is postponed until some future date.

Deficiency judgment A court order to pay the balance owed on a loan if the proceeds from the sale of the security are insufficient to pay off the loan. Not allowed in all states.

Delinquent The status of a loan with a payment past due.

Delivery The legal, final, and absolute transfer of a deed from seller to buyer in such a manner that it cannot be recalled by the seller; a necessary requisite to the transfer of title; in mortgage lending, the physical transfer of loan documents to an investor or agent in conformance with the commitment.

Demand deposit A checking account or transaction deposit that can be withdrawn without any prior notice to the institution, as opposed to time deposit.

Department of Housing and Urban Development (HUD) The department of the federal government that is responsible for administering government housing and urban development programs.

Department of Veterans Affairs (DV) is under the department of Housing and urban development. It is the agency that oversees VA loans.

Depository Institutions Deregulation Committee (DIDC) A committee established by the U.S. Congress in 1980 to oversee the orderly phasing out of interest rate ceilings in depository institutions.

Depreciation A loss of value in real estate property brought about by age, physical deterioration, or functional or economic obsolescence. Broadly, a loss in value from any cause. The opposite of *appreciation*.

Developer A person or entity who prepares raw land for building sites and sometimes builds on the sites.

Direct endorsement A lender has the authority to fund a loan without going to the Federal Housing Administration (FHA) for approval. This is in contrast to automatic funding, which is for DVA loans.

Direct mail advertising A promotional medium sent directly to a target market by using the postal service.

Disbursements The payment of monies on a previously agreed-upon basis, such as construction loan draws or a title company payoff of an existing loan principal at the close of escrow.

Disclosure To reveal and make known specific facts about the property, the loan terms, environmental issues, or material facts that affect the value or desirability to complete a real estate transaction.

Discount In loan obligations, an amount withheld from loan proceeds by a lender. In secondary market sales, the amount by which the sale price of a note is less than the face value. The purpose is to adjust the yield upward, whether in lieu of interest or in addition to interest. The discount depends on money market conditions, the credit of the borrower, and the rate and terms of the note.

Discount point See *Point*.

Document correction compliance agreement A form signed by a prospective borrower allowing changes to be made to correct minor errors on documents.

Documentary transfer tax A tax applied to the transfer of real property. Notice of payment is usually entered on the face of the deed.

Down payment Of the purchase, the cash portion paid by a buyer from her or his own funds, as opposed to the amount financed.

Drawing docs The final step in drawing loan documents by the lender/investor.

DRE An acronym used to identify the Department of Real Estate.

Due-on-sale clause A type of acceleration clause calling for a debt under a loan to be due in its entirety upon transfer of ownership of the secured property. See *Alienation clause.*

DVA qualifications *Guidelines used in qualifying a veteran buyer.*

E

Earnest money See *Deposit.*

Earthquake disclosure A booklet entitled *The Homeowners Guide to Environmental Hazards and Earthquake Safety,* which includes the federal lead booklet. Approved by the California Seismic Safety Commission to comply with applicable government codes, which must be given to a prospective home purchaser in a real estate transaction.

Easement Right or interest in the land of another entitling the holder to a specific limited use, privilege, or benefit, such as utility company access.

Economics The study of the production of goods and services as related to real property.

Eminent domain The right of a government to take private property for public use upon payment of its fair value.

Employee A person who performs acts under the direction and supervision of an employer.

Encumbrance Anything that affects or limits the fee simple title to property, such as real estate loans, leases, easements, or restrictions.

Endorsement The act of the holder of a note, bill, check, or other negotiable instrument in assigning said instrument by signing the back of the instrument, with or without qualifications.

Energy Efficient Mortgage (EEM) A loan program intended to make the existing home stock more efficient through financing the installation of energy-saving improvements.

Environmental hazards A mandatory disclosure for potential hazards, including asbestos, lead-based paint and contaminates, methane, radon, other gases, fuel, oil or chemical storage tanks, contaminated soil or water, hazardous waste, waste disposal sites, electromagnetic fields, nuclear sources, and other substances, materials, products, or conditions. See *Earthquake disclosure.*

Equal Credit Opportunity Act (ECOA) A federal law that requires lenders and creditors to make credit equally available without discrimination based on race, color, religion, national origin, age, sex, marital status, receipt of income from public assistance programs, or reliance on any consumer protection law. Also known as Regulation B.

Equity financing Lender finances a high-ratio loan in exchange for a percentage of ownership and the right to share in the property's cash flow.

Equity loan A loan in the form of an extension of revolving credit on which real property serves as collateral.

Equity of redemption The common-law right to redeem property during the foreclosure period.

Errors and omissions (E&O) insurance A form of liability insurance that seeks to protect brokers and salespeople from errors, omissions, and mistakes made during the day-to-day course of business.

Escrow A transaction in which a third party, acting as the agent for the parties, carries out instructions for each party and assumes the responsibilities of handling the paperwork, accounting, and disbursement of funds.

Escrow instructions Instructions that are signed by each principal that enable an escrow agent to carry out the procedures necessary to enact business.

Escrow payment That portion of a loan payment held by the lender to pay for taxes, hazard insurance, mortgage insurance, lease payments, and other items as they become due. Known as *impounds.*

Estate The ownership interest of an individual in property.

Ethics A moral code that treats the duties a member of a profession or trade owes to the public, clients, partner, and professional peers; accepted standards of right and wrong.

Eviction The lawful expulsion of an occupant from real property.

Exceptions Matters excepted from the property conveyed, such as oil and gas rights or easements for specified purposes.

Exchange The trading of equity in a piece of property for the equity of another.

Execute To complete, make, perform, do, follow out; to execute or make a deed, including especially signing, sealing, and delivering; to execute a contract is to perform the contract; to follow out to the end; complete.

Extended coverage title Insurance coverage that extends beyond the basic coverage.

F

Face value The value of notes, loans, as stated on the face of the instrument and not considering any discounting.

Fair Credit Reporting Act A federal law giving a person the right to see his or her credit report.

Fair lending notice This document notifies the consumer of various credit-related laws and the rights of the individual under each of these laws.

Fair market value The price at which property is transferred between a willing buyer and a willing seller, each of whom has a reasonable knowledge of all pertinent facts and neither of whom is under any undue influence to buy or sell. Also called *arm's length transaction.*

Fannie Mae See *Federal National Mortgage Association (FNMA).*

Farmers Home Administration (FmHA) An agency within the Department of Agriculture that provides financing to farmers who are unable to obtain loans elsewhere. Funds are borrowed from the U.S. Treasury.

Federal Deposit Insurance Corporation (FDIC) The federal corporation insures against loss of deposits in banks, up to a maximum amount (currently $100,000 per account) or per authorized signator for multiple accounts in the same institution.

Federal home loan bank Provides credit reserves systems for member state and federal savings and loan associations.

Federal Reserve Board A seven-member board of governors, appointed by the president, along with the twelve Federal Reserve District banks, each with its own president, to oversee and administer the federal reserve system created under the Federal Reserve Act of 1913 (Web site http://www.federalreserve.gov).

Federal Trade Commission (FTC) A government agency that establishes rigid rules for advertising and labeling.

Fee simple An estate under which the owner is entitled to unrestricted powers to dispose of the property and that can be left by will or inherited; the greatest interest a person can have in real estate.

FHA mortgage A loan that is insured by the Federal Housing Administration.

FHA qualifications Guidelines used when qualifying an FHA buyer.

FHLMC See *Freddie Mac.*

FICO A credit score method developed by the Fair, Isaac Company. Used industrywide in determining the creditworthiness of a borrower.

Fictitious business name A company name in an unincorporated business.

Fidelity bond A security posted for the discharge of an obligation of personal services.

Fiduciary A person in a position of trust and confidence for another.

Finance company A limited-purpose financing entity organized and controlled by a builder for the purpose of facilitating the issuance of bonds.

Financial intermediary A financial institution that acts as an intermediary between savers and borrowers by selling its own obligations or serving as a depository and in turn lending the accumulated funds to borrowers.

Finder's fee A fee or commission paid to a broker for obtaining a loan for a client, referring a loan to a broker, or locating a property.

Fire insurance A hazard policy that covers losses to property caused by fire, smoke, or windstorm. May include endorsements or indemnification against perils for liability insurance, or contents.

Firm commitment A lender's agreement to make a loan to a specific borrower on a specific property.

FIRREA Financial Institutions Reform, Recovery, and Enforcement Act; federal legislation passed in 1989 to change the regulatory framework of financial institutions and appraisal practices; created the Savings Association Insurance Fund (SAIF) and the Bank Insurance Fund (BIF), both administered by the Federal Deposit Insurance Corporation (FDIC). The legislation also created the Resolution Trust Corporation (RTC), the agency charged with the management and sale of assets of failed savings and loans.

First mortgage or deed of trust A loan having priority over all other voluntary liens against certain property.

First-time home-buyers loan program A nongovernment, conventional loan program that requires a very low down payment to qualified borrowers, and income to debt ratios are higher.

Fixed-rate loan (FRM or FRL) A loan term in which the interest rate does not change.

Fixture Personal property that becomes real property.

Flipping The illegal act that involves repeated refinancing of a loan by rolling the balance of an existing loan into a new loan with new charges and fees.

Float The time between a lender's collection of payments from borrowers and the remittance of those funds to an investor.

Flood disaster insurance Insurance indemnifying against loss by flood damage. Required by lenders (usually banks) in areas federally designated as potential flood areas. The insurance is private but federally subsidized.

FNMA See *Fannie Mae.*

Foreclosure An authorized procedure taken by a lender under the terms of a loan for the purpose of having the property sold and the proceeds applied to the payment of a defaulted debt and authorized costs to sale.

Forfeiture Loss of money or anything else of value due to failure to perform.

Forgery A false signature of material alteration with intent to defraud. The forged signature of the grantor will not pass title regardless of recording or lack of knowledge by the grantee or future grantees.

Fraud The intentional and successful employment of any cunning, deception, collusion, or artifice used to circumvent, cheat, or deceive another person whereby that person acts upon it to the loss of property and to legal injury.

Fraud audit form A form used by underwriters to detect possible fraud in a loan file. A checklist.

Freddie Mac See *Federal Home Loan Mortgage Corporation.*

Front-end ratio House payment divided by the borrower's monthly gross income. Total housing payment is referred to as the "front-end ratio."

Full disclosure In real estate, a licensee must reveal known facts that materially affect the value or desirability of a property that may affect the decision of a buyer. A builder must give to a potential buyer the facts on a new development.

Full documentation file A loan file that has all documentation, 1003, credit report, appraisal, preliminary title report, VOD, VOE, VOM, pay stubs, W-2s.

Fully indexed note rate As related to adjustable-rate mortgages, the index value at application plus the gross margin stated in the note.

Fund into the month When a loan does not close by the end of the month, the lender is allowed to "fund into the next month," up to 5 days of the new month.

Funder A person within the lending institution who handles the final step in "funding" the loan for the lender/investor.

Funding The disbursement of funds to complete a transaction. In mortgage finance, it occurs when the lender provides money to close a real estate sale and when an investor transfers funds to the lender to purchase a mortgage loan.

G

Garnishment A proceeding that applies specified monies, wages, or property to a debt or creditor by proper statutory process against a debtor.

General lien (1) A lien such as a tax lien or judgment lien that attaches to all property of the debtor. (2) The right of a creditor to hold personal property of a debtor for payment of a debt not associated with the property being held.

Gift letter Required when part of the down payment is from other than the borrower's funds. It must state that the gift does not have to be repaid.

GI loans Also known as DVA loans. Common term for loans guaranteed by the Department of Veterans Affairs for qualified veterans. See *Department of Veterans Affairs.*

Ginnie Mae See *Government National Mortgage Association (GNMA).*

GNMA See *Government National Mortgage Association (GNMA).*

GNMA II Similar to GNMA certificates, except that the loans within the pool may have interest rates that may vary within 100 basis points.

Good faith Something done with good intentions, without knowledge of fraudulent circumstances, or reason to inquire further.

Government National Mortgage Association (GNMA) Handles government-backed real estate loan securities pooled on the secondary money market. Popularly known as *Ginnie Mae.*

Graduated equity or rapid amortization Fixed-rate long-term loan (25–40 years). The payments, however, are increased annually in negotiated amounts. The additional dollars are allocated to the outstanding principal, thereby paying the mortgage off earlier than planned (12–15 years).

Grant To transfer an interest in real property, either the fee or a lesser interest, such as an easement.

Grant deed A document used to transfer ownership title in real property that warrants against prior conveyances or encumbrances.

Grantee The person to whom an interest in real property is conveyed.

Grantor The person conveying an interest in real property.

Gross income Total income from property before any expenses are deducted, or the total income for a borrower, with no federal, state, or local taxes removed.

Gross margin With regard to an adjustable-rate mortgage, an amount expressed as percentage points, stated in the note, that is added to the current index value on the rate-adjustment date to establish the new note rate.

Gross rent multiplier (GRM) A figure used to compare rental properties to determine value. It gives the relationship between the gross rental income and the sales price.

Growing equity mortgage (GEM) A real estate loan that has monthly payments increasing according to an agreed-upon schedule to reduce the principal sooner for a shorter payoff.

Guaranteed loan A note to secure a loan guaranteed by DVA, FmHA, or other interested party.

H

Hard money loan A loan given in return for cash.

Hardship letter A letter written by the borrower, when funding into the first of the month, stating that it would create a severe hardship if the loan is not closed at once.

Hazard insurance A contract whereby an insurer, for a premium, undertakes to compensate the insured for loss on a specific property because of certain hazards.

Holder in due course One who has taken a note, check, or bill of exchange in due course (1) before it was overdue, (2) in good faith and for value, (3) without knowledge that it has been previously dishonored without notice of any defect when it was negotiated to him or her.

HOME A loan program that provides federal assistance to participating jurisdictions for housing rehabilitation, assistance to first-time homebuyers, and new construction or needed rental housing.

Home equity conversion mortgage The FHA 255 loan program by the Housing and Community Development Act that insures reverse mortgages, RAM, reverse annuity mortgage, for borrowers who are 62 or older. This allows older homeowners to convert their home equity into spendable dollars.

Home equity line of credit (HELOC) loan – This is a 2nd mortgage on your property. You can use the money for anything and deduct the interest. (A home equity line of credit (HELOC) is a form of revolving credit in which the property serves as collateral.)

Homeowners association (1) An association of people who own units in a given area, formed for the purpose of improving or maintaining the quality of the area; usually managed by a board of directors, often under recorded articles of incorporation, frequently with delegated duties contracted to a professional property management company. (2) An association formed by the builder of condominiums or planned-unit developments and required by statute in some states. The builder's participation and the duties of the association are controlled by statute.

Home ownership counseling A workshop conducted by FHA for first-time homebuyers to ensure that home ownership is right for them.

Homeowners Association An organization of the homeowners in a particular subdivision, planned unit development, or condominium: generally for the purpose of enforcing deed restrictions or managing the common elements of the development.

Homeowners insurance A multiple-peril policy commonly called a "package policy." It is available to owners of private dwellings and covers the dwelling and contents in case of fire or wind damage, theft, liability for property damage, and personal liability.

Homestead estate The property occupied by an owner that is protected by law up to a certain amount from attachment and sale for the claims of creditors.

HOP A loan program under the community development commission created to provide home ownership to low-income households in specific California counties.

HOPE Federal assistance for participating jurisdictions to help lower-income persons to acquire or rehabilitate single-family properties at affordable prices.

Housing affordability index Measures whether or not a typical family could qualify for a mortgage loan on a typical home.

Housing expense Those expenses that directly relate to the house payment: PITI, association dues, flood insurance, earthquake insurance, leased land payments.

Housing Financial Discrimination Act The lender must provide a fair lending notice to the applicant. The notice explains that it is illegal to discriminate on the basis of race, color, religion, sex, marital status, national origin, or ancestry.

HUD The Department of Housing and Urban Development, which is responsible for the implementation and administration of rentals, loans, and home purchase programs. The broad range of programs includes community planning and development, housing production and mortgage credit (FHA), equal opportunity in housing, and research and technology.

Hypothecate To give a thing as security without the necessity of giving up possession of it; to pledge property on the promise to repay.

I

Impound account Account held by a lender for payment of items such as property taxes, hazard insurance, and mortgage insurance. The debtor pays a portion of the anticipated yearly expense with each monthly payment. The lender pays the actual bill from the accumulated funds. See *Escrow payment.*

Income That which can be verified by a neutral third party is classified as income. Examples are wages, rents, interest and dividend income, and social security compensation.

Income approach to value The appraisal technique used to estimate real property value by capitalizing net income. See *Capitalization.*

Income property Real estate developed or improved to produce income.

Income ratio The monthly payment on a loan, including principal and interest, taxes, and insurance, divided by the borrower's monthly gross income.

Incompetent A person who is unable to care for himself or herself, such as a minor; one who is declared incompetent by a court. A contract with an incompetent person is void.

Independent contractor A person who acts for another but who sells final results and whose methods of achieving those results are not subject to the control of another.

Index An economic measurement that is used to measure periodic interest rate adjustments for an adjustable-rate loan.

Installment loan The regular periodic payment that a borrower agrees to make to the lender or to the loan-servicing agency.

Institutional lender Financial institutions such as a savings banks, life insurance companies, commercial banks, and savings and loan associations.

Instrument Any writing having legal form and significance, such as a deed, mortgage, will, or lease.

Insurance A contract for indemnification against loss.

Insured loan A loan insured by FHA or a private mortgage insurance company.

Interest Consideration in the form of money paid for the use of money, usually expressed as an annual percentage. Also, a right, share, or title in property.

Interest-only loan A straight nonamortized loan in which only interest is paid. Interest can be paid periodically when the principal is paid in a lump sum. See *Straight note.*

Interest-only note The monthly payment will consist of interest-only payments and no principal. At the term of the note, all of the principal is due.

Interest rate The percentage of an amount of money that is paid for its use for a specified time to the investors as a return on the investment. Usually expressed as an annual percentage.

Intermediary Financial institutions that act as middlemen for savers, depositors, and investors.

Intestate To die leaving no valid will.

Inventory The loans a lender has closed but has not yet delivered to an investor.

Investor The holder of a real estate loan or the permanent lender for whom a real estate lender services the loan. Any person or institution investing in real estate lenders.

J

Joint protection policy A policy of title insurance that insures both the owner and the lender under the same policy.

Joint tenancy An equal undivided ownership of property by two or more persons whose survivors take the interest upon the death of any one of them.

Joint venture An association between two or more parties to own or develop real estate formed for a specific purpose and duration.

Judgment That which has been adjudicated, allowed, or decreed by a court.

Judgment lien A lien upon the property of a debtor, resulting from the decree of a court.

Jumbo loan Amount of loan exceeding the maximum *FNMA* and *FHLMC* loan limits. See *Nonconforming loan.*

L

Land contract A contract ordinarily used in connection with the sale of property if the seller does not wish to convey title until all or a certain part of the purchase price is paid by the buyer.

Landlord Owner or lessor of real property.

Lane Guide A publication used to locate employers, banks, and savings and loans to ensure the proper delivery of verifications for employment or loan information.

Late fee An additional charge a borrower is required to pay as penalty for failure to pay a regular installment when due.

Lead-based paint A warning statement required to be given to every purchaser or tenant of residential property built prior to 1978 that may present exposure to lead from paint.

Lease A written document under which the possession, use, and quiet enjoyment to property is given by the owner to another for a stated period for a stated consideration under specific conditions.

Leasehold An interest in real property held by virtue of a lease; less-than-freehold.

Lease purchase agreement Buyer makes a deposit for the future purchase of a property, with the right to lease the property during the interim.

Legal description A property description recognized by law that is sufficient to locate and identify the property without oral testimony.

Lessee (tenant) The person(s) holding right of possession and use of property under terms of a lease.

Lessor (landlord) The one leasing property to a lessee.

Leverage The use of borrowed money to increase the return on a cash investment. For leverage to be profitable, the rate of return on the investment must be higher than the cost of the money borrowed (interest plus amortization).

Liability A general term encompassing all types of debts and obligations.

Lien A legal hold or claim of one person on the property of another as security for a debt or charge; the right given by law to satisfy a debt.

Life insurance company A business that collects a person's savings by selling contracts (policies) paid for through periodic premiums to provide cash payment upon death.

Limited partnership A business entity that consists of one or more general partners who are fully liable, along with one or more limited partners who are liable only up to the amount of their investment.

Line of credit An agreement by a financial institution to extend credit up to a certain amount for a certain time to a specific borrower.

Liquid assets Cash or assets immediately convertible to cash.

Liquidity Cash position based on assets that can readily be converted to cash.

Listing An employment contract between principal and agent authorizing the agent to perform services for the principal involving the owner's property. Listing contracts are entered into for the purpose of securing persons to buy, lease, or rent property. Employment of an agent by a prospective purchaser or lessee to locate property for purchase or lease may be considered a listing, called a buyer-broker agreement.

Loan A sum of money loaned, often called principal balance.

Loan administration Mortgage bankers not only originate loans but also "service" them from origination to maturity of the loan.

Loan assumption Agreement by a buyer to assume the liability under an existing note secured by a real estate loan. The lender usually must approve the new debtor in order to release the existing debtor (usually the seller) from liability.

Loan commitment Lender's contractual commitment to a loan based on the appraisal and underwriting.

Loan committee A committee or one individual in a lending institution who reviews loan applications and either approves or disapproves.

Loan correspondent See *Correspondent.*

Loan docs A term used when referring to the loan documents.

Loan doc audit sheet A form used in the loan document department of a lender/investor to ensure that all items are in a loan file and that the documents are in compliance with all rules and regulations.

Loan fee A charge made by a lender for originating the loan; included in closing costs.

Loan limits The maximum amount of money that can be loaned under a specific loan program.

Loan package The file of all items necessary for the lender to decide to give or not give a loan. These items include the information on the prospective borrower (loan application, credit report, financial statement, employment letters, etc.) and information on the property (appraisal, survey, etc.). There may be a charge for "packaging" the loan.

Loan submission A package of pertinent papers and documents about a specific property or properties. It is delivered to a prospective lender for review and consideration for the purpose of making a mortgage loan.

Loan-to-value ratio (LTV) The ratio of the loan principal (amount borrowed) to the property's appraisal value (selling price). On a $100,000 home with a loan principal of $80,000, the LTV is 80%.

Loan underwriting The process of approving or disapproving loan applications.

Loan verifier The person who completes the loan title insurance company wire transfer instruction form; the individual who indicates that each item required is completed.

London Inter-Bank Offering Rate An international rate compiled in London by using the interest rates of ARMs sold in Europe.

M

Margin ratio The number of basis points a lender adds to an index to determine the interest rate of an adjustable-rate loan.

Market approach or market comparison An appraisal method to establish value.

Market value The highest price that a buyer, willing but not compelled to buy, would pay and the lowest a seller, willing but not compelled to sell, would accept.

Marketable title A title that a well-informed and prudent buyer of real estate would accept.

Marketing Any type of message that promotes communication of a product, service, or idea.

Maturity The terminating or due date of a note, time, draft, acceptance, bill of exchange, or bond. The date a time instrument or indebtedness becomes due and payable.

Maximum loan amount That maximum loan amount that may be set by the loan program that the borrower is applying for (FNMA/FHLMC, FHA, DVA).

Mechanic's lien A lien, created by statute, that exists against real property in favor of persons who have performed work or furnished materials for the improvement of the real property.

Mello-Roos A method of financing government entities (city, counties, school districts, and other special districts) by the use of bond money. Bond is usually 20 to 40 years and is not tax deductible.

Memorandum items Items placed into escrow instructions for information purposes only. The escrow company does not accept any liability for the items placed into the escrow instructions.

MGIC Referred to as Magic; a vehicle to provide a mortgage to borrowers with less than 20% available as a down payment. Mortgage Guarantee Insurance Corporation sells an insurance policy to the lender, paid for by the borrower, to protect the lender in the event of default.

Minor All persons under 18 years of age.

Misrepresentation A false or misleading statement or assertion.

Mobile home As defined in the Business and Professions Code Section 10131.6(c), a structure transportable in one or more sections, designed and equipped to contain not more than two dwelling units to be used with or without a foundation system; it does not include a recreational vehicle.

Modification The act of changing any of the terms of a real estate note.

Mortgage An instrument given by a borrower (mortgagor) to a lender (mortgagee) in real property given as security for the payment of a debt.

Mortgage-backed securities Bondlike investment securities representing an undivided interest in a pool of real estate loans. Income from the underlying loan is used to pay off the securities. See *GNMA mortgage-backed securities.*

Mortgage banker A firm or individual active in the field of mortgage banking. Mortgage bankers, as local representatives of regional or national institutional lenders, act as correspondents between lenders and borrowers. Mortgage bankers need to borrow the funds they lend.

Mortgage banking The packaging of real estate loans secured by real property to be sold to a permanent investor with servicing retained for the life of the loan for a fee. The origination, sale, and servicing of mortgage loans by a firm or individual. The investor correspondent system is the foundation of the mortgage banking industry.

Mortgage broker A firm or individual bringing the borrower and lender together and receiving a commission. A mortgage broker does not retain servicing.

Mortgage company A private corporation (sometimes called a *mortgage banker*) whose principal activity is the origination and servicing of mortgage loans that are sold to other financial institutions.

Mortgage credit certificate (MCC) A loan program that offers a first-time homebuyer a federal income tax credit, which reduces the amount of federal taxes the holder of the certificate pays.

Mortgage guaranty insurance Insurance against financial loss, available to mortgage lenders from private mortgage insurance companies.

Mortgagee A person or firm to whom property is conveyed as security for a real estate mortgage loan. The lender under a mortgage.

Mortgage insurance The function of mortgage insurance, whether government or private, is to insure a mortgage lender against loss caused by a mortgagor's default. This insurance may cover a percentage or virtually all the mortgage loan, depending on the type of mortgage insurance.

Mortgage insurance premium (MIP) The consideration paid by a borrower for mortgage insurance either to FHA or a private mortgage insurance (PMI) company; required on FHA loans to insure the lender against loss. Annual premium is ½% of the loan balance each year, divided by 12 and collected monthly with the loan payment.

Mortgage loan disclosure statement A document that provides a prospective borrower with information about loan features, such as a balloon payment on a short-term loan; limits the amount of commission and fees charged for relatively small loan amounts. See *Article 7*.

Mortgage note A written promise to pay a sum of money at a stated interest rate during a specified term. It is secured by a mortgage.

Mortgagor One who borrows money, giving a mortgage on real property as security (a debtor).

Multifamily housing Buildings with five or more residential units.

Mutual mortgage insurance (MMI) One of four FHA insurance funds into which all mortgage insurance premiums and other specified revenue of the FHA are paid and from which any losses are met.

Mutual savings bank A savings bank originated in the New England states in which the depositors place their savings, with the right to borrow money for home loans; there are no mutual savings banks in California.

My Community Mortgage Loan is an FNMA community home-buyer loan that offers low mortgage insurance, with no additional loan-level price adjustment.

N

Negative cash flow Cash expenditures of an income-producing property in excess of the cash receipts.

Negotiable Capable of being negotiated; assignable or transferable in the ordinary course of business.

Net income The difference between effective gross income and expenses, including taxes and insurance. The term is qualified as net income before depreciation and debt service.

Net worth The value of all assets, including cash, less total liabilities. It is often used as an underwriting guideline to indicate an individual's creditworthiness and financial strength.

Net yield The part of gross yield that remains after the deduction of all costs, such as servicing, and any reserves for losses.

News release Information given to the press to promote the name or recognition of an individual or a firm.

Nominal interest rate The percentage of interest stated in loan documents.

Non-conforming loan Any loan that exceeds FNMA or FHLMC loan limits.

Noninstitutional lender Lenders on real estate loans other than banks, insurance companies, and savings and loan associations.

Nontraditional mortgage credit report A credit report used in place of a traditional credit report. Generally used when the borrower has not established any form of traditional credit.

Notary public An appointed officer with authority to take the acknowledgment of persons executing documents, to sign the certificate, and to affix a seal (notarize).

Note A signed instrument acknowledging a debt and a promise to repay per the items outlined.

Note rate This rate determines the amount of interest charged annually to the borrower; also called the accrual rate, contract rate, or coupon rate.

Note repurchase When a mortgage loan has gone bad that was submitted by a mortgage broker, the mortgage broker may be required to purchase it back from the lender/investor.

Notice (1) Actual notice is express or implied knowledge of a fact; (2) constructive notice is a fact, imputed to a person by law, that should have been discovered because of the person's actual notice of circumstances and the inquiry that a prudent person would have been expected to make; (3) legal notice is information required to be given by law.

Notice of default (NOD) A notice recorded after the occurrence of a default under a real estate loan or a notice required by an interested third party insuring or guaranteeing a loan.

Notice of delinquency (NOD) CC Section 2924e allows a junior lien holder to file a "request for notice of delinquency" with any senior lien holder on one to four units to be advised if the borrower becomes delinquent on the loan payment; permission of the borrower is required.

Notice of sale (NOS) A public notice given when a property that has gone into foreclosure is now going to the final sale.

Null and void Of no legal validity or effect.

O

Obsolescence The loss of value of a property occasioned by going out of style, by becoming less suitable for use, or by other economic influences.

Occupancy affidavit A document signed by borrowers stating that they will occupy a property within a certain period of time from the date of closing the loan.

OREA (Office of Real Estate Appraisal) State of California agency that handles the licensing of real estate appraisers.

Office layout The placement of furniture, fixtures, and equipment to facilitate the workflow of loan personnel.

Omnibus Reconciliation Act An act that limited housing revenue bond tax exemptions for certain loans.

Option A contract agreement granting a right to purchase, sell, or otherwise contract for the use of a property at a stated price during a stated period of time.

Origination The process by which the lender brings into being a loan secured by real property; the process of originating real estate loans. Solicitation may be from individual borrowers, builders, or brokers.

Origination fee A fee or charge for the work involved in the evaluation, preparation, and submission of a proposed real estate loan.

Originator A person who solicits builders, brokers, and others to obtain applications for mortgage loans.

P

Package loan A real estate loan that includes items that are technically personal property, called chattels, such as appliances, carpeting, and drapery.

Packing Requiring high-cost fees, such as high-cost credit insurance, as a term of the loan.

Paper Term used by real estate agents, investors, and others to designate promissory notes, usually secured by trust deeds and mortgages.

Par or par pricing The cost of a loan in which the loan broker does not have to pay the lender or investor to receive a certain interest rate, nor does the broker receive a rebate for delivering a loan to the lender or investor at a higher yield above par.

Participation Also called equity participation or revenue sharing. An agreement in which the property owner and the lender agree that the lender will share in some future income from the property; may be a part of the sales price or income generated. In addition to base interest on mortgage loans on income properties, a percentage of gross income is required, sometimes predicated on certain conditions being fulfilled, such as a minimum occupancy or a percentage of net income after expenses, debt service, and taxes.

Payment adjustment date With regard to an adjustable-rate loan, the date the borrower's monthly principal and interest payment may change.

Payment cap With regard to an adjustable-rate loan, a limit on the amount of increase in the borrower's monthly principal and interest at the payment adjustment date, if the principal and interest increase called for by the interest rate increase exceeds the payment cap percentage. This limitation is often at the borrower's option and may result in negative amortization.

Payment factor A factor used to calculate the monthly principal and interest payment on a mortgage. Example: The payment factor for a 30-year mortgage at 7.0% interest rate is 6.653025 per thousand of the loan amount. (Take the payment factor, 6.653025 times the loan amount, $145,000 = 96468862 *or* $964.69 PI per month).

Penalty An extra payment or charge required of the borrower for deviating from the terms of the original loan agreement. Usually levied for being late in making a regular payment or for paying off the loan before it is due.

Periodic Caps Used in adjustable rate loans. The interest rate will have specific dates in which the interest rate can go up and there will be a cap to the rate.

Personal property Any property that is not real property.

P&I (principal and interest) Also called debt service; that part of a mortgage payment that consists of payment of some principal and some interest on the loan.

PITI (principal, interest, taxes, and insurance) The principal and interest payment on most loans is fixed for the term of the loan; the tax and insurance portion may be adjusted to reflect changes in taxes or insurance costs.

Planned-unit development (PUD) A real estate project in which each unit owner has title to a residential lot and building and nonexclusive easement on the common areas of the project.

Pledge The depositing of personal property by a debtor with a creditor as security for a debt or engagement.

Point An amount equal to 1% of the principal amount of an investment or note. Loan discount points are a one-time charge assessed at closing by the lender to increase the yield on the mortgage loan to a competitive position with other types of investments.

Pool A group of real estate loans that back an issue of mortgage-backed securities. Also, the act of packaging loans with similar characteristics for sale in the secondary mortgage market.

Portfolio Investments (including real estate loans and securities) held by an individual or institution. The term also refers to real estate loans held by a lender prior to their sale in the secondary market to lenders for investment purposes and to loans that a lender continues to service for investors.

Preapproval A loan broker's submission of verified income and expenses plus cash on hand to an investor to receive preapproval for a loan based on specific guidelines of a given loan program.

Predatory lending Abusive practice of targeting subprime borrowers, the elderly, and low-income communities by charging excessive fees and interest rates far beyond the risk incurred. Practices include steering, unnecessary insurance, flipping, hidden balloon, and prepayment penalties.

Preliminary title report (prelim) A report issued by the title company as a worksheet for escrow, such as listing all liens of record, judgments, CC&Rs, and delinquent property taxes.

Premium The amount, often stated as a percentage, paid in addition to the face value of a note or bond.

Prepayment Payment in full on a real estate loan, due either to a sale of the property or to foreclosure and, in either case, before the loan has been fully amortized.

Prepayment penalty A fee charged a borrower who prepays a loan before it is due. Not allowed for FHA or DVA loans; is charged on Cal Vet loans paid off during the first years; may be charged on conventional loans. Often calculated as six months' interest on the unpaid loan balance after 20% is first deducted. The formula is 80% × unpaid loan amount × loan interest rate/6 mo = prepayment penalty. Also referred to as a "transaction fee."

Prepayment privilege The right given a purchaser to pay all or part of a debt prior to its maturity. The mortgagee cannot be compelled to accept any payment other than those originally agreed to.

Prequalifying The act performed by a lender to determine the creditworthiness of a prospective borrower prior to formal loan application; may be based upon a credit report and preliminary income and expense data.

Present value The lump sum value today of an annuity.

Price level adjusted mortgage (PLAM) A loan program in which the outstanding principal balance is adjusted in constant dollars, with adjustments in both the monthly payment and the outstanding principal, on an annual basis.

Primary loan insurance Type of insurance for loans with minimal down payments, usually less than 20%. Provided by the Federal Housing Administration or private mortgage insurance companies.

Primary mortgage market The market in which lenders originate real estate loans by making direct loans to homebuyers. See also *Secondary mortgage market.*

Prime rate The minimum interest rate charged by a commercial bank on short-term loans made to its largest and strongest clients, with the highest credit standing; used as a base rate for loans; determined by the rates banks pay for money they lend to their prime borrowers.

Principal Amount of debt, not including interest. The face value of a note or loan.

Principal balance The outstanding balance of a loan, exclusive of interest and any other charges.

Principle The laws, doctrines, rules of conduct and written norms of real estate practice.

P&I (principal and interest) That portion of a homebuyer's monthly payments to the lender that composes the debt service on the loan. See *T&I.*

Prior to documents Conditions in which the mortgage company receives the loan approval, in which the investor has made stipulation on the loan, which are items needed, before drawing the loan documents. For example, current pay stubs, possible corrections to an appraisal.

Prior to funding Conditions set by the investor of items needed before funding the loan. For example, quality control review, telephone verifications, and backup credit report. See *Prior to documents.*

Priority As applied to claims against property, status of being prior or having precedence over other claims. Priority is usually established by filing or recordation in point of time but may be established by statute or agreement.

Privacy Act First enacted in 1976 and revised in 2001. Discloses who has access to financial records held by a financial institution or department store.

Private mortgage insurance (PMI) Insurance written by a private company protecting the mortgage lender against loss occasioned by a mortgage default; used on conventional loans to insure the lender against loss. Generally, all loans above an 80% loan-to-value (LTV) ratio require PMI.

Processing The steps taken to prepare a loan file for submission to an underwriter, including ordering all verifications.

Profit and loss statement An official quarterly or annual financial document published by a public company, showing earnings, expenses, and net profit.

Promissory note See *Note.*

Promotional note A lien on real property in a subdivision made by a real property securities dealer.

Property Assessed Clean Energy (PACE) Enable local governments to finance renewable energy and energy efficiency projects on private property, including residential, commercial, and industrial properties.

Property profile A packet furnished by the title company on a subject property that lists ownership, liens recorded, demographics of the area, and recent property sales information.

Proposition 13 A property tax initiative that set the base tax rate for residential and commercial properties.

Proration Adjustments of interest, taxes, and insurance on a pro rata basis as of the closing date.

Public Employees Retirement System (PERS) A California loan program for employees of public entities for purchase or refinance of a home.

PUD See *planned-unit development.*

Purchase money A loan given by a lender to a purchaser of real property to finance the purchase of real estate; often an extension of credit to the borrower by the seller.

Purpose of loan letter When you are refinancing a property and receiving more than $1,000 cash back, the investor will generally require a written statement from the borrowers on what the additional funds will be used for.

Q

Qualifying worksheet A document used by mortgage brokers to work up income and expenses for a potential borrower.

Quality control A system of safeguards to ensure that all loans are originated, processed, underwritten, closed, and serviced according to the lender's and an investor's standards.

Quit claim deed A deed that transfers (with no warranty) only such interest, title, or right a grantor may have at the time the conveyance is executed.

R

Rate lock The lender will "lock" the interest rate for a period of time.

Rate of return The yield expressed as a percentage of the total investment.

Rate reduction refinance A DVA program in which the veteran may transfer entitlement used on an existing loan to a new DVA loan at a reduction in the interest rate. The veteran may receive no cash proceeds.

Ratio A formula used to ascertain whether a borrower would qualify for a specific loan program, after determining the percentage of down payment; for example, 32/38 with a 20% down payment.

Real estate investment trust (REIT) A financial intermediary that can own and hold loans on real estate and pass on earnings from these assets free of income tax to the corporation but taxable to shareholders.

Real estate law See *Business and Professions Code.*

Real estate owned (REO) A term frequently used by lending institutions as applied to ownership of real property acquired for investment or as a result of foreclosure.

Real property Land appurtenances, including anything of a permanent nature, such as structures, trees, minerals, and the interest, benefits, and inherent rights thereof.

Real property security Formerly under DRE Article 6, is now regulated by DOC; regulates the sales of notes to investors.

Realtor® A real estate broker or an associate holding active membership in a local real estate board affiliated with the National Association of Realtors®.

Reconciliation The step in which the broker verifies the bank statement with the accounting system to balance entries, which must be performed at least once every 30 days.

Reconveyance The transfer of the title of land from one person to the immediately preceding owner. It is used when the performance of debt is satisfied under the terms of a deed of trust.

Record date The date that determines who is the holder of record entitled to receive payment of principal, interest, and any prepayment from the servicer or custodian.

Recorder The public official in a political subdivision who keeps records of transactions affecting real property in the area. Sometimes known as the county clerk.

Recording The noting in the registrar's office of the details of a properly executed legal document, such as a deed, mortgage, a satisfaction of mortgage, or an extension of mortgage, thereby making it a part of the public record.

Recourse The right of the holder of a note secured by a real estate loan to look personally to the borrower or endorser for payment, not just to the property. In the secondary mortgage market, the forced repurchase of a defaulted loan or note by the seller.

Red flags A list of items developed by the Federal National Mortgage Association (FNMA) to detect possible fraud in a loan application.

Referral fee A fee paid to a licensed person for referring business to the lender.

Refinance (1) Renewal of an existing loan with the same borrower and lender; (2) a loan on the same property by either the same lender or same borrower; (3) the selling of loans by the original lender.

Regulation B See *Equal Credit Opportunity Act (ECOA)*.

Regulation C Home Mortgage Disclosure Act (HMDA).

Regulation X A federal law enforced by HUD that requires lenders to provide loan applicants with five types of disclosures relating to settlement costs in connection with applications for federally related mortgage loans used to purchase or refinance one- to four-unit residential property and the principal residence of the borrower.

Regulation Z See *Truth-in-lending*.

Reinstate Cure a default under a note secured by a deed of trust.

REIT See *Real estate investment trust*.

Release clause Stipulation that upon the payment of a specific sum of money to the holder of a trust deed or mortgage, the lien of the instrument as to a specific described lot or area shall be removed from the blanket lien on the whole area involved.

Relief provision A formal arrangement designed to help a borrower resolve a delinquency.

Rent Consideration paid for use or occupancy of property, buildings, or dwelling units.

Rent with option A contract that gives one the right to lease property at a certain sum with the option to purchase at a future date.

Required yield An investor's required yield. It is quoted on a net basis; that is, it does not include the lender's servicing fee.

Rescission The cancellation or annulment of a transaction or contract by the operation of law or by mutual consent.

Reserves See *Escrow payment*.

Reserve requirement (1) Under bank regulations, sets the minimum reserves each bank must hold to customer deposits and notes, influencing the country's economy, borrowing, and interest rates; (2) under lender criteria, requires the borrowers have a cash reserve that is used as an indicator of financial stability for the loan.

Residence A place where someone lives.

Residential home loan A real estate loan covering a one- to four-family dwelling; larger residential buildings are classified as multifamily housing loans.

Residential loan application Also known as the 1003 and the URLA. This is the application that is completed by a borrower(s) to apply for a real estate loan.

Residual income Under DVA loans, residual income is that income that is left over for family support after all debts have been accounted for, PITI, and long-term debts.

Resolution Trust Corporation (RTC) See *FIRREA*.

Restriction A limitation on the use of real property. Property restrictions fall into two general classifications: public and private. Zoning ordinances are examples of the former type. Restrictions may be created by private owners, typically by appropriate clauses in deeds or in agreements or in general plans of entire subdivisions. Usually, they assume the form of a covenant, or promise, to do or not to do a certain thing.

Return Profit from an investment; the yield.

Reverse annuity mortgage (RAM) A type of loan for an owner-occupied property, with a borrower at least 62 years of age, based on the equity in the property.

Reversion A right to future possession retained by an owner at the time of a transfer of an owner's interest in real property.

Reviewer An individual employed to verify the credit, source of funds, vesting, preliminary title report, liens, legal description, and appraisal report; duties may be performed by reviewer, processor, or junior underwriter.

S

Sales contract Another name for a sales agreement or purchase agreement; not to be confused with a land contract, which is a conditional sales contract.

Salesperson A person working under a DRE broker and performing acts for which a license is required.

Satisfaction Discharge of a mortgage or trust deed from the records upon payment of the debt.

Savings and loan association A mutual or stock association chartered and regulated by either the federal government or a state. S&Ls accept time deposits and lend funds primarily on residential real estate.

Savings Association Insurance Fund (SAIF) See *FIRREA.*

Second See *Junior lien.*

Secondary financing Financing real estate with a loan or loans subordinate to a first mortgage or first trust deed.

Secondary mortgage market A market in which existing real estate loans are bought and sold. It contrasts with the primary mortgage market, in which mortgages are originated. See *Primary mortgage market.* Also known as the secondary money market.

Second mortgage/second trust Junior mortgage or junior lien; an additional loan imposed on property with a first mortgage, generally at a higher interest rate and for a shorter term than a first mortgage.

Secured party The party holding a security interest or lien; on real estate, referred to as the mortgagee or beneficiary.

Securities and Exchange Commission (SEC) The federal agency that regulates securities and the securities business. It is involved in real estate lending.

Securities dealer An individual who undertakes to transact business on behalf of another for loans secured by real property notes.

Security The collateral given, deposited, or pledged to secure the fulfillment of an obligation or payment of a debt.

Security instrument The mortgage or trust deed evidencing the pledge of real estate security as distinguished from the note or other credit instrument.

Security interest According to the Uniform Commercial Code, security interest designates the interest of the creditor in the property of the debtor in all types of credit transactions. It thus replaces such terms as chattel mortgage, pledge, trust receipt, chattel trust, equipment trust, conditional sale, and inventory lien.

Seller carryback loans (soft money) The money to be financed as part of the purchase price in which the seller is the beneficiary and the buyer is the trustor. See *Purchase money.*

Seller concessions On a DVA loan, a seller may pay for veteran-buyer closing costs. Anything of value added to the transaction by the seller for which the buyer pays no additional amount and for which the seller is not normally required to pay or provide.

Servicer An entity who has the responsibility for collecting payments, reporting credit information, relating loan delinquency to the investor, and maintaining impound account records.

Servicing fee The compensation a lender receives from an investor each month for servicing loans on its behalf.

Servicing loans The duties of the lender as a loan correspondent as specified in the servicing agreement, for which a fee is received. The collection for an investor of payments, interest, principal, and trust items such as hazard insurance and taxes on a note by the borrower in accordance with the terms of the note. Servicing also consists of operational procedures covering accounting, bookkeeping, insurance, tax records, loan payment follow-up, delinquency loan follow-up, and loan analysis.

Servicing retained Retention of the rights to service a loan when the loan is sold in the secondary market.

Settlement See *Closing.*

Shared appreciation mortgage (SAM) Type of loan in which the borrower and lender share in the appreciation upon the sale of the property. If a purchase price is $125,000 with a loan of $100,000 and then the property is sold for $175,000 with a loan of $95,000, the borrower and lender would share in the $80,000 profit from appreciation.

Shared equity mortgage (SEM) Type of loan in which the borrower and lender share in the equity in the property upon its sale. If the purchase price is $125,000 with a loan of $100,000 and the property is sold for $175,000 with a remaining loan balance of $95,000, the borrower and lender would share in the $5,000 equity, 50-50. The appreciation of $50,000 would remain with the lender. Note: True equity is derived by the principal reduction of the mortgage.

Small Business Administration (SBA) A nonprofit organization that will help small businesses get started.

Smoke detector compliance California law for every single-family dwelling unit sold or rented after January 1, 1986, to have an operable smoke detector (Health and Safety Code 13113.8).

Southern California Home Financing Authority Created by the Community Development Commission to provide tax-exempt mortgage revenue bonds that are sold to Fannie Mae to provide financing for first-time homebuyers.

Special assessment A tax levied against property to pay for all or part of an improvement that will benefit the property being assessed.

Specific performance A remedy in a court of equity compelling the defendant to carry out the terms of an agreement or contract.

Spread The difference between the average rate at which money can be borrowed and the average rate at which it can be lent.

Standard commitment An agreement to sell or swap loans based on an investor's posted yields, rather than on negotiated terms.

Standard refinance loan A DVA loan to refinance an existing loan in which the veteran may receive cash proceeds if the new loan amount does not exceed 90% of the CRV.

Statement of information (SI) Also known as a statement of identity. A document that covers the last 10 years of residence and employment, used by the title company to eliminate any derogatory items that may show up in the public records. Very helpful when people with common names are involved.

Steering Deliberately placing a borrower with good credit into a loan with high interest.

Straight note A loan with periodic payments of interest only; the principal sum is due in one lump sum upon maturity. No payment due until maturity at which time the entire principle and interest is due.

Streamline documentation file When a borrower has a current FHA loan and wishes to reduce the interest rate, the new FHA loan is called a "streamline" loan, with or with an appraisal.

"Subject to" When a purchaser buys "subject to" the existing loan(s) but does not endorse the same or assume to pay the loans. See *Assumption.*

Subject to conditions An underwriter can approval a loan "subject to conditions," meaning additional documentation is needed to furnish final loan approval.

Subordinate To make subject to or junior to.

Subordination The act of a party acknowledging by written recorded instrument that a debt due is inferior to the interest of another in the same property. Subordination may apply not only to real estate loans but also to leases, real estate rights, and any other type of debt instruments.

Subprime loan A loan made to a property or to a borrower that does not meet standard lending guidelines. Property located on land that is not zoned for its use. A borrower who may have credit information that is not suited for a particular lender.

Swap The exchange of loans for real estate loans backed by securities rather than cash.

Swing loan Used to assist in the purchase of a replacement house before the sale of the original house is completed.

T

T-bill rate An indicator of the cost of money that the government is paying on interest for borrowed money.

Takeout loan The loan arranged by the owner or builder-developer for a buyer. The construction loan made for construction of the improvements is usually paid in full from the proceeds of the more permanent mortgage loan.

Tax deed A deed on property purchased at public sale for nonpayment of taxes.

Tax lien A claim against property for the amount of its due and unpaid taxes.

Tax service A fee paid to a tax service agency that each year reviews the records of taxing bodies and reports any delinquencies to the lender. The fee is usually paid by the borrower.

Taxes The amount and status of past unpaid real estate taxes, if any, and current year's taxes, paid or unpaid, or taxes that are a lien but not yet payable.

Tenancy A holding of real estate under any kind of right or title. Used alone, tenancy implies a holding under a lease.

Tenancy in common In law, the type of tenancy or estate created when real or personal property is granted, devised, or bequeathed to two or more persons in the absence of expressed words creating a joint tenancy. There is no right of survivorship. See *Joint tenancy.*

Tenant One who is not the owner but occupies real property under consent of the owner and in subordination to the owner's title. The tenant is entitled to exclusive possession, use, and enjoyment of the property, usually for a rent specified in the lease.

Term The period of time between the commencement date and termination date of a note, loan, legal document, or other contract.

Threshold reporting The DRE requirement to submit forms by DRE brokers who, in a successive 12-month period, perform certain acts, such as negotiate transactions for the sale or exchange of notes secured by real property.

T&I (taxes and insurance) That portion of a homebuyer's monthly payments to the lender that goes into an escrow fund to pay property taxes, the homeowner's insurance premiums, and mortgage insurance, if applicable.

Tier credit A formula developed by the Federal National Mortgage Association (FNMA) for those borrowers who do not have any of the standard forms of credit. See *Chapter 7*.

Time-saver documentation file A loan program that requires less documentation for completion.

Title The evidence of the right to ownership in property. In the case of real estate, the documentary evidence of ownership is the title deed, which specifies in whom the legal state is vested and the history of ownership and transfers.

Title 1 loan A loan program specifically designed for home improvements under FHA.

Title insurance policy A contract by which the insurer, usually a title insurance company, agrees to pay the insured a specified amount for any loss caused by defects of title to real estate, wherein the insured has an interest as purchaser, lender, or otherwise.

Title report A report that discloses the condition of the title, made by a title company preliminary to issuance of a title insurance policy.

Total debt The PITI payment plus all long-term debt, installment and revolving, is referred to as the borrower's total debt.

Total housing debt The total housing payment, PITI, HOA dues, flood insurance, lease land payment, and any other item that may be in the house payment is referred to as the total housing debt.

True equity True equity is derived from the principal reduction of the mortgage. Example: You have a loan amount of $315,000 at 7.0% interest for 30 years. The PI payment would be $2,095.70. The interest for the month would be $1,837.50. Therefore, the true equity would be: $258.20 for the month. The borrower and lender would share the $258.20 50-50.

Trust account (bank); trust fund An account separate and apart and physically segregated from a broker's own funds, in which the broker is required by law to deposit all funds collected for clients.

Trust deed The instrument given by a borrower (trustor) to a trustee vesting title to a property in the trustee as security for the borrower's fulfillment of an obligation. See *Deed of trust*.

Trustee One who holds title to a real property under the terms of a deed of trust.

Trustor A borrower under a trust deed who deeds property to trustee as security for the repayment of the debt.

Truth-in-Lending (TIL) A federal law designed to show a borrower the total cost of a loan. The annual percentage rate (APR) is the term used to disclose the effective rate of interest. See *Regulation Z*.

U

Underwriter The person who makes the final decision about whether to make the loan, generally after years of experience in evaluating loan files.

Underwriting The analysis and matching of risk to an appropriate rate and term. The process of deciding whether to make a real estate loan.

Underwriting guidelines Loan guidelines set down by each investor for the lenders to follow, ensuring that the lender will be able to market the loan to an investor.

Underwriting worksheet Worksheet used by the underwriter to ensure that the processor has submitted the file correctly.

Undue influence Use of a fiduciary or confidential relationship to obtain a fraudulent or unfair advantage over another's weakness of mind, distress, or necessity.

Uniform Commercial Code (UCC) A comprehensive law regulating commercial transactions. It has been adopted, with modification, by all states.

Uniform residential appraisal report (URAR) one of the most common forms used in real estate **appraisal** which was created to allow for standard reporting and analysis of single family dwellings or single family dwellings with an "accessory unit".

Uniform residential loan application (URLA) Also known as the 1003, the standard loan application used for conventional, FHA, and DVA loans.

Uniform standards of professional appraisal practice (USPAP) With deregulation that followed, many problems arose with the mismanagement of some of the institutions. Significant changes were brought about in 1986 as a result of the Financial Institution's Reform and Recovery Act (FIRREA). The Uniform Standards of Professional Appraisal Practice (USPAP) were generated, which included specific guidelines and appraisal ethics on most federally related transactions.

Uniform underwriting and transmittal summary (1008) A form used by mortgage brokers to submit a loan to a lender. This form will give a quick review of the loan package being submitted.

Unsecured A loan that is not secured by a trust deed, mortgage, or other property.

Up-front mortgage insurance premium (UPMIP) A mortgage insurance premium paid at closing that amounts to 1.5% of the loan amount. The premium is reduced for first-time homebuyers and inner-city buyers who complete a homebuyer education program.

URAR Uniform residential appraisal report (See *Appraisal report*).

Usury Charging more for the use of money than allowed by law.

Utility line extensions Effective July 1, 1995, the Public Utilities Commission (PUC) adopted a stipulation and settlement agreement for electric and gas lines. Water and telephone lines are excluded. The new rule imposes a per-foot charge to bring in gas or electricity from the source.

V

VA certificate of reasonable value The DVA issues a certificate of reasonable value at a specific figure, agreeing to guarantee a loan to an eligible qualified veteran buyer upon completion and sale of the house. The veteran must be aware of the VA's appraised value of the property.

VA no-no A qualified veteran may purchase a property with no cash down payment and no cash closing costs. Allowable costs are included in the loan amount.

Valuation See *Appraisal.*

Variable Interest Rate (VIR) This is also an ARM loan. VIR loans were with a State chartered lender and a ARM loan was with a federally chartered lender.

Variable rate An agreement that allows for adjustment of the interest rate in keeping with a fluctuating market and terms agreed upon in the note.

Variable Rate Mortgage (VRM) A long-term Mortgage loan applied to residences, under which the Interest Rate may be adjusted on a 6-month basis over the term of the loan.

Vendee The party to whom personal or real property is sold.

Verification Sworn statement before a duly qualified officer as to correctness of contents of an instrument.

Verification of deposit (VOD) Document mailed out to a borrower's banks and savings and loans to verify all monies on deposit.

Verification of employment (VOE) Document mailed out to current and previous employers to verify employment. Generally covers 2 years of continued employment.

Verification of mortgage (VOM) Document mailed out to current lenders to verify the borrower's payment record on a mortgage.

Verification of rent (VOR) Document mailed out to a borrower's landlord to verify the borrower's payment record on rent.

Vesting Names(s) in which title to property is held.

W

Waive Relinquish or abandon; forgo a right to enforce or require anything.

Warehousing The holding of a real estate loan on a short-term basis pending either a sale to an investor or other long-term financing. These loans may be used as collateral security with a bank to borrow additional funds. A builder "warehouses" loans by taking back a note from a homebuyer and holding the loan for a period.

Warranty deed A deed in which the grantor or seller warrants or guarantees that good title is being conveyed.

Water heater bracing California state law requiring all new and replacement water heaters for residential property to braced, anchored, or strapped to resist falling or horizontal displacement due to earthquake motion. Health and Safety Code 19211.

Wholesale broker agreement A written contract between the mortgage broker and the lender/ investor.

Will A written document providing for the distribution of property at death.

Wire transfer The electronic transfer of funds directly from one source of funds to another, which can expedite the closing.

WORK One of the six traits needed to succeed in the Mortgage business. WORK = Wealth: Opportunities: Rewards: Knowledge

Y

Yield In real estate, the effective annual amount of income that is being accrued on an investment, expressed as a percentage of the price originally paid.

Yield spread premium (YSP) A premium paid to a mortgage broker by a lender/investor for bringing a loan to the lender/investor at a yield above "par."

Z

Zero tolerance A property that is used for illegal activity can be taken by an agency of the federal government. Consult an attorney for further information.

Zoning The act of city or county authorities specifying the type of use to which property may be put in specific areas.

Index

S